SWORD AND SHIELD

THIRD EDITION

A Practical Approach to Section 1983 Litigation

Editors
Mary Massaron Ross
Edwin P. Voss, Jr.

ABA Section of State and Local Government Law

ABA
Defending Liberty
Pursuing Justice

Cover design by ABA Publishing.

Printed in the United States of America

10 09 08 07 06   5 4 3 2 1

Library of Congress Cataloging-in-Publication Data

Sword and shield : a practical approach to Section 1983 litigation /edited by Mary Massaron Ross, Edwin P. Voss, Jr. -- 3rd ed.

p. cm.

Prev. ed.: Sword & shield revisited / edited by Mary Massaron Ross. c1998.

Includes index.

ISBN 1-59031-766-1

1. Tort liability of municipal corporations--United States. 2. Stateaction (Civil rights)–United States. I. Ross, Mary Massaron, 1951- II.Voss, Edwin P. III. American Bar Association. State and Local GovernmentLaw Section. IV. Sword & shield revisited.

KF1325.C58S96 2006
342.7308'8--dc22

2006024431

Discounts are available for books ordered in bulk. Special consideration is given to state bars, CLE programs, and other bar-related organizations. Inquire at Book Publishing, American Bar Association, 750 N. Lake Shore Drive, Chicago, Illinois 60611.

DEDICATION

To my father, who gave all of his children a sense of justice, and my mother (in memory), who taught us the power and beauty of language, and to my brothers and sisters, Nora, Mark, Eric, David, Karen, John, and Steve (in memory), who have put those lessons to use each in their own way.

Mary Massaron Ross

To my close friends and law partners, Terrence S. Welch, Kent S. Hofmeister, Mark S. Houser, Robert F. Brown and Mark E. Goldstucker.

Edwin P. Voss, Jr.

ACKNOWLEDGMENTS

Thanks on my part to my co-editor, Edwin P. Voss, Jr., for all his work to make this new edition of the book a reality. I also echo the thanks offered by Ed to the writers who worked so hard on updating or writing new chapters. Thanks also should go to Section Chair Thomas E. Roberts, whose support for this and other projects in the Section over the years has made my involvement in them a source of joy despite the hard work required. The head of the Section's book publications program, Donna Pugh, deserves special thanks for her efforts to get this new edition off the ground. And thanks as always to the ABA Publications staff, especially Rick Paszkiet.

Mary Massaron Ross

The State and Local Government Law Section of the ABA is the preeminent bar organization for those interested in government law. I want to thank both Mary Massaron Ross and the Section for the opportunity to work on this project, for patience during the delays in its completion, and for such a rewarding experience.

I also thank the authors who gave so much of their time to complete this project. Writing in this area is particularly difficult because the law changes quickly, and because there are so many opinions that can make it overwhelming to stay abreast of emerging issues. The complexity of § 1983 litigation demands attention to numerous nuances and detail, requiring much thought and analysis. The writers, without whom this book would not exist, are deserving of special thanks and gratitude for their knowledge, their patience, and their willingness to contribute to this worthwhile and helpful publication in such an important area of the law. It is no wonder that § 1983 litigation takes up such a substantial part of the federal and state courts' dockets.

Edwin P. Voss, Jr.

TABLE OF CONTENTS

FOREWORD

In 1983, the ABA published *Section 1983: Sword and Shield,* an anthology that explored the expanding scope of 42 U.S.C. § 1983 liability. In a series of articles, the authors analyzed the history of § 1983 litigation, the scope of potential liability, available defenses, remedies, and policy implications, after the bellwether case of *Monell v. Department of Social Services.*[1] After more than fifteen years had elapsed since that effort, in 1998, a second edition was published, entitled *Sword and Shield Revisited, A Practical Approach to Section 1983. Sword and Shield Revisited* addressed the reality that practicing lawyers, academics, and judges are as hard-pressed to keep up with the twists and turns in this changing area of law as they were in the 1980s. Whether tracing the lines of authority that set forth the parameters for an illegal search and seizure claim, or examining the emerging retaliation theories brought by public employees, § 1983 claims are as legally and factually complex as ever. Grounded in the Constitution, this area of law affects every aspect of life in our constitutional democracy, from birth to death.[2]

The continued growth of § 1983 litigation over the years only confirms the reality that every official policy or conduct of a state or local government is potentially subject to suit on some constitutional or statutory theory of liability. The effect of § 1983 remains broad: every public employee, government official, citizen, or student in public and private schools is entitled to bring suit to vindicate his or her civil rights. For example, a small town is forced to permit nude dancing in a local bar; a politician is prohibited from firing his political enemy when he takes office; a citizen's property development is limited due to government land use regulations; a jailer does not provide proper medical care to a prisoner or fails to protect him from other inmates who are threatening him; a police officer tries to arrest a suspected drug dealer or to search his house. Nowhere is the scope of potential lawsuit liability more apparent than in the area of § 1983 jurisprudence.

With this new and updated volume of *Sword and Shield,* the reader will see the framework for § 1983 litigation as it has developed into the new millennium. Professor Martin Schwartz starts with a comprehensive review of

---

1 436 U.S. 658 (1978).

2 *See* Vacco V. Quill, 521 U.S. 793 (1997); Cruzan v. Director, Missouri Dep't of Health, 497 U.S. 261 (1990); Webster v. Reproductive Health Services, 492 U.S. 490 (1989).

the fundamentals of § 1983 litigation. From that overview, the reader can learn the procedural intricacies of § 1983 litigation in federal court from Jane K. Swanson's chapter. Ms. Swanson identifies important procedural issues that may arise in § 1983 litigation, including ripeness, forum choice, and removal, and sets forth numerous procedural considerations pertaining to damages, the jury charge, discovery, and waivable defenses.

Professor Steven H. Steinglass then provides a comprehensive overview into § 1983 litigation in state court. Starting with its historical background, Professor Steinglass provides a discussion of state court jurisdiction, forum choice considerations, the methodology of state court § 1983 litigation, and § 1983 remedial issues. Michael S. Bogren next presents a more defense-oriented view of municipal liability, reviews the methods for showing that a municipality is liable, and explains recent Supreme Court decisions defining the critical proofs necessary to present a case establishing an unlawful policy, practice, or custom.

Professor Kathryn R. Urbonya's article discusses police misconduct claims in the context of the complex search and seizure rules that police officers must follow under the Fourth Amendment. Perhaps no other subject generates as much § 1983 law enforcement litigation as this one police operational area. A good argument could be made, however, that § 1983 employment litigation in and of itself is causing the courts' dockets to swell. In the chapter addressing public employees, co-editor Mary Massaron Ross sets forth the constitutional rights of public employees—rights that limit public employers substantially when dealing with their work force. Another set of issues that is causing a lawsuit boom concern property rights cases. Professor Thomas E. Roberts discusses the § 1983 land use case from its inception to the Supreme Court's recent expansion of the rights of property owners, particularly as these rights are affected by procedural issues. Professor Roberts also provides insight into takings law and the recent hot-button case of *Kelo v. City of New London*.[3]

Margaret-Ann F. Howie tells readers about a student's constitutional rights in the public school setting, a topic that demonstrates that the reach of § 1983 litigation can be felt in almost every area of American life. Robert F. Brown provides an overview of the individual immunity defenses available for legislators, prosecutors, judges, and other public employees and officials sued under § 1983. Immunity issues provide much fodder for both substantive and procedural lawsuit battles, sometimes confounding judge and practitioner alike.

---

3 125 S. Ct. 2655 (2005).

The procedural and substantive issues discussed in the various chapters of this updated version of *Sword & Shield* are sometimes repeated, both for emphasis as well as for instruction about how those matters apply in different contexts. For instance, the *Rooker-Feldman*[4] doctrine is an important procedural consideration, in general, and also finds particular life in land use litigation, in both Chapters 2 and 7. Immunity issues require serious procedural and substantive attention, and are addressed in Chapters 1, 2 and 9. In this book, the authors continue the interrelated focus of previous editions, and provide a timely analysis of practical considerations necessary to practice effectively in this technically difficult and ever-evolving area of law.

Mary Massaron Ross
Edwin P. Voss, Jr.

4 Rooker v. Fidelity Trust Co., 263 U.S. 413 (1923), and District of Columbia Court of Appeals v. Feldman, 460 U.S. 462 (1983).

ABOUT THE EDITORS

Mary Massaron Ross, of Plunkett & Cooney, P.C., concentrates her practice on appellate law, civil rights, land use, and government liability. A former clerk for Justice Boyle on the Michigan Supreme Court, she has briefed and argued cases before the Michigan Supreme Court, the Michigan Court of Appeals, and the Sixth Circuit Court of Appeals. Notable cases that she has handled include *Mason v. Wayne County, Ortman v. Thomas, McBride v. Village of Michiana,* and *Kevorkian v. Thompson.*

Ms. Massaron Ross has chaired the Appellate Practice Section of the State Bar of Michigan, and is a past chair of the Defense Research Institute's Appellate Advocacy Committee. She also co-chairs the Michigan Appellate Bench Bar Conference Foundation, an organization of appellate lawyers and judges in Michigan. She has been active in the Appellate Advocacy Committee of the Tort and Insurance Practice Section of the ABA, serving as a past co-chair of its subcommittee on appellate rules of procedure, and is currently the chair of the ABA Standing Committee on Amicus Briefs, the five-member committee that oversees preparation of ABA briefs for filing in the United States Supreme Court and other courts. She was recently appointed by the Chief Judge of the Michigan Court of Appeals to its Internal Operating Procedures Task Force. Ms. Massaron Ross has served in the leadership of the State and Local Government Law Section of the ABA and has served as a member of its governing council. She also has chaired the Tort and Insurance Practice Section's Governmental Liability Committee.

Ms. Massaron Ross graduated second in her law school class from Wayne State University in 1990, where she served as an editor on the law review and was nominated to membership in the Order of the Coif. Ms. Massaron Ross has published numerous articles dealing with appeals, government law, zoning and land use, election law, and civil rights. A frequent lecturer, Ms. Massaron Ross has spoken at seminars around the country on such topics as preserving the record on appeal, the constitutional rights of public employees, and land use law. She is admitted to practice in all Michigan and New York state courts, the United States Supreme Court, the U.S. Court of Appeals for the Third, Sixth, Seventh and Federal Circuits, and the United States District Courts for the Eastern and Western Districts of Michigan.

Edwin P. Voss, Jr., of Brown & Hofmeister, L.L.P., practices municipal law, focusing on civil rights defense, employment and Title VII defense, land use, zoning and ordinance defense, construction and personal injury. Mr. Voss has represented numerous clients in the United States District Courts for the Northern, Eastern and Western Districts of Texas, as well as in the Fifth Circuit Court of Appeals, in addition to Texas state trial courts, Texas Courts of Appeals, and the Texas Supreme Court. Mr. Voss has handled § 1983 litigation for local governments, special districts, and government officials during the bulk of his legal career. Mr. Voss is a member of the Section of State and Local Government Law of the American Bar Association, is currently Committee Coordinator for the Section, and is on the Section's National Council. He is also Chair of the State and Local Government Relations Section of the Federal Bar Association. He has served on various federal court committees, and has over two dozen reported cases. He is Board Certified in Civil Appellate Law by the Texas Board of Legal Specialization, is a member of the Appellate Section of the State Bar of Texas, and is also a member of the Appellate Section of the Dallas Bar Association.

Mr. Voss has lectured numerous times on the subjects of § 1983 liability, employment law and ethics. He is has authored numerous articles concerning those same subjects, and recently published a chapter regarding immunity issues, in *A Defense Lawyer's Guide to Appellate Practice,* published by the Defense Research Institute. He received his B.A. and J.D. degrees from Baylor University.

ABOUT THE CONTRIBUTORS

Michael S. Bogren is a shareholder in the Detroit-based firm of Plunkett & Cooney, P.C., and is the managing partner of the firm's Kalamazoo, Michigan, office. He specializes in the representation of municipal defendants in civil rights litigation in both federal and state courts.

Mr. Bogren is the author of several articles on civil rights litigation and constitutional law. He has lectured on civil rights litigation for the Michigan ICLE and also lectures for the Michigan Municipal League on civil rights issues. Mr. Bogren is a member of the ABA, the Michigan Defense Trial Counsel, the Michigan Association of Municipal Attorneys, and the Kalamazoo County Bar Association. He earned his B.A. from Western Michigan University and his J.D. from the University of Detroit.

Robert F. Brown is a partner in the Richardson, Texas, firm of Brown & Hofmeister, L.L.P, where he specializes in an active litigation and appellate practice, with an emphasis on municipal law, including constitutional law, civil rights, and zoning and land use matters.

In addition to his litigation practice, Mr. Brown acts as city attorney for a number of municipalities in the North Texas area. He has chaired the Federal Litigation Section of the Federal Bar Association, and has served on the Government Liability Committee of the State and Local Government Law Section of the ABA. Mr. Brown is a frequent author and speaker on civil rights and land use matters with numerous articles and presentations to his credit, including co-authorship of *Seeking Terra Firma in Complex Zoning Litigation: The Defense Practitioner's Perspective,* published by Matthew Bender & Company in its 1994 Institute on Planning, Zoning and Eminent Domain.

Mr. Brown received his law degree from Texas Tech University School of Law and his B.B.A. from Texas A&M University.

Margaret-Ann F. Howie is counsel to the superintendent of the Baltimore County Public Schools. In this capacity, she advises the superintendent of schools and senior staff on a variety of issues involving employment, students' rights, and collective bargaining. She previously worked as director of Legal and Legislative Services for the Maryland Association of Boards of Education.

Ms. Howie is a member of the board of directors of the National School Boards Association's Council of School Attorneys and has served as chair of the council's Urban Law Committee. She has spoken and written nationally on legal issues related to student discipline and school violence.

Ms. Howie received her J.D. from Columbia University School of Law, her M.A. from Middlebury College, and her B.A. from John Hopkins University.

Thomas E. Roberts is a professor of law at the Wake Forest University School of Law, where he teaches real estate and land use law. Professor Roberts is a nationally recognized authority in land use law, particularly concerning property rights litigation. He has written numerous articles, book chapters and book reviews concerning land use and takings issues, and has authored and edited several books on those topics. Most recently, Professor Roberts edited *Taking Sides on Takings Issues: The Impact of Tahoe-Sierra,* published by the ABA.

Professor Roberts has served as an Assistant Dean and adjunct Professor of Law at the Ohio State University College of Law, and was in private practice in Columbus, Ohio.

Professor Roberts received his B.A. degree from Hanover College, and his J.D. from Ohio State University. Prior to law school, Professor Roberts served in the Peace Corps in Ecuador.

Martin A. Schwartz is a professor of law at Touro Law Center in Huntington, New York. Professor Schwartz has written numerous publications on civil rights issues. He is the author of a multi-volume treatise on § 1983 litigation, *Section 1983 Litigation: Claims and Defenses* (Aspen, 3d ed., 1997); author of Section 1983 *Litigation: Federal Evidence* (Aspen, 3d ed., 1999); and co-author of *Section 1983 Litigation: Jury Instructions* (Aspen 2000).

Professor Schwartz is the author of a semi-monthly column in the *New York Law Journal* on public interest law. Professor Schwartz is co-chair of the Practicing Law Institute's annual program on § 1983 litigation. A legal services attorney from 1968 to 1984, Professor Schwartz has argued three cases before the United States Supreme Court.

Steven H. Steinglass is dean emeritus and professor of law at the Cleveland-Marshall College of Law, Cleveland State University, where he has taught since 1980. He teaches Civil Procedure, Federal Jurisdiction, § 1983 Litigation, and State Constitutional Law. He lectures throughout the country on § 1983 issues at continuing legal and judicial education programs. Professor Steinglass, who writes frequently on § 1983 issues, is the author of *Section*

1983 Litigation in State Courts, a two-volume treatise published by Clark Boardman Callaghan.

Professor Steinglass, a member of the Ohio and Wisconsin bars, practiced in Wisconsin from 1969 to 1980 with Legal Action of Wisconsin, Inc., and its predecessor legal services organizations, and he had argued two § 1983 cases in the United States Supreme Court, *Board of Regents v. Roth* and *Felder v. Casey.* Professor Steinglass is a graduate of the Wharton School of the University of Pennsylvania, and received his J.D. from the Columbia University School of Law.

Jane K. Swanson practices in Woodlands, Texas, with the Law Offices of Jane K. Swanson. She is a former managing attorney and litigation director of East Texas Legal Services and a former project director of Wyandotte-Leavenworth Legal Services in Kansas City, Kansas.

In her legal services and private practice career, Ms. Swanson has litigated a wide variety of § 1983 claims on behalf of indigent clients in both the federal and state court systems. She has been a frequent speaker on civil rights issues at seminars for legal services and other public interest attorneys, and has lectured on the topic "Procedural Issues in Section 1983 Litigation" for the ABA.

Ms. Swanson is admitted to practice before the United States Supreme Court, the Fifth and Tenth Circuit Courts of Appeals, the United States District Courts for the Eastern and Southern Districts of Texas, and received her J.D. degree from the University of Houston Law Center.

Kathryn R. Urbonya, a professor at William and Mary School of Law, has written numerous articles about search and seizure and the use of force by governmental officials, and the availability of the qualified immunity defense for constitutional torts. She has lectured at conferences sponsored by the ABA, Defense Research Institute, Federal Judicial Center, Georgetown University Law Center, Practicing Law Institute, and the U.S. Information Agency.

Prior to teaching, Professor Urbonya was a law clerk for Justice Gerald W. VandeWalle of the North Dakota Supreme Court, and Federal District Judge G. Ernest Tidwell in Atlanta. She is co-author of a treatise on civil rights litigation published by West Publishing, *Section 1983 Litigation.* Professor Urbonya received her undergraduate degree from Beloit College, and her masters and J.D. degrees from the University of North Dakota

Chapter 1

FUNDAMENTALS OF SECTION 1983 LITIGATION

*by Professor Martin A. Schwartz**

*The author expresses an appreciation for the valuable assistance of Ryan Browning and Kathleen Clair, students at William and Mary College of Law, in the preparation of this chapter.

I. INTRODUCTION

Section 1983 of Title 42 (42 U.S.C. § 1983) is the most important civil statute in American law. It authorizes private parties to enforce their federal constitutional rights, and some federal statutory rights, against defendants who acted under color of state law. These defendants are principally state and municipal officials and municipalities. Large numbers of § 1983 claims are filed in federal and state courts on an ongoing basis by a wide array of claimants, including victims of police misconduct, prisoners, present and former public employees and licensees, property owners, and applicants and recipients of public benefits.

Section 1983 litigation is multifaceted and complex. A § 1983 case may involve the interpretation of the federal Constitution, federal statutes (including § 1983 itself), and even state law. The mere fact that the plaintiff establishes a violation of a federally protected right does not necessarily mean that she will obtain relief. This is because the law of § 1983 has numerous defenses that may defeat recovery: jurisdictional defenses such as lack of standing and mootness, a variety of immunities (Eleventh Amendment as well as absolute and qualified immunity), the statute of limitations, preclusion, and the various abstention doctrines.

The law of § 1983 litigation develops on an ongoing basis. The lower court decisional law is voluminous. The goal of this chapter is to analyze the fundamental principles of § 1983 litigation.

II. ELEMENTS OF THE SECTION 1983 CLAIM, FUNCTIONAL ROLE OF SECTION 1983, PLEADING, AND JURISDICTION

A. Elements of the Section 1983 Claim

Section 1983 authorizes the assertion of a claim for relief against a person who, acting under color of state law, violated the claimant's federally protected rights. The U.S. Supreme Court stated that there are two elements of a § 1983 claim. The plaintiff must allege: (1) a deprivation of a federal right, and (2) that the person who deprived him of that right acted under color of state law.[1] However, in the author's view there are at least four major elements of a § 1983 claim. The plaintiff must establish

a. conduct by a "person";
b. who acted under "color of state law";
c. proximately causing;
d. a deprivation of a federally protected right.

In addition, if the plaintiff is seeking to establish municipal liability, she must show that the deprivation of her federal right was attributable to the enforcement of a municipal custom or policy. *See* Part IX, *infra.* The plaintiff bears the burden of establishing each element of the claim for relief by a preponderance of the evidence.[2]

1. Gomez v. Toledo, 446 U.S. 635, 640 (1980). *Accord* West v. Atkins, 487 U.S. 42 (1988); Flagg Bros. v. Brookes, 436 U.S. 147 (1978).
2. Larez v. Holcomb, 16 F.3d 1513, 1517–18 (9th Cir. 1994); Shaw v. Leatherberry, 706 N.W. 2d 299 (Wis. 2005). *See also* Crawford-El v. Britton, 523 U.S. 574 (1998) (rejecting imposition of clear and convincing evidence burden on plaintiffs

Section 1983 has no particular state-of-mind requirement.[3] However, the particular personal constitutional right may require a showing that the defendant had a certain state of mind when she engaged in the contested conduct. For example, to establish a due process violation, it must be shown that a state or local official intentionally or deliberately caused a deprivation of life, liberty or property; negligent conduct will not suffice.[4] A claim under the Equal Protection Clause alleging racial or gender-based discrimination will invoke heightened judicial scrutiny only if the plaintiff establishes intentional discrimination.[5] And, the denial of adequate medical care to a prisoner violates the Eighth Amendment only if the plaintiff demonstrates deliberate indifference to a serious medical need.[6] In other words, medical malpractice is not a constitutional violation merely because the plaintiff is a prisoner. A wide range of federal constitutional rights may be enforced under § 1983.[7] Each constitutional claim must be evaluated to determine whether it requires a showing that the defendant acted with a particular state of mind.

B. Functional Role of Section 1983

Section 1983 does not itself create or establish any federally protected rights. Rather, § 1983 authorizes the assertion of a claim for relief to enforce federal rights created by either the federal Constitution or, in some cases, by a federal statute (other than § 1983).[8] This means that the § 1983 plaintiff must establish that the defendant violated a federally protected right created either by the Constitution or by some federal statute other than § 1983. Section 1983 fulfills the procedural or remedial function of authorizing the assertion of the claim for relief. It is well established that when the plaintiff asserts a violation of a federal constitutional right against a defendant who acted under color of state law, § 1983 provides the exclusive available

---

who assert wrongful motive claim subject to qualified immunity defense raised on summary judgment); Clark v. Mann, 562 F.2d 1104, 1117 (8th Cir. 1977) (§ 1983 plaintiffs "ordinarily retain the burden of proof throughout the trial.").

3. Parratt v. Taylor, 451 U.S. 527 (1981).
4. Daniels v. Williams, 474 U.S. 327 (1986). *See also* Davidson v. Cannon, 474 U.S. 344 (1986).
5. *See, e.g.,* Arlington Heights v. Metropolitan Housing Dev. Corp., 429 U.S. 252 (1977) (race); Personnel Adm'r v. Feeney, 442 U.S. 256 (1979) (gender).
6. Estelle v. Gamble, 429 U.S. 97, 106 (1976).
7. *See* Wilson v. Garcia, 471 U.S. 261, 273 (1985).
8. Albright v. Oliver, 510 U.S. 266 (1994); Graham v. Connor, 490 U.S. 386 (1989); Chapman v. Houston W.R.O., 441 U.S. 600, 608 (1979) (§ 1983 "creates no substantive rights; it merely provides remedies for deprivations of rights established elsewhere."); Baker v. McCollan, 443 U.S. 137 (1979).

remedy. Thus, plaintiff may not seek to avoid the limitations of the § 1983 claim for relief by asserting a claim directly under the Constitution.[9]

C. Pleading Section 1983 Claims

Federal court § 1983 complaints are governed by notice pleading. Federal Rule of Civil Procedure 8(a) provides that the complaint must set forth "(1) a short and plain statement of the grounds on which the court's jurisdiction depends," "(2) a short and plain statement of the grounds showing that the pleader is entitled to relief, and (3) a demand for judgment for the relief the pleader seeks."[10] Although FED. R. CIV. P. 9 requires that certain issues be pled "with particularity" (e.g., fraud and mistake), there is no requirement that § 1983 claims be pleaded with particularity. In fact, Rule 9(a) provides that "[m]alice, intent knowledge, and other conditions of mind of a person may be averred generally."

In *Leatherman v. Tarrant County*,[11] the Supreme Court rejected a "heightened" pleading requirement for § 1983 municipal liability claims, because it is not authorized by Rules 8 and 9. The Court found that § 1983 municipal liability claims are governed by the notice pleading standard of Rule 8. "This requirement is by no means onerous; instead, it is designed to ensure that the complaint will give the defendant fair notice of what the plaintiff's claim is and the grounds upon which it rests."[12]

---

9. Jett v. Dallas Independent S.D., 491 U.S. 701, 735 (1989); Wax 'n Works v. St. Paul, 213 F.3d 1016 (8th Cir. 2000); Baxter v. Vigo County School Corp., 26 F.3d 728, 732 n.3 (7th Cir. 1994); Azul-Pacitico, Inc. v. City of Los Angeles, 973 F.2d 704, 705 (9th Cir. 1992), *cert. denied,* 506 U.S. 1081 (1993); Santiago v. New York State Dep't of Correctional Servs., 945 F.2d 25 (2d Cir. 1991); Thomas v. Shipka, 818 F.2d 496 (6th Cir. 1987); Tarpley v. Greene, 654 F.2d 1 (D.C. Cir. 1982); Pauk v. Board of Trustees of City Univ. of New York, 654 F.2d 856, 865 (2d Cir. 1981).

10. Pro se complaints: The Supreme Court holds that pro se complaints are subject to "less stringent standards than formal pleadings drafted by lawyers," and should be liberally construed in the plaintiff's favor. Hughes v. Rowe, 449 U.S. 5, 9 (1980); Haines v. Kerner, 404 U.S. 519 (1972). District courts should "read the pleadings of a pro se plaintiff liberally and interpret them to raise the strongest arguments that they suggest." Burgos v. Hopkins, 14 F.3d 787, 790 (2d Cir. 1994). *Accord* McPherson v. Coombe, 174 F.3d 276 (2d Cir. 1999). However, pro se status does not exempt a party from compliance with procedural rules. Traguth v. Zuck, 710 F.2d 90, 96 (2d Cir. 1983).

11. 507 U.S. 144, 163 (1993).

12. Slade v. Hampton Roads Regional Jail, 407 F.3d 243 (4th Cir. 2005) (quoting Conley v. Gibson, 355 U.S. 41, 47 (1957)).

In *Swierkiewicz v. Sorema, N. A.*,[13] the Supreme Court rejected a heightened pleading standard for Title VII and Age Discrimination in Employment Act (ADEA) claims. As in *Leatherman* the Court found that Title VII and ADEA claims are governed by the Rule 8 notice pleading standard. The Court in *Swierkiewicz* also reaffirmed that federal courts may "dismiss a complaint only if it is clear that no relief could be granted under any set of facts that could be consentient with the allegations."[14] The decision in *Swierkiewicz* clearly applies to § 1983 claims.[15]

The Court in *Leatherman* left open whether a heightened pleading may be imposed on personal capacity claims subject to the defense of qualified immunity. Applying the rationale of *Leatherman* and *Swierkiewicz,* the great majority of circuit courts hold that, like other § 1983 claims, personal capacity claims subject to qualified immunity are governed by notice pleading.[16] The courts have several tools to eliminate meritless personal capacity claims early in the litigation, including ordering the plaintiff to file either a detailed reply to the defendant's answer, FED. R. CIV. P. 7, or a more definite statement, FED. R. CIV. P. 12(e), or tailoring discovery to protect the defendant from unnecessary embarrassments or burdens, under FED. R. CIV. P. 26(c).[17]

The federal courts have traditionally imposed a heightened pleading standard for § 1983 conspiracy claims on the theory that these claims are easy to plead but difficult to prove.[18] It is arguable that under *Leatherman* and *Swierkiewicz* these claims too should be governed by notice pleading.[19]

---

13. 534 U.S. 506 (2002).
14. Hishon v. King & Splading, 467 U.S. 69, 73 (1984).
15. *See, e.g.,* Educadores Puertorriqueños v. Hernandez, 367 F.3d 61 (1st Cir. 2004); Walker v. Thompson, 288 F.3d 1005 (7th Cir. 2002). *See also* Hill v. McDonough, 126 S. Ct. 2096 (2006).
16. *See, e.g.,* Evancho v. Fisher, 423 F.3d 347 (3d Cir. 2005); Doe v. Cassel, 403 F.3d 986 (8th Cir. 2005); Educadores Puertorriqueños En Accion v. Rey Hernandez, 367 F.3d 61 (1st Cir. 2004); Goad v. Mitchell, 297 F.3d 497 (6th Cir. 2002); Currie v. Doran, 242 F.3d 905 (10th Cir.), *cert. denied,* 534 U.S. 1019 (2001). *Contra* GJR Investments Inc. v. County of Escambia, 132 F.3d 1359 (11th Cir. 1998).
17. *See, e.g.,* Crawford-El v. Britton, 523 U.S. 574 (1988); Schultea v. Wood, 47 F.3d 1427 (5th Cir. 1995) (en banc); Doe v. Cassel, 403 F.3d 986 (8th Cir. 2005).
18. *See* MARTIN A. SCHWARTZ, 1 SECTION 1983 LITIGATION: CLAIMS AND DEFENSES, ("SCHWARTZ") § 1.06 (4th ed. 2004). *See, e.g.,* Ciambriello v. County of Nassau, 292 F.3d 307, 325 (2d Cir. 2002) ("complaints containing only conclusory, vague, or general allegations that defendants have engaged in a conspiracy to deprive the plaintiff of his constitutional rights are properly dismissed; diffuse and expansive allegations are insufficient, unless amplified by specific instances of misconduct."); Burns v. County of King, 883 F.2d 819, 821 (9th Cir. 1989).
19. *See* Walker v. Thompson, 288 F.3d 1005 (7th Cir. 2002).

D. Federal Court Jurisdiction

Section 1983 does not grant the federal courts subject matter jurisdiction. Nevertheless, federal district courts clearly have jurisdiction over § 1983 claims. Federal court jurisdiction over §1983 claims is authorized by either 28 U.S.C. § 1343 (a)(3)[20] or by the general federal question jurisdiction statute, 28 U.S.C. § 1331.[21] Nevertheless, the federal court's jurisdiction may be defeated by some other jurisdictional doctrine, such as the *Rooker-Feldman* doctrine (discussed below), the Eleventh Amendment (*see* Part XIII), or abstention (*see* Part XX).

1. Rooker-Feldman *Doctrine*

In some federal court § 1983 actions, a party who lost in state court may try to "make a federal case of it" by seeking to overturn the state court judgment in a federal court § 1983 action. This stratagem is normally doomed to fail. In most cases, a federal suit that seeks to overturn a state court judgment will be barred by the *Rooker-Feldman* doctrine, named after the Supreme Court's decisions in *Rooker v. Fidelity Trust Co.*[22] and *District of Columbia v. Feldman.*[23] This doctrine holds that a federal district court does not have jurisdiction to overturn a state court judgment, even when the federal court complaint alleges that the state court judgment violates the plaintiff's federal constitutional rights. The rationale is that since the federal district courts have only original jurisdiction, they do not have appellate jurisdiction to review state judgments. Federal court appellate jurisdiction over state court judgments is vested exclusively in the U.S. Supreme Court.[24]

The lower federal courts have struggled to determine the contours of the *Rooker-Feldman* doctrine.[25] In *Exxon Mobil Corporation v. Saudi Basic Industries Corporation,*[26] the U.S. Supreme Court found that some lower federal courts had interpreted the *Rooker-Feldman* doctrine "far beyond" its intended contours by "overriding Congress' conferral of federal-court jurisdiction concurrent with the jurisdiction exercised by state courts, and superseding the ordinary application of preclusion law pursuant to 28 U.S.C.

20. *See* Chapman v. Houston W.R.O., 441 U.S. 600 (1978).
21. A federal court with subject matter jurisdiction over a § 1983 claim may decline to exercise that jurisdiction over one or more of the abstention doctrines. See Part XX, *infra.*
22. 263 U.S. 413 (1923).
23. 460 U.S. 462 (1983).
24. 28 U.S.C. § 1257.
25. *See* SCHWARTZ, *supra* note 18, § 1.07.
26. 544 U.S. 280, 125 S. Ct. 1517 (2005) (non-§ 1983).

§ 1738."[27] The Court in *Exxon Mobil* clarified that the *Rooker-Feldman* doctrine is confined to federal court actions "bought by state-court losers complaining of injuries caused by state-court judgments rendered before the district court proceedings commenced."[28] The Court in *Exxon Mobil* made clear that the *Rooker-Feldman* doctrine does not apply merely because "parallel" suits have been filed in state and federal court, even if the state suit comes to judgment during the pendency of federal suit. The Court said that "the pendency of an action in the State Court is no bar to proceedings concerning the same matter in the federal court having jurisdiction."[29]

The Court's statement that "[s]ince *Feldman*, this Court has never applied *Rooker-Feldman* to dismiss an action for want of jurisdiction"[30] seems designed to emphasize the narrowness of the doctrine. The Court in *Exxon Mobil* acknowledged that *Rooker-Feldman* does not "override or supplant" preclusion and abstention doctrines, and that these doctrines may be relevant when the federal court action parallels a state court suit. Unfortunately, the decision in *Exxon Mobil* provided no guidance on the issue that has given the lower federal courts the most difficulty, namely, determining whether the federal court complaint contests the validity of a state court judgment. The critical inquiry is "whether the injury alleged by the federal plaintiff resulted from the state court judgment itself or is distinct from that judgment."[31] This principle is easy to state though often difficult to apply.

The Supreme Court has recognized that the *Rooker-Feldman* doctrine may apply even when the federal court claim that is the subject of federal suit was not determined in the state court proceeding, if that claim was "inextricably intertwined" with the state court judgment.[32] The lower federal courts have experienced difficulties in applying this concept.[33]

The *Rooker-Feldman* doctrine does not apply to a federal suit brought by a plaintiff who was not a party to the state court proceeding.[34] Nor does

---

27. *Exxon Mobil*, 125 S. Ct. at 1517, 1527.
28. 125 S. Ct. at 1521–22. *Accord* Lance v. Dennis, 126 S. Ct. 1198 (2006).
29. *Id.* at 1526–27 (quoting McClellan v. Carland, 217 U.S. 268, 282 (1910)).
30. *Id.* at 1523.
31. Garry v. Geils, 82 F.3d 1362, 1365 (7th Cir. 1996). *Accord* Guttman v. Khalsa, 410 F.3d 1170 (10th Cir. 2005); Kenman Engineering v. City of Union, 314 F.3d 468 (10th Cir. 2002).
32. *Exxon Mobil*, 125 S. Ct. at 1523 n.1 (citing District of Columbia Court of Appeals v. Feldman, 460 U.S. 462 (1983)).
33. A federal claim is "inextricably intertwined" with the state court judgment when "the federal claim succeeds to the extent that the state court wrongly decided the issues before it." Allstate Ins. Co. v. W. Va. State Bar, 233 F.3d 813, 816 (4th Cir. 2000).
34. Johnson v. De Grandy, 512 U.S. 997 (1994); Holiday Amusement v. South Carolina, 400 F.3d 534 (4th Cir. 2005); Twin City Fire Ins. Co. v. Adkins, 400 F.3d 293

the *Rooker-Feldman* doctrine apply when the federal court plaintiff seeks review of a state administrative or executive determination.[35]

2. *Supplemental Jurisdiction*

In many § 1983 actions the federal court plaintiff seeks to assert one or more state law claims along with the § 1983 claim. In these § 1983 actions the plaintiff normally is unable to establish diversity jurisdiction over the state law claim because the parties usually are not citizens of different states. Nevertheless, the state law claim may come within the federal court's supplemental jurisdiction. The supplemental jurisdiction statute, 28 U.S.C. § 1367, codifies the *United Mine Workers v. Gibbs*[36] doctrine of pendent jurisdiction. Section 1367(a) grants the federal district courts supplemental jurisdiction "over all other claims that are so related to claims" over which the federal district court has original jurisdiction "that they form part of the same case or controversy under Article III. . . ." In *United Mine Workers v. Gibbs* the Supreme Court held that a pendent claim is part of the same Article III controversy when the pendent claim arises out of the "same nucleus of operative fact" as the jurisdictional conferring claim.

Like pendent jurisdiction, supplemental jurisdiction is a matter of both power and discretion. Thus, § 1367(c) provides that the district court may *decline* to exercise its supplemental jurisdiction when the supplemental claim "raises a novel or complex issue of state law"; the state law claim "substantially predominates over" the jurisdiction conferring claim; the district court has dismissed the jurisdiction conferring claim; or in other "exceptional circumstances."

Assume that the plaintiff asserts a non-insubstantial § 1983 constitutional claim against Officer Jones. Under § 1367, the plaintiff may assert a "supplemental" state law claim arising out of the same incident against Jones. Or, the plaintiff might choose to assert a "supplemental" state law claim against a new "supplemental party" defendant, for example, a state law vicarious liability claim against the city, even though there is no independent jurisdictional basis for the claim against the city.[37] In other words, the supplemental jurisdiction statute encompasses both pendent claim and

---

(6th Cir. 2005). *See also* Lance v. Dennis, 126 S. Ct. 1198 (2006) (*Rooker-Feldman* doctrine not applicable when federal court plaintiff was not party to state judgment, even if, for purpose of preclusion federal plaintiff was in privity with party to state judgment).

35. Verizon of Md., Inc. v. Public Serv. Comm'n of Md., 535 U.S. 635, 644 n.3 (2002).
36. 383 U.S. 715, 725 (1966).
37. *See* Jinks v. Richland County, 538 U.S. 456 (2003) (supplemental jurisdiction may be asserted in § 1983 actions against municipalities).

pendent party jurisdiction.[38] It also encompasses counterclaims, cross-claims, and impleader claims.[39]

The Supreme Court held that a state court judicial review claim may come within the district court's supplemental jurisdiction.[40] On the other hand, the Court has held that the supplemental jurisdiction statute does not override the Eleventh Amendment and thus does not authorize district courts to exercise supplemental jurisdiction over claims against nonconsenting states.[41]

Section 1367(d) of the supplemental jurisdiction statute provides for the tolling of the limitations period for supplemental claims while they are pending in federal court and for 30 days following a federal court's dismissal of a supplemental claim, unless state law provides for a longer tolling period.[42] The Supreme Court held that the supplemental jurisdiction tolling provision does not apply when a federal court dismisses a supplemental claim against a state on Eleventh Amendment grounds.[43] The tolling provision does apply to claims against municipal entities.[44]

3. *Removal Jurisdiction*

State court defendants who are sued under § 1983 may remove the action to federal court.[45] A state court complaint alleging a § 1983 federal constitutional claim and a state law claim may be removed to federal court and the federal court *may* exercise supplemental jurisdiction over the state law claim.[46] When a state court complaint asserts a § 1983 personal capacity

---

38. *See* Exxon Mobil Corporation v. Allapattah 125 S. Ct. 2611, 2620–21 (2005) (Court recognized that § 1367 overturned decision in Finley v. United States, 490 U.S. 545 (1989) rejecting pendent party jurisdiction, in actions under the Federal Tort Claims Act: "The last sentence of § 1367 makes it clear that the grant of supplemental jurisdiction extends to claims involving joinder or intervention of additional parties. . . . § 1367(a) is a broad jurisdictional grant with no distinctions drawn between pendent-claim and pendent-party cases. . . . The terms of §1367 do not acknowledge any distinctions between pendent jurisdiction and so-called ancillary jurisdiction.").
39. *Id.*
40. *See* Chicago v. Int'l College of Surgeons, 522 U.S. 156 (1997).
41. Raygor v. Regents of University of Minnesota, 534 U.S. 533 (2002). *Cf.* Jinks v. Richland County, 538 U.S. 456 (2003) (supplemental jurisdiction may be asserted in § 1983 action against municipality).
42. *See* Jinks v. Richland County, 538 U.S. 456 (2003) (§ 1367(d) tolling provision is within Congress's legislative power, does not impermissibly intrude upon states' rights, and encompasses claims against municipal entities).
43. Raygor v. Regents of University of Minnesota, 543 U.S. 533 (2002).
44. Jinks v. Richland County, 538 U.S. 459 (2003)
45. 28 U.S.C. § 1441(a) and (b).
46. *Supra* note 40.

claim and a claim against a state entity that is barred by the Eleventh Amendment, the action is removable to federal court, which can hear the nonbarred claims.[47] The state's removal of a state court suit to federal court waives the state's Eleventh Amendment immunity from liability on a state law claim to which the state had waived its sovereign immunity in the state court.[48]

E. State Court Jurisdiction

State courts have concurrent jurisdiction over § 1983 claims.[49] When federal claims are asserted in state court, "federal law takes the state courts as it finds them."[50] This means that "[s]tates may establish the rules of procedure governing litigation in their own courts[,]" for example, neutral rules of procedure governing service of process and substitution of parties.[51] On the other hand, state courts may not apply state rules that unduly burden, frustrate, or discriminate against the federal claim for relief. For example, the Supreme Court has held that a state court may not apply a state notice-of-claim requirement to a § 1983 claim, because notice-of-claim provisions discriminate and unduly burden a plaintiff with claims against governmental entities.[52]

The elements of the § 1983 claim for relief and the defenses to the § 1983 claim are matters of federal law, and they may not be modified on the basis of state law.[53] The Supreme Court in *Howlett v. Rose*[54] held that state law immunity defenses may not be applied to state court § 1983 claims. In U.S. Supreme Court decisions arising from state court § 1983 actions, the Court has normally held that the same rules that govern the liti-

---

47. Wisconsin Dep't of Corrections v. Schacht, 524 U.S. 381 (1998).

48. Lapides v. Board of Regents, 535 U.S. 613 (2002). See Part XIII (Eleventh Amendment).

49. National Private Truck Council v. Oklahoma Tax Comm'n, 515 U.S. 582 (1995); Howlett v. Rose, 496 U.S. 356 (1990); Felder v. Casey, 487 U.S. 131 (1988); Arkansas Writers' Project v. Ragland, 481 U.S. 221 (1987); Patsy v. Bd. of Regents, 457 U.S. 496 (1982). *See* S. STEINGLASS, SECTION 1983 LITIGATION IN STATE COURTS (West), and Chapter 3, *infra,* for a more detailed discussion of this subject.

50. S. STEINGLASS, SECTION 1983 LITIGATION IN STATE COURTS, § 10.1, p. 10-1 (quoting Hart, *The Relations Between State and Federal Law,* 54 COLUM. L. REV. 489, 508 (1954)).

51. Felder v. Casey, 487 U.S. 131, 138, 145 (1988).

52. Felder v. Casey, 487 U.S. 131 (1988) (state notice-of-claim rule not applicable to § 1983 claims). *See generally* Brown v. Western Ky., 338 U.S. 294, 296–99 (1949) (local practice rules may not unduly burden the federal right).

53. Howlett v. Rose, 496 U.S. 956 (1990).

54. *Id.*

gation of § 1983 actions in federal court also govern the litigation of § 1983 actions in state court.[55]

---

55. *See* National Private Truck Council v. Oklahoma Tax Comm'n, 515 U.S. 582 (1995) (policies of Tax Injunction Act apply in state court § 1983 actions challenging state tax policies); Howlett v. Rose, 496 U.S. 956 (1990) (state law immunity defense is not applicable to § 1983 municipal liability claim); Felder v. Casey, 487 U.S. 131 (1987) (state notice-of-claim rules are not applicable in state or federal court § 1983 actions); Will v. Michigan Department of State Police, 491 U.S. 58 (1989) (state liability under § 1983: whether § 1983 claim is filed in state or federal court, states and state entities are not § 1983 persons). However, state courts are not obligated to grant § 1983 defendants a right of interlocutory appeal from the denial of qualified immunity even when there is a right to an interlocutory qualified immunity appeal in federal court. Johnson v. Frankel, 520 U.S. 911 (1997) (*See* Part XV, *infra*).
Pleadings: It is unclear whether state courts are required to apply the federal court's liberal notice pleading standards in state court § 1983 actions. It has been suggested that "state courts that desire to apply strict pleading requirements should be able to do so only if their pleading rules do not burden § 1983." Steinglass, *Litigating Section 1983 Actions in State Courts,* p. 41 (2003), in 20TH ANNUAL SECTION 1983 CIVIL RIGHTS LITIGATION (Practicing Law Institute Course Handbook H-700, 2003). The Supreme Court stated: "Should this Court fail to protect federally created rights from dismissal because of over-exacting local requirements for meticulous pleadings, desirable uniformity in adjudication of federal rights could not be achieved." Brown v. Western Railway of Alabama, 338 U.S. 294, 299 (1950) (action under Federal Employers' Liability Act).
Burden of Proof: Shaw v. Leatherberry, 706 N.W. 2d 299 (Wis. 2005) (federal preponderance of evidence standard that governs federal court § 1983 excessive force claims governs these claims in state court as well).
Discovery: Some state court decisions hold that discovery in state court § 1983 actions is governed by the Federal Rules of Civil Procedure rather than by state law. Mann v. Alvarez, 242 A.D. 2d 318, 661 N.Y.S. 2d 250 (2d Dept. 1997) (discovery of police officer personnel files is governed by the Federal Rules of Civil Procedure rather than by New York Civil Rights Law § 50-a). *See also* Svaigsen v. City of New York, 203 A.D. 2d 32, 609 N.Y.S. 2d 894 (1st Dept. 1994). In the author's view, discovery in state court § 1983 actions should be governed by neutral state discovery rules unless the state discovery rule unduly burdens, frustrates, discriminates against, or otherwise conflicts with the § 1983 claim for relief.
Preclusion: State courts sometimes have to decide whether a determination in a federal court § 1983 action precludes litigation of a state law claim in state court. *See* 1A SCHWARTZ, SECTION 1983 LITIGATION: CLAIMS AND DEFENSES, ch. 11 (4th ed. 2005). Federal preclusion principles generally apply in these circumstances. If a federal court rejects a state law claim on the merits, that determination will normally preclude relitigation of that claim in state court. *Id.* What if the state claim was not asserted in the federal court action? When a § 1983 claim was litigated in federal court, and no state law claim was asserted in federal court, whether the

III. SECTION 1983 PLAINTIFFS

A wide range of plaintiffs are considered "persons" who are entitled to sue under § 1983. The right to sue under § 1983 is not limited to U.S. citizens. Legal and even illegal aliens are entitled to sue under § 1983.[56] Nor is the right to sue limited to individuals. Both profit and nonprofit organizations may sue under § 1983.[57] However, the Supreme Court held that a Native American tribe that sought to vindicate its sovereign status was not entitled to sue under § 1983.[58] The Court reasoned that "Section 1983 was designed to secure private rights against government encroachment, not to advance a sovereign's prerogative to withhold evidence relevant to a criminal investigation."[59]

Whether the plaintiff is a "person" entitled to sue under § 1983 is a question separate and distinct from whether the plaintiff has standing to sue. For example, Michael Newdow, who sought to challenge the constitutionality of a school policy requiring teacher-led recitation of the Pledge of Allegiance, was clearly a "person" entitled to sue under § 1983, but the Supreme Court held that he did not have standing to challenge the constitutionality of the Pledge of Allegiance.[60] There is extensive decisional law governing standing to sue in federal court. This decisional law establishes three Article III standing requirements: (1) actual or threatened injury; (2) fairly traced to the defendant's conduct; and (3) a sufficient likelihood that the injury will be redressed by a favorable decision on the merits.[61] In addition to the Article III requirements, the Supreme Court has formulated "prudential" standing requirements. The most important of the prudential rules is the rule

---

federal court judgment precludes litigation of the state law claim in state court will normally depend upon the likelihood that the federal court would have asserted supplemental jurisdiction over the state law claim. *Id.*

56. *See* 1A Schwartz, Section 1983 Litigation: Claims and Defenses, ch. 2 (4th ed. 2005).

57. *Id.*

58. Inyo County v. Pauite-Shoshone Indians, 538 U.S. 701, 712 (2003) (citing Will v. Michigan Dep't of State Police, 491 U.S. 58, 66 (1989)).

59. *Id. See also* Skokomish Indian Tribe v. United States, 410 F.3d 506, 514–15 (9th Cir. 2005) (en banc) (plaintiff Tribe asserted "communal fishing rights reserved to it, as a sovereign, by a treaty it entered into with the United States"; circuit court held that the Tribe could not assert its treaty-based rights under § 1983, because Tribe is not a "person" entitled to sue under §1983 for violation of a sovereign prerogative; nor were the tribe members entitled to sue, because the asserted fishing treaty rights were communal rights of the Tribe, even though the individual members benefit from these rights).

60. Elk Grove United School District v. Newdow, 542 U.S. 1 (2004).

61. *See, e.g.*, Allen v. Wright, 468 U.S. 737 (1984); Warth v. Seldin, 422 U.S. 490 (1975). *Accord* Daimler Chrysler Corp. v. Cuno, 126 S. Ct. 1854, 1861 (2006).

against third-party standing that generally requires the plaintiff to assert her own rights and not the rights of a third party.[62]

To establish standing to seek prospective relief, the plaintiff must demonstrate a realistic probability that she will again be subjected to the same injurious conduct.[63] In *Los Angeles v. Lyons*,[64] the plaintiff sought an injunction against the use of chokeholds by Los Angles police officers where the police were not threatened with serious harm. The Supreme Court held that "Lyons' standing to seek the injunction requested depended on whether he was likely to suffer future injury from the use of the chokehold by police officers."[65] Because Lyons could not demonstrate a substantial likelihood that he would again be subjected to the chokehold, he did not have standing to seek prospective relief. Of course, Lyons did have standing to seek damages for past harm from being subjected to the chokehold.

IV. CONSTITUTIONAL RIGHTS ENFORCEABLE UNDER SECTION 1983

A very wide range of federal constitutional rights may be enforced under § 1983 against defendants who acted under color of state law. These rights encompass the Fourteenth Amendment rights to substantive and procedural due process and to the equal protection of the laws. The provisions of the Bill of Rights that have been incorporated into the Due Process Clause of the Fourteenth Amendment may be enforced under § 1983. These incorporated rights include the rights protected by the First Amendment free speech and religion clauses (the free exercise and establishment clauses), the Fourth Amendment protection against unreasonable searches and seizures, and the Eighth Amendment protection against cruel and unusual punishment.

Section 1983 is not limited to the enforcement of Fourteenth Amendment rights. In *Dennis v. Higgins*,[66] the Supreme Court held that the Dormant Commerce Clause, also referred to as the "negative implications" of the commerce clause, is enforceable under § 1983. The Dormant Commerce Clause imposes constitutional limitations on the power of the states to regulate interstate commerce.

---

62. *See* E. Chemerinsky, Federal Jurisdiction, § 2.3.4 (4th ed. 2003). Exceptions to the rule against third-party standing allow a party to assert the rights of a third party when the rights of the litigant before the court and the third party are closely related (e.g., physician and patient) or where an obstacle prevents the third party from asserting her own claim. Singleton v. Wulff, 428 U.S. 106 (1976).
63. Los Angeles v. Lyons, 461 U.S. 95 (1983).
64. *Id.*
65. *Id.* at 105.
66. 498 U.S. 439 (1991).
67. 493 U.S. 103 (1989).

In *Golden State Transportation Corporation v. Los Angeles*,[67] however, the Supreme Court held that the Supremacy Clause does not create rights that are enforceable under § 1983. Rather, the Supremacy Clause dictates that state and local laws that are in conflict with federal statutes are unenforceable. When state action is alleged to violate a federal statute, the pertinent issue is whether the particular federal statute creates rights enforceable under § 1983.[68]

Whether the plaintiff has alleged a proper constitutional claim under § 1983 depends upon an interpretation of the particular constitutional provision at issue, not upon an interpretation of § 1983. For example, in *Graham v. Connor*,[69] the Supreme Court held that claims of excessive force during an arrest, investigatory stop, or other seizure are evaluated under a Fourth Amendment objective reasonableness standard.[70] The Court in *Graham* rejected the existence of "a generic 'right' to be from excessive force, grounded . . . in 'basic principles of § 1983 jurisprudence.'"[71] "In addressing an excessive force claim brought under § 1983, analysis begins by identifying the specific constitutional right allegedly infringed by the challenged application of force."[72]

Large numbers of Fourth Amendment challenges to warrantless arrests are asserted under § 1983. The key issue in these cases is whether the arresting officer had probable cause. Probable cause exists when the facts and cir-

---

68. *See* Part V, *infra.*
69. 490 U.S. 386 (1989).
70. The Court in *Graham* held that "*all* claims that law enforcement officers have used excessive force—deadly or not—in the course of an arrest . . . should be analyzed under the Fourth Amendment and its 'reasonableness' standard." Graham, 490 U.S. at 395. *See also* Tennessee v. Garner, 471 U.S. 1 (1995) (deadly force). In determining whether the use of force was objectively reasonable, courts consider, inter alia, the severity of the crime, whether the suspect poses an immediate threat to the safety of the officer or others, and whether the suspect is attempting to resist or evade arrest. Graham, 490 U.S. at 396. "The calculus of reasonableness must embody allowance for the fact that police officers are often forced to make split-second judgments—in circumstances that are tense, uncertain, and rapidly evolving—about the amount of force that is necessary in a particular situation." *Id.* at 396–97. Fourth Amendment excessive force claims are subject to qualified immunity. Saucier v. Katz, 533 U.S. 194 (2001) (*See* Part XV, *infra*).
71. Graham, 490 U.S. at 393.
72. *Id.* at 394. Excessive force claims asserted by convicted prisoners are governed by the Eighth Amendment prohibition against cruel and unusual punishment. To establish an Eighth Amendment violation, the plaintiff must show that the force was applied "maliciously and sadistically to cause harm" rather than "in a good-faith effort to maintain or restore discipline." Hudson v. McMillian, 503 U.S. 1, 7 (1992); Whitley v. Albers, 475 U.S. 312 (1986). Excessive force claims asserted by pretrial detainees are governed by the substantive due process prohibition against the infliction of "punishment" on pretrial detainees. *See generally* Bell v. Wolfish, 441 U.S. 520 (1979).

cumstances known to the officer would lead a reasonably prudent person to conclude that the suspect committed, or was committing, an offense.[73] Because probable cause is a wholly objective standard, the officer's subjective belief or intent is irrelevant.[74] Probable cause is a complete defense to a § 1983 Fourth Amendment unconstitutional arrest claim.[75]

Large numbers of § 1983 claims allege free speech retaliation claims. These claims frequently give rise to difficult legal issues and sharply contested factual issues.[76] The majority of these claims are asserted by present and former public employees (*see* Chapter 6, *infra*). First Amendment retaliation claims are also asserted by individuals subject to criminal prosecution, government contractors, prisoners, and landowners, among others. The key issues in these cases are (1) whether the plaintiff spoke out on a matter of public concern; (2) if so, whether the defendant took adverse action against the plaintiff for doing so; and (3) whether the governmental interest outweighs the plaintiff's free speech interests.[77]

Violations of state law are not enforceable under § 1983.[78] When governmental conduct is not proscribed by a textually explicit provision of the Bill of Rights, the Supreme Court has generally rejected substantive due

---

73. Michigan v. Defillipo, 443 U.S. 31 (1979); Beck v. Ohio, 379 (1964). *See also* Maryland v. Pringle, 124 S. Ct. 795 (2003). The Fourth Amendment is satisfied so long as the arresting officer had probable cause to arrest for *any* crime; there need not be probable cause for the offense articulated by the arresting officer or even for an offense "closely related" to the articulated offense. Devenpeck v. Alford, 543 U.S. 146 (2004). Because § 1983 false arrest claims are subject to qualified immunity, the officer will be protected from personal liability so long as she reasonably though mistakenly believed there was probable cause. *See generally* Anderson v. Creighton, 483 U.S. 635 (1981) (*See* Part XV, *infra*). Stated differently, for the purpose of qualified immunity it is sufficient that the officer had "arguable" probable cause.
74. Whren v. United States, 517 U.S. 806 (1996).
75. Weyant v. Okst, 101 F.3d 845 (2d Cir. 1996); Singer v. Fulton County Sheriff, 63 F.3d 110 (2d Cir. 1995), *cert. denied,* 517 U.S. 1189 (1996).
76. *See* 1 Schwartz, Section 1983 Litigation: Claims and Defenses, ch. 3 (4th ed. 2005).
77. *Id.*
78. *See, e.g.,* Baker v. McCollan, 443 U.S. 137, 146 (1979) ("Just as '[m]edical malpractice does not become a constitutional violation merely because the victim is a prisoner,' Estelle v. Gamble, 429 U.S. 97, 106 (1976), false imprisonment does not become a violation of the Fourteenth Amendment merely because the defendant is a state official."); Voytickey v. Village of Timberlake, 412 F.3d 669 (6th Cir. 2005) (intentional infliction of emotional distress does not itself give rise to § 1983 constitutional claim). Violations of state constitutional rights are not enforceable under § 1983. *See, e.g.,* Raadvansky v. City of Olmstead Falls, 395 F.3d 291, 314 (6th Cir. 2005) ("[A] claimed violation of a state constitutional right is not cognizable under § 1983."); Bookman v. Shubzda, 945 F. Supp. 999 (N.D. Tex. 1996).

process protections and left the plaintiff to available state tort remedies.[79] For example, in *Baker v. McCollan*[80] the Court held that "[f]alse imprisonment does not become a violation of the Fourteenth Amendment merely because the defendant is a state official." Similarly in *Paul v. Davis*,[81] the Court held that defamation by a government official does not itself violate the Federal Constitution. The Court in *Paul* stated that § 1983 is not a "font

---

79. *See, e.g.,* Collins v. Harker Heights, 503 U.S. 115 (1992) (safe working conditions); DeShaney v. Winnebago County Dep't of Social Services, 489 U.S. 189 (1989) (protection of children from parental abuse); Paul v. Davis, 424 U.S. 693 (1976) (defamation). The Supreme Court recognized substantive due process protection in high-speed police pursuit cases, but imposed a very demanding burden on plaintiffs. County of Sacramento v. Lewis, 523 U.S. 833 (1998) (passengers killed or injured as result of high-speed police pursuit may assert substantive due process claim under "shocks the conscience standard" and must show pursuing officer acted with intent to cause harm).

In *DeShaney,* the Supreme Court held that as a general rule the state does not have a due process duty to protect a private individual from being harmed by another private individual, even when the state knows of the risk of harm and has taken some action to protect the individual in the past. The state does have a due process duty to protect persons in state custody, such as convicted prisoners, Farmer v. Brennan, 511 U.S. 825 (1994), and involuntarily committed mental patients. Youngberg v. Romeo, 457 U.S. 307 (1982). Lower courts consistently hold that the state has a due process duty to protect children it places in foster care. *See, e.g.,* Nicini v. Morra, 212 F.3d 798 (3d Cir. 2000) (en banc); Lintz v. Skipski, 25 F.3d 304 (6th Cir.) *cert. denied,* 513 U.S. 988 (1994); Norfleet v. Dep't of Social Services, 989 F.2d 289 (8th Cir. 1993); Yvonne L. v. Dep't of Human Services, 959 F.2d 883 (10th Cir. 1992); Taylor v. Ledbetter, 818 F.2d 791 (11th Cir. 1987) (en banc), *cert. denied,* 489 U.S. 1065 (1989); Doe v. Dep't of Social Services, 649 F.2d 134 (2d Cir. 1981), *cert. denied,* 464 U.S. 864 (1983). Most circuit courts have held that due process is violated when the state enhances the risk of an individual being harmed by another private individual. *See* 1 SCHWARTZ, SECTION 1983 LITIGATION: CLAIMS AND DEFENSES, § 3.09.

A claim that state or municipal officials have breached a contact does not give rise to § 1983 claim. Lujan v. G & G Fire Sprinklers, Inc., 532 U.S. 189, 196 (2001) (breach of contract by state did not give rise to procedural due process claim, because state law provided "ordinary breach-of-contract suit"); Redondo-Borges v. U.S. Dep't of Housing & Urban Dev., 421 F.3d 1 (1st Cir. 2005); Dover Elevator Co. v. Ark. State Univ., 64 F.3d 442, 446 (8th Cir. 1995) ("it is well established that 'a simple breach of contract does not give rise to the level of a constitutional deprivation.'") (quoting Medical Laundry Servs. v. Board of Trustees of Univ. of Ala., 906 F.3d 571, 573 (11th Cir. 1990)); Gannett Flemming West, Inc. v. Village of Angel Fire, 375 F. Supp.2d 1104 (D.N.M. 2004); Bock Assoc. v. Chronister, 951 F. Supp. 969 (D. Kan. 1996).

80. 443 U.S. 137, 146 (1979).

81. 424 U.S. 693 (1976).

of tort law to be superimposed upon whatever system may already be administered by the states."[82]

In *Collins v. Harker Heights*,[83] the Supreme Court held that a claim that the city breached its duty of care to its employees by failing to provide a safe working environment was "analogous to a fairly typical state law tort claim" and was not cognizable under § 1983. The Court stated:

> Because the Due Process Clause does not purport to supplant traditional tort law in laying down rules of conduct to regulate liability for injuries that attend living together in society . . . we [reject] claims that the Due Process Clause should be interpreted to impose federal duties that are analogous to those traditionally imposed by state tort law.[84]

However, in some cases state law may have a significant, even decisive, impact on a federal constitutional right. For example, whether the plaintiff has a protected property interest for the purpose of the Due Process Clause of the Fourteenth Amendment depends upon whether state law creates a reasonable expectation in the particular interest. In *Board of Regents v. Roth*[85] the Supreme Court held that "[p]roperty interests . . . are not created by the Constitution. Rather, they are created and their dimensions are defined by existing rules or understandings that stem from an independent source such as state law-rules or understandings. . . ." Further, under the *Parratt/Hudson* doctrine, when the deprivation of property or liberty results from "random and unauthorized" governmental action, the availability of an adequate post-deprivation remedy will satisfy procedural due process.[86]

V. ENFORCEMENT OF FEDERAL STATUTES UNDER SECTION 1983

Some federal statutory rights may be enforced under § 1983. In *Maine v. Thiboutot*,[87] the Supreme Court rejected the argument that only federal statutes dealing with "equal rights" or "civil rights" are enforceable under § 1983. The Court in *Thiboutot* held that § 1983's reference to "laws" of the

82. *Id.* at 701.
83. 503 U.S. 115, 128 (1992).
84. 503 U.S. 115, 128 (1992) (citing Daniels v. Williams, 474 U.S. 327, 332–33 (1986); Baker v. McCollan, 443 U.S. 137, 146 (1979); Paul v. Davis, 424 U.S. 693 (1976)).
85. 408 U.S. 564, 577 (1972).
86. Hudson v. Palmer, 468 U.S. 517 (1984); Parratt v. Taylor, 451 U.S. 527 (1981). It is not always easy to determine whether the deprivation resulted from "random and unauthorized" governmental action. *See, e.g.,* Zinnelman v. Burch, 494 U.S. 113 (1990).
87. 448 U.S. 1 (1980).

United States means what it says and, therefore, all federal statutes are enforceable under § 1983 against defendants who acted under color of state law. However, subsequent Supreme Court decisions substantially cut back the decision in *Thiboutot* by holding that not all federal statutes are enforceable under § 1983.[88]

For a federal statute to be enforceable under § 1983, "a plaintiff must assert the violation of a federal *right*, not merely a violation of federal *law*."[89] The Supreme Court has identified three factors to determine whether a particular federal statutory provision creates a federal right:

> First, Congress must have intended that the provision in question benefit the plaintiff.[90]
>
> Second, the plaintiff must demonstrate that the right assertedly protected by the statute is not so "vague and amorphous" that its enforcement would strain judicial competence.[91]
>
> Third, the statute must unambiguously impose a binding obligation on the States. In other words, the provision giving rise to the asserted right must be couched in mandatory rather than precatory terms.[92]

The pertinent issue is not whether the federal statutory scheme creates enforceable rights, but whether the *specific* federal statutory provision at issue creates enforceable rights.[93]

If the plaintiff demonstrates that a federal statute creates an enforceable right, there is "a rebuttable presumption that the right is enforceable under § 1983."[94] Defendant has the burden of rebutting the presumption by showing that Congress intended to preclude enforcement under § 1983.[95] Con-

---

88. *See, e.g.,* City of Rancho Palos Verdes v. Abrams, 544 U.S. 113 (2005); Gonzaga University v. Doe, 536 U.S. 273 (2002); Suter v. Artist M., 503 U.S. 347 (1992); Middlesex County Sewerage Authority v. National Sea Clammers Ass'n, 453 U.S. 1 (1981).
89. Blessing v. Freestone, 520 U.S. 329, 340 (1997) (citing Golden State Transit Corp. v. Los Angeles, 493 U.S. 103 (1989)). *Accord* Gonzaga University v. Doe, 536 U.S. 273 (2002).
90. *Blessing,* 520 U.S. at 340 (quoting Wright v. Roanoke Redevelopment and Housing Authority, 479 U.S. 418, 430 (1987)).
91. *Blessing,* 520 U.S. at 340–41 (quoting *Wright,* 479 U.S. at 430).
92. *Blessing,* 520 U.S. at 341 (citing Wilder v. Virginia Hospital Ass'n, 496 U.S. 498, 500 (1990); Pennhurst State School and Hospital v. Halderman, 451 U.S. 1 (1981)).
93. Blessing v. Freestone, 520 U.S. 329 (1997).
94. *Blessing,* 520 U.S. at 341. *Accord* City of Rancho Palos Verdes v. Abrams, 544 U.S. 113 (2005).
95. *See* Smith v. Robinson, 468 U.S. 992 (1984). *See also* City of Rancho Palos Verdes v. Abrams, 544 U.S. 113 (2005).

gress may preclude enforcement under § 1983 either expressly or impliedly by creating a remedial scheme that is so comprehensive as to demonstrate a congressional intent to preclude enforcement under § 1983.[96] A congressional remedy that is very specific and circumscribed may also imply a congressional intent to preclude enforcement under § 1983.[97]

In recent years the Supreme Court has tightened up the standards for enforcing federal statutes under § 1983.[98] In *Gonzaga University v. Doe*,[99] the Court stated that to create an enforceable federal statutory right, Congress "must do so in clear and unambiguous terms—no less and no more than is required for Congress to create new rights under an implied right of action." The Court in *Gonzaga University* also strongly indicated that federal statutes enacted under the Spending Clause are unlikely to create private enforceable rights. The Court in *Gonzaga University* pointed out that it has found Spending Clause legislation enforceable under § 1983 only twice.[100]

The lower federal courts are in disagreement as to when a federal regulation is enforceable under § 1983.[101] Most of the recent decisions hold that "a federal regulation alone may not create a right enforceable through section 1983 not already found in the enforcing statute."[102] Under this view, "regulations give rise to a right of action [under § 1983] only insofar as they construe a personal right that a statute creates."[103] This position finds support in the Supreme Court's statement in *Alexander v. Sandoval*[104] that "language in a regulation may invoke a private right of action that Congress through statutory text created, but it may not create a right that Congress has not."

---

96. Middlesex County Sewerage Authority v. National Sea Clammers Ass'n, 453 U.S. 1 (1981).
97. City of Rancho Palos Verdes v. Abrams, 544 U.S. 113 (2005).
98. City of Rancho Palso Verde v. Abrams, 544 U.S. 113 (2005); Gonzaga University v. Doe, 536 U.S. 273 (2002); Blessing v. Freestone, 520 U.S 329 (1997); Suter v. Artist M., 503 U.S. 347 (1992).
99. 536 U.S. 273, 290 (2002).
100. *See* Wilder v. Virginia Hospital Ass'n Authority, 496 U.S. 498 (1990); Wright v. Roanoke Redevelopment and Housing Authority, 479 U.S. 418 (1987).
101. *See* 1 SCHWARTZ, SECTION 1983 LITIGATION: CLAIMS AND DEFENSES, § 4.04[A] (4th ed. 2005).
102. South Camden Citizens in Action v. New Jersey Dep't of Envt'l Protection, 274 F.3d 771, 790 (3d Cir. 2001), *cert. denied,* 536 U.S. 939 (2002). *See also* Wright v. Roanoke Redevelopment and Housing Authority, 479 U.S. 418 (1987); Harris v. James, 127 F.3d 993 (11th Cir. 1997).
103. Three Rivers Center for Independent Living v. Housing Authority of Pittsburgh, 382 F.3d 412, 424 (3d Cir. 2004).
104. 532 U.S. 275, 291 (2001).

VI. SECTION 1983 DEFENDANTS

Section 1983 authorizes assertion of a claim for relief against a "person" who acted under color of state law. A suable § 1983 "person" encompasses state and local officials sued in their personal capacities, municipal entities, municipal officials sued in an official capacity, but not states and state entities.

In *Will v. Michigan Department of State Police*,[105] the Supreme Court held that a suable "person" under § 1983 does not include a state, a state agency, or a state official sued in her official capacity for damages. However, the Court in *Will* ruled that a state official sued in an official capacity is a § 1983 "person" when sued for prospective relief.[106] In *Hafer v. Melo*,[107] the Supreme Court held that a state official sued for damages in her personal capacity is a § 1983 person, even though the claim for relief arose out of the official's official responsibilities. In its landmark decision in *Monell v. Department of Social Services*,[108] the Supreme Court held that municipalities and municipal officials sued in an official capacity are suable § 1983 persons.[109] Since a claim against a municipal official in her official capacity is tantamount to a suit against the municipal entity, when claims are asserted against both the municipal entity and a municipal official in her official capacity, federal courts typically dismiss the official capacity claim as "redundant" to the municipal entity claim.

Courts sometimes have to decide whether an official is a state as opposed to municipal policymaker in a particular subject area or on a particular issue. This is an important issue because municipal entities are suable § 1983 persons while state entities are not. In addition, Eleventh Amendment sovereign immunity protects state entities from federal court liability but provides no protection for municipal entities.[110] In *McMillian v. Monroe County*,[111] the Supreme Court held that whether an official is a state or municipal policymaker is "dependent on an analysis of state law." The Court in *McMillian* recognized that a particular official (e.g., the county sheriff) may be considered a state official in one state and a municipal official in another state. Furthermore, an official may be considered a state official for the purpose of one function and a municipal official for the purpose of another function. For example, district attorneys are normally considered

105. 491 U.S. 58 (1989).
106. Will, 491 U.S. at 71 n.10.
107. 502 U.S. 21 (1991).
108. 436 U.S 658 (1978).
109. "The District of Columbia is a municipality for the purpose of § 1983." People for Ethical Treatment of Animals v. Gittens, 396 F.3d 416, 425 (D.C. Cir. 2005).
110. *See* Part XIII, *infra*.
111. 510 U.S. 781, 786 (1997). See Part X, *infra*.

state officials when prosecuting crimes, but they are considered municipal officials when carrying out their administrative duties such as training staff.

It should be noted that municipal departments, offices, and commissioners are normally not considered suable entities. This is a matter of form rather than substance. It means simply that, for example, instead of naming the "police department" as a party defendant, the plaintiff should name as defendant the municipality (city, town, or village) of which the department is a part.

VII. COLOR OF STATE LAW AND STATE ACTION

An essential ingredient of a § 1983 claim is that the defendant acted under color of state law.[112] Furthermore, the Fourteenth Amendment imposes limitations only upon state action; it does not reach the conduct of private parties, no matter how discriminatory or harmful.[113] Neither § 1983 nor the Fourteenth Amendment reaches the conduct of federal officials or of purely private persons. "[P]ersons victimized by tortious conduct of private parties must ordinarily explore other avenues of redress."[114]

The Supreme Court and the lower courts have generally treated color of state law and state action as meaning the same thing.[115] A finding that the defendant was engaged in state action means that the defendant acted under color of state law. If the defendant was not engaged in state action, the Fourteenth Amendment is not implicated, and there is no reason for a court to determine whether the defendant acted under color of state law.

A. State and Local Officials

The clearest case of state action (and action under color of state law) is a public official who carried out her official responsibilities in accordance with state law. *Polk County v. Dodson*[116] is the only Supreme Court case that found that a state or local official who carried out her official responsibilities was not engaged in state action. The Court in *Polk County* held that a public defender's representation of an indigent criminal defendant was not under color of state law.[117] The Court reasoned that although the public defender is employed and paid by the state, when representing a criminal

112. Flagg Bros. v. Brooks, 436 U.S. 149 (1978).

113. Brentwood Academy v. Tennessee Secondary School Athletic Ass'n, 531 U.S. 288 (2001); American Manufacturers Mutual Insurance Co. v. Sullivan, 526 U.S. 40 (1999); Jackson v. Metropolitan Edison Co., 419 U.S. 345 (1974).

114. Roche v. John Hancock Mutual Life Ins. Co., 81 F.3d 249, 253 (1st Cir. 1996).

115. Lugar v. Edmonson Oil Co., 457 U.S. 922 (1982).

116. 454 U.S. 312 (1981).

117. *See* West v. Atkins, 487 U.S. 42, 50 (1988) (discussing *Polk County*).

defendant she acts not for the state, but as an adversary of the state, and not under color of state law, but pursuant to the attorney-client relationship with undivided loyalty to her client.

In *West v. Atkins*,[118] the Supreme Court held that a private physician who provides medical services to prisoners pursuant to a contract with the state acts under color of state law. Unlike the public defender in *Polk County*, the prison physician is not an adversary of the state. *West* seems to have been based primarily upon the fact that the prison physician performs a governmental function and carries out the state's constitutional obligation of providing medical care to prison inmates.[119]

1. Abuse of State Power

State and local officials who abuse their official power act under color of state law. The governing principle is that "'[m]isuse of power, possessed by virtue of state law and made possible only because the wrongdoer is clothed with the authority of state law, is action taken "under color of" state law.'"[120]

Courts often must determine whether an official abused governmental power or acted as a private individual (e.g., as an irate spouse). The issue often arises with respect to off-duty police officers. To determine whether an off-duty police officer acted under color of state law, courts consider such factors as whether an ordinance deemed the officer as being on duty for 24 hours; the officer identified herself as a police officer; the officer had or showed her service revolver or other police department weapon; the officer flashed her badge; the officer conducted a search or made an arrest; the officer intervened in an existing dispute pursuant to police department regulations (as opposed to instigating a dispute).[121]

B. State Action Tests

Courts frequently must determine whether a private party's involvement with state or local government justifies the conclusion that the party was engaged in "state action" for the purpose of the Fourteenth Amendment.

---

118. 487 U.S. 42 (1988).

119. *See* American Manufacturers Mutual Insurance Co. v. Sullivan, 526 U.S. 40, 55–58 (1999) (discussing West v. Atkins).

120. Monroe v. Pape, 365 U.S. 167, 184 (1961) (quoting United States v. Classic, 313 U.S. 299, 325–26 (1946)).

121. *See, e.g.,* Pickrel v. City of Springfield, 45 F.3d 1115 (7th Cir. 1995); Pitchell v. Callahan, 13 F.3d 545 (2d Cir. 1994); United States v. Tarpley, 945 F.2d 806 (5th Cir. 1991), *cert. denied,* 504 U.S. 917 (1992); Bonsignore v. City of New York, 683 F.2d 635 (2d Cir. 1982); Layne v. Sampley, 627 F.2d 12 (6th Cir. 1980); Stengel v. Belcher, 522 F.2d 438 (6th Cir. 1975), *cert. dismissed,* 429 U.S. 118 (1976).

The Supreme Court state action decisional law has advanced the following state action tests:

- symbiotic relationship
- public function
- close or joint nexus
- joint participation
- pervasive entwinement

The fact that these tests can be culled from the Supreme Court state action decisional law does not mean that all Supreme Court state action holdings have been based upon one of the above doctrines. At times, the Supreme Court has found state action based upon ad hoc evaluations of a variety of connections between the private party and the state.[122]

1. Symbiotic Relationship

The Supreme Court's decision in *Burton v. Wilmington Parking Authority*[123] is often cited to support the principle that state action is present when the state and private party have a symbiotic relationship.[124] Although the decision in *Burton* has not been overruled, the Supreme Court read *Burton* very narrowly as supporting a finding of state action only when the state profited from the private wrong.[125] Furthermore, the Supreme Court denigrated *Burton* as one of its "early" state action decisions containing "vague" "joint participation" language.[126]

2. Public Function

Supreme Court decisions state that there is state action when a private party carries out a function that has been historically and traditionally the "exclusive" prerogative of the state.[127] This is a very demanding standard that

---

122. *See* Georgia v. McCollum, 505 U.S. 42 (1992) (criminal defense lawyer's exercise of race-based preemptory challenge); Edmonson v. Leesville Concrete Co., 500 U.S. 614 (1991) (private civil litigants exercise at race-based preemptory challenge); West v. Atkins, 487 U.S. 42 (1988) (private physician's provision of medical care to inmates). *See also* Brentwood Academy v. Tennessee Secondary School Athletic Ass'n, 531 U.S. 288 (2001).

123. 365 U.S. 715 (1961).

124. *See* Moose Lodge v. Irvis, 407 U.S. 163, 175 (1972) (describing holding in *Burton*).

125. Rendell-Baker v. Kohn, 457 U.S. 830 (1982); Blum v. Yaretsky, 457 U.S. 991 (1982).

126. American Manufacturers Mutual Insurance Co. v. Sullivan, 526 U.S. 40 (1999).

127. Flagg Brothers v. Brooks, 436 U.S. 149 (1978); Jackson v. Metropolitan Edison Co., 419 U.S. 345 (1974).

§ 1983 plaintiffs find very difficult to satisfy. While many functions may be historically and traditionally governmental functions, very few are "exclusively" governmental functions. The Supreme Court has found state action under the public function doctrine in cases involving political primaries,[128] and has stated that eminent domain is an example of an exclusively governmental power.[129] The Supreme Court's decision in *West v. Atkins*[130] that a private physician's provision of medical care to prison inmates constitutes state action was based in part upon the fact that the physician carries out a governmental function of providing medical care to inmates.[131]

The Supreme Court has held that the following functions do not satisfy the public function doctrine, because they are not "exclusively" governmental functions:

a. insurance companies' suspension of workers' compensation benefits pending utilization committee review;[132]
b. education of maladjusted children;[133]
c. nursing-home care;[134]
d. coordination of amateur athletics;[135]
e. dispute resolution through forced sale of goods by a warehouse company to enforce a possessory lien;[136]
f. operation of a shopping mall;[137] and
g. provision of utility services.[138]

These decisions demonstrate that the fact that a function is an important government function is not sufficient to satisfy the public function test.

3. *Close Nexus Test*

Under the "sufficiently close nexus" test, state action is present if the state has ordered the private conduct, "exercised coercive power or has provided such significant encouragement, either overt or covert, that the choice must

128. Terry v. Adams, 345 U.S. 461 (1953).
129. *See* discussion in Jackson v. Metropolitan Edison Co., 419 U.S. 345, 353 (1974).
130. 487 U.S. 42 (1988).
131. *See* American Manufacturers Mutual Insurance Co., 526 U.S. at 55–58 (discussing *West*).
132. American Manufacturers Mutual Ins. Co. v. Sullivan, 526 U.S. 40 (1999).
133. Rendell-Baker v. Kohn, 457 U.S. 830 (1982).
134. Blum v. Yaretsky, 457 U.S. 991 (1982).
135. San Francisco Arts & Athletics v. U.S. Olympic Committee, 483 U.S. 522 (1987). *See also* National Collegiate Athletic Ass'n v. Tarkanian, 488 U.S. 179 (1988).
136. Flagg Bros. v. Brooks, 436 U.S. 149 (1970).
137. Hudgens v. NLRB, 424 U.S. 507 (1976).
138. Jackson v. Metropolitan Edison Co., 419 U.S. 345 (1974).

in law be deemed to be that of the State."[139] The federal courts have held that the following are not sufficient to satisfy this test:

a. state authorization of private conduct;[140]
b. a private party's use of a state furnished dispute resolution mechanism;[141]
c. a private party's request for police assistance;[142]
d. a private party's attempt to influence governmental action;[143]
e. state licensing and regulation, even if pervasive;[144] and
f. state financial assistance, even if extensive.[145]

The Supreme Court has found no state action even when several of these indicia of government involvement coalesced in the same case. The Court has held that private parties (such as a utility company, private school, and a nursing home) that were extensively regulated by the state, received substantial governmental assistance, carried out an important societal function, and acted pursuant to state authority were not engaged in state action.[146]

4. Joint Participation

A private party who jointly participates in the alleged constitutional wrongdoing with a state or local official is engaged in state action.[147] Joint participation requires (1) some type of conspiracy, agreement, or concerted action between the state and private party; (2) a showing that the state and private party shared common goals; and (3) conduct pursuant to the conspiracy, agreement, or concerted action that violated the plaintiff's federally protected rights. In *Dennis v. Sparks*,[148] the Supreme Court held that

---

139. Blum v. Yaretsky, 457 U.S. 991, 1004 (1982).
140. Flagg Bros. v. Brooks, 436 U.S. 149 (1978); Jackson v. Metropolitan Edison Co., 419 U.S. 345 (1974).
141. American Mutual Manufacturers Insurance Co. v. Sullivan, 526 U.S. 40 (1999).
142. *See, e.g.,* Ginsberg v. Healy Car & Truck Leasing, 189 F.3d 268 (2d Cir. 1999).
143. NCAA v. Tarkanian, 488 U.S. 179 (1988).
144. Rendell-Baker v. Kohn, 457 U.S. 830 (1982); Blum v. Yaretsky, 457 U.S. 991 (1982); Jackson v. Metropolitan Edison Co., 419 U.S. 345 (1974).
145. Rendell-Baker v. Kohn, 457 U.S. 830 (1982) (no state action even though educational institution received almost all of its funding from state). *See also* Jackson v. Metropolitan Edison Co., 419 U.S. 345 (1974) (state grant or monopoly power).
146. *See* Rendell-Baker v. Kohn, 45 U.S. 830 (1982) (school); Blum v. Yaretsky, 457 U.S. 991 (1982) (nursing home); Jackson v. Metropolitan Edison Co., 419 U.S. 345 (1974) (utility company).
147. *See* Lugar v. Edmonson Oil Co., 457 U.S. 922 (1982); Dennis v. Sparks, 449 U.S. 24 (1980); Adickes v. S. H. Kress & Co., 398 U.S. 144 (1970).
148. 449 U.S. 24 (1980).

private parties who corruptly conspire with a judge act under color of state law, even though the judge is protected by judicial immunity. In *National Collegiate Athletic Ass'n v. Tarkanian*,[149] the Supreme Court held that there was no joint action between the NCAA, a private entity, and the state university because they had diametrically opposite goals. The NCAA's goal was that the university's head basketball coach be suspended while the university sought to retain its prominent head coach.

5. *Pervasive Entwinement*

In *Brentwood Academy v. Tennessee Secondary School Athletic Ass'n*,[150] the Supreme Court held that a statewide interscholastic athletic association was engaged in state action because the state was "pervasively entwined" with the association. The Court relied heavily upon the fact that because almost all of the state's public schools were members of the association, there was a "largely overlapping identity" between the association and the state's public schools. The Court also relied upon the facts that the association's governing board was dominated by public school officials, most association revenue was derived from governmental funds, and the association carried out a function that otherwise would have to be carried out by the state board of education.

VIII. CAUSATION

Section 1983 by its terms authorizes the imposition of liability only upon a defendant who "subjects, or causes to be subjected, any citizen . . . or other person . . . to the deprivation of any rights" guaranteed by federal law. This language has been read by the Supreme Court as imposing a proximate cause requirement on § 1983 claims.[151] The great weight of judicial authority equates § 1983's causation requirement with common-law proximate cause.[152] This reading of § 1983 is consistent with the fundamental principle that § 1983 should be interpreted "against the background of tort liability that makes a [person] responsible for the natural consequences of his actions."[153]

---

149. 488 U.S. 179 (1988).

150. 531 U.S. 288 (2001).

151. Martinez v. California, 444 U.S. 277 (1980).

152. Murray v. Earle, 405 F.3d 278 (5th Cir. 2005) (proximate cause under § 1983 is evaluated under common-law standards); McKinley v. City of Mansfield, 404 F.3d 418, 438 (6th Cir. 2005) ("causation in the constitutional sense is no different than causation in the common law sense"). Questions of causation "are generally best left to the jury. . . ." Young v. City of Providence, 404 F.3d 4, 23 (1st Cir. 2005) (citing Wortley v. Camplin, 333 F.3d 288, 295 (1st Cir. 2003)).

153. Monroe v. Pape, 365 U.S. 167, 187 (1961). *Accord* Malley v. Briggs, 475 U.S. 335, 344 n.7 (1986).

A § 1983 defendant may be held liable for "reasonably foreseeable consequences attributable to intervening forces, including acts of third parties."[154] On the other hand, a § 1983 defendant may not be held liable when an intervening cause was not reasonably foreseeable, or when the link between the defendant's conduct and the plaintiff's injuries is too remote, tenuous, or speculative.[155] "In the context of criminal law enforcement, courts have differed as to the circumstances under which acts of subsequent participants in the legal system are superseding causes that avoid liability of an initial actor."[156]

Causation frequently plays a significant role in § 1983 municipal liability claims based upon inadequate training, supervision, or hiring practices.[157] For these municipal liability claims, Supreme Court decisional law states that the municipal policy or practice must be the "moving force," "closely related," "direct causal link," or "affirmatively linked" to the deprivation of the plaintiff's federally protected rights.[158] It is unclear whether these standards are alternative ways of articulating common-law proximate cause or are intended to impose a more stringent causation requirement.

IX. CAPACITY OF CLAIM

A claim against a state or municipal official in her official capacity is treated as a claim against the entity itself.[159] By contrast, a personal (or individual) capacity claim seeks monetary recovery payable out of the responsible official's personal finances.[160]

In *Hafer v. Melo*,[161] the Supreme Court outlined the distinctions between personal and official capacity suits:

1. In official capacity suits, the plaintiff must show that enforcement of the entity's policy or custom caused the violation of the plaintiff's federally protected right.

---

154. Warner v. Orange County Dep't of Probation, 115 F.3d 1068, 1071 (2d Cir. 1996).
155. *See, e.g.,* Martinez v. California, 444 U.S. 277 (1980); Murray v. Earle, 405 F.3d 278 (5th Cir. 2005); Townes v. City of New York, 176 F.3d 138 (2d Cir.), *cert. denied,* 528 U.S. 964 (1999).
156. Zahrey v. Coffey, 221 F.3d 342, 351 (2d Cir. 2000).
157. Board of County Commissioners of Bryan County v. Brown, 520 U.S. 397 (1997); City of Canton v. Harris, 489 U.S. 378 (1989).
158. *Id.*
159. Kentucky v. Graham, 473 U.S. 159 (1985); Brandon v. Holt, 469 U.S. 464 (1985); Monell v. New York City Dep't of Social Services, 436 U.S. 658, 690 n.55 (1978).
160. Hafer v. Melo, 502 U.S. 21 (1991).
161. *Id.* at 25.

2. In official capacity suits, the defendant may assert only those immunities the entity possesses, such as the states' Eleventh Amendment immunity and municipalities' immunity from punitive damages.
3. Liability may be imposed against defendants in personal capacity suits even if the violation of the plaintiff's federally protected right was not attributable to the enforcement of a governmental policy or practice. "[T]o establish *personal* liability in a § 1983 action, it is enough to show that the official, acting under color of state law, caused the deprivation of a federal right."[162]
4. Personal-capacity defendants may assert common-law immunity defenses, that is, either an absolute or qualified immunity.[163]

The § 1983 complaint should clearly specify the capacity (or capacities) in which the defendant is sued. Unfortunately, many § 1983 complaints fail to do so. When the capacity of a claim is ambiguous, most courts look to the "course of proceedings" to determine the issue.[164] For example, when a municipal official is sued under § 1983, assertion of a claim for punitive damages is a strong indicator that the claim was asserted against the official in her personal capacity, because municipalities are immune from punitive damages under § 1983. By the same token, when the defendant official asserts an absolute or qualified immunity as a defense, this strongly indicates that the claim was asserted against the official personally, because these defenses are available only against personal capacity claims.

X. MUNICIPAL LIABILITY

In the landmark decision *Monell v. New York City Department of Social Services*,[165] the Supreme Court held that municipal entities are subject to § 1983 liability, but not on the basis of respondeat superior.[166] Therefore, a municipality may not be held liable under § 1983 solely because it hired an employee who became a constitutional wrongdoer. *Monell* established that a municipality is subject to liability under § 1983 only when the violation of

162. *Hafer*, 502 U.S. at 25 (quoting Kentucky v. Graham, 473 U.S. 159 (1985)).

163. *See* Parts XIV (Absolute Immunities) and XV (Qualified Immunity), *infra*.

164. 1 Schwartz, Section 1983 Litigation: Claims and Defenses, § 6.05. Some courts, however, have held that when the capacity in which the defendant is sued is ambiguous, there is a presumption against personal capacity claims. *Id.*

165. 436 U.S. 658 (1978).

166. State law cannot authorize respondeat superior under § 1983. Coon v. Town of Springfield, 404 F.3d 683, 687 (2d Cir. 2005) ("Just as states cannot extinguish municipal liability under §1983 via state law, they cannot enlarge it either.").

the plaintiff's federally protected right can be attributable to the enforcement of a municipal policy, practice, or decision of a municipal policymaker.[167] "[I]t is when execution of a government's policy or custom, whether made by its lawmakers or by those whose edicts or acts may fairly be said to represent official policy, inflicts injury that the government as an entity is responsible under § 1983."[168]

The Supreme Court in *Owen v. City of Independence*,[169] held that a "municipality may not assert the good faith of its officers or agents as a defense to liability under § 1983." "[U]nlike governmental municipal officials, municipalities do not enjoy immunity from suit—either absolute or qualified under § 1983."[170] Although compensatory damages and equitable relief may be awarded against a municipality under § 1983,[171] the Court in *City of Newport v. Fact Concerts*[172] held that municipalities are immune from punitive damages. The Court in *City of Newport* found that because an award of punitive damages against a municipality would be payable from taxpayer funds, the award would not further the deterrent and punishment goals of punitive damages. These goals are best accomplished by awards of punitive damages against an official in her personal capacity. As discussed in Part XXI, *infra*, punitive damages may be awarded under § 1983 against a state or municipal official in her individual capacity.

Under Supreme Court decisional law, municipal liability may be based upon (1) an express municipal policy, such as an ordinance, regulation, or policy statement; (2) a "widespread practice that, although not authorized by written law or express municipal policy, is 'so permanent and well settled as

---

167. A suit against a municipal official in his or her official capacity is considered a suit against the municipality itself. Brandon v. Holt, 469 U.S. 464 (1985). *Accord* Kentucky v. Graham, 473 U.S. 159 (1985). *See* Part IX, *supra*.

168. *Monell,* 436 U.S. at 694. The municipal policy or practice requisite is often very difficult to satisfy. *See* Wimberly v. City of Clovis, 375 F. Supp. 2d 1120, 1127 (D.N.M. 2004) ("the *Monell* standard is very difficult for any plaintiff to reach. Even plaintiffs that proceed to trial against individual defendants often are unable to keep the municipality in the case.").

169. 445 U.S. 622, 638 (1980).

170. Leatherman v. Tarrant County, 507 U.S. 163, 166 (1993). *See, e.g.,* Burge v. Parish of Tammany, 187 F.3d 452 (5th Cir. 1999) (absolute prosecutorial immunity not available in official capacity suit); Goldberg v. Town of Rocky Hill, 973 F.2d 70 (2d Cir. 1992) (municipality may not assert legislative immunity). Further, state law immunities may not be asserted by municipalities sued under § 1983. Howlett v. Rose, 496 U.S. 356 (1990) (state court § 1983 action). *See also* Alden v. Maine, 527 U.S. 706, 740 (1994) (reaffirming *Howlett*).

171. Monell v. Department of Social Services, 436 U.S. 658 (1978).

172. 453 U.S. 247 (1981).

to constitute a custom or usage' with the force of law";[173] or (3) the decision of a person with "final policymaking authority."[174] The following types of municipal policies and practices may give rise to § 1983 liability:

1. deliberately indifferent training;[175]
2. deliberately indifferent supervision or discipline;
3. deliberately indifferent hiring;[176]
4. deliberately indifferent failure to adopt policies necessary to prevent constitutional violations.[177]

There must be a sufficient causal connection between the enforcement of the municipal policy or practice and the violation of the plaintiff's federally protected right. A municipality may be held liable under § 1983 only when the enforcement of the municipal policy or custom was the "moving force" behind the violation of plaintiff's federally protected right.[178] The courts have also described this causal connection as a "direct causal link," "closely related," and "affirmatively linked."[179]

In *Collins v. City of Harker Heights*,[180] the Supreme Court stressed that the issue of whether there is a basis for imposing municipal liability for the violation of the plaintiff's federally protected rights is an issue separate and distinct from the issue of whether there was a violation of plaintiff's federal rights. The Court stated that a "proper analysis requires [the separation of] two different issues when a § 1983 claim is asserted against a municipality: (1) whether the plaintiff's harm was caused by a constitutional violation, and (2) if so, whether the city is responsible for that violation."[181]

A. Municipal Policymakers

Some bases of § 1983 municipal liability warrant special discussion. Supreme Court decisional law holds that municipal liability may be based upon a single

173. St. Louis v. Praprotnik, 485 U.S. 112, 127 (1988) (quoting Adickes v. S. H. Kress & Co., 398 U.S. 144, 167–68 (1970)).
174. *Praprotnik*, 485 U.S. at 123. *See also* Pembaur v. Cincinnati, 475 U.S. 469 (1986).
175. City of Canton v. Harris, 489 U.S. 378 (1989).
176. Board of County Commissioners of Bryan County v. Brown, 520 U.S. 397 (1997).
177. *See, e.g.*, Oviatt v. Pearce, 954 F.2d 1470 (9th Cir. 1992).
178. Board of County Commissioners v. Brown, 520 U.S. 397 (1997); City of Canton v. Harris, 489 U.S. 378 (1989).
179. City of Canton v. Harris, 489 U.S. 378, 385 (1989) (there must be "a direct causal link between a municipal policy or custom and the alleged constitutional deprivation.").
180. 503 U.S. 115 (1992).
181. *Id.* at 120.

decision by a municipal official who has final policymaking authority.[182] Whether an official has final policymaking authority is an issue of law to be determined by the court by reference to state and local law.[183] The mere fact that a municipal official has discretionary authority is not a sufficient basis for imposing municipal liability.[184] It is not always easy to determine whether a municipal official has policymaking authority or merely discretionary authority.

Another potentially difficult issue is whether an official is a state or municipal policymaker. In *McMillian v. Monroe County*,[185] the Supreme Court held that this issue, too, is determined by reference to state law. The Court in *McMillian* acknowledged that an official may be a state policymaker for one purpose and a municipal policymaker for another purpose. For example, courts commonly hold that district attorneys are state policymakers when prosecuting criminal cases, but they are municipal policymakers for purposes of carrying out administrative and supervising functions, such as training of assistant district attorneys.[186]

B. Inadequate Training

In *City of Canton v. Harris*,[187] the Supreme Court held that § 1983 municipal liability may be based upon deliberately indifferent training that was the moving force of the violation of the plaintiff's federally protected right. The plaintiff must demonstrate *specific* training deficiencies, and either (1) a pattern of constitutional violations of which policymaking officials are charged with knowledge, *or* (2) a showing that training is obviously necessary to avoid constitutional violations (e.g., the constitutional limits on a police officer's use of deadly force). Plaintiff must show that "the need for more or different training was so obvious, and the inadequacy so likely to result in the violation of constitutional rights" as to amount to a municipal policy of deliberate indifference to citizens' constitutional rights.[188] The Court in *City*

---

182. St. Louis v. Praprotnik, 485 U.S. 112 (1988); Pembaur v. Cincinnati, 475 U.S. 469 (1986).
183. *See* Jett v. Dallas Indep. School Dist., 491 U.S. 701 (1989); St. Louis v. Praprotnik, 485 U.S. 112 (1988).
184. *Pembaur,* 475 U.S. at 481.
185. 520 U.S. 781 (1997).
186. *See, e.g.,* Carter v. Philadelphia, 181 F.3d 339 (3d Cir.), *cert. denied,* 528 U.S. 1005 (1999); Walker v. City of New York, 974 F.2d 293 (2d Cir. 1992), *cert. denied,* 507 U.S. 961 (1993); Baez v. Hennessey, 853 F.2d 73 (2d Cir. 1988), *cert. denied,* 488 U.S. 1014 (1989).
187. 489 U.S. 378 (1989).
188. *City of Canton,* 489 U.S. at 390.

of Canton held that negligent or even grossly negligent training does not give rise to a § 1983 municipal liability claim. Plaintiff must also demonstrate a sufficiently close causal connection between the deliberately indifferent training and the deprivation of the plaintiff's federally protected right.[189]

The *City of Canton* "objective obviousness" deliberate indifference standard employed for municipal liability inadequate training claims differs from the Eight Amendment *Farmer v. Brennan*[190] deliberate indifference standard under which the official must be "subjectively" aware of the risk of harm to a prisoner. The Court in *City of Canton* employed an "objective obviousness" deliberate indifference standard "for the purpose of identifying the threshold for holding a city responsible for the constitutional rights committed by its inadequately trained agents."[191]

City of Canton's fault ("deliberate indifference") and causation ("moving force") standards are stringent. The Court in *Canton* expressly stated that federal courts should not lightly second-guess municipal training policies. Although numerous municipal liability claims based upon allegedly inadequate training have been brought, a relatively small percentage succeeded.

C. Inadequate Screening

In *Board of Commissioners of Bryan County v. Brown*,[192] the Supreme Court held that municipal liability can be premised upon a municipality's deliberately indifferent deficient hiring of a constitutional wrongdoer, but only if the plaintiff demonstrates that the hired officer "was highly likely to inflict the *particular* injury suffered by the plaintiff." The Court in *Brown* acknowledged that the fault and causation standards for inadequate hiring claims are even more stringent than for inadequate training claims.

---

189. The Second Circuit held that to establish municipal liability based upon deliberately indifferent failure to train, the plaintiff must show:

> [1] That a policymaker knows "to a moral certainty" that her employees will confront a given situation. . . . Thus, a policymaker does not exhibit deliberate indifference by failing to train employees for rare or unforeseen events.
>
> [2] That the situation either presents the employee with a difficult choice of the sort that training or supervision will make less difficult or that there is a history of employees mishandling the situation.
>
> [3] The plaintiff must show that the wrong choice by the city employee will frequently cause the deprivation of a citizen's constitutional rights.

Walker v. City of New York, 974 F.2d 293, 297 (2d Cir. 1992) (citations omitted).

190. 511 U.S. 825, 829 (1994).

191. Collins v. City of Harker Heights, 503 U.S. 115, 124 (1992).

192. 520 U.S. 397, 412 (1997).

D. Pleading

In *Leatherman v. Tarrant County*,[193] the Supreme Court held that federal courts may not impose a heightened pleading requirement for § 1983 municipal liability claims. This means that the Federal Rules of Civil Procedure notice pleading standard governs § 1983 municipal liability claims. However, even after *Leatherman*, some courts reject wholly conclusory allegations of municipal policy or practice.[194]

XI. SUPERVISORY LIABILITY

In many § 1983 actions the plaintiff seeks to impose liability not only upon the officer who directly engaged in the unconstitutional conduct (e.g., a police officer) but also upon a supervisory official (e.g., the chief of police). The supervisory liability claim is normally premised upon allegations that the supervisor knew or should have known about the danger that the subordinate would engage in the unconstitutional conduct, had the authority to take steps to prevent it, yet failed to do so.

Like municipal liability claims, supervisory liability claims normally seek to impose liability upon one party (the supervisor) for a wrong directly inflicted by another party (the subordinate). The reference to "normally" reflects the fact that in some cases a supervisor may have directly inflicted the harm. Like § 1983 municipal liability, § 1983 supervisory liability may not be based upon respondeat superior but only upon the supervisor's own wrongful acts or omissions. And, like municipal liability, there must be sufficient causal link or nexus between the supervisor's wrongful conduct or failure to act and the violation of the plaintiff's federally protected right.

On the other hand, there are important differences between supervisory liability and municipal liability:

1. Supervisory liability is a form of personal liability; municipal liability is a form of entity liability.
2. Because supervisory liability is personal liability, supervisors may assert a common-law absolute or qualified immunity defense.[195] Municipalities may not assert these defenses, although it should be

---

193. 507 U.S. 163 (1993).

194. *See, e.g.,* Spriller v. Texas City, 130 F.3d 162 (5th Cir. 1997). For further discussion of municipal liability issues, please see Chapter 4.

195. *See* Poe v. Leonard, 282 F.3d 123 (2d Cir. 2002) (supervisory official is protected by qualified immunity unless both federal right and basis of supervisory liability were clearly established); Camilo-Robles v. Hoyos, 151 F.3d 1, 6 (1st Cir. 2005)

recalled that municipalities sued under § 1983 are absolutely immune from punitive damages.

3. A municipal entity may be liable under § 1983 only when the violation of the plaintiff's federal right is attributable to the enforcement of a municipal policy or practice. By contrast, supervisory liability does not depend upon a municipal policy or practice.

The U.S. Supreme Court has yet to formulate culpability standards for supervisory liability. The circuit courts have articulated supervisory liability standards. Although these standards differ somewhat from circuit to circuit, they generally require a showing that the supervisory defendant either acquiesced in or was deliberately indifferent to the subordinate's unconstitutional conduct and that the supervisor's action or inaction was "affirmatively linked" to the deprivation of the plaintiff's federal rights.[196]

(when supervisory official asserts qualified immunity, plaintiff will prevail only if it is shown that (1) the subordinate's actions violated a clearly established federal right, and (2) "it was clearly established that a supervisor would be liable for constitutional violations perpetrated by his subordinates in that context."), *cert. denied,* 525 U.S. 1105 (1999).

196. **First Circuit:** Matos v. Toledo, 135 F.3d 182 (1st Cir. 1998) (supervisory encouragement, condemnation, acquiescence, or deliberate indifference). *See also* Wilson v. Town of Mendon, 294 F.3d 1 (1st Cir. 2002); Camilo-Robles v. Hoyos, 151 F.3d 1 (1st Cir. 1998), *cert. denied,* 525 U.S. 1105 (1999).

Second Circuit: Colon v. Coughlin, 58 F.3d 865 (2d Cir. 1995) (direct participation in wrongdoing, failure to remedy wrong after informed of it, creation of policy or custom, grossly negligent supervision, or deliberately indifferent failure to act on information about constitutional violations). *See also* Hernandez v. Keane, 341 F.3d 137 (2d Cir. 2003); Poe v. Leonard, 282 F.3d 123 (2d Cir. 2002).

Third Circuit: Rode v. Dellarciprete, 845 F.3d 1195 (3d Cir. 1988) (supervisor must have had knowledge of and acquiesced in unlawful conduct). *Accord* Baker v. Monroe Township, 50 F.3d 1186 (3d Cir. 1995).

Fourth Circuit: Carter v. Morris, 164 F.3d 215 (4th Cir. 1999) (actual or constructive knowledge of risk or constitutional injury and deliberate indifference). *See also* Randall v. Prince George's County, 302 F.3d 188 (4th Cir. 2002).

Fifth Circuit: Atteberry v. Nocona General Hospital, 430 F.3d 245, 254 (5th Cir. 2005) ("[S]upervisors may be liable for constitutional violations committed by subordinate employees when supervisors act, or fail to act, with *deliberate indifference* to violations of others' constitutional rights committed by their subordinates"; court adopted Farmer v. Brennan, 511 U.S. 825 (1994) definition of deliberate indifference); Roberts v. City of Shreveport, 397 F.3d 287 (5th Cir. 2005) (supervisory liability requires showing of deliberately indifferent training or supervision);. Doe v. Dallas Independent S.D., 153 F.3d 211 (5th Cir. 1998) (deliberate indifference).

Sixth Circuit: Doe v. City of Roseville, 296 F.3d 431, 440 (6th Cir. 2000) ("'Supervisor liability [under § 1983] occurs either when the supervisor personally participates in the alleged constitutional violation or when there is a causal connection between actions of the supervising official and the alleged constitutional deprivation.

XII. RELATIONSHIP BETWEEN INDIVIDUAL AND MUNICIPAL LIABILITY

When claims are brought against both a state or local official in her personal capacity and against a municipal entity, the district court has discretion either to bifurcate the claim or to try them jointly.[197] Section 1983 plaintiffs generally favor a joint trial, because in a joint trial the plaintiff may be

---

The causal connection can be established when a history of widespread abuse puts the responsible supervisor on notice of the need to correct the alleged deprivation, and he [she] fails to do so. The deprivations that constitute widespread abuse sufficient to notify the supervising official must be obvious, flagrant, rampant, and of continued duration, rather than isolated occurrences'") (quoting Brady v. Fla. Dep't of Labor & Empl. Sec., 133 F. 3d 797, 802 (11th Cir. 1998)), Sehehee v. Luttrell, 199 F.3d 295 (6th Cir. 1999) (supervisory liability cannot be based upon mere failure to act; the supervisor must have at least implicitly authorized, approved, or knowingly acquiesced in unconstitutional conduct of subordinate officers); Poe v. Haydon, 853 F.2d 418 (6th Cir. 1988); Hays v. Jefferson County, 668 F.2d 869 (6th Cir.), *cert. denied,* 459 U.S. 833 (1982). *See also* Combs v. Wilkinson, 315 F.3d 548 (6th Cir. 2002).

Seventh Circuit: Jones v. Chicago, 856 F.2d 985 (7th Cir. 1988) (conduct of subordinate must have occurred with supervisor's knowledge, consent, or deliberate indifference). *See also* Gossmeyer v. McDonald, 128 F.3d 481 (7th Cir. 1997).

Eighth Circuit: Green v. Branson, 108 F.3d 1296 (8th Cir. 1997) (deliberate indifference); Andrews v. Fowler, 98 F.3d 1069, 1078 (8th Cir. 1996) ("deliberately indifferent to or tacitly authorized the attending acts").

Ninth Circuit: Cunningham v. Gates, 229 F.3d 1271, 1292 (9th Cir. 2000) ("Supervisors can be held liable for: (1) their own culpable action or inaction in the training, supervision or control of subordinates; (2) their acquiescence in the constitutional deprivation in which a complaint is made; or (3) for conduct that showed a reckless or callous indifference to the rights of others.")

Tenth Circuit: Lankford v. City of Hobart, 73 F.3d 283 (10th Cir. 1996) ("personal direction" or actual knowledge of wrongdoing and acquiescence).

Eleventh Circuit: Cottone v. Jenne, 326 F.3d 1352 (11th Cir. 2003) (supervisor either (1) personally participated in unconstitutional conduct; (2) failed to correct widespread violations; (3) initiated custom or policy that was deliberately indifferent to constitutional rights; or (4) directed subordinates to act unconstitutionally or knew they would do so, yet failed to stop them from doing so). *See also* Dalrymple v. Reno, 334 F.3d 991 (11th Cir. 2003); Brady v. Fla. Dep't of Labor & Empl. Sec., 133 F. 3d 797, 802 (11th Cir. 1998).

D.C. Circuit: Int'l Action Center v. United States, 365 F.3d 20 (D.C. Cir. 2004) (actual or co-instructive knowledge of past transgressions or responsible or aware of "clearly deficient" training); Haynesworth v. Miller, 820 F.2d 1245 (D.C. Cir. 1987) (breach of duty to instruct subordinate to prevent constitutional harm).

197. Fed. R. Civ. P. 42(b). *See, e.g.,* Amato v. City of Saratoga Springs, 170 F.3d 311 (2d Cir. 1999). *See also* 1A Schwartz, Section 1983 Litigation: Claims and Defenses, § 7.14 (4th ed. 2005).

allowed to introduce evidence of wrongdoing by other officers or by the municipal entity, albeit with limiting instructions. Section 1983 defendants normally seek bifurcation in order to thwart this stratagem.

In *Los Angeles v. Heller*,[198] plaintiff asserted § 1983 false arrest and excessive force claims. The complaint alleged personal capacity and municipal liability claims. The Supreme Court held that a determination in the first phase that the individual officer defendant did not violate the plaintiff's federally protected rights required dismissal of the municipal liability claim. This is because the municipal liability claim was premised on the city's allegedly having adopted a policy of condoning excessive force in making arrests. The Court in *Heller* reasoned that the city could not be liable under § 1983 unless some official (or officials) violated the plaintiff's federally protected rights.

Some courts have read *Heller* broadly as meaning that if the personal capacity claim is dismissed, the municipal liability claim *must* be dismissed. However, other courts have recognized that there may be situations in which the named subordinate defendant(s) did not violate plaintiff's federally protected rights, but the plaintiff's rights were violated by the joint action of a group of officers, or by a nondefendant, or by policymaking officials. Under these circumstances, dismissal of the claim against the individual officer defendant should not result in dismissal of the municipal liability claim.[199]

The fact that the plaintiff's claim against the individual officer defendant is defeated by qualified immunity should not automatically result in dismissal against the municipality, because an officer who is protected by qualified immunity may have violated the plaintiff's federally protected rights. The qualified immunity determination may mean only that the defendant did not violate the plaintiff's *clearly established* federally protected rights.[200] It should be recalled that while qualified immunity may be asserted by an official sued in her personal capacity, it may not be asserted by a municipal entity.

The interplay of the rules governing qualified immunity and municipal liability results in a cost allocation scheme among the municipality, the individual officer, and the plaintiff whose federally protected rights were violated. The U.S. Supreme Court in *Owen v. City of Independence*[201] explained how the "costs" are allocated.

---

198. 475 U.S. 796 (1986).

199. *See* Fairley v. Luman, 281 F.3d 913 (9th Cir. 2002); Speer v. City of Wynne, 276 F.3d 980 (8th Cir. 2002); Barrett v. Orange County, 194 F.3d 341 (2d Cir. 1999); Anderson v. Atlanta, 778 F.2d 678 (11th Cir. 1985); Garcia v. Salt Lake City, 768 F.2d 303 (10th Cir. 1985).

200. *See, e.g.,* Doe v. Sullivan County, 956 F.2d 545 (6th Cir.), *cert. denied,* 506 U.S. 864 (1992). For more discussion regarding qualified immunity, see Part XV.

201. 445 U.S. 622, 657 (1980).

1. The municipality will be held liable when the violation of the plaintiff's federally protected right is attributable to enforcement of a municipal policy or practice.
2. The individual officer will be held liable when she violated plaintiff's clearly established federally protected right and, therefore, is not shielded by qualified immunity.
3. The plaintiff whose federally protected right was violated will not be entitled to recovery and will "absorb the loss" when the violation of her right is not attributable to a municipal policy or practice and the individual officer did not violate plaintiff's clearly established federal rights.

XIII. STATE LIABILITY: THE ELEVENTH AMENDMENT

The Eleventh Amendment grants the states sovereign immunity from federal court liability. Although the language of the Eleventh Amendment refers to a suit brought by a citizen of one state against *another* state, the Supreme Court has interpreted the Eleventh Amendment as granting the states sovereign immunity protection even when a state is sued in federal court by one of its own citizens.[202] The Supreme Court also holds that the Eleventh Amendment applies to § 1983 claims because, in enacting the original version of § 1983, Congress did not intend to abrogate the states' Eleventh Amendment immunity.[203] A federal court award of § 1983 damages against a state, state agency, or state official sued in an official capacity is barred by the Eleventh Amendment.[204]

A. *Young* Prospective Relief

Under the doctrine of *Ex parte Young*,[205] prospective relief against a state official in her official capacity to prevent future federal constitutional or federal statutory violations is not barred by the Eleventh Amendment. The

202. Hans v. Louisiana, 134 U.S. 1 (1890). *See* Seminole Tribe v. Florida, 517 U.S. 44 (1996) (reaffirming *Hans*).

203. Quern v. Jordan, 440 U.S. 332 (1979).

204. Edelman v. Jordan, 415 U.S. 651 (1974). "[W]hen the action is in essence one for the recovery of money from the state, the state is the real, substantial party in interest and is entitled to invoke its [Eleventh Amendment] sovereign immunity from suit even though individual officials are nominal defendants." Ford Motor Co. v. Dep't of Treasury, 323 U.S. 459, 464 (1945). Even if the federal government agrees to indemnify the state, the Eleventh Amendment will protect the state from a monetary judgment. Regents of University of California v. Doe, 519 U.S. 425 (1997).

205. 209 U.S. 123 (1908).

Court in *Ex parte Young* reasoned that a state official who violated federal law is "stripped of his official or representative character" and therefore did not act for the state, but as an individual. Because the Eleventh Amendment protects states and state entities, and not individuals, the claim for prospective relief is not barred by the Eleventh Amendment. The rationale behind the *Young* doctrine is fictitious because *Young* prospective relief operates in substance against the state and may impact substantially upon the state treasury. The *Young* fiction was born of necessity to enable the federal courts to insure prospective compliance by the states with federal law.

To come within the *Young* doctrine, the plaintiff must establish ongoing violations of federal law and seek prospective relief. To determine whether the plaintiff has alleged a *Young* claim, the court "need only conduct a 'straightforward inquiry into whether [the] complaint alleges an ongoing violation of federal law and seeks relief properly characterized as prospective.'"[206] In addition, the plaintiff must name as defendant the state official who is responsible for enforcing the contested statute in her official capacity; a claim for prospective relief against the state itself, or a state agency, will be barred by the Eleventh Amendment.[207] Declaratory relief is within the *Young* doctrine, but only when there are ongoing or threatened violations of federal law.[208]

When a federal court grants *Young* prospective relief, it has power to enforce that relief, including by ordering monetary sanctions payable out of the state treasury.[209] Similarly, a federal court's enforcement against a state of a consent decree that is based upon federal law does not violate the Eleventh Amendment.[210] Federal courts are not relegated to granting prospective relief and hoping for compliance.

In *Pennhurst State School and Hospital v. Halderman*,[211] the Supreme Court held that the *Young* doctrine does not apply to state law claims that are pendent ("supplemental") to the § 1983 claim. Therefore, a supplemental state law claim that seeks to compel the state to comply with state law is barred by the Eleventh Amendment. The Court in *Pennhurst* reasoned that

---

206. Verizon of Md., Inc. v. Public Serv. Comm'n of Md., 535 U.S. 635, 645 (2002) (quoting Idaho v. Coeur d'Alene Tribe of Idaho, 521 U.S. 261 296 (1997) (O'Connor, S., concurring)).
207. Alabama v. Pugh, 438 U.S. 781 (1978).
208. Green v. Mansour, 474 U.S. 64 (1985).
209. Hutto v. Finney, 437 U.S. 678 (1978).
210. Frew v. Hawkins, 540 U.S. 431 (2004).
211. 465 U.S. 89 (1984).

the *Young* fiction was born out of the necessity of federal supremacy to enable the federal courts to compel state compliance with federal law, a factor not present when the plaintiff claims a violation of state law. The Court in *Pennhurst* viewed federal court relief requiring a state to comply with state law as a great intrusion on state sovereignty.

B. Personal Capacity Claims

The Eleventh Amendment does not encompass a § 1983 claim for damages against a state official in her personal capacity.[212] The monetary relief awarded on such a claim would not be payable out of the state treasury, but would be payable out of the state official's personal funds, which are not protected by the Eleventh Amendment. The fact that the state agreed to indemnify the state official for a personal capacity monetary judgment does not create Eleventh Amendment immunity, because the decision to indemnify is a voluntary policy choice of state government; it is not compelled by mandate of the federal court.[213]

C. Municipal and Hybrid Entities

The Eleventh Amendment does not protect municipalities.[214] Thus, in contrast to a § 1983 federal court damage award against a state entity, a § 1983 damage award against a municipal entity is not barred by the Eleventh Amendment. Many entities have attributes of both state and local entities. For example, an entity may receive both state and local funding. An entity that carries out a local function may be subject to state oversight. Federal courts frequently have to determine whether these "hybrid" entities should be treated as an arm of the state or of local government.[215] In making this determination the most important factor is whether the federal court judgment can be satisfied from state or municipal funds. This makes sense because the Eleventh Amendment is designed to protect the *state* treasury.

---

212. Hafer v. Melo, 502 U.S. 21 (1991).

213. *See, e.g.,* Stoner v. Wisconsin Dep't of Agriculture, 50 F.3d 481 (7th Cir. 1995).

214. Missouri v. Jenkins, 495 U.S. 33, 56 n.20 (1990); Monell v. Dep't of Soc. Servs., 436 U.S. 658, 690 n.54 (1978); Mt. Healthy City S.D. v. Doyle, 429 U.S. 274 (1977). *See also* Northern Ins. Co. of N.Y. v. Chatham County, 126 S. Ct. 1689 (2006). "The District of Columbia is a municipality for the purpose of §1983." People for Ethical Treatment of Animals v. Gittens, 396 F.3d 416, 425 (D.C. Cir. 2005).

215. *See* Mt. Healthy City S.D. v. Doyle, 429 U.S. 274 (1977). 1A Schwartz, Section 1983 Litigation: Claims and Defenses, § 8.10.

D. Waiver

A state may voluntarily waive its Eleventh Amendment immunity, but these waivers are relatively rare. The Supreme Court invokes a strong presumption against such a waiver and holds that waiver will be found only by the clearest of language in which the state agrees to subject itself to liability in federal court. In *Lapides v. Board of Regents*,[216] the Supreme Court held that a state removal of a state's court suit to federal court waives the state's Eleventh Amendment immunity from liability on a state law claim to which the state had waived its sovereign immunity in the state court.

E. Appeals

In *Puerto Rico Aqueduct & Sewer Authority v. Metcalf & Eddy*,[217] the Supreme Court held that a district court's denial of Eleventh Amendment immunity is immediately appealable to the court of appeals. The Court in *Metcalf & Eddy* relied upon the fact that the Eleventh Amendment grants states not only immunity from liability but also "immunity from suit," that is, from the burdens of litigation. The Court found that an immediate appeal was necessary to vindicate this immunity as well as the states' "dignitary interests."

XIV. PERSONAL CAPACITY CLAIMS: ABSOLUTE IMMUNITIES

A. Absolute versus Qualified Immunity: The Functional Approach

Officials sued for monetary relief in their personal capacities may be entitled to assert a common-law defense of absolute or qualified immunity. In general, absolute immunity may be asserted by judges, prosecutors, witnesses, and legislators, while executive and administrative officials may assert qualified immunity. However, whether an official is entitled to assert an absolute immunity as opposed to qualified immunity depends upon "the nature of the function performed, not the identity of the actor who performed it."[218] Thus, an official may be entitled to absolute immunity for carrying out one function and qualified immunity for another. For example, a judge may assert absolute judicial immunity for carrying out her judicial functions, but only

216. 535 U.S. 613 (2002).
217. 506 U.S. 139 (1993).
218. Kalina v. Fletcher, 522 U.S. 118, 127 (1997) (quoting Forrester v. White, 484 U.S. 219, 229 (1988)).

qualified immunity for carrying out administrative and executive functions, such as hiring and firing court employees.[219] As discussed below, prosecutors may claim absolute prosecutorial immunity for their advocacy functions, but only qualified immunity for their investigatory and administrative functions.

B. Judicial Immunity

Absolute judicial immunity protects judges from liability for damages for their judicial acts, so long as they do not act in the clear absence of all jurisdictions.[220] A judge does not lose absolute immunity simply because she acted in excess of jurisdiction; absolute immunity is lost only when the judge either did not perform a judicial act, or when the judge acted in the clear absence of all jurisdiction (e.g., a surrogate court judge who tries a felony). A judge who acts in excess of jurisdiction, or without personal jurisdiction, or who makes grave procedural errors does not necessarily act in the clear absence of all jurisdiction. To determine whether the judge performed a "judicial act," consideration is given to whether the judge engaged in action normally performed by a judge, and whether the parties dealt with the judge in her judicial capacity.[221]

Administrative hearing officers may claim absolute quasi-judicial immunity if they are sufficiently independent (politically) and if the hearing affords sufficient procedural safeguards so that the administrative process fairly resembles the judicial process.[222] On the other hand, the Supreme Court has held that court reporters may not assert absolute immunity, because they do not engage in the kind of discretionary decision making or exercise of judgment protected by judicial immunity.[223] Circuit court authority holds that judicial law clerks may claim absolute immunity.[224]

---

219. *See* Forrester v. White, 484 U.S. 219 (1988).

220. Mireles v. Waco, 502 U.S. 9 (1991); Stump v. Sparkman, 435 U.S. 349 (1978); Pierson v. Ray, 386 U.S. 547 (1967); Bradley v. Fisher, 80 U.S. 335 (1871).

221. Mireles v. Waco, 502 U.S. 9 (1991) (judge who ordered bailiff to use excessive force to bring lawyer to courtroom performed judicial act); Stump v. Sparkman, *supra* note 220 (acts are judicial even though informal and irregular, e.g., no docket number, no filing with clerk's office, and no notice to minor subject to sterilization order).

222. *Compare* Butz v. Economou, 438 U.S. 478 (1978) (federal hearing officers found entitled to assert absolute immunity) *with* Cleavinger v. Saxner, 474 U.S. 193 (1985) (prison officials who held disciplinary hearings were not entitled to claim absolute immunity because of lack of independence and insufficient procedural safeguards).

223. Antoine and Byers v. Anderson, 508 U.S. 429 (1993).

224. Moore v. Brewster, 96 F.3d 1240 (9th Cir. 1996), *cert. denied,* 519 U.S. 1118 (1997); Olivia v. Heller, 839 F.2d 37 (2d Cir. 1988).

C. Prosecutorial Immunity

Prosecutors are absolutely immune when acting "as an advocate for the State" by engaging in conduct that is "intimately associated with the judicial phase of the criminal process."[225] Supreme Court decisional law holds that "acts undertaken by a prosecutor in preparing for the initiation of juridical proceedings or for trial, and which occur in the course of his role as an advocate for the state, are entitled to the protection of absolute immunity."[226] Prosecutorial immunity protects the prosecutor even if she acted "with an improper state of mind or improper motive."[227] Prosecutors are absolutely immune for carrying out such advocacy actions as

- deciding whether to prosecute;
- pretrial litigation activities concerning applications for arrest and search warrants, opposing bail applications, and opposing suppression motions;
- preparation for trial, including interviewing witnesses and evaluating evidence;
- plea bargaining.

Prosecutors, however, may not claim absolute immunity for investigative and administrative functions. Thus, prosecutors may assert only qualified immunity for such administrative and investigative functions as

- holding a press conference;[228]
- engaging in investigative activity prior to the establishment of probable cause to arrest;[229]
- advising the police in the investigative phase that there "probably" was probable cause to arrest.[230]

It is often difficult to determine whether the prosecutor's actions should be characterized as advocacy as opposed to investigative or administrative. The courts have drawn some very fine distinctions.[231] For example, in

225. Imbler v. Pachtman, 424 U.S. 409, 430–31 (1976).
226. Buckley v. Fitzsimmons, 509 U.S. 259, 272 (1993).
227. Shmueli v. City of New York, 424 F.3d 231, 237 (2d Cir. 2005) (citing Bernard v. County of Suffolk, 356 F.3d 495 (2d Cir. 2004)).
228. Buckley v. Fitzsimmons, 509 U.S. 259 (1993).
229. *Id.*
230. Burns v. Reed, 500 U.S. 478 (1991).
231. Buckley v. Fitzsimmons, 509 U.S. 259, 273 (1993) (citation omitted) ("There is a difference between the advocate's role in evaluating evidence and interviewing witnesses as he prepares for trial, on the one hand, and the detective's role in searching for the clues and corroboration that might give him probable cause to recommend

Kalina v. Fletcher,[232] the Supreme Court held that the prosecutor was protected by absolute prosecutorial immunity for preparing and filing a motion for an arrest warrant, because these were advocacy functions, but not for certifying facts to support probable cause, because that is the function of a complaining witness. A useful rule of thumb is that "[t]he more distant a function is from the judicial process, the less likely absolute immunity will attach."[233]As discussed below, complaining witnesses are not protected by absolute immunity.

D. Witness Immunity

In *Briscoe v. LaHue*,[234] the Supreme Court held that witnesses, including police officers who testify in judicial proceedings, are protected by absolute immunity, even if the witness gave perjured testimony. Denying absolute immunity might make some witnesses reluctant to testify or cause them to distort their testimony because of fear of liability.[235] The Court found that "[s]ubjecting . . . police officers to damages liability under § 1983 for their testimony might undermine not only their contribution to the judicial process but also the effective performance of their other public duties."[236] Complaining witnesses, however, are not protected by absolute immunity.[237] "[T]he term 'complaining witness' is something of a misnomer, as the complainant need not testify as a witness so long as he played a significant role in initiating or procuring the prosecution."[238]

E. Legislative Immunity

State and local legislators enjoy absolute immunity for their legislative acts.[239] Under the functional approach the critical issue is whether the official

---

that a suspect be arrested, on the other hand. When a prosecutor performs the investigative functions normally performed by a detective or police officer, it is "neither appropriate nor justifiable that, for the same act, immunity should protect the one and not the other.").

232. 522 U.S. 118 (1997).

233. Snell v. Tunnell, 920 F.2d 673, 687 (10th Cir. 1990).

234. 460 U.S. 325 (1983).

235. *Id.* at 333.

236. *Id.* at 343.

237. *See* Malley v. Briggs, 475 U.S. 335, 340 (1986); Cervantes v. Jones, 188 F.3d 805 (7th Cir. 1999), *cert. denied,* 528 U.S. 1154 (2000); White v. Frank, 855 F.2d 956 (2d Cir. 1988).

238. Cervantes v. Jones, 188 F.3d 805, 810 (7th Cir. 1999), *cert. denied,* 528 U.S. 1154 (2000).

239. Bogan v. Scott-Harris, 523 U.S. 44 (1998); Tenney v. Brandhove, 341 U.S. 367 (1951).

was engaged in legislative activity.[240] "Whether an act is legislative turns on the nature of the act, rather than on the motive or intent of the official performing it."[241] Courts frequently must distinguish between legislative action and executive action. Legislative action involves the formulation of policy while executive action enforces and applies the policy in particular circumstances.[242]

For a more detailed discussion of individual immunities, see Chapter 9.

XV. PERSONAL LIABILITY: QUALIFIED IMMUNITY

Qualified immunity may well be the most important issue in § 1983 litigation. It is very frequently asserted as a defense to § 1983 personal capacity claims for damages. Furthermore, courts decide a high percentage of § 1983 personal capacity claims for damages in favor of the defendant on the basis of qualified immunity. Supreme Court decisional law holds that qualified immunity is not just an immunity from liability, but an "immunity from suit," that is, from the burdens of having to defend the litigation.[243]

Qualified immunity protects an official who violated the plaintiff's federally protected right so long as the official did not violate clearly established federal law. Therefore, when qualified immunity is asserted as a defense, the critical issue is whether the defendant official violated federal law that was clearly established at the time she acted.[244] That the official may have violated clearly established *state* law is generally irrelevant.[245]

Qualified immunity protects officials who acted in an objectively reasonable manner. An official who violated clearly established federal law did

240. *See, e.g.,* Bogan v. Scott-Harris, *supra* (city council member who introduced budget eliminating plaintiff's employment position and mayor who signed bill into law were protected by absolute immunity); Supreme Court of Virginia v. Consumers Union, 446 U.S. 719 (1980) (state judges' promulgation of lawyer professional responsibility rules were protected by absolute immunity); Tenney v. Brandhove, 341 U.S. 367 (1951) (legislators who carried out legislative investigation were protected by absolute immunity).

241. Brogan v. Scott-Harris, 523 U.S. 44, 54 (1998). *See also* Torress-Rivera v. Calderon-Serra, 412 F.3d 205 (1st Cir. 2005) (governor's signing of bill into law was protected by abortive immunity, regardless of his motive or intent.).

242. *See* 1A SCHWARTZ, SECTION 1983 LITIGATION: CLAIMS AND DEFENSES, § 9.08 [B] [5] (4th ed. 2005).

243. *See* Mitchell v. Forsyth, 472 U.S. 511 (1985). *Accord* Saucier v. Katz, 533 U.S. 194 (2002). *See also* Chapter 9, *infra.*

244. Harlow v. Fitzgerald, 457 U.S. 800 (1982). *See also* Groh v. Ramirez, 540 U.S. 551 (2004); Hope v. Pelzer, 536 U.S. 730 (2002); Saucier v. Katz, 533 U.S. 194 (2001); Wilson v. Layne, 526 U.S. 603 (1999); Anderson v. Creighton, 483 U.S. 635 (1987).

245. Davis v. Scherer, 468 U.S. 183 (1984).

not act in an objectively reasonable manner, while an official who violated federal law, but not clearly established federal law, did not act in an objectively reasonable manner. The official's subjective motivation is irrelevant to the qualified immunity defense, but may be relevant to the constitutional claim asserted.[246]

The Supreme Court has described the qualified immunity test as a "fair warning" standard; that is, if the federal law was clearly established, the official is on notice that violation of the federal law may lead to personal monetary liability.[247] Under qualified immunity, public officials "are not liable for bad guesses in grey areas; they are liable for transgressing bright lines."[248] In *Hope v. Pelzer*,[249] the Supreme Court held that under the particular circumstances the defendant prison officials' cuffing an inmate to a hitching post for a lengthy period of time while shirtless in the hot Alabama sun violated clearly established Eighth Amendment standards. The Supreme Court in *Hope* found that the Eleventh Circuit had erred in applying a rigid rule that for the federal law to be clearly established the facts of the existing precedent must be "materially similar" to the facts of the instant case. "[O]fficials can still be on notice that their conduct violates established law even in novel factual circumstances."[250] The Court in *Hope* found that the defendants had fair warning that their conduct was unconstitutional from (a) the reasoning of Eleventh Circuit authority, although not factually on all fours; (b) a regulation of the State Department of Corrections relating to use of the hitching post that had been ignored by prison officials; and (c) a U.S. Justice Department transmittal to the State Department of Corrections advising it that its use of the hitching post was unconstitutional. The Supreme Court relied upon this last factor even though the record did not show that the Department of Justice's position had been communicated to the defendant state officials.[251]

---

246. Crawford-El v. Britton, 523 U.S. 574 (1998).

247. Hope v. Pelzer, 536 U.S. 730 (2002); United States v. Lanier, 520 U.S. 259 (1997).

248. Maciariello v. Sunner, 973 F.2d 295, 298 (4th Cir. 1992). *Accord* Abdouch v. Burger, 426 F.3d 982, 987 (8th Cir. 2005); Littrell v. Franklin, 388 F.3d 578, 582 (8th Cir. 2004).

249. 536 U.S. 730 (2002).

250. *Hope*, 536 U.S. at 741.

251. The fact that an official claims to have acted on advice of counsel or pursuant to orders of a superior normally will not protect the official if she violated clearly established federal law. *See* 1A Schwartz, Section 1983 Litigation: Claims and Defenses, ch. 9 A (4th ed. 2005). *See, e.g.*, Lawrence v. Reed, 406 F.3d 1224 (10th Cir. 2005). An official who acted pursuant to a presumptively constitutional state statute will very likely be protected by qualified immunity. *See, e.g.*, Connecticut v. Crotty, 346 F.3d 84 (2d Cir. 2003).

A. Who May Assert Qualified Immunity?

State and local officials who carry out executive and administrative functions may assert qualified immunity.[252] So far the Supreme Court has not allowed private party state actors to assert qualified immunity. In *Richardson v. McKnight*,[253] the Supreme Court held that private prison guards are not entitled to assert qualified immunity. In *Wyatt v. Cole*,[254] the Court held that a creditor who employed a state replevin procedure could not assert qualified immunity. However, the Supreme Court in *Richardson* and *Wyatt* left open whether the defendants in those cases were entitled to assert a good-faith defense. Some lower courts have allowed a private party state actor defendant to assert a good-faith defense that implicates the defendant's subjective intent.[255]

The Court in *Richardson* and *Wyatt* did not resolve whether private party state actors who carry out public functions, such as mental evaluations or civil commitments, may assert qualified immunity.[256] An important factor

---

252. *See, e.g.,* Brosseau v. Hougen, 543 U.S. 194 (2004); Groh v. Ramirez, 540 U.S. 551 (2004); Saucier v. Katz, 533 U.S. 194 (2001); Anderson v. Creighton, 483 U.S. 633 (1987); Malley v. Briggs, 475 U.S. 335 (1986).

253. 521 U.S. 399 (1997).

254. 504 U.S. 158 (1992).

255. *See* Vector Research v. Howard & Howard, 76 F.3d 692 (6th Cir. 1996); Jordan v. Fox, Rothschild, O'Brien, & Frankel, 20 F.3d 1250 (3d Cir. 1994); Wyatt v. Cole, 994 F.2d 1113 (5th Cir.), *cert. denied,* 510 U.S. 977 (1993).

256. For post–*Richardson v. McKnight, supra* note 253, decisions, *compare, e.g.,* Burke v. Town of Walpole, 405 F.3d 66 (1st Cir. 2005) (forensic odontologist retained by district attorney's office to evaluate bite mark evidence as part of criminal investigation was engaged in state action and entitled to assert qualified immunity), and Camilo-Robles v. Hoyos, 151 F.3d 1 (1st Cir. 1998) (psychiatrists under contract with state to assist police department in evaluating police officers entitled to assert qualified immunity because they performed necessary function within police department), *cert. denied,* 525 U.S. 1105 (1999), *with* Jensen v. Lane County, 222 F.3d 570 (9th Cir. 2000) (private physician who provided services to county relating to civil commitment not entitled to assert qualified immunity) and Halvorsen v. Baird, 146 F.3d 680 (9th Cir. 1998) (private not-for-profit organization providing municipality with involuntary commitment services for inebriates not entitled to assert qualified immunity; the fact that organization was not-for-profit was not a sufficient basis for distinguishing *Richardson*).

The Second Circuit held that a private defendant who conspired with government officials is not entitled to assert qualified immunity. Toussie v. Powell, 323 F.3d 178 (2d Cir. 2003).

For pre-*Richardson* decisions allowing the private-party defendant to assert qualified immunity, *see* Young v. Murphy, 90 F.3d 1225 (7th Cir. 1996) (private doctor

may be whether the defendant acted under government supervision. In *Richardson v. McKnight*, the Supreme Court regarded the lack of government supervision over the private prison guards as an important factor justifying denial of the right to assert qualified immunity.

B. Clearly Established Federal Law

Normally, a controlling precedent of either the U.S. Supreme Court, the particular circuit, or the highest court in the state is necessary to clearly establish the federal law. The right must be clearly established in a "fairly particularized sense: the contours of the right must be sufficiently clear that a reasonable official would understand that what he is doing violates that right. That is not to say that an official action is protected by qualified immunity unless the very action has been held unlawful, but it is to say that in light of preexisting law the unlawfulness must be apparent."[257] For federal law to be clearly established, there must be fairly close factual correspondence between the prior precedents and the case at hand.[258] Federal law is less likely to be clearly established when it depends on an ad hoc balancing of competing interests.[259] Decisions from outside the controlling jurisdiction do not clearly establish federal law absent "a consensus of cases of persuasive authority such that a reasonable officer could not have believed that his actions were lawful."[260] In some cases, the federal law might be clearly established even in the absence of controlling precedent. For example, the type of conduct engaged in by the defendant may be so obviously unconstitutional that there was no need to litigate the issue previously.[261] A conflict in the lower court is a strong indicator that the federal law was not clearly established.[262]

The qualified immunity objective reasonableness defense applies even to Fourth Amendment challenges to arrests and searches where the constitutional

---

hired by county to evaluate individual's mental competency); Sherman v. Four County Counseling Center, 987 F.2d 397 (7th Cir. 1993) (private hospital that accepted and treated mental patients pursuant to court order). *See* 1A Schwartz, Section 1983 Litigation: Claims and Defenses, § 9.15.

257. Anderson v. Creighton, 483 U.S. 635, 639–40 (1987) (quoting Davis v. Scherer, 468 U.S. 183, 195 (1984)) (citation omitted).

258. Anderson v. Creighton, 483 U.S. 633 (1987).

259. *See* Dorheim v. Sholes, 430 F.3d 919, 926 (8th Cir. 2005); Manzano v. South Dakota Dep't of Soc. Servs., 60 F.3d 505, 510 (8th Cir. 1995).

260. *Wilson*, 526 U.S. at 617.

261. *See* Wilson v. Layne, 526 U.S. 603, 620–21 (1999) (Stevens, J., dissenting). *See also* Hope v. Pelzer, 536 U.S. 730 (2002).

262. Wilson v. Layne, 526 U.S. 603 (1999).

standard itself is objective reasonableness.[263] Similarly, the qualified immunity objective reasonableness test applies to Fourth Amendment excessive force arrest claims that are governed by the *Graham v. Connor*[264] objective reasonableness standard.[265] Applying *Harlow-Anderson* qualified immunity to constitutional claims litigated under an objective reasonableness standard gives the official two layers of reasonableness protection: one under the Fourth Amendment and another under qualified immunity. This can lead to the awkward conclusion that the officials acted in a reasonable manner for immunity purposes though unreasonably for constitutional purposes. Courts typically try to avoid the linguistic awkwardness of an official acting "reasonably unreasonably" by asking whether the official had *arguable* probable cause, or whether the officer reasonably believed there was probable cause, or whether a reasonable officer could have mistakenly concluded there was probable cause.[266] In excessive force arrest cases, police officers who make reasonable mistakes in evaluating whether a particular use of force is legal in the circumstances are protected by qualified immunity.[267]

There is a potential tension between a constitutional claim that implicates the defendant's subjective intent, such as a free speech retaliation claim, and qualified immunity, which is an objective reasonableness standard under which defendant's subjective intent is irrelevant. The Supreme Court in *Crawford-El v. Britton*[268] held that when the constitutional claim implicates the defendant official's subjective intent, the lower courts should follow the Federal Rules of Civil Procedure and not place special burdens on plaintiffs who are faced with summary judgment qualified immunity motions. The Court in *Crawford* said that the federal courts should not rewrite the Federal Rules of Civil Procedure, that placing unduly harsh burdens on plaintiffs may rob meritorious claims of their fair day in court, and that existing pleading, motion, and discovery rules and the Prison Litigation Reform Act adequately protect defendants against insubstantial constitutional claims.

C. Procedural Aspects of Qualified Immunity

Qualified immunity is normally raised on a motion for summary judgment, sometimes on a motion to dismiss, and sometimes on a Rule 50 motion for

---

263. Anderson v. Creighton, 483 U.S. 635 (1987).

264. 490 U.S. 386 (1989).

265. Brosseau v. Haugen, 543 U.S. 194 (2004); Saucier v. Katz, 533 U.S. 194 (2001).

266. *See, e.g.,* Hunter v. Bryant, 502 U.S. 224, 227 (1987).

267. Brosseau v. Haugen, 543 U.S. 194 (2004); Saucier v. Katz, 533 U.S. 194 (2001).

268. 523 U.S. 574 (1988).

judgment as a matter of law.[269] The Supreme Court's goal in defining qualified immunity in wholly objective terms is to enable the district courts to resolve qualified immunity, to the greatest extent possible, as a matter of law, pretrial and even prediscovery.[270] However, in many cases disputed issues of fact must be resolved in order to determine whether the official violated clearly established federal law. If qualified immunity cannot be decided until material factual disputes are resolved, the district court may allow limited discovery on facts relevant to the immunity defense. In *Crawford-El v. Britton*,[271] the Supreme Court described various options that the district court can invoke when facts concerning the defendant's alleged retaliatory motive are in dispute:

1. allow the plaintiff to take a "focused deposition" of the defendant on the issue of retaliatory motive;
2. allow discovery only on "historical facts" before allowing discovery on the defendant's motive;
3. order the plaintiff to file a reply or grant defendant's motion for a more definite statement requiring specific factual allegations of defendant's conduct and motive before allowing any discovery.

When facts relevant to qualified immunity are in dispute, it may be proper for the district court to either submit the factual issues and the immunity defense to the jury under proper instructions that (a) tell the jury what the clearly established federal law is, and (b) describe the nature of qualified immunity; or, alternatively, submit the factual issues that are material to qualified immunity to the jury by special verdicts, while the district court reserves for itself the power to determine the immunity defense in light of the jury's responses to the special verdicts. Most courts have chosen this second option because it seems to best reflect the jury's function as finder of fact and the court's expertise in determining the law.[272]

---

269. The great weight of lower court authority rejects a heightened pleading standard for personal capacity claims subject to qualified immunity. *See* Part II, *supra.*

270. *See* Hunter v. Bryant, 502 U.S. 224 (1991). *See also* Anderson v. Creighton, 483 U.S. 635, 646 n.6 (1987).

271. 523 U.S. 574 (1988).

272. *See, e.g.,* Willingham v. Crooke, 412 F3d 583, 590 (4th Cir. 2005); Littrell v. Franklin, 388 F.3d 578 (8th Cir. 2004); Carswell v. Borough of Homestead, 381 F.3d 235 (3d Cir. 2004); Stephenson v. Doe, 332 F.3d 68 (2d Cir. 2003); Johnson v. Breeden, 280 F.3d 1308 (11th Cir. 2002). *But see* McCoy v. Hernandez, 203 F.3d 371 (5th Cir. 2000) (jury may decide qualified immunity defense); Presley v. City of Benbrook, 4 F.3d 405 (5th Cir. 1993) (same).

Supreme Court decisional law holds that when qualified immunity is asserted as a defense, the court must first determine if the complaint states a violation of federally protected rights.[273] The rationale for this methodology is that if courts always took qualified immunity up first, it would be hard for constitutional standards to develop. "Deciding the constitutional question before addressing the qualified immunity . . . question promotes clarity in the legal standards for official conduct."[274]

D. Qualified Immunity Appeals

When the district court denies qualified immunity on a summary judgment motion, the defendant may take an immediate appeal from the denial of qualified immunity to the court of appeals *if* the immunity appeal can be decided as a matter of law.[275] However, it is not always clear whether a qualified immunity appeal presents an issue of law or fact. If the district court denies a defendant's summary judgment qualified immunity motion because there are disputed issues of material fact, defendant may not take an immediate appeal that contests the district court's factual determinations.[276] However, even when the district court denies a summary judgment qualified immunity motion on the ground that there are disputed issues of material fact, the defendant may take an immediate appeal if the appeal can be decided as a matter of law. Thus, an immediate qualified immunity appeal lies when the appellant

1. contests the materiality of a disputed issue of fact found by the district court; or
2. claims entitlement to qualified immunity even on the basis of the facts alleged by the plaintiff.

Furthermore, an immediate appeal may be taken from the denial of qualified immunity raised on a motion to dismiss, because in this circum-

---

273. Hope v. Pelzer, 536 U.S. 730 (2002); Saucier v. Katz, 533 U.S. 194 (2001); Wilson v. Layne, 526 U.S. 603 (1999); Conn v. Gabbert, 526 U.S. 286 (1999); County of Sacramento v. Lewis, 523 U.S. 833 (1998); Siegert v. Gilley, 500 U.S. 226 (1991).

274. Wilson v. Layne, 526 U.S. 603 (1999). *See also* Saucier v. Katz, 533 U.S. 194 (2001). Nevertheless, some courts at times prefer to reach the immunity issue first. *See, e.g.*, Brosseau v. Haugen, 543 U.S. 194 (2004); Horne v. Coughlin, 178 F.3d 603 (2d Cir. 1999).

275. Behrens v. Pelletier, 516 U.S. 299 (1996); Johnson v. Jones, 515 U.S. 304 (1995); Mitchell v. Forsyth, 472 U.S. 511 (1985).

276. Johnson v. Jones, 515 U.S. 304 (1995).

stance the appeal presents an issue of law—namely, whether, assuming the facts alleged by the plaintiff to be true, the defendant is entitled to qualified immunity.[277] Circuit courts at times find that they have jurisdiction over parts of an immunity appeal raising questions of law, though not over other parts raising questions of fact.

A § 1983 defendant may be entitled to take multiple interlocutory qualified immunity appeals. In *Behrens v. Pelletier*,[278] the Supreme Court held that the defendant may take an immediate appeal from the denial of qualified immunity raised on a motion to dismiss and, if still unsuccessful, from a subsequent denial of qualified immunity raised on summary judgment, provided the summary judgment immunity appeal can be decided as a matter of law.

Qualified immunity appeals are very costly to civil rights plaintiffs in terms of litigation resources and delay of litigation. Qualified immunity appeals normally stay proceedings in the district court. However, the plaintiff may ask the district court to certify that an interlocutory immunity appeal is frivolous.[279] "This practice . . . enables the district court to retain jurisdiction pending summary disposition of the appeal and thereby minimizes disruption of the ongoing proceedings."[280]

XVI. EXHAUSTION OF STATE REMEDIES

A. State Judicial Remedies

State judicial remedies generally need not be exhausted in order to bring a § 1983 action. "The federal [§ 1983] remedy is supplementary to the state remedy, and the latter need not be first sought and refused before the federal one is invoked."[281]

Under the *Parratt-Hudson*[282] doctrine, when a deprivation of liberty or property results from "random and unauthorized" official conduct, the availability of an adequate post-deprivation judicial remedy satisfies procedural due process. The *Parratt-Hudson* doctrine does not apply when the deprivation

---

277. *See, e.g.,* McKenna v. Wright, 386 F.3d 432 (2d Cir. 2004).

278. 516 U.S. 299 (1996).

279. *Behrens,* 516 U.S. at 310–11; Chan v. Wodnicki, 67 F.3d 137 (7th Cir. 1995); Yates v. City of Cleveland, 941 F.2d 444 (6th Cir. 1991); Apostol v. Gallion, 870 F.2d 1335 (7th Cir. 1989).

280. *Behrens,* 516 U.S. at 310–11.

281. Monroe v. Pape, 365 U.S. 167, 183 (1961).

282. Hudson v. Palmer, 468 U.S. 517 (1984); Parratt v. Taylor, 451 U.S. 527 (1981).

results from enforcement of the established state procedure,[283] or from actions by officials with authority to both cause deprivations and provide pre-deprivation process.[284] *Parratt-Hudson* is not an exhaustion doctrine: when the *Parratt-Hudson* doctrine is applicable, it results in rejection of procedural due process claims on the merits, not for failure to exhaust. A post-deprivation remedy may be adequate under *Parratt-Hudson* even if it does not afford all of the relief available under § 1983, such as an award of attorneys' fees.[285]

1. The **Preiser-Heck** *Doctrine*

In *Preiser v. Rodriguez*,[286] the Supreme Court held that a prisoner's constitutional claim that challenges the fact or duration of her confinement and seeks immediate or speedier release must be brought under federal habeas corpus, following exhaustion of state remedies, even though such a claim may come within the literal terms of § 1983. In these circumstances federal habeas corpus is the exclusive remedy. The Court in *Preiser* reasoned that the more specific federal habeas remedy should prevail over the more general § 1983 remedy, and that prisoners should not be allowed to evade the federal habeas exhaustion requirement by filing the claim under § 1983.

The decision in *Preiser*, however, does not preclude prisoners from utilizing § 1983 to either challenge the conditions of their confinement or to enforce procedural due process protections. In *Wilkinson v. Dotson*,[287] the Supreme Court held that the prisoners' challenge to parole release procedures may be made under § 1983 because the prisoners sought only enhanced process. They did not challenge either the fact or length of their confinement and did not seek immediate or speedier release from confinement. If successful, the plaintiffs at most could obtain new parole release hearings. In *Nelson v. Campbell*,[288] the Supreme Court held that a death row inmate may assert a § 1983 challenge to the constitutionality of a medical procedure that would have been a precursor to his lethal injection.[289] The Court viewed the claim as a condition of confinement medical treatment claim. The

283. Logan v. Zimmerman Brush Co., 455 U.S. 422 (1982).
284. Zinerman v. Burch, 494 U.S. 113 (1990).
285. Parratt v. Taylor, 451 U.S. 527 (1981).
286. 411 U.S. 475 (1973).
287. 544 U.S. 74 (2005).
288. 540 U.S. 749 (2004).
289. *Accord* Hill v. McDonough, 126 S. Ct. 2096 (2006) (challenge to three-drug sequence used for lethal injection to carry out execution may be asserted under § 1983).

Court in *Nelson* did not decide whether a challenge to the method of execution itself (e.g., lethal injection) may be asserted under § 1983.

Under the doctrine of *Heck v. Humphrey*,[290] in order to seek damages on a § 1983 claim that necessarily implicates the constitutionality of the claimant's conviction or sentence, the claimant must show that the conviction or sentence has been overturned, either judicially or by executive order. Strictly speaking, *Heck* is not an exhaustion doctrine. In fact, the *Heck* doctrine is more onerous than an exhaustion requirement because, unless and until the conviction is overturned, the § 1983 claim is not cognizable. Lower courts often have a difficult time determining whether a § 1983 claim "necessarily implicates" the validity of a conviction.[291] The *Heck* doctrine has implications for the date of accrual for the purpose of the statute of limitations because a § 1983 claim that necessarily implicates the validity of a conviction or sentence is not cognizable and thus does not accrue until the conviction has been overturned.

In *Edwards v. Balisok*,[292] the Supreme Court held that the doctrine of *Heck v. Humphrey* applies to prisoner procedural due process claims that necessarily implicate the validity of a prison disciplinary sanction. On the other hand, in *Muhammad v. Close*,[293] the Supreme Court held that a prisoner's challenge to some aspect of a prison disciplinary proceeding that does not implicate either the finding of "guilt" or the sanction is not governed by the *Heck* doctrine.

In *Spencer v. Kemna*,[294] five Justices in concurring and dissenting opinions took the position that the *Heck* doctrine does not apply to § 1983 claimants who are not in state custody and, therefore, cannot seek relief in a federal habeas corpus proceeding. The lower courts are in conflict over whether the positions of these five Justices should be viewed as binding precedent.[295]

B. State Administrative Remedies

In *Patsy v. Board of Regents*,[296] the Supreme Court held that state administrative remedies need not be exhausted in order to bring suit under § 1983. The Court stressed that in enacting the original version of § 1983, Congress

---

290. 512 U.S. 477 (1994).
291. *See* 1A Schwartz, Section 1983 Litigation: Claims and Defenses, § 10.06.
292. 520 U.S. 641 (1997).
293. 540 U.S. 749 (2004).
294. 523 U.S. 1 (1998).
295. *See* 1A Schwartz, Section 1983 Litigation: Claims and Defenses, § 10.06[F].
296. 457 U.S. 496 (1989).

sought to guarantee individuals immediate access to the federal courts. However, under the Prison Litigation Reform Act (PLRA), prisoners are required to exhaust administrative remedies before bringing suit to contest the conditions of confinement.[297]

In *Booth v. Churner*,[298] the Supreme Court held that prisoners who seek money damages judicially must satisfy the PLRA exhaustion requirement even when the available administrative procedures do not afford a monetary remedy, so long as some type of relief is available administratively. In *Porter v. Nussle*,[299] the Supreme Court held that prisoner excessive force claims are challenges to conditions of confinement and thus subject to the PLRA exhaustion requirement. The Court in *Porter* found "that the PLRA's exhaustion requirement applies to all inmate suits about prison life, whether they involve general circumstances or particular episodes, and whether they allege excessive force or some other wrong."[300]

C. Notice of Claim

In *Felder v. Casey*,[301] the Supreme Court held that state notice-of-claim rules may not be applied to § 1983 claims. Because a notice-of-claim rule is not a universally recognized rule necessary for fair procedure, such as a statute of limitations, the absence of a federal notice-of-claim rule is not a "deficiency" in the federal law requiring resort to state law under 42 U.S.C. § 1988(a). Furthermore, the Court in *Felder* found that state notice-of-claim rules unduly burden and discriminate against civil rights claimants. However, as the Court in *Felder* acknowledged, state notice-of-claim rules may be applied to state law claims that are supplemental to § 1983 claims.

D. Ripeness

In *Williamson County Regional Planning Comm'n v. Hamilton Bank*,[302] the Supreme Court imposed stringent two-prong ripeness requirements for

---

297. 42 U.S.C. § 1997e(a). Dismissal of a prisoner's complaint for failure to comply with the PLRA exhaustion requirement generally should be without prejudice. Steele v. Fed. Bureau of Prisoners, 355 F.3d 1204, 1212–13 (10th Cir. 2003); Walker v. Thompson, 288 F.3d 1005 (7th Cir. 2002).
298. 532 U.S. 731 (2001).
299. 534 U.S. 516 (2002).
300. *Id.* at 532. In Woodford v. Ngo, 126 S. Ct. 2378 (2006), the Court held that to satisfy the PLRA exhaustion requirement, the prisoner must comply with the prison grievance deadlines and other procedural rules. The Court left open whether there should be an exception for procedures designed to "trip up" prisoners.
301. 487 U.S. 131 (1988).
302. 473 U.S. 172 (1985).

§ 1983 regulatory takings claims. First, *Williamson* requires that the § 1983 takings plaintiff obtain a final determination from land use authorities concerning the permissible use of the property. This requirement is satisfied when the permissible uses of the property are known to a reasonable degree of certainty.[303] The second *Williamson* ripeness prong requires the plaintiff to obtain a final determination from state court of the right to just compensation. When the § 1983 takings claimant has pursued a claim for just compensation in state court in order to satisfy this second requirement, normal preclusion principles will apply in the federal court § 1983 action.[304] The interplay of ripeness and preclusion is a potentially lethal "Catch-22" for § 1983 takings claimants.

XVII. PRECLUSION DEFENSES

Under the full faith and credit statute, 28 U.S.C. § 1738, federal courts in § 1983 actions must give state court judgments the same preclusive effect they would receive in state court under state law.[305] This principle controls so long as the federal litigant against whom preclusion is asserted had a full and fair opportunity to litigate her federal claims in state court. A full and fair opportunity to be heard requires only that state judicial procedures meet minimal procedural due process requirements.[306]

The full faith and credit statute governs even with respect to federal claims asserted by involuntary state court litigants, like criminal defendants;[307] and takings claimants who were required to pursue a state court just compensation remedy.[308] Furthermore, the full faith and credit statute governs even if the federal court § 1983 claimant has no alternative federal court remedy, as when a Fourth Amendment claim is not assertable in a federal habeas corpus proceeding under *Stone v. Powell*.[309] The full faith and credit statute applies even as to claims that could have been, but were not, litigated in the state court proceeding, if state preclusion law encompasses the doctrine of claim preclusion.[310]

---

303. Palazzolo v. Rhode Island, 533 U.S. 606 (2001).

304. San Remo Hotel v. San Francisco, 125 S. Ct. 2491 (2005). See Part XVII, *supra*.

305. San Remo Hotel v. San Francisco, 125 S. Ct. 2491 (2005); Migra v. Warren City Sch. Dist., 465 U.S. 75 (1984); Allen v. McCurry, 449 U.S. 90 (1980). *See also* Haring v. Prosise, 462 U.S. 306 (1983).

306. Kremer v. Chemical Const. Corp., 456 U.S. 461 (1982); Allen v. McCurry, 449 U.S. 90 (1980).

307. Allen v. McCurry, 449 U.S. 90 (1980).

308. San Remo Hotel v. San Francisco, 125 S. Ct. 2491 (2005).

309. 428 U.S. 465 (1976). *See* Allen v. McCurry, 449 U.S. 90 (1980).

310. Migra v. Warren City Sch. Dist., 465 U.S. 75 (1984).

A. Administrative Res Judicata

Although § 1983 plaintiffs are not required to exhaust state administrative remedies, many § 1983 plaintiffs in fact choose to do so. In *University of Tennessee v. Elliott*,[311] the Supreme Court held that an agency's fact findings may preclude relitigation in a § 1983 action. Under *Elliott*, "when a state agency 'acting in a judicial capacity . . . resolves disputed issues of fact properly before it which the parties have had an adequate opportunity to litigate', . . . federal courts must give the agency's fact finding the same preclusive effect to which it would be entitled in the State's courts."[312] The decision in *Elliott* was not based upon the full faith and credit statute, but upon federal common-law preclusion principles.

B. Arbitration Decisions

In *McDonald v. City of West Branch*,[313] the Supreme Court held that arbitration decisions are not entitled to preclusive effect in § 1983 actions. The Court in *McDonald* found that an arbitration proceeding is not a judicial proceeding within the meaning of the full faith and credit statute. Furthermore, Congress intended § 1983 to be judicially enforced, and arbitration is not an adequate substitute for judicial enforcement.

XVIII. STATUTE OF LIMITATIONS

A. Limitations Period

There is no federal statute of limitations for § 1983 claims. Given this deficiency in federal law, 42 U.S.C. § 1988(a) requires federal courts to borrow a state's limitations period. In *Wilson v. Garcia*,[314] the Supreme Court held that the federal court should borrow the state's limitations period for personal injury actions, so long as the period is not inconsistent with the policies of § 1983. This means that the governing limitations period for federal court § 1983 actions may differ from state to state. A state's unduly short limitations period (e.g., six months) is inconsistent with the policies of § 1983.[315] "[W]here state law provides multiple statutes of limitations for

---

311. 478 U.S. 788 (1986).
312. *University of Tennessee*, 478 U.S. at 799.
313. 466 U.S. 284 (1984).
314. 471 U.S. 261 (1985).
315. *See* Burnett v. Grattan, 468 U.S. 42 (1984).

personal injury actions, courts . . . should borrow the general or residual statute for personal injury actions."[316]

B. Relation Back

Whether an amended complaint "relates back" to the filing of the original complaint for limitations purposes is governed by FED. R. CIV. P. 15(c). Under Rule 15, the amended complaint will relate back to the filing of the original complaint if the claim in the amended complaint arose out of the same conduct or transaction in the original complaint. If the amended complaint "changes" the defendant, the amended complaint will relate back to the filing of the original complaint if the amended complaint arose out of the same conduct as the original complaint, the newly named defendant, within the period of service of the summons and complaint, received notice of the institution of the action that will avoid prejudice in defending the action, and the newly named defendant "knew or should have known that, but for a mistake concerning the identity of the proper party, the action would have been brought against the party."[317] Rule 15(c) provides that when, as in §1983 actions, state law governs the limitation period, a state law relations back doctrine that is more forgiving than the Rule 15(c)'s relation back doctrine will govern the issue.[318]

Most courts hold that an amendment of a complaint substituting a John Doe defendant with the names of the actual officers does not relate back to the filing of the original complaint.[319] The rationale of these decisions is that lack of knowledge about the names of alleged wrongdoer defendants is not a "mistake" within the meaning of Rule 15(c).[320]

C. Accrual

Unlike the selection of the limitations period, which is determined by reference to state law, the accrual of a § 1983 claim is a question of federal law.

---

316. Owens v. Okure, 488 U.S. 235, 236 (1989).

317. FED. R. CIV. P. 15(a).

318. *See* Advisory Committee note to 1991 Amendment to FED. R. CIV. P. 15.

319. Garrett v. Fleming, 362 F.3d 692, 696–97 (10th Cir. 2004); Wayne v. Jarvis, 197 F.3d 1098 (11th Cir. 1999), *cert. denied,* 529 U.S. 1115 (2000); Jacobsen v. Osborne, 133 F.3d 315 (5th Cir. 1998); Cox v. Treadway, 75 F.3d 230 (6th Cir. 1996), *cert. denied,* 519 U.S. 821 (1996); Barrow v. Wethersfield Police Dept., 66 F.3d 466 (2d Cir. 1995), *modified,* 74 F.3d 1366 (2d Cir. 1996).

320. *But see* Singletary v. Pennsylvania Department of Corrections, 266 F.3d 186 (3d Cir. 2001) (rejecting lack of mistake rationale, but denying relation back because newly named official had not received notice of action within requisite time period).

Section 1983 claims generally accrue when the plaintiff knows or has reason to know of the injury that is the basis of her claim.[321] In applying this standard, courts seek to determine "what event should have alerted the typical lay person to protect his or her rights."[322] In employment termination cases, for example, the § 1983 claim accrues when the employee is notified of the termination, not when the termination became effective.[323]

XIX. SURVIVORSHIP AND WRONGFUL DEATH

A. Survivorship

The survivorship of § 1983 claims is not covered by federal law. In *Robertson v. Wegmann*,[324] the Supreme Court held that to remedy this deficiency in federal law, 42 U.S.C. § 1988(a) requires federal courts to borrow state survivorship law, as long as the state survivorship policy is not inconsistent with the policies of § 1983. The Court in *Robertson* ruled that the mere fact that the particular plaintiff's § 1983 claim abates under state law does not mean that the state law is inconsistent with the policies of § 1983. Rather, whether state survivorship law is compatible with the policies of § 1983 depends upon whether that state law is generally hospitable to the survival of § 1983 claims.[325]

B. Wrongful Death

The Supreme Court has not resolved whether a wrongful death claim may be brought under § 1983. There is considerable disagreement on this issue in the lower courts.[326] Some courts, viewing this as a deficiency in federal law, have borrowed state wrongful death law. Other courts have inquired whether the defendant's conduct, which caused the death of A, violated the

---

321. *See* 1C Schwartz, Section 1983 Litigation: Claims and Defenses, § 12.04.

322. Dixon v. Anderson, 928 F.2d 212, 215 (6th Cir. 1991). *See also* United States v. Kubrick, 444 U.S. 111, 121–22 (1979) (non-§ 1983) (patient's medical malpractice claim accrued when he was "aware of his injury and its cause"; accrual should not be further delayed until plaintiff learns of his legal rights regarding the claim).

323. Chardon v. Fernandez, 454 U.S. 6 (1981).

324. 436 U.S. 584 (1978).

325. *See, e.g.*, Banks v. Yokemick, 177 F. Supp. 2d 239 (S.D.N.Y. 2001) (New York survivorship law, which denies recovery for loss of enjoyment of life, is inconsistent with § 1983 policies of compensation and deterrence).

326. *See* Carringer v. Rogers, 333 F.3d 844, 850 n.9 (11th Cir. 2003) (the "right to wrongful death recoveryunder § 1983 has generated considerable debate among our sister circuits").

constitutionally protected rights of survivor B. There is also an argument that § 1983 itself authorizes a wrongful death remedy.[327] Of course, the § 1983 plaintiff may attempt to assert a state law wrongful death claim under the federal court's supplemental jurisdiction.

XX. ABSTENTION DOCTRINES

A. *Pullman* Abstention

A federal court § 1983 action may be defeated by one or more of the abstention doctrines. Under *Pullman* abstention, named after *Railroad Commission of Texas v. Pullman*,[328] a federal court may abstain when the contested state law is ambiguous and susceptible to a state court interpretation that may avoid or modify the federal constitutional issue. When a federal court invokes *Pullman* abstention, the § 1983 claimant must seek a state court interpretation of the state law from the highest court in the state. In some cases this may be accomplished expeditiously pursuant to a state certification procedure.[329] After completion of state court proceedings, the § 1983 claimant may return to federal court, unless she has voluntarily litigated her federal claims fully in state court.[330] The plaintiff may make an "*England* reservation" on the state court record of the right to litigate the federal claim in federal court.[331]

B. *Younger* Abstention

The most frequently invoked abstention doctrine in § 1983 actions is *Younger* abstention, named after the leading case of *Younger v. Harris*.[332] *Younger* abstention generally prohibits the federal courts from granting relief that interferes with pending state criminal prosecutions, or with pending state civil proceedings that implicate important state interests.[333] In *Middlesex*

327. The various theories are discussed in 1B SCHWARTZ, SECTION 1983 LITIGATION: CLAIMS AND DEFENSES, §§ 13.03–13.07. *See also* STEVEN H. STEINGLASS, WRONGFUL DEATH ACTIONS AND SECTION 1983, 60 IND. L.J. 559 (1985).

328. 312 U.S. 496 (1941).

329. *See* Arizonans for Official English v. Arizona, 520 U.S. 43 (1997).

330. England v. State Board of Medical Examiners, 375 U.S. 411 (1964).

331. *Id.*

332. 401 U.S. 37 (1971).

333. Younger v. Harris, 401 U.S. 37 (1971). *See also* Pennzoil Co. v. Texaco, 481 U.S. 1 (1987) (federal court may not interfere with enforcement of state civil judgment); Moore v. Sims, 442 U.S. 415 (1979) (child abuse proceedings); Trainor v. Hernandez,

County Ethics Comm'n v. Garden State Bar Ass'n,[334] the Supreme Court stated that three inquiries are relevant to *Younger* abstention:

1. is there an "ongoing" state judicial proceeding;
2. does the state proceeding implicate "important state interests;" and
3. "is there an adequate opportunity in the state proceedings to raise constitutional challenges."

Younger abstention also applies to quasi-judicial administrative proceedings implicating important state interests, so long as there is an adequate opportunity to litigate federal claims either in the administrative proceeding or in a state court judicial review proceeding.[335]

There are very narrow exceptions to the *Younger* doctrine. The most important exception requires a showing that the state prosecution was undertaken in bad faith, meaning not to secure a valid conviction but to retaliate against or chill the exercise of constitutionally protected rights. There is also an exception when the pending state proceedings fail to afford a full and fair opportunity to litigate the federal claim, but this is rarely found to be the case.[336]

C. *Colorado River* Abstention

Under *Colorado River* abstention, named after *Colorado River Water Conservation District v. United States*,[337] a federal court may abstain when there is a "parallel" proceeding pending in state court. Even when a "parallel" state court proceeding is pending, a federal court should invoke *Colorado River* abstention only in "exceptional" circumstances. The federal court's task "is not to find some substantial reason for the *exercise* of federal jurisdiction," but to determine whether special circumstances "justify the *surrender* of that jurisdiction."[338]

---

431 U.S. 434 (1977) (attachment of welfare benefits allegedly obtained by fraud); Juidice v. Vail, 430 U.S. 327 (1977) (civil contempt proceeding); Huffman v. Pursue, 420 U.S. 592 (1975) (quasi-criminal nuisance proceeding to enjoin allegedly obscene movie).

334. 457 U.S. 423, 432 (1982).

335. Ohio Civil Rights Comm'n v. Dayton Christian Sch., 477 U.S. 619 (1986).

336. Plaintiff bears the burden of showing that state procedural law barred presentation of her constitutional claim. Pennzoil Co. v. Texaco, Inc. 481 U.S. 1, 14 (1987); Moore v. Sims, 442 U.S. 415, 432 (1997).

337. 424 U.S. 800 (1976).

338. Moses H. Cone Memorial Hosp. v. Mercury Constr. Corp., 460 U.S. 1, 25–26 (1983) (emphasis in original).

D. *Burford* Abstention

Under *Burford* abstention, named after *Burford v. Sun Oil Co.*,[339] a federal court may abstain when federal court relief will disrupt a complex state regulatory scheme and the state's effort to centralize judicial review in a unified state court of special competence.[340] In *New Orleans Public Service, Inc. v. Council of New Orleans*,[341] the Supreme Court stated that under the

> *Burford* doctrine [w]here timely and adequate state-court review is available, a federal court sitting in equity must decline to interfere with the proceedings or orders of state administrative agencies: (1) when there are "difficult questions of state law bearing on policy problems of substantial public import whose importance transcends the result in the case then at bar"; or (2) where the "exercise of federal review of the question in a case and in similar cases would be disruptive of state efforts to establish a coherent policy with respect to a matter of substantial public concern."

E. Domestic Relations Doctrine

The "domestic relations" doctrine generally prohibits federal court adjudication of a domestic relations matter, such as custody, support, or alimony.[342] It is unclear whether this doctrine applies to § 1983 constitutional claims. In fact, federal courts have routinely adjudicated the constitutionality of state policies pertaining to family law matters.[343]

---

339. 319 U.S. 315 (1943).

340. New Orleans Public Service Inc. v. Council of New Orleans, 491 U.S. 350 (1989).

341. *Id.* at 362. (quoting Colorado River Water Conservation District v. United States, 424 U.S. 800, 814 (1976)).

342. *See, generally,* Akenbrandt v. Richards, 504 U.S. 689 (1992).

343. *See* Troxel v. Granville, 530 U.S. 57 (2000); Clarke v. Jeter, 486 U.S. 456 (1988); Lehr v. Robertson, 463 U.S. 248 (1983); Pickett v. Brown, 462 U.S. 1 (1983); Mills v. Habluetzel, 456 U.S. 91 (1982); Santosky v. Kramer, 455 U.S. 745 (1982); Lassiter v. Department of Social Servs., 452 U.S. 18 (1981); Little v. Streeter, 452 U.S. 1 (1981); Caban v. Mohammed, 441 U.S. 380 (1979); Orr v. Orr, 440 U.S. 268 (1979); Quilloin v. Walcott, 434 U.S. 246 (1978); Smith v. Organization of Foster Families for Equality & Reform, 431 U.S. 816 (1977); Sosna v. Iowa, 419 U.S. 393 (1975); Stanley v. Illinois, 405 U.S. 645 (1972). Given these decisions, it is hard to conclude that the domestic relations doctrine extends to all federal questions arising in the family law area. *See* Flood v. Braaten, 727 F.2d 303 (3d Cir. 1984). The Supreme Court's decision in Lehman v. Lycoming County Children's Servs., 458

F. Tax Injunction Act

The Tax Injunction Act prohibits federal courts from interfering with state and local tax collection, so long as the state provides a plain, speedy, and efficient remedy.[344] However, in *Hibbs v. Winn*,[345] the Supreme Court held that the Tax Injunction Act does not apply to a constitutional challenge to a state tax credit policy because such a claim does not interfere with the collection of state taxes.

XXI. MONETARY RELIEF

A. Compensatory Damages

Compensatory damages under § 1983 are normally determined according to common-law tort principles. In *Memphis Community School Dist. v. Stachura*[346] and *Carey v. Piphus*,[347] the Supreme Court held that compensatory damages for a constitutional violation under § 1983 must be based upon the actual injuries suffered by the plaintiff. The Court in *Memphis Community School District* and *Carey* ruled that when a § 1983 plaintiff suffers a violation of constitutional rights, but no actual injuries, she is entitled to an award of only $1 nominal damages.[348] Like common-law tort plaintiffs, § 1983 plaintiffs are required to take reasonable steps to mitigate their damages.

B. Punitive Damages

In *Smith v. Wade*,[349] the Supreme Court held that a § 1983 plaintiff may recover punitive damages against an official in her personal capacity, if the

---

U.S. 502 (1982), that federal habeas corpus is not available to contest the involuntary termination of parental rights, is based upon the fact that Congress did not intend that the federal habeas corpus statutes encompass child custody cases.

344. 28 U.S.C. § 1341. *See* California v. Grace Brethren Church, 457 U.S. 393 (1982); Rosewell v. La Salle National Bank, 450 U.S. 503 (1981). *See also* National Private Truck Council v. Oklahoma Tax Comm'n, 515 U.S. 582 (1995) (policies of § 1341 apply to state court § 1983 equitable actions contesting state tax policies); Fair Assessment in Real Estate v. McNary, 454 U.S. 100 (1981) (policies of § 1341 pertain to claims for damages).

345. 542 U.S. 88 (2004).

346. 477 U.S. 299 (1986) (First Amendment claim).

347. 435 U.S. 247 (1978) (procedural due process claim).

348. Corpus v. Bennett, 430 F.3d 912 (8th Cir. 2005) ("[O]ne dollar is recognized as an appropriate value for nominal damages.").

349. 461 U.S. 30 (1983).

official acted with a malicious or evil intent or in callous disregard of the plaintiff's federally protected rights.[350] "Although the specific intent to violate plaintiff's federally protected right will support a punitive damages award, 'reckless indifference' towards a plaintiff's federally protected right also suffices to authorize liability for punitive damages under § 1983."[351] The *Smith v. Wade* standard does not require a showing that the defendant engaged in "egregious" misconduct.[352] The burden is on defendant to introduce evidence of his financial circumstances.[353]

In *City of Newport v. Fact Concerts*,[354] the Supreme Court held that punitive damages may not be awarded against a municipal entity. Eleventh Amendment state sovereign immunity would bar a federal court award of punitive damages payable out of the state treasury.[355] Furthermore, as discussed in Part VI, *supra*, states and state entities are not suable "persons" within the meaning of § 1983.

Supreme Court decisional law holds that punitive damage awards that are "grossly excessive" violate substantive due process.[356] To determine whether the award is "grossly excessive," consideration must be given to (1) the degree of reprehensibility of defendant's conduct—the most important factor; (2) the ratio between the harm or potential harm to plaintiff and the punitive damages award; and (3) the disparity between the punitive damages award and civil penalties authorized or imposed in comparable cases.[357] The Supreme Court stated that "in practice, few [punitive damages] awards exceeding a single-digit ratio between punitive and compensatory damages, to a significant degree, will satisfy due process."[358] However, the Court also recognized that a larger ratio "may comport with due process when a

350. Punitive damages may also be based upon "oppressive" conduct when the defendant misused authority or exploited plaintiff's weakness. Dang v. Cross, 422 F.3d 800 (9th Cir. 2005).

351. Powell v. Alexander, 391 F.3d 1, 19 (1st Cir. 2004).

352. Kolstad v. American Dental Ass'n, 527 U.S. 526 (1999).

353. Tapalian v. Tusino, 377 F.3d 1, 8 (1st Cir. 2004); Mason v. Oklahoma Turnpike Authority, 182 F.3d. 1212, 1214 (10th Cir. 1999); Zarcone v. Perry, 572 F.3d 52, 56 (2d Cir. 1978).

354. 453 U.S. 247 (1981).

355. *See* Part XIII, *supra.*

356. State Farm Mutual Automobile Insurance Co. v. Campbell, 538 U.S. 408 (2003); BMW of North America v. Gore, 517 U.S. 559 (1996).

357. *Id.*

358. State Farm Mutual Automobile Insurance Co. v. Campbell, 538 U.S. 408, 425 (2003).

particularly egregious act has resulted in only a small amount of economic damages."[359] These principles apply in § 1983 actions.[360]

C. Release Dismissal Agreements

Section 1983 damage claims may be settled, waived, or released. A recurring issue in § 1983 actions concerns the validity of "release dismissal agreements" pursuant to which law enforcement authorities agree to dismiss criminal charges in exchange for the release of § 1983 claims. In *Town of Newton v. Rumery*,[361] the Supreme Court held that these agreements are not automatically invalid. Rather, the validity of a release-dismissal agreement should be evaluated on a case-by-case basis to determine whether the agreement (1) was voluntary, (2) is the product of prosecutorial overreaching or other misconduct, and (3) adversely affects the public interest.

D. Indemnification

An important issue in many § 1983 cases is whether the relevant governmental entity will indemnify the defendant official for her monetary liability. Indemnification is not covered by federal law; it is strictly a matter of state or local law.

XXII. ATTORNEYS' FEES

The Civil Rights Attorney's Fees Awards Act of 1976, 42 U.S.C. § 1988(b), authorizes courts, in their discretion, to award reasonable attorneys' fees to the prevailing party in a § 1983 action. Section 1988 fees are an "integral part" of § 1983 remedies.[362] The Supreme Court has admonished the lower

359. *Id.* at 419 (quoting BMW of North America v. Gore, 517 U.S. 559, 582 (1996)).
360. *See, e.g.,* Tapalian v. Tusino, 377 F.3d 1 (1st Cir. 2004); Williams v. Kaufman County, 352 F.3d 994 (5th Cir. 2003); DiSorbo v. Hoy, 343 F.3d 172 (2d Cir. 2003); Bogle v. McClure, 332 F.3d 347 (11th Cir. 2003); Lee v. Edwards, 101 F.3d 805 (2d Cir. 1996); Morgan v. Woessner, 997 F.2d 1244 (9th Cir.1993), *cert. dismissed,* 510 U.S. 1033 (1994).
361. 480 U.S. 386 (1985).
362. Maine v. Thiboutet, 448 U.S. 1, 11 (1980). *See also* Hudson v. Michigan, 126 S. Ct. 2159, 2167 (2006) ("Since some civil-rights violations would yield damages too small to justify the expense of litigation, Congress has authorized attorney's fees for civil rights plaintiffs.").

federal courts that a "request for [§ 1988(b)] attorney's fees should not result in a second major litigation."[363] Nevertheless, § 1988(b) fee disputes often do result in a "second major litigation."[364] Fee litigation "can turn a simple civil case into two or even more cases—the case on the merits, the case for fees, the case for fees on appeal, the case for fees for proving fees, and so on ad infinitum or at least ad nauseam."[365] The goal of avoiding a second major litigation "has proved a somewhat pious and forlorn hope. In view of the complexities the Supreme Court and the lower courts have grafted onto the fee calculation process, federal courts are today enmeshed in an inordinately time consuming and ultimately futile search for a fee that reflects market forces in the absence of a relevant market."[366]

A. Prevailing Parties

The courts interpret the § 1988 fee shifting statute to mean that attorneys' fees should be awarded to a prevailing plaintiff almost as a matter of course. Fees should be denied to a prevailing plaintiff only when "special circumstances" would make a fee award unjust. The fiscal impact of a fee award upon a municipality is not a special circumstance.[367] Defendant's good faith is not a special circumstance justifying denial of fees to a prevailing plaintiff.[368] The fact the fees will ultimately be paid by taxpayers is not a special circumstance justifying either a denial or reduction of fees.[369] However, plaintiff's grossly inflated fee application may be a special circumstance justifying the denial of fees.[370]

Unlike prevailing plaintiffs, prevailing defendants are not presumptively entitled to fees. Prevailing defendants are entitled to attorneys' fees only

---

363. Hensley v. Eckerhart, 461 U.S. 424, 437 (1983). *Accord* Webb v. Bd. of Educ., 471 U.S. 234, 244 n.20 (1985); Blum v. Stenson, 465 U.S. 886, 902 n.19 (1984).

364. Doe v. Ward, 282 F. Supp.2d 323, 329 n.4 (W.D.Pa. 2003) (principle that fees should not result in major litigation "is one of the emptiest phrases in our jurisprudence" because fee questions "most definitely constitute major litigation").

365. Ustrak v. Fairman, 851 F.2d 983, 987 (7th Cir. 1988). *See also* Divane v. Krull Electric Co., 319 F.3d 307, 314 (7th Cir. 2003) (ERISA suit).

366. System Management, Inc. v. Loiselle, 154 F. Supp.2d 195, 207 (D.Mass 2001).

367. Aware Woman Clinic v. Cocoa Beach, 629 F.2d 1146, 1149–50 (5th Cir. 1980).

368. *See, e.g.,* Williams v. Hanover Housing Auth., 113 F.3d 1294 (1st Cir. 1997).

369. *See, e.g.,* Ramos v. Lamm, 713 F.3d 546 (10th Cir. 1983).

370. 2 Schwartz & Kirklin, Section 1983 Litigation: Statutory Attorneys' Fees, § 3.14 (3d ed. 1997).

when the plaintiff's action was "frivolous, unreasonable, or groundless, or . . . the plaintiff continued to litigate after it clearly became so."[371]

The plaintiff will be considered a prevailing party when she succeeds on "any significant issue" that achieves some of the benefit sought in bringing suit.[372] To be a prevailing party, the plaintiff must obtain some judicial relief as a result of the litigation; the mere fact that the court expressed the view that plaintiff's constitutional rights were violated does not qualify the plaintiff as a prevailing party.[373] The mere fact that the plaintiff prevailed on a procedural issue during the course of the litigation, such as by obtaining an appellate decision granting a new trial, does not qualify the plaintiff as a prevailing party.[374] "[A] plaintiff 'prevails when actual relief on the merits of [her] claim materially alters the legal relationship between the parties by modifying the defendant's behavior in a way that directly benefits the plaintiff.'"[375]

In *Farrar v. Hobby*,[376] the Supreme Court held that a § 1983 plaintiff who recovers only nominal damages is nevertheless a prevailing party eligible to recover attorneys' fees under § 1988(b); but usually a reasonable fee in these circumstances is either no fees or very low fees. Justice O'Connor's concurring opinion in *Farrar* urged courts to consider the difference between the damages sought and the damages recovered, the significance of the legal issues on which plaintiff claims to have prevailed, and the public purpose served by the litigation. The lower federal courts have generally relied upon the O'Connor concurrence in evaluating the fee issue in nominal damages cases.[377]

A plaintiff who asserts a § 1983 claim that is not insubstantial and obtains relief on a "pendent" (i.e., "supplemental") state law claim is a prevailing party eligible for fees under § 1988, even though the § 1983 claim is

---

371. Hughes v. Rowe, 449 U.S. 5, 14 (1978); Christiansburg Garment Co. v. EEOC, 434 U.S. 412, 422 (1978). Sullivan v. School Board of Pipellas County, 773 F.2d 1182, 1189 (11th Cir. 1985) (There are no "hard-and-fast rules" for determining whether plaintiff's claim was frivolous; courts may consider (1) whether plaintiff established prima facie case; (2) whether defendant offered to settle; and (3) whether district court dismissed case before trial or after trial on merits).

372. Hensley v. Eckerhart, 461 U.S. 424, 433 (1983); Texas State Teacher's Ass'n v. Garland Indep. S.D., 489 U.S. 782 (1989).

373. Hewitt v. Helms, 482 U.S. 755 (1987).

374. Hanrahan v. Hampton, 446 U.S. 754 (1980).

375. Farrar v. Hobby, 506 U.S. 103, 111–12 (1992).

376. 506 U.S. 103 (1992).

377. *See, e.g.*, Mercer v. Duke Univ., 401 F.3d 199 (4th Cir. 2005); Gudenkauf v. Stauffer Communications, Inc., 158 F.3d 1078 (10th Cir. 1998).

not decided on the merits.[378] The plaintiff, however, is not entitled to fees if the § 1983 claim is insubstantial.[379]

The plaintiff may be a prevailing party even though she did not prevail on all of her claims. In *Hensley v. Eckerhart*,[380] the Supreme Court held that when plaintiff prevails on some but not all claims arising out of common facts, the results obtained determine whether the fees should be reduced because of lack of success on some claims. The Court said that in determining the amount of the fee award, "the most critical factor is the degree of success obtained."[381] The Court in *Hensley* also ruled that when the plaintiff prevails on some but not all claims that are not interrelated, the plaintiff should be awarded fees only for the successful claims.[382] However, when the successful and unsuccessful claims are interrelated, the district court should focus on the overall results achieved. If the plaintiff achieved "excellent results," she should recover a full compensatory fee award. If the plaintiff achieved "only partial or limited success," the district court should consider whether the lodestar fee amount (reasonable hours multiplied by reasonable rates) is excessive. The district court should award only that amount of fees that is "reasonable in relation to the results obtained."[383]

In *Buckhannon Board and Care Home v. West Virginia Department of Health and Human Services*,[384] the Supreme Court held that the fact that the lawsuit was a catalyst in causing the defendant to alter its conduct to the plaintiff does not qualify the plaintiff as a prevailing party. The Court said that to be a prevailing party, the plaintiff must secure a favorable judgment on the merits or a court-ordered consent decree. The decision in *Buckhannon* overturned the catalyst doctrine that had been adopted by eleven circuits and rejected only by the Fourth Circuit. Under *Buckhannon,* only "enforceable judgments on the merits and court-ordered consent decrees create the 'material alteration of the legal relationship of the parties necessary

378. Maher v. Gagne, 448 U.S. 122 (1980); Milwe v. Cavuoto, 653 F.2d 80 (2d Cir. 1981).

379. *See, e.g.,* United States v. Washington, 813 F.2d 1020 (9th Cir. 1987), *cert. denied,* 485 U.S. 1034 (1988).

380. 461 U.S. 424 (1983).

381. *Id.* at 436. *Accord* Farrar v. Hobby, 506 U.S. 103 (1992).

382. "[W]ork on an [unrelated] unsuccessful claim cannot be deemed to have been expended in pursuit of the ultimate result achieved. The congressional intent to limit awards to prevailing parties requires that these unrelated claims be treated as if they had been raised in separate lawsuits, and therefore no fee may be awarded for services on the unsuccessful claim." *Hensley,* 461 U.S. at 435.

383. *Hensley*, 461 U.S. at 440.

384. 532 U.S. 598 (2001).

to permit an award of attorney's fees."[385] Dictum in *Buckhannon* states that private settlements not embodied in a judicial decree will not qualify the plaintiff as a prevailing party because "[p]rivate settlements do not entail the judicial approval and oversight involved in consent decrees."[386]

The decision in *Buckhannon* has generated a great deal of lower court litigation, raising such issues as whether a preliminary injunction or "so ordered" settlement qualifies the plaintiff as a prevailing party. A "stipulation and order of discontinuance," combined with court retention of jurisdiction over the settlement for enforcement purposes, may qualify the plaintiff as a prevailing party.[387]

A pro se plaintiff is not eligible to recover attorney's fees, even if the plaintiff is a lawyer.[388] Thus, only a prevailing plaintiff who is represented by counsel is eligible to recover fees.

B. Computation of Fee Award

Fees awarded under § 1988 are generally computed under the lodestar method of multiplying reasonable hours by reasonable hourly market rates for lawyers in the community with comparable backgrounds and experience.[389] The underlying goal of a § 1988 (b) fee award is to "attract competent counsel."[390] The Supreme Court has generally disapproved of the use of upward adjustments to the lodestar.[391] In very rare cases an upward adjustment may be made on the basis of superior quality of representation.[392] Fees may also be adjusted upward to compensate the prevailing party for delay in payment, either by using current market rates rather than historic rates or by adjusting historic rates to account for inflation.[393] The lodestar should not be enhanced to compensate for the risk of nonsuccess when plaintiff's

---

385. *Buckhannon*, 532 U.S. at 604.
386. *Id.* at 604 n.7.
387. Roberson v. Giuliani, 346 F.3d 75 (2d Cir. 2003).
388. Kay v. Ehrler, 499 U.S. 432 (1991).
389. Blum v. Stenson, 465 U.S. 886 (1984).
390. Hensley v. Eckerhart, 461 U.S. 424, 430 (1983).
391. Blum v. Stenson, 465 U.S. 886 (1984).
392. Pennsylvania v. Delaware Valley Citizens' Council, 478 U.S. 546 (1986); Blum v. Stenson, 465 U.S. 886, 889 (1984). ("The quality of representation, . . . generally is reflected in the reasonable hourly rate. It, therefore, may justify an upward adjustment only in the rare case where the fee applicant offers specific evidence to show that the quality of service rendered was superior to that one reasonably should expect in light of the hourly rates charged and that the success was exceptional.")
393. Missouri v. Jenkins, 491 U.S. 274 (1989).

lawyer was retained on a contingency basis.[394] In *City of Riverside v. Rivera*,[395] the Supreme Court held that the fees awarded need not be proportional to the damages recovered by the plaintiff. The approximately $245,000 fees awarded in *City of Riverside* substantially exceed the $33,350 damages plaintiff recovered. "Because damages awards do not reflect fully the public benefit advanced by civil rights litigation, Congress did not intend for fees in civil rights cases . . . to depend on obtaining substantial monetary relief."[396]

The fees awarded under § 1988 are not limited to the amount of fees recoverable by counsel pursuant to a contingency fee agreement.[397] Conversely, the fees collectable under a contingency agreement may exceed the fees awarded under § 1988.[398]

Fees generally may not be awarded for work performed on administrative proceedings that preceded the § 1983 action.[399] In addition, expert witnesses expenses are not recoverable as part of the § 1988 fee award in § 1983 actions.[400]

Legal services and other nonprofit organizations are entitled to have fee awards computed on the basis of reasonable market rates rather than upon the lower salaries paid to the organization's lawyers.[401]

C. Other Fee Issues

When prospective relief is awarded against state officials under the doctrine of *Ex parte Young*, an award of fees payable out of the state treasury is not barred by the Eleventh Amendment.[402] The Eleventh Amendment does not bar an upward adjustment in the lodestar to compensate for delay in payment.[403]

---

394. City of Burlington v. Dague, 505 U.S. 557 (1992).
395. 477 U.S. 561 (1986).
396. *Id.* at 575.
397. Blanchard v. Bergeron, 489 U.S. 87 (1989).
398. Venegas v. Mitchell, 495 U.S. 82 (1990).
399. Webb v. Bd. of Educ., 466 U.S. 935 (1984).
400. West Virginia Univ. Hosp. v. Casey, 499 U.S. 83 (1991). An amendment to § 1988 authorized on an award of expert witness fees only in actions under 42 U.S.C. § 1981 or § 1981 (a).
401. Blum v. Stenson, 465 U.S. 886 (1984). *Accord* Washington v. Seattle School Dist., 458 U.S. 457, 487 n.31 (1982).
402. Hutto v. Finney, 437 U.S. 678 (1979).
403. Missouri v. Jenkins, 491 U.S. 274 (1989).

Fed. R. Civ. P. 68 provides that "a party defending a claim may serve upon the adverse party an offer to allow judgment to be taken against the defending party for the money . . . specified in the offer, with costs then accrued." If the offeree rejects the offer, and "the judgment finally obtained by the offeree is not more favorable than the offer, the offeree must pay the costs incurred after making the offer." In *Marek v. Chesney*,[404] the Supreme Court held that the "costs" referred to in Rule 68 encompass § 1988(b) attorneys' fees. Therefore, under Rule 68, even though the plaintiff was the prevailing party, if the plaintiff did not obtain more favorable relief than she had been offered under Rule 68, she may not recover from the defendant any § 1988(b) fees that accrued after the rejected offer of judgment.

Marek did not address whether a defendant who makes a successful Rule 68 offer is entitled to § 1988 fees that accrued after the date of the offer. The great weight of lower court authority holds that although Rule 68 authorizes an award of post-offer "costs" to the defendant, these costs do not include § 1988 fees to a nonprevailing defendant.[405]

In *Evans v. Jeff D.*,[406] the Supreme Court held that an offer by defendant to settle plaintiff's claim on the merits and the claim for fees simultaneously is not necessarily unethical. The Court in *Evans* said that a claim for § 1988 fees is considered part of "the arsenal of remedies available to combat violations of civil rights, a goal not invariably inconsistent with conditioning settlement on the merits on a waiver of statutory attorney's fees."[407]

---

404. 473 U.S. 1 (1985).

405. Champion Produce, Inc. v. Ruby Robinson Co., 342 F.3d 1016 (9th Cir. 2003) (non-§ 1983); Payne v. Milwaukee County, 288 F.3d 1021 (7th Cir. 2002); Harbor Motor Co. v. Arnell Chevrolet-Geo, 265 F.2d 638 (7th Cir. 2001) (non-§ 1983); O'Brien v. City of Greers Ferry, 873 F.2d 1115 (8th Cir. 1989); Crossman v. Maccoccio, 806 F.2d 329 (1st Cir. 1986), *cert. denied,* 481 U.S. 1029 (1987). *Contra* Jordan v. Time, Inc., 111 F.3d 102 (11th Cir. 1997).

406. 475 U.S. 717 (1986).

407. *Id.* at 731–32.

Chapter 2

PROCEDURAL GUIDE TO SECTION 1983 LITIGATION IN FEDERAL COURT

by Jane K. Swanson

I. INTRODUCTION

The aim of this chapter is to identify and briefly examine some of the specialized procedural and tactical issues involved in the litigation of a § 1983 case. It presents these issues in the order in which they typically must be dealt within the litigation process. Chapter 3 of this book focuses specifically on § 1983 litigation in state courts. So, this chapter will for the most part deal with § 1983 procedural issues as they occur in the federal court system, with some brief references to state court differences where applicable.

II. PRE-LITIGATION CONSIDERATIONS FOR PLAINTIFF'S COUNSEL

For any federal case, Federal Rule of Civil Procedure 11 requires at least a general "inquiry reasonable under the circumstances." For a § 1983 case, an intelligent case acceptance decision requires much more (i.e., an examination of more varied and complex factors than are immediately obvious).

A. Advisable Factual and Legal Investigation Before Case Acceptance

If the client's objective is money damages, counsel will need to consider how the doctrine of qualified immunity[1] can reasonably be expected to

---

1. *See* Chapter 9, "Individual Immunity Defenses under Section 1983."

affect the client's likelihood of being able to impose damages liability on a defendant. This in turn calls for a factually specific description of the defendant's conduct and a comparison of it to the standards set by the U.S. Supreme Court and the relevant circuit court in comparable cases.

Similarly, as § 1983 liability may not be imposed on a respondeat superior basis, counsel should conduct a more particularized evaluation of the potential liability of the governmental unit on whose behalf the individual defendant acted.[2] This may entail, for example, an examination of relevant state law to determine which officials had policymaking authority for which issues on behalf of the governmental unit in question. Then, counsel will need to evaluate if and how the policies set by these officials were the "moving force" that caused the client's damages.[3] Most possible bases of governmental unit liability require extensive factual development as to the policies, procedures, customs, and practices of the governmental unit in question and the ways in which they brought about the deprivation of the client's constitutional or statutory rights.

The Supreme Court's opinion in *Leatherman v. Tarrant County,*[4] discussed below, has eliminated the need for plaintiff's counsel to be able to plead a detailed factual basis for governmental liability in the initial complaint without even the benefit of discovery. But, that case has not changed the practical economic advisability of evaluating the relevant governmental unit's potential § 1983 liability as carefully as possible, before deciding whether to accept a case and commit large amounts of time and other resources to it. Counsel should also investigate governmental policies about indemnifying employees, either voluntarily or by state or local law.

Typically, the prospective client will have almost none of the factual information that would bear on the issue of governmental unit liability. In order to develop such information, it is worthwhile to check at the courthouse, and in available computer-accessible data banks, for similar litigation filed against the same governmental unit. It is also worthwhile to review discovery materials in similar litigation, and to confer with lawyers involved in those cases. Additionally, the state equivalent of the Freedom of Information Act (such as the Texas Public Information Act[5]) can be very useful in obtaining documents about the history of the governmental unit concerning the type of problem the client alleges.

---

2. See Chapter 4, "Municipal Liability under Section 1983."
3. *See* Board of County Comm'rs of Bryan County, Oklahoma v. Brown, 520 U.S. 397, 407–08 (1997). *See also* Chapter 4, "Municipal Liability under Section 1983."
4. 507 U.S. 163 (1993).
5. Texas Gov't Code, ch. 552.

B. Explanations to Client

A thorough examination of these factors will permit a better-reasoned case acceptance decision. It will also facilitate a more realistic and thorough explanation to the client about the difficulties, complexities, costs, and chances of success. Clients with potential § 1983 claims are unlikely to be familiar with any standard of employer or supervisory liability other than respondeat superior. So, they may have unrealistic expectations if not given a basic explanation of what standards are applicable to this determination in a § 1983 case. Potential procedural complications, such as the possibility of an interlocutory appeal on immunity grounds, should be considered and explained at this stage as well. This will allow the accompanying delay and cost factors to be weighed together with other relevant considerations. Then lawyer and client can reach a realistic decision about whether to make the necessary time and cost commitment to go forward with the case.

C. Fee Agreement with Plaintiff

Whatever fee agreement is reached with the client, § 1983 litigation is almost invariably done with the goal of ultimately collecting attorneys' fees from the defendant pursuant to 42 U.S.C. § 1988. The Supreme Court has held that the fee agreement between a plaintiff and her counsel is not determinative of the amount of the defendant's §1988 fee liability, if the plaintiff prevails.[6] The converse is also true; that is, if the plaintiff agrees to a fee contract that would result in payment of a higher fee than the court awards against the defendant, the plaintiff remains responsible for the higher fee if it is otherwise proper.[7]

Plaintiff's counsel should be aware that some local federal court rules require ultimate court approval of the plaintiff's attorneys' fees. Some also specify how expenses are to be calculated in arriving at plaintiff's final liability on a contingent fee contract. Thorough familiarity with the local rules of the jurisdiction in which the case is to be filed may avoid later embarrassment on this point.

If the sole or primary aim of the case is to obtain declaratory and/or injunctive relief, counsel should be aware at this stage of the *Evans v. Jeff D.*[8] holding and its implications for attorneys' fees recovery. In *Jeff D.*, the Supreme Court, in effect, gave its stamp of approval to a defendant's tactic

---

6. Blanchard v. Bergeron, 489 U.S. 87, 95–96 (1989).
7. Venegas v. Mitchell, 495 U.S. 82, 90 (1990).
8. 475 U.S. 717, 729–30 (1986).

of offering to agree to the requested declaratory and injunctive relief on condition that the plaintiff waive all potential attorneys' fees recovery from the defendant.

There is no easy solution to the potential problems raised by this scenario for the plaintiff and the plaintiff's counsel. But, a frank discussion about this possibility prior to filing the case provides a much greater possibility of an acceptable resolution than one that takes place only after such an offer has been made and after plaintiff's counsel has expended substantial time on the case. If dealing with a potential plaintiff who will not have the financial resources to pay a reasonable fee, and whose primary aim is injunctive and/or declaratory relief, counsel should consider reaching some agreement as to the handling of a future *Evans v. Jeff D.* situation, and incorporating the agreement into the written fee contract with the plaintiff.

D. Readiness of Claims for Court

While a complete exploration of any of these three issues would be well beyond the scope of this chapter, some discussion is appropriate at this point. It may be possible, at this stage, to correct situations that could otherwise be stumbling blocks later in the litigation process.

1. Ripeness

This is not ordinarily a disputed issue in actions for damages outside the land use setting. It is always a requirement to consider, however, when planning a suit for injunctive relief. The purpose of the ripeness requirement is to assure that the constitutional Article 3 "case or controversy" requirement is met. That is, it assures that the parties have a real, not merely a hypothetical, dispute that will not be a waste of judicial resources.

Practically speaking, the ripeness requirement focuses on the requirement that the defendant's challenged action, or refusal to act, be definite and final, so that the court process initiated to correct it is really needed. Frequently, plaintiff's counsel can avoid or minimize ripeness concern in lawsuits seeking declaratory and/or injunctive relief by postponing litigation until the litigant has made all reasonable attempts to obtain defendant's definitive and provable refusal to provide the relief that the plaintiff is seeking. For example, in *Georgia Advocacy Office v. Camp,*[9] the Advocacy staff sought to enjoin managers of a care home for the mentally ill from denying their access to residents. The Advocacy Office was funded to serve this

9. 172 F.3d 1294 (11th Cir. 1999).

population, and regulations secured their right of access to provide legal information and advocacy. The Eleventh Circuit found this claim not to be ripe for court review, however, because the plaintiffs could not prove a clear request and a clear refusal of their right to visit for this purpose.

The plaintiffs in *Georgia Advocacy Office* may well have been correct in thinking that a request to see the care home residents for the purposes they had in mind would have had no realistic chance of success. However, a clear, provable attempt to do so would have been relatively simple to accomplish and might have saved a great deal of lawyer time later. Consideration of this type of ripeness concern before filing suit for injunctive relief is not to be confused with a need to exhaust administrative remedies or to comply with locally created notice requirements for damage claims.

Plaintiffs in § 1983 land use litigation have encountered particularly complex and troublesome ripeness problems.[10] One component of this issue is the question of whether the regulatory entity has reached a truly final determination about what development it will permit. The Supreme Court in *Williamson County Regional Planning Commission v. Hamilton Bank*[11] carefully distinguished land use "ripeness" considerations from administrative exhaustion requirements, which theoretically may not be imposed on § 1983 plaintiffs. According to the Court, ripeness requires only that "the initial decisionmaker has arrived at a definitive position on the issue that inflicts an actual concrete injury"; exhaustion, in contrast, refers to "procedures by which an injured party may seek review of an adverse decision by a third party, in the hope of obtaining a remedy."[12] Exactly what a landowner must do to secure a determination the courts would accept as "definitive" and "concrete" was open to substantial question after *Williamson*.

Palazzolo v. Rhode Island[13] clarified the Court's "ripeness" doctrine in a way that provided some relief for landowners. The *Palazzolo* Court reversed the Rhode Island Supreme Court's decision that a landowner's "takings" claim based on regulatory prohibition of development was unripe. The court held that "once it becomes clear that the agency lacks the discretion to permit any development, or the permissible uses of the property are known to a reasonable degree of certainty, a takings claim is likely to have ripened."[14] "Landowners must explore development opportunities only if there is uncertainty as to the land's permitted use."[15]

---

10. This topic is more fully addressed in Chapter 7, "The Section 1983 Land Use Case."
11. 473 U.S. 172 (1985).
12. 473 U.S. at 193.
13. 533 U.S. 606 (2001).
14. 533 U.S. at 620.
15. 533 U.S. at 622.

2. *Exhaustion Requirements and Related Concerns*

Exhaustion issues, in general terms, involve statutory or court-imposed requirements that other administrative or judicial remedies be pursued unsuccessfully to their conclusion, before filing a § 1983 claim in court. This section attempts only to mention the basic characteristics of more-commonly encountered exhaustion requirements. This should alert counsel to situations in which further research is required before proceeding with a § 1983 court action.

a. Requirements specified by statute. In a few instances, a specific federal statute controls the question of what, if any, alternate remedies must be pursued to their conclusion before seeking court relief for violations of federal constitutional or statutory rights. One example is the federal habeas corpus statute for prisoners, which requires prior exhaustion of state judicial remedies.[16] The U.S. Supreme Court has held that any prisoner action seeking declaratory or injunctive relief from the *fact* or *duration* of current confinement (as opposed to its conditions) is in effect a habeas corpus action.[17] So, however the prisoner seeks to categorize the case, it requires exhaustion. Additionally, the Civil Rights of Institutionalized Persons Act[18] requires that potential § 1983 claims of adult inmates of state and local correctional facilities be first asserted through administrative grievance procedures.

Another example of a statutorily imposed exhaustion requirement applicable to claimed violations of federal constitutional and statutory rights is the 1986 amendment to the Individuals with Disabilities Education Act (IDEA). This statute addresses the circumstances under which students and their parents may assert alternate or additional causes of action (apparently including § 1983 actions) in fact situations to which the IDEA would apply. It provides that nothing in the IDEA restricts the assertion of such alternate or additional claims. However, plaintiffs asserting them to seek relief that would also be available through the IDEA must exhaust its administrative remedies.[19]

b. State judicial remedies. In 1961, the Supreme Court clearly indicated in *Monroe v. Pape*[20] that a § 1983 plaintiff need not either exhaust the possibilities of obtaining relief in state court or demonstrate the inadequacy of available state court procedures as a prerequisite to filing a federal court § 1983 action. In fact, to attempt to do so would invite res judicata problems.

---

16. 28 U.S.C. § 2254(b)–(c).
17. Preiser v. Rodriguez, 411 U.S. 475, 496–500 (1973).
18. 42 U.S.C. § 1997e.
19. 20 U.S.C. § 1415 (l).
20. 365 U.S. 167, 173–80 (1961).

This is still basically good law, but plaintiff's counsel should be aware of some circumstances in which the federal courts now impose a directive that sounds on the surface like an exhaustion requirement. In fact, it is something even worse. A § 1983 plaintiff trying to use a federal constitutional due process theory to vindicate harm not brought about by the application of established state procedures will encounter the growing body of case law deferring to state-created tort remedies. If these state-law-based remedies are theoretically available and at least minimally adequate at providing compensation for the harm, a would-be § 1983 plaintiff cannot state a valid claim for deprivation of due process under color of state law.[21] This, of course, is not an exhaustion requirement, but instead a court-imposed mandatory detour away from constitutional law and toward state common-law tort claims.

Would-be § 1983 land use plaintiffs will encounter similar issues with "takings" as well as with procedural due process claims. Ordinarily, landowners must first attempt to obtain compensation through any available state-created judicial remedies, such as inverse condemnation.[22] Reasoning that pre-deprivation compensation is not required by the "taking" clause, the Supreme Court has held that "the State's action here is not 'complete' . . . until the State fails to provide adequate compensation for the taking" through its available procedures.[23]

In *Heck v. Humphrey*[24] the Supreme Court announced another doctrine that superficially resembles a judicial exhaustion requirement. The Court held that a § 1983 damages action for harm caused by an allegedly unlawful criminal conviction or imprisonment has certain prerequisites. That is, the conviction must have already been invalidated through reversal on appeal or expungement by executive order, or called into question by a federal court's issuance of a writ of habeas corpus. The Court stated, however:

> We do not engraft an exhaustion requirement upon § 1983, but rather deny the existence of a cause of action.[25]

As in the procedural due process situation described above, such a plaintiff does not have a § 1983 claim if he pursues these alternate remedies unsuccessfully to their conclusion.

---

21. Hudson v. Palmer, 468 U.S. 517, 533–36 (1984); Parratt v. Taylor, 451 U.S. 527, 543–44 (1981).
22. *See Williamson County,* 473 U.S. at 194–95.
23. 473 U.S. at 195.
24. 512 U.S. 477 (1994).
25. 512 U.S. at 489.

Counsel should also be aware that a related state judicial proceeding pending at the time the plaintiff wishes to file his federal court § 1983 action will probably create *Younger* problems.[26] These must be thoroughly researched before a decision can be made about such filing.

c. State administrative remedies. In the absence of a specific statutory requirement such as the examples mentioned above, a § 1983 plaintiff need not exhaust state administrative remedies prior to filing a § 1983 claim.[27] A related state administrative proceeding pending at the time the plaintiff wishes to file a § 1983 court action may create *Younger* problems similar to those caused by pending state judicial proceedings.[28] This issue must also be researched, if such circumstances exist.

d. "Notice of claim" requirements. Some state and local governmental entities have created an array of procedural notice requirements, frequently with very short time deadlines. The statute or regulation imposing these provisions frequently requires compliance with them as a prerequisite to filing a claim against the governmental entity in state court.

In *Felder v. Casey*,[29] the Supreme Court held that a state's application of such a notice requirement to § 1983 claims filed in state courts violated the Supremacy Clause. These requirements are impermissible if they significantly burden plaintiffs' right to seek redress for § 1983 violations through the state court system. The Court found it incompatible with the Supremacy Clause that highly restrictive procedural requirements would predictably cause different outcomes for § 1983 claims, depending on whether they were brought in federal or state court.[30] Further, the Court viewed the "notice of claim" prerequisite, as applied to § 1983 actions, to be an impermissible state-imposed exhaustion requirement. Since § 1983 is a federally created cause of action and Congress imposed no such general requirement on it, the state's attempt to do so was impermissible.[31]

Of course, such "notice of claim" hurdles may still be required for some state-created causes of action that a § 1983 plaintiff may wish to raise as pendent claims.

---

26. *See* Younger v. Harris, 401 U.S. 37 (1971), and the discussion of this doctrine in the sources listed as "Suggestions for Further Reading" at the end of this chapter.
27. Patsy v. Board of Regents, 457 U.S. 496, 515–16 (1982).
28. *See* Ohio Civil Rights Comm'n v. Dayton Christian Schools, 477 U.S. 619, 625–29 (1986), and note 26, *supra.*
29. 487 U.S. 131, 150–53 (1988).
30. 487 U.S. at 153.
31. 487 U.S. at 146–50.

III. STRUCTURING THE LAWSUIT

After reviewing the facts and legal issues thoroughly and deciding to proceed with the § 1983 claim, the next step is to determine how best to structure the lawsuit. This requires consideration of potential defendants and of whether they will be sued in their individual or official capacities.

A. "Every Person"

Section 1983 provides for the liability of "every person" who subjects the plaintiff or causes the plaintiff to be subjected to the deprivation of federal constitutional or statutory rights "under color of any statute, ordinance, regulation, custom, or usage, of any State or Territory or the District of Columbia." With one important exception, both natural persons and entities such as corporations and governmental units are "persons" who are proper defendants in § 1983 cases. The state itself has been held not to be a "person" that may be named as a § 1983 defendant, either in federal or in state court.[32] This holding also applies to specific agencies of the state.

If the plaintiff seeks injunctive relief against the state pursuant to § 1983, it is still possible to properly plead for it through the "*Ex parte Young* fiction."[33] This involves naming the appropriate state officers in their official capacities as defendants and pleading only for injunctive relief, not damages. This artifice permits the courts to effectuate the Supremacy Clause by bringing the state into compliance with federal law, while still recognizing the state's specially protected status.

B. "Official Capacity" vs. "Individual Capacity"

Suit against a governmental officer or employee in his or her "official capacity" is, in effect, a suit against the governmental entity that person represents.[34] Suing an officer or employee in this manner for damages does not seek the individual's personal liability, but rather recovery from the funds of the governmental unit.[35] Death or replacement of the named official-capacity defendant during the pendency of the action will not affect its status. The

32. Will v. Michigan Dep't of State Police, 491 U.S. 58, 69–71 (1989).
33. 491 U.S. at 71 n.10, *citing* Kentucky v. Graham, 473 U.S. at 167 n.14 (1985); *and* Ex parte Young, 209 U.S. 123, 159–60 (1908); *see also* Frew v. Hawkins, 540 U.S. 431, 437 (2004).
34. Kentucky v. Graham, 473 U.S. 159, 165 (1985), *citing* Monell v. Dep't of Social Services, 436 U.S. 658, 690 n.55 (1978).
35. 473 U.S. at 166.

successor official will be automatically substituted as the named defendant; the action continues, in effect, against the governmental unit. Other than the *Ex parte Young* situation, in which official capacity suits are necessary to obtain injunctive relief from state agencies' violations of federal law, it is probably less confusing to simply name the governmental unit itself as the defendant when seeking relief from it.

It is also important to understand that suing a governmental unit by naming an officer in his official capacity is merely a pleading device. It does not effect any substantive changes in the requirements for governmental liability, or the immunities from it. For example, suing a state officer in his or her official capacity for damages pursuant to § 1983 is not permissible. This is so both because the state is not a "person" suable under § 1983 and because the state can claim Eleventh Amendment immunity from such a suit. Naming a particular state officer in his or her official capacity as defendant does not cure either of these problems. The suit is still an impermissible attempt to obtain a monetary recovery against the state, so it is barred by the doctrines explained above.[36]

In contrast, a § 1983 claim against a governmental officer or employee in her "individual capacity" or "personal capacity" is not a suit against the governmental unit. Instead, it is an attempt to impose personal liability against this individual for actions taken under color of state law.[37] Individual immunities will be applicable to this type of claim, not the liability requirements and immunities that would apply if the governmental unit on whose behalf the officer acted were the defendant.[38] It is best for counsel to clearly state in the caption and body of the complaint the capacity in which each defendant is sued. Defendants may be sued in both their official and individual capacities, if the plaintiff can show an entitlement to both types of relief.

C. Overview of the Status of Several Types of Individuals and Entities as "Persons" Subject to Section 1983 Liability

1. State Officers and Employees

State officers and employees sued in their *individual capacities* for damages are still "persons" and therefore proper § 1983 defendants.[39] Although not protected from such claims by the Eleventh Amendment, these persons may

---

36. *See Will,* 491 U.S. at 71.
37. *Kentucky,* 473 U.S. at 165–68.
38. 473 U.S. at 166–68.
39. Hafer v. Melo, 502 U.S. 21, 27–29 (1991).

be able to assert either absolute or qualified "individual" immunity for their challenged actions.[40]

2. *Local Governmental Officers and Employees*

Officers and employees of counties, municipalities, school districts, and other local governmental units are also "persons" for § 1983 purposes, and therefore proper § 1983 defendants. Like state employees, however, they may be entitled to assert either absolute or qualified individual immunity.

Occasionally, plaintiff's counsel is unaware or uncertain of the identity of one or more persons who should be sued in their individual capacities. For example, the plaintiff may have descriptions but not names of police officers who used excessive force. It may be possible to list these defendants as "John Does" in the original complaint. The unknown defendants and the fact situation giving rise to their liability should be described in as much detail as possible in order to place counsel on notice to prepare a defense for them. Plaintiff's counsel should then immediately commence discovery to determine their identities.

It is safest to amend and substitute the correct identities of all defendants before the expiration of the statute of limitations, if at all possible. If it is not possible, FED. R. CIV. P. 15(c)(3) may be of help in arguing that an amended complaint filed during the period permitted for service of process[41] "relates back" to the date of the original complaint.

3. *Local Governmental Units*

Counties, municipalities, school districts, and other local governmental bodies are "persons" for § 1983 purposes, and therefore proper § 1983 defendants.[42] However, they are not liable for the actions of their officers and employees solely on the basis of respondeat superior.[43] These governmental units do not have qualified immunity from compensatory damage claims, as do some individual defendants, but they are absolutely immune from liability for punitive damages.[44]

---

40. See Chapter 9, "Individual Immunity Defenses under Section 1983."
41. *See* FED. R. CIV. P. 4(m).
42. Monell v. Dep't of Social Services, 436 U.S. 658, 690–95 (1978).
43. See Chapter 4, "Municipal Liability under Section 1983," for a full discussion of the way in which § 1983's causation standard is applied with respect to governmental unit liability.
44. Owen v. City of Independence, 445 U.S. 622, 650–58 (1980); City of Newport v. Fact Concerts, Inc., 453 U.S. 247, 258–71 (1981).

4. *Other Potential Defendants*

Occasionally, individuals who are not governmental officers, agents, or employees have acted under color of state law to deprive the plaintiff of federally protected rights. They may either have conspired with governmental actors to do so, or they may have used state-created procedures that deprived the plaintiff of federally protected rights. In such situations, these individuals are appropriate § 1983 defendants, even if any governmental representative with whom they acted is absolutely immune from suit.[45] These nongovernmental actors are not entitled to qualified immunity from suit for damages, but may be entitled to a "good faith" defense against damage claims.[46]

IV. INITIAL SELECTION OF FORUM

A. Concurrent Federal and State Jurisdiction over Section 1983 Claims

Section 1983 creates a cause of action that, in general, may properly be filed in either federal or state court. The Supreme Court has held that the Supremacy Clause prevents a state from using its sovereign immunity laws to block § 1983 claims from being litigated in its courts.[47] The related attorney's fee statute, 42 U.S.C. § 1988, is as applicable to § 1983 claims filed in state court as to those filed in federal court.[48]

Because § 1983 is a federally created remedy, its litigation in state court produces many thorny questions as to exactly how the extensive body of federal law interpreting and applying it interacts with the forum state's rules. This is the mirror image of the classic *Erie Railroad v. Tompkins*[49] issue. *Erie* arose in the context of state-created causes of action being litigated in federal courts, through their diversity jurisdiction. As can be seen from *Felder v. Casey*,[50] it is not a simple matter of distinguishing between what is "substantive" and what is "procedural." A state-created "procedural" rule may not be applied to § 1983 claims if it substantially burdens or thwarts the assertion of these claims in a manner inconsistent with § 1983's purpose. Many of these "converse *Erie*" questions that arise in the context of state court § 1983 litigation are examined in Chapter 3 of this volume.

---

45. Dennis v. Sparks, 449 U.S. 24, 27–32 (1980).
46. Wyatt v. Cole, 504 U.S. 158 (1992).
47. Howlett v. Rose, 496 U.S. 356, 375–83 (1990).
48. Maine v. Thiboutot, 448 U.S. 1, 8–11 (1980).
49. 304 U.S. 64 (1938).
50. 487 U.S. 131, 147–51 (1988).

B. Limitations on Section 1983 Plaintiff's Choice of Forum

1. Removal

The most significant limitation on the § 1983 plaintiff's opportunity to choose the forum is defendant's removal option. That is, if the plaintiff chooses to file a § 1983 claim in state court, defendants have a statutory right to remove it to federal court.[51] This is because the § 1983 claim arises under the "Constitution, treaties or laws of the United States" and therefore falls within the original jurisdiction of the federal courts. The mechanics of defendants' exercise of this right are discussed below.

In looking ahead to the possibility of removal, plaintiff's counsel should be aware that once an action is properly removed to federal court, there is no sure way of returning it to state court. Even voluntarily dismissing the § 1983 claim and retaining only pendent claims based on state law may not accomplish this.[52] The Supreme Court's opinion in *Carnegie-Mellon University v. Cohill* holds that a federal court has discretion to remand a removed case to state court if all federal claims have been dismissed. However, one of the factors the court should consider as weighing against a possible remand is the presence of deliberate "forum manipulation" by the plaintiff's counsel.[53]

Therefore, if plaintiff's counsel would consider it a grave calamity to try a particular case in the federal court to which it would be removed, he or she should consider pleading only claims based on state law. These might include state constitutional provisions or individual rights statutes, and common-law tort remedies. If plaintiff's counsel does this, defendants do not have a removal right, even though on the same facts the plaintiff *could* have pled a § 1983 claim or other federal remedy.[54]

2. The **Pennhurst** *Situation*

A plaintiff seeking declaratory or injunctive relief against state officials based on both § 1983 and pendent state law claims will be faced with particularly difficult procedural choices. Counsel in this situation will have to either file the entire action in state court, drop the state law claims in order

---

51. 28 U.S.C. § 1441 (a)–(b).

52. *See* Carnegie-Mellon Univ. v. Cohill, 484 U.S. 343, 357 (1988).

53. 484 U.S. at 357.

54. *See, e.g.,* Merrell Dow Pharmaceuticals v. Thompson, 478 U.S. 804, 809 n.6 (1986), and cases cited therein.

to file in federal court, or bifurcate the case, with all the attendant risks and complications.

The Supreme Court dealt with this issue in *Pennhurst State School and Hospital v. Halderman.*[55] In *Pennhurst,* the Court said the rationale of *Ex parte Young* does not extend to the enforcement of state-created rights. Therefore, the Court reasoned, the Eleventh Amendment bars federal courts from enjoining state officials to effectuate state-created rights. This is so even when rights created by state law are asserted as pendent claims to causes of action over which the federal court has primary jurisdiction.[56]

3. Abstention

While a substantive discussion of abstention issues is beyond the scope of this chapter, counsel should be aware that there are fact situations in which abstention is such a strong possibility that it may be best to file in state court and avoid the probability of a time-consuming procedural battle on this topic.[57]

C. Factors to Consider in Forum Choice

Although there are exceptions, the general rule is that the § 1983 plaintiff has a choice, at least initially, of the federal or the state court system. This choice should be exercised thoughtfully. Even though removal is the defendant's option, if the defendant is either unable to agree (with another defendant about removal) or does not act quickly enough (within 30 days) to effect it, the plaintiff's forum choice will be the final one.

Assuming that the plaintiff has a choice of forum based on the substantive law applicable to the case, the following are examples of some practical factors to consider in making the choice:

1. Federal court personnel still have much more familiarity with § 1983 claims. However, familiarity does not necessarily mean receptivity. The records of specific judges to whom the case may be assigned are always a consideration.
2. Increasingly, some state supreme courts interpret constitutional rights more broadly than do the federal appellate courts. It is

55. 465 U.S. 89, 103–06 (1984).

56. 465 U.S. at 117–21; *see also* Silver v. Baggiano, 804 F.2d 1211, 1213–15 (11th Cir. 1986).

57. *See, e.g.,* Younger v. Harris, 401 U.S. 37 (1971); Railroad Comm'n v. Pullman Co., 312 U.S. 496 (1941). *See also* the sources listed at the end of this chapter as "Suggestions for Further Reading," and Chapter 1, *supra.*

advisable to investigate rulings on any constitutional issue raised by the fact situation before making a forum choice.

3. Counsel should compare the breadth and volume of discovery available in each potential forum. Many states have altered their discovery rules to more closely resemble the federal model, but some still have major differences. Due to relatively recent modifications to the Federal Rules, discovery will sometimes be more broadly available in state court.[58] However, early availability of the material that must be provided in federal court initial disclosures can be extremely helpful.[59] States may also differ from federal courts with respect to the use of depositions at trial.
4. If a jury trial is likely, counsel should consider such variables as geographical area from which the jury array will be summoned, voir dire and argument procedures, and civil verdict requirements in both the federal and state forums. For example, less than a unanimous verdict may be permitted in state court. In some states, voir dire is always performed by counsel rather than the court. Time constraints for voir dire and final argument can vary significantly.
5. Docket congestion, and therefore the length of time required to get to trial, may vary markedly between the federal and the state court system. If counsel will be seeking preliminary injunctive relief, availability of court time to schedule a hearing of reasonable length in the near future may be very different in the two systems as well. This in turn may influence the probability of obtaining such relief.
6. If it appears likely that a temporary restraining order must be sought, counsel should investigate the actual practices of both forums in handling such requests. Bond setting standards may also vary a great deal. In these procedural areas, there are likely to be local traditions and standard practices that are not official or even written. So, it is highly advisable for inexperienced counsel to consult at this point with one or more lawyers who have practiced for some time in the forums being considered.
7. Particularly in the case of small governmental entities that do not often have § 1983 claims raised against them, the choice of forum may actually determine defendant's choice of counsel. Filing in a federal forum will almost always trigger the immediate hiring of

---

58. *See, e.g.*, FED. R. CIV. P. 33(a).
59. *See* FED. R. CIV. P. 26(a)(1).

counsel who are knowledgeable and experienced concerning § 1983 claims, while filing in state court may not. Even if the case is later transferred to counsel more experienced in defending against civil rights claims, some time-limited options, such as removal to federal court, may have been lost. On the other hand, the possibility of reaching a speedy, reasonable settlement of a well-founded claim because of the advice of a knowledgeable defense counsel may have been lost as well.

V. JURISDICTION AND VENUE IN FEDERAL COURT

The following is a discussion of the basic jurisdictional and venue provisions that apply to § 1983 cases filed in federal court.

A. Primary Jurisdiction

Section 1983 cases always invoke general "federal question" jurisdiction, pursuant to 28 U.S.C. § 1331. The other jurisdictional statute commonly invoked for § 1983 actions is 28 U.S.C. § 1343(a)(3). It provides for federal jurisdiction over cases brought to:

> redress the deprivation, under color of any State law, statute, ordinance, regulation, custom or usage, of any right, privilege or immunity secured by the Constitution of the United States or by any Act of Congress providing for equal rights of citizens or of all persons within the jurisdiction of the United States; . . .[60]

This statute covers all § 1983 actions based on constitutional deprivations, and some § 1983 actions based on statutory provisions that confer "equal rights." This provision has not been interpreted as broadly as § 1983's "laws" provision, however. So, there are some statutory sections, such as certain parts of the Social Security Act, that may be enforced through § 1983 but do not fit within §1343(a)(3) jurisdiction.[61] This is not a barrier to federal court access, because § 1331 "federal question" jurisdiction is always applicable. Since the Federal Question Jurisdictional Amendment Act of 1980, § 1331 has no minimum jurisdictional amount requirement.[62]

---

60. 28 U.S.C. § 1343(a) (3).

61. *Compare* Maine v. Thiboutot, 448 U.S. 1, 4–8 (1980), *with* Chapman v. Houston Welfare Rights Org., 441 U.S. 600, 615–23 (1979).

62. 28 U.S.C. § 1331.

B. Supplemental Jurisdiction

If a complaint properly invokes federal court jurisdiction for at least one of its claims, the next jurisdictional question involves "pendent" claims. That is, what other claims may the complaint properly bring before the federal court if those claims by themselves would not trigger federal jurisdiction?

The Judicial Improvements Act of 1990, codified at 28 U.S.C. § 1367, markedly expanded the federal courts' supplemental or "pendent" jurisdiction. Even before the enactment of this statute, federal courts could take jurisdiction over a "pendent" state law claim against the same defendant if the claim arose from the "same nucleus of operative fact" as the claim(s) over which the federal court had primary jurisdiction.[63] However, federal courts were much less likely to take jurisdiction in a "pendent party" situation, in which the plaintiff sought to include a defendant against whom only a state law claim existed. This was true even if the state law claim arose from the same factual nucleus as federal claims against the other defendants.[64]

The Judicial Improvements Act of 1990 broadened the range of circumstances in which a federal court must exercise its pendent or "supplemental" jurisdiction over both claims and parties.[65] For "federal question" cases such as § 1983 actions, this act mandates that a federal court with appropriate "primary" jurisdiction over one of the plaintiff's claims must almost always assume "supplemental" jurisdiction of all other claims the plaintiff seeks to assert, if they form "part of the same case or controversy under Article III of the United States Constitution."[66] This Article III "same case or controversy" standard has been interpreted to mean that the claims arise from a "common nucleus of operative fact" such that they would ordinarily be expected to be tried in the same proceeding.[67]

There are only a few exceptions to the statutory presumption favoring the federal court's exercise of its "supplemental jurisdiction." Exceptions include claims raising a "novel or complex issue of State law," case situations in which a state claim "substantially predominates" over the federal claim(s), cases in which all claims over which the court had primary juris-

---

63. United Mine Workers v. Gibbs, 383 U.S. 715, 724–25 (1966).
64. *See* Aldinger v. Howard, 427 U.S. 1, 14–19 (1976).
65. 28 U.S.C. § 1367.
66. 28 U.S.C. § 1367(a).
67. Owen Equip. and Erection Co. v. Kroger, 437 U.S. 365, 371–72 (1978); United Mine Workers v. Gibbs, 383 U.S. 715, 724–25 (1966).

diction have been dismissed, and "exceptional circumstances" in which there are "other compelling reasons for declining jurisdiction."[68]

This expansion of federal courts' supplemental jurisdiction to include most "pendent party" situations permits plaintiffs to include defendants against whom a § 1983 claim could not be stated. They may be included if they are appropriate defendants for a pendent state law claim arising from the same "case or controversy." For example, this could include a defendant's employer who has respondeat superior liability for the employee's tort pursuant to state law, but not enough culpability to trigger § 1983 liability. It permits the inclusion of "pendent party plaintiffs" as well, for example, spouses of § 1983 plaintiffs asserting state law claims for loss of consortium.[69]

Powerful though it is, the Judicial Improvements Act does not eliminate the Eleventh Amendment barrier that prevents pendent state law claims from being asserted in federal court against state officials.[70]

C. Federal Venue

For "federal question" cases, such as those including § 1983 claims, venue options are set out in 28 U.S.C. § 1391(b). This statute provides that, "except as otherwise provided by law," the suit may be filed in the following locations:

1. If all defendants reside in the same state, the suit may be filed in any judicial district in which a defendant resides.[71] (For venue purposes, a corporation "resides" in any judicial district with which it has sufficient contacts to be subject to personal jurisdiction at the time the action is commenced.)[72]
2. Alternatively, the suit may be brought in any judicial district in which a "substantial part of the events or omissions giving rise to the claim occurred, or a substantial part of property that is the subject of the action is situated."[73] The Second Circuit case *Bates v. C&S Adjusters*[74] provides an instructive analysis of this provision

68. 28 U.S.C. § 1367(c).
69. *See, e.g.*, Niehus v. Liberio, 973 F.2d 526, 532 (7th Cir 1992).
70. *See* Pennhurst v. Halderman, 465 U.S. 89, 117–21 (1984); Silver v. Baggiano, 804 F.2d 1211, 1213–15 (11th Cir. 1986).
71. 28 U.S.C. § 1391(b) (1).
72. 28 U.S.C. § 1391(c).
73. 28 U.S.C. § 1391(b) (2).
74. 980 F.2d 865, 866–68 (2d Cir. 1992).

and its history, interpreting it to authorize multiple venue possibilities—assuming that the defendant is subject to personal jurisdiction in each. The *Bates* opinion also interprets § 1391(b) to mean that the federal courts no longer must resolve venue disputes by attempting to select the location with the greatest "weight of contacts."

3. If neither of the above provisions can be applied to authorize a filing location, then the suit may be filed in any judicial district "in which any defendant may be found" (again assuming that the defendant(s) may be subjected to personal jurisdiction there).[75]

There are special provisions for the venue of suits against foreign individual defendants, foreign countries, and U.S. agencies or their officers.[76]

Even if venue is proper in the district where the case is originally filed, the district court in which it is filed may exercise its sound discretion to transfer it to any other district in which it could have been brought, either on a party's motion or on the court's own initiative. This consideration should be based largely on "the convenience of parties and witnesses."[77]

VI. PLEADING AND FILING THE SECTION 1983 LAWSUIT

A. Drafting the Complaint

A few cautionary considerations are appropriate here, looking ahead to attorneys' fees claims. Although any substantive discussion of attorneys' fees claims is beyond the scope of this chapter, there are a few basic principles of which plaintiff's counsel should be aware when drafting initial pleadings. The Supreme Court's decisions about attorneys' fees awards make it clear that plaintiff's counsel is not well advised either to inflate damage claim amounts for dramatic effect or to use a shotgun-type approach in pleading causes of action and claims for relief. This is not to suggest that such a strategy might be appropriate or effective for any other purpose. It simply means that the likely boomerang effect on a later attorneys' fees claim is particularly clear.

The Supreme Court's holding in *Hensley v. Eckerhart*[78] is one precedent with which counsel should be familiar at the complaint drafting stage. It indicates that a victorious plaintiff's counsel should not ordinarily be com-

75. 28 U.S.C. § 1391(b)(3).
76. 28 U.S.C. § 1391(d)–(f).
77. 28 U.S.C. § 1404(a).
78. 461 U.S. 424, 434–37 (1983).

pensated for time spent on unsuccessful claims that are not "substantially related" to the successful ones.[79] In practice, it may be very difficult to clearly distinguish such time, and the presence of several unsuccessful claims may result in a substantial overall discounting of plaintiff's counsel's fee.[80]

Another very instructive opinion for plaintiff's counsel at the complaint drafting stage is *Farrar v. Hobby*.[81] The Supreme Court held that a plaintiff who obtained only nominal damages was a prevailing party; however, no attorneys' fees were appropriate because of the lack of significance of this relief. The result might well have been the same if the plaintiff's counsel had not sought $17 million from six defendants, but it is notable that this damage demand amount is mentioned four times in the ten-page majority opinion.[82] It is also a major focus of Justice O'Connor's concurrence.[83]

Whatever the substantive import of these cases, familiarity with them should influence complaint drafting as well. What can reasonably be gathered from them is that, not surprisingly, plaintiff's own initial pleadings are a major factor in shaping the court's later view of the success of the litigation, or the lack thereof. So, in the long run, caution is probably more advisable than exaggeration.

B. Heightened Pleading Requirements for Section 1983 Complaints in Federal Court

Before the Supreme Court's 1993 opinion in *Leatherman v. Tarrant County*,[84] the federal courts were imposing increasingly stringent and demanding specificity requirements for § 1983 plaintiffs' initial pleadings. They applied this technique in a variety of case situations. The unanimous and remarkably forceful *Leatherman* opinion initiated some change, but there has been uncertainty about the scope of its application. In 1998, *Crawford-El v. Britton*[85] provided further guidance to district courts engaged in the difficult balancing exercises that occur at the pleading and discovery

79. However, the fee to a successful plaintiff's counsel should not be reduced simply because the court did not fully accept all contentions raised. 461 U.S. at 435.

80. For example, please see the Fourth Circuit's total denial of fees to a successful plaintiff's counsel in Fair Housing Council v. Landow, 999 F.2d 92, 97–98 (4th Cir. 1993).

81. 506 U.S. 103 (1992).

82. 506 U.S. at 105–116.

83. 506 U.S. at 116–22.

84. 507 U.S. 163 (1993).

85. 523 U.S. 574 (1998).

stages of many § 1983 cases. That is, the court must strive to protect governmental defendants from groundless and insubstantial suits as early in cases as possible without using a "blunt instrument" that crushes legitimate constitutional claims as well.[86] A closer look at the background and development of this area of § 1983 law may help put the current situation in better perspective.

1. *Pre*-Leatherman

Federal Rule of Civil Procedure 8, which specifies standard requirements for federal pleadings, calls for only "a short and plain statement of the claim showing that the pleader is entitled to relief."[87] It also states: "No technical forms of pleading or motions are required."[88] The Supreme Court has held that the appropriate test of most federal pleadings' sufficiency is the "fair notice" standard.[89] That is, the court looks at whether the action is pled with sufficient concreteness and clarity to give the opposing party fair notice of its basis and enable him or her to properly prepare a responsive pleading. In *Conley v. Gibson*, the Court explained:

> [W]e have no doubt that petitioners' complaint adequately set forth a claim and gave the respondents fair notice of its basis. The Federal Rules reject the approach that pleading is a game of skill in which one misstep by counsel may be decisive to the outcome.[90]

Despite these generally applicable principles, the approach expressly rejected by the *Conley* Court was an excellent description of the prevailing situation in § 1983 cases before *Leatherman*. As discussed below, in some respects, it remains a good description.

There has always been tension between the pure "notice pleading" standard and the goal of quickly eliminating cases in which the plaintiff will not be able to assert in good faith each essential element of the cause of action. The recurring tension between these competing goals has been the major underlying theme in the developing case law about § 1983 pleading requirements. In these cases, the policy considerations involved in protecting certain defendants from unfiltered exposure to the litigation process are at their

---

86. 523 U.S. at 595.
87. Fed. R. Civ. P. 8(a)(2).
88. Fed. R. Civ. P. 8(e)(1).
89. Conley v. Gibson, 355 U.S. 41, 47–48 (1957); *cf.* McLain v. Real Estate Board, 444 U.S. 232, 246–47 (1980).
90. 355 U.S. at 48.

strongest. But so are the values reflected in Rule 8, concerning the practical availability of the federal courts.

Before *Leatherman*, the overall trend in § 1983 litigation was one of increasingly radical departure from the generally applicable federal notice pleading standard, in more and more types of cases. In cases against individual defendants with potential claims of absolute or qualified immunity, many circuits required plaintiffs to include in their initial complaints specific facts negating this immunity.[91] Allegations of conspiracy also have triggered a heightened pleading requirement in some courts.[92]

Similarly, when an individual defendant's state of mind or motive was an element of plaintiff's cause of action (e.g., in a First Amendment retaliatory termination case), many courts required specific factual allegations supporting this claim.[93] Until the Supreme Court directed otherwise in *Crawford-El*, the District of Columbia Circuit carried this even further. This circuit required not only factually specific supporting evidence of improper motive but also direct, not circumstantial, factually specific supporting evidence—a requirement not even present at trial in a criminal case.[94]

Some circuits subjected § 1983 complaints asserting damage claims against municipalities or other governmental units to very exacting pleading requirements. Plaintiffs were required to state, without benefit of discovery, detailed factual allegations specifying the precise way in which the policies, established customs, training deficiencies, etc. of the governmental unit brought about the deprivation of the plaintiff's rights.[95]

2. Leatherman v. Tarrant County—*Rule 8 Means What It Says*

The *Leatherman* case involved § 1983 plaintiffs' claims of municipal and county liability, based largely on alleged failure to properly train law enforcement officers. The district court granted a motion to dismiss the complaints, based on lack of specificity in the plaintiffs' pleadings about alleged defects in the governmental units' training policies and procedures.[96] The Fifth

91. *See, e.g.,* Sawyer v. County of Creek, 908 F.2d 663, 665–68 (10th Cir. 1990); Elliott v. Perez, 751 F.2d 1472, 1477–82 (5th Cir. 1985).
92. Streetman v. Jordan, 918 F.2d 555, 557 (5th Cir. 1990); Sooner Products Co. v. McBride, 708 F.2d 510, 512 (10th Cir. 1983).
93. *See, e.g.,* Branch v. Tunnell, 937 F.2d 1382, 1386–88 (9th Cir. 1991).
94. *See* Siegert v. Gilley, 895 F.2d 797, 800–05 (D.C. Cir. 1990), *aff'd on other grounds,* 500 U.S. 226 (1991).
95. *See, e.g.,* Palmer v. City of San Antonio, 810 F.2d 514, 516–17 (5th Cir. 1987); Strauss v. City of Chicago, 760 F.2d 765, 767–70 (7th Cir. 1985).
96. 755 F. Supp. 726, 729–31 (1991).

Circuit affirmed, relying on its established heightened pleading standard for civil rights complaints against municipalities.[97]

In an opinion as striking for its forcefulness and unanimity as for its actual holding, the Supreme Court reversed.[98] The Court indicated that it needed to "resolve a conflict among the Courts of Appeals concerning the applicability of a heightened pleading standard to § 1983 actions alleging municipal liability." It struck down the Fifth Circuit's rigorous pleading standard for such claims.[99] In so ruling the Court held, in effect, that Rule 8 means what it says.

Defendants argued that the degree of factual specificity required by Rule 8 should vary according to the complexity of the cause of action being asserted. The Supreme Court, however, rejected this analysis of what it meant to "state a claim" pursuant to Rule 8(a)(2). Referencing its prior holdings requiring only "notice pleading" of claims, not factually detailed pleading, the Court reasoned that these general standards must also be applied to civil rights claims. The Court also found it significant that the federal rules expressly listed a few types of claims that required more-detailed pleadings. This, they reasoned, indicated that types of claims not so listed were not intended to have to meet such a requirement.[100]

The Court also considered and rejected defendants' argument that more-relaxed pleading standards would overburden governmental entities by requiring them to respond to discovery in every § 1983 case, whether or not well founded. They found a city's lack of susceptibility to respondeat superior liability under § 1983 to be very different, for this purpose, from an individual defendant's immunity from suit. To ultimately establish liability, of course, the plaintiff must still prove how the "municipal policy or custom caused the constitutional injury."[101] For initial pleading, however, broad, global allegations to this effect were found acceptable.

The *Leatherman* Court carefully noted that the case situation before it was not one involving claims against individual governmental employees. Therefore, the Court had no occasion to rule on the application of heightened pleading requirements in cases where there were assertions of absolute or qualified immunity.

---

97. 954 F.2d 1054, 1057-58 (1992).
98. 507 U.S. 163 (1993).
99. 507 U.S. at 166–68.
100. 507 U.S. at 168, citing Fed. R. Civ. P. 9(b).
101. 507 U.S. at 166.

3. Schultea v. Wood *and* Crawford-El v. Britton—*How Courts Can Use Rules 7 and 12(e) to Protect Individual Defendants*

Although the voice of the Court seemed unusually strong and clear in *Leatherman*, it produced an amazing cacophony of responses. Much dissension centered on whether *Leatherman's* relaxed pleading standard should be applied in cases against individual defendants with potential immunity claims.[102] In addition, some opinions demonstrated internal inconsistencies, accepting the language but not the substance of *Leatherman*. See, for example, *Hill v. City of New York*, in which the Second Circuit gave lip service to applying *Leatherman* in connection with conspiracy allegations, but then proceeded to reverse the district court's decision not to dismiss such claims, holding that the plaintiff "has not alleged facts sufficient to support this charge."[103]

Meanwhile the Fifth Circuit, sitting en banc, regrouped its forces and repackaged its heightened pleading requirement for use in cases against individual defendants. This repackaged version changed the form of the requirement but retained its substance. *Schultea v. Wood*[104] involved a § 1983 damages complaint against city councilmen, who moved to dismiss based on alleged failure to state a claim. The trial court denied defendants' motion. A Fifth Circuit panel reversed in part, but remanded to give the plaintiff an opportunity to amend his pleading. The Fifth Circuit then granted rehearing en banc in order to prescribe the pleading standards to which the plaintiff should be held on remand.

The en banc court began by acknowledging that qualified immunity is a defense, so the burden to raise it is on the defendant. Accordingly, the court shifted its focus away from Rule 8's and Rule 9's requirements for stating claims. It focused instead on Rule 7's provisions about replies to pleadings. The majority held that if a defendant asserts qualified immunity, the plaintiff should be required to reply in detail, refuting this defense.[105] This requirement could be initiated either through a defendant's motion or on the court's own initiative. Deftly manipulating the *Leatherman* Court's analysis of the federal pleading rules, the *Schultea* majority found Rule 8(a)(2)'s

102. *Compare, e.g.*, Black v. Lane, 22 F.3d 1395, 1399 (7th Cir. 1994), *with* Edgington v. Missouri Dept. of Corrections, 52 F.3d 777, 779 n.3 (8th Cir. 1995), and Branch v. Tunnell, 14 F.3d 449, 455–57 (9th Cir.), *cert. denied,* 512 U.S. 1219 (1994).

103. Hill v. City of New York, 45 F.3d 653, 664 (2d Cir. 1995).

104. 47 F.3d 1427 (5th Cir. 1995) (en banc).

105. 47 F.3d at 1432–34, citing Fed. R. Civ. P. 7(a).

"short and plain statement" standard inapplicable to Rule 7 replies, because Rule 8 does not expressly reference them.[106]

Throughout their analysis, the majority emphasized their belief that these procedural protections were necessary to effectuate the rights of defendants with well-founded immunity claims. Noting that the *Schultea* opinion was "our answer to *Leatherman,*" they provided several suggestions for district court judges about how to implement their "answer." These included requiring a complaint that "rests on more than conclusions alone," routinely requiring a detailed reply from the plaintiff if the defendant raises qualified immunity, either banning or limiting discovery until "sufficient precision and factual specificity" is present in the reply, and then "consider[ing]" summary judgment motions pursuant to Rule 56.[107]

The Supreme Court's 1998 *Crawford-El v. Britton*[108] opinion adopted some of the *Schultea* opinion's reasoning with respect to cases involving immunity claims. Crawford-El alleged in his suit that prison officials retaliated against him to punish and deter his exercise of First Amendment rights and to deter his right of access to the courts. His complaint was dismissed because it did not allege "direct" as opposed to circumstantial evidence of defendants' unconstitutional motives. After the D.C. Circuit issued en banc opinions about this and other procedural issues in the case, the Supreme Court granted certiorari.

The Court reiterated its *Leatherman* refusal to permit special pleading requirements for initial 1983 complaints. However, it expressly approved one of the filtering methods suggested in *Schultea* and added another possibility as well.[109] An individual defendant could, for example, use Fed. R. Civ. P. 7(a) to require a reply to his assertion of qualified immunity, or Fed. R. Civ. P. 12(e)[110] to move for a more definite statement of plaintiff's claim. Under either rule, the plaintiff could be required to plead "specific, nonconclusory factual allegations" to support his claims. So, while condemning lower courts' practice of creating new pleading rules to effectuate immunity

106. 47 F.3d at 1433. The more general rule governing the content of pleadings, Rule 8(e)(1), which the majority acknowledged to be applicable, prescribes "simple, concise, and direct" pleadings. This sounds a great deal like the same thing, but apparently not to the Fifth Circuit.

107. 47 F.3d at 1433–34.

108. 523 U.S. 574 (1998).

109. 523 U.S. at 598.

110. Despite the Court's affinity for it, the use of Rule 12(e) is still explicitly disfavored by many local rules; *e.g.,* Local Rule 12.1 United States District Court for the Northern District of Texas.

guarantees, the Court encouraged more-expansive use of existing ones for this purpose.[111]

4. *Heightened Pleading Requirements in State Courts*

Pleading requirements are ordinarily considered "procedural." But, they can quite obviously be outcome determinative, as they were in many of the above-cited cases. This should mean that state courts may not impose them more stringently than federal courts, in a way that significantly burdens plaintiffs' right to pursue § 1983 claims in state court.[112] This and related topics are discussed in Chapter 3.

C. In Forma Pauperis Filing

A case may be filed without payment or security for court costs if the plaintiff files a motion for permission to do so, together with an affidavit listing his assets and swearing he is unable, due to poverty, to pay or post security.[113] The case must be permitted to proceed unless it appears to the court that the allegation of poverty is untrue, or the court determines that the action is frivolous or malicious, fails to state a claim, or seeks damages from a defendant immune from damage claims.[114] The primary effect of in forma pauperis filing status is to permit filing of the suit without prepayment of the filing fee. It also places a duty on court officers to serve required legal process without charge. It does not excuse the payment of witness fees and expenses or place the responsibility for such payment on the government.[115]

The Supreme Court has held that only natural persons, not associations or other artificial entities, are eligible to file in forma pauperis.[116] Another limitation on the availability of in forma pauperis status is that it is not fully available to prisoners, due to the Prison Litigation Reform Act.[117] Also, a

111. *Crawford-El* also has implications for discovery and summary judgment in § 1983 cases. These are discussed below.
112. *See* Felder v. Casey, 487 U.S. 131, 150–53 (1988).
113. 28 U.S.C. § 1915(a)(1).
114. 28 U.S.C. § 1915(e)(2).
115. *See, e.g.,* Malik v. Lavalley, 994 F.2d 90 (2d Cir. 1993).
116. Rowland v. California Men's Colony, 506 U.S. 194 (1993).
117. 28 U.S.C. § 1915(b). That is, they must pay the filing fee through an assessment against their institutional trust fund.

prisoner who has brought three previous suits termed frivolous, malicious, or that have failed to state a claim may no longer use in forma pauperis status at all except in emergency circumstances.[118]

1. Nature and Standard of Review for Frivolousness

Filing a complaint in forma pauperis requires clearing an additional hurdle, although this should not ordinarily be a problem for well-founded claims. In contrast to the trial court's scope of review in ruling on a FED. R. CIV. P. 12(b)(6) motion to dismiss, a trial court applying § 1915 may "pierce the veil of the complaint's factual allegations" and dismiss complaints based upon "fantastic or delusional scenarios."[119] However, it is not appropriate for a trial court to dismiss simply because the complaint's allegations are unlikely or improbable.[120]

The Fifth Circuit's en banc *Schultea* opinion states that *Leatherman* should have no effect on trial courts' review of in forma pauperis complaints. This review may include a consideration of whether "it is clear that the defendants are immune from suit."[121]

Dismissal of an in forma pauperis complaint pursuant to § 1915(d) does not have a res judicata effect precluding the filing of a paid complaint raising the same claims. But, it may preclude subsequent consideration of the same allegations again raised in forma pauperis.[122] Appellate review of a trial court's § 1915(d) dismissal is for abuse of discretion, not de novo.[123]

2. Defendant's Options

Defense counsel who have occasion to deal with in forma pauperis complaints should familiarize themselves with the Tenth Circuit's opinion in *Lemmons v. Morris and Morris.*[124] In *Lemmons,* the appellate court reviewed for abuse of discretion a trial court's dismissal of an inmate's § 1983 complaint pursuant to § 1915. Acting without the benefit of a response or briefing

---

118. 28 U.S.C. § 1915(g).
119. Neitzke v. Williams, 490 U.S. 319, 327–28 (1989); *see also* Denton v. Hernandez, 504 U.S. 25 (1992).
120. *Denton,* 504 U.S. at 33.
121. Schultea v. Wood, 47 F.3d 1427, 1434 (5th Cir. 1995), quoting Neitzke v. Williams, 490 U.S. 319, 327 (1989).
122. *Denton,* 540 U.S. at 34.
123. 540 U.S. at 33.
124. 39 F.3d 264, 268–69 (10th Cir. 1994).

by defendants, the Tenth Circuit reversed. The opinion demonstrates that, although defendants are not required to respond at all until the § 1915 issue is settled, there are times when it may be wise to do so.

VII. INITIAL CONSIDERATIONS FOR DEFENDANT'S COUNSEL

A. Deciding Whom to Represent—Conflicts of Interest in Section 1983 Defense Work

All situations in which counsel is asked to represent more than one defendant present at least some potential for ethical problems. For defense counsel in § 1983 litigation, decisions about whether to represent two or more defendants can be particularly complex and troublesome. If, for example, a lawyer is asked to defend both an individual government employee and his employer against a suit for damages, there are many obvious and not so obvious ways in which the interests of these potential clients may diverge.

The interest of a governmental entity defendant may well be in showing that the defendant employee did not act in accordance with its established policies and procedures. Instead, he acted erratically and unpredictably in such a manner that it would be unjustified to impose liability for his actions on the governmental unit. Conversely, the interest of the employee may be best served by showing that he followed an accepted, standard, approved course of conduct sanctioned by the policies of his employer.

A less common but just as troublesome example is that of the governmental employee who has clearly committed an unlawful act for which the plaintiff seeks to impose liability on his employer based on "failure to train." One possible strategy for defending the governmental unit would be to attempt to defeat causation by establishing that the employee was (unknown to his employers) so bent on committing misconduct that no amount of training would have made any difference.[125] Of course, such an argument could not be made by a lawyer who also represents the individual employee.

There are several reported cases in which appellate courts have been faced with disgruntled individual defendants after trials in which defense counsel undertook multiple representation. Some of these courts have issued opinions about whether the apparent conflict of interest required a new trial, and about whether the trial judge was obligated to warn individual defendants

---

125. For example, would it have helped to send Mark Fuhrman to racial and gender diversity classes?

about the hazards of joint representation.[126] The real significance of these cases for defense counsel, though, is not the courts' various findings about whether a retrial was required. Rather, it is the extent of the troubles that accrued to defense counsel as a result of the joint representation.[127]

It may be possible to avoid the worst potential conflicts through governmental unit decisions to fully indemnify individual employees, or through stipulations about some issues that could otherwise create conflicts.[128] However, even these situations may expose defense counsel to increased risks. Therefore, they call for careful communication and file documentation. This should include such things as informing all clients of litigation risks and settlement offers, diligence in following up on evidentiary leads suggested by clients, etc.[129] It is clear that mere boilerplate, pro forma "disclosure" and "consent" are not enough.[130] In addition to exercising caution about the acceptance of joint representation in the first place, counsel should also remain on the alert as the case develops for unexpected circumstances that increase the seriousness of potential conflicts. These may mandate the hiring of separate counsel, even if it must be at the expense of the governmental unit.

Interestingly, these practical problems in providing counsel for individual defendants in civil rights cases may have had an influence on the development of the law about such claims. In *Kimberlin v. Quinlan*, one D.C. Circuit judge stated:

> Of course, in *Bivens* cases, individual governmental officers are sued personally, and are sometimes obliged to pay attorneys' fees out of modest government salaries. That is why the court has recognized that early dismissal of all but the few obviously meritorious cases is desirable.[131]

B. Removal

After the decision about whom to represent, the next choice defense counsel must usually make is whether to remove to federal court, if the case is filed

---

126. *Compare, e.g.,* Dunton v. County of Suffolk, 729 F.2d 903, 907–10 (2d Cir. 1984), *modified on other grounds,* 748 F.2d 69; *with* Rodick v. City of Schenectady, 1 F.3d 1341, 1349–50 (2d Cir. 1993); *see also* Gordon v. Norman, 788 F.2d 1194, 1198–99 (6th Cir. 1986).

127. *See, e.g.,* Gordon v. Norman, 788 F.2d 1194, 1198–99 nn.4 and 5 (6th Cir. 1986).

128. *See, e.g., id.* at 1198; Manganella v. Keyes, 613 F. Supp. 795, 798–99 (D. Conn. 1985).

129. *See, e.g.,* Rodick v. City of Schenectady, 1 F.3d 1341, 1350–51 (2d Cir. 1993); Gordon v. Norman, 788 F.2d 1194, 1198 (6th Cir. 1986).

130. *See, e.g., Dunton,* 729 F.2d at 909.

131. 17 F.3d 1525, 1526 (D.C. Cir. 1994). (Silberman, J., concurring in denial of rehearing en banc.)

in state court. Defendants have the ultimate choice of forum in § 1983 cases, if they are aware of it and know how to exercise it. This choice should be governed by an analysis similar to that suggested above for plaintiff's counsel's decision about where to file. Some governmental defendants still feel more at home at the state courthouse; others may be more attracted to favorable procedural factors in the federal court system. For example, interlocutory appeal from denial of immunity claims is not uniformly available in the state courts at this time.

The substance of defendant's removal right is governed by 28 U.S.C. § 1441, while the procedure for its exercise is governed by 28 U.S.C. § 1446. Section 1446(a) provides for the filing of a "notice of removal" in the federal district court where the action is pending, together with copies of all the state court papers served on the defendant. The notice should contain a "short and plain statement of the grounds for removal." It is no longer necessary to file a bond, and the notice need not be verified—rather, it must simply be "signed pursuant to Rule 11."[132]

The defendant then gives written notice of the removal to all adverse parties, and sends a copy of the removal notice to the clerk of the state court. No hearing or other consideration of the removal notice may take place in the state court—the removal is automatic upon compliance with these steps. The state court then loses jurisdiction, and any consideration of remand must take place in the federal court.[133]

1. *Pitfall Alert on Removal Procedures*

Although § 1446 appears on the surface to be relatively simple to understand and comply with, this is cruelly deceptive. In fact, various forms of technical peril lurk therein.[134] Further, it is strictly construed against removing defendants; procedural defects, including failure to meet applicable time limits, will probably be held to waive the right to remove.

The major traps for unwary defense counsel are computation of the time limit for filing the removal notice, especially in multiple defendant cases, and the standards for complying with the requirement that all defendants who have been served must join in this notice. It would be impossible to cover herein all the potential complications of either. So, counsel unfamiliar with this area of law are simply warned to be wary of these issues,

---

132. 28 U.S.C. § 1446(a).

133. 28 U.S.C. § 1446(d); *see, e.g.,* Libhart v. Santa Monica Dairy Co., 592 F.2d 1062, 1064 (9th Cir. 1979).

134. *See, e.g.,* Local Union No. 172 v. P. J. Dick, Inc., 253 F. Supp.2d 1022, 1025–26 (S.D. Ohio 2003); Sonoma Falls Developers v. Nevada Gold & Casinos, 272 F. Supp.2d 919, 925–27 (N.D. Cal. 2003).

and are urged to familiarize themselves with the relevant Wright and Miller sections referenced in the "Suggestions for Further Reading," as well as a broader range of cases construing the statute cited above.[135]

C. Waivable "Procedural" Defenses in Federal Court

If the case is to be litigated in federal court, defense counsel must next determine whether the facts support any potential defense that will be waived if not asserted very early in the litigation process. Pursuant to FED. R. CIV. P. 12(h)(1), there are four such initial "procedural" defenses:

(1) lack of personal jurisdiction over the defendant;

(Note: a suggestion that the court lacks subject matter jurisdiction of the case, unlike a claim of lack of personal jurisdiction over the defendant, may be raised at any time during the litigation, even on appeal.)[136]

(2) improper venue;

(3) insufficiency of process; or

(4) insufficiency of service of process.

(Note: The defense of "insufficiency of service of process" includes objections to the timeliness of service. These objections will be waived unless raised at the time and in the manner described below.[137])

These four easily waivable procedural defenses may ordinarily be raised either through a pre-answer motion, or in the original answer itself.[138] But, if defendant's counsel files a Rule 12 motion of any type before or at the same time as an answer, all the above-listed procedural defenses present at

---

135. Counsel for state agency defendants should also familiarize themselves with *Lapides v. Board of Regents,* 535 U.S. 613 (2002). Therein, the Court held that Georgia's removal of a case to federal court waived the state's immunity from being forced to defend against certain pendent state law claims in federal court. The Court limited the effect of its ruling to claims for which the state's legislature had waived its immunity in state court.

136. FED. R. CIV. P. 12(h)(3); *see, e.g.,* Tongkook America, Inc. v. Shipton Sportswear Co., 14 F.3d 781, 786 (2d Cir. 1994).

137. Santos v. State Farm Fire and Casualty Co., 902 F.2d 1092, 1096 (2d Cir. 1990); Kersh v. Derozier, 851 F.2d 1509, 1511–12 (5th Cir. 1988).

138. FED. R. CIV. P. 12(b).

that time *must* be included in it. Otherwise, they will be waived—that is, they cannot be included either in a later motion or in the defendant's answer.[139]

The defendant may seek leave of court later in the case to amend his answer and assert additional defenses of many types. A later-amended answer may not be used, however, to assert for the first time any of these four Rule 12(h)(1) defenses, unless it is filed within the time for amendment as of right, pursuant to Rule 15(a).[140]

D. Motions to Dismiss for Failure to State a Claim

Defendants may use Fed. R. Civ. P. 12(b)(6) to seek the dismissal of a complaint that fails to state an actionable claim. It may also be used to challenge a complaint that reveals the presence of a bar to recovery, such as the statute of limitations. The target of this motion is the pleading only, not the evidence that might or might not support the pleading. The distinction between a motion to dismiss and a motion for summary judgment does not depend on what title is used for the motion. Rather, it hinges on whether the court considers materials outside the pleadings in ruling on it.[141] If either party submits materials outside the pleadings and the court considers them, the motion must be treated as one for summary judgment. Rule 56 procedures, therefore, must be followed, including giving all parties the opportunity to submit evidentiary materials in response. See Part VII herein for a discussion of summary judgment motions in the § 1983 context.

Defendants may make requests to dismiss pursuant to Rule 12(b)(6) either in their answer or by separate motion. Failure to assert it in initial pleadings will not waive the opportunity to do so later.[142] Usually, 12(b)(6) challenges are raised early in the case, but Rule 12 provides that a request to dismiss for failure to state an actionable claim may be made in any pleading, in a motion for judgment on the pleadings during the pendency of the case, or even at trial.[143] Not surprisingly, the Sixth Circuit has held that filing a pre-answer Rule 12 motion without an assertion of qualified immunity

---

139. Fed. R. Civ. P. 12(g) and (h)(1); Albany Insurance Co. v. Almacenadora Somex, 5 F.3d 907, 909–10 (5th Cir. 1993); Pardazi v. Cullman Medical Center, 896 F.2d 1313, 1314–17 (11th Cir. 1990).

140. Fed. R. Civ. P. 12(h)(1); *see, e.g.*, Konigsberg v. Shute, 435 F.2d 551, 552 (3d Cir. 1970).

141. Fed. R. Civ. P. 12(b).

142. Fed. R. Civ. P. 12(h)(2).

143. Fed. R. Civ. P. 12(h)(2). This does not override the trial court's power to control its docket by setting its own deadlines for dispositive motions.

did not waive the defendant's right to seek dismissal on this ground in a later pleading or in a post-answer motion.[144]

Because their focus is solely on pleadings, the practical value of Rule 12(b)(6) motions in § 1983 litigation is somewhat limited. First, their usefulness with respect to § 1983 claims against governmental units was substantially reduced by *Leatherman*. Also, their practical value is limited by the usual procedure of permitting the plaintiff an opportunity to amend if the complaint is found insufficient.

Although immunity defenses may be raised through a 12(b)(6) motion, this places only the pleadings—and no evidentiary materials—before the court. The plaintiff's factual allegations must be taken as true for purposes of ruling on the motion.[145] For an example of use of a motion to dismiss to raise a qualified immunity claim, see the Seventh Circuit's *McMath v. City of Gary, Indiana*.[146]

VIII. DISCOVERY AND SUMMARY JUDGMENT ISSUES

A. The Impact of Federal Rule Changes on Discovery

The Supreme Court amended Federal Rule 26(a) in 2000 to narrow the scope of mandatory and automatic disclosure. This rule provides for early disclosure by all parties of basic information about supporting witnesses and documents, without a discovery request. The Court eliminated Rule 26(a)'s previous reference to matters "alleged with particularity in the pleadings." This removed the incentive for either side to initially plead with more particularity than otherwise necessary in order to trigger an opponent's broader disclosure obligation. Also, only those witnesses and documents that the disclosing party "may use to support its claims or defenses" must now be disclosed, rather than any witness or document with relevant information.[147] The 2000 amendments also eliminated some of the local "opt-out" provisions previously present in the discovery rules, in an effort to create more procedural uniformity in the federal courts.[148]

The boundaries of routinely discoverable information have been affected by Federal Rule changes as well. Matters "relevant to the claim or

144. English v. Dyke, 23 F.3d 1086, 1089–91 (6th Cir. 1994).

145. *See, e.g.,* United States v. Mississippi, 380 U.S. 128, 143 (1965); Canadyne-Georgia Corp. v. Nations Bank, 183 F.3d 1269, 1275 (11th Cir. 1999).

146. 976 F.2d 1026, 1031 (7th Cir. 1992).

147. Fed. R. Civ. P. 26(a)(1)(A) and (B).

148. These procedures are still subject to modification through "case-specific orders." *See, e.g.,* Fed. R. Civ. P. 26(a)(1) and (2).

defense" of any party are discoverable without court intervention.[149] For "good cause" the court can authorize broader discovery of matters "relevant to the subject matter" of the action. This represents a significant narrowing of the material available as of right, and empowers the court to limit discovery in ways it could not previously.[150]

B. The Role of Discovery and Summary Judgment in Section 1983 Litigation after *Leatherman* and *Crawford-El*

The Court in *Harlow v. Fitzgerald* expressed its abiding concern that governmental officers sued personally for damages would be substantially impaired in the performance of their job duties by the litigation process itself, whatever the outcome.[151] Of course, one of the major burdens of the litigation process is the obligation to respond to discovery. This obligation was described by the *Harlow* Court as potentially "wide-ranging, time-consuming, and not without considerable cost."[152]

The Court has repeatedly emphasized its determination to protect governmental officials with well-founded immunity claims from the litigation process, not just from monetary liability. But, it has also proscribed the imposition of special, heightened pleading or proof standards for civil rights cases as a tool to accomplish this purpose.[153] Rather than erecting special hurdles, district courts must somehow apply existing procedural rules in a way that effectuates immunity claims. Although *Leatherman* did not involve an immunity claim, its guidance to district courts has practical usefulness for this purpose. According to the *Leatherman* opinion, lower courts should "rely on summary judgment and control of discovery to weed out unmeritorious claims sooner rather than later."[154]

In *Crawford-El v. Britton*,[155] the Supreme Court ventured again into these trenches. The Court's *Crawford-El* opinion is an attempt to guide lower courts toward effectuating *Harlow* without smothering large numbers

---

149. Fed. R. Civ. P. 26(b)(1).

150. *See* Advisory Committee notes regarding 2000 amendments to Fed. R. Civ. P. 26(b)(1)—"The Committee intends that the parties and the court focus on the actual claims and defenses involved in the action."

151. 457 U.S. 800, 815–18 (1982).

152. *Id.* at 817 n.29, quoting Halperin v. Kissinger, 606 F.2d 1192, 1214 (D.C. Cir. 1979).

153. *See* Crawford-El v. Britton, 523 U.S. 574, 594–97 (1998). *See also* the reasoning of *Leatherman,* 507 U.S. at 167–68 (1993), regarding civil rights claims against governmental entities.

154. 507 U.S. at 168–69.

155. 523 U.S. 574 (1998).

of well-founded civil rights claims in their infancy. As in *Leatherman,* the Court rejected an appellate court's attempt to craft its own special procedural rules to short-circuit § 1983 cases.[156] In doing so, the Court reiterated its preference for procedural rules enacted "either by the rulemaking process or the legislative process" and not by the courts. However, the *Crawford-El* opinion suggested several ways to apply existing Federal Rules to test claims against public officials early in the litigation process. The Court advised that lower courts use Fed. R. Civ. P. 7(a) (court may order a reply to defendant's answer) and Fed. R. Civ. P. 12(e) (court may grant motion for a more definite statement) "prior to permitting any discovery at all."[157]

The *Crawford-El* opinion also emphasized the "many options" district judges have to control the discovery process through Rule 26(b), (c), and (d). For example, narrowing initial discovery and dictating the sequence of discovery in appropriate cases may facilitate early resolution of immunity claims. So, although restrained from crafting their own special rules to quickly dispose of nonmeritorious § 1983 cases, district courts have been encouraged to make aggressive use of existing procedural rules to do this. Although scrutiny can begin at the pleading stage, discovery and summary judgment rulings are at the heart of this process.

C. Summary Judgments in Federal Court—Background and Application

FED. R. CIV. P. 56 authorizes either party to seek summary judgment on any issue about which he claims no material fact is in dispute, and on which he claims to be entitled to judgment as a matter of law.[158] Summary judgment is not a test of the sufficiency of the pleadings of the opposing party. Instead, it probes for the existence of some proof that an actual factual dispute is present and that, therefore, a trial on the merits is required.[159]

The aggressive use of summary judgment motions to test the sufficiency of litigants' claims has for many years been an important part of the federal judicial process for all types of cases. In many state court systems summary judgment is a disfavored device, regarded with heavy skepticism by trial court judges. In the federal court system, however, it is a favored tool for

---

156. 523 U.S. at 594–97.

157. 523 U.S. at 598.

158. FED. R. CIV. P. 56(a) and (b).

159. FED. R. CIV. P. 56(c) and (e). *See e.g.,* Zweig v. Hearst Corp., 521 F.2d 1129, 1133 (9th Cir.), *cert. denied,* 423 U.S. 1025 (1975).

avoiding unnecessary trials and for narrowing the issues that require trial.[160] The *Crawford-El* Court reaffirmed it as "the ultimate screen" for § 1983 cases in which qualified immunity is an issue.[161]

D. *Celotex Corp. v. Catrett*

Through its 1986 *Celotex* opinion, the Supreme Court clarified the analysis district courts should apply in ruling on summary judgment motions.[162] In doing so, the Court made these motions an even more powerful tool for defendants. Or, more precisely, they were made a more powerful tool for parties who do not have the burden of proof with respect to the matter at issue in the motion.

The defendant in *Celotex* used a summary judgment motion to, in effect, test whether the plaintiff could come forward with some proof of each essential element of her cause of action. The defendant did not produce any definitive proof of its own negating any element of the plaintiff's case. Rather, the defendant used the summary judgment motion as a device to force the plaintiff to come forward with proof in order to avoid summary judgment being granted for the defendant. The plaintiff was unable to provide acceptable proof of one essential element of her claim, and the court granted defendant's summary judgment motion.[163]

The Supreme Court approved the granting of summary judgment in these circumstances. But, the Court noted that the plaintiff did not necessarily have to produce evidence that would be admissible at trial in order to avoid summary judgment. Rather, she only needed to submit "some evidence," such as an affidavit.[164] The Court also recognized the potential problem with premature consideration of such motions. According to the Court, Rule 56(f) could be applied to prevent such premature disposition.[165] This subpart of Rule 56 provides that a summary judgment motion may be denied, or a hearing on the motion continued until after further discovery is made, if the responding party cannot "for reasons stated" present summary

160. *See, e.g.,* McEwen v. Delta Air Lines, 919 F.2d 58, 60 (7th Cir. 1990); Freeman v. Continental Gin Co., 381 F.2d 459, 467–70 (5th Cir. 1967).

161. 523 U.S. at 600.

162. Celotex Corp. v. Catrett, 477 U.S. 317, 322–23 (1986).

163. 477 U.S. at 320–21.

164. 477 U.S. at 324. She did produce three documents that were discounted as not meeting the requirements of admissible materials as defined by Rule 56(c) and (e).

165. 477 U.S. at 326.

judgment evidence when the motion is first considered.[166] The *Celotex* Court interpreted this to indicate that a ruling may be postponed "if the nonmoving party has not had an opportunity to make full discovery."[167]

E. Summary Judgment/Discovery Issues in Suits Against Governmental Entities

One of the most notable effects of *Leatherman* was to move the first major battle between the civil rights plaintiff and the governmental entity defendant a bit further into the litigation process. That is, it is now more likely to happen at the discovery/summary judgment stage, rather than at the initial pleading/motion-to-dismiss stage. The practical implication of *Leatherman* seemed to be that § 1983 plaintiffs no longer had to develop key aspects of their case through informal discovery before filing it, in order to survive an early motion to dismiss. As a corollary, trial courts could be expected to face increasing numbers of discovery battles between plaintiffs and governmental unit defendants.

Crawford-El did not involve a claim against a governmental entity, but some of the opinion's language may still be useful in defending against such a claim. The *Crawford-El* Court indicated that a Rule 12(e) Motion for a More Definite Statement might be appropriate before the court permits any discovery.[168] Also, *Crawford-El* emphasized the district court's broad discretion to protect defendants appropriately by controlling discovery, based on the individual case circumstances. Governmental entity defendants should make as much use as possible of *Crawford-El*'s helpful hints during the discovery phase of § 1983 cases against them.

Also, although most governmental unit defendants have no claim of immunity from the litigation process itself, they can certainly make early and aggressive use of *Celotex*-type summary judgment motions. This may be especially effective if the case development efforts of plaintiffs' counsel are not diligent, expeditious, and clearly focused, as discussed below.

The *Celotex* opinion refers to the nonmoving party's "opportunity to make full discovery" before summary judgment consideration, pursuant to FED. R. CIV. P. 56(f).[169] However, this subsection of Rule 56 provides a

166. FED. R. CIV. P. 56(f).

167. 477 U.S. at 326.

168. 523 U.S. at 598. Although the Court apparently views FED. R. CIV. P. 12(e) with affection, many sets of local rules do not; *see, e.g.*, U.S. District Court for the Northern District of Texas, Local Rule 12.1.

169. 477 U.S. at 326.

fairly amorphous guideline. Typically, district courts have been held to have a good deal of discretion as to how, exactly, it is to be applied.[170] Courts that strongly supported heightened pleading requirements before *Leatherman* may now be inclined to exercise this discretion by prematurely granting defendants' summary judgment motions, after little or no discovery. In this way, they accomplish the same goal as do heightened pleading requirements without directly flouting the *Leatherman* mandate. Indeed, *Leatherman* and *Crawford-El's* rather ominous references to discovery control as a way to "weed out unmeritorious claims sooner rather than later" provide some support for district courts' active screening efforts at the discovery stage.[171]

For a § 1983 plaintiff, there is little practical difference between the effects of a motion to dismiss and those of a prematurely considered summary judgment motion. The motion to dismiss seeks to dispose of the case based on the pleadings before the plaintiff has had an opportunity to obtain discovery to flesh out the pleadings. A premature summary judgment motion seeks to dispose of his case before he has had an opportunity to obtain discovery to effectively oppose the motion.

Unless and until the Supreme Court further clarifies the ground rules for this increasingly critical stage of the battle, plaintiffs' lawyers must plan carefully in order not to be vulnerable to a premature summary judgment motion. First, counsel are still well advised to perform as much informal discovery as possible before naming a governmental unit as a defendant. This should assist in responding to summary judgment motions without the benefit of extensive discovery, if this becomes necessary. It should also help to provide a careful and specific focus for the discovery efforts that are made.

Second, many reported opinions have focused on the need for specificity in Rule 56(f) affidavits. They have rejected broad, global allegations that more time is needed for discovery, and that further discovery is expected to produce "relevant information."[172] If a Rule 56(f) affidavit is necessary, plaintiff's counsel should state as specifically as possible what further discovery is requested. Counsel should also state what information she expects to develop through it and describe the indications that the needed information is actually available from these sources. Finally, counsel

---

170. *See* Sheinkopf v. Stone, 927 F.2d 1259, 1263–64 (1st Cir. 1991); Pittman v. Gaines, 905 F.2d 199, 201 (8th Cir. 1990); *but see* Dean v. Barber, 951 F.2d 1210, 1213–14 (11th Cir. 1992).

171. *Leatherman,* 507 U.S. at 168–69; *Crawford-El,* 523 U.S. at 597–99.

172. *See, e.g.,* Lewis v. City of Ft. Collins, 903 F.2d 752, 758–59 (10th Cir. 1990).

should explain how this information will be probative of a material fact issue in the case, so as to make the entry of summary judgment inappropriate.[173]

Additionally, plaintiff's counsel should proceed as expeditiously with discovery as the rules permit. Any unavoidable delays in doing so should be explained to the court in the Rule 56(f) affidavit.[174] Defendant's counsel should be on the alert from the beginning of the case for any deviation from these standards. If one occurs, defendant's counsel should make effective use of it in a summary judgment motion.

F. Summary Judgment/Discovery Issues in Suits Against Individual Defendants

The general summary judgment principles outlined above also apply in cases against individual defendants. Additionally, such cases implicate policy issues that favor the early, aggressive use of summary judgment motions and the imposition of discovery limits.

The issue with respect to qualified immunity claims is whether the defendant violated "clearly settled law." At first glance, this looks like a strictly legal question, easily lending itself to disposition by summary judgment motion. Also, the early use of a summary judgment motion to resolve this issue furthers important policy considerations. That is, it protects governmental employees with sound immunity claims from the full hardships of the legal process.[175]

This approach sounds logical in the abstract and is understandably favored by the Supreme Court on policy grounds, but in practice it has proven to be extraordinarily difficult for lower courts to implement in a consistent and fair manner. Many times disputed factual issues simply must be resolved in order for the trial court to rule properly on qualified immunity claims. The question of what law was clearly settled at the time of the defendant's challenged actions is always a legal matter for the court to determine, while at the same time, in most cases, defendants' actions and their circumstances are hotly disputed. If, under plaintiff's version of the facts, defendant did things that no reasonable official in his position could have believed to be lawful, and under defendant's version of the facts he did

---

173. *See, e.g.,* United States v. Leong Chinese Merchants Ass'n Bldg., 918 F.2d 1289, 1294–95 (7th Cir. 1990), *cert. denied,* 502 U.S. 809 (1991).

174. *See, e.g.,* Sofo v. Pan-American Life Ins. Co., 13 F.3d 239, 242 (7th Cir. 1994), in which the court held that ongoing settlement negotiations did not provide an effective excuse for plaintiff's failure to pursue discovery for ten months.

175. *See, e.g.,* Harlow v. Fitzgerald, 457 U.S. 800, 814–18 (1982).

only things that a reasonable official in his position *could* have believed to be lawful, a material factual dispute exists. This should preclude resolution by summary judgment.[176]

One of the Supreme Court's most strongly worded opinions about the use of summary judgment to resolve qualified immunity claims is the 1991 case *Hunter v. Bryant*.[177] This was a *Bivens* lawsuit in which Fourth Amendment damage claims were raised against Secret Service agents, who claimed qualified immunity for their actions in arresting the plaintiff. The trial court denied defendants' summary judgment motion, and the Ninth Circuit partially upheld this decision. The Ninth Circuit panel thought there was a "more reasonable interpretation" of the plaintiff's actions than the threatening one defendants used to justify his arrest. The panel held the plaintiff's wrongful arrest claim could not properly be disposed of by summary judgment unless there was "only one reasonable conclusion a jury could reach" about whether a reasonable officer could have believed he had probable cause.[178]

The Supreme Court reversed the Ninth Circuit, and described the analysis that should be applied to a summary judgment motion based on qualified immunity. Emphasizing that qualified immunity protects governmental officers who reasonably could have thought they were not violating the law, the Court held that summary judgment should have been granted on the facts of the *Hunter* case. The Court summarized by stating, "[I]mmunity ordinarily should be decided by the court long before trial."[179]

Crawford-El provides a useful road map for defense counsel seeking to effectuate a governmental employee's well-founded immunity claim. In addition to using federal pleading rules 7 and 12(e), as discussed above, counsel should ordinarily assert immunity through a summary judgment motion early in the litigation process. Counsel may simultaneously move to stay all discovery, including the "automatic disclosure" obligation referenced above, pending a ruling on the summary judgment motion.[180] Discovery against the defendant should then be limited to those fact issues, if any, that must be further developed in order to rule on the legal issues raised by his immunity claim.[181]

---

176. *See, e.g.,* Harper v. Harris County, 21 F.3d 597, 600–02 (5th Cir. 1994).

177. 502 U.S. 224 (1991).

178. 502 U.S. at 228.

179. *Id.*

180. *Cf., e.g.,* Anderson v. Creighton, 483 U.S. 635, 646–47 (1987).

181. *See, e.g., Anderson,* 483 U.S. at 646–47 n.6; Gaines v. Davis, 928 F.2d 705, 707 (5th Cir. 1991).

Plaintiff's counsel faced with this type of motion should respond by showing the court exactly what factual material is necessary to refute the defendant's immunity claim, and how any requested discovery relates to that determination. An overly broad discovery order at this stage may be subject to interlocutory appeal by a defendant claiming immunity.[182]

IX. INTERLOCUTORY APPEALS

Since Chapter 3 deals with procedural issues in state court litigation of § 1983 claims, this section will focus exclusively on interlocutory appeal issues as they occur in the federal court system. Disputes about availability and scope of interlocutory appellate jurisdiction for immunity claims are among the most hotly debated, heavily litigated matters in § 1983 law. The Supreme Court has produced three major opinions on this topic within the past decade: *Swint v. Chambers County*, *Johnson v. Jones*, and *Behrens v. Pelletier*, all of which are discussed below.[183]

A. Background and Rationale

The availability of interlocutory appeals to certain defendants in § 1983 litigation reflects a judicially created exception to the "finality" rule. That is, except in a few statutorily enumerated circumstances, as a rule only final orders are immediately appealable.[184] The exception frequently used in § 1983 cases stems from the "collateral order" doctrine. The courts have recognized that certain orders, although interlocutory, determine with finality important claims separate and independent from those on which the litigation is based. These "collateral" claims cannot be fully vindicated if appealed at the conclusion of the entire litigation.[185]

Individual defendants' claims of either qualified or absolute immunity seem to fit well within this rationale because the asserted right is immunity from suit, not just from liability. This right could never be effectively vindicated after the suit is over.[186] In *Mitchell v. Forsyth*, the Supreme Court held that trial courts' denials of individual defendants' summary judgment

182. *See, e.g., Gaines,* 928 F.2d at 706–07.
183. Swint v. Chambers County, 514 U.S. 35 (1995); Johnson v. Jones, 515 U.S. 304 (1995); Behrens v. Pelletier, 516 U.S. 299 (1996).
184. Mitchell v. Forsyth, 472 U.S. 511, 524–30 (1985).
185. Cohen v. Beneficial Indus. Loan Corp., 337 U.S. 541, 546 (1949).
186. *Mitchell,* 472 U.S. at 526–27.

motions based on immunity claims are immediately appealable "collateral orders" for this reason.[187]

The *Mitchell* Court, apparently reassuring itself that it was not creating a monster, reasoned that it would be unnecessary for an appellate court to resolve disputed facts in this type of interlocutory appeal: "on the contrary, all it need determine is an issue of law."[188] As with some of the Court's other pronouncements about how individual immunities are to be implemented, this opinion led to uncertainty for litigants and chaos in the lower courts. Some but not all of the confusion has been resolved by later Supreme Court cases.

B. What Legal Claims Trigger a Defendant's Right to Interlocutory Appeal?

For the reasons outlined above, an individual defendant whose dispositive motion based on qualified or absolute immunity is denied has a right to interlocutory appeal if the denial implicates a legal issue, as opposed to a purely factual dispute.[189] The difficulty, of course, is in sorting out what is really denial of a qualified immunity claim on legal grounds, and what is denial of a claim of "I didn't do it" or "I didn't do it like that" from a defendant whose case situation includes qualified immunity issues.[190]

As described by the *Mitchell* Court, the issue on appeal is whether, accepting the plaintiff's version of the facts, "the legal norms allegedly violated by the defendant were clearly established at the time of the challenged actions." Or, if the trial court denied summary judgment for the defendant on the ground that even under the defendant's version of the facts his conduct violated clearly established law, "whether the law clearly proscribed the actions the defendant claims he took."[191]

An interlocutory appeal is not available, however, to challenge the district court's determination of what fact issues are "genuine." Most cases in which defendants claim qualified immunity involve hotly disputed facts about defendants' actions and their circumstances. These disputed fact issues are frequently closely intertwined with the issue of qualified immunity, if

187. 472 U.S. at 530.

188. 472 U.S. at 528.

189. Johnson v. Jones, 515 U. S. 304 (1995); Mitchell v. Forsyth, 472 U.S. 511 (1985).

190. *See Johnson,* 515 U.S. at 313–15.

191. *Mitchell,* 472 U.S. at 528.

not nearly identical with it, for example, in excessive force cases.[192] In these cases, defendants can move for summary judgment on various grounds—some involving the "clearly settled" law applicable to their conduct, some alleging that fact issues unrelated to qualified immunity must be resolved in their favor as a matter of law. And, some motions raise harder-to-classify summary judgment claims, grounded in qualified immunity and involving disputed facts. Many of these appellate situations are clearly far afield from the superficial simplicity and clarity of *Mitchell v. Forsyth*'s analysis.

Before *Johnson v. Jones*, the circuits had reached varying results in their attempts to sort out the situations in which denials of qualified immunity claims would trigger interlocutory appellate jurisdiction.[193] One major question was whether individual defendants claiming qualified immunity could properly invoke interlocutory appellate jurisdiction when their "evidence sufficiency" summary judgment claims were denied. In *Johnson v. Jones*, the Supreme Court said no.

The *Johnson v. Jones* interlocutory appeal centered on three individual defendants' summary judgment contentions in an excessive force case. These defendants argued that there was no evidence they were involved in beating the plaintiff, or even that they observed anyone else doing so. The district court denied their motion, and the Seventh Circuit dismissed their appeal. The Seventh Circuit panel reasoned that this type of "evidence sufficiency" dispute simply did not trigger interlocutory appellate review, despite defendants' claims that their qualified immunity from suit would be irretrievably lost without it.[194]

The Supreme Court affirmed. In doing so, the Court reviewed and explained the nature and purpose of interlocutory appellate jurisdiction in cases involving immunity claims. According to the Court, this jurisdiction is properly usable to determine what law was "clearly established" at the time of defendants' actions when this would control the outcome of their summary judgment motion.[195] However, interlocutory appellate jurisdiction may not properly be invoked to review whether factual disputes are "genuine" for summary judgment purposes. To find otherwise would contradict the

---

192. Even so, the qualified immunity question cannot properly be compressed into the issue of whether a constitutional violation occurred. Saucier v. Katz, 533 U.S. 194, 204–06 (2001).

193. *Compare, e.g.,* Elliott v. Thomas, 937 F.2d 338, 341–42 (7th Cir. 1991), *cert. denied,* 502 U.S. 1074 (1992); *with* Kelly v. Bender, 23 F.3d 1328, 1330 (8th Cir. 1994).

194. 515 U.S. at 308.

195. 515 U.S. at 313.

rationale and purpose of the collateral order doctrine as originally applied to immunity claims in *Mitchell*. Also, it would create an unnecessary and burdensome chore for the appellate courts. That is, they would frequently be faced with a detailed examination of complex evidentiary materials in order to rule on factual issues, a task for which trial courts are better suited. In many cases, the appellate court would probably have to look at the same case's factual record twice—once on interlocutory appeal and later, in a more developed state, after trial.

The main thrust of the Court's *Johnson* opinion is a renewed emphasis on the language of *Mitchell v. Forsyth*. The Court spoke in *Mitchell* of an interlocutory appellate procedure available for the resolution of legal, not factual, disputes. In effect, the Court ratified the view of the circuits that contended all along the interlocutory appellate process was not properly used to entertain claims of "We didn't do it."[196] The Court acknowledged that its relatively narrow view of the circumstances in which interlocutory appellate jurisdiction was available would serve to limit the practical enforceability of immunities; but, it indicated, this was unavoidable.[197]

The *Johnson* opinion encouraged trial courts ruling on qualified immunity summary judgment motions to include a list of facts they took to be established for the purpose of their ruling. This, the Court thought, would aid the appellate courts in their threshold determination of whether they had interlocutory appellate jurisdiction.

But, what if the district court does not do so? Should the appeals court sort out the factual record for itself and arrive at a determination of what facts are established, viewed in the form most favorable to the respondent? Or, should it focus on what the district court "likely assumed"? In *Winfield v. Bass*,[198] the en banc Fourth Circuit wrestled with such a situation. The majority held that the court must examine the factual record itself, and reach a determination (in the light most favorable to the respondent) of what has been established. Then the court should make legal conclusions based on these findings.

The label the district court gives to its decision (i.e., "legal" or "factual") does not determine whether interlocutory appeal will be allowable. Rather, if the appellate court concludes that a legal issue controls the outcome of the defendant's immunity claim, interlocutory appeal is proper. This is true whether or not the district court approached the case in this manner.[199]

---

196. *See, e.g., Elliott,* 937 F.2d at 342.

197. *Johnson,* 515 U.S. at 317–18.

198. 106 F.3d 525 (4th Cir. 1997) (en banc).

199. *See, e.g.,* Christophel v. Kukulinsky, 61 F.3d 479, 485 (6th Cir. 1995).

For example, in *Sanderfer v. Nichols*,[200] the district court denied a defendant's qualified immunity claim. The court's stated basis was that "more than a scintilla" of evidence supported the plaintiff's version of events. The Sixth Circuit nevertheless found it had interlocutory appellate jurisdiction. In the appellate panel's view the plaintiff's version of the facts, even if true, failed to state a constitutional violation.[201] This ruling therefore served to protect a defendant's correctly asserted right not to be subject to the litigation process. This was an appropriate use of interlocutory appellate jurisdiction, despite the district court's characterization of the matter as a factual dispute.

Defendants whose summary judgment motions are denied based on "material disputed fact issues" should, if justified, argue that the disputed facts are not material to the qualified immunity determination. Whether they are or are not is a question of law, appropriate for interlocutory appeal.[202] The Supreme Court recently placed its stamp of approval on this reasoning in *Behrens v Pelletier.*[203] As the Sixth Circuit explained in *Christophel v Kukulinsky:* "A defendant's right to appeal the denial of qualified immunity does not turn on the phrasing of the district court's order." [204]

The Supreme Court has held that denial of an Eleventh Amendment sovereign immunity claim is reviewable by interlocutory appeal.[205] The Court declined to distinguish cases in which the claimed Eleventh Amendment immunity was "bound up in factual complexities" from those in which the relevant facts were undisputed.[206]

Local governmental units are not liable on a respondeat superior basis for the unlawful conduct of their employees. But this does not mean they have an immunity from *suit*, as do the state and some individual defendants. Rather, they just cannot be found liable unless and until certain facts are established.[207] Therefore, local governmental units have no valid collateral appellate entitlement that would be permanently defeated unless the appellate court acted to protect it while the case is pending.[208]

---

200. 62 F.3d 151 (6th Cir. 1995).
201. 62 F.3d at 153 and n.2.
202. Chiu v. Plano Indep. Sch. Dist., 260 F.3d 330 (5th Cir. 2001); Boyd v. Baeppler, 215 F.3d 594 (6th Cir. 2000).
203. 516 U.S. at 312–13.
204. 61 F.3d at 485.
205. Puerto Rico Aqueduct & Sewer Auth. v. Metcalf & Eddy, Inc., 506 U.S. 139 (1993).
206. 506 U.S. at 147.
207. *See Swint,* 514 U.S. at 43; *Leatherman,* 507 U.S. at 166.
208. *Id.; compare Mitchell,* 472 U.S. at 526.

For this reason, the Supreme Court held in *Swint v. Chambers County* that the defendant county could not invoke interlocutory appellate jurisdiction to appeal denial of its summary judgment motion. The motion had argued the county could not be found liable, because the official whose conduct was at issue was not its policymaker.[209] Presumably, this reasoning would be applicable to denial of a summary judgment motion by a local governmental unit asserting its nonliability on any other grounds, as well.

C. What Procedural Circumstances Trigger the Right to Interlocutory Appeal?

Assuming the presence of an appropriate legal issue, what exactly does the trial court have to do, or fail to do, in order to trigger defendant's right to invoke interlocutory appellate jurisdiction?

1. Denial of Motion for Summary Judgment

This is the most common procedural scenario through which a defendant's immunity claim can properly reach the appellate court before the conclusion of the case.[210]

2. Denial of Motion to Dismiss

This also triggers interlocutory appellate jurisdiction, given the presence of an appropriate legal issue.[211]

3. "De facto" Denial of Motion for Summary Judgment or to Dismiss: Permitting Overly Broad Discovery

Defendants are entitled to rulings on their immunity claim, when presented through dispositive motions. Occasionally, rather than rule squarely on such claims, the trial court will defer the ruling until further discovery is accomplished, or indefinitely, or "until trial."[212] If the court's refusal to act on, or

---

209. 514 U.S. at 39.

210. *See, e.g.,* Anderson v. Creighton, 483 U.S. 635, 638 (1987).

211. Mitchell v. Forsyth, 472 U.S. 511, 527 (1985); *see also, e.g.,* McMath v. City of Gary, Indiana, 976 F.2d 1026, 1030–31 (7th Cir. 1992). The issue of whether more than one interlocutory appeal may be taken in the same case by the same defendant is discussed below.

212. *See, e.g.,* Workman v. Jordan, 958 F.2d 332, 335–36 (10th Cir. 1992); Gaines v. Davis, 928 F.2d 705, 707 (5th Cir. 1991).

delay in acting on, the motion has the effect of depriving a defendant of an asserted immunity from suit, the defendant may invoke interlocutory appellate jurisdiction to review it at that time, without relying on the extraordinary remedy of mandamus.[213]

If a defendant's immunity claim turns on a disputed fact issue, however, the court may permit further development of that issue through specifically tailored discovery. Such an order has been held not to trigger interlocutory appellate jurisdiction.[214] In contrast, if a court defers its ruling on a dispositive immunity-based motion until after broader discovery is completed, interlocutory appeal has been held to be available.[215] Apparently, the key factor is whether the court allows plaintiff's discovery to explore areas not necessary to rule on defendants' immunity claims.

4. *Denial of Motion for Summary Judgment or to Dismiss Regarding Damage Claims, When Claims for Injunctive Relief Are Also Pending*

Qualified immunity is immunity from damage claims, not from claims for injunctive relief. So, if a defendant faces both types of claims, suit may continue against him even if his dispositive motion based on qualified immunity is granted. That is, he would still face claims for injunctive relief. However, all circuits have now held that interlocutory appeal is available to challenge the denial of a dispositive motion based on qualified immunity, even if claims for injunctive relief against the same defendant will remain pending.[216]

D. Scope of Review on Interlocutory Appeal

When a circuit court properly exercises its interlocutory appellate jurisdiction to consider an immunity claim, what other issues in the case may it review? Consideration of this question requires an examination of *Siegert v. Gilley*, which reached the Supreme Court on review of an interlocutory

---

213. *Workman,* 958 F.2d at 334–36, and cases cited therein. *See also* Valiente v. Rivera, 966 F.2d 21, 23 (1st Cir. 1992), in which a trial court's refusal to permit a defendant to file his qualified immunity summary judgment motion was held to be an appealable event.

214. Lion Boulos v. Wilson, 834 F.2d 504, 507–10 (5th Cir. 1987). *See* Smith v. Reagan, 841 F.2d 28, 31 (2d Cir. 1988).

215. *See, e.g.,* Gaines v. Davis, 928 F.2d 705, 707–10 (5th Cir. 1991); Smith v. Reagan, 841 F.2d 28, 30–31 (2d Cir. 1988).

216. *See, e.g.,* Young v. Lynch, 846 F.2d 960, 961 (4th Cir. 1988); *see also* Acierno v. Cloutier, 40 F.3d 597, 607–09 (3d Cir. 1994) (en banc).

qualified immunity decision by the D.C. Circuit.[217] The Court looked first at the "threshold issue" of whether the facts alleged by plaintiff amounted to the violation of a clearly established constitutional right. Ruling that they did not, the Court found no need to look further.[218]

Siegert itself was a narrowly focused holding. Nonetheless, it seemed to spawn a plethora of circuit court decisions taking broader views of what issues could be considered on interlocutory appeal, once an immunity issue provided primary appellate jurisdiction.[219] The concept of "pendent appellate jurisdiction," furthering the goal of "judicial economy," was used to support these wide-ranging holdings. The boundaries of pendent appellate jurisdiction were seen as discretionary. The emphasis was on resolving as many issues as reasonably possible while the case was in the appellate court, in order to better direct the subsequent course of the litigation.[220] Because of this, there were many instances in which an interlocutory appeal filed to champion a qualified immunity defense resulted in a decision on some grounds other than, or in addition to, qualified immunity. This trend continued unabated until the Supreme Court's 1995 holding in *Swint v. Chambers County*.[221]

In *Swint*, the plaintiffs sued two individual police officers, a county sheriff, a city, and a county for alleged misconduct in connection with law enforcement raids on a nightclub. All the defendants filed summary judgment motions. The individual defendants claimed qualified immunity from suit. The county claimed it could not be found liable, because the sheriff who authorized the raid was allegedly not the county's law enforcement policymaker. After the trial court denied all defendants' summary judgment motions, the individual defendants appealed, invoking classic *Mitchell v. Forsyth* interlocutory appellate jurisdiction.

The county also appealed, contending that its alleged right not to be found liable for the sheriff's actions entitled it to interlocutory appeal from denial of its summary judgment motion. Alternatively, the county argued that "pendent appellate jurisdiction" empowered the circuit court to entertain its appeal in the interest of "judicial economy," because the appeals of the individual defendants were already properly before the court.[222]

---

217. 500 U.S. 226 (1991).
218. 500 U.S. at 232.
219. *See, e.g.*, Schmelz v. Monroe County, 954 F.2d 1540, 1542–43 (11th Cir. 1992); O'Bar v. Pinion, 953 F.2d 74, 79–81 (4th Cir. 1991).
220. *Id.; see also* Stewart v. Baldwin County, 908 F.2d 1499, 1509 (11th Cir. 1990).
221. 514 U.S. 35 (1995).
222. 514 U.S. at 39.

An Eleventh Circuit panel held that the county's defenses would not by themselves have triggered interlocutory appellate jurisdiction. But, the panel thought, the issues it raised were within the reach of "pendent appellate jurisdiction." So, they proceeded to rule on the county's claims. The Supreme Court agreed with the Eleventh Circuit's determination that the county's summary judgment motion did not assert an immunity from suit. Rather, it claimed a "mere defense to liability." Therefore, it did not in itself trigger an entitlement to interlocutory appeal.[223] The Court then stated that broad "pendent party appellate jurisdiction" in the interest of "judicial economy" simply did not exist in the form that many appellate courts seemed to think.[224] Rather, only limited power to review anything other than the immunity issue itself was present on interlocutory appeal.

The Court acknowledged that review of "threshold issues" or issues inextricably intertwined with immunity was sometimes unavoidable. But, any broader extension of "pendent appellate jurisdiction" might not pass muster. In *Swint*, the order the county sought to appeal involved a clearly separate issue, in fact, a separate party. So, the Court found it easy to determine there was no pendent jurisdiction over the county's interlocutory appeal.[225]

The *Swint* decision does not answer all questions about the circumstances in which appellate courts should resolve any issue other than the specific immunity claims before them on interlocutory appeal. But, it does significantly narrow the scope of interlocutory appellate review. Probably, the eventual guideline will be close to the following recommendation, which the Court quoted with approval:

> Only where essential to the resolution of properly appealed collateral orders should courts extend their *Cohen* jurisdiction to rulings that would not otherwise qualify for expedited consideration.[226]

Post-*Swint*, circuit courts have consistently considered and resolved "threshold issues" such as whether plaintiffs have stated a constitutional claim. Rulings about what issues are "inextricably intertwined" have been more varied.[227]

---

223. 514 U.S. at 43.
224. 514 U.S. at 50–51.
225. 514 U.S. at 51.
226. 514 U.S. at 51, *quoting* Riyaz A. Kanji, *The Proper Scope of Pendent Appellate Jurisdiction in the Collateral Order Context,* 100 Yale L.J. 511, 530 (1990).
227. *See, e.g.,* Toussie v. Powell, 323 F.3d 178 (2d Cir. 2003) (defining "inextricably intertwined" as having substantial factual overlap); Okruhlik v. University of Arkansas, 255 F.3d 615 (8th Cir. 2001) ("inextricably intertwined" means "coterminous with, or subsumed in").

E. Effect of Interlocutory Appeals on Proceedings in the Trial Court

The filing of a notice of interlocutory appeal has been held to divest the trial court of jurisdiction to conduct further proceedings on "those aspects of the case involved in the appeal."[228] How, exactly, is the trial court to distinguish between an aspect of the case that is so involved, and one that is not? And what, if anything, can the plaintiff's counsel and the trial court do to prevent this powerful defense tool from being used in a dilatory or manipulative manner?

Ordinarily, any trial court proceeding that would have the effect of thwarting the immunity claim being asserted on appeal should not be permitted while appellate review is pending. As the Seventh Circuit stated in *Apostol v. Gallion*, "It makes no sense for trial to go forward while the court of appeals cogitates on whether there should be one."[229] Similarly, it would make no sense for broad discovery against individual defendants to proceed while the court of appeals considers whether they should be immune from it.[230] However, there are many questions that are not so clearly answerable. What about discovery against other defendants not raising immunity defenses? What about the availability of preliminary injunctive relief from the trial court, while interlocutory appeal of immunity from damage claims is pending? What about discovery necessary to support the request for preliminary injunctive relief? In many circumstances the required separability of the "collateral" issue raised in an interlocutory appeal permits easy determination of what matters are "involved in the appeal." But, as the Court acknowledged in *Johnson v. Jones*, separability has always been the weak link in attempts to bring immunity issues within the established analytical framework of interlocutory appellate jurisdiction.[231]

While not all of the above questions have definitive answers, there have been some useful guidance from the circuit courts about what will and will not be permitted to take place in the trial court while an interlocutory appeal is pending. Further, recognizing the risks of harm stemming from misuse of interlocutory appeals, many circuits have established procedures that help plaintiffs deal with some of the most problematical situations.

---

228. Griggs v. Provident Consumer Discount Co., 459 U.S. 56, 58 (1982); Stewart v. Donges, 915 F.2d 572, 574–76 (10th Cir. 1990); Apostol v. Gallion, 870 F.2d 1335, 1337–40 (7th Cir. 1989).

229. 870 F.2d at 1338.

230. *See, e.g.,* Gaines v. Davis, 928 F.2d 705, 707–10 (5th Cir. 1991).

231. 515 U.S. at 314–15.

One of the most thorough examinations of these interlocutory appellate procedural issues occurred in *Stewart v. Donges*, a 1990 Tenth Circuit case.[232] In *Stewart*, a defendant police officer filed an interlocutory appeal from denial of his summary judgment motion based on qualified immunity. The trial court also denied the defendant's motion to vacate the trial setting and stay further trial court proceedings. The defendant did not seek a stay from the appellate court. The plaintiff did not ask the trial court to certify the defendant's appeal as frivolous, nor did the trial court issue its own order to this effect. The case proceeded to trial during the pendency of the officer's interlocutory appeal, and a judgment for damages was rendered against him. He then took a second appeal, which was consolidated with the still-pending interlocutory one.

The Tenth Circuit held that the trial proceeding, conducted while the officer's interlocutory appeal was pending, was "a nullity."[233] The court explained that, because the defendant's immunity claim was a claim of immunity from the entire proceeding against him, the divestiture of trial court jurisdiction over the defendant during his appeal on immunity grounds was virtually total.[234]

The *Stewart* panel recognized that this doctrine could potentially facilitate abuse of the interlocutory appellate process for purposes of delay or manipulation. So, the panel suggested a procedure through which a trial court, believing an interlocutory appeal to be frivolous, might certify it as such and therefore retain jurisdiction over the case.[235] However, the court indicated it would not be effective for the district court simply to say later that it retained jurisdiction because the appeal was frivolous. Rather, it must formally certify to the court of appeals that the appeal is frivolous or forfeited on procedural grounds (as described more fully in the next section, below).

The Tenth Circuit panel considered it the plaintiff's burden to obtain such a determination from the trial court, if he wished to continue with proceedings against a defendant who has filed a notice of interlocutory appeal. As a corollary, the defendant need not move for a stay in the trial court in order to effectively preserve this right. The stay would be, in effect, automatic unless a trial court certified the "frivolousness or forfeiture" of the

232. 915 F.2d 572 (10th Cir. 1990).

233. 915 F.2d at 574.

234. 915 F.2d at 576. This result should be different if a claim for injunctive relief, from which the defendant could not claim immunity, remained pending in the trial court.

235. 915 F.2d at 576–77, *citing* United States v. Hines, 689 F.2d 934, 936–37 (10th Cir. 1982) (a double jeopardy claim) and Apostol v. Gallion, 870 F.2d 1335, 1338 (7th Cir. 1989).

appeal to the appellate court.[236] The certification had to be made before any further proceedings took place in the trial court; it could not be entered retroactively to validate proceedings that had already taken place.[237] The panel emphasized the need for district courts making such a certification to use one of the key words "frivolous" or "forfeited," and to include findings supporting their conclusion.[238]

The Supreme Court briefly discussed this matter in *Behrens v. Pelletier*, in which it approved the practice of filing more than one interlocutory appeal per case in appropriate circumstances. The solution, according to the Court, is for the district court to certify a frivolous appeal as such, and thereby "retain jurisdiction."[239]

According to other courts that have addressed this type of situation, the remedy for a defendant whose interlocutory appeal has been improperly certified as frivolous is to seek a stay of further trial court proceedings. He must first seek it from the trial court. If unsuccessful there, he should seek a stay from the appellate court, supporting his request with persuasive argument that the trial court's "frivolous" label is clearly wrong.[240]

F. Timing, Forfeiture, and Frequency Issues for Interlocutory Appeals: How Late Is Too Late? How Often Is Too Often?

1. Timing and Forfeiture of Interlocutory Appeals

Given the renowned ability of interlocutory appeals to bring trial court proceedings to a screeching halt, the courts have understandably been concerned that defendants will use this important procedural right in a dilatory or manipulative manner. Indeed, it does appear to have been so used in several reported instances. For example, defendants filed a motion for summary judgment on immunity grounds five years after suit was brought and days

---

236. 915 F.2d at 577–78 and n.6.

237. 915 F.2d at 578 n.8; *see also* Chuman v. Wright, 960 F.2d 104, 105 (9th Cir. 1992); *but see* Rivera-Torres v. Ortiz Velez, 341 F.3d 86, 96 (1st Cir. 2003), *cert. denied,* 541 U.S. 972 (2004) (a frivolous appeal does not divest the trial court of jurisdiction, even in the absence of formal certification as such).

238. *See, e.g., Stewart,* 915 F.2d at 577–79.

239. 516 U.S. at 310–11. The *Behrens* majority cites cases from the Sixth, Seventh, Ninth, and Tenth Circuits as reflecting use of this practice.

240. Fed. R. App. P. 8; *see* Chuman v. Wright, 960 F.2d at 105 n.1 and *Apostol,* 870 F.2d at 1339.

before the trial setting, and then sought interlocutory appellate review of the trial court's denial.[241]

Appellate courts seem to agree that there is a need to control misuse of interlocutory appeals. They also agree that the way to do so is to impose a forfeiture of the right to take an interlocutory appeal on defendants who attempt to use this right in a dilatory or manipulative manner.[242] Relevant appellate opinions confer on the trial court the first-line responsibility for determining when to impose such a forfeiture. Currently there are no bright-line rules for this determination, but a few guiding principles have emerged. For example, trial courts may subject summary judgment motions based on qualified immunity to the same "motion deadlines" as other similar motions. If they do this, they may appropriately certify as "forfeited" interlocutory appeals from refusals to consider subsequently filed motions.[243] Also, the generally applicable rules of appellate procedure are not suspended for interlocutory appeals based on immunity. Therefore, the time limit prescribed by these rules for filing the notice of appeal applies; a later-filed appeal is time-barred.[244]

It is important to note that the "forfeiture" discussed here is forfeiture of the right to take an interlocutory appeal, not forfeiture of the right to claim qualified immunity. If a defendant does not seek summary judgment on his qualified immunity claim, or seeks it so late in the case that the trial court certifies his interlocutory appeal from its denial as forfeited, what he has forfeited is the right to take an interlocutory appeal. He has not forfeited the right to claim qualified immunity at trial, assuming he has pled this defense in a timely and adequate manner.[245]

2. *Frequency of Interlocutory Appeals*

Theoretically, if the frequency of interlocutory appeals is not limited, defendants could file an unlimited number of dispositive motions claiming immu-

---

241. Yates v. City of Cleveland, 941 F.2d 444, 448-49 (6th Cir. 1991); *see also* Spann v. Rainey, 987 F.2d 1110 (5th Cir. 1993).

242. *See, e.g., Yates,* 941 F.2d at 449; Apostol v. Gallion, 870 F.2d 1335, 1339–40 (7th Cir. 1989).

243. *See, e.g.,* Kennedy v. City of Cleveland, 797 F.2d 297, 300–01 and n.6 (6th Cir. 1986), *cert. denied,* 479 U.S. 1103 (1987).

244. Fed. R. App. P. 4(a); *see, e.g.,* Taylor v. Carter, 960 F.2d 763, 764 (8th Cir. 1992); Kennedy v. City of Cleveland, 797 F.2d 297, 301 (6th Cir. 1986), *cert. denied,* 479 U.S. 1103 (1987).

245. *See, e.g.,* Taylor v. Carter, 960 F.2d 763, 764 (8th Cir. 1992); Apostol v. Gallion, 870 F.2d 1335, 1339 (7th Cir. 1989).

nity and seek interlocutory appellate review of each. From the defendant's perspective, this would have the benefit of delaying trial interminably and in the process bankrupting the plaintiff and/or the plaintiff's counsel. In response to this type of manipulation, trial courts can certify too-frequent or repetitive interlocutory appeals as "forfeited," thereby retaining jurisdiction. Indeed, some appellate courts, faced with successive interlocutory appeals in the same case, responded with bright-line rules authorizing a particular number of such appeals and no more.[246]

Before the Supreme Court's decision in *Behrens v. Pelletier,* the Ninth Circuit had been particularly emphatic in its holdings that a defendant seeking a pretrial ruling on immunity claims got only one chance per case at an interlocutory appeal on this issue.[247] In *Behrens*,[248] the Supreme Court struck down the Ninth Circuit's ad hoc "one interlocutory appeal" rule. One interlocutory appeal might not be enough, the Court reasoned, because "the legally relevant factors bearing upon the *Harlow* question will be different on summary judgment than on an earlier motion to dismiss."[249] At the motion-to-dismiss stage, the issue is whether the plaintiff's pleadings state violations of clearly established law. Summary judgment, in contrast, requires an examination of the evidence.

The Court dealt with concerns about abuse of the interlocutory appeal process by pointing out that appellate courts are empowered to deal summarily with frivolous appeals.[250] Also, as noted above, district courts can label interlocutory appeals "frivolous" when appropriate, and retain jurisdiction while the appeal is pending.

G. Summarizing Interlocutory Appeal Issues

Based on the above-described case law, defendants are well advised to use their powerful weapon of interlocutory appeal only within the limits currently prescribed by the appellate courts. This area of law is in a stage of

---

246. *See, e.g.,* Pelletier v. Fed. Home Loan Bank, 968 F.2d 865, 870–71 (9th Cir. 1992) (one); Feliciano-Angulo v. Rivera-Cruz, 858 F.2d 40, 48 n.8 (1st Cir. 1988) (one); Kennedy v. City of Cleveland, 797 F.2d 297, 299 (6th Cir. 1986), *cert. denied,* 479 U.S. 1103 (1987) (two).

247. *See* Nelson v. Silverman, 999 F.2d 417, 418 (9th Cir. 1993); Pelletier v. Fed. Home Loan Bank of San Francisco, 968 F.2d 865, 870–71 (9th Cir. 1992).

248. 516 U.S. at 309–11.

249. 516 U.S. at 309.

250. As almost any practitioner would agree, that does not mean they exercise this power expeditiously.

active development and will probably remain so for at least the next several years. So, up-to-date research on these issues is particularly important.

Plaintiffs, on the other hand, should not assume that every interlocutory appeal filed by a defendant is properly before the appellate court, and proceed to briefing the merits. Rather, they should carefully consider whether the appeal, or part of it, may not be within the court's interlocutory appellate jurisdiction. If it is not, plaintiffs should file a motion to dismiss in the appellate court. Further, plaintiffs should consider whether the appeal may be appropriately labeled "frivolous" or "forfeited." If so, plaintiffs should file a motion in the trial court seeking to have it declared as such so that the case may continue to progress there.

X. PROCEDURAL ISSUES AT TRIAL

A. Which Issues Are for the Court to Decide, and Which Should Be Submitted to the Jury?

At trial, the interwoven legal and factual material about several commonly hard-fought issues, such as qualified immunity, raise a whole new set of procedural complexities. Which issues are to be determined by the trial court judge? Which must be submitted to a jury, and how are they to be submitted?

1. Who Are the Policymakers?

The question of who a governmental unit's "policymakers" are, with respect to a particular subject area, has been held to be an issue of law, primarily state law. The trial court judge, not the jury, makes this determination.[251] The jury should be instructed about the court's findings, and then asked about causation, according to the Supreme Court in *Jett v. Dallas Independent School District*.

The *Jett* opinion builds on the Court's previous plurality holding in *Praprotnik v. City of St. Louis*.[252] In *Praprotnik* the Court emphasized the pivotal importance of state law to the identification of a city's policymakers with respect to particular issues.[253]

251. Jett v. Dallas Indep. Sch. Dist., 491 U.S. 701, 737 (1989).
252. 485 U.S. 112, 124–26 (1988).
253. 485 U.S. at 124–26.

2. *Policy, Custom, or Decision of Governmental Unit*

The jury should be told who the governmental unit's policymakers are with respect to the matters at issue.[254] Then, they should be asked whether the plaintiff was deprived of federally protected rights as a direct result of a "custom, policy, ordinance, regulation or decision" of these policymakers.[255] *Board of County Commissioners of Bryan County, Oklahoma v. Brown,*[256] discussed in the following paragraph, has also affected the way in which this question must be approached.

3. *Failure to Screen, Train, or Supervise*

In *Bryan County,* the plaintiff alleged that she was subjected to excessive force as a result of a sheriff's decision to hire a deputy without adequately checking his background. The Supreme Court used this case to further restrict the circumstances in which juries may be permitted to consider governmental liability for policymakers' failure to screen, train, or supervise subordinates. If a policymaker did not personally direct or authorize the violation, the controlling question is whether the policymaker was deliberately indifferent to the fact that deprivation of particular federally protected rights would be a "plainly obvious consequence" of his actions.[257] Unless a reasonable jury could find this, the court must direct a verdict in favor of the governmental unit.

4. *Qualified Immunity*

The import of *Hunter v. Bryant,* discussed above, may be to give the ultimate qualified immunity determination always to the trial court judge. As the *Hunter* opinion emphasizes, it is controlled by a question of law (i.e., what law was "clearly established" at the time of the defendant's actions).[258] But, although controlled by a question of law, qualified immunity is frequently still entangled in a web of facts. Some appellate courts have suggested that trial court judges handle this commonly occurring situation by

---

254. *See generally* McMillian v. Monroe County, Alabama, 520 U.S. 784–85 (1997).
255. *Jett,* 491 U.S. at 737.
256. 520 U.S. 397 (1997).
257. 520 U.S. at 415.
258. 502 U.S. 224 (1991).

submitting separate special interrogatories about key fact issues to the jury. After the jury answers these questions, the court should apply the law to their factual determinations.[259] This sounds much more workable in the abstract than it actually is in practice. One appellate judge has referred to such handling of qualified immunity claims as "a fearful tangle" and another as "a way that will cause procedural nightmares."[260] However, alternate possibilities have complications as well.

The Fifth Circuit pattern jury instructions still provide, post-*Hunter*, for the jury to make the ultimate determination about qualified immunity if the underlying facts about defendant's conduct are disputed. The judge is to instruct them about what relevant law was clearly settled at the time of defendants' challenged actions.[261]

In *Saucier v. Katz*,[262] the Court made it clear that, even in excessive force cases, the qualified immunity question may not be compressed into the issue of whether there has been a constitutional violation. These are separate inquiries, that is, whether the force used was objectively unreasonable (if so, a constitutional violation), and whether it would have been clear to a reasonable officer that his challenged conduct would be unlawful in the circumstances he confronted (if so, no qualified immunity).

B. Damages—Elements/Measures/Requirements—What Comes from Tort Law and What Does Not

1. Compensatory Damages—Overview

State common-law tort concepts have been said to be the "appropriate starting point" in defining the elements and prerequisites of § 1983 compensatory damages.[263] They are definitely not the final word on these topics, however. Rather, the courts must effectuate § 1983's remedial purpose by applying damage standards that are broad and consistent, as opposed to varying from state to state based on the idiosyncrasies of state tort law.[264]

---

259. *See, e.g.,* Stone v. Peacock, 968 F.2d 1163, 1166 (11th Cir. 1992); Warren v. Dwyer, 906 F.2d 70, 76 (2d Cir. 1990), *cert. denied,* 498 U.S. 967 (1990).

260. Mahoney v. Kesery, 976 F.2d 1054, 1059 (7th Cir. 1992); ACT Up/Portland v. Bagley, 988 F.2d 868, 875 (9th Cir. 1993) (J. Norris, dissenting).

261. http://www.lb5.uscourts.gov/juryinstructions/2004CIVIL.htm

262. 533 U.S. 194 (2001). The *Saucier* appeal arose from the denial of a defendant's summary judgment motion on the grounds that the excessive force and qualified immunity questions were inseparable.

263. Carey v. Piphus, 435 U.S. 247, 257–58 (1978).

264. *See* Carey, 435 U.S. at 257–59; *see also, e.g.,* Bolden v. Southeastern Pennsylvania Transp. Auth., 21 F.3d 29, 35 (3d Cir. 1994).

Statute 42 U.S.C. § 1988 provides the general framework for determining whether to apply federal or state rules to particular § 1983 remedies issues. That statute requires courts to look first to federal laws "so far as such laws are suitable to carry [§ 1983] into effect."[265] If there is no suitable federal law, courts should look next to state "common law, as modified and changed by the constitution and statutes" of the forum state. Federal courts are to apply state law, however, only to the extent it is "not inconsistent with the Constitution and laws of the United States."[266]

Some of the most complex applications of these principles in § 1983 cases have arisen in the context of survival and wrongful death damage claims. While an examination of these matters is beyond the scope of this chapter, counsel facing any such issues should be aware that further research is necessary, and that detailed information is available from the sources listed in "Suggestions for Further Reading" at the end of this chapter.

2. *Some Particular Compensatory Damages Issues*

a. Joint and several liability for indivisible injuries. Several circuits have held that federal rather than state standards apply to apportionment of liability for compensatory damages in a § 1983 case. Although the statute itself is silent on this topic, an increasing body of federal common law establishes joint and several liability for § 1983 defendants. That is, each defendant whose actions or omissions proximately cause indivisible harm to the plaintiff is jointly and severally liable for the full amount of that harm.[267] This is true even when different standards for damage apportionment apply in the state where the case is tried. However, a few circuit courts have applied state damage apportionment standards, finding them not inconsistent with the remedial goals of § 1983.[268]

b. Compensatory damages for emotional distress. In § 1983 cases, emotional distress damages may be awarded, based on appropriate supporting testimony, without regard for the required elements of proof of such damages in the courts of the state where the action is tried.[269]

265. 42 U.S.C. § 1988(a).
266. *Id.; see* Burnett v. Grattan, 468 U.S. 42, 47–48 (1984).
267. *See, e.g.,* Northington v. Marin, 102 F.3d 1564 (10th Cir. 1996); Weeks v. Chaboudy, 984 F.2d 185, 188–89 (6th Cir. 1993); Watts v. Laurent, 774 F.2d 168, 179 (7th Cir. 1985), *cert. denied,* 475 U.S. 1085 (1986).
268. *See, e.g.,* Hinshaw v. Doffer, 785 F.2d 1260, 1268–69 (5th Cir. 1986).
269. *See, e.g.,* Bolden v. Septa, 21 F.3d 29, 35 (3d Cir. 1994).

c. Prejudgment interest. Similarly, prejudgment interest has been held to be awardable to a § 1983 plaintiff whether or not it would be awardable on a tort claim in the courts of the state in which the trial takes place.[270] The First Circuit has held that such a request must be submitted to the jury; several other circuits have ruled that it is within the discretion of the trial court.[271]

3. *Punitive Damages*

a. General requirements. The federal standard expressed in *Smith v. Wade* controls punitive damages requirements. That is, the trier of fact must find that the defendant acted either with "evil motive or intent" or "reckless or callous indifference to [the plaintiff's] federally protected rights."[272] Punitive damages are available whether or not compensatory damages are awarded; this does not vary based upon the law of the state in which the trial takes place.[273] Punitive damages are not awarded jointly and severally but must be specifically considered and awarded with respect to each defendant.[274] Local governmental units are immune from punitive damages awards.[275]

b. Appellate review. Within the past decade the Supreme Court has devoted considerable attention to defining how federal appellate courts must review punitive damages awards in all types of federal litigation, including § 1983 cases. Also, several due process challenges to state court punitive damages awards have reached the Court.[276] These opinions are instructive

270. Savarese v. Agriss, 883 F.2d 1194, 1207 (3d Cir. 1989).

271. *Compare* Savarese, 883 F.2d at 1207 *with* Cordero v. De Jesus-Mendez, 922 F.2d 11, 13 (1st Cir. 1990); *see also* Gierlinger v. Gleason, 160 F.3d 858, 873–74 (2d Cir. 1998) (abuse of discretion not to award prejudgment interest on compensation for lost wages).

272. 461 U.S. 30, 56 (1983). *See also* Kolstad v. American Dental Association, 527 U.S. 526 (1999), a Title VII case in which the Court applied what it described as a *Smith v. Wade* standard. In *Kolstad,* the Court said that to trigger punitive damages liability, a defendant must have acted "in the face of a perceived risk that [his] actions [would] violate federal law" (527 U.S. at 536). That is, he must have demonstrated at least a reckless or careless indifference to the prospect that his conduct might be unlawful.

273. *See, e.g.,* King v. Macri, 993 F.2d 294, 297–98 (2d Cir. 1993), and cases cited therein.

274. *See, e.g.,* McFadden v. Sanchez, 710 F.2d 907, 913 (2d Cir. 1983), *cert. denied,* 464 U.S. 961.

275. City of Newport v. Fact Concerts, Inc., 453 U.S. 247, 258–71 (1981).

276. *See, e.g.,* BMW v. Gore, 517 U.S. 559 (1996); Pacific Mutual Life Insurance Co. v. Haslip, 499 U.S. 1 (1991).

for federal court litigation as well, since of course due process requirements are equally applicable in federal court.

Before the trial of any case in which a large punitive damages award is a real possibility, counsel for both sides should carefully review *State Farm v. Campbell*,[277] *Cooper Industries v. Leatherman Tool Group*,[278] *B.M.W. v. Gore*,[279] *TXO Production Corp. v. Alliance Resources Corp.*,[280] and *Pacific Mutual Life Insurance Co. v. Haslip*.[281]

Haslip (1991) was one of the Court's seminal ventures into using the due process clause to screen state courts' punitive damages awards. The opinion's focus is primarily procedural. It sets out minimum guidelines that must be used in submitting punitive damages issues to juries, and in rendering and reviewing judgments based on juries' verdicts. The *Haslip* opinion indicates that defendant's due process rights may be violated unless: (1) the jury instructions adequately inform the jury of the purposes of punitive damages; (2) there are adequate posttrial procedures for state trial court review of punitive damages awards; and (3) there are substantive state appellate review standards for such awards.[282]

In its 1993 *TXO* opinion, the Court applied a seemingly more relaxed constitutional analysis in reviewing a state court punitive damages award. The *TXO* jury had awarded $19,000 in compensatory damages and $10 million in punitive damages. First, a plurality of the Court found that such a ratio of compensatory to punitive damages did not in itself create constitutional infirmity, despite its suggestion to the contrary in *Haslip*. Second, the plurality approved the jury's consideration of "potential harm" that could have resulted from the defendant's conduct as a factor in determining a punitive damages award.[283] The opinion contains some rumblings about the potential constitutional implications of the jury argument and instructions' emphasis on the defendant's wealth. But, there was no ruling on those issues, because of the Court's holding that defense counsel waived them.[284]

The *BMW* case was the Court's next and perhaps most definitive instance of constitutional punitive damages jurisprudence. Therein, the Court reviewed a state court jury verdict for $4,000 in compensatory damages and

277. 538 U.S. 408 (2003).
278. 532 U.S. 424 (2001).
279. 517 U.S. 559 (1996).
280. 509 U.S. 443 (1993).
281. 499 U.S. 1 (1991).
282. 499 U.S. at 17–24.
283. 509 U.S. at 460.
284. 509 U.S. at 464.

$4 million in punitive damages.[285] The Court focused on the notice component of due process in the context of punitive damages awards. That is, defendants must receive adequate notice not only of what conduct is subject to punishment in the form of punitive damages but also of how severe a penalty could be imposed. The Court identified three "guideposts" for how severe the penalty could be, in the guise of adjudicating whether BMW had received constitutionally adequate notice of its potential liability. These guideposts were listed by the Court: (1) degree of reprehensibility of a defendant's conduct;[286] (2) ratio between compensatory and punitive damages awarded; and (3) comparison of the punitive damages awarded with the civil or criminal sanctions the state could impose for similar misconduct. By these standards, the Gore award was "grossly excessive" and violative of the due process clause. The Court was particularly concerned that the state of Alabama not penalize conduct that did not affect Alabama residents and was not illegal in the states in which it occurred.[287]

In *Cooper Industries*, a federal jury awarded the plaintiff $50,000 in actual damages and $4.5 million in punitive damages. Both the district court and the Ninth Circuit affirmed, rejecting defendant's argument that the verdict violated *BMW v. Gore*'s due process standards. The Ninth Circuit used an abuse of discretion standard in reviewing the district court's decision granting judgment on the verdict. The Supreme Court, however, held that the correct standard for appellate review of punitive damages awards was de novo. That is, the appellate court must make a "thorough, independent review" of the relevant criteria, as specified in *BMW v. Gore*.[288] This, the Court reasoned, was more likely to "stabilize the law." That, in turn, should help fulfill the due process clause's requirement for clear notice of the potential consequences of various types of punishable conduct.

In *State Farm*, state court plaintiffs obtained a verdict of $2.6 million in compensatory damages and $145 million punitive damages. The district court reduced it to $1 million and $25 million, respectively. The state supreme court then reinstated the $145 million punitive damages award, and the U.S. Supreme Court granted certiorari. The Court ostensibly applied the three *BMW* factors for evaluating whether a punitive damages award vio-

285. The Alabama Supreme Court reduced the punitive damages award to $2 million.

286. Suggested evaluative factors included whether the harm was economic as opposed to injurious to health or safety, whether deceit was involved as opposed to simple negligence, and whether defendant made an affirmative misrepresentation as opposed to concealing a pertinent fact.

287. 517 U.S. at 577–79.

288. 532 U.S. at 441.

lated defendant's due process rights: (1) reprehensibility of the defendant's conduct;[289] (2) ratio of the compensatory damages award to the punitive damages award; and (3) the difference between the punitive damages award and civil penalties or fines that could be imposed in comparable cases. Reprehensibility must be evaluated by considering only conduct within the state where the trial occurs, unless out-of-state conduct has a direct connection to the harm the plaintiff suffered. Other malfeasance within the state must also be excluded from consideration if the actions are different in any significant respect from the conduct that injured the plaintiff. There are "no rigid benchmarks," but ratios between compensatory damages and punitive damages should ordinarily be no more than "single-digit multipliers"—not 145 to 1, as in the State Farm case.[290]

The *State Farm* decision drew an unlikely coalition of dissenters—Justices Scalia, Thomas, and Ginsburg. Justice Scalia and Justice Ginsburg expressed concern that the Court was misusing the due process clause to venture into jurisprudence as arbitrary and capricious as any challenged jury verdict.

C. Jury Charge

Reported cases are replete with instances in which erroneous jury instructions or issues were submitted to the detriment of a party, but the error was waived through failure to object, or failure to object with sufficient clarity.[291] It is important to review, well in advance of trial, the relevant law of the circuit in which the case is to be tried. Counsel can then be prepared to tender a proposed charge in substantially correct form and to object appropriately on the record to any incorrect submissions.

The starting point for preparation of a § 1983 jury charge is now the website of the circuit court for the area in which the trial will take place. The other references suggested at the end of this chapter are useful, as well, but all of these materials may still require modification based on the individual case situation. When preparing to try a case before an unfamiliar judge, it is also a good idea to determine well in advance whether he or she has "personal favorite" standard instructions or issues for the type of case to be tried. So, if counsel has strong objections to any of them, there will be time to compile the research and arguments to raise these objections effectively.

---

289. Although State Farm's actions were not shown to have physically harmed anyone, they did give a whole new dimension to the term "consumer fraud." *See* 538 U.S. at 412–15, 431–36.

290. 538 U.S. at 425–26.

291. *See, e.g.,* King v. Macri, 993 F.2d 294, 297–98 (2d Cir. 1993); Taken Alive v. Litzau, 551 F.2d 196, 199 n.4 (8th Cir. 1977).

XI. CONCLUSION

Section 1983 litigation provides some of the most complex and hotly debated procedural issues litigated in the federal court system. These procedural issues, for example, court-imposed "heightened pleading requirements" and aggressive use of *Celotex*-type summary judgment motions, have determined the outcome of many § 1983 cases. With its decisions in *Leatherman*, *Swint*, and *Johnson v. Jones*, the Supreme Court has eroded at least some of the procedural barriers to the litigation of well-founded § 1983 claims. The Court is still struggling to fully effectuate the promise of *Harlow* and *Mitchell* for litigants with sound immunity defenses. But, *Crawford-El* provided a usable road map for the lower courts with front-line responsibility for making this promise a workable reality. The continued development of the law with respect to these and other procedural issues discussed herein will be crucial to effectuating the substantive rights of § 1983 plaintiffs and defendants.

XII. SUGGESTIONS FOR FURTHER READING

Sheldon H. Nahmod, Civil Rights and Civil Liberties Litigation, Shepard's (McGraw-Hill 4th ed. 2004).

Martin A. Schwartz, Section 1983 Litigation (Aspen Publishers 4th ed. 2003).

C. Wright, A. Miller, and E. Cooper, Federal Practice and Procedure: Jurisdiction; and Related Matters, §§ 3501–5000 (West Publishing 2nd ed. 1984); and volume 20: Federal Practice Deskbook (2002).

Websites of U.S. Courts of Appeals for each circuit, for example, http://www.ca1.uscourts.gov/, *et seq.* for pattern jury instructions.

Chapter 3

AN INTRODUCTION TO STATE COURT SECTION 1983 LITIGATION

by Steven H. Steinglass

I. INTRODUCTION

The federal cause of action contained in 42 U.S.C. § 1983[1] permits persons whose federal rights are violated by defendants acting under color of state law to bring civil suits for both damages and injunctions. The statute is not a source of substantive rights, but it is the principal civil remedy for the private enforcement of the federal Constitution against state and local governments and their employees.

Most § 1983 litigation has taken place in federal courts since 1961, when the U.S. Supreme Court in *Monroe v. Pape*[2] resurrected this seldom used legacy of Reconstruction. Before *Monroe*, § 1983 suits against state and local governmental defendants were relatively rare because of the narrow construction that the Supreme Court had given to § 1983[3] and because of the existence of few constitutional limitations on the states.[4] *Monroe* established § 1983 as a supplementary federal remedy and refused to require § 1983 plaintiffs to first seek relief under even adequate state remedies.[5]

1. 42 U.S.C. § 1983 (2000), as amended by the Federal Courts Improvement Act of 1996, Pub. L. No. 104–317, § 309(c), 110 Stat. 3847 (1996). The statute, in its entirety, provides as follows:

   > Every person who, under color of any statute, ordinance, regulation, custom, or usage, of any State or Territory or the District of Columbia, subjects, or causes to be subjected, any citizen of the United States or other person within the jurisdiction thereof to the deprivation of any rights, privileges, or immunities secured by the Constitution and laws, shall be liable to the party injured in an action at law, suit in equity, or other proper proceeding for redress, except that in any action brought against a judicial officer for an act or omission taken in such officer's judicial capacity, injunctive relief shall not be granted unless a declaratory decree was violated or declaratory relief was unavailable. For the purposes of this section, any Act of Congress applicable exclusively to the District of Columbia shall be considered to be a statute of the District of Columbia.

2. 365 U.S. 167 (1961).
3. *See* Michael G. Collins, *"Economic Rights," Implied Constitutional Actions, and the Scope of Section 1983,* 77 GEO. L.J. 1493, 1499–1506 (1989).
4. *See* Louise Weinberg, *The Monroe Mystery Solved: Beyond the "Unhappy History" Theory of Civil Rights Litigation,* 1991 BYU L. REV. 737, 745–57 ("The decade immediately following *Monroe* was marked by increasing absorption of the Bill of Rights into the fourteenth amendment.").
5. 365 U.S. at 183 ("The federal remedy is supplementary to the state remedy, and the latter need not be first sought and refused before the federal one is invoked.").

Consequently, § 1983 plaintiffs may go directly to federal court,[6] and the volume of § 1983 litigation in the federal courts has increased more than one hundredfold in the last four decades.[7]

Under the presumption of concurrent jurisdiction, state courts may exercise jurisdiction over § 1983 cases,[8] and since the early 1980s there has been a sharp increase in the volume of state court § 1983 litigation throughout the country. The precise number of state court § 1983 cases is unclear,[9] but a review of appellate court decisions makes clear that for a variety of ad hominem, doctrinal, and tactical reasons, an increasing number of § 1983 plaintiffs are forsaking the federal courts and seeking relief in state courts.[10]

Commentators have recognized the importance of state court § 1983 litigation,[11] and the Supreme Court has begun to pay greater attention to state court § 1983 cases.[12] Nonetheless, most scholarly and practice-oriented writing on § 1983 focuses on the federal courts. This chapter fills this void by providing lawyers and judges with an introduction to state court § 1983 litigation. This

---

6. *See* Patsy v. Board of Regents, 457 U.S. 496, 504 (1982) (construing § 1983 as providing "immediate access to the federal courts notwithstanding any provision of state law to the contrary"); *but see* Williamson County Reg'l Planning Comm'n v. Hamilton Bank of Johnson City, 473 U.S. 172 (1985) (requiring exhaustion of state judicial compensation remedies as a condition of bringing § 1983 taking claims in federal court).
7. *See* Steven H. Steinglass, *Section 1983 Litigation in the Ohio Courts: An Introduction for Ohio Lawyers and Judges,* 41 CLEV. ST. L. REV. 407, 409 n.7 (1993) [hereinafter Steinglass, *Section 1983 Litigation in Ohio*]; *see also* Steven H. Steinglass, *The Emerging State Court § 1983 Action: A Procedural Review,* 38 U. MIAMI L. REV. 381, 393 n.52, 435 (1984) [hereinafter Steinglass, *Emerging State Court § 1983 Action*].
8. *See infra* notes 47–49 and accompanying text.
9. *See* Steinglass, *Section 1983 Litigation in Ohio, supra* note 7, at 424 n.95.
10. For a discussion of choice of forum considerations, see *infra* notes 87–126 and accompanying text.
11. *See, e.g.*, Susan N. Herman, *Beyond Parity: Section 1983 and the State Courts,* 54 BROOK. L. REV. 1057, 1057 (1989) ("State court is the new frontier of civil rights litigation."); *cf.* William B. Rubenstein, *The Myth of Superiority,* 16 CONST. COMMENT. 599 (1999) (discussing forum selection aspects of the parity debate in the context of gay rights litigation); *but see* Burt Neuborne, *Parity Revisited: The Uses of a Judicial Forum of Excellence,* 44 DEPAUL L. REV. 797 (1995); Burt Neuborne, *The Myth of Parity,* 90 HARV. L. REV. 1105 (1977).
12. *See, e.g.,* Johnson v. Fankell, 520 U.S. 911 (1997); National Private Truck Council, Inc. v. Oklahoma Tax Comm'n, 515 U.S. 582 (1995); Dennis v. Higgins, 498 U.S. 439 (1991); Howlett v. Rose, 496 U.S. 356 (1990); National Collegiate Athletic Ass'n v. Tarkanian, 488 U.S. 179 (1988); Felder v. Casey, 487 U.S. 131 (1988); Maine v. Thiboutot, 448 U.S. 1 (1980); Martinez v. California, 444 U.S. 277 (1980).

chapter also addresses a number of the unique procedural and remedial issues that have arisen, or are likely to arise, in § 1983 litigation in the state courts.

II. RECONSTRUCTION BACKGROUND

Section 1983, which has its origins in the post–Civil War Reconstruction Era, is the current version of § 1 of the Civil Rights Act of 1871.[13] The act was a broad proposal, introduced on March 28, 1871, by Representative Shellabarger at the request of the Grant Administration to address the state of lawlessness throughout much of the South[14] and to enforce the Fourteenth Amendment.[15] Section one created a civil remedy to enforce federal constitutional provisions against state or local officials who violated the "rights, privileges, or immunities" of persons within the United States.[16] Ironically in light of its current prominence, § 1983 was a minor, and not heavily debated,[17] provision of a more far-reaching statute designed to restore federal supremacy in the face of a widespread breakdown of law and order in the southern and border states.[18]

Congress enacted the predecessor to § 1983 during the period that marked the sharpest permanent expansion of federal court jurisdiction in the nation's history,[19] and the Supreme Court in *Mitchum v. Foster*[20] characterized § 1983 as

---

13. Act of April 20, 1871, ch. 22, § 1, 17 Stat. 13 (current version at 42 U.S.C. § 1983 (2000)).
14. *See* CONG. GLOBE, 42d Cong., 1st Sess. 236 (1871) (President Grant's message to Congress urgently recommended legislation to deal with "[a] condition of affairs . . . in some of the States of the Union rendering life and property insecure.").
15. *See* Monroe v. Pape, 365 U.S. 167, 171 (noting that the "purpose [of § 1983] is plain from the title of the legislation, 'An Act to enforce the Provisions of the Fourteenth Amendment to the Constitution of the United States, and for other Purposes'").
16. Civil Rights Act of 1871, § 1. This civil cause of action was patterned after the criminal provision contained in § 2 of the Civil Rights Act of 1866, ch. 31, 14 Stat. 27 (1866). *See* Briscoe v. LaHue, 460 U.S. 325, 360–61 (1983) (Marshall, J., dissenting). Section two's modern equivalent can be found at 18 U.S.C. § 242 (2000). For a discussion of this criminal provision, see United States v. Lanier, 520 U.S. 259 (1997).
17. *See* Monell v. Department of Soc. Servs., 436 U.S. 658, 665 (1978); *see also Briscoe,* 460 U.S. at 361 (Marshall, J., dissenting).
18. *See generally Monroe,* 365 U.S. at 174–83. For a further discussion of the events leading to the passage of the Civil Rights Act of 1871, *see Developments in the Law—Section 1983 and Federalism,* 90 HARV. L. REV. 1133, 1141–56 (1977).
19. *See* William M. Wiecek, *The Reconstruction of Federal Judicial Power 1863–1876,* 13 AM. J. LEGAL HIST. 333 (1969).
20. 407 U.S. 225 (1972).

> a product of a vast transformation from the concepts of federalism that had prevailed in the late 18th century . . . . The very purpose of § 1983 was to interpose the federal courts between the States and the people, as guardians of the people's federal rights—to protect the people from unconstitutional action under color of state law, "whether that action be executive, legislative, or judicial."[21]

Given the origins of § 1983 in a period marked by a profound distrust of the state courts and by a major change in the relationship between state and federal courts, the emergence of state courts as the forum of choice for many parties who believe that their federal rights have been violated is ironic. It is even more ironic that many state court § 1983 defendants now take advantage of the liberal federal question removal statute to veto plaintiffs' choice of state courts and remove § 1983 cases to federal courts.[22] Nonetheless, despite the increasing importance of federal question removal in § 1983 litigation, a substantial number of § 1983 cases are litigated in the state courts.

III. THE SECTION 1983 REMEDY

A. Nature of the Section 1983 Remedy

Section 1983 is a remedial statute that authorizes a civil action only against defendants who act under color of state law and violate rights secured by federal law. The Supreme Court has made clear that § 1983 confers no substantive rights,[23] and state and federal courts have consistently recognized this principle.[24] Thus, for there to be a viable § 1983 claim, there must be a violation of a substantive or rights-conferring provision of federal law.

B. Color of Law Requirement

The Supreme Court has construed § 1983's color of law requirement to reach not only conduct that is authorized by state law but also conduct that

---

21. *Id.* at 241 (quoting *Ex parte* Virginia, 100 U.S. 339, 346 (1879)).
22. *See generally infra* notes 391–97 and accompanying text (discussing removal).
23. *See* Chapman v. Houston Welfare Rights Org., 441 U.S. 600, 618 (1979) ("Standing alone, § 1983 clearly provides no protection for civil rights since, as we have just concluded, § 1983 does not provide any substantive rights at all.").
24. For state court cases recognizing this principle, *see* STEVEN H. STEINGLASS, SECTION 1983 LITIGATION IN STATE COURTS § 3:2 n.1 (Thomson/West rev. ed. 2005) [hereinafter STEINGLASS, SECTION 1983 LITIGATION IN STATE COURTS].

is unauthorized (or even barred) by state law. Thus, in *Monroe v. Pape*,[25] the Court rejected the argument that § 1983 was available only as a remedy for officially sanctioned conduct and held that police officers who conducted an unreasonable search and seizure in violation of state law also could be sued under § 1983 for violating the Fourth Amendment.[26]

C. Deprivations of Federal Rights

In addition to an act taken under color of state law, a proper § 1983 claim requires the existence of a "deprivation of . . . rights, privileges, or immunities secured by the Constitution and laws. . . ."[27] This language is quite broad, and the Court has not limited § 1983 to the types of conduct that led to the passage of the Civil Rights Act of 1871.

1. Constitutional Rights

Despite the close nexus between the Civil Rights Act of 1871 and the Fourteenth Amendment, the reference to "rights, privileges, or immunities secured by the Constitution" in the original version of § 1983 is not, by its terms, limited to Fourteenth Amendment rights. Indeed, the Supreme Court has not limited § 1983 to Fourteenth Amendment claims,[28] and in *Dennis v. Higgins*[29] the Court held that dormant Commerce Clause claims were actionable under § 1983. As a result, it is likely that § 1983 can also be used to enforce non–Fourteenth Amendment claims having their origin in the Obligation of Contracts Clause,[30] the Ex Post Facto Clause,[31] and the Article IV Privileges and Immunities Clause.[32]

---

25. 365 U.S. 167 (1961); *but see id.* at 202 (Frankfurter, J., dissenting) (arguing that § 1983 was limited to official conduct); *see also* Eric H. Zagrans, *"Under Color of" What Law: A Reconstructed Model of Section 1983 Liability,* 71 VA. L. REV. 499 (1985) (defending the Frankfurter position).
26. *See generally* Steven L. Winter, *The Meaning of "Under Color of" Law,* 91 MICH. L. REV. 323 (1992).
27. 42 U.S.C. § 1983 (2000).
28. *But see Collins, supra* note 3, at 1502–04 (describing the earlier use of a narrow definition of what rights are "secured" under § 1983).
29. 498 U.S. 439 (1991).
30. U.S. CONST. art. I, § 10.
31. U.S. CONST. art. I, § 9, cl. 2, § 10.
32. U.S. CONST. art. IV.

2. *Statutory Rights*

As enacted in the Civil Rights Act of 1871, the cause of action that became § 1983 did not contain any reference to deprivations of federal statutory rights.[33] In 1874, however, in the course of codifying the federal statutes, Congress separated the cause of action in § 1 of the act from the jurisdictional counterpart in the same section and added the phrase "and laws" to the cause of action.[34] The significance of this change remained unclear for more than a century, but in *Maine v. Thiboutot*,[35] a state court § 1983 case, the Supreme Court construed the phrase "and laws" to reach all federal statutes.[36]

Despite the broad holding of *Thiboutot*, the Court subsequently restricted the use of § 1983 to enforce federal statutes by defining narrowly when federal statutes contain judicially enforceable rights[37] and by implying limitations on the scope of § 1983 from the existence of private remedies.[38]

D. State-of-Mind Requirement

In *Monroe v. Pape*[39] the Supreme Court rejected the existence of a "specific intent" requirement in § 1983 and construed § 1983 against principles of tort law.[40] This use of tort principles raised the question of whether § 1983 was available in cases involving only negligent conduct, but in *Parratt v.*

---

33. *See* Civil Rights Act of 1871, ch. 22, § 1, 17 Stat. 13 (1871).
34. *See Chapman,* 441 U.S. at 608–09.
35. 448 U.S. 1 (1980).
36. *See id.* at 6–8.
37. *See* Gonzaga Univ. v. Doe, 536 U.S. 273 (2002) (holding that § 1983 is not available to enforce students' right to privacy under the Family Educational Rights and Privacy Act); and Pennhurst State Sch. & Hosp. v. Halderman, 451 U.S. 1 (1981) (§ 1983 not available to enforce the Developmentally Disabled Assistance and Bill of Rights Act because the act does not create enforceable rights and obligations).
38. *See also* City of Rancho Palos Verdes v. Abrams, 544 U.S. 113 (2005) (refusing to authorize a § 1983 suit to enforce claims for permits under the Telecommunications Act of 1996 even though the federal statute unambiguously confers enforceable rights); Middlesex County Sewerage Auth. v. National Sea Clammers Ass'n, 453 U.S. 1, 20 (1981) ("When the remedial devices provided in a particular Act are sufficiently comprehensive, they may suffice to demonstrate congressional intent to preclude the remedy of suits under § 1983.").
39. 365 U.S. 167 (1961).
40. *Id.* at 187 (observing that the statute "should be read against the background of tort liability that makes a man responsible for the natural consequences of his actions").

Taylor[41] the Court held that § 1983 does not contain a state-of-mind requirement. Nonetheless, the federal rights that are actionable under § 1983 often contain state-of-mind requirements,[42] and the defendant's state of mind is often an issue in § 1983 litigation.[43]

IV. STATE COURT JURISDICTION

A. Concurrent Jurisdiction

Unlike § 1983, which is only a cause of action, § 1 of the Civil Rights Act of 1871 contained both a cause of action and a jurisdictional provision.[44] The latter was necessary because in 1871 there was no general federal question jurisdictional provision for the federal courts.[45] In the 1874 codification of the U.S. Statutes, however, Congress separated the jurisdictional provision from the cause of action,[46] and this division continues today. Thus, it is necessary to look someplace other than § 1983 to determine whether state or federal courts have jurisdiction over § 1983 actions.

Federal courts are courts of limited jurisdiction, and there must be an affirmative grant of subject matter jurisdiction before a federal court may entertain a civil action.[47] State courts, however, are courts of general

41. 451 U.S. 527 (1981).

42. *See, e.g.,* Daniels v. Williams, 474 U.S. 327 (1986) (negligent conduct not sufficient to state a due process claim); Estelle v. Gamble, 429 U.S. 97 (1976) (negligent denial of medical care by prison officials not actionable under § 1983, but the Eighth Amendment is available for claims involving deliberate indifference to inmates' serious medical needs).

43. Although not directly relevant to the availability of immunities, *see infra* notes 203–07 and accompanying text, the defendant's state of mind is relevant to claims for punitive damages. *See infra* notes 308–09 and accompanying text.

44. The jurisdictional language provided that "such proceedings to be prosecuted in the several district or circuit courts of the United States, with and subject to the same rights of appeal, review upon error, and other remedies provided in like cases in such courts. . . ." Civil Rights Act of 1871, ch. 22, § 1, 17 Stat. 13 (1871).

45. The predecessor to 28 U.S.C. § 1331 (2000), the general federal question jurisdiction statute, was adopted in the Act of March 3, 1875, ch. 137, § 1, 18 Stat. 470 (1875).

46. *See Chapman,* 441 U.S. at 608–09.

47. *See* Charles Alan Wright & Mary Kay Kane, Law of Federal Courts 480 (6th ed. 2002). The Federal Rules of Civil Procedure recognize that federal courts are courts of limited jurisdiction and require the party seeking to invoke federal court jurisdiction to include in his or her pleading "a short and plain statement of the grounds upon which the court's jurisdiction depends." Fed. R. Civ. P. 8(a)(1).

jurisdiction,[48] and the Supreme Court has relied on the presumption of concurrent jurisdiction[49] that characterizes our system of judicial federalism to hold that state courts have concurrent jurisdiction over § 1983 actions.[50]

B. The Nondiscrimination Principle, Valid Excuses, and the Affirmative Duty to Entertain Section 1983 Suits

The Supreme Court has provided only limited guidance as to whether state courts are obligated to exercise their concurrent jurisdiction over § 1983 suits. The Court has treated the nondiscrimination principle as preventing state courts from excluding § 1983 claims on a discriminatory basis, but it has not decided whether federal law requires states to create forums that can

---

48. Although some state courts are courts of limited jurisdiction, all states have courts of general jurisdiction. State pleading rules reflect the different status of state courts, and unlike their federal counterpart, generally do not require pleading the existence of subject matter jurisdiction for suits filed in courts of general jurisdiction. *See, e.g.*, ALA. R. CIV. P. 8(a); COLO R. CIV. P. 8(a); MINN. R. CIV. P. 8.01; OHIO R. CIV. P. 8(A); WIS. R. CIV. P. 802.10(a)(1); *but see* ARIZ. R. CIV. P. 8(a)(1); FLA. R. CIV. P.1.110(b).
49. Under this presumption, state courts may exercise jurisdiction over federal causes of action as long as Congress has not explicitly or implicitly made federal court jurisdiction exclusive. An implied exclusivity can result from an "unmistakable implication from legislative history, or by a clear incompatibility between state-court jurisdiction and federal interests." Gulf Offshore Co. v. Mobile Oil Corp., 453 U.S. 473, 478 (1981) (citations omitted); *see also* Claflin v. Houseman, 93 U.S. 130, 136 (1876) ("[W]here jurisdiction may be conferred on the United States courts, it may be made exclusive where not so by the Constitution itself; but, if exclusive jurisdiction be neither express nor implied, the State courts have concurrent jurisdiction whenever, by their own constitution, they are competent to take it."); *see generally* Martin H. Redish & John E. Muench, *Adjudication of Federal Causes of Action in State Courts,* 75 MICH. L. REV. 311 (1976); STEINGLASS, SECTION 1983 LITIGATION IN STATE COURTS, *supra* note 24, at §§ 9:2–9:6. The Supreme Court has unanimously relied on the presumption to permit state court jurisdiction of Title VII and civil RICO actions, *see* Yellow Freight Sys., Inc. v. Donnelly, 494 U.S. 820 (1990) (Title VII employment discrimination actions); Tafflin v. Levitt, 493 U.S. 455 (1990) (civil RICO actions), and the only criticism on the Court of the presumption comes from Justices who would strengthen it. *See Tafflin,* 493 U.S. at 469 (Scalia, J., concurring) (questioning whether concurrent state court jurisdiction can ever be rebutted by implication from legislative history or by findings of incompatibility).
50. *See Thiboutot,* 448 U.S. at 3 n.1; Martinez v. California, 444 U.S. 277, 283 n.7 (1980); *see also* Felder v. Casey, 487 U.S. 131, 147 (1988) (reaffirming concurrent state court jurisdiction over § 1983 actions).

entertain § 1983 claims[51] or whether state courts are under an affirmative obligation to treat § 1983 suits more favorably than analogous state law claims.

The nondiscrimination principle has its roots in litigation in the earlier part of the twentieth century involving the refusal of state courts to entertain suits under the Federal Employers' Liability Act (FELA). Some state courts were reluctant to entertain FELA claims, but the Court relied upon the nondiscrimination principle to impose an obligation on state courts to entertain FELA and ultimately other federal causes of action.

In *Mondou v. New York, New Haven & Hartford Railroad*,[52] the Court held that the state courts of Connecticut could not refuse to exercise jurisdiction over FELA cases. Building on cases establishing the principle of concurrent jurisdiction, the Court stated that "[t]he existence of the jurisdiction creates an implication of duty to exercise it, and that its exercise may be onerous does not militate against that implication."[53]

In *McKnett v. St. Louis & San Francisco Railway*,[54] the Court elevated the principle of nondiscrimination from a rule of statutory construction to a constitutional principle in holding that Alabama could not refuse to hear transitory FELA actions between nonresidents on out of state accidents when it heard similar transitory actions under state law as well as nontransitory FELA actions. Thus, state courts of general jurisdiction may not refuse to hear claims solely because they are brought under federal law.

In *Testa v. Katt*,[55] the Rhode Island state courts refused to hear actions under the Federal Emergency Price Control Act because the actions included claims for treble damages. Previously, the Court had upheld nondiscriminatory refusals to entertain a subclass of federal causes of action

51. *See* Howlett v. Rose, 496 U.S. 356, 378 (1990) ("This case does not present the questions whether Congress can require the States to create a forum with the capacity to enforce federal statutory rights or to authorize service of process on parties who would not otherwise be subject to the court's jurisdiction."); *see also id.* at 378 n.20 ("We have no occasion to address in this case the contention[]. . . that the States need not establish courts competent to entertain § 1983 claims."); National Private Truck Council, Inc. v. Oklahoma Tax Comm'n, 515 U.S. 582, 588 n.4 (1995) (characterizing the obligation of state courts to entertain § 1983 actions as an open issue and, observing that "[w]e have never held that state courts must entertain § 1983 suits").

52. 223 U.S. 1 (1912).

53. *Id.* at 58.

54. 292 U.S 230 (1934).

55. 330 U.S. 386 (1947).

when states had "valid excuses" for such partial exclusions.[56] The *Testa* Court, however, held that the failure to enforce "penal" statutes of other jurisdictions, including those of the United States, was not a valid excuse when the state court entertained the "same type" of state law claims as well as double-damage claims under other federal statutes.

The Supreme Court has applied the nondiscrimination principle to state court § 1983 litigation. In *Martinez v. California*,[57] the Court reserved the question of whether state courts are obligated to entertain § 1983 actions, but it relied on the nondiscrimination principle in observing that "where the same type of claim, if arising under state law, would be enforced in the state courts, the state courts are generally not free to refuse enforcement of the federal claim."[58]

In *Howlett v. Rose*,[59] the Court unanimously rejected an argument that sovereign immunity represented a jurisdictional limitation on the power of the Florida courts. Comparing § 1983 actions to the tort claims against state entities that Florida entertained in its courts of general jurisdiction, and looking at the exercise of jurisdiction by Florida courts over § 1983 actions against individuals, the *Howlett* Court held that federal law required the Florida courts to entertain § 1983 actions against local school boards.[60] In taking this position, the Court defined broadly the comparison to be made under the nondiscrimination principle and made clear that states that opened their courts to § 1983 actions may not pick and choose among the § 1983 actions they wished to entertain by classifying state policies as jurisdictional.[61]

Given the breadth of the nondiscrimination principle, state courts are, in effect, required to hear § 1983 actions. To exclude § 1983 cases, a state would have to close its courts to similar actions authorized by state and federal law against state and local governmental bodies and their employees.

---

56. *See* Douglas v. New York, N.H. & H.R. Co., 279 U.S. 377, 387–88 (1929) (approving evenhanded exclusion of FELA actions by nonresidents on out-of-state accidents); *see also* Missouri *ex rel.* Southern Ry v. Mayfield, 340 U.S. 1 (1950) (permitting the nondiscriminatory use of forum non conveniens to exclude FELA actions by nonresidents on out-of-state accidents).
57. 444 U.S. 277 (1980).
58. *Id.* at 283 n.7.
59. 496 U.S. 356 (1990).
60. *Id.* at 379–80.
61. *See id.* at 381; *see also* Willbourn v. City of Tulsa, 721 P.2d 803, 805 (Okla. 1986) (relying on the nondiscrimination principle to hold that state courts must entertain § 1983 actions).

Although such wholesale exclusions of legal challenges to governmental action are theoretically possible, they are so implausible that one commentator has concluded that the nondiscrimination principle imposes a "de facto obligatory jurisdiction" on state courts.[62] Moreover, the Court has never approved a total exclusion of a particular federal cause of action by state courts.

Although the Court has not squarely decided whether state courts are under an affirmative duty to hear § 1983 causes of action where they exclude analogous state causes of action, the Court in *Howlett* noted that "[v]irtually every state has expressly or by implication opened its courts to § 1983 actions and there are no state court systems that refuse to hear § 1983 cases."[63] This willingness of state courts to open their doors voluntarily to § 1983 claims has made it unlikely that the Court will have to address the ultimate question of whether a state may refuse to hear § 1983 actions.

Nonetheless, the Court has given state courts the theoretical option of refusing to entertain § 1983 and other federal causes of action when they have a "valid excuse."[64] The *Howlett* Court alluded to this possibility when it noted that "[a] state court may not deny a federal right, when the parties and controversy are properly before it, in the absence of 'valid excuse.'"[65] Although acknowledging that in some circumstances state courts may rely on neutral state policies to refuse to exercise jurisdiction over federal cases, the Court defined narrowly the type of jurisdictional and other rules that it would accept as "valid excuses":

> The fact that a rule is denominated jurisdictional does not provide a court an excuse to avoid the obligation to enforce federal law if the rule does not reflect the concerns of power over the person and competence over the subject matter that jurisdictional rules are designed to protect.[66]

The *Howlett* Court also noted that the cases in which it had found valid excuses for state court refusals to entertain federal causes of action involved the application of neutral rules of judicial administration, including state

---

62. *See* Burt Neuborne, *Toward Procedural Parity in Constitutional Litigation,* 22 WM. & MARY L. REV. 725, 759 (1983).
63. *See Howlett,* 496 U.S. at 378 n.20 (citing STEINGLASS, SECTION 1983 LITIGATION IN STATE COURTS, supra note 24).
64. *See supra* note 56.
65. 496 U.S. at 369 (quoting *Douglas,* 279 U.S. at 387–88).
66. *Howlett,* 496 U.S. at 381.

policies involving forum non conveniens, the jurisdiction of state courts of limited jurisdiction, and access to state courts by nonresidents.[67] Finally, the Court concluded that it "is quite inadmissible" for states to decline jurisdiction over federally created causes of action because of disagreements with federal policy.[68]

In *National Private Truck Council, Inc. v. Oklahoma Tax Commission,*[69] a state court § 1983 challenge to state tax policies, the Court held that § 1983 did not authorize an action challenging a state tax where the state provided an adequate legal remedy. Because this ruling went to the scope of § 1983 regardless of forum, the Court did not have to reach the jurisdictional issues the case posed. Nonetheless, the Court noted that in some circumstances the Supremacy Clause obligated state courts to entertain § 1983 and other federal causes of action. Referring to the period before the creation of federal question jurisdiction, the Court observed that state courts at that time were under an obligation to entertain federal claims:

> As petitioners note, it was not until 1875 that Congress provided any kind of general federal-question jurisdiction to the lower federal courts. . . . "Until that time, the state courts provided the only forum for vindicating many important federal claims." Because of the Supremacy Clause, state courts could not have refused to hear cases arising under federal law merely to ensure "uniformity" between state and federal courts located within a particular state.[70]

Although state courts may not be obligated to entertain *every* § 1983 case that comes before them, the jurisdictional principles summarized in *Howlett* establish that state courts must do more than refrain from discriminating against federal causes of action. Even when state courts apply their own policies evenhandedly to state-created and § 1983 actions, states should be able to deny § 1983 claimants a state forum only when the states have a sufficiently strong interest in the administration of their judicial system to justify the use of state policies. Even though the Supreme Court has upheld the use of state policies governing which federal actions will be heard based on the identity of parties and the relation of the parties and the cause of action to the forum, the existence of a strong state interest in such state policies does not ipso facto justify the refusal of state courts to entertain partic-

67. *See id.* at 371.

68. *Id.*

69. 515 U.S. 582 (1995).

70. *Id.* at 588–89 (quoting Palmore v. United States, 411 U.S. 389, 401 (1973)).

ular § 1983 actions,[71] especially where the state has already opened its courts to other § 1983 actions.

C. Selective Refusals to Exercise Jurisdiction

Although no state court system categorically excludes § 1983 cases from its courts, some states exclude subclasses of § 1983 cases. Such selective exclusions, however, are improper when they are not based on neutral rules of judicial administration.[72]

The most flagrant example of a state court system selectively excluding § 1983 cases is the refusal of the New York courts to entertain § 1983 actions against state correctional officials. Under New York law, state courts may not hear damage suits brought against correctional officers for acts taken within the scope of the latter's employment.[73] In *Cepeda v. Coughlin*,[74] the New York appellate court construed state law as denying the New York courts subject matter jurisdiction in such cases. The court then held that the evenhanded application of the exclusion both to state and federal claims made it proper.[75]

The Supreme Court's decision in *Howlett* undercuts the New York policy of precluding suits against correctional officers. The state policy is based on a substantive judgment that the state, as contrasted to state employees, should be liable for certain wrongful acts; but this state policy is not a neutral rule of judicial administration. Moreover, the willingness of New York to entertain other § 1983 suits, including individual capacity § 1983 suits against other state employees, implicates the suggestion in *Howlett* that a state that opens its courts to some § 1983 suits may not bar other § 1983 suits.[76]

The proper approach to these jurisdictional issues is illustrated by the decision of the Ohio Court of Appeals in *Weinfurtner v. Nelsonville-York*

---

71. *Cf.* Felder v. Casey, 487 U.S. 131 (1988) (state interest in notice-of-claim requirement does not support its application to § 1983 actions).
72. *See supra* notes 55–61 and accompanying text.
73. *See* N.Y. CORRECTION LAW § 24(1) (McKinney 1987).
74. 513 N.Y.S.2d 528 (App. Div.), *appeal denied,* 512 N.E.2d 560 (N.Y. 1987).
75. *See also* Faulkner-King v. Wicks, 590 N.E.2d 511, 518 (Ill. App. Ct.) (treating state Human Rights Act as precluding state circuit courts from exercising subject matter jurisdiction over § 1983 gender-based employment discrimination claim), *appeal denied,* 602 N.E.2d 450 (Ill. 1992), *cert. denied,* 507 U.S. 960 (1993).
76. New York, however, may immunize state correctional officers (and other state officials) from suit under state law whether such suits are brought in state or federal courts. *See* Baker v. Coughlin, 77 F.3d 12 (2d Cir. 1996).

School District Board of Education.[77] Relying on *Howlett*, the court held that the state policy of providing the State Employment Relations Board with exclusive jurisdiction over disputes involving unfair labor practice charges was not a neutral rule of judicial administration and, thus, was not a valid excuse for divesting Ohio courts of subject matter jurisdiction over § 1983 claims arising out of such disputes.[78]

D. Courts of Limited Jurisdiction and Joinder of Claims

States have some leeway in determining which courts they will open to federal causes of action,[79] but states may not adopt jurisdictional policies that burden the litigation of § 1983 or other federal claims.[80]

Some § 1983 suits involving relatively small damage claims are appropriate for consideration by small claims courts, but state courts are split as to whether they must open their small claims courts to § 1983 suits. In *Terry v. Kolski*,[81] the Wisconsin Supreme Court, relying principally on state law, held that small claims courts in Wisconsin may entertain § 1983 claims. On the other hand, in *City of Cleveland v. A.J. Rose Manufacturing Company*,[82] the Ohio Court of Appeals concluded that the Cleveland Municipal Court could not entertain a § 1983 counterclaim because municipal courts were not courts of general jurisdiction.[83]

Related issues arise when plaintiffs join § 1983 claims with special state proceedings for judicial review of administrative decisions. Some states per-

77. 602 N.E.2d 318 (Ohio Ct. App. 1991).

78. *Id.* at 321–22; *accord* East Mississippi State Hosp. v. Callens, 892 So.2d 800 (Miss. 2004) (permitting state employees to bring § 1983 individual capacity suits against state officials without going through the Employee Appeals Board, the statutorily mandated administrative remedy available to state employees); Thomas v. Allen, 837 S.W.2d 631, 632–33 (Tex. 1992) (relying on *Howlett* and the absence of a neutral rule of judicial administration to reverse a trial court's discretionary refusal to assume jurisdiction over an inmate's § 1983 claim against correctional officers).

79. *Cf.* Herb v. Pitcairn, 324 U.S. 117 (city court of limited jurisdiction may decline to exercise jurisdiction over FELA actions on the ground that the action arose outside its territorial jurisdiction), *supplemental opinion,* 325 U.S. 77 (1945); Manning v. Ohio State Library Bd., 577 N.E.2d 650 (Ohio 1991) (holding that Ohio courts may entertain Title VII employment discrimination actions against the state, but only in the Court of Claims).

80. *See generally* STEINGLASS, SECTION 1983 LITIGATION IN STATE COURTS, *supra* note 24, at § 11:2.

81. 254 N.W.2d 704 (Wis. 1977).

82. 624 N.E.2d 245, 249 (Ohio Ct. App. 1993).

83. For a discussion of this issue, *see* Steinglass, *Section 1983 Litigation in Ohio*, *supra* note 7, at 119–22.

mit such joinders,[84] while others do not.[85] For example, in *Maisonet v. New Jersey Department of Human Services*,[86] the Appellate Division of the New Jersey Superior Court refused to exercise original jurisdiction over a § 1983 claim raised only in a notice of claim filed by a party who also sought judicial review of a decision of a state administrative agency. Although upholding the Appellate Division's refusal to exercise original jurisdiction as based on a neutral rule of judicial administration, the New Jersey Supreme Court found a creative way to permit petitioners to pursue both their § 1983 and judicial review claims. Recognizing the importance of providing federal access to state forums that can adjudicate all claims, including federal claims, the court required the appellate court to transfer the § 1983 claim to a state trial court.

V. CHOICE OF FORUM CONSIDERATIONS

Most choice of forum discussions focus at least initially on plaintiffs because they are responsible for choosing the court in which to file a suit. Defendants, however, have an equal interest in which court will hear a case. Accordingly, the factors that may convince some § 1983 plaintiffs to select state courts often lead defendants to seek ways to avoid remaining in state courts. Given the liberal federal question removal statute, state court defendants who prefer to defend § 1983 claims in federal court can almost always remove such cases, and they are increasingly doing so.[87]

A full review of choice of forum considerations is beyond the scope of this chapter,[88] but some of the more important factors deserve mention. At first, however, a caveat: at best, any choice of forum discussion only identifies factors that should be considered. Which direction these factors point

---

84. *See, e.g.*, Stratos v. Department of Pub. Welfare, 439 N.E.2d 778 (Mass. 1982); Thiboutot v. State, 405 A.2d 230 (Me. 1979), *aff'd on other grounds sub nom.*, Maine v. Thiboutot, 448 U.S. 1 (1980); Maldonado v. Nebraska Dep't of Pub. Welfare, 391 N.W.2d 105 (Neb. 1986).
85. *See, e.g.*, Orvis Co. Inc. v. Tax Appeals Tribunal, 612 N.Y.S.2d 503 (App. Div. 1994), *aff'd on other grounds,* 654 N.E.2d 954 (N.Y.), *cert. denied,* 516 U.S. 989 (1995); Spencer v. South Carolina Tax Comm'n, 316 S.E.2d 386 (S.C. 1984), *aff'd by an equally divided court,* 471 U.S. 82 (1985); *cf.* Human Development of Erie, Inc. v. Zoning Hearing Bd. of Millcreek Township, 600 A.2d 658 (Pa. Commw. Ct. 1991).
86. 657 A.2d 1209 (N.J. 1995).
87. For a discussion of removal, see *infra* notes 391–97 and accompanying text.
88. For general review of choice-of-forum considerations and for a choice-of-forum checklist, *see* STEINGLASS, SECTION 1983 LITIGATION IN STATE COURTS, *supra* note 24, at chs. 5–9 & App. G.

will vary based on the nature of the case, the identity and attitudes of the parties and lawyers, the relief sought, the identity of the judge, and the respective roles of the judge and the jury. In addition, the body of relevant precedents as well as a myriad of tactical considerations influence choice of forum decisions.

A. The Decision Makers

1. The Judges

The identity of the judge who will hear a case is one of the more important choice of forum factors, but it is difficult to generalize as to how differences between state and federal judges influence choice-of-forum decisions in specific cases. Moreover, because it is not possible to know which judge in a multijudge district or division will be assigned to a particular case (or will keep a case through trial), initial judgments about the attractiveness of the state or federal benches are necessarily collective judgments.[89]

Federal trial judges clearly have better jobs than their state counterparts do. They have higher wages, better working conditions, and greater job security, including a guarantee of life tenure that enables them to remain not only above partisan politics but also independent of the bar, the public, and the media.[90] State court judges, on the other hand, lack the independence that characterizes the federal bench, especially in states that have rejected "merit selection" and have retained the tradition of a politicized and partisan elected state judiciary.[91]

Federal judges also have the institutional support to give their cases adequate attention. Their caseloads are significantly lighter than those of state trial judges, and their resources are invariably more substantial than those available to their state court counterparts.

These generalizations do not do justice to the subtle forces that influence individual judges. Many state court judges, despite their lack of resources, efficiently manage their caseloads. Likewise, many federal court judges,

---

89. Unlike plaintiffs' lawyers, who rarely know which judge will be assigned to their case, state court defendants obviously know the identity of the state court judge to whom a case has been assigned and may effectively divest a particular state court judge of jurisdiction by removing the case to federal court.

90. *See generally* RICHARD A. POSNER, THE FEDERAL COURTS: CRISIS AND REFORM 30–48 (1985).

91. This is not to suggest that all federal judges have left their political or partisan concerns behind after their confirmation. Nor does it suggest that all state court judges lack independence. Rather, it is easier for federal judges to remain independent.

despite their institutional advantages, do not.[92] Thus, like collective judgments about the competence or attitudes of the state or federal judiciary, generalizations about efficiency or capacity have little relevance as to how an individual judge will act in a specific case.

2. *The Juries*

There are significant differences in the composition of juries in the state and federal courts as well as in their mode of selection and method of operation. State court juries are typically selected from a venire representing a single county, unlike multicounty federal juries.[93] Thus, state court juries more closely resemble the county in which a suit is filed. Lawyers in many state courts conduct the voir dire and thus play a greater role in selecting juries than do lawyers in the federal courts. Finally, juries in most state court systems decide civil cases by a nonunanimous vote rather than by the unanimous vote required in federal court under both the Seventh Amendment and the Federal Rules of Civil Procedure.[94]

B. Doctrinal Limitations on Federal Courts

Federal courts are courts of limited jurisdiction, and federal practice is characterized by restrictive policies on such justiciability requirements as standing, mootness, and ripeness. Likewise, the various abstention doctrines limit the equitable power of federal courts.

Despite the suggestions that have been made by some academic commentators who have argued that state courts should be required to follow federal policies when entertaining federal claims,[95] it is well established that state courts operate independently of federal constraints and may hear federal

---

92. The Judicial Improvements Act of 1990 attempted to improve the efficiency of the federal bench by requiring all federal districts to adopt "a civil justice expense and delay reduction plan." Pub. L. No. 101-650, § 103(a), 104 Stat. 5098 (1990) (creating 28 U.S.C. § 471 (2000)).

93. *See* Steinglass, *Emerging State Court § 1983 Action*, *supra* note 7 at 418–21.

94. *See* American Publishing Co. v. Fisher, 166 U.S. 464, 467–68 (1897); *see also* FED. R. CIV. P. 48.

95. *See* Paul J. Katz, *Standing in Good Stead: State Courts, Federal Standing Doctrine, and the Reverse-*Erie *Analysis,* 99 NW. U. L. REV 1315 (2005); William A. Fletcher, *The "Case or Controversy" Requirement in State Court Adjudication of Federal Questions,* 78 CAL. L. REV. 263 (1990); *but see* Brian A. Stern, *An Argument Against Imposing the Federal "Case or Controversy" Requirement on State Courts,* 69 N.Y.U. L. REV. 77 (1994).

claims that federal courts cannot hear.[96] For example, in *Texas Association of Business v. Texas Air Control Board*,[97] the Texas Supreme Court looked to state law as the source of a broader standing doctrine than that used in federal courts:[98]

> The differences between our Texas Constitution and the Federal Constitution not only justify, but also require, that citizen groups be accorded a broader right of access to our state courts. The Texas Constitution contains no express limitation of courts' jurisdiction to "cases" or "controversies," as provided by the federal charter. . . . Instead, it affirmatively protects the rights of litigants to gain access to our judicial system. . . .[99]

Consistent with these principles, many state courts, unlike federal courts, make broad use of taxpayer standing.[100] Also, unlike federal courts, state courts have rejected the narrow federal mootness[101] and ripeness[102] doc-

---

96. *See* City of Los Angeles v. Lyons, 461 U.S. 95, 113 (1983) ("[T]he state courts need not impose the same standing or remedial requirements that govern federal court proceedings. The individual states may permit their courts to use injunctions to oversee the conduct of law enforcement authorities on a continuing basis."); *see also* Langford v. Superior Court (Gates), 729 P.2d 822, 833 n.6 (Cal.) (noting that "California's [standing] requirements are less stringent than those imposed by federal law"), *cert. denied,* 484 U.S. 824 (1987); *but cf.* Girard v. Wagenmaker, 470 N.W.2d 372, 387 n.14 (Mich. 1991) (citing Supreme Court cases on standing based on Article III of the U.S. Constitution, but observing that "Michigan law embodies a similar requirement of an 'actual controversy'").
97. 852 S.W.2d 440 (Tex. 1993).
98. In ASARCO Inc. v. Kadish, 490 U.S. 605, 622–23 (1989), however, the Supreme Court held that it is not bound by the same justiciability requirements that apply in federal trial courts at the outset of litigation. In expanding its power to review state court judgments, the Court permitted losing state court defendants to rely on the state court judgment itself for the injury that meets the case or controversy requirement and, thus, permits Supreme Court review.
99. 852 S.W.2d at 471–72.
100. *Compare* Streight v. Ragland, 655 S.W.2d 459 (Ark. 1983) (taxpayer has standing to challenge the constitutionality of state income tax exemptions on retirement income of state and federal pensioners); Mendoza v. County of Tulare, 180 Cal. Rptr. 347 (Ct. App. 1982) (taxpayer has standing to challenge conditions of jail); Mandel v. Hodges, 127 Cal. Rptr. 244 (Ct. App. 1976) (taxpayer has standing to challenge released time given state employees for Good Friday observance); Noyola v. Board of Educ. of City of Chicago, 592 N.E.2d 165, 167 (Ill. App. Ct.) (concluding that "it would serve no useful purpose to further expand the concept of standing in Illinois beyond the present requirement that the plaintiff show an injury in fact to a legally cognizable interest"), *appeal denied,* 602 N.E.2d 458 (Ill. 1992); Doremus v. Board of Educ., 75 A.2d 880, 881–82 (N.J. 1950), *appeal dismissed,* 342 U.S.

trines and have refused to apply the strict federal standing requirements involving third-party standing,[103] and causation and redressibility.[104]

On the other hand, state courts may be limited in their ability to refuse to hear § 1983 claims that federal courts could hear. For example, a narrow state court interpretation of what controversies are justiciable may not be an

---

429 (1952), *with* United States v. Richardson, 418 U.S. 166 (1974) (denying taxpayer and citizen standing to challenge secrecy concerning expenditures of the Central Intelligence Agency as inconsistent with a federal constitutional provision requiring a regular statement and account of public funds).

101. *Compare* Duhon v. Gravett, 790 S.W.2d 155 (Ark. 1990) (relying on considerations of public interest and the prevention of future litigation to decide an otherwise moot § 1983 action challenging the constitutionality of the state post-judgment execution law); Shapiro v. Columbia Union Nat'l Bank & Trust Co., 576 S.W.2d 310 (Mo. 1978) (en banc) (permitting female student's challenge to a charitable trust for "deserving boys" attending private universities permitted despite her graduation because the question was one of great public importance and involved public rights), *cert. denied,* 444 U.S. 831 (1979); Wickham v. Fisher, 629 P.2d 896, 899 (Utah 1981) (permitting courts to hear issues that are moot as to the litigant but are of wide concern, affect the public, and are likely to recur in a similar manner); Milwaukee Prof'l Firefighters Local 215 v. City of Milwaukee, 253 N.W.2d 481, 488 (Wis. 1977) (permitting decision of constitutional issues in otherwise moot actions) *with* Weinstein v. Bradford, 423 U.S. 147 (1975) (limiting capable of repetition yet evading review of mootness exception to cases in which the named party may again be affected).

102. *Compare* Thomas v. Anchorage Equal Rights Comm'n, 102 P.3d 937 (Alaska 2004) (holding that a challenge by landlords to a ban on housing discrimination on the basis of marital status as an infringement of the landlords' religious freedom was ripe and rejecting a contrary ripeness decision by the Ninth Circuit), *with* Thomas v. Anchorage Equal Rights Comm'n, 220 F.3d 1134 (9th Cir. 2000) (holding that challenge to housing discrimination ban was not ripe), *cert. denied,* 531 U.S. 1143 (2001).

103. *See, e.g.,* Parrish v. Civil Serv. Comm'n, 425 P.2d 223 (Cal. 1967) (social worker terminated because of refusal to participate in early morning raids on homes of welfare recipients may raise rights of recipients in his own proceeding for reinstatement); State Bd. for Cmty. Colleges and Occupational Educ. v. Olson, 687 P.2d 429, 434–36, 440–41 (Colo. 1984) (faculty advisor to student-run newspaper has third-party standing to raise rights of students in challenging termination of funding); Right to Choose v. Byrne, 450 A.2d 925 (N.J. 1982) (plaintiffs challenging state restrictions on abortion funding permitted to raise free exercise claim under state constitution because New Jersey standing rules are more liberal than federal rules).

104. *See, e.g.,* Stocks v. City of Irvine, 170 Cal. Rptr. 724 (Ct. App. 1981); Southern Burlington County NAACP v. Township of Mount Laurel, 336 A.2d 713 (N.J. 1975).

adequate state ground on which to base a judgment and preclude Supreme Court review of a state court case rejecting a federal claim.[105]

C. Tactical Differences

State and federal courts often have different procedural policies governing civil litigation. Despite the widespread adoption of rules of civil procedure patterned after the Federal Rules of Civil Procedure, many states have resisted the influence of the Federal Rules. Indeed, some states, including several of the most populous ones, retain systems of code pleading and do not fully embrace the philosophy of notice pleading that characterizes the Federal Rules.[106] Moreover, even states that follow the lead of the Federal Rules sometimes reject federal policies. Finally, some states that have adopted identical rules have construed the rules differently from the federal courts.

Rule 11 of the Federal Rules of Civil Procedure and the willingness of federal judges to use (or to threaten to use) Rule 11 and other sanctions may deter some plaintiffs from filing § 1983 cases in federal courts.[107] In state courts, however, the analogous rules generally have far fewer teeth.[108] Even more importantly, state trial court judges are often reluctant to use sanctions aggressively against lawyers whose support they may need to retain their jobs.

Federal case management procedures are also more demanding than analogous state procedures, especially in the age of "civil justice reform."[109]

---

105. *See infra* notes 149–58 and accompanying text.

106. This includes such code-pleading states as California, Illinois, and New York. *See generally* John B. Oakley & Arthur F. Coon, *The Federal Rules in State Courts: A Survey of State Court Systems of Civil Procedure,* 61 WASH L. REV. 1367 (1986); *but see* Thomas O. Main, *Procedural Uniformity and the Exaggerated Role of Rules: A Survey of Intra-State Uniformity in Three States That Have Not Adopted the Federal Rules of Civil Procedure,* 46 VILL. L. REV. 311 (2001) (discussing procedural issues in Illinois, Nebraska, and Pennsylvania).

107. Under FED. R. CIV. P 11(b), as amended in 1993, a lawyer signing a pleading, motion, or other paper is deemed to have certified that the filing is not being presented for any improper purpose and that there is a proper basis for the legal and factual contentions.

108. *See generally* Byron C. Keeling, *Toward a Balanced Approach to "Frivolous" Litigation: A Critical Review of Federal Rule 11 and State Sanctions Provisions,* 21 PEPP. L. REV. 1067 (1994).

109. *See generally* Judicial Improvements Act of 1990, Pub. L. No. 101-650, § 105, 104 Stat. 5098 (1990).

Because moving cases to trial quickly is one of plaintiffs' goals, one might think that plaintiffs would prefer judges who have both the tools and the inclination to accomplish this. Nonetheless, some plaintiffs resist what they believe to be overly demanding case management requirements, and they often have concerns about the interventionist approach of many federal judges.

Discovery rules in the state and federal courts are becoming less similar. The federal courts have made major changes in discovery, moving to a system of uniform mandatory pretrial disclosure;[110] state courts, however, have moved in multiple directions, with some having embraced mandatory disclosure and an expanded role for trial judges in the pretrial process while others have adhered to the traditional discovery model.[111]

State and federal courts also have different policies concerning litigation against defendants whose identity is unknown at the time the suit is filed—an issue that often arises in § 1983 litigation. The federal rules, consistent with the approach followed in most states, do not treat the naming of a fictitious Doe defendant (whose real identity is unknown) as a "mistake" sufficient to justify relation back (for statute of limitations purpose) of an amended complaint naming the real defendant.[112] However, some states permit the use of Doe defendants to allow plaintiffs to amend otherwise timely complaints to join previously unknown defendants after the expiration of the limitations period.[113] The 1991 amendment of Rule 15 of the Federal Rules of Civil Procedure added a provision that expressly permits federal courts to borrow state policies authorizing the relation back of amended pleadings

---

110. Under FED. R. CIV. P. 26(a)(1), as amended in 2000, federal district courts may no longer adopt local rules to opt out of or modify the national uniform mandatory disclosure procedures, and half of the federal districts have adopted local rules opting out of mandatory disclosure. *See* Advisory Committee on Civil Rules (commenting on FED. R. CIV. P. 26(a)(1)) (2000).

111. *See generally* Seymour Moskowitz, *Rediscovering Discovery: State Procedural Rules and the Level Playing Field,* 54 RUTGERS L. REV. 595 (2002).

112. *See* Barrow v. Wethersfield Police Dep't, 74 F.3d 1366 (2d Cir. 1996) (construing FED. R. CIV. P. 15(c)(3)(B) and refusing to permit amendment substituting Doe Defendants to relate back when failure to name police officers was due to lack of knowledge of their identity), *modifying* 66 F.3d 466 (2d Cir. 1995); Worthington v. Wilson, 8 F.3d 1253 (7th Cir. 1993) (same); *see generally* Howard M. Wasserman, *Civil Rights Plaintiffs and John Doe Defendants: A Study in Section 1983 Procedure,* 25 CARDOZO L. REV. 793 (2003).

113. *See, e.g.,* ALA. R. CIV. P. 9(h & 15(c)(4)); CAL. CIV. PROC. CODE § 474; 735 ILL. COMP. STAT. § 5 2-413; N.J. CIV. PRAC. R. 4: 26-4; OHIO R. CIV. P. 3(A) & 15(D).

naming new defendants,[114] and some federal courts borrow the policies of their forum states and permit the relation back of Doe defendant complaints.[115] On the other hand, some federal courts have construed begrudgingly this borrowing provision and refused to permit amended complaints to relate back.[116] Consequently, the choice of a federal forum may not serve the interests of § 1983 plaintiffs in jurisdictions that are unwilling to borrow forgiving state policies, and state court defendants may have an incentive to remove such cases to federal courts in these jurisdictions.

The federal offer of judgment rule[117] also represents a difference between federal and state civil procedure. Though used only occasionally, this rule is a powerful weapon for federal court defendants. It provides leverage to force settlements by limiting defendants' exposure to fee awards in § 1983 suits.[118] There is no analogous provision under the law of many states.[119] Finally, the clear availability in the federal courts of interlocutory appeals of trial court decisions denying § 1983 immunity, as contrasted to

---

114. *See* FED. R. CIV. P. 15(c)(1) ("An amendment of a pleading relates back to the date of the original pleading when . . . relation back is permitted by the law that provides the statute of limitations applicable to the action . . . ."); *see also* Advisory Committee Notes on 1991 Amendments (describing 15(c)(1) as "intended to make it clear that the rule does not apply to preclude any relation back that may be permitted under the applicable limitations law").

115. *See, e.g.,* Saxton v. ACF Indus., Inc., 254 F.3d 959, 963 (11th Cir. 2001) (en banc); Wilson v. City of Atlantic City, 142 F.R.D. 603 (D. N.J. 1992) (permitting use of state relation back rules under 1991 amendments); *cf.* Cabrales v. Los Angeles County, 864 F.2d 1454 (9th Cir. 1988) (interpreting the pre-1991 version of FED. R. CIV. P. 15(c) to permit the use of state relation back rules), *vacated on other grounds,* 490 U.S. 1087 (1989).

116. *See, e.g.,* Lovelace v. O'Hara, 985 F.2d 847, 851 (6th Cir. 1993) (refusing to borrow state relation back policies because the Kentucky Rules of Civil Procedure, not the state statute providing the relevant statute of limitations, permitted relation back); *Worthington,* 8 F.3d at 1256–57 (applying the "mistake" requirement in 15(c)(3) as applicable to the old and the amended rule without considering the independent significance of 15(c)(1)); Oros v. Hull & Assocs., 217 F.R.D. 401, 404 & 404 n.2 (N.D. Ohio 2003) (describing a split in the Circuits on the construction of 15(c)(1) and refusing to borrow state relation back policy contained in state rules of civil procedure); *but see Saxton,* 254 F.3d at 963 (construing 15(c)(1) broadly to permit borrowing of state relation back policies even when contained in state rules of civil procedure).

117. FED. R. CIV. P. 68.

118. *See* Marek v. Chesny, 473 U.S. 1 (1985) (construing FED. R. CIV. P. 68 to permit the use of rejected offers of judgment to limit awards of attorneys' fees to plaintiffs under 42 U.S.C. § 1988).

119. *See, e.g.,* OHIO R. CIV. P. 68 (barring the use of rejected offers of judgment to determine costs).

the absence of the right of such nonfinal appellate review in some state courts,[120] is another reason § 1983 plaintiffs may prefer state courts.

Differences between state and federal practice are often more than simply a question of comparing the text of the relevant rules. One of the most significant areas of difference for purposes of choice of forum decisions involves the availability of summary judgment. Some states have expressly rejected the federal model of summary judgment,[121] but even when states maintain summary judgment rules patterned after the federal model, federal judges are far more likely than state court judges to dismiss § 1983 claims on summary judgment. In part, this is a result of U.S. Supreme Court decisions that encourage greater use of summary judgment,[122] especially in § 1983 cases,[123] but it also may be a function of the greater resources that federal courts can bring to the task of addressing complex, document-intensive motions for summary judgment. Independent of doctrine, it is often easier for state court judges to deny summary judgment and set a case for trial rather than to produce a written opinion granting summary judgment. Federal judges, on the other hand, are more likely to refer the stack of depositions, affidavits, and briefs to a law clerk (or law student intern), a luxury available to few state trial courts.

D. Federal Law and the Law of the Circuit

State courts often look to the U.S. Court of Appeals for the federal circuit in which their state is located for guidance in construing § 1983. Even though the same body of federal law governs § 1983 actions in state and federal courts, it is well established that state courts are not obligated to follow the law of their federal circuit.[124] Although this may appear somewhat surprising, this is consistent with the structure of the federal judicial system in which only the U.S. Supreme Court is responsible for resolving conflicts

---

120. *See infra* notes 248–58 and accompanying text.

121. *See* Steinglass, Section 1983 Litigation in State Courts, *supra* note 24, at § 8:5.

122. *See* Celotex Corp. v. Catrett, 477 U.S. 317, 322 (1986) ("[T]he plain language of Rule 56(c) mandates the entry of summary judgment, after adequate time for discovery and upon motion, against a party who fails to make a showing sufficient to establish the existence of an element essential to that party's case, and on which that party will bear the burden of proof at trial."); *see also* Anderson v. Liberty Lobby, 477 U.S. 242 (1986); Matsushita Elec. Indus. Co. v. Zenith Radio Corp., 475 U.S. 574 (1986).

123. *Cf.* Harlow v. Fitzgerald, 457 U.S. 800 (1982) (adopting an almost exclusively objective qualified immunity standard).

124. *See* United States *ex rel.* Lawrence v. Woods, 432 F.2d 1072, 1075–76 (7th Cir. 1970), *cert. denied,* 402 U.S. 983 (1971).

between state and federal courts on the meaning of federal law.[125] Thus, when state and federal courts differ on their interpretations of important elements of the § 1983 remedy or the underlying substantive law enforceable through § 1983, both plaintiffs and defendants should consider the impact of such conflicts on their choice of forum decisions.[126]

VI. METHODOLOGY OF STATE COURT SECTION 1983 LITIGATION

As the volume of § 1983 state court litigation increases, state courts have had to address a number of novel issues. State courts that entertain § 1983 actions tend to apply familiar state policies, including state rules of practice and procedure. This application of state policies raises a range of discrete state and federal law issues, including whether the state policies apply to § 1983 claims as a matter of state law, and, if so, whether such applications are consistent with federal law.

The Supreme Court requires state courts to use federal standards to define the elements of the § 1983 cause of action.[127] States may not go beneath this federal floor to reject federal policies on such matters as the available immunities, the absence of exhaustion requirements, and the availability of attorneys' fees to prevailing parties,[128] nor may states adopt policies that discriminate against or burden § 1983 actions.[129] On the other hand, when the policies applicable to federal court § 1983 litigation are not

---

125. *See generally* Steinglass, Section 1983 Litigation in State Courts, *supra* note 24, at § 5.8; *see also* Lockhart v. Fretwell, 506 U.S. 364, 376 (1993) (Thomas, J., concurring) ("The Supremacy Clause demands that state law yield to federal law, but neither federal supremacy nor any other principle of federal law requires that a state court's interpretation of federal law give way to a (lower) federal court's interpretation. In our federal system, a state trial court's interpretation of federal law is no less authoritative than that of the federal court of appeals in whose circuit the trial court is located."); Graham v. Scissor-Tail, Inc., 623 P.2d 165, 179 (Cal. 1981) ("[T]his court is in any event under no obligation to follow federal lower court precedents interpreting acts of Congress when we find those precedents unpersuasive."); Gayety Books, Inc. v. City of Baltimore, 369 A.2d 581, 585 (Md. 1977) ("The courts of this State . . . are not bound by the holdings of a federal district court or of a federal circuit court of appeals.").

126. For example, the Sixth Circuit has interpreted federal law as requiring the use of a two-year statute of limitations for § 1983 cases, but some Ohio Courts of Appeals have selected a four-year limitations period. *See* Steinglass, *Section 1983 Litigation in Ohio, supra* note 7, at 490–92.

127. *See infra* notes 136–40 and accompanying text.

128. *See infra* notes 187–91, 332–45, and 379–90 and accompanying text.

129. *See infra* notes 142–45 and accompanying text.

derived from § 1983 itself, such as with the jury unanimity requirement of the Seventh Amendment or the case or controversy requirement of Article III, state courts are generally free to follow their own policies.[130]

A. The Meaning of State Law

State courts must initially determine whether state law applies to § 1983 actions. By addressing this issue first, state courts may sometimes be able to avoid reaching federal issues. For example, in *Terry v. Kolski*[131] the Wisconsin Supreme Court relied on principles of state court jurisdiction to hold that state law required small claims courts to entertain § 1983 actions otherwise within their jurisdiction. The *Terry* court therefore had no reason to reach the ultimate question of whether federal law required the same result.[132]

In many cases, however, state statutes are not clear as to whether they apply to § 1983 actions, and this lack of clarity raises difficult issues of state statutory construction. In such cases, state courts often assume that state policies apply to § 1983 claims *as a matter of state law*.[133] An alternative approach to this threshold state law issue is followed by the Supreme Judicial Court of Massachusetts. In *Mellinger v. Town of West Springfield*,[134] the court adopted a "clear statement rule" under which it refused to apply the Massachusetts notice-of-claim requirement to § 1983 claims "in the absence of a clear legislative statement that § 1983 claimants must comply" with the state policy.[135] Because state legislators rarely have § 1983 or other federal causes of action in mind when they adopt policies to govern state court litigation, the Massachusetts rule of statutory construction seems more sound than a rule that presumptively applies state substantive policies (or state procedural policies that have a substantive impact) to federal causes of action.

B. A Federal Definition of Section 1983

When states voluntarily open their courts to federal causes of action, they must give plaintiffs "the benefit of the full scope of these [federally created]

130. *See generally* Steinglass, Section 1983 Litigation in State Courts, *supra* note 24, at § 10:2.

131. 254 N.W.2d 704 (Wis. 1977).

132. *See id.* at 713.

133. *See, e.g.,* Felder v. Casey, 408 N.W.2d 19 (Wis. 1987) (construing state statute providing that "no action may be brought . . . unless" a claimant complies with the state notice-of-claim requirement as applying to § 1983 actions), *rev'd on other grounds,* 487 U.S. 131 (1988).

134. 515 N.E.2d 584 (Mass. 1987).

135. *Id.* at 589.

rights."[136] This principle requires state courts to apply the federal definition of the § 1983 cause of action.[137] In *Howlett v. Rose*,[138] the Supreme Court applied this principle and rejected the availability of state sovereign immunity as a defense to a § 1983 suit against a local school board. Noting that "[t]he elements of, and the defenses to, a federal cause of action are defined by federal law,"[139] the Court made clear the primacy of federal standards in defining § 1983:

> [A]s to persons that Congress subjected to liability, individual States may not exempt such persons from federal liability by relying on their own common-law heritage. If we were to uphold the immunity claim in this case, every State would have the same opportunity to extend the mantle of sovereign immunity to "persons" who would otherwise be subject to § 1983 liability. States would then be free to nullify for their own people the legislative decisions that Congress has made on behalf of all the People.[140]

In *Shaw v. Leatherberry*,[141] the Wisconsin Supreme Court held that the middle burden of proof (i.e., the clear and convincing standard) does not as a matter of federal law apply to a § 1983 excessive force claim against police officers. Wisconsin applies this heightened burden to state-created excess force claims against police officers, but the state court characterized the burden of proof as "substantive" and held that state courts entertaining § 1983 actions were required to follow federal substantive law and use the preponderance of the evidence standard.

C. The Nondiscrimination Principle

The Supreme Court has relied on the nondiscrimination principle to limit the ability of state courts to exclude § 1983 actions from their courts.[142]

---

136. Garrett v. Moore-McCormack Co., 317 U.S. 239, 249 (1942).
137. *See generally* Steinglass, Section 1983 Litigation in State Courts, *supra,* note 24, at §§ 10:3, 15:7; *see also* Martinez v. California, 444 U.S. 277, 284 n.8 (1980) (states may not narrow § 1983 cause of action by immunizing conduct wrongful under § 1983).
138. 496 U.S. 356 (1990).
139. *Id.* at 375.
140. *Id.* at 383.
141. 706 N.W.2d 299 (Wis. 2005).
142. *See supra* note 51 and accompanying text.

This jurisdictional principle, however, also prevents states from singling out federal causes of action and applying policies not followed in analogous state-created actions.[143] Moreover, in *Felder v. Casey*[144] the Court broadened the nondiscrimination principle by treating as discriminatory policies that the state imposed "only upon those who seek redress for injuries resulting from the use or misuse of governmental authority."[145]

D. State Policies and Burdens on Section 1983 Litigation

The purposes of § 1983 are compensation and deterrence.[146] State policies that are inconsistent with those purposes, or that burden the litigation of § 1983 claims, should be rejected in § 1983 litigation in both state and federal courts. Thus, federal law bars the use of state policies in state court § 1983 litigation even when state courts apply those policies evenhandedly to both state and federal causes of action.

In *Felder* the Court gave content to the compensation purpose of § 1983 by holding that state policies that limited the right of recovery for the purpose of minimizing governmental liability were inconsistent with federal law.[147] In addition, the Court held that state policies applicable only to state court § 1983 actions must be rejected not only when they are inconsistent with federal policies concerning immunities, exhaustion, and statutes of limitations but also when they impose "unnecessary" burdens on state court § 1983 litigation.[148]

Although state court judgments based on state procedural doctrines are insulated from Supreme Court review under the adequate state ground

---

143. *See generally* Steinglass, Section 1983 Litigation in State Courts, *supra,* note 24, at §10:4.
144. 487 U.S. 131 (1988).
145. *Id.* at 141 (rejecting the application to § 1983 of a state notice-of-claim requirement that the state applied only on a specific class of plaintiffs—those who sue governmental defendants, the archetypical § 1983 defendant.)
146. *See* Robertson v. Wegmann, 436 U.S. 584, 590–91 (1978) ("The policies underlying § 1983 include compensation of persons injured by deprivation of federal rights and prevention of abuses of power by those acting under color of state law.").
147. 487 U.S. at 153.
148. *Id.* at 150 ("Federal law takes state courts as it finds them only insofar as those courts employ rules that do not 'impose unnecessary burdens upon rights of recovery authorized by federal laws.'") (quoting Brown v. Western Ry. of Ala., 338 U.S. 294, 298–99 (1949)).

doctrine,[149] the adequacy of the state ground is itself a federal question. For example, in Federal Employers' Liability Act (FELA) litigation, the Supreme Court observed that "the forms of local practices" cannot defeat the federal right,[150] and further stated that "[s]trict local rules of pleading cannot be used to impose unnecessary burdens upon rights of recovery authorized by federal laws."[151] States may not use procedural doctrines that discriminate against federal causes of action to refuse to reach the merits of federal claims; nor may they give their courts unlimited discretion to determine when to overlook procedural defaults and reach federal issues.[152]

In *Howlett* the Supreme Court reviewed the adequate state ground doctrine in the course of rejecting the use of the state-created doctrine of sovereign immunity to protect local school boards that would have been subject to suit under § 1983 in federal court. Noting "the concern that the state court may be evading federal law and discriminating against federal causes of action," the Court stated that "[t]he adequacy of the state law ground to support a judgment precluding litigation of the federal claim is itself a federal question which we review *de novo*."[153] The Court then stated that it "is within our province to inquire not only whether the [federal] right was denied in express terms, but also whether it was denied in substance and effect, as by putting forward nonfederal grounds of decision that were without any fair or substantial support."[154]

State courts have followed these principles to reject the application of policies that burden § 1983 litigation. For example, in *Barcik v. Kubiaczyk*[155] the Oregon Supreme Court refused to apply stringent state justiciability standards to a § 1983 action that could have been heard in federal court under federal standards. Relying, in part, on the fact that the Oregon mootness

---

149. Under the adequate state ground doctrine, the Supreme Court cannot review a decision resting on an adequate and independent state ground because the Court's review of the federal issue would not affect the state court judgment and, thus, would be only an advisory opinion. *See* Michigan v. Long, 463 U.S. 1032, 1040–41 (1983). For a discussion of the adequacy of state procedural doctrines grounds as a bar to Supreme Court review of state court § 1983 decisions, *see* STEINGLASS, SECTION 1983 LITIGATION IN STATE COURTS, *supra* note 24, at § 10.6.

150. *Brown,* 338 U.S. at 286.

151. *Id.* at 298.

152. *See* Sullivan v. Little Hunting Park, Inc., 396 U.S. 229 (1969) (state rule concerning notice for reviewing a transcript on appeal deemed discretionary and not an adequate state ground to prevent Supreme Court review of federal issues in a § 1982 case).

153. 496 U.S. at 366.

154. *Id.*

155. 895 P.2d 765 (Or. 1995).

policy was not a "neutral procedural rule," the state court concluded that "an Oregon court cannot apply state standards of mootness and justiciability to a section 1983 claim brought in state court if application of those standards would preclude a plaintiff's federal claim, but application of federal standards would not."[156]

Thus, state courts that maintain case or controversy requirements that are narrower than their federal counterparts may not be able to apply these requirements to § 1983 claims. Such limitations of what controversies are justiciable under state law may not be an adequate state ground on which to base a judgment and deny Supreme Court review of otherwise reviewable federal issues.[157] Similarly, state courts have rejected the application of strict state pleading requirements, state heightened proof standards, and state limitations on discovery.[158]

E. Intrastate Uniformity and the "Reverse-*Erie*" Approach

In *Felder* the Court also rejected the use of "outcome determinative" state policies in state court § 1983 litigation.[159] In doing so, the Court relied heavily on the federal interest in "intrastate uniformity" and the principles developed in diversity cases under the *Erie* doctrine. "Just as federal courts are constitutionally obligated to apply state law to state claims, . . . so too the Supremacy Clause imposes on state courts a constitutional duty 'to proceed in such manner that all the substantial rights of the parties under controlling federal law [are] protected.'"[160] Because the notice-of-claim requirement did not apply to § 1983 claims filed in the federal courts, the application of the requirement to § 1983 state court actions would permit the choice of forum to dictate the outcome and thus would encourage the type of forum shopping that the *Erie* doctrine was intended to limit.[161]

---

156. *Id.* at 772; *cf.* Liner v. Jafco, Inc., 375 U.S. 301 (1964) (treating a decision based on state mootness grounds as not resting on an adequate state ground).

157. *See generally* Steinglass, Section 1983 Litigation in State Courts, *supra* note 24, at §§ 10.6, 13.2, and 13:4.

158. *See infra* notes 180–81, 321–23, and 370–77 and accompanying text (discussing the use of state pleading, state standards of proof, and state discovery policies).

159. *Felder,* 487 U.S. at 151–52.

160. *Id.* at 151 (quoting Garrett v. Moore-McCormack Co., 317 U.S. 239, 245 (1942)).

161. *Accord* Shaw v. Leatherberry, 706 N.W.2d 299 (Wis. 2005) (following *Felder* and rejecting the use of the clear and convincing burden of proof in § 1983 excessive force actions against police officers because its use was outcome-determinative and disrupted the federal interest in uniformity).

Nonetheless, *Felder* gave states some room to adopt policies that differ from federal policies and are more congenial to § 1983 claims.[162] Thus, federal policies that are not derived from § 1983 itself, such as policies involving jury unanimity or the standing and other justiciability requirements applicable in federal courts, need not be followed by state courts in § 1983 actions.

In *National Private Truck Council, Inc. v. Oklahoma Tax Commission,*[163] the Court did not rely on the principle of "intrastate uniformity" in the course of a decision barring state taxpayers from bringing a § 1983 case involving state taxes in state court. Recognizing that the plaintiffs could not have brought a similar case in the federal court because of abstention-related doctrines, the Court nonetheless stated that the principle of "intrastate uniformity" was not a basis for state court refusals to entertain federal causes of action.[164] Instead, the Court construed § 1983 itself as not reaching challenges to the constitutionality of state taxes (whether in state or federal courts) where the state had an adequate legal remedy.

Similarly, the Court refused to rely on the doctrine of "intrastate uniformity" in *Johnson v. Fankell*[165] when it permitted a state to deny § 1983 defendants the right to interlocutory appeals of denials of qualified immunity even though federal court defendants were entitled to such interlocutory appeals.

These Supreme Court cases—*Felder, Howlett, National Private Truck,* and *Fankell*—establish that when limitations on § 1983 are derived from the Court's interpretation of § 1983 itself, those limitations are equally applicable in state and federal courts. Thus, on issues such as the appropriate immunities, the no-exhaustion principle, the availability of attorneys' fees, and the unavailability of § 1983 in state tax cases, the Court has applied the same policies to state and federal court § 1983 litigation. When limitations on the § 1983 cause of action come not from the Court's interpretation of the cause of action but from jurisdictional and other limitations on the power of federal courts, such limitations will not ex proprio vigore apply to § 1983 actions in state courts, and the Court expects state courts to ask whether the use of the state policies burdens § 1983.

---

162. 487 U.S. at 151 ("States may make the litigation of federal rights as congenial as they see fit . . . because such congeniality does not stand as an obstacle to the accomplishment of Congress' goals.").
163. 515 U.S. 582 (1995).
164. *Id.* at 588 ("Nor can a desire for 'intrastate uniformity' permit state courts to refuse to award relief merely because a federal court could not grant such relief.")
165. 520 U.S. 911 (1997).

VII. SECTION 1983 REMEDIAL ISSUES

A. Pleading

Plaintiffs in § 1983 cases need only plead that some person, acting under color of state law, deprived them of federal rights secured by § 1983. It is not necessary to allege that defendants acted in bad faith or abused their qualified immunities, and defendants must raise such "confession and avoidance" defenses affirmatively.[166] Despite this liberal approach to pleading, most federal courts, until recently, had applied a strict or heightened pleading requirement to § 1983 complaints.[167] This had been most common on immunity issues, but some federal courts had extended the heightened pleading requirement to nonimmunity issues such as municipal liability.[168] The Supreme Court, however, in *Leatherman v. Tarrant County Narcotics Intelligence and Coordination Unit*,[169] rejected the application of strict pleading requirements to § 1983 claims against municipalities.

Leatherman did not resolve the application of strict pleading requirements to § 1983 cases involving qualified immunity issues. In *Crawford-El v. Britton*,[170] however, the Court effectively rejected the use of strict or heightened pleading requirements on qualified immunity issues, while making clear that on a case-by-case basis federal courts could require § 1983 plaintiffs to "'put forward specific, nonconclusory factual allegations' that establish improper motive causing cognizable injury in order to survive a prediscovery motion for dismissal or summary judgment."[171] Subsequently, in *Swierkiewicz v. Soreman*[172] the Court rejected the applicability of a requirement for particularity in pleading in federal employment discrimination cases, and federal courts have concluded that the Supreme Court has

---

166. *See* Gomez v. Toledo, 446 U.S. 635, 640–41 (1980).
167. *See* Hobson v. Wilson, 737 F.2d 1, 30 n.87 (D.C. Cir. 1984), *cert. denied,* 470 U.S. 1084 (1985), and cases cited therein.
168. *See, e.g.*, Sivard v. Pulaski County 959 F.2d 662, 667 (7th Cir. 1992) ("This Court demands that plaintiffs suing a municipal body under § 1983 plead with greater specificity than might ordinarily be required."); *accord* Palmer v. City of San Antonio, 810 F.2d 514, 516–17 (5th Cir. 1987); Strauss v. City of Chicago, 760 F.2d 765, 767 (7th Cir. 1985).
169. 507 U.S. 163 (1993).
170. 523 U.S. 574 (1998).
171. *Id.* at 598 (quoting Siegert v. Gilley, 500 U.S. 226, 236 (1991) (Kennedy, J., concurring in judgment).
172. 534 U.S. 506 (2002).

finally clearly rejected the use of strict or heightened pleading requirements in § 1983 cases.[173] In so ruling the Court relied on the normal pleading requirements of the Federal Rules and the failure of the drafters to extend the special pleading requirements of Rule 9(b) of the Federal Rules of Civil Procedure to § 1983 or other civil rights complaints.[174]

Before *Leatherman*, a number of state courts had relied on federal cases as authority for the use of strict pleading requirements.[175] *Leatherman* and the Court's subsequent pleading decisions undercut federal support for an across-the-board strict pleading requirement for § 1983 cases, but they do not answer whether states may independently, as a matter of state law, impose strict pleading requirements on § 1983 or other federal civil rights claims.

---

173. *See* Educadores Puertorriqueños en Acción v. Hernández, 367 F.3d 61, 67 (1st Cir. 2004) (rejecting the application of heightened pleading standards for § 1983 cases and stating that "[t]he rule that we announce today is not contingent on the type of civil rights case, the capacity in which a particular defendant is sued, the availability vel non of a qualified immunity defense, or the need (or lack of need) for proof of illegal motive"), and cases cited therein.

174. *See* 507 U.S. at 168 (noting that Fed. R. Civ. P. 9(b) imposes a particularized pleading requirement for averments of fraud and mistake).

175. *See, e.g.,* Kyle v. Civil Serv. Comm'n, 588 So. 2d 1154, 1160 (La. Ct. App. 1991) (expressing concern about permitting plaintiffs to state § 1983 claims with "vague, broadly worded complaints," and, relying on Fifth Circuit decisions, imposing a stringent pleading requirement under which "to commence a lawsuit against a public official for acts for which he is potentially immune, the complaint must allege with particularity all material facts on which [the claimant] contends . . . that the plea of immunity cannot be sustained") (internal quotations omitted), *writ denied,* 595 So. 2d 654 (La. 1992); Henschke v. Borough of Clayton, 598 A.2d 526, 530 (N.J. Super. Ct. App. Div. 1991) (relying on Third Circuit cases and stating that "a plaintiff is required to set forth specific conduct by the state or its officials which violated the constitutional rights of the plaintiff . . . [and] is required to establish with specificity that defendant deprived him of a right secured by the Constitution and that such a deprivation was caused by a person acting under color of law"); *cf.* Black v. Rouse, 587 So. 2d 1359, 1361 (Fla. Dist. Ct. App. 1991) (applying Florida strict pleading rules requiring the pleading of a "short and plain statement of the ultimate facts showing that the pleader is entitled to relief" to a § 1983 complaint), *review denied,* 598 So. 2d 75 (Fla. 1992); International Soc'y for Krishna Consciousness v. City of Evanston, 411 N.E.2d 1030 (Ill. App. Ct. 1980) (applying Illinois strict pleading rules to § 1983 complaints), *cert. denied,* 454 U.S. 878 (1981); *but cf.* Cunha v. City of Algona, 334 N.W.2d 591, 596 (Iowa 1983) (rejecting strict pleading standard for § 1983 cases); Casteel v. Vaade, 481 N.W.2d 476 (Wis. 1992) (applying liberal pleading standards to pro se § 1983 complaints).

Under the nondiscrimination principle, a state may not impose heightened pleading requirements on federal claims, if it does not impose the same standards on state claims,[176] but a different question arises when a state evenhandedly applies strict state pleading rules to state and federal claims. The Supreme Court has not directly addressed this issue in § 1983 litigation, but in *Brown v. Western Railway of Alabama*,[177] a FELA case, the Court stated that "[s]trict local rules of pleading cannot be used to impose unnecessary burdens upon rights of recovery authorized by federal laws."[178] The *Brown* Court further observed that it would not "fail to protect federally created rights from dismissal because of over-exacting local requirements for meticulous pleadings. . . ."[179] Some state courts have relied on these principles to reject the application of state pleading requirements to § 1983 complaints,[180] and a number of state courts have relied on *Leatherman* and *Crawford-El* to reject the application of strict pleading requirements to § 1983 cases.[181]

A recurring pleading issue in state court § 1983 litigation is whether plaintiffs must specifically plead that they are relying upon § 1983.[182] Federal courts have not imposed such a pleading requirement,[183] and state

---

176. *See supra* notes 142–45 and accompanying text.
177. 338 U.S. 294 (1949).
178. *Id.* at 298.
179. *Id.* at 299.
180. *See, e.g.,* Bach v. County of Butte, 195 Cal. Rptr. 268, 272–74 (Ct. App. 1983) (relying on *Brown* and federal standards to determine the sufficiency of a § 1983 complaint); Kay v. David Douglas Sch. Dist., 719 P.2d 875 (Or. Ct. App. 1986) (holding state rule requiring specific pleading of attorneys' fees inapplicable to § 1983 actions), *rev'd as moot,* 738 P.2d 1389 (Or. 1987), *cert. denied,* 484 U.S. 1032 (1988).
181. *See, e.g.,* Fulwood v. Porter, 639 A.2d 594, 598 n.7 (D.C. 1994) (noting similarity in language between state rule and FED. R. CIV. P. 8(a)(2) and treating *Leatherman* as authoritative in the District of Columbia); Ennis v. Dasovick, 506 N.W.2d 386, 390 (N.D. 1993) (relying on *Leatherman* and rejecting application of heightened pleading standard to a prisoner's § 1983 claim alleging deliberate indifference to serious medical needs); *see also* McCormick v. Board of County Comm'rs of Shawnee County, 35 P.3d 815, 825 (Kan. 2001) (relying on *Crawford-El* and rejecting the applicability of a heightened pleading requirement to § 1983 claims involving qualified immunity issues).
182. Plaintiffs who prevail only on state law claims may sometimes recover attorneys' fees if the suit also included a § 1983 claim. *See infra* notes 388–89 and accompanying text. Thus, the issue of whether a claim was brought under § 1983 often arises at the end of litigation when a prevailing plaintiff seeks a fee award.
183. *See, e.g.,* Americans United for Separation of Church and State v. School Dist. of Grand Rapids, 835 F.2d 627, 635 (6th Cir. 1987).

courts have generally taken the same position.[184] Although courts generally look to the course of the litigation to determine whether a suit included a § 1983 claim, a number of state courts that have not required the pleading of § 1983 have nonetheless observed that the "better practice is to specifically plead" reliance on § 1983.[185]

Unlike the refusal of federal and state courts to require specific pleading of § 1983, some federal courts have strictly required plaintiffs to plead whether § 1983 claims are being brought against defendants in their individual or official capacities. The use of such a pleading standard, however, even if occasionally appropriate in federal courts of limited jurisdiction, seems inappropriate in state courts of general jurisdiction.[186]

B. Official Immunities

Section 1983, by its terms, is silent about the availability of any immunities for officials who violate federal law. Nonetheless, the Supreme Court has established an elaborate system of absolute and qualified immunities to protect government officials and employees from personal liability under § 1983. It has done this by reading § 1983 against the background of the common law that existed in 1871. When an immunity was well established at that time, the Court has been unwilling to assume that Congress would have overridden the immunity without expressly providing so.[187]

The immunities applicable to federal court § 1983 claims also apply in state courts, and the Supreme Court, in *Martinez v. California*,[188] held that federal, not state, law governed their availability:

> Conduct by persons acting under color of state law which is wrongful under 42 U.S.C. § 1983 . . . cannot be immunized by state law.

---

184. *See, e.g.,* Gumbhir v. Kansas State Bd. of Pharmacy, 646 P.2d 1078 (Kan. 1982), *cert. denied,* 459 U.S. 1103 (1983); Rzeznik v. Chief of Police of Southampton, 373 N.E.2d 1128, 1134 n.8 (Mass. 1978); L.K. v. Gregg, 425 N.W.2d 813 (Minn. 1988); Marx v. Truck Renting and Leasing Ass'n, 520 So. 2d 1333 (Miss. 1987); Tarkanian v. National Collegiate Athletic Ass'n, 741 P.2d 1345 (Nev. 1987*), rev'd on other grounds,* 488 U.S. 179 (1988); Packard v. Gordon, 537 A.2d 140 (Vt. 1987); Boldt v. State, 305 N.W.2d 133 (Wis.), *cert. denied,* 454 U.S. 973 (1981).

185. *Gumbhir,* 646 P.2d at 1085; *accord Rzeznik,* 373 N.E.2d at 1134 n.8; *L.K.,* 425 N.W.2d at 820.

186. This issue comes up most often in § 1983 suits against state officials. *See infra* notes 283–96 and accompanying text.

187. *See generally* Pierson v. Ray, 386 U.S. 547, 554–55 (1967); Tenney v. Brandhove, 341 U.S. 367, 376 (1951).

188. 444 U.S. 277 (1980).

> A construction of the federal statute which permitted a state immunity defense to have controlling effect would transmute a basic guarantee into an illusory promise; and the [S]upremacy [C]lause of the Constitution insures that the proper construction may be enforced. . . . The immunity claim raises a question of federal law.[189]

State courts have widely accepted the *Martinez* principle. For example, in *Cooperman v. University Surgical Associates*,[190] the Ohio Supreme Court noted that "[i]mmunity, for purposes of a federal claim, is clearly a question of federal law."[191] The Supreme Court, however, has provided only limited guidance on the extent to which, or even whether, states may develop their own policies for the administration of federal immunities.[192] Thus, it is unclear whether state courts entertaining § 1983 claims are required to follow the lead of federal courts and limit discovery, make expanded use of summary judgment, and restrict the role of the jury.

1. Absolute Immunities

The Supreme Court maintains a presumption against absolute immunity and has been "quite sparing" in recognizing it.[193] Most governmental officials, including governors and executive branch officials, have only a qualified immunity from § 1983 damage suits,[194] but some § 1983 defendants may claim an absolute immunity from suit based on the governmental functions they are performing. For example, state legislators have absolute immunity

---

189. *Id.* at 284 n.8 (citations and quotations omitted); *see also* Felder v. Casey, 487 U.S. 131, 139 (1988) ("[A] state law that immunizes government conduct otherwise subject to suit under § 1983 is preempted, even where the federal civil rights litigation takes place in state court, because the application of the state immunity law would thwart the congressional remedy, . . . which of course already provides certain immunities for state officials.").
190. 513 N.E.2d 288 (Ohio 1987).
191. *Id.* at 296.
192. *Cf.* Johnson v. Fankell, 520 U.S. 911 (1997) (holding that states need not provide § 1983 defendants with a right to an interlocutory or nonfinal appeal of a denial of qualified immunity).
193. Burns v. Reed, 500 U.S. 478, 487 (1991) (quoting Forrester v. White, 484 U.S. 219, 224 (1988)).
194. *See* Scheuer v. Rhodes, 416 U.S. 232 (1974); *see also* Harlow v. Fitzgerald, 457 U.S. 800, 807 (1982) (observing that qualified immunity represents the norm for executive officials).

from § 1983 damage and injunctive suits for their legislative acts,[195] as do regional[196] and local legislators.[197] Likewise, state court judges and prosecutors have absolute immunity from § 1983 damage claims involving their judicial or prosecutorial functions.

Absolute immunity, however, is limited. Judges only have absolute immunity from § 1983 damage suits for judicial acts taken within their jurisdiction,[198] and they may be liable for their administrative decisions.[199] They may also be sued under § 1983 for injunctive relief (on claims for which they have an absolute immunity from damage suits), and they are subject to liability for attorneys' fees.[200]

Similarly, prosecutors have absolute quasi-judicial immunity when performing prosecutorial functions intimately associated with the judicial phase of the criminal process,[201] but they are not entitled to absolute immunity for either investigative or other nonprosecutorial activities. [202]

---

195. *See* Tenney v. Brandhove, 341 U.S. 367 (1951); s*ee also* Supreme Court of Virginia v. Consumers Union, 446 U.S. 719, 732 (1980) ("Although *Tenney* involved an action for damages under § 1983, its holding is equally applicable to § 1983 actions seeking declaratory or injunctive relief.").
196. *See* Lake Country Estates, Inc. v. Tahoe Reg'l Planning Agency, 440 U.S. 391 (1979).
197. *See* Bogan v. Scott-Harris, 523 U.S. 44 (1998).
198. *See* Stump v. Sparkman, 435 U.S. 349 (1978) (absolute judicial immunity for ordering sterilization of a "somewhat retarded" fifteen-year-old girl); Pierson v. Ray, 386 U.S. 547 (1967) (absolute judicial immunity for unconstitutionally convicting persons challenging segregated interstate bus terminal facilities).
199. *See* Forrester v. White, 484 U.S. 219 (1988) (no absolute judicial immunity for the nonjudicial administrative act of demoting and dismissing a court-attached probation officer).
200. In Pulliam v. Allen, 466 U.S. 522 (1984), the Supreme Court held that the doctrine of judicial immunity did not preclude suits against state court judges for injunctive relief and the award of attorneys' fees to prevailing parties in such suits against state court judges. In the Federal Courts Improvement Act of 1996, Pub. L. No. 104-317, § 309(c), 110 Stat. 3847 (1996), however, Congress partially limited the availability of injunctive relief in § 1983 actions against judicial officers acting in their judicial capacity to those cases in which judicial officers either violated a declaratory judgment or in which declaratory relief was unavailable. The Act also overruled *Pulliam* by amending 42 U.S.C. § 1988(b) to limit the availability of awards of attorneys' fees. *See infra* note 380.
201. *See* Imbler v. Pachtman, 424 U.S. 409, 430 (1976).
202. *See* Buckley v. Fitzsimmons, 509 U.S. 259 (1993) (denying absolute immunity to prosecutors for fabricating evidence during a preliminary investigation and for making false statements at a press conference announcing the return of an indictment); Burns v. Reed, 500 U.S. 478 (1991) (denying absolute immunity to a prosecutor for providing legal advice to police officers concerning the hypnotizing and questioning of a suspect).

2. *Qualified Immunities*

The Supreme Court has held that public officials who are not entitled to absolute immunity may still be immune from § 1983 damage suits when their performance of discretionary functions violates federal law.[203] In 1975, in *Wood v. Strickland*,[204] the Supreme Court initially defined the § 1983 qualified immunity in both objective and subjective terms. Seven years later, however, in *Harlow v. Fitzgerald*,[205] a *Bivens* action,[206] the Court eliminated the subjective leg and defined qualified immunity in objective terms by asking whether the defendants violated clearly established federal law.[207]

In *Anderson v. Creighton*,[208] the Court held that the determination of whether the law was clearly established required a particularized definition of the issue of federal law that must be clearly established:

> [T]he right the official is alleged to have violated must have been "clearly established" in a more particularized, and hence more relevant, sense: The contours of the right must be sufficiently clear that a reasonable official would understand that what he is doing violates that right. This is not to say that an official action is protected by qualified immunity unless the very action in question has previously been held unlawful, . . . but it is to say that in the light of pre-existing law the unlawfulness must be apparent.[209]

Anderson requires courts addressing qualified immunity issues to define the underlying right with a high degree of particularity, thus expanding the

---

203. *See* Scheuer v. Rhodes, 416 U.S. 232, 246–49 (1974); Pierson v. Ray, 386 U.S. 547, 564 (1967); *cf.* Wyatt v. Cole, 504 U.S. 158 (1992) (holding that private defendants who relied on a state replevin statute subsequently declared unconstitutional were not entitled to an objectively defined qualified immunity).
204. 420 U.S. 308 (1975).
205. 457 U.S. 800 (1982).
206. *Bivens* actions are suits brought against federal officials directly under the federal constitution. *See* Bivens v. Six Unknown Named Agents, 403 U.S. 388 (1971). Many of the Court's most important qualified immunity decisions arose in *Bivens,* not § 1983, actions; but the Court has applied the same immunity policies to both actions. *See Harlow,* 457 U.S. at 818 n.30; Butz v. Economou, 438 U.S. 478, 504 (1978).
207. *Harlow,* 457 U.S. at 818–19 ("If the law was clearly established [at the time the action occurred], the immunity defense ordinarily should fail, since a reasonably competent public official should know the law governing his conduct."); *see also* Davis v. Scherer, 468 U.S. 183 (1984) (holding that federal, not state, law must be clearly established to deny defendants a qualified immunity).
208. 483 U.S. 635 (1987).
209. *Id.* at 640.

utility of qualified immunity for § 1983 defendants.[210] The Court, however, has not provided guidance as to how courts should determine whether federal law is clearly established,[211] and state and federal courts have disagreed as to where they should look to determine whether federal law is clearly established.[212]

3. *Administering the Section 1983 Qualified Immunity*

In the more than two decades since its 1982 decision in *Harlow v. Fitzgerald*,[213] the Court has addressed a range of administrative issues involving qualified immunity, including issues concerning pleading, the sequencing of the decision-making process, discovery, summary judgment, the jury, and interlocutory appeals. The Court's decisions have invariably assumed the litigation of § 1983 actions in the federal courts, and the Court has only once directly addressed the administrative and analytical issues that arise when qualified immunity issues arise in state courts. In *Johnson v. Fankell*,[214] the Court unanimously held that federal law did not require states to permit immediate appeals of denials of qualified immunity. In so ruling, the Court treated the right to an immediate appeal in federal court as not derived from § 1983 but rather as a "federal procedural right that simply does not apply in a nonfederal forum."[215]

The *Fankell* Court also emphasized that the "outcome" it had in mind when it adapted the outcome-determinative test to § 1983 claims in *Felder v. Casey*[216] was the ultimate disposition of the case and not simply some aspect of the litigation. Thus, the *Johnson* Court did not require states to abandon their own neutral jurisdictional policies and permitted states to deny immediate appellate review of trial court decisions rejecting qualified immunity defenses.

---

210. *Cf.* Elliott v. Thomas, 937 F.2d 338, 341 (7th Cir. 1991) ("By sleight of hand you can turn any defense on the merits into a defense of qualified immunity."), *cert. denied*, 502 U.S. 1074 & 1121 (1992).
211. *See generally* Karen M. Blum, *Qualified Immunity: A User's Manual,* 26 IND. L. REV. 187, 203–05 (1993); Kit Kinports, *Qualified Immunity in Section 1983 Cases: The Unanswered Questions,* 23 GA. L. REV. 597, 605 n.41 (1989).
212. For a discussion of the role of state law in determining whether federal law is clearly established, see Richard B. Saphire, *Qualified Immunity in Section § 1983 Cases and the Role of State Decisional Law,* 35 ARIZ. L. REV. 621 (1993).
213. 457 U.S. 800 (1982).
214. 520 U.S. 911 (1997).
215. *Id.* at 921; *see also id.* at 923 n.13 ("We have made it quite clear that it is a matter for each State to decide how to structure its judicial system.")
216. 487 U.S. 131 (1988).

a. Pleading. The Supreme Court has made clear that federal courts may not impose strict or heightened pleading requirements on § 1983 qualified immunity issues.[217] Had the Court taken the bold step and held that federal immunity from trial was "sufficiently" substantive to override the liberal pleading requirements of the federal rules,[218] state court plaintiffs would not be able to resist the argument that federal law also overrode liberal state pleading requirements. However, the rejection of a heightened pleading requirement for federal court § 1983 suits against individuals means that state courts may only apply strict state pleading requirements to § 1983 claims if the application of the state pleading rules does not burden § 1983.[219]

b. Sequencing of decision making. In *Siegert v. Gilley*,[220] a *Bivens* action by a former federal employee involving an alleged deprivation of a liberty interest without due process,[221] the Court stated that "[q]ualified immunity is a defense that must be pleaded by a defendant official"[222] and held that the initial inquiry was not whether the plaintiff alleged a violation of federal law that was clearly established at the time of the defendant's action but whether the plaintiff alleged the violation of any constitutional right at all.[223]

---

217. *See supra* notes 170–74 and accompanying text. For an interesting approach to this issue, however, see the Fifth Circuit Court of Appeals' decisions, calling for the use of a reply procedure from FED. R. CIV. P. 7(a), in Reyes v. Sazan, 168 F.3d 158 (5th Cir. 1999); and Schultea v. Wood, 47 F.3d 1427 (5th Cir. 1995) (en banc).
218. Under 28 U.S.C. § 2072 (2000), the Court may not adopt rules that "abridge, enlarge, or modify any substantive right." This delegation of rule-making to the Court is quite broad, *see* Hanna v. Plummer, 380 U.S. 460 (1965), and the Court has never rejected a federal rule because of a conflict with the substantive law. *See* GENE R. SHREVE & PETER RAVEN-HANSEN, UNDERSTANDING CIVIL PROCEDURE § 7.04[3][b] 186 (3d ed. 2002). The Court, however, has often construed a federal rule narrowly to avoid such a conflict. *See Hanna,* 380 U.S. at 472. Given the relatively recent characterization of the qualified immunity as an immunity from suit, *see* Harlow v. Fitzgerald, 457 U.S. 800 (1982), it is difficult to argue that the drafters of the federal rules did not intend the liberal pleading requirements to apply to suits against public officials.
219. *See supra* notes 146–58 and accompanying text.
220. 500 U.S. 226 (1991).
221. The plaintiff in *Siegert* claimed that his supervisor's writing a defamatory letter deprived him of procedural due process.
222. *Id.* at 231.
223. *Id.* at 233.

Before *Siegert,* federal courts often assumed the existence of a violation of the underlying federal right but disposed of cases on qualified immunity grounds because the federal right was not clearly established.[224] *Siegert* rejected this approach and foreshadowed the Court's approach to the sequencing of the discrete decisions that courts must make in addressing qualified immunity issues. Ultimately, in *Saucier v. Katz*[225] the Court made clear that lower federal courts should first decide whether the plaintiffs had alleged a violation of federal law and only then the issue of whether the plaintiff had alleged the violation of clearly established federal law.[226] When § 1983 cases are being heard in state courts, it is difficult to imagine that federal law governs the order in which state courts must address the various federal issues that are before them.

c. Discovery. In *Harlow v. Fitzgerald,*[227] the Court treated the existence of qualified immunity as a threshold legal issue based on whether the federal right in question was clearly established at the time of the alleged violation.[228] The *Harlow* Court then required federal courts to stay discovery until the threshold issue is resolved.[229]

Despite this preference for resolving qualified immunity issues early in the litigation, the Court, in *Anderson v. Creighton,*[230] opened the door to limited discovery, at least when the immunity issue is fact specific. In *Anderson,* the Court recognized that "the determination whether it was objectively legally reasonable to conclude that [the alleged conduct was legal] . . . will often require examination of the information possessed by" the defendants.[231] "The relevant question . . . is the objective (albeit fact-specific) question whether a reasonable officer could have believed [the defendant's

224. *See, e.g.,* Danese v. Asman, 875 F.2d 1239 (6th Cir. 1989) (not reaching the merits of a § 1983 jail suicide claim because the underlying law was not clearly established), *cert. denied,* 494 U.S. 1027 (1990).

225. 533 U.S. 194 (2001).

226. *But see* Brosseau v. Haugen, 543 U.S. 194 (2004) (per curiam) (disposing of case summarily but on the merits because alleged conduct did not violate clearly established federal law without reviewing whether conduct violated federal law).

227. 457 U.S. 800 (1982).

228. *Id.* at 817–19.

229. *Id.* at 818 ("Until this threshold immunity question is resolved, discovery should not be allowed."); *but cf.* Shilpa Shah, *An Application of Federal Rule of Civil Procedure 26(a)(1) to Section 1983 Actions: Does Rule 26(a)(1) Violate the Rules Enabling Act?* 43 CLEV. ST. L. REV. 115 (1995).

230. 483 U.S. 635 (1987).

231. *Id.* at 641.

conduct] . . . to be lawful, in light of clearly established law and the information the [defendant] . . . possessed. [The defendant's] . . . subjective beliefs . . . are irrelevant."[232] The *Anderson* Court also acknowledged that when the factual allegations of the parties differ, "discovery may be necessary before [the defendant's] . . . motion for summary judgment . . . can be resolved."[233]

It is unclear whether these limitations on discovery apply with equal force to state court § 1983 litigation. Even given the characterization of the § 1983 immunity as an immunity from suit, it is difficult to accept the proposition that federal law requires states to organize their judicial systems to mirror the federal model. Some state court systems might rely heavily on summary judgment and limit discovery, while others might downplay summary judgment, expand discovery, and rely more heavily on trials.[234] While a state that imposed cumulative burdens on the qualified immunity available to individual § 1983 defendants might violate federal law,[235] the interest of states in the administration of their judicial systems may outweigh the relevant federal interest and give state courts some leeway in managing discovery in § 1983 cases.[236]

d. Summary judgment. In redefining qualified immunity, the *Harlow* Court expressly relied on its concern about the difficulty of resolving qualified immunity issues on summary judgment.[237] As with other issues involving the administration of § 1983 qualified immunities, however, it is unclear whether states must follow the federal model or whether they may apply summary judgment standards that place a greater burden on defendants seeking to assert an immunity from suit. Although many state courts have embraced aspects of the federal summary judgment model, it is difficult to imagine federal law requiring state trial courts to make greater use of summary judgment on § 1983 qualified immunity issues than state law otherwise permits.

---

232. *Id.*

233. *Id.* at 646 n.6.

234. States are involved in a number of experiments to make civil litigation more efficient. *See, e.g.*, Robert D. Myers, *MAD Track: An Experiment in Terror*, 25 Ariz. St. L.J. 11 (1993) (discussing Arizona's Mandatory Alternative Discovery Track program for reducing discovery costs and minimizing the time involved in getting civil cases through the system).

235. *See supra* notes 368–78 and accompanying text.

236. *But cf.* Felder v. Casey, 487 U.S. 131, 145 (1988) (rejecting the argument that sound notions of public administration justified the application of a state notice-of-claim requirement to state court § 1983 litigation).

237. *Harlow*, 457 U.S. at 815–18.

e. Role of the jury. The Supreme Court's treatment of qualified immunity as raising an objective legal question in *Harlow* expanded the role of trial court judges at the expense of the jury, but there remains a great deal of confusion over the respective roles of the judge and the jury on qualified immunity issues. In *Hunter v. Bryant*,[238] the Court summarily reversed a Ninth Circuit decision because the lower court had framed the qualified immunity issue for the jury in terms of whether a reasonable officer could have believed there was probable cause to make a warrantless arrest. The *Hunter* Court concluded that this routinely placed the question of qualified immunity in the hands of the jury, whereas "[i]mmunity ordinarily should be decided by the court long before trial" by the court "ask[ing] whether the [defendants] acted reasonably under settled law in the circumstances. . . ."[239]

Federal court judges are responsible for determining what is clearly established federal law for qualified immunity purposes, but some federal courts view qualified immunity as requiring the court to determine not only whether the law was clearly established but also the "objective legal reasonableness of the defendants' conduct."[240] For example, in *Scott v Henrich*[241] the Ninth Circuit treated the standard for analyzing excessive force claims the same as the qualified immunity standard, but it noted that "even though reasonableness traditionally is a question of fact for the jury, . . . defendants can still win on summary judgment if the district court concludes, after resolving all factual disputes in favor of the plaintiff, that the officer's use of force was objectively reasonable under the circumstances."[242]

Hunter does not eliminate the role for juries in performing the fact-finding that is relevant to qualified immunity issues. For example, in *Wash-*

---

238. 502 U.S. 224 (1991) (per curiam).

239. *Id.* at 228.

240. *See, e.g.*, Biddle v. Martin, 992 F.2d 673, 675 (7th Cir. 1993). The *Harlow* Court treated the qualified immunity inquiry as a single question and assumed that if the law was clearly established, a reasonable public official would be aware of this and act accordingly. *See Harlow,* 457 U.S. at 818–19 ("If the law was clearly established, the immunity defense ordinarily should fail, since a reasonably competent public official should know the law governing his conduct.").

241. 39 F.3d 912 (9th Cir. 1994), *cert. denied,* 515 U.S. 1159 (1995).

242. *Id.* at 915; *see also* Feathers v. Aey, 319 F.3d 843, 847–48, 851 (6th Cir. 2003) (asking whether police officers' conduct was objectively unreasonable in light of clearly established federal law); ActUp!/Portland v. Bagley, 988 F.2d 868, 873 (9th Cir. 1993) (modified opinion) (interpreting *Hunter* "to hold that the question of whether a reasonable officer could have believed probable cause (or reasonable suspicion) existed to justify a search or an arrest is 'an essentially legal question,' that should be determined by the district court at the earliest possible point in the litigation").

ington v. Newsom,[243] a case involving the use of deadly force, the Sixth Circuit recognized the factual nature of the qualified immunity question by pointing out that the question of whether an objectively reasonable police officer would have known that the decedent was not armed depended upon the factual question of the precise information possessed by the officers.

Under the practices generally followed in state and federal courts, juries apply the law to the facts.[244] In the area of determining entitlement to qualified immunity, the Court has made clear that the judge, not the jury, is responsible for identifying the clearly established federal law, but the Court has not explained why it has deviated from the prevailing policies that typically govern whether the judge or the jury will be responsible for applying the law to the facts.[245] Nor has the Court explained how either the Seventh Amendment or sound principles of judicial administration support giving federal trial judges responsibility for determining whether § 1983 defendants acted reasonably in violating clearly established federal law.

Even assuming that federal court judges, not juries, are responsible for determining whether § 1983 defendants acted unreasonably in failing to follow federal law, states may not be precluded by federal law from following their traditional practices in allocating decision-making authority between judges and juries,[246] and a number of state courts appear to treat the question of whether the defendant acted reasonably in light of the applicable legal principles as raising a factual issue for the jury.[247]

---

243. 977 F.2d 991 (6th Cir. 1992), *cert. denied,* 507 U.S. 1031 (1993).

244. *See generally* W. PAGE KEETON ET AL., PROSSER AND KEETON ON THE LAW OF TORTS § 37, at 235–38 (5th ed. 1984) (discussing the functions of the court and the jury in negligence cases); *see also* FLEMING JAMES, JR. ET AL., CIVIL PROCEDURE § 7.18, at 353–56 (4th ed. 1992) (discussing the role of the jury in assessing the legal consequences of the facts).

245. *See Bagley,* 988 F.2d at 874 (Norris, J., dissenting) (dissenting from failure to rehear case en banc) (describing the panel opinion as "def[ying] our common law tradition, which since time immemorial has considered the reasonableness of human conduct to be a quintessential jury question").

246. *But cf.* Dice v. Akron, Canton & Youngstown R.R., 342 U.S. 359 (1952) (treating the allocation of responsibility between judge and jury as a matter of federal law in a state court FELA action).

247. *See, e.g.*, Carroll v. Robinson, 874 P.2d 1010 (Ariz. Ct. App. 1994) (treating the question of whether the legal right allegedly violated was clearly established as a question of law, but treating the question of whether a reasonable official would know that he or she was violating that clearly established law as a question for the jury); Fulwood v. Porter, 639 A.2d 594, 599 (D.C. 1994) (noting that in cases where qualified immunity is asserted, the factual circumstances necessary to decide the immunity issue should be presented to the jury, but the court should decide the

f. Interlocutory appeals. Under the final judgment rule[248] federal appellate courts, with limited statutory exceptions not relevant here,[249] have jurisdiction only over appeals from final decisions of district courts. There is, however, a judicially developed collateral order exception to the final judgment rule, and in *Cohen v. Beneficial Industrial Loan Corporation*[250] the Supreme Court permitted the immediate appeal of district court decisions that fall within "that small class which finally determine claims of right separable from, and collateral to, rights asserted in the action, too important to be denied review and too independent of the cause itself to require that appellate consideration be deferred until the whole case is adjudicated."[251] The Court has applied this collateral order exception to the *immunity from suit* provided by absolute and qualified immunity,[252] and individual § 1983 defendants[253] may immediately appeal trial court decisions denying them either type of immunity.[254]

---

purely legal issue of whether a right was clearly established, but in "failure to act" cases, the issues are inseparable, and therefore, "the question . . . of whether [the defendant–police chief] violated clearly established rights of which he should have known—the immunity issue—and the question whether he exhibited deliberate indifference to the violation of constitutional rights by street-level officers—the liability issue—are effectively the same"); Lee v. Greene, 442 S.E.2d 547 (N.C. Ct. App. 1994) (holding that highway patrol officers did not violate clearly established rights in entering arrestee's house to make an arrest, but that genuine issues of historical fact respecting the officers' conduct or its reasonableness under the circumstances precluded summary judgment on the issue of whether highway patrol officers were entitled to qualified immunity on a § 1983 excessive force claim).

248. 28 U.S.C. § 1291 (2000) ("The courts of appeals . . . shall have jurisdiction of appeals from all final decisions of the district courts of the United States. . . .").

249. *See, e.g.*, 28 U.S.C. § 1292(a)(1) (2000) (permitting interlocutory appeals from orders granting or denying preliminary injunctions); 28 U.S.C. § 1292(b) (2000) (permitting interlocutory appeals from otherwise nonappealable orders certified as involving controlling questions of law).

250. 337 U.S. 541 (1949).

251. *Id.* at 546.

252. *See* Mitchell v. Forsyth, 472 U.S. 511, 530 (1985) (construing 28 U.S.C. § 1291 to permit immediate appeals of the "denial of a claim of qualified immunity, to the extent that it turns on an issue of law"); *see also* Nixon v. Fitzgerald, 457 U.S. 731, 742–43 (1982) (permitting immediate appeal of denials of absolute immunity).

253. Municipalities, on the other hand, are not entitled to an immediate appeal of federal trial court decisions forcing them to go to trial. *See* Swint v. Chambers County Comm'n, 514 U.S. 35, 43 (1995); *but see* Puerto Rico Aqueduct and Sewer Auth. v. Metcalf & Eddy, Inc., 506 U.S. 139 (1993) (permitting immediate appeals by defendants claiming an Eleventh Amendment immunity from suit in federal court).

254. *But cf.* Johnson v. Jones, 515 U.S. 304 (1995) (denying immediate appeals of fact-based decisions rejecting the availability of qualified immunity).

State courts had been sharply divided on whether federal law requires states to provide an immediate appeal of trial court denials of qualified or absolute immunity,[255] but the Supreme Court in *Johnson v. Fankell*[256] unanimously held that federal law did not require such immediate appeals.[257] Nonetheless, many state courts continue to follow the federal model and provide immediate appeals to defendants who have been denied qualified immunity.[258]

C. Municipal Liability

In *Monroe v. Pape*,[259] the Supreme Court held that cities were not "persons" within the meaning of § 1983 and thus were not amenable to suit. In *Monell v. Department of Social Services*,[260] however, the Court reversed this aspect of *Monroe* and held that cities could be sued under § 1983, but the Court rejected respondeat superior as a basis for liability.[261] Nonetheless, municipalities and other units of local government may be liable under § 1983 for violations of federal rights when the challenged actions are (1) based on official policies made by the municipality's lawmakers,[262] (2) taken by other official policymakers,[263] (3) the result of inadequate training or other policies that reflect a deliberate indifference to the constitutional rights of persons with whom municipal employees come into contact,[264] or (4) part of

---

255. *See* STEINGLASS, SECTION 1983 LITIGATION IN STATE COURTS, *supra* note 24, at § 8:19.
256. 520 U.S. 911 (1997).
257. *See supra* notes 214–16 and accompanying text for a discussion of *Johnson.*
258. *See* STEINGLASS, SECTION 1983 LITIGATION IN STATE COURTS, *supra* note 24, at § 8:19.
259. 365 U.S. 167 (1961).
260. 436 U.S. 658 (1978).
261. *Id.* at 691 ("[A] municipality cannot be held liable *solely* because it employs a tortfeasor—or, in other words, a municipality cannot be held liable under § 1983 on a *respondeat superior* theory.").
262. *Id.* at 694.
263. *See* Jett v. Dallas Indep. Sch. Dist., 491 U.S. 701, 737–38 (1989); *see also* City of St. Louis v. Praprotnik, 485 U.S. 112 (1988); Pembaur v. City of Cincinnati, 475 U.S. 469 (1986).
264. *See* City of Canton v. Harris, 489 U.S. 378 (1989). A single unconstitutional act by a municipal employee, standing alone, may not be the basis for inferring an improper training policy. *See* City of Oklahoma City v. Tuttle, 471 U.S. 808 (1985). However, when combined with sufficient evidence of inadequate policies of training or supervision, a single act may be the basis for imposing § 1983 liability on a municipality. *See id.,* 471 U.S. at 821–22; *cf. Pembaur,* 475 U.S at 480 ("[I]t is plain that [§ 1983] municipal liability may be imposed for a single decision by municipal policymakers under appropriate circumstances.").

the custom or practice of the municipality.[265] In all cases, however, there must be a causal connection between the action or inaction of the municipality and the resulting injury.[266]

The Supreme Court treats "the identification of those officials whose decisions represent the official policy of the local governmental unit . . . [as] a legal question to be resolved by the trial judge *before* the case is submitted to the jury."[267] The determination of who is an official policymaker may involve not only an analysis of "state and local positive law" *but also* "custom or usage having the force of law."[268] Although the Supreme Court apparently expects federal judges to do whatever fact-finding is necessary to identify the official policymakers, state courts may have more authority to assign such fact-finding to the jury.

Unlike individual governmental employees, municipalities and other political subdivisions cannot claim a qualified immunity under § 1983.[269] As a result, § 1983 plaintiffs often join municipalities or other governmental entities to assure the presence of a defendant that lacks an immunity and is capable of satisfying a judgment. The joinder of political subdivisions in § 1983 suits, however, can complicate § 1983 litigation, especially when entity liability is based either on inadequate training or supervision or on the existence of a custom.[270]

Plaintiffs may sometimes avoid these difficulties in states that permit suits to be brought directly against political subdivisions based on respon-

---

265. *See* Bordanaro v. McLeod, 871 F.2d 1151 (1st Cir.), *cert. denied,* 493 U.S. 820 (1989); Leach v. Shelby County Sheriff, 891 F.2d 1241, 1246–48 (6th Cir. 1989), *cert. denied,* 495 U.S. 932 (1990).

266. *See* Jett, 491 U.S at 737 ("Once those officials who have the power to make official policy on a particular issue have been identified, it is for the jury to determine whether *their* decisions have caused the deprivation of rights at issue. . . ."); *see also* Board of Comm'rs of Bryan County v. Brown, 520 U.S. 397 (1997) (requiring a strong causal connection between deliberately indifferent hiring policies and the resulting injury).

267. *Jett,* 491 U.S. at 737.

268. *Id.* (internal quotations omitted) (quoting *Praprotnik,* 485 U.S. at 124 n.1).

269. *See* Owen v. City of Independence, 445 U.S. 622 (1980); *see also* Berkley v. Common Council of the City of Charleston, 63 F.3d 295 (4th Cir. 1995) (en banc) (rejecting argument that municipalities are immune from suit under § 1983 for legislative decisions), *cert. denied,* 516 U.S. 1073 (1996).

270. Section 1983 claims against governmental entities often represent a case within a case and can significantly lengthen and complicate a trial. Thus, a number of federal judges bifurcate § 1983 claims and hear the claims against the individual defendants first. *See generally* Douglas L. Colbert, *Bifurcation of Civil Rights Defendants: Undermining* Monell *in Police Brutality Cases,* 44 HASTINGS L.J. 499 (1993).

deat superior or that maintain liberal indemnification policies under which judgments against employees are paid by the governmental entity.[271]

D. Suits Against States

Cities and other units of local government are "persons" for purposes of suit under § 1983, but in *Will v. Michigan Department of State Police*[272] the Supreme Court held that states are not. Thus, the Court immunized states from § 1983 suits in state courts.[273]

Federal, not state, law, however, governs whether a political subdivision must be considered the state for purposes of § 1983; and in *Howlett v. Rose*,[274] the Court held that local school boards in Florida were subject to suit under § 1983 in the Florida state courts.[275]

Even before *Will*, unconsenting states could not be sued in federal court under § 1983 because of the Eleventh Amendment.[276] State officials, however, have long been subject to § 1983 official capacity suits in federal court for prospective injunctive relief even though such relief really runs against the state.[277] *Will* made clear that § 1983 was equally available in state courts for suits against state officials for prospective injunctive relief,[278] and state courts have recognized this.[279]

---

271. *See, e.g.*, Hibma v. Odegaard, 769 F.2d 1147 (7th Cir. 1985) (construing WIS. STAT. ANN. § 895.46); Cameron v. City of Milwaukee, 307 N.W.2d 164 (Wis. 1981) (same); *see generally* STEINGLASS, SECTION 1983 LITIGATION IN STATE COURTS, *supra* note 24, at § 15:16.
272. 491 U.S. 58 (1989).
273. In rejecting the availability of § 1983 as a basis for obtaining relief against the state in state courts, the *Will* Court imported the distinctions used in federal court for purposes of the Eleventh Amendment into the definition of "person" under § 1983. *See Will*, 491 U.S. at 66–67 ("[I]n deciphering congressional intent as to the scope of § 1983, the scope of the Eleventh Amendment is a consideration, and we decline to adopt a reading of § 1983 that disregards it.").
274. 496 U.S. 356 (1990).
275. *See also* Blades v. Woods, 667 A.2d 917 (Md. Ct. App. 1995) (rejecting the argument that the Baltimore City Police Department is a state agency for purposes of § 1983).
276. *See* Quern v. Jordan, 440 U.S. 332 (1979).
277. *See generally* Edelman v. Jordan, 415 U.S. 651 (1974); *cf. Ex parte* Young, 209 U.S. 123 (1908) (creating a fiction under which state officers could be sued for injunctive relief directly under the constitution despite the Eleventh Amendment).
278. 491 U.S. at 71 n.10 ("Of course a state official in his or her official capacity, when sued for injunctive relief, would be a person under § 1983 because 'official-capacity actions for prospective relief are not treated as actions against the State.'").
279. *See generally* STEINGLASS, SECTION 1983 LITIGATION IN STATE COURTS, *supra* note 24, at § 15:17.

E. Suits Against State Officials

In contrast to the availability of § 1983 suits seeking prospective injunctive relief against state officials, § 1983 is not available in official capacity damage actions against state officials. Nonetheless, in *Hafer v. Melo*[280] the Supreme Court held that state officials were subject to personal liability in individual capacity § 1983 damage claims for acts taken as part of their official duties.

The implications that flow from the characterization of a § 1983 damage suit against a state official as an individual or official capacity suit are significant. State officials have a potential qualified immunity in individual capacity damage suits, and neither state nor federal courts may entertain official capacity damage claims against state officials.[281] Therefore, a threshold question in any § 1983 suit naming a state official is the determination of the capacity in which the official is sued.[282]

When plaintiffs fail to state clearly the capacity in which they are bringing § 1983 damage suits against state officials, most federal courts look to the "course of proceedings" to determine whether the suit is a permissible individual capacity suit or an impermissible official capacity suit.[283] The Eighth Circuit, on the other hand, has adopted a bright-line test under which it treats complaints that do not specify the capacity in which defendants are

---

280. 502 U.S. 21 (1991).

281. In federal court, state officials can avoid such suits by relying on their Eleventh Amendment immunity from official capacity damage suits, while in state court they can rely on the Court's limited definition as to who is a "person" under § 1983.

282. Similar issues arise in § 1983 suits against local governmental officials. Such individual capacity defendants, like state officials, may assert a qualified or an absolute immunity, but local governments do not share that immunity. *See supra* note 269. Because an official capacity § 1983 suit against a local governmental official is really another way of naming the entity, *see* Brandon v. Holt, 469 U.S. 464 (1985), the entity may not claim an immunity. On the other hand, to prevail in an official capacity § 1983 damage suit against a local governmental official, a § 1983 plaintiff must meet *Monell* standards and prove that an official policy of the entity caused the deprivation of federal law. *See supra* notes 260–68 and accompanying text.

283. *See* Powell v. Alexander, 391 F.3d 1, 22 (1st Cir. 2004) (noting that "the other circuits have, with virtual unanimity, adopted the 'course of proceedings' test as the better approach"); *see also* Moore v. City of Harriman, 272 F.3d 769, 772 (6th Cir. 2001) (en banc), *cert. denied,* 536 U.S. 922 (2002); Miller v. Smith, 220 F.3d 491, 494 (7th Cir. 2000); Melo v. Hafer, 912 F.2d 628, 635 (3d Cir. 1990), *aff'd on other grounds,* 502 U.S. 21, 24 n.* (1991).

sued as official capacity suits, [284] and the Sixth Circuit, until recently,[285] agreed with the Eighth Circuit and went so far as to treat the capacity issue as jurisdictional in cases against state officials.[286]

The Supreme Court did not reach the pleading issue in *Hafer*[287] and thus did not decide whether the Third Circuit acted properly in looking to the proceedings below to determine whether the § 1983 damage suit was brought against the state official in her official or her personal capacity.[288] Nonetheless, the *Hafer* Court agreed with the Third Circuit's observation that "[i]t is obviously preferable for the plaintiff to be specific in the first instance to avoid any ambiguity."[289]

Despite the Supreme Court's failure to reach this issue and its obvious preference for clarity in pleading, the Court has approached the issue of determining the capacity in which a § 1983 suit has been brought by looking to the course of the proceedings.[290] Moreover, the Court's willingness to permit the *Hafer* suit to go forward suggests that the pleading of individual capacity is not jurisdictional.

A policy treating capacity as jurisdictional, even if proper for suits against state officials in federal court, is inapplicable to state court § 1983

---

284. Nix v. Norman, 879 F.2d 429, 431 (8th Cir. 1989).

285. *See* Rodgers v. Banks, 344 F.3d 587 (6th Cir. 2003) (construing en banc decision in *Moore v. City of Harriman, supra,* as requiring the application of the "course of proceeding" approach even in § 1983 actions against state officials).

286. *See* Wells v. Brown, 891 F.2d 591, 592 (6th Cir. 1989) ("[B]ecause the Eleventh Amendment places a jurisdictional limit on federal courts in civil rights cases against states and state employees, we understand Rule 9(a) to *require* plaintiffs to properly allege capacity in their complaint."); *but see* Moore v. City of Harriman, *supra* (adopting a "course of proceedings" approach without expressly overruling *Wells*).

287. *See Hafer,* 502 U.S. at 24 n.*.

288. *See* Melo v. Hafer, 912 F.2d 628, 635–36 (3d Cir. 1990), *aff'd,* 502 U.S. 21 (1991). Other circuits following this approach and cited by the Court are Conner v. Reinhard, 847 F.2d 384, 394 n.8 (7th Cir.), *cert. denied,* 488 U.S. 856 (1988); Houston v. Reich, 932 F.2d 883, 885 (10th Cir. 1991); Lundgren v. McDaniel, 814 F.2d 600, 603–04 (11th Cir. 1987). The Court cited the Sixth and Eighth Circuit decisions in *Wells* and Nix v. Norman, 879 F.2d 429, 431 (8th Cir. 1989), as imposing more rigid pleading requirements.

289. *See Hafer,* 502 U.S. at 24 n.* (quoting 912 F.2d at 636 n.7).

290. *See* Kentucky v. Graham, 473 U.S. 159, 167 n.14 (1985) (observing that "[i]n many cases, the complaint will not clearly specify whether officials are sued personally, in their official capacity, or both. 'The course of proceedings' in such cases typically will indicate the nature of the liability sought to be imposed.") (quoting Brandon v. Holt, 469 U.S. 464, 469 (1985)).

claims. In *Carrillo v. State*,[291] the leading state court case addressing the construction of § 1983 complaints that are ambiguous as to the capacity in which individuals are being sued, the Arizona Court of Appeals recognized the "important repercussions" of treating a § 1983 suit as a personal capacity as contrasted to an official capacity suit.[292] Nonetheless, the court rejected a requirement that plaintiffs plead that they are suing a defendant in his or her personal or individual capacity.[293]

Viewing the strict pleading approach as derived, in part, from the jurisdictional requirements of the Eleventh Amendment, the Arizona court refused to impose such a requirement on state court § 1983 plaintiffs:

> [A] plaintiff should allege specifically the capacity in which he is suing the official. Such specificity both relieves courts from the difficulty inherent in interpreting an ambiguous complaint and gives the defendant clear notice of his possible personal liability for damages. We decline to hold, however, that failure to allege specifically official or personal capacity will be the death knell of a § 1983 action or that an allegation of capacity, standing alone, is determinative of this issue. Such a conclusion would result in a harsh elevation of form over substance.[294]

Instead, the court applied an "interpretive" approach, which it found supported by the Supreme Court's decision in *Brandon v. Holt*.[295] Following this approach, the state court reviewed the pleadings and the course of the proceedings to determine that the case before it was a § 1983 personal capacity suit.[296]

---

291. 817 P.2d 493 (Ariz. Ct. App. 1991).
292. The court defined the "repercussions" as follows:

> The plaintiff in a § 1983 action can recover monetary damages, including punitive damages, only against a defendant named in his personal capacity. Balanced against that right of recovery, however, is the right of a defendant named in his personal capacity to assert a defense of qualified or absolute immunity, a defense not available to one named in his official capacity.

293. 817 P.2d at 496–497.
294. *Id.* at 497. The court *also* relied on Ariz. R. Civ. P. 9(a), which limits required allegations of capacity to those going to jurisdiction. *Id.* at 497 n.3. *But cf.* Ashton v. Brown, 660 A.2d 447, 468 (Md. 1995) (distinguishing *Hafer* from suits against local governmental officials, who cannot claim an Eleventh Amendment immunity from official capacity suits, and refusing to treat § 1983 claims against the latter as individual capacity claims when they relate to actions taken to implement governmental law, policy, or custom).
295. 469 U.S. 464, 469 (1985).
296. *Carrillo,* 817 P.2d at 497.

F. Damages

1. Compensatory Damages

In *Carey v. Piphus*,[297] the Supreme Court looked to the federal principle of compensation as the source of a uniform § 1983 damage policy that would not vary from state to state. The Court also made clear that § 1983 damages are not limited to those available in 1871, when the predecessor to § 1983 was enacted, but are based on evolving federal standards.[298] Finally, the Court rejected the availability of presumed damages for procedural due process violations.[299]

Under federal principles, a broad range of damages may be awarded in § 1983 cases,[300] including damages for mental and emotional distress.[301] In *Memphis Community School District v. Stachura*,[302] however, the Court rejected the availability of presumed damages to supplement § 1983 damage awards but permitted such damages as a substitute when traditional damages are difficult to prove.[303] Thus, in the typical § 1983 case, a plaintiff may not recover damages for the value of the constitutional right itself.

The damage policies in § 1983 actions are based on the common law but are not dependent upon the law of the forum state.[304] For example, the Sixth Circuit has held that the federal doctrine of joint and several liability

---

297. 435 U.S. 247 (1978).

298. *Id.* at 257–59.

299. *Id.* at 260–64.

300. State law, on the other hand, governs the survival of § 1983 claims, *see* Robertson v. Wegmann, 436 U.S. 584 (1978), and the damage policies applicable to § 1983 survival and wrongful death claims, unlike the typical § 1983 damages policies, involve a certain amount of borrowing from the law of the forum state. For a detailed discussion of § 1983 survival and wrongful death issues, see Steven H. Steinglass, *Wrongful Death Actions and Section 1983*, 60 IND. L.J. 559 (1985) [hereinafter Steinglass, *Wrongful Death Actions*]; *see also* STEINGLASS, SECTION 1983 LITIGATION IN STATE COURTS, *supra* note 24, at ch. 21.

301. *Carey*, 435 U.S. at 263 & 264 n.20.

302. 477 U.S. 299 (1986).

303. *Id.* at 310–11.

304. *See* Basista v. Weir, 340 F.2d 74, 86 (3d Cir. 1965) ("We believe that the benefits of the [Civil Rights] Acts were intended to be uniform throughout the United States, that the protection to the individual to be afforded by them was not intended by Congress to differ from state to state, and that the amount of damages to be recovered by the injured individual was not to vary because of the law of the state in which the federal court suit was brought.").

applies to § 1983 claims.[305] Likewise, most federal courts apply a federal, not a state, collateral source doctrine to determine whether reductions should be made to § 1983 damage awards.[306] State courts have generally followed federal policies to determine the damage policies applicable to § 1983 claims.[307]

2. *Punitive Damages—Generally*

Punitive damages are available in federal court § 1983 litigation when defendants act intentionally or with reckless or callous disregard for plaintiffs' rights.[308] Furthermore, under federal common-law principles, punitive damages are available against individual defendants even absent actual damages,[309] and it is the responsibility of the jury to determine eligibility for and amount of punitive damages under the traditional civil burden of proof:

---

305. Weeks v. Chaboudy, 984 F.2d 185, 188–89 (6th Cir. 1993) (holding that there is a federal rule of joint and several liability in § 1983 cases and reversing the apportionment of liability for compensatory damages among the defendant and other prison personnel who were not parties to the action).
306. *See* Linda L. House, *Section 1983 and the Collateral Source Rule,* 40 CLEV. ST. L. REV. 101, 112–13 (1992).
307. *See, e.g.*, Sundholm v. City of Bettendorf, 389 N.W.2d 849 (Iowa 1986) (following federal law to permit punitive damages under § 1983 despite the absence of actual damages); Janda v. City of Detroit, 437 N.W.2d 326 (Mich. Ct. App. 1989) (applying federal standards to affirm a § 1983 award of punitive damages despite the unavailability of punitive damages for punishment under state law); Rogers v. Saylor, 760 P.2d 232 (Or. 1988) (rejecting the application of the $100,000 damage ceiling of the Oregon Tort Claims Act and the immunity of governmental employees from awards of punitive damages to § 1983 actions); Orr v. Crowder, 315 S.E.2d 593 (W. Va. 1983) (following federal law to uphold a § 1983 damages award for mental anguish absent physical injury), *cert. denied,* 469 U.S. 981 (1984); Thompson v. Village of Hales Corners, 340 N.W.2d 704 (Wis. 1983) (holding that the state $25,000 damage ceiling on municipal liability does not apply to § 1983 actions under principles of federal law).
308. *See* Smith v. Wade, 461 U.S. 30, 51 (1983) ("[R]eckless or callous disregard for the plaintiff's rights, as well as intentional violations of federal law, should be sufficient to trigger a jury's consideration of the appropriateness of punitive damages."); *cf.* State Farm Mut. Auto. Ins. Co. v. Campbell, 538 U.S. 408 (2003) (holding that as a matter of substantive due process the reprehensibility of the defendant's conduct is the most important factor in determining the amount of punitive damages).
309. *See* King v. Macri, 993 F.2d 294, 297 (2d Cir. 1993); Erwin v. County of Manitowoc, 872 F.2d 1292, 1299 (7th Cir. 1989); Wilson v. Taylor, 658 F.2d 1021, 1023 (5th Cir. 1981); Basista v. Weir, 340 F.2d 74, 87–88 (3d Cir. 1965).

the preponderance of the evidence standard.[310] Municipalities, however, are not subject to § 1983 claims for punitive damages.[311]

A number of states have limited the availability of punitive damages by requiring the showing of actual malice[312] or by requiring the plaintiff to satisfy the state's clear and convincing standard of proof.[313] A few states have reduced the role of the jury by limiting the inquiry to determining whether the plaintiff is entitled to an award of punitive damages but leaving determination of the amount of any award to the judge.[314]

The Supreme Court has not directly addressed what damages are available when § 1983 cases are heard in state courts, but the damages available in § 1983 actions are part of the federal definition of the § 1983 cause of action.[315] Consequently, state courts have generally relied upon uniform federal, not state, policies to determine the punitive damages policies applicable to § 1983 claims.[316]

---

310. *See* Bird v. Figel, 725 F. Supp. 406 (N.D. Ind. 1989); *cf. Karnes v. SCI Colorado Funeral Servs. Inc.*, 162 F.3d 1077 (10th Cir. 1998) (holding that the preponderance of the evidence standard is the proper standard for determining whether to award punitive damages under Title VII of the 1964 Civil Rights Act and rejecting the Colorado beyond a reasonable doubt standard).
311. *See* City of Newport v. Fact Concerts, Inc., 453 U.S. 247 (1981). The Court in *Fact Concerts* left a small opening for the award of punitive damages against municipalities under § 1983 in an "extreme situation where the taxpayers are directly responsible for perpetrating an outrageous abuse of constitutional rights." *Id.* at 267 n.29. Courts have generally rejected the availability of § 1983 punitive damage awards against municipalities even in egregious circumstances. *See* STEINGLASS, SECTION 1983 LITIGATION IN STATE COURTS, *supra* note 24, at § 16:6.
312. *See, e.g.,* OHIO REV. CODE ANN. § 2315.21(C)(1) (LexisNexis 2005) (requiring showing of "malice or aggravated or egregious fraud").
313. *See* Pacific Mut. Life Ins. Co. v. Haslip, 499 U.S. 1, 23 n.11 (1991) (citing and speaking favorably of state statutes that require a higher burden of proof for punitive damages awards).
314. *See, e.g.*, KAN. STAT. ANN § 60-3702 (1994); Ohio Rev. Code Ann. § 2315.21(C) (Anderson 1991). The Ohio statute was repealed in response to the Ohio Supreme Court decision in Zoppo v. Homestead Ins. Co., 644 N.E.2d 397 (Ohio 1984). *See* 2001 Ohio Laws, S. 108, § 2.2 & 3.
315. *See supra* notes 136–41 and accompanying text.
316. *See, e.g.*, Porter v. City of Manchester, 849 A.2d 103, 120 (2004) (noting that "[i]t is well-established that 'a jury [is] permitted to assess punitive damages in an action under § 1983 when the defendant's conduct is shown to be motivated by evil motive or intent, or when it involves reckless or callous indifference to the federally protected rights of others.'") (citing Smith v. Wade, 461 U.S. 30, 56 (1983)); *see also* Booze v. City of Alexandria, 637 So.2d 91 (La. 1994) (overturning earlier decision and holding that punitive damages are recoverable in § 1983 suits filed in Louisiana courts).

The Court, however, has provided some indirect guidance on the standard of proof for awarding punitive damages under § 1983 in state courts. In *Price Waterhouse v. Hopkins*,[317] the Court characterized the preponderance of the evidence standard as the traditional civil burden of proof, and in *American Dredging Co. v. Miller*,[318] the Court characterized a 1942 maritime case (that arose in the state courts) as having treated the burden of proof on the validity of releases as "'inher[ing] in . . . [the] cause of action,'" as "'part of the very substance of . . . [the] claim'" and not "'a mere incident of a form of procedure.'"[319] Moreover, federal courts entertaining diversity actions treat the burden of proof as part of the definition of the element of damages and apply state policies under the *Erie* doctrine.[320]

Until recently, the Supreme Court of Colorado applied the state's unusual "beyond a reasonable doubt" burden of proof to § 1983 claims for punitive damages.[321] The better view, however, is that the available damages are part of the § 1983 remedy and that state courts entertaining § 1983 claims are required to provide the full range of damages that are available under federal standards, and in *Community Hospital v. Fail*[322] the Colorado court expressly overruled its earlier decision and rejected the application of the "beyond a reasonable doubt" standard to § 1983 punitive damage claims. Instead, the court held that the proper standard to be applied in state *and* federal courts to claims under § 1983 is the federal preponderance of the evidence standard.[323]

Because the burden of proof is bound up with the element of damages, state courts entertaining § 1983 claims should apply the traditional preponderance of the evidence burden of proof rather than the state clear and convincing standard to punitive damage claims.[324] Moreover, the use of

---

317. 490 U.S. 228, 235 (1989) (noting that "parties to civil litigation need only prove their case by a preponderance of the evidence").
318. 510 U.S. 443 (1994).
319. *Id.* at 454 (quoting Garrett v. Moore-McCormack Co., 317 U.S. 239, 249 (1942)).
320. *See, e.g.,* Mattison v. Dallas Carrier Corp., 947 F.2d 95 (4th Cir. 1991); Galjour v. General American Tank Car Corp., 764 F. Supp. 1093 (E.D. La. 1991); *cf.* Palmer v. Hoffman, 318 U.S. 109, 117 (1943) (holding that the burden of proof in diversity cases is allocated according to state law).
321. *See* Boulder Valley Sch. Dist. R-2 v. Price, 805 P.2d 1085 (Colo. 1991).
322. 969 P.2d 667 (Colo. 1998).
323. *Accord* Nelson v. Emerald People's Util. Dist., 862 P.2d 1293 (Or. 1993) (refusing to apply the state clear and convincing standard to a § 1983 claim); Janda v. City of Detroit, 437 N.W.2d 326 (Mich. Ct. App. 1989) (same).
324. *See* Steinglass, Section 1983 Litigation in State Courts, *supra* note 24, at § 16:6.

"outcome determinative" state policies to govern the availability of punitive damages in state court § 1983 litigation is inconsistent with the federal interest in "intra-state uniformity" and the "reverse-*Erie*" principle that the Supreme Court applied to state court § 1983 cases in *Felder v. Casey*.[325]

3. Punitive Damages and Jury Trials

In *Feltner v. Columbia Pictures Television, Inc.*,[326] the Supreme Court held that the Seventh Amendment required the jury to determine the *amount* of statutory damages. *Feltner* was a copyright infringement case, but its significance for § 1983 litigation is the Court's holding that the traditional question of the amount of damages is an issue for the jury even when the cause of action is statutory. Federal courts entertaining § 1983 cases have recognized that the Seventh Amendment gives the jury responsibility for determining both eligibility for punitive damages and the amount of such damages.[327]

The Seventh Amendment is not applicable to state courts,[328] but federal statutory causes of action often have their own jury trial guarantees.[329] In *City of Monterey v. Del Monte Dunes at Monterey, Ltd.*,[330] however, the Supreme Court held that there is no statutory right to trial by jury in § 1983 cases. Therefore, neither the U.S. Constitution nor § 1983 prevents state

---

325. 487 U.S. 131 (1988); *see also supra* notes 159–65 and accompanying text.
326. 523 U.S. 340 (1998).
327. *See* Morgan v. Woessner, 997 F.2d 1244, 1258–59 (9th Cir. 1993), *cert. dismissed,* 510 U.S. 1033 (1994); *see also* McKinnon v. City of Berwyn, 750 F.2d 1383, 1392 (7th Cir. 1984) (reversing a district court's remittitur of punitive damages, without option of a new trial, in a § 1983 case, and noting that the "Seventh Amendment reserves the determination of damages, in jury trials within its scope, to the jury"); *cf.* Hetzel v. Prince William County, 523 U.S. 208 (1998) (per curiam) (limiting the role of federal appellate courts in second-guessing juries on the amount of damages and holding that a decision reducing damages was in the nature of a remittitur thus entitling the plaintiff to a new trial); Defender Indus., Inc. v. Northwestern Mut. Life Ins. Co., 938 F.2d 502, 507 (4th Cir. 1991) (en banc) ("An assessment by a jury of the amount of punitive damages is an inherent and fundamental element of the common-law right to trial by jury."); *but cf.* Tull v. United States, 481 U.S. 412 (1987) (holding that the Seventh Amendment does not guarantee a jury trial to assess civil penalties under a federal statute).
328. *See* Walker v. Sauvinet, 92 U.S. 90 (1875).
329. *See, e.g.,* Civil Rights Act of 1991, Pub. L. No. 102-166, §102, 105 Stat. 1071, 1072–73 (1991) (creating a new cause of action for intentional employment discrimination, 42 U.S.C. §1981A, under which the right to trial by jury extends to any party in a case in which "a complaining party seeks compensatory or punitive damages").
330. 526 U.S. 687 (1999).

courts from denying the jury a role in determining eligibility for (or the amount of) punitive damages in § 1983 cases.[331]

G. No-Exhaustion Policy

In *Patsy v. Board of Regents*[332] the Supreme Court applied a general no-exhaustion policy to § 1983 actions and held that § 1983 plaintiffs need not exhaust state administrative remedies. A number of state courts, however, initially viewed the *Patsy* no-exhaustion policy as applicable only in federal courts,[333] but in *Felder v. Casey*[334] the Court applied the no-exhaustion policy to state court § 1983 actions in the course of holding that state courts could not apply notice-of-claim requirements to § 1983 claims. Most state courts have recognized that *Felder* goes beyond notice-of-claim requirements and construed it to bar the use of exhaustion of administrative remedy requirements in state court § 1983 litigation.[335]

The *Patsy-Felder* no-exhaustion policy must be contrasted with *Parratt v. Taylor*.[336] In *Parratt* the Court held that in cases involving random and unauthorized actions, states can meet their obligation to provide procedural due process by having adequate post-deprivation remedies.[337] *Parratt*, however, does not impose an exhaustion requirement with which plaintiffs must comply before filing § 1983 suits. Rather, it is an interpretation of the requirements of procedural due process and a recognition that in limited circumstances in which it is not feasible to provide pre-deprivation reme-

---

331. Some states, however, prohibit limitations on the jury under their state constitutions. *See, e.g.*, Zoppo v. Homestead Insurance Co., 644 N.E.2d 397 (Ohio 1994) (holding that a state statute giving the judge, not the jury, responsibility for determining the amount of punitive damages violates the right to trial by jury guarantee in Art. I, §5 of the Ohio Constitution), *cert. denied*, 516 U.S. 809 (1995); *but see, e.g.*, Smith v. Printup, 866 P.2d 985 (Kan. 1993) (upholding the validity under § 5 of the Kansas Constitution of a statute requiring the judge to determine the amount of punitive damages).

332. 457 U.S. 496 (1982).

333. *See* STEINGLASS, SECTION 1983 LITIGATION IN STATE COURTS, *supra* note 24, § 17:5.

334. 487 U.S. 131 (1988).

335. *See* STEINGLASS, SECTION 1983 LITIGATION IN STATE COURTS, *supra* note 24, § 17:9.

336. 451 U.S. 527 (1981).

337. *See also* Hudson v. Palmer, 468 U.S. 517 (1984) (applying the *Parratt* requirement to intentional acts); *but see* Logan v. Zimmerman Brush Co., 455 U.S. 422 (1982) (holding *Parratt* inapplicable to established state policies).

dies,[338] the state may meet its constitutional obligation by providing adequate post-deprivation remedies.[339]

Despite the general no-exhaustion policy applicable to § 1983 claims, there are limited circumstances in which Congress has authorized exhaustion of administrative remedies requirements. For example, in § 1983 suits by prisoners, the Civil Rights of Institutionalized Persons Act,[340] as amended by the Violent Crime Control and Law Enforcement Act of 1994[341] and the Prison Litigation Reform Act,[342] requires courts to stay judicial proceedings while prisoners use available prison administrative proceedings.[343] The Act does not expressly apply to state courts, but the Court in *Felder* assumed that the limited statutory exhaustion requirement for prisoners also applied in state courts in the course of rejecting the use of a notice-of-claim requirement in state court § 1983 cases,[344] and state courts have generally applied this special exhaustion requirement to state court prisoner § 1983 suits.[345]

---

338. *See* Zinermon v. Burch, 494 U.S. 113 (1990) (limiting *Parratt* to cases in which it is not feasible to provide pre-deprivation remedies); *but see* Albright v. Oliver, 510 U.S. 266, 283–86 (1994) (Kennedy, J., concurring) (arguing that *Parratt* is inapplicable to establish state policies).
339. *Cf.* Williamson County Reg'l Planning Comm'n v. Hamilton Bank of Johnson City, 473 U.S. 172 (1985) (requiring exhaustion of state compensation judicial remedies as a condition of bringing a taking claim in federal court).
340. Pub. L. No. 96-247, 94 Stat. 352 (1980) (current version at 42 U.S.C. § 1997e (2000)).
341. Pub. L. No. 103-322, § 20416, 108 Stat. 1796, 1833–34 (1994).
342. Pub. L. No. 104-134, § 803(d), 110 Stat. 1321 (1996).
343. The 1996 legislation imposed a more demanding exhaustion requirement and no longer limited the courts to staying proceedings for 180 days and no longer requires that prison administrative procedures be "plain, speedy and effective." *See* 42 U.S.C § 1997e(a) (2000). In Porter v. Nussle, 534 U.S. 516, 532 (2002), the Court construed the PLRA prisoner exhaustion requirement broadly to apply to "general circumstances or particular episodes, and whether they allege excessive force or some other wrong."
344. *See Felder,* 487 U.S. at 148–49; *but see id.* at 159 (O'Connor, J., dissenting) (treating the prisoner exhaustion requirement as applying only in federal courts and concluding that "Congress has never concerned itself with the application of exhaustion requirements in *state* courts") (emphasis added).
345. *See, e.g.,* Baker v. Rolnick, 110 P.3d 1284, 1287–88 (Ariz. Ct. App. 2005); Kellogg v. Nebraska Dep't of Corr. Servs., 690 N.W.2d 574 (Neb. 2005); Casteel v. Vaade, 481 N.W.2d 476 (Wis. 1992); *but see* Pendleton v. Mills, 73 S.W.3d 115 (Tenn. Ct. App. 2001) (holding that PLRA did not preempt state law and that state courts could entertain § 1983 suits brought by prisoners who had not exhausted state prison remedies). For a fuller discussion, *see* STEINGLASS, SECTION 1983 LITIGATION IN STATE COURTS, *supra* note 24, at § 17:6.

H. Statutes of Limitations

Section 1983 does not contain a statute of limitations, but the Supreme Court has applied the borrowing principles authorized by 42 U.S.C. § 1988,[346] the civil rights choice-of-law statute,[347] to fill this gap in federal law with state statutes of limitations. Under *Wilson v. Garcia*,[348] courts must select a single statute of limitations for § 1983 claims in each state, and this is the personal injury limitations period.[349] Some states, however, have multiple limitations periods for personal injury actions; but in *Owens v. Okure*,[350] the Supreme Court held that in such cases the relevant period is found in the "general or residual statute for personal injury actions."[351]

The Supreme Court has not addressed whether the same federal principles that apply to the selection of § 1983 statutes of limitations in federal

---

346. 42 U.S.C. § 1988 (2000). For a discussion of this complex statute, see STEINGLASS, *Wrongful Death Actions, supra* note 300, at 612–25.

347. Although § 1988, by its terms, appears to be addressed to federal courts, the Supreme Court has treated it as applicable to state courts. *See* Sullivan v. Little Hunting Park, Inc., 396 U.S. 229, 240 (1969); *see also* STEINGLASS, SECTION 1983 LITIGATION IN STATE COURTS, *supra* note 24, at § 10:5. *Cf.* Maine v. Thiboutot, 448 U.S. 1 (1980) (applying the attorneys'-fees provision of 42 U.S.C. § 1988 to state court § 1983 litigation).

348. 471 U.S. 261 (1985).

349. *Id.* at 279–80.

350. 488 U.S. 235 (1989). The *Owens* Court also rejected the use of the statute of limitations for intentional torts. *Id.* at 249.

351. *Id.* at 250. The *Owens* Court, however, reaffirmed the Court's earlier rejection of the residual limitations periods, while allowing the use of the residual *personal injury* limitations period.

> Our decision today is fully consistent with *Wilson*'s rejection of a state residual, or "catch-all," limitations provision as the appropriate one for § 1983 actions. In *Wilson,* we rejected recourse to such provisions in the first instance, a position we continue to embrace. Courts should resort to residual statutes of limitations only where state law provides multiple statutes of limitations for personal injury actions and the residual one embraces, either explicitly or by judicial construction, unspecified personal injury actions.

Id. at 250 n.12.

court apply in state courts, but most state courts that have assumed that they do,[352] and this position seems correct.[353]

I. Preclusion

Under the full faith and credit statute,[354] federal courts are required to give state court judgments the same preclusive effect that state courts give them, and this principle is applicable to § 1983 litigation.[355] Thus, both state and federal courts entertaining § 1983 actions look to state law to determine the preclusive effect of prior state court judgments. When prior judgments are rendered by federal courts, on the other hand, the relevant preclusion policies come from federal law. The principle that the court rendering a judgment determines the scope of the judgment has guided federal courts in developing a federal law of preclusion,[356] and the Supreme Court has interpreted federal law as requiring state courts to give federal judgments the same full faith and credit that federal courts give them.[357]

Some state courts, however, inappropriately look to their own law of preclusion, rather than federal law, when determining the preclusive effect of prior federal court judgments. Usually, this does not result in different

352. *See Felder,* 487 U.S. at 154 (White, J., concurring), and cases cited therein; *see also* Hemberger v. Bitzer, 574 N.W.2d 656 (Wis. 1998) (applying the Wisconsin six-year general and residual personal injury statute of limitations to § 1983 claims); Putter v. Montpelier Pub. Sch. Sys. 697 A.2d 354, 356 (Vt. 1997) (recognizing that the Supreme Court has required the application of a single statute of limitations to § 1983 claims in each state).

353. *Cf.* Engel v. Davenport, 271 U.S. 33 (1926) (barring states from applying shorter statutes of limitations to FELA claims); *but see* Herman, *supra* note 11, at 1082 n.106 (1989) (suggesting that § 1988 does not apply in state courts and that states may adopt longer statutes of limitations for § 1983 actions than those applicable in federal court).

354. *See* 28 U.S.C. § 1738 (2000).

355. *See* Migra v. Warren City Sch. Dist., 465 U.S. 75 (1984) (claim preclusion); Allen v. McCurry, 449 U.S. 90 (1980) (issue preclusion).

356. *See* RESTATEMENT (SECOND) OF JUDGMENTS § 87 (1982) ("Federal law determines the effects under the rules of res judicata of a judgment of a federal court."); *see generally* Stephen B. Burbank, *Interjurisdictional Preclusion, Full Faith and Credit and Federal Common Law: A General Approach,* 71 CORNELL L. REV. 733 (1986); Ronan E. Degnan, *Federalized Res Judicata,* 85 YALE L.J. 741 (1971).

357. *See* Limbach v. Hooven & Allison Co., 466 U.S. 353, 361–63 (1984); *see also* International Bd. of Elec. Workers v. Hawaiian Tel. Co., 713 P.2d 943, 955 n.17 (Haw. 1986) ("In a subsequent state court action, the collateral estoppel effect of a federal law ruling in a prior federal court adjudication is a question of federal

outcomes; but in states that define "claim" narrowly, the use of the state law of claim preclusion can limit the preclusive effect of earlier federal court judgments.[358]

Preclusion issues often arise in § 1983 litigation when federal court plaintiffs split their claims and do not join their state law claims with their federal claims under the doctrine of supplemental jurisdiction.[359]

When federal courts lack the power to exercise supplemental jurisdiction over certain state law claims, state courts should exercise jurisdiction over the state law claims. For example, the Supreme Court's decision in *Pennhurst State School and Hospital v. Halderman*[360] erected an Eleventh Amendment bar to the litigation of state claims for injunctive relief against state officials. Accordingly, plaintiffs who face potential *Pennhurst* problems in federal court should be able to bifurcate their claims and file their state claims in state court and their federal claims in federal court. In such circumstances, state courts should not require federal court litigants to go through the futile task of attempting to join their state law claims in federal court. If the state law claims go to judgment first, however, federal courts will borrow the state law of claim preclusion and in most cases will refuse to hear the federal claims that could have been joined in the original state court action.

---

law."); Veiser v. Armstrong, 688 P.2d 796, 799 (Okla. 1984) ("Federal law governs both the preclusive and res judicata effect of the prior federal-court judgment. . . .").

358. *See, e.g.,* Lamartiniere v. Allstate Ins. Co., 415 So. 2d 499 (La. Ct. App.) (narrowly defining a "cause of action" for purposes of res judicata and permitting plaintiffs to bifurcate their claims and bring a state court tort suit after the dismissal of their federal court § 1983 claim), *writ denied,* 420 So. 2d 442 (La. 1982); Cranwill v. Donahue, 426 N.E.2d 337 (Ill. App. Ct. 1981) (relying on state definition of cause of action to permit litigation of pendent state law claims dismissed on jurisdictional grounds by federal court); *but see* Reeder v. Succession of Palmer, 623 So.2d 1268, 1271 (La. 1993) (relying on the RESTATEMENT (SECOND) OF JUDGMENTS and recognizing that the preclusive effect of a federal court judgment rendered by a federal court exercising federal question jurisdiction is governed by federal law), *cert denied,* 510 U.S. 1165 (1994).

359. The judge-made doctrine of pendent jurisdiction, *see generally* United Mine Workers v. Gibbs, 383 U.S. 715 (1966), was renamed and partially codified as "supplemental jurisdiction" in Title III of the Judicial Improvements Act of 1990, which contains the Federal Courts Study Committee Implementation Act of 1990. Pub. L. No. 101-650, 104 Stat. 5089 (1990) (creating 28 U.S.C. § 1367 (2000)). Under § 1367, plaintiffs may invoke the supplemental jurisdiction of the federal courts to join § 1983 and state law claims in a single civil action. *See generally* STEVEN H. STEINGLASS, *State Courts and Supplemental Jurisdiction Under the Civil Rights Act of 1991,* in THE CIVIL RIGHTS ACT OF 1991 (American Law Institute-American Bar Association Committee on Continuing Professional Education 1993).

360. 465 U.S. 89 (1984).

When federal courts exercise discretion and refuse to hear joined state law claims, most state courts will entertain the unaddressed state law claims.[361] On the other hand, when federal court plaintiffs do not attempt to join state law claims that are arguably within the supplemental jurisdiction of the federal courts, state courts will generally refuse to hear the state law claims. In such cases, state courts are generally reluctant to assume that the federal courts will exercise discretion to decline to hear the state law claims. Thus, state courts often require plaintiffs either to have attempted to join the state law claims in federal court or to make a strong showing that it would have been futile to do so.[362] Although some state courts have excused plaintiffs who did not even attempt to join state law claims in earlier federal court litigation,[363] plaintiffs who wish to preserve access to a federal forum without running the risk of losing their state law claims should attempt to join their state law claims in the federal court proceeding even if there is a significant chance that the federal court will decline to exercise supplemental jurisdiction.

---

361. *See, e.g.*, Terrell v. City of Bessemer, 406 So. 2d 337, 339–340 (Ala. 1981); DeLaurentis v. City of New Haven, 597 A.2d 807 (Conn. 1991); *see also* Rennie v. Freeway Transp., 656 P.2d 919, 924 n.8 (Or. 1982), and cases cited therein; *but see* Mattson v. City of Costa Mesa, 164 Cal. Rptr. 913 (Ct. App. 1980) (refusing to hear a state law claim brought by a plaintiff who had earlier proceeded to trial in federal court on federal claims after the federal court declined to exercise pendent jurisdiction over the state law claim); City of Los Angeles v. Superior Court, 149 Cal. Rptr. 320, 324 (Ct. App. 1978) (observing that "a litigant cannot avoid the impact of the rule against splitting causes of action by choosing for his first foray a tribunal of limited jurisdiction").

362. *See, e.g., Terrell supra*; Merry v. Coast Cmty. Coll. Dist., 158 Cal. Rptr. 603, 607–08 (Ct. App. 1979) (concluding that "since it clearly appears that the federal court would have declined to exercise its pendent jurisdiction to adjudicate plaintiff's state claims had they been raised, the . . . [federal court] summary judgment is not a bar to the maintenance of the instant action"); Anderson v. Phoenix Inv. Counsel of Boston, Inc., 440 N.E.2d 1164, 1168–69 (Mass. 1982) (following the Restatement (Second) of Judgments § 25, comment e, illustration 10 (1982), and requiring state court to dismiss state law claim unless it is clear that the federal court would not have had pendent jurisdiction or, having jurisdiction, clearly would have declined to exercise it as a matter of discretion); Rennie v. Freeway Transp., 656 P.2d 919, 924 (Or. 1982).

363. *See, e.g.*, City and County of Denver v. Block 173 Assoc., 814 P.2d 824 (Colo. 1991) (relying on the consistent refusal of federal courts to exercise pendent jurisdiction over state law claims after the dismissal of federal claims to refuse to apply claim preclusion to bar a state law claim after a federal court dismissed factually identical federal claim at summary judgment); Pope v. City of Atlanta, 240 S.E.2d 241, 243 (Ga. 1977) (refusing to apply claim preclusion to state law claim after concluding that federal court would "most likely" not have exercised pendent jurisdiction), *cert. denied,* 440 U.S. 936 (1979).

Preclusion issues also arise in state court § 1983 litigation because federal courts do not adhere to the requirements of mutuality, and the Supreme Court has permitted both the offensive and defensive use of issue preclusion.[364] Consequently, federal courts entertaining § 1983 actions have permitted nonparties to earlier litigating to take advantage of issue preclusion and have prohibited parties (to the earlier litigation) from relitigating issues that were resolved against them.[365]

In states that have not abandoned the doctrine of mutuality, nonparties to earlier litigation may not use findings of fact and conclusions of law against parties from earlier litigation in whose case both legal and factual issues were resolved.[366] When the earlier litigation was in federal court, however, state courts must give the federal court judgment the same preclusive effect that federal courts would give it. Thus, some state courts may be required by *federal* law to ignore their own preclusion policies and apply federal issue preclusion policies under which nonparties may take advantage of earlier judgments rendered against their adversaries.[367]

J. Discovery

When § 1983 cases are brought in federal court, questions concerning the scope of discovery are governed by federal law, and federal courts reject the use of state policies to limit discovery.[368] State courts, not surprisingly, gen-

---

364. *See* Parklane Hosiery Co. Inc. v. Shore, 439 U.S. 322 (1979) (permitting offensive use of issue preclusion); Blonder-Tongue Lab., Inc. v. University of Ill. Found., 402 U.S. 313 (1971) (permitting defensive use of issue preclusion).

365. *See, e.g.*, McDuffie v. Estelle, 935 F.2d 682 (5th Cir. 1991) (applying offensive collateral estoppel against prison officials on some, but not all, § 1983 claims).

366. *See generally* Michael J. Waggoner, *Fifty Years of* Bernhard v. Bank of America *Is Enough: Collateral Estoppel Should Require Mutuality but Res Judicata Should Not,* 12 Rev. Litig. 391 (1993); Janet Schmitt Ellis, *Nonmutuality: Taking the Fairness Out of Collateral Esptoppel,* 13 Ind. L. Rev. 563 (1980).

367. *See, e.g.,* Edwards v. First Fed. Sav. & Loan Ass'n, 696 P.2d 484 (N.M. Ct. App. 1985) (permitting defensive use of collateral estoppel of a federal judgment despite state adherence to mutuality).

368. *See* Kelly v. City of San Jose, 114 F.R.D. 653, 656 (N.D. Cal 1987) ("If state law controlled, state authorities could effectively insulate themselves from constitutional norms simply by developing privilege doctrines that made it virtually impossible for plaintiffs to develop the kind of information they need to prosecute their federal claims."); *see also* Frankenhauser v. Rizzo, 59 F.R.D. 339 (E.D. Pa. 1973) (identifying factors to be considered in addressing the scope of discovery of investigative files in police misconduct cases).

erally apply their own discovery policies in litigation in their courts,[369] but state courts are split on whether they are obligated to ignore state discovery policies in favor of federal policies when entertaining § 1983 claims. This issue has come up most starkly in § 1983 cases involving the discovery of internal police investigatory files.

In *Henneman v. City of Toledo*,[370] the Supreme Court of Ohio stated broadly that "[w]here a particular claim is based on the United Stated Constitution or federal statutes, federal law controls on the question of evidentiary privilege."[371] The court then ruled that internal affairs reports in § 1983 police misconduct cases were discoverable in camera despite state statutory exception for "confidential law enforcement investigatory records." Likewise, in *Svaigsen v. City of New York*[372] the New York Appellate Division, relying on *Felder v. Casey*,[373] stated that "[w]hen a state court entertains a Federally created cause of action, 'the federal right cannot be defeated by the forms of local practice.' "[374] The New York court then held that the trial court was required to follow federal discovery policies concerning the discovery of police investigatory documents despite the state statutory exemption of such documents from discovery.

On the other hand, the California Court of Appeals in *Denari v. Superior Court (County of Kern)*[375] ruled that state courts entertaining § 1983 actions must follow state discovery policies and refused to set aside a California constitutionally based right to privacy that shielded police personnel records from discovery. In so ruling, the California court concluded that the state privilege (1) did not conflict in its "purpose and effects with the remedial objectives of § 1983"; (2) did not "immunize[] government conduct otherwise subject to suit" under § 1983; (3) did not burden the "civil rights victims who seek redress in state courts"; (4) did not "frequently and predictably produce different outcomes in federal civil rights litigation based solely on whether that litigation takes place in state or federal court"; and (5) was a "neutral and uniformly applicable rule of procedure" rather than a substantive rule.[376]

369. *But cf.* CHARLES ALAN WRIGHT & MARY KAY KANE, LAW OF FEDERAL COURTS 673 (6th ed. 2002) (noting that state law of privilege generally applies in federal courts when state law supplies the rule of decision such as in diversity cases).
370. 520 N.E.2d 207 (Ohio 1988).
371. *Id.* at 209.
372. 609 N.Y.S.2d 894 (N.Y. App. Div. 1994).
373. 487 U.S. 131 (1988).
374. *Svaigsen,* 609 N.Y.S.2d at 894 (quoting *Felder,* 497 U.S. at 138, quoting *Brown v. Western Ry,* 338 U.S. 29, 296 (1949)).
375. 264 Cal. Rptr. 261 (1989).
376. *Id.* at 1498 (quoting *Felder*).

These three discovery decisions involved the application of state privileges that would not be applicable to § 1983 litigation in federal courts, but the state court decisions in Ohio and New York requiring the application of federal discovery policies to state court § 1983 claims seem overly broad. Professor Hart's famous statement that "federal law takes the state courts as it finds them"[377] surely has some applicability to rules of discovery that are "among the universally familiar aspects of litigation considered indispensable to any scheme of justice,"[378] and the federalization of state discovery goes too far. Nonetheless, specific state discovery policies may have a substantive impact on the litigation of § 1983 claims, and the use of such policies could be seen as burdening § 1983 claims. Moreover, when the state policies at issue give special weight to the governmental interests that are most often at stake in § 1983 litigation, the principles announced by the Court in *Felder* may override the state limitations on discovery. Thus, a strong argument can be made that the California court in *Denari*, despite the quality of its opinion, may not have ruled correctly in insulating police investigative reports from discovery in state court § 1983 cases involving allegations of police misconduct, while the New York and Ohio courts may have reached the right result in the particular cases despite the breadth of their conclusions about the use of federal discovery policies in state courts.

K. Attorneys' Fees

Prevailing plaintiffs in § 1983 actions are entitled to attorneys' fees as a result of the Civil Rights Attorney's Fees Awards Act of 1976,[379] which added fee-authorizing language to 42 U.S.C. § 1988.[380] The Fees Act was

---

377. Henry Hart, *The Relations Between State and Federal Law,* 54 COLUM. L. REV. 489, 508 (1954). Professor Hart also stated that state rules need not be applied when they "are . . . so rigorous as, in effect, to nullify the asserted rights." *Id.*

378. *Felder,* 487 U.S. at 144–45 (noting that although the state "notice-of-claim statute does not discriminate between state and federal causes of action against local governments, . . . the law's protection extends only to governmental defendants and thus conditions the right to bring suit against the very persons and entities Congress intended to subject to liability.").

379. Pub. L. No. 94-559, 90 Stat. 2641 (1976).

380. 42 U.S.C. § 1988(b) (2000) ("In any action or proceeding to enforce a provision of sections 1981, 1981a, 1982, 1983, 1985, and 1986 of this title, title IX of Public Law 92-318, the Religious Freedom Restoration Act of 1993, the Religious Land Use and Institutionalized Person Act of 2000, title VI of the Civil Rights

adopted to overrule *Alyeska Pipeline Service Co. v. Wilderness Society*,[381] a Supreme Court case holding that federal courts did not have an inherent power to award fees to prevailing parties under a private attorneys general theory. The language in the Act, however, is not limited to federal court litigation; and in *Maine v. Thiboutot*,[382] the Supreme Court characterized the availability of attorneys' fees as an "integral" part of the § 1983 remedy[383] and applied the Fees Act to state court § 1983 litigation.[384]

State courts have recognized the applicability of the Fees Act to state court § 1983 litigation and have generally followed federal standards in applying the Act.[385] Thus, in addressing the availability of fees, most state courts have followed federal standards under which prevailing plaintiffs are presumptively entitled to fee awards except in rare cases in which defendants can point to special circumstances that justify the denial of fees.[386] Likewise, state courts have generally followed federal standards in determining the amount of fee awards.[387]

Act of 1964, or section 13981 of this title, the court, in its discretion, may allow the prevailing party, other than the United States, a reasonable attorney's fee as part of the costs, except that in any action brought against a judicial officer for an act or omission taken in such officer's judicial capacity such officer shall not be held liable for any costs, including attorney's fees, unless such action was clearly in excess of such officer's jurisdiction."). The Fees Act was amended by the Federal Courts Improvement Act of 1996, Pub. L. No. 104-317, § 309(c), 110 Stat. 3847 (1996), to limit the availability of attorneys' fees in cases against judicial officers.

381. 421 U.S. 240 (1975).

382. 448 U.S. 1 (1980).

383. *Id.* at 11.

384. For a discussion of the application of the Fees Act in state courts, *see* STEINGLASS, SECTION 1983 LITIGATION IN STATE COURTS, *supra* note 24, at §§ 22:10–22:13.

385. *See, e.g.*, Ferdinand v. City of Fairbanks, 599 P.2d 122, 125 (Alaska 1979) (holding that "federal guidelines appl[y] in ascertaining an appropriate fee award"); International Soc'y for Krishna Consciousness v. Colorado State Fair and Indus. Exposition Comm'n, 673 P.2d 368 (Colo. 1983); Johnson v. Blum, 448 N.E.2d 449 (N.Y. 1983); Thompson v. Village of Hales Corners, 340 N.W.2d 704 (Wis. 1983).

386. *See, e.g.*, Henderson v. District of Columbia, 493 A.2d 982 (D.C. 1985); O'Connors v. Helfgott, 481 A.2d 388 (R.I. 1984); Jacobsen v. City of Seattle, 658 P.2d 653 (Wash. 1983).

387. *See, e.g.*, Henderson v. District of Columbia, *supra;* Holden Arboretum v. City of Kirtland, 483 N.E.2d 167 (Ohio Ct. App. 1984).

State courts have also been willing to award fees to plaintiffs who prevailed on state law claims that were joined with substantial federal claims,[388] although some state courts have been uncomfortable with the prospect of doing so when state law does not authorize fee awards.[389]

State courts have approved fee awards in a number of circumstances in which federal courts either have abstained or probably would have applied an abstention or other door-closing doctrine.[390]

---

388. *See, e.g.,* Davis v. Everett, 443 So.2d 1232 (Ala. 1983); Allison v. Board of County Comm'rs of Johnson County, 737 P.2d 6 (Kan. 1987); Crane v. Commissioner of Pub. Welfare, 400 Mass. 46, 507 N.E.2d 751 (Mass. 1987); Stratos v. Department of Pub. Welfare, 439 N.E.2d 778 (Mass. 1982); Thomasel v. Perales, 585 N.E.2d 359 (N.Y. 1991); Doe v. Cuddy, 487 N.E.2d 914 (Ohio Ct. App. 1985); International Ass'n of Machinists v. Affleck, 504 A.2d 468 (R.I. 1986); Lorenc v. Call, 789 P.2d 46 (Utah Ct. App.), *cert. denied,* 795 P.2d 1138 (Utah 1990); *cf.* Filipino Accountants v. State Bd. of Accounting, 204 Cal. Rptr. 913 (Ct. App. 1984) (applying federal standards to award fees in a § 1981 action to party who prevailed on state grounds). For a discussion of the availability of fees to § 1983 plaintiffs who prevail on state law claims, *see* STEINGLASS, SECTION 1983 LITIGATION IN STATE COURTS, *supra* note 24, at ch. 23.

389. *See,* e.g., Still v. Personnel Bd. of Jefferson County, 406 So.2d 860 (Ala. 1981), *cert. denied,* 455 U.S. 1020 (1982); Gumbhir v. Kansas State Bd. of Pharmacy, 646 P.2d 1078 (Kan. 1982), *cert. denied,* 459 U.S. 1103 (1983); Jackson v. Inhabitants of the Town of Searsport, 456 A.2d 852 (Me. 1983), *cert. denied,* 464 U.S. 825 (1983); Oregon State Police Officers Ass'n, Inc. v. State, 783 P.2d 7 (Or. 1989), *cert. denied,* 498 U.S. 810 (1990).

State courts may refuse to award fees to plaintiffs who prevail on state law claims when the joined constitutional claims are wholly insubstantial, *see* County Executive of Prince George's County v. Doe, 479 A.2d 352 (Md. 1984), or when the particular constitutional claim cannot be raised under § 1983, *see* Dennis v. State, 451 N.W.2d 676 (Neb. 1990), *rev'd on other grounds,* 498 U.S. 439 (1991), but some state courts confuse the question of "substantiality" with the merits of the constitutionally based fee claim. *See, e.g.,* Slawik v. State, 480 A.2d 636 (Del. 1984).

390. *See, e.g.,* Robinson v. City of Omaha, 495 N.W.2d 281 (Neb. 1993) (holding that a plaintiff who filed a state court suit presenting only a state law claim to the state courts after a federal court *Pullman* abstention is a prevailing party and entitled to a fee award under § 1988); *cf.* Crane v. Commissioner of Pub. Welfare, 400 Mass. 46, 507 N.E.2d 751 (Mass. 1987); Stratos v. Department of Pub. Welfare, 439 N.E.2d 778 (Mass. 1982) (authorizing a fee award to plaintiffs who obtained prospective relief under § 1983 in federal court and retroactive relief under state law in state court).

VIII. REMOVAL

Given the liberal federal question removal statute,[391] state court defendants who prefer to defend § 1983 claims in federal court can almost always remove such cases, and they are increasingly doing so.[392]

Removal of state court § 1983 cases is not available when the state court defendant fails to meet the timeliness and other procedural requirements of removal[393] or when the federal court "lacks subject matter jurisdiction" over the case.[394]

Because state courts are not required to follow the justiciability requirements of Article III of the U.S. Constitution, defendants may not remove § 1983 cases that meet state, but not federal, justiciability requirements.[395] Likewise, federal courts do not have removal jurisdiction over § 1983 cases that are barred from federal court by the Eleventh Amendment.[396] When

---

391. 28 U.S.C. § 1441(a) (2000) (permitting defendants to remove federal question cases to federal court if the action could have been filed originally in federal court). *See generally* Dorsey v. City of Detroit, 858 F.2d 338 (6th Cir. 1988) (applying § 1441 to permit removal of § 1983 cases).

392. This conclusion about the increase in the removal of state court § 1983 actions is based on the author's analysis of raw statistical data from the Administrative Office of the U.S. Courts, from discussions with practicing lawyers throughout the country, from the increasingly frequent references to removal in federal court § 1983 opinions, and from the general increase in the number of state court cases removed under federal question removal. *Cf.* Neal Miller, *An Empirical Study of Forum Choices in Removal Cases Under Diversity and Federal Question Jurisdiction,* 41 AM. U. L. REV. 369, 389 n.86 (1992) (documenting the increase in federal question removal).

393. Defendants wishing to remove state court § 1983 cases must file a notice of removal "within thirty days after receipt by the defendant, through service or otherwise, of a copy of the initial pleading . . . or within thirty days after service of summons. . . ." 28 U.S.C. § 1446(b) (2000); *see* Murphy Bros., Inc. v. Michetti Pipe Stringing, Inc., 526 U.S. 344 (1999) (holding that the removal period begins with the formal service of the summons).

394. *See* 28 U.S.C. § 1447(c) (2000).

395. *See* International Primate Prot. League v. Administrators of Tulane Educ. Fund, 500 U.S. 72, 88–89 (1991) (noting that "plaintiff's lack of Article III standing would not necessarily defeat its standing in state court").

396. *See* Lapides v. Board of Regents of Univ. Sys. of Georgia, 535 U.S. 613 (2002) (holding that the removal of a claim from state to federal court was a waiver of a state's Eleventh Amendment immunity but making clear that its holding did not apply to § 1983 claims against the state because states were not "persons" within the meaning of § 1983).

cases are removed to federal courts that lack subject matter jurisdiction, federal courts are required to remand the cases to state courts.[397]

IX. CONCLUSION

As this review of § 1983 litigation in the state courts suggests, § 1983 litigation is no longer exclusively the province of the federal courts. And that is how it should be in a system of judicial federalism. As former Supreme Court Justice William J. Brennan, Jr., himself a former state court judge, once observed, "[o]ne of the strengths of our federal system is that it provides a double source of protection for the rights of our citizens."[398] In part, this means that state courts should pay close attention to their own constitutions, but it also suggests the important role that state courts should play in enforcing federal law.

397. *See* 28 U.S.C. § 1447(c) (2000); *see also* Henry v. Metropolitan Sewer Dist., 922 F.2d 332 (6th Cir. 1990) (treating a § 1983 official capacity claim as a suit against the state that is barred by the Eleventh Amendment and ordering a remand but retaining jurisdiction over the § 1983 individual capacity claim). For a further discussion of jurisdictional issues in removed § 1983 cases, *see* STEINGLASS, SECTION § 1983 LITIGATION IN STATE COURTS, *supra* note 24, § 24.4.

398. William J. Brennan, Jr., *State Constitutions and the Protection of Individual Rights,* 90 HARV. L. REV. 489, 503 (1977).

Chapter 4

MUNICIPAL LIABILITY UNDER SECTION 1983

by Michael S. Bogren

I. INTRODUCTION

Section 1983 is the descendant of § 1 of the Civil Rights Act of 1871, 17 Stat. 13. The bill was introduced on March 28, 1871, as H.R. 320. Section 1 of the bill, now § 1983, was debated on a limited basis and was passed without amendment.[1] The Act, also known as the Ku Klux Klan Act, grew out of a message sent to Congress by President Ulysses Grant on March 23, 1871.[2] The bill was designed, inter alia, to provide a federal remedy where a state-created remedy was in existence, but was not available in practice.[3] The scope of that remedy has only recently taken more concrete form, particularly as it relates to municipal liability.

II. FRAMEWORK CASES

A. *Monroe v. Pape*

In 1961 the U.S. Supreme Court issued its decision in *Monroe v. Pape*.[4] *Monroe* greatly expanded the scope of official conduct actionable under § 1983 by holding that state officials acted "under color of law" even when they violated state or federal law. The plaintiff, Monroe, alleged that thirteen Chicago police officers broke into his home without a warrant while he and his wife were in bed, made them stand naked in the living room, and ransacked every room in the house. The complaint further alleged that Mr. Monroe was taken to the police station and detained for ten hours while he was interrogated about a murder. He was subsequently released without criminal charges being filed against him. The complaint alleged that the police officers had no search warrant and no arrest warrant, but that they acted under color of law.[5]

The plaintiffs filed suit in federal court, alleging a violation of their constitutional rights. The defendant police officers argued that the phrase "under color of law" excluded acts of a state official who could point to no legal authority authorizing his actions. In addressing this argument, the Supreme Court first held that the federal remedy was supplementary to any state remedy, and that the state remedy need not be exhausted before the federal remedy could be utilized.[6] In rejecting the defendants' construction

---

1. Monell v. Department of Social Services, 436 U.S. 658, 664–65 (1978).
2. Monroe v. Pape, 365 U.S. 167, 172 (1961).
3. *Monroe,* 365 U.S. at 174.
4. 365 U.S. 167 (1961).
5. *Monroe,* 365 U.S. at 169.
6. *Id.* at 183.

of the phase "under color of law," the Court relied on *United States v. Classic*[7] and *Screws v. United States*,[8] cases that analyzed 18 U.S.C. § 242, the criminal counterpart to § 1983. The Court followed the holdings in *Classic* and *Screws*, and held that "misuse of power, possessed by virtue of state law and made possible only because the wrongdoer is clothed with the authority of state law, is action taken 'under color' of state law."[9]

The *Monroe* Court refused, however, to allow claims under § 1983 to be asserted against municipal corporations. The Court stated: "[W]e are of the opinion that Congress did not undertake to bring municipal corporations within the ambit of [Section 1983]."[10] The Supreme Court relied on the legislative history of the Ku Klux Klan Act, and specifically the rejection of the Sherman Amendment, to find municipal corporations excluded from § 1983. The Sherman Amendment, as originally proposed, included a provision that would have made the inhabitants of a municipality in which certain acts of violence occurred liable to pay full compensation to the person damaged.[11] The version of the Sherman Amendment that was finally adopted deleted all provisions for municipal liability.[12] The Supreme Court concluded its discussion of municipal liability in *Monroe* by stating:

> The response of the Congress to the proposal to make municipalities liable for certain actions being brought within federal purview by the Act of April 20, 1871, was so antagonistic that we cannot believe that the word "person" was used in this particular Act to include [municipal corporations]. Accordingly, we hold that the motion to dismiss the complaint against the City of Chicago was properly granted.[13]

Municipal corporations were beyond the purview of liability under § 1983 until 1978.

B. *Monell v. Department of Social Services*

In *Monell v. Department of Social Services*,[14] the Supreme Court revisited the holding of *Monroe v. Pape*, that municipal corporations could not be

---

7. 313 U.S. 299 (1941).
8. 325 U.S. 91 (1945).
9. *Monroe,* 365 U.S. at 183.
10. *Id.* at 187.
11. Cong. Globe, 42d Cong., 1st Sess., p. 663.
12. *Monroe,* 365 U.S. at 190.
13. *Id.* at 191–92 (footnote omitted).
14. 436 U.S. 658 (1978).

held liable under § 1983. Reexamining the debate in the 42nd Congress on the Civil Rights Act of 1871, and examining historical rulings that treated municipal corporations as natural persons for virtually all purposes of constitutional and statutory analysis,[15] the Supreme Court overruled *Monroe* and held that Congress *did* intend municipalities to be included among those "persons" to whom § 1983 applied.[16] That holding has spawned litigation that has resulted in conflicting circuit court decisions, fractured Supreme Court rulings, and few concrete rules to guide the practitioner.

III. PRELIMINARY MATTERS

Prior to examining the bases of liability against municipalities under § 1983, it is necessary to understand various concepts that can come into play in litigating such claims. Practitioners seeking to prosecute or defend a municipality in an action under § 1983 must be familiar with these concepts.

A. Eleventh Amendment

The Eleventh Amendment states:

> The Judicial power of the United States shall not be construed to extend to any suit in law or equity, commenced or prosecuted against one of the United States by Citizens of another State, or by Citizens or Subjects of any Foreign State.

To the uninitiated, the Eleventh Amendment appears to be of very limited terms. As the Supreme Court explained in *Hans v. Louisiana*,[17] however, the Amendment deprives a federal court of jurisdiction to entertain a suit brought by a citizen against his or her own state, as well as another state. The Supreme Court held that the history of Article III of the Constitution and the preexisting common law did not contemplate federal jurisdiction over any suits against unconsenting states.[18] In spite of this jurisdictional bar, a state may waive Eleventh Amendment immunity and consent to suit against it in federal court.[19] In determining whether a state has waived its constitutional protection under the Eleventh Amendment, the courts will

---

15. *Monell,* 436 U.S. at 665–89.
16. *Id.* at 690.
17. 134 U.S. 1 (1890).
18. *Hans,* 134 U.S. at 15.
19. Pennhurst State School and Hospital v. Halderman, 465 U.S. 89, 99 (1984).

find waiver only where stated by express language or by such overwhelming implications from the text of a statute that there is no room for any other reasonable construction.[20]

Congress has the power to abrogate Eleventh Amendment immunity consistent with the provisions of Section 5 of the Fourteenth Amendment.[21] However, just as statutes are strictly construed when determining whether a state has consented to suit, so too must the congressional intent to abrogate Eleventh Amendment immunity be unequivocal.[22] The Supreme Court held in *Quern v. Jordan*[23] that § 1983 does not explicitly abrogate the immunity of the states, nor does it have a history that would lead to such a conclusion. Thus, the Court held that Eleventh Amendment immunity barred federal courts from obtaining jurisdiction over states in § 1983 actions.

It can become confusing to determine proper application of the Eleventh Amendment because § 1983 creates liability on the part of every "person" who—under color of any statute, ordinance, regulation, custom, or usage of any state, territory, or the District of Columbia—causes a deprivation of any rights, privileges, or immunities secured by the Constitution or laws of the United States. This requirement is generally referred to as "state action," and defendants in § 1983 actions are typically referred to as "state actors."

Eleventh Amendment immunity from suit in federal courts extends to the states themselves and state agencies, but does not typically extend to counties and other political subdivisions, especially municipal corporations.[24] The issue to be determined in applying Eleventh Amendment immunity is whether the defendant is the state itself or, in the words of *Monell*, a "local government unit." This determination must be made by examining state law. The Supreme Court held in *Mount Healthy* that a board of education was not entitled to assert Eleventh Amendment immunity, because under Ohio law the "state" did not include "political subdivisions," while "political subdivisions," in turn, *did* include local school districts.[25]

A determination must be made on a state-by-state basis as to whether a particular governmental entity is protected by Eleventh Amendment immunity. See *Fordyce v. City of Seattle*[26] (under Washington law a municipal

---

20. Edelman v. Jordan, 415 U.S. 651, 673 (1974).
21. Fitzpatrick v. Bitker, 427 U.S. 445 (1976).
22. Pennhurst State School and Hospital, 465 U.S. at 99.
23. 440 U.S. 332, 345 (1979).
24. Mount Healthy City School District Board of Education v. Doyle, 429 U.S. 274, 280 (1977); *Monell,* 436 U.S. at 690 n.54.
25. *Mount Healthy,* 429 U.S. at 280.
26. 55 F.3d 436, 442 (9th Cir. 1995).

corporation, such as the city of Seattle, is not a state agency); *Eaglesmith v. Ward*[27] (under California law County Office of Education [COE] is a state agency for Eleventh Amendment purposes, as is a county school district); and *Roach v. West Virginia Regional Jail and Correctional Facility Authority*[28] (under West Virginia law a regional jail and correctional facility authority is a state agency for purposes of Eleventh Amendment immunity). This can lead to the rather anomalous result of a similar agency or office being both "state" and "local" in the same circuit, depending upon which state is involved.[29] The circuits have developed various standards to determine whether an agency or officer is "state" or "local." Ultimately, the determining factor is whether the agency or officer is acting as an "arm of the state."[30]

---

27. 73 F.3d 857, 860 (9th Cir. 1996).
28. 74 F.3d 46, 48 (4th Cir. 1996).
29. *Compare* Hufford v. Rodgers, 912 F.2d 1338 (11th Cir. 1990) (holding Florida sheriffs are local) *with* Parker v. Williams, 862 F.2d. 1471 (11th Cir. 1989) (holding Alabama sheriffs to be state-level officers).
30. For example, the Third Circuit has established a three-factor test to determine whether an entity is an arm of the state: (1) whether payment of a judgment resulting from the suit would come from the state treasury, (2) the status of the entity under state law, and (3) the entity's degree of autonomy. Chisolm v. McManimon, 275 F.3d 315, 323 (3d Cir. 2001). The Fourth Circuit has adopted a similar test, although the principal factor to be considered is whether a judgment against the government entity would have to be paid from the state's treasury. If so, Eleventh Amendment immunity is found. However, even if the state treasury will not be used to satisfy a judgment, immunity can still be found if the relationship of the entity with the state is close enough to implicate the dignity of the state as a sovereign. The Fourth Circuit applies three additional factors in that determination: (1) the degree of control that the state exercises over the entity, (2) whether the entity deals with local rather than statewide concerns, and (3) the manner in which state law treats the entity. Kitchen v. Upshaw, 286 F.3d 179, 184 (4th Cir. 2002). The Fifth Circuit uses a six-factor test to determine whether the state is the real party in interest: (1) whether the state statutes and case law view the agency as an arm of the state, (2) the source of the entity's funding, (3) the entity's degree of local autonomy, (4) whether the entity is concerned primarily with local as opposed to statewide issues, (5) whether the entity has the authority to sue and be sued in its own name, and (6) whether the entity has the right to hold and use property. Cozzo v. Tangipahoa Parish, 279 F.3d 273, 281 (5th Cir. 2002). The Ninth Circuit examines five factors in making a determination of whether a governmental entity is an arm of the state for Eleventh Amendment purposes: (1) whether a money judgment would be satisfied out of state funds, (2) whether the entity performs central governmental functions, (3) whether the entity may sue or be sued, (4) whether the entity has the power to take property in its own name or only in the name of the

The Eleventh Amendment does not bar a claim where the action under § 1983 is brought in state court, since the Amendment, by its explicit terms, restrains only the "Judicial power of the United States."[31] Section 1983 actions may be brought in state court.[32] Thus, a plaintiff bringing suit against a state or state agency under § 1983 can avoid Eleventh Amendment immunity by filing suit in state court.[33] However, as will be discussed, the state is not a "person" for purposes of § 1983. So, the fact that Eleventh Amendment immunity does not bar a § 1983 claim brought in state court against the state does not give a plaintiff a claim that is free from defenses.

The Eleventh Amendment has also been held to apply to a suit seeking injunctive relief, as the language of the Eleventh Amendment speaks of suits "in law or equity."[34] There is an important exception to Eleventh Amendment immunity with respect to injunctive relief. A suit challenging the constitutionality of a state official's action is not deemed to be one against the state, and prospective injunctive relief may be issued by a federal court under such circumstances.[35] The Supreme Court has held, however, that while a federal court may award an injunction that governs the state official's future conduct, it still may not award monetary damages.[36] Thus, the

---

state, and (5) the corporate status of the entity. Savage v. Glendale Union High School, 343 F.3d 1036, 1040 (9th Cir. 2003). The Eleventh Circuit employs a four-factor inquiry, taking into account: (1) how state law defines the entity, (2) what degree of control the state maintains over the entity, (3) the source of the entity's funds, and (4) who bears financial responsibility for judgments entered against the entity. Abusaid v. Hillsbrough County Board of Commissioners, 405 F.3d 1298, 1303 (11th Cir. 2005).

31. Maine v. Thiboutot, 448 U.S. 1, 9 n.7 (1980).
32. Martinez v. California, 444 U.S. 277 (1980).
33. Defendants have a right to remove actions arising under the Constitution and statutes of the United States to federal court. 28 U.S.C. § 1331; 28 U.S.C. § 1441. Once the case is removed, the defendant has, in all likelihood, waived Eleventh Amendment immunity. In Lapides v. Board of Regents, 535 U.S. 613, 624 (2002), the Supreme Court held that removal is a form of voluntary invocation of a federal court's jurisdiction that constitutes a waiver of Eleventh Amendment immunity. Although Lapides limits the effect of its decision to suits based on state law claims to which the state has waived immunity in its own courts, the Courts of Appeals have nearly unanimously applied the reasoning to the removal of federal question cases as well. Meyers v. Texas, 410 F.3d 236, 247 (5th Cir. 2005); Embury v. King, 361 F.3d 562, 564 (9th Cir. 2004); Estes v. Wyoming Dep't of Transp., 302 F.3d 1200, 1206 (10th Cir. 2002).
34. Cory v. White, 257 U.S. 85, 91 (1982).
35. *Ex parte* Young, 209 U.S. 123, 160 (1908).
36. Edelman v. Jordan, 415 U.S. 651, 666 (1974).

federal courts may award *prospective* injunctive relief against a state official in a suit challenging the constitutionality of the official's action.[37]

The Supreme Court has also held that an award of attorneys' fees to a prevailing plaintiff under § 1988 is not barred by the Eleventh Amendment.[38] Therefore, a prevailing plaintiff who obtains prospective injunctive relief against a state official will be entitled to an award of attorneys' fees payable from the state treasury.

B. Official Capacity Suits and Personal Capacity Suits

It is necessary to understand the distinction between official capacity suits and personal capacity suits. In *Brandon v. Holt*,[39] the Supreme Court held that a suit brought against a public official "in his official capacity" imposed liability on the entity that person represented, rather than on the individual himself. As the Supreme Court further explained in *Kentucky v. Graham*:[40]

> Personal-capacity suits seek to impose personal liability upon a government official for actions he takes under color of state law. Official-capacity suits, in contrast, "generally represent only another way of pleading an action against an entity of which an officer is an agent." As long as the government entity receives notice and an opportunity to respond, an official-capacity suit is, in all respects other than name, to be treated as a suit against the entity. It is not a suit against the official personally, for the real party in interest is the entity. Thus, while an award of damages against an official in his personal capacity can be executed only against the official's personal assets, a plaintiff seeking to recover on a damages judgment in an official-capacity suit must look to the government entity itself.

It is oftentimes difficult to ascertain whether a plaintiff seeks to sue an individual in his or her individual or official capacity. The Supreme Court has observed that "it is obviously preferable for the plaintiff to be specific in the first instance to avoid any ambiguity."[41] In the absence of an explicit statement in the complaint, however, the circuits are split as to how to determine whether a claim should be treated as an individual capacity claim or an official capacity claim. The First, Second, Third, Fourth, Fifth, Sixth,

---

37. *Pennhurst State School and Hospital,* 465 U.S. at 103.
38. Hutto v. Finney, 437 U.S. 678, 697 (1978).
39. 469 U.S. 464, 471–72 (1985).
40. 473 U.S. 159, 165–66 (1985).
41. Hafer v. Melo, 502 U.S. 21, 24 n.* (1991).

Seventh, Ninth, Tenth, and Eleventh Circuits have adopted the approach of looking to the substance of the plaintiff's claim, the relief sought, and the "course of proceedings" to determine the nature of a § 1983 suit when a plaintiff fails to allege capacity. One circuit, the Eighth, has adopted a bright-line rule that where the complaint is silent as to individual or official capacity, it is presumed that a defendant has been sued only in his or her official capacity.

The majority view in the circuits, which looks to the course of proceedings to determine the nature of the suit, is fairly consistent in its application. In *Powell v. Alexander,*[42] the First Circuit recently adopted the "course of proceedings" test (relief sought in the complaint, particularly claim for punitive damages, defenses raised by the individual defendants, particularly qualified immunity, the plaintiff's failure to assert that the defendant followed a policy or custom of the city, and the failure of the complaint to specify that the defendant was being sued solely in her official capacity, gave the defendant fair notice that she was being sued in her personal capacity). The other circuits applying the "course of proceedings" test have reached similar conclusions.[43]

---

42. 391 F.3d 1 (1st Cir. 2004).

43. Rodriguez v. Phillips, 66 F.3d 470, 482 (2d Cir. 1995) (relief sought in the complaint, defenses raised by the individual defendants, and the fact that the plaintiff continued the claim against the individual who was no longer employed rather than substituting the current officeholder led to a determination that the suit was a personal capacity suit); Melo v. Hafer, 912 F.2d 628, 636 (3d Cir. 1990), *aff'd on other grounds,* 502 U.S. 21 (1991) (claims asserted in the complaint together with defenses raised compel conclusion that defendant was sued in both her official and individual capacities); Biggs v. Meadows, 66 F.3d 56, 61 (4th Cir. 1995) (relief requested in the complaint together with defenses raised demonstrate that the plaintiff intended to sue the defendants in their individual capacity); Adrian v. Regents of the University of California, 363 F.3d 398, 403 (5th Cir. 2004) (where defendants clearly stated in their motion to dismiss that the individual employees should be dismissed because they were named only in their official capacity, and the plaintiff never challenged that assertion, the employees were named only in their official capacities); Shockley v. Jones, 823 F.2d 1068, 1071 (7th Cir. 1987) (presumption favoring official-capacity suit is not conclusive; "a court must look to the manner in which the parties have treated the suit"); Shoshone-Bannock Tribes v. Fish & Game Commission, Idaho, 42 F.3d 1278, 1284–85 (9th Cir. 1994) (where state officials are named in a complaint seeking damages under § 1983, it is presumed that the officials are being sued in their individual capacity. However, since the plaintiff explicitly named one official in his individual capacity, the other officials were entitled to assume that they were being sued only in their official capacity); Reames v. Oklahoma, 411 F.3d 1164, 1168 (10th Cir. 2005) (where the plaintiff did not seek

In *Egerdahl v. Hibbing Community College*,[44] the Eighth Circuit continued to follow its previously announced rule that if a plaintiff's complaint is silent about the capacity in which an individual is being sued, the complaint is interpreted as including only official capacity claims. The Sixth Circuit originally announced the same bright-line test in *Wells v. Brown*.[45] However, the Sixth Circuit has abandoned the bright-line test and adopted the "course of proceedings" test in *Moore v. City of Harriman*.[46]

As the Supreme Court noted in *Hafer v. Melo*, *supra*, the preferable approach is for a plaintiff to unequivocally state whether an individual is being sued in his or her individual capacity, official capacity, or both. This places no greater burden on the plaintiff, clearly identifies the nature of the claim upon which a defendant is being called to defend, and avoids confusion. Most important from the practitioner's standpoint, this practice will avoid the potential loss of a viable cause of action if it is not properly pled.

Apart from Eleventh Amendment immunity issues, the capacity of an individual defendant is important for determining what claims may be brought against the defendant and what defenses can be raised. For example, while qualified immunity is available to an individual defendant sued in his or her individual capacity,[47] a municipality may not assert the qualified immunity of its officers or agents as a defense to liability from damages.[48] Thus, an individual sued in his or her official capacity could not raise the defense of qualified immunity, since the suit is, in fact, a claim against the governmental entity.

By the same token, while punitive damages can be assessed against a defendant sued in his or her individual capacity,[49] a municipality has immunity from imposition of punitive damages.[50] Therefore, an official-capacity

---

to impose liability on employees of state agencies independent of the actions of the agencies, the plaintiff treated the lawsuit from its inception as a suit against the state, not an individual capacity suit); Hobbs v. Roberts, 999 F.2d 1526, 1531 (11th Cir. 1993) (allegation of "several" liability among defendants, dismissal of official who became successor in office after the date alleged in the complaint, and defenses raised demonstrated that individuals were sued in both their official and individual capacity).

44. 72 F.3d 615, 619–20 (8th Cir. 1995).
45. 891 F.2d 591, 593 (6th Cir. 1989) ("It is not too much to ask that if a person or entity is to be subject to suit, the person or entity should be properly named and clearly notified of the potential for payment of damages individually."). *See also* Lovelace v. O'Hara, 985 F.2d 847, 850 (6th Cir. 1993).
46. 272 F.3d 769, 772 n.1 (6th Cir. 2001).
47. Anderson v. Creighton, 483 U.S. 635 (1987).
48. Owen v. City of Independence, 445 U.S. 622, 638, 657 (1980).
49. Smith v. Wade, 461 U.S. 30 (1983).
50. City of Newport v. Fact Concerts, Inc., 453 U.S. 247, 271 (1981).

claim asserted against an individual would not allow the imposition of punitive damages, but an individual capacity claim asserted against an individual state actor would.

Finally, and most important, to establish personal liability in a § 1983 action a plaintiff must show that the official, acting under color of state law, caused the deprivation of a federal right.[51] In an official capacity action, however, the governmental entity's policy or custom must have caused the violation of federal law.[52] (The requirements for establishing liability against a governmental entity under *Monell* are discussed in detail in Part IV *infra.*)

When a plaintiff is determining the capacity in which an individual defendant is sued, it must be kept foremost in mind that a suit against an individual in his or her official capacity will require the same elements and standard of proof as would be required to establish liability against the entity itself, because an official capacity suit *is* a suit against the entity.

C. The State Is Not a "Person" Under Section 1983

In *Will v. Michigan Department of State Police*,[53] the Supreme Court addressed the issue of whether a state (or one of its agencies) is a person under § 1983. The Supreme Court held that a state is not a "person" within the meaning of § 1983. Using its decision in *Quern v. Jordan*, *supra*, as a starting point, the Court relied on the legislative history of § 1983 and the long-established doctrine of sovereign immunity.[54] The Court concluded that neither a state nor its officials acting in their official capacities are "persons" under § 1983.[55] The Supreme Court's ruling in *Will* created some confusion with respect to state officials. Defendants attempted to argue that when a plaintiff alleged that a state official was *acting* in "official capacity," as opposed to being *sued* in "official capacity," *Will* automatically barred the claim.

This confusion was resolved in *Hafer v. Melo*. The defendant in *Hafer* asserted that she could not be held personally liable for discharging employees of the state of Pennsylvania. In rejecting this contention, the Supreme Court stated:

> Of course, the claims considered in *Will* were official-capacity claims; the phrase "acting in their official capacities" is best understood as a reference to the capacity in which the state actor is sued,

51. Kentucky v. Graham, 473 U.S. 159, 166 (1985).

52. *Id.*

53. 491 U.S. 58 (1989).

54. *Will,* 491 U.S. at 67–68.

55. *Id.* at 71.

> not the capacity in which the officer inflicts the alleged injury. To the extent that *Will* allows the construction Hafer suggests, however, we now eliminate that ambiguity.
>
> * * *
>
> Hafer seeks to overcome the distinction between official- and personal-capacity suits by arguing that Section 1983 liability turns not on the capacity in which state officials are sued, but on the capacity in which they acted when injuring the plaintiff. Under *Will*, she asserts, state officials may not be held liable in their personal capacity for actions they take in their official capacity.[56]

The Court rejected Hafer's argument, stating:

> The requirement of action under color of state law means that Hafer may be liable for discharging respondents precisely because of her authority as auditor general. We cannot accept the novel proposition that this same official authority insulates Hafer from suit.[57]

The Court concluded by holding:

> We hold that state officials, sued in their individual capacities, are "persons" within the meaning of Section 1983. The Eleventh Amendment does not bar such suits, nor are state officers absolutely immune from personal liability under Section 1983 solely by virtue of the "official" nature of their acts.[58]

One of the significant results of *Will* is that Eleventh Amendment immunity, which had no effect on a § 1983 claim brought against a state in state court, became relatively unimportant. Since a state was not a "person" under § 1983, it could not be sued for damages under § 1983 in either state or federal court. The practical effect of *Will* was explained by the Sixth Circuit:[59]

> Thus, in an effort to get a "deep pocket," the plaintiff in *Brandon* sued the Director in his official capacity. A public official is only a "deep pocket," however, if the governmental unit will pay the judgment. This may or may not occur. In order to provide the plaintiff in *Brandon* with the "deep pocket" he would have had post-*Monell*,

---

56. *Hafer,* 502 U.S. at 26–27.
57. *Id.* at 27–28.
58. *Id.* at 31.
59. Ritchie v. Wickstrom, *supra,* 938 F.2d at 691.

> the Supreme Court simply declared that a suit against a public official in his "official capacity" is a suit against the governmental unit.

What goes around comes around, however, and the "deep pocket" feeling of euphoria felt by plaintiffs post-*Brandon* was dampened somewhat when the Supreme Court issued its opinion in *Will v. Michigan Department of State Police*, 491 U.S. 58, 109 S. Ct. 2304, 105 L.Ed.2d 45 (1989). In *Will*, the Supreme Court determined that states are not "persons" within the meaning of § 1983 and that "a suit against a state official in his or her official capacity is not a suit against the official, but rather is a suit against . . . the state itself."

Thus, at least for causes of action brought under § 1983, a plaintiff will fare no better in state court attempting to assert an official capacity suit against a state official than he would in federal court. Practitioners representing states or state agencies and officials must bear in mind that Eleventh Amendment immunity is quasi-jurisdictional in that it can be waived. It is an affirmative defense that can be waived when the state appeals and defends the action without raising the immunity as a defense.[60] A more detailed discussion of this issue can be found in Chapter 3.

D. Prerequisites for a Claim Under Section 1983

The deprivation of a federally protected right is the essence of a claim under § 1983. The claim may be a federal statutory right[61] or rights protected by the U.S. Constitution. Rights protected by the Constitution are the more prevalent claim asserted under § 1983.[62] It must be kept in mind that § 1983 creates no substantive rights. As the Supreme Court stated in *Chapman v. Houston Welfare Organization*:[63]

> [I]t remains true that one cannot go into court and claim a "violation of § 1983"—for § 1983 by itself does not protect anyone against anything.

In other words, § 1983 is not self-executing. It cannot be the federal statute that is claimed to have been violated. Section 1983 merely provides a remedy for the violation of any underlying federally protected right.

---

60. Atascadero State Hospital v. Scanlon, 475 U.S. 234 (1985).
61. Maine v. Thiboutot, 448 U.S. 1 (1980); Chapman v. Houston Welfare Rights Organization, 440 U.S. 600 (1979).
62. Wilson v. Garcia, 471 U.S. 261, 278 (1985).
63. 441 U.S. at 617.

The existence of a constitutional violation (or the violation of certain federal statutes) is a fundamental prerequisite to hold a municipality liable under § 1983. In *City of Los Angeles v. Heller*,[64] the Supreme Court addressed the requirement of a constitutional violation. In a bifurcated trial the jury returned a verdict in favor of a defendant police officer and against the plaintiff, Heller, on an excessive force claim. The district court then dismissed the action against the city of Los Angeles, concluding that since the officer had been exonerated by the jury, there could be no basis for liability against the city. The Ninth Circuit reversed.[65]

The Supreme Court reversed the Ninth Circuit, stating: "[The city and its police commission] were sued only because they were thought legally responsible for [Officer] Bushey's actions; if the latter inflicted no constitutional injury on respondent, it is inconceivable that petitioners could be liable to respondent."[66] The Court concluded by stating:

> If a person has suffered no constitutional injury at the hands of the individual police officer, the fact that the departmental regulations might have authorized the use of constitutionally excessive force is quite beside the point.[67]

---

64. 475 U.S. 796 (1986).
65. *Heller,* 475 U.S. at 798.
66. *Id.* at 799.
67. *Id.* All of the circuits have followed the holding in *Heller. See* Young v. City of Providence, 404 F.3d 4 (1st Cir. 2005); Curley v. Village of Suffern, 268 F.3d 65 (2d Cir. 2001); Bright v. West Morland County, 380 F.3d 729 (3d Cir. 2004); Grayson v. Peed, 195 F.3d 692 (4th Cir. 1999); Leatherman v. Tarrant County, 28 F.3d 1388 (5th Cir. 1994); Voyticky v. Village of Timberlake, 412 F.3d 669 (6th Cir. 2005); Treece v. Hochstetler, 213 F.3d 360 (7th Cir. 2000); Schulz v. Long, 44 F.3d 643 (8th Cir. 1995); Dixon v. Wallowa County, 336 F.3d 1013 (9th Cir. 2003); Trigalet v. City of Tulsa, 239 F.3d 1150 (10th Cir. 2001); Hardim v. Hayes, 52 F.3d 934 (11th Cir. 1995). The Third Circuit's holding in *Bright* and the Tenth Circuit's holding in *Trigalet* moved those circuits in line with the other circuits on this issue. In Fagan v. City of Vineland, 22 F.3d 1283 (3d Cir. 1994) the Third Circuit had previously held that a finding that an individual officer did not inflict a constitutional injury on the plaintiff did not automatically foreclose a claim against the municipality that employed the individual. Similarly, in Williams v. City of Denver, 99 F.3d 1009 (10th Cir. 1996) the Tenth Circuit held that a city could be liable for it own conduct even in the absence of constitutional conduct by an individual officer. Now, however, the circuits are unanimous in their approach to this issue.

    It should be pointed out, however, that both the Second Circuit and the Eighth Circuit have qualified their holdings. In *Curley, supra,* the Second Circuit stated that *Heller* would not bar a claim "where alleged injuries are not solely attributable to the actions of named individual defendants." 268 F.3d at 71. The Eighth Circuit

The holding in *Heller* should not be misconstrued as a ruling that the dismissal of claims against individual defendants on the basis of qualified immunity will insulate a municipality from liability. *Heller* was based upon the fact that a determination was made that a police officer had not inflicted a constitutional injury upon the plaintiff. The Supreme Court was careful to point out that qualified immunity was not an issue in the case.[68]

An individual defendant dismissed on the basis of qualified immunity stands in a different position than one who has been dismissed on a finding that no constitutional violation occurred. A detailed discussion of qualified immunity can be found in Chapter 9. For purposes of this discussion, however, it is enough to state that qualified immunity shields an individual defendant from liability and suit where there may have been a violation of the plaintiff's constitutional rights because the law was not "clearly established" that the defendant's actions were improper.[69]

While the Supreme Court has not explicitly addressed what impact qualified immunity of an individual defendant has on claims of municipal liability, it has held that qualified immunity does not apply to municipalities.[70] The Circuits that have addressed the issue are unanimous in holding that a municipality does not escape liability for a § 1983 violation based solely upon the qualified immunity of an officer who committed the violation.[71]

---

announced a similar caveat in Speer v. City of Wynne, 276 F.3d 980, 986 (8th Cir. 2002): "However, situations may arise where the combined actions of multiple officials or employees may give rise to a constitutional violation, supporting municipal liability, but where no one individual's actions are sufficient to establish personal liability for the violation."

68. *Heller,* 475 U.S. at 798.
69. *See, generally,* Anderson v. Creighton, 483 U.S. 635 (1987).
70. Owen v. City of Independence, *supra,* note 48.
71. Walker v. Walthan Housing Authority, 44 F.3d 1042, 1047 (1st Cir. 1995) ("Perhaps a municipality might in rare cases be liable for a constitutional violation, even though the individual who acted for it was protected by qualified immunity."); Cowan v. Breen, 352 F.3d 756, 765 (2d Cir. 2003) ("Even if [Officer] Breen was entitled to qualified immunity, if Cooper's constitutional rights were violated, the town could still be liable."); Babb v. Dorman, 33 F.3d 472, 476 n.7 (5th Cir. 1994) (affirming dismissal of conspiracy claim against municipality, but rejecting trial court's reasoning that a city could not conspire with a person who was qualifiedly immune, stating that municipal liability could be upheld notwithstanding the qualified immunity of the individual defendants); Gray v. City of Detroit, 399 F.3d 612, 617 (6th Cir. 2005) ("it is possible that city officials may be entitled to qualified immunity for certain actions while the municipality may nevertheless be held liable for the same actions."); Kuha v. City of Minnetonka, 365 F.3d 590, 603 (8th Cir. 2004) ("even though we find that the defendant officers are entitled to qualified

IV. MUNICIPAL LIABILITY AFTER *MONELL*

A. The Holding in *Monell*

As previously discussed, *Monell* overruled *Monroe v. Pape* to the extent that *Monroe* held that municipalities were not "persons" subject to suit under § 1983. *Monell*'s explicit holding was:

> Our analysis of the legislative history of the Civil Rights Act of 1871 compels the conclusion that Congress *did* intend municipalities and other local government units to be included among those persons to whom § 1983 applies. Local governing bodies, therefore, can be sued directly under § 1983 for monetary, declaratory, or injunctive relief where, as here, the action that is alleged to be unconstitutional implements or executes a policy statement, ordinance, regulation, or decision officially adopted and promulgated by that body's officers. Moreover, although the touchstone of the § 1983 action against a government body is an allegation that official policy is responsible for a deprivation of rights protected by the Constitution, local governments, like every other § 1983 "person," by the very nature of the statute, may be sued for constitutional deprivations visited pursuant to governmental "custom" even though such a custom has not received formal approval through the body's official decisionmaking channels.[72]

---

immunity protection, we must still address the question of municipal liability. This is so because 'a municipality that operates under a policy or custom that unconstitutionally deprives a citizen of his or her rights may be liable under § 1983. This is true even if the arresting officers are not held responsible because of some good faith belief, meriting qualified immunity.'"); Gibson v. County of Washoe, 290 F.3d 1175, 1186 n.7 (9th Cir. 2002) ("For example, a municipality may be liable if an individual officer is exonerated on the basis of the defense of qualified immunity, because even if an officer is entitled to immunity a constitutional violation might still have occurred."); Jiron v. City of Lakewood, 392 F.3d 410, 419 n.8 (10th Cir. 2004) ("Plaintiff is correct that some dismissals against the officers on the basis of qualified immunity do not preclude a suit against the municipality (citation omitted). However, when a finding of qualified immunity is based on a conclusion that the officer has committed no constitutional violation—i.e., the first step of the qualified immunity analysis—a finding of qualified immunity *does* preclude the imposition of municipal liability.").

72. *Monell,* 436 U.S. at 690–91 (emphasis in original).

However, after holding that a municipality was a "person" under § 1983 and could be sued for an officially adopted policy, or for a governmental custom that is the moving force behind a constitutional injury, the Court explicitly rejected liability on the basis of respondeat superior:

> On the other hand, the language of § 1983, read against the background of the same legislative history, compels the conclusion that Congress did not intend municipalities to be held liable unless action pursuant to official municipal policy of some nature caused a constitutional tort. In particular, we conclude that a municipality cannot be held liable *solely* because it employs a tortfeasor—or, in other words, a municipality cannot be held liable under § 1983 on a *respondeat superior* theory.[73]

Tying the two holdings together, the Court concluded:

> We conclude, therefore, that a local government may not be sued under § 1983 for an injury inflicted solely by its employees or agents. Instead, it is when execution of a government's policy or custom, whether made by its lawmakers or those whose edicts or acts may fairly be said to represent official policy, inflicts the injury that the government as an entity is responsible under § 1983. Since this case unquestionably involves official policy as the moving force of the constitutional violation found by the District Court . . . we must reverse the judgment below. In so doing, we have no occasion to address, and do not address, what the full contours of municipal liability under § 1983 may be. We have attempted only to sketch so much of the § 1983 cause of action against the local government as is apparent from the history of the 1871 Act and our prior cases, and we expressly leave further development of this action to another day.[74]

The full contours of municipal liability under § 1983 remain unclear. The Supreme Court has, in some instances, attempted to define some of those contours. The Courts of Appeals have been left to address municipal liability where the Supreme Court has not. In both situations, the result has been inconsistent, leaving practitioners with few clear benchmarks.

---

73. *Id.* at 691 (emphasis in original).
74. *Id.* at 694–95.

B. The Search for "Policy" or "Custom"

To avoid imposition of liability under a theory of respondeat superior, the Supreme Court has consistently required a plaintiff to identify a municipal "policy" or "custom" that caused the constitutional injury. There are three ways that a plaintiff can establish a policy that could result in municipal liability:

1. A policymaker promulgates a generally applicable statement of policy, and the implementation of that policy results in a constitutional deprivation;
2. A course of action tailored to a particular situation, and not intended to have general application, when the action is taken by a policymaker or at the direction of a policymaker;
3. Where a policymaker has failed to act when the need to take action to control governmental agents is so obvious that the policymaker can be said to have been deliberately indifferent to the need.[75]

All three areas require, as an initial step, the identification of a policymaker.

V. POLICYMAKERS

A. Final Authority to Make Policy Under State Law

The policymaker is most easily identified in situations where the legislative body of the entity acts. There, unquestionably, the policymaker has established policy.[76] It is when the legislative body has not acted that difficult questions arise.

In *Pembaur v. City of Cincinnati*,[77] the Court in a plurality opinion held that officials other than the properly constituted legislative body of a municipality could create municipal policy. The Court stated:

> If the decision to adopt that particular course of action is properly made by that government's authorized decisionmakers, it surely represents an act of official government "policy" as that term is commonly understood.[78]

---

75. Liability for a "custom" that has not been formally approved by a policymaker but that subjects a municipality to liability on the theory that the practice is so widespread as to have the force of law (Addickes v. S.H. Cress & Company, 398 U.S. 144, 167–68 (1970)) is typically analyzed under the third basis for finding a municipal policy.
76. *See* City of Newport v. Fact Concerts, 453 U.S. 247 (1981).
77. 475 U.S. 469 (1986).
78. *Pembaur*, 475 U.S. at 481 (footnote omitted).

Justice Brennan's plurality opinion went on to state:

> Having said this much, we hasten to emphasize that not every decision by municipal officers automatically subjects the municipality to § 1983 liability. Municipal liability attaches only where the decisionmaker possesses final authority to establish municipal policy with respect to the action ordered. The fact that a particular official—even a policymaking official—has discretion in the exercise of particular functions does not, without more, give rise to municipal liability based on an exercise of that discretion. The official must also be responsible for establishing final government policy respecting such activity before the municipality can be held liable. Authority to make municipal policy may be granted directly by a legislative enactment or may be delegated by an official who possesses such authority, and of course, whether an official had final policymaking authority is a question of state law.
>
> Thus, for example, the County Sheriff may have discretion to hire and fire employees without also being the county official responsible for establishing county employment policy. If this were the case, the Sheriff's decisions respecting employment would not give rise to municipal liability, although similar decisions with respect to law enforcement practices, over which the Sheriff is the official policymaker, would give rise to municipal liability. Instead, if county employment policy was set by the Board of County Commissioners, only that body's decisions would provide a basis for county liability. This would be true even if the Board left the Sheriff discretion to hire and fire employees and the Sheriff exercised that discretion in an unconstitutional manner; the decision to act unlawfully would not be a decision of the Board. However, if the Board delegated its power to establish final employment policy to the Sheriff, the Sheriff's decisions would represent county policy and could give rise to municipal liability.[79]

The Supreme Court attempted to clarify the issue of final authority to make municipal policy the following year in *City of St. Louis v. Praprotnik*.[80] Unfortunately, a deeply divided Court again resulted in a plurality

79. *Id.* at 481–82 (footnotes omitted).
80. 485 U.S. 112 (1988).

opinion. Relying heavily upon Justice Brennan's opinion in *Pembaur*, the Supreme Court reversed a finding of liability against the city of St. Louis for alleged retaliation in the disciplining and ultimate layoff of a city employee.[81]

The Court reiterated that identifying policymakers with final authority was not a question of federal law, but a question of state law. Moreover, the Court stated that the identification of policymakers was not a question of fact, but is a question for the Court to determine as a matter of law.[82] Acknowledging that there would be "a rich variety of ways in which the power of government is distributed," the Court was confident that "state law (which may include valid local ordinances and regulations) will always direct a court to some official or body that has the responsibility for making law or setting policy in any given area of a local government's business."[83]

The Court then touched upon the issue that has given rise to some of the most difficult determinations in this area: when a municipal policymaker has delegated policymaking authority to another official. The Court stated that the mere exercise of discretion by an employee will not give rise to a constitutional violation, as that result would be indistinguishable from respondeat superior liability. The Court also acknowledged, however, that policymakers could not insulate a municipality from liability simply by delegating their policymaking authority to others.[84] The Court then outlined guiding principles in addressing the issue.

The Court, relying upon *Pembaur*, stated that the relevant authority to make municipal policy for *Monell* liability was necessarily the authority to make *final* municipal policy.

> When an official's discretionary decisions are constrained by policies not of that official's making, those policies, rather than the sub-

81. The employee, James Praprotnik, alleged that he had been first transferred and then laid off in retaliation for appealing an earlier suspension. The St. Louis legislative body was charged with enacting ordinances. It had created a civil service commission whose function was to hear appeals from city employees who believed that their rights had been violated by employment decisions. Praprotnik was disciplined by his supervisors, transferred to another unit, and ultimately laid off purportedly due to a lack of funding. All of the employment decisions were made by his immediate supervisors. Praprotnik had been able to obtain relief from some of the adverse decisions from the Civil Service Commission. His appeal to the Civil Service Commission for the layoff was postponed when Praprotnik filed suit in federal court challenging his layoff on the basis of a First Amendment violation.

82. *Praprotnik,* 485 U.S. at 124.

83. *Id.* at 125 (footnote omitted).

84. *Id.* at 126.

> ordinate's departures from them, are the act of the municipality. Similarly, when a subordinate's decision is subject to review by the municipality's authorized policymakers, they have retained the authority to measure the official's conduct for conformance with *their* policies. If the authorized policymakers approve a subordinate's decision and the basis for it, their ratification would be chargeable to the municipality because their decision is final.[85]

Rejecting the Court of Appeals' conclusion that Praprotnik's supervisors were policymakers, the Court stated that simply going along with discretionary decisions made by subordinates was not a delegation to the subordinates to make policy. As the Court noted, "It is equally consistent with the presumption that the subordinates are faithfully attempting to comply with the policies that are supposed to guide them."[86]

The Court observed that it would be a different matter if a particular decision made by a subordinate was in the form of a policy statement and was then expressly approved by the policymaker. It would also be a different matter, the Court stated, if a series of decisions by a subordinate manifested a custom or usage of which the policymaker must have been aware, but failed to act. The Court then concluded by stating:

> But the mere failure to investigate the basis of a subordinate's discretionary decisions does not amount to a delegation of policymaking authority, especially where (as here) the wrongfulness of the subordinate's decision arises from a retaliatory motive or other unstated rationale. In such circumstances, the purpose of § 1983 would not be served by treating a subordinate employee's decision as if it were a reflection of municipal policy.[87]

The Supreme Court finally rendered a majority opinion on the issue of policymakers in *Jett v. Dallas Independent School District*.[88] The Court held that municipal policy could only be established by:

> [T]hose officials or governmental bodies who speak with final policymaking authority for the local government actor concerning the action alleged to have caused the particular constitutional or statutory violation at issue.[89]

---

85. *Id.* at 127 (emphasis added).
86. *Id.* at 130.
87. *Id.* at 130.
88. 491 U.S. 701 (1989).
89. *Jett,* 491 U.S. at 737.

Given the Supreme Court's struggle to create a coherent standard, it is not surprising that this has proven to be one of the more difficult areas in § 1983 litigation. It is difficult to reconcile successive sentences in some of the Supreme Court's opinions. What the Court gives on the one hand, it apparently takes away with the other. The Courts of Appeals have fared little better in their attempts to create a uniform standard.

In *Young v. City of Providence*, 404 F.3d 4 (1st Cir. 2005), the First Circuit declined to determine whether a chief of police was a final policymaker for the City of Providence on police department training issues, finding that even if the chief were not such a final policymaker, the commissioner of public safety was. The First Circuit found that the commissioner had been delegated broad policymaking authority over Providence Police Department procedures by the municipality, and his promulgation and approval of policies constituted official policy of the City of Providence. In *Back v. Hastings on Hudson Union Free School Dist.*, 365 F.3d 107, 128–29 (2d Cir. 2004), the Second Circuit held that the Board of Education was the final policymaker for a school district on employment matters, but the plaintiff failed to demonstrate that the school board approved of discriminatory views held by administrators, or acted with delivered indifference to the plaintiff's allegations of discrimination.

The Third Circuit's decision in *McGreevy v. Stroup*, 413 F.3d 359 (3d Cir. 2005), demonstrates the difficulty in reconciling the seemingly conflicting statements from *Pembaur* and *Praprotnik*. McGreevy was employed as the school nurse at the Bermudian Springs School District Elementary School. McGreevy began publicly advocating on behalf of the mother of two orthopedically disabled children in order to gain special assistance for them. She communicated with the Pennsylvania Department of Health and the Office for Civil Rights. She also contacted the Bureau of Compliance of the Pennsylvania Department of Education. These communications resulted in a meeting between Gerald Soltis, the superintendent; Roger Stroup, the principal of the elementary school; the former assistant superintendent; and McGreevy. Subsequently, McGreevy filed a complaint with the Pennsylvania Department of Agriculture regarding unlicensed spraying of pesticide in the school that had resulted in both students and teachers becoming ill. Due to that complaint, the school district was fined by the Department of Agriculture. McGreevy then learned that she had been listed as the middle school nurse for the school district as well. She contacted the Pennsylvania Department of Health and informed the department that she was not the middle school nurse. As a result, the Auditor General's office began an investigation and eventually ordered withholding of future reimbursements to the district from the Department of Health for School Nurse Services. At the end of that school year, McGreevy received her lowest employee evaluation. McGreevy alleged that she became the target of constant criticism and harassment, especially at the hands of the superintendent and principal. McGreevy tendered a letter of resignation to the district. McGreevy filed suit against the district under 42 U.S.C. § 1983 alleging violations of her First Amendment rights.

A district court granted the school district's motion for summary judgment, holding that only the school board was a final policymaker and that the plaintiff had failed to prove any policy, practice, or custom of the school board that violated her First Amendment rights. Reversing, the Third Circuit held that the fact that McGreevy could have appealed her employment ratings to the school board was not determinative. Rather, a state statute providing that the ratings were to be done under the supervision of the superintendent rendered the superintendent a final policymaker. The school district, therefore, could be liable if the jury determined that McGreevy's ratings were adopted by the superintendent in retaliation for exercise of her First Amendment rights.[90]

In apparent contrast to the Third Circuit's reasoning in *McGreevy*, the Fourth Circuit in *Kirby v. City of Elizabeth City*, 388 F.3d 440, 451 (4th Cir. 2004) held that a chief of police lacked final authority with regard to the motion because the decision was subject to review by the City's Personnel Appeals Committee. The Third Circuit held that the availability of an appeal process was irrelevant to determining a final policymaker, since there is no exhaustion requirement in § 1983 claims and since the plaintiff did not actually appeal.[91] Under Fourth Circuit precedent, however, when a municipal official's discretionary action is subject to review by the municipality's authorized policymakers, those policymakers are deemed to have retained the authority to measure that conduct for conformance with official policies.[92]

The Fifth Circuit drew a distinction between an officially promulgated policy and the official who enforces that policy. In *Communication Workers of America v. Ector County Hospital District*, 392 F.3d 733, 739 (5th Cir. 2004), plaintiff Herrera was disciplined for wearing a "Union Yes" lapel button, in violation of the hospital's dress code. Herrera was disciplined by his immediate supervisor, Durham. The hospital argued that Durham had "no policymaking authority, much less final policymaking authority." The hospital, therefore, argued that it could not be liable for the actions of an

90. *McGreevy,* 413 F.3d at 368–69.
91. *Id.* at 369.
92. *Kirby,* 388 F.3d at 451, citing Riddick v. School Board, 238 F.3d 518, 523 (4th Cir. 2000).

official who lacked final policymaking authority. In rejecting the argument, the Fifth Circuit held that a municipality can be liable if it causes a constitutional tort through a policy statement officially adopted and promulgated by a final policymaking body or official, even if the official who enforces the policy has no final policymaking authority. "This last fact does not change the character of the alleged injury or the policy under which that injury occurred."[93] The Fifth Circuit explained that the crucial question was whether the dress code was an official policy of the hospital, not whether the hospital employee who enforced the terms of the policy had final policymaking authority.[94]

The Sixth Circuit narrowly applied *Pembaur* and *Praprotnik* in *Miller v. Calhoun County*.[95] In *Miller*, the personal representative of the estate of a prison detainee who died of a brain tumor while in pretrial custody at the county jail alleged deliberate indifference to the detainee's medical needs. The plaintiff argued that the on-call doctor was a final policymaker, and his decision to delay treatment became the policy of the county. The plaintiff argued that the sheriff and jail administrator delegated final policymaking authority to the on-call doctor.[96] In rejecting this argument, the Sixth Circuit noted that policymaking implies the power to "formulate plans for the implementation of broad goals," and that a policymaker's decisions "are final and unreviewable and are not constrained by the official policies of superior officials."[97]

The Sixth Circuit noted that the on-call doctor contracted with the county to provide on-site services for eight hours a week, and to be on call twenty-four hours a day. There was no evidence that the doctor was involved in setting or influencing medical policy at the jail. In contrast, the sheriff testified that, pursuant to his authority, he appointed a training coordinator, sought accreditation for the jail, requested bids for medical services, changed medical providers, formulated policy for medical care, and initiated an investigation into the detainee's death.[98] On the record, the Sixth Circuit found that final policymaking authority clearly rested with the sheriff, not with the on-call doctor. Similar to the Fifth Circuit's holding in *Ector County Hospital*, the Seventh Circuit, in *Killinger v. Johnson*,[99] held that in

93. 392 F.3d at 739.
94. *Id.*
95. 408 F.3d 803, 818 (6th Cir. 2005).
96. *Id.* at 817–18.
97. *Id.* at 818.
98. *Id.*
99. 389 F.3d 765, 771 (7th Cir. 2004).

order to have final policymaking authority, an official must possess "responsibility for making law or setting policy," that is, "authority to adopt rules for the conduct of government." The Court stated that the mere authority to implement preexisting rules is not the authority to set policy.

The plaintiff, David Killinger, sued the mayor and the Village of Port Byron after the mayor had temporarily closed Killinger's bar, suspended the liquor license, and imposed a fine for underage drinking. The plaintiff alleged that the mayor's decision, which was exercised pursuant to the state Liquor Act, constituted municipal authority. The Seventh Circuit rejected the argument, finding that there was no state or local law that gave the mayor authority to adopt rules relevant to the case. The court noted that the plaintiff's argument that the mayor failed to observe the procedures mandated by the Liquor Act defeated the claim. The court noted that it was the Illinois General Assembly, not the mayor, that established the procedures applicable to temporary closings, suspensions, and fines under the Act. The Court stated that "if the mayor violated these procedures, he was acting contrary to—not setting—the policy of the State. Because the mayor does not hold final policymaking authority to establish procedural rules, Port Byron is not liable for his actions."[100]

The lack of clarity in this area is again demonstrated by the Eighth Circuit's decision in *Ware v. Jackson County, Missouri*.[101] The plaintiff, Sylvia Ware, was an inmate who was raped by a corrections officer. The plaintiff alleged, in part, that the Director of the Jackson County Jail was a final policymaker for the County. The plaintiff argued that the Director's failure to discipline the corrections officer was a direct causal link to her rape. The County argued that the Director was not a final policymaker. The County argued that the Director's decisions were subject to review by both the County Executive and the Director of Administration. The County asserted that the Director merely possessed discretionary authority that was constrained by policies of the County. In rejecting the County's argument, the Eighth Circuit found the Director to be a final policymaker on jail personnel matters. The court noted that the Director had authority to promulgate jail policy, including the rules of conduct for personnel; the Director directly handled disciplinary actions in the case; the County Executive lacked a proven mechanism through which he could review the Director's decisions regarding discipline; and the Director was in charge of more than 260 employees.[102]

---

100. 389 F.3d at 772.
101. 150 F.3d 873 (8th Cir. 1998).
102. 150 F.3d at 886–87.

In *Lytle v. Carl*,[103] the Ninth Circuit held that a school superintendent was a final policymaker where the school board had explicitly delegated full authority over employee discipline to the superintendent. District policy explicitly provided that the school board "does not have the authority to discipline employees. Discipline is a right reserved to the superintendent and other administrators in accordance with the applicable negotiated agreements, laws, board policies, and regulations."

In *Dill v. City of Edmond*,[104] the Tenth Circuit held that where the city charter and policies were silent as to which official had authority for discipline and transfer within the police department, the chief of police was a final policymaker. The city argued that only the city council and the city manager could be determined to be a final policy maker. The Tenth Circuit found that under the circumstances, however, final policy in the area of the discipline and transfer of police officers had been given to the chief of police.

Diametrically opposed to the Seventh Circuit's decision in *Killinger*, that a local official enforcing a state law was not a final policymaker who could subject a municipality to liability, is the Eleventh Circuit's decision in *Cooper v. Dillon*.[105] At issue in *Cooper* was a Florida statute that made it a misdemeanor for a participant in an internal investigation of a law enforcement officer to disclose any information obtained pursuant to the investigation before it becomes a public record. The plaintiff published a free weekly newspaper that was distributed in several hundred locations in Key West, Florida. In a series of articles the plaintiff reported that an internal affairs investigator with the Key West Police Department failed to investigate a complaint filed with the Florida Department of Law Enforcement. The plaintiff filed a formal complaint against the internal affairs investigator. The plaintiff subsequently received two letters from the Florida Department of Law Enforcement. The plaintiff published an article in his newspaper disclosing his complaint and the correspondence from the Florida Department of Law Enforcement. When the article was published, defendant Dillon, the Chief of Police of the Key West Police Department, obtained a warrant for the plaintiff's arrest for violation of the nondisclosure statute.[106]

The Eleventh Circuit found that Dillon, as Chief of Police, was the ultimate policymaker for police procedure in the City of Key West.[107] The Eleventh Circuit further found that the fact that Dillon was enforcing an

---

103. 382 F.3d 978, 983 (9th Cir. 2004).
104. 153 F.3d 1193, 1211 (10th Cir. 1998).
105. 403 F.3d 1208 (11th Cir. 2005).
106. *Id.* at 1212–13.
107. *Id.* at 1222.

unconstitutional state statute did not shield the city from liability, because Dillon was in a policymaking position.[108] The Eleventh Circuit slightly recharacterized the chief's authority, finding that he was "clothed with final policymaking authority for law enforcement matters in Key West and in this capacity he chose to enforce the statute against Cooper."[109] Thus, the court ultimately determined that Dillon's single decision subjected the City of Key West to liability.

Conceptually this is one of the most difficult areas in § 1983 litigation. The practitioner must be aware of the distinction between policymaking authority and discretion in the execution of policy. The courts are reluctant to ascribe policymaking authority to a high-level official with discretion to act, in the absence of a clear statement under state or local law that the official is, in fact, a policymaker. Thus it is also an area that is sufficiently unsettled that practitioners can be creative in advancing novel theories of liability and defenses.

B. Rules for Determining Policymakers

In *Jett*, the Supreme Court clarified two interrelated points from *Pembaur* and *Praprotnik* related to the issue of determining where policymaking authority lies. The Court held:

> Whether a particular official has 'final policymaking authority' is a question of state law; and
>
> The identification of a policymaker is a legal question to be resolved by the trial court before the case is submitted to the jury.[110]

---

108. *Id.* at 1223. This decision is difficult to reconcile with *Monell.* The Eleventh Circuit determined that the chief of police was the ultimate policymaker *for police procedures* in the city. However, a decision to make an arrest is not a procedural decision. The effect of the Eleventh Circuit's decision is that any chief of police who actively participates in law enforcement activities (as most chiefs of police do in small towns), creates automatic liability for the municipality if they make an incorrect decision regarding probable cause, use of force, etc. While the individual chief may well be exonerated on the basis of qualified immunity, the status of the chief under *Cooper* as "the ultimate policymaker" has the effect of creating respondeat superior liability to the city. Not only is this result directly at odds with the Seventh Circuit's decision in *Killinger,* but it appears to be directly contrary to the policy behind *Monell.*

109. *Id.*

110. *Jett,* 491 U.S. at 737.

As the Supreme Court readily admitted in *Praprotnik*, the "rich variety" of local government models can create some difficulty in identifying who a policymaker is in a given situation. Since the courts may look beyond state statutes to local ordinances and regulations, however, the Court was confident that the law will ultimately direct the trial court to some official or body "that has the responsibility for making law or setting policy in any given area of a local government's business."[111]

Based upon this analysis, it is doubtful that prior decisions from a particular federal district court or circuit will be binding in terms of identifying a policymaker in subsequent cases. Unless the identical municipal entity is involved, a holding that the city manager of a given city is a policymaker is unlikely to be binding authority for determining that a city administrator is a policymaker in another lawsuit involving a different municipality.

It is also unclear from the Supreme Court the method by which the trial court determines who a policymaker is. One thing that is clear is that this effort determines who a policymaker is. Another thing that is clear is that this determination is to be made by the court, not the jury. The preferable way to make the determination would seem to be by way of a motion for summary judgment, either by the defendant challenging the identification of certain individuals as policymakers, or by the plaintiff seeking a determination that a given individual is a policymaker. In the absence of motions for summary judgment, however, the trial court must be provided with sufficient information by the parties to make the determination prior to submitting the case to the jury. It remains for the jury to determine whether the decisions of the policymaker have caused the deprivation of rights at issue.[112] Thus, the court must make the determination as to who a policymaker is before the case is submitted to the jury. Both plaintiffs and defendants should give early attention to either agreeing upon the identity of the policymaker or gathering the appropriate state and local laws, ordinances, and regulations that will allow the court to make that determination.

C. Single Decision of Policymaker Is Policy

In *City of Oklahoma City v. Tuttle*,[113] the Supreme Court held that proof of a single incident of unconstitutional activity is not sufficient to impose liability on a municipality unless the plaintiff could prove that the incident was caused by an existing unconstitutional policy that could in turn be attributed

---

111. *Praprotnik,* 485 U.S. at 125.
112. *Jett,* 491 U.S. at 737.
113. 471 U.S. 808 (1985).

to a municipal policymaker.[114] The Court went on to hold that where a policy is not itself unconstitutional, more proof than a single incident would be necessary to establish municipal liability.[115] In *Pembaur*, the Supreme Court held that a single decision by a policymaker could result in municipal liability:

> If the decision to adopt that particular course of action is properly made by that government's authorized decisionmakers, it surely represents an act of official government "policy" as that term is commonly understood. More importantly, where action is directed by those who establish government policy, the municipality is equally responsible whether that action is to be taken only once or to be taken repeatedly.[116]

Where a municipal policy is itself unconstitutional, a single application of that policy will result in municipal liability. By the same token, where a municipal policymaker makes a single decision, and that decision is applied, municipal liability will result. Where there is no policy established by a policymaker, however, and the plaintiff attempts to impose liability on the basis of custom or practice, a single action by a municipal employee will not result in liability. As the court explained in *Tuttle*, the word "policy" implies a course of action chosen from among various alternatives. A single action on the part of a non-policymaking employee is insufficient to create a policy attributable to the municipality.

VI. CUSTOM OR PRACTICE

In addition to imposing liability upon municipalities for the actions of policymakers that cause constitutional deprivations, a municipality can also be liable under § 1983 when its custom or practice causes constitutional deprivations. The Supreme Court in *Monell* explicitly recognized that municipalities could be liable for custom or practice:

> Local governments, like every other § 1983 "person," by the very terms of the statute, may be sued for constitutional deprivations visited pursuant to governmental "custom" even though such a custom has not received formal approval through the body's official decisionmaking channels. . . . Congress included customs and usages in § 1983 because of the persistent and widespread discriminatory

---

114. *Tuttle,* 471 U.S. at 824.

115. *Id.*

116. *Pembaur,* 475 U.S. at 481 (footnote omitted).

> practices of state officials. . . . Although not authorized by written law, such practices of state officials could well be so permanent and well settled as to constitute a "custom or usage" with the force of law.[117]

The courts have required substantial proof to support a claim of a municipal custom or policy. For example, in *Doe v. Claiborne County*,[118] the Sixth Circuit rejected a claim that a school board had a custom of failing to act to prevent the sexual abuse of students. The court stated that a custom must have "the force of law" and be a "legal institution" not memorialized by written law.[119] While the cases rejecting attempts to impose liability upon custom or practice far outnumber those imposing liability, there are numerous cases in which custom or practice was the basis for municipal liability.[120]

There are no bright-line rules that will establish when a custom or practice exists. It is clear that there must be more than one event to give rise to a custom or practice. Additionally, the practice must be "long-standing" and "pervasive." Beyond that, the determination is subject to ad hoc review by the courts.

VII. CAUSATION AND CULPABILITY

A. Causation

Even assuming that a plaintiff can establish the existence of a municipal policy or custom, that does not end the inquiry. Before liability can be imposed upon a municipality, a plaintiff must establish causation between the policy and the constitutional deprivation. This link was established in *Monell*, where the Court stated that "the touchstone of the § 1983 action

---

117. *Monell,* 436 U.S. at 690–91 (footnote omitted).
118. 103 F.3d 495 (6th Cir. 1996).
119. *Doe,* 103 F.3d at 507–08.
120. *See, e.g.,* Scott v. Moore, 85 F.3d 230, 334 (5th Cir. 1996) (Ten-year practice at jail to have unsupervised male jailer present with female detainees constituted custom or practice sufficient to impose liability.); Bordanarro v. McLeod, 871 F.2d 1151, 1155 (1st Cir. 1989) (Police department had long-standing practice, engaged in by virtually all officers, of breaking down doors without a warrant when arresting a felon.); Jones v. City of Chicago, 856 F.2d 985, 995 (7th Cir. 1988) (Police officers' keeping of "street files" was pervasive and long-standing, entitling jury to find that it had been approved by policymakers for the police department.); Leach v. Shelby County Sheriff, 891 F.2d 1241, 1247 (6th Cir. 1989) (Deliberate indifference to medical needs of physically incapacitated prisoners was so pervasive as to constitute custom and practice for the county sufficient to impose liability.).

against a government body is an allegation that official policy is *responsible* for the deprivation of rights"[121] under the Constitution. The Court also pointed out that "Congress did not intend municipalities to be held liable unless action pursuant to official municipal policy of some nature *caused* a constitutional tort."[122] The connection between policy and constitutional deprivation has been reiterated by the Supreme Court in every case since *Monell* when municipal liability has been addressed.

In *Bryan County v. Brown*,[123] the plaintiff brought a claim for damages under § 1983, alleging that a county deputy used excessive force in arresting her and that the county was liable based on the sheriff's decision to hire the deputy, who had a misdemeanor assault conviction. The plaintiff obtained judgment at the district court level, and the judgment was affirmed by the Fifth Circuit.[124] The Supreme Court reversed, concluding that "Congress did not intend to impose liability on a municipality unless deliberate action attributable to the municipality itself is the 'moving force' behind the Plaintiff's deprivation of federal rights."[125]

The plaintiff's claims against Bryan County arose out of the sheriff's decision to hire a reserve officer without adequately checking his criminal background. The reserve officer had pleaded guilty to various driving-related offenses and other misdemeanors, including assault and battery, resisting arrest, and public drunkenness.

While Oklahoma law did not preclude the hiring of an individual as a police officer who had a misdemeanor conviction, the plaintiff asserted that the hiring policy of Bryan County, as instituted by its policymaker, Sheriff Moore, was so inadequate that it amounted to deliberate indifference to the plaintiff's constitutional rights.[126] The county stipulated that Sheriff Moore was the policymaker for the county regarding the sheriff's department. The Court stated that it is not enough, however, for a § 1983 plaintiff to merely identify conduct attributable to the municipality. Additionally, the plaintiff must demonstrate "a direct causal link between the municipal action and the deprivation of federal rights."[127]

Distinguishing situations where a municipality's legislative body has intentionally deprived a plaintiff of a federally protected right, the Court

121. *Monell,* 436 U.S. at 690 (emphasis added).
122. *Id.* at 691 (emphasis added).
123. 520 U.S. 397 (1997).
124. 67 F.3d 1174 (5th Cir. 1995).
125. *Bryan County,* 520 U.S. at 399–400.
126. *Id.* at 401.
127. *Id.* at 404.

required "rigorous standards" of causation to be applied in Bryan County, where a plaintiff claimed that the municipality had not directly inflicted injury but had caused an employee to do so.[128] Since every injury at the hands of a municipal employee can be traced to a hiring decision in a "but-for" sense (but for the decision to hire the employee, the plaintiff would not have suffered an injury), the Supreme Court stated that "a court must carefully test the link between the policymaker's inadequate decision and the particular injury alleged."[129] The Court required that a plaintiff prove that a particular employee was "highly likely" to inflict the particular injury suffered by the plaintiff before municipal liability could attach. The Court explained that:

> [A] finding of culpability simply cannot depend on the mere probability that any officer inadequately screened will inflict any constitutional injury. Rather, it must depend on a finding that this officer was highly likely to inflict the particular injury suffered by the plaintiff. The connection between the background of the particular applicant and the specific constitutional violation alleged must be strong.[130]

After "carefully testing" the link between Sheriff Moore's hiring decision and the plaintiff's injury, the Court found the plaintiff's proofs to be inadequate. The Court concluded that the reserve deputy's criminal record was simply not of a nature that the sheriff would necessarily have determined that the use of excessive force would have been a plainly obvious consequence of the hiring decision.[131] Concluding, the Court held:

> Bryan County is not liable for Sheriff Moore's isolated decision to hire Burns without adequate screening, because respondent has not demonstrated that his decision reflected a conscious disregard for a high risk that Burns would use excessive force in violation of respondent's federally protected right.[132]

After *Bryan County*, the plaintiff who seeks to impose liability on a municipality for an injury inflicted by a non-policymaking employee bears a significant burden on the issue of causation.

---

128. *Id.* at 405.
129. *Id.* at 410.
130. *Id.* at 412.
131. *Id.* at 412–13.
132. *Id.* at 415–16.

The issue of causation is often tied to the issue of fault. As the Supreme Court explained in *Bryan County*, proof that a policymaker had intentionally deprived a plaintiff of a federally protected right necessarily establishes municipal liability. Similarly, where the action taken or directed by the policymaker violates federal law, the plaintiff will necessarily establish that the action was the moving force behind the injury. It is in the case where some intervening act on the part of a lower-level employee inflicts the injury that the issue of causation arises.

The most common situation that falls within this category of cases is "failure to train." In *City of Canton v. Harris*,[133] the Supreme Court held that there are limited circumstances in which a "failure to train" can be the basis for liability under § 1983. In outlining those "limited circumstances," the Court again focused on the issue of causation. The Court held that a municipality could be liable under § 1983 only where its policy of failing to train was the "moving force" behind the constitutional violation.

In explaining the parameters for municipal liability, the Court held that a plaintiff would have to show much more than that the existing training program represented a policy for which the city is responsible. The Court held that the municipality must choose an inadequate training program from among various alternatives. Giving as an example the need to train police officers in the constitutional limitations on the use of deadly force, the Court stated that in light of the duties assigned to police officers, the need for more or different training may become so obvious, and the inadequacy of the training so likely to result in constitutional violations, that the policymakers can reasonably be said to have been deliberately indifferent to the need for more or different training.[134]

The Court then emphasized that before liability can attach, an identified deficiency in a training program "must be closely related to the ultimate injury."[135] The plaintiff must prove that the deficiency actually caused the particular constitutional deprivation.[136] Implicitly, the fact that a deficiency in a training program could be said to lead to a higher likelihood of constitutional deprivations generally would be insufficient. Similarly, if the evidence in a particular case demonstrates that the same result would have occurred regardless of the training program, municipal liability would not attach. It is only when an identifiable deficiency in the training program can

---

133. 489 U.S. 378 (1989).
134. *City of Canton*, 489 U.S. at 390.
135. *Id.* at 391.
136. *Id.*

be proven to have resulted in the specific constitutional violation that municipal liability can attach.

Circuit decisions on the issue of causation which predate *Bryan County* also required a strong showing of causation. For example, in *Walker v. City of New York*,[137] the Second Circuit rejected a claim of failure to train officers not to commit perjury on the basis of causation. While the court acknowledged that there had not been a training program with respect to the obligation not to commit perjury, the Second Circuit found the obligation not to commit perjury was so obvious to all without training that the failure to train was not "so likely" to produce a constitutional violation that the city could be held liable.[138]

In *Jones v. Wellham*,[139] the Fourth Circuit held that there was not the necessary affirmative link between a city policy and a violation where a police officer had been disciplined, but not discharged, for a sexual assault ten years before committing a sexual assault on the plaintiff. The Fourth Circuit's standard for the connection between the policy and the injury was that the specific injury be "almost bound to happen, sooner or later, rather than merely likely to happen in the long run."[140]

In *Gazette v. City of Pontiac*,[141] the Sixth Circuit accepted the plaintiff's facts as true, but found no causal link between the municipal policy and the constitutional deprivation. The plaintiff alleged that when her mother was reported missing under circumstances that suggested foul play, the police assured her that they were taking appropriate action, but in fact did nothing. The mother was found murdered several days later, and the plaintiff claims that, had the police not lied to her, she could have investigated her mother's disappearance and found her before the murder.

In rejecting this argument, the Sixth Circuit Court stated that there was "no close causal connection between the police officers' lies and Bandy's death because many factors could have prevented the police officers, or Bandy's family and friends, from locating Bandy. The causal connection between the police officers' lies and Bandy's death simply is not sufficient to sustain a § 1983 claim."[142]

In *Ricketts v. City of Columbia*,[143] the Eighth Circuit found no causal link in a case where the plaintiff claimed that the casual treatment of

137. 974 F.2d 293 (2d Cir. 1992).
138. *Walker,* 974 F.2d at 299–300.
139. 104 F.3d 620 (4th Cir. 1997).
140. *Jones,* 104 F.3d at 625.
141. 41 F.3d 1061 (6th Cir. 1994).
142. *Gazette,* 41 F.3d at 1066.
143. 36 F.3d 775 (8th Cir. 1994).

domestic abuse cases by police resulted in her and her mother being attacked by her estranged husband. Specifically, the plaintiff alleged that had her estranged husband been arrested for previous domestic assaults, he would not have raped her and murdered her mother on the date in question. Rejecting this claim, the Eighth Circuit stated that such speculation could not "establish causation because it is equally plausible that an arrest for the prior harassment might as easily have spawned retaliatory violence from Sonny."[144]

The Supreme Court's decision in *Bryan County* establishes a significant hurdle for plaintiffs to overcome. In situations where the municipal policy is not directly tied to the constitutional injury (primarily in failure to train in negligent hiring cases), a plaintiff must now prove that the specific constitutional injury is directly related to the municipal policy and that the former would be a "plainly obvious consequence" of the latter. It should be anticipated that the courts will not be lenient in assessing this nexus in light of *Bryan County*.

B. Deliberate Indifference: The Standard of Culpability

Closely related to the issue of causation is the issue of culpability. As with the issue of causation, where the municipal policy itself is unconstitutional, culpability is a given. For example, when a city's legislative body violates a First Amendment right through a legislative enactment (*Newport v. Fact Concerts, Inc.*[145]), liability is established when the decision itself is found to be unconstitutional. Similarly, where a municipal employee is discharged without procedural due process (*Owen v. Independence*[146]), the formal decision of the municipal legislative body discharging the employee without a hearing resulted in liability.

Claims not involving an allegation that the municipal action itself violated the Constitution present different issues of fault. In the examples of First Amendment violations and procedural due process violations, the "state of mind" requirement was all that was necessary to establish the underlying constitutional violation. That was true because the plaintiff was challenging the decision of the legislative body itself. However, where a plaintiff seeks to establish liability on the theory that a facially lawful municipal policy or action has led an employee to violate the plaintiff's constitutional rights, the plaintiff must demonstrate that the municipal action was taken with "deliberate indifference," quite apart from the underlying constitutional claim.

---

144. *Ricketts,* 36 F.3d at 780.
145. 453 U.S. 247 (1981).
146. 445 U.S. 622 (1980).

The simplest examples are found in *City of Canton* and *Bryan County*. In *City of Canton*, the plaintiff claimed that the individual police officer deprived her of due process by failing to obtain adequate medical care for her mental condition while she was in policy custody. In *Bryan County*, the plaintiff claimed that the individual police officer violated her Fourth Amendment rights. The claims against the municipal employer, however, were premised upon a policy of failing to train and a policy of improper hiring procedures. Thus, proving a due process violation in *City of Canton* or a Fourth Amendment violation in *Bryan County* against the individual officer would not speak to the city's culpability.

In *City of Canton*, the Court held that liability could attach to a municipality where the failure to train amounted to deliberate indifference to the rights of persons with whom the police come into contact.[147] The deliberate indifference required a finding that the municipality made a deliberate choice to follow a course of action from among various alternatives.[148] The Court stated, "That a particular officer may be unsatisfactorily trained will not alone suffice to fasten liability on the city, for the officer's shortcomings may have resulted from factors other than a faulty training program."[149]

The Court also rejected the idea that liability could attach if the plaintiff proved that an injury could have been avoided if better or different training had been given. The Court observed that such a claim could be made about almost any encounter resulting in injury, yet would "not condemn the adequacy of the program to enable officers to respond properly to the usual and recurring situations with which they must deal."[150]

In *Bryan County,* the Supreme Court held that the sheriff's failure to thoroughly review a deputy's criminal record prior to hiring him was not enough to establish deliberate indifference. The Court stated:

> In layman's terms, inadequate screening of an applicant's record may reflect "indifference" to the applicant's background. For purposes of a legal inquiry into municipal liability under § 1983, however, that is not the relevant "indifference." A plaintiff must demonstrate that a municipal decision reflects deliberate indifference to the risk that a violation of a particular constitutional or statutory right will follow the decision. Only where adequate scrutiny of an applicant's background would lead a reasonable policymaker to conclude that the plainly obvious consequences of the decision to hire the applicant

---

147. *City of Canton,* 489 U.S. at 388.
148. *Id.* at 389.
149. *Id.* at 390–91.
150. *Id.* at 391.

would be deprivation of a third party's federally protected right can the official's failure to adequately scrutinize the applicant's background constitute "deliberate indifference."[151]

In light of *Bryan County*, it is likely that the issue of culpability will receive greater scrutiny in the future. This has been an area in which the circuits have been inconsistent. Many times, after struggling with the difficult concepts of who is a policymaker and causation, the courts essentially assume culpability. The Supreme Court in *Bryan County*, however, makes clear that culpability is a separate issue, and a significant one to be addressed with careful scrutiny.

The decision in *Bryan County* reaffirms the circuit decisions that predated it. *Bryan County* demonstrated that the "deliberate indifference" standard is the standard by which essentially all claims of municipal liability will be addressed. The circuits have traditionally required a showing of deliberate indifference before imposing municipal liability for a policy that is not facially invalid. However, prior to *Bryan County*, the circuits varied widely in what constituted "deliberate indifference."

For example, in *San Filippo v. Bongiovanni*,[152] the Third Circuit held that Rutgers University could be liable if it was deliberately indifferent to the plaintiff's First Amendment rights by approving a recommendation that the plaintiff be dismissed. The Third Circuit's discussion, however, did not appear to require a great deal of culpability on the part of the university before the deliberate indifference standard could be met. The court stated that the university could not be liable for a "mere failure to investigate" the rationale behind a recommendation to terminate.[153]

The court went on to state that the university "had reason to suspect" that the plaintiff's protected activities had been a motivating factor in the decision to initiate dismissal proceedings.[154] Finally, the court stated that the university was required to "tread with a certain amount of care to avoid the possibility of *inadvertently* punishing someone for exercising his First Amendment rights."[155] These facts led the Third Circuit to conclude that a factual issue existed as to whether the university had been deliberately indifferent.

In contrast, in *Jones v. Wellham*,[156] the Fourth Circuit held that there was no deliberate indifference as a matter of law for the actions of the chief

151. *Bryan County,* 520 U.S. at 411.
152. 30 F.3d 424 (3d Cir. 1994).
153. *San Filippo,* 30 F.3d at 446.
154. *Id.*
155. *Id.* at 446 n.26.
156. 104 F.3d 620 (4th Cir. 1997).

of police. The chief had disciplined, but not discharged, a police officer in 1979 for a sexual assault. After six months, the chief returned the officer to street duty. In 1990, the same officer raped the plaintiff. In finding that the chief's actions did not constitute deliberate indifference, the Fourth Circuit stated that, with the benefit of hindsight, the chief's actions were "clearly unfortunate, might perhaps be thought to be imprudent, or even be found legally negligent, but that does not suffice; only decisions taken with deliberate indifference to the potential consequences of known risks suffices to impose municipal liability."[157]

In *Gonzalez v. Ysleta Independent School District*,[158] the Fifth Circuit rejected the plaintiff's claim that the school district had been deliberately indifferent by transferring a teacher to another school in the face of allegations of sexual abuse. In seeking to satisfy the *City of Canton* test, the plaintiff argued that the school district made a deliberate choice from among various alternatives, such as suspending the teacher, ordering further investigation, scheduling a hearing, issuing a more severe reprimand, or providing for classroom monitoring. Instead, the school district chose to transfer the teacher to another school, where he sexually abused the plaintiff's daughter.

The Fifth Circuit rejected this approach, stating that municipal liability "must be predicated upon a showing of 'fault,' not merely 'responsibility'."[159] The court went on to state that in order for municipal liability to attach, "plaintiffs must offer evidence of not simply a decision, but a 'decision by the city itself to violate the Constitution.'"[160] The Fifth Circuit then held as a matter of law that the actions of the board in reassigning the teacher did not amount to deliberate indifference because the board did not "ignore or turn a blind eye" to the complaint against the teacher, but undertook an investigation, and thus the school district could not be deliberately indifferent to the constitutional rights of the plaintiff. Even though the failure to impose a more severe sanction was not only negligent but also inconsistent with the school district's handling of other similar cases, the Fifth Circuit concluded that such facts simply did not give rise to deliberate indifference as a matter of law.[161]

---

157. *Jones,* 104 F.3d at 627.
158. 996 F.2d 745 (5th Cir. 1993).
159. *Gonzalez,* 996 F.2d at 757.
160. *Id.* at 759.
161. *Id.* at 762.

In a factually similar case, the Sixth Circuit reached the same result in *Doe v. Claiborne County*.[162] There, a high school student had been sexually assaulted by one of her teachers in 1992. In 1989, an allegation of sexual misconduct was made against the same teacher; and in 1990, complaints were made that the teacher had sexually abused nine different girls at a middle school. An investigation was undertaken by a state agency at the school district's request, and the teacher was initially not rehired by the board for the following school year. Shortly thereafter, however, a new superintendent was hired and the school board approved the decision to rehire the teacher. After being rehired, the teacher sexually abused the plaintiff.

In finding that the plaintiff had failed to demonstrate deliberate indifference as a matter of law, the court observed that the board members "might have been recklessly passive in the performance of their duties," and that it could be argued that "they were reckless in their failure, collectively, to inquire further into the allegations."[163] However, such conduct did not reach the level of deliberate indifference.

While the law will continue to develop as the circuits apply the *Bryan County* holding to specific cases, it appears that the Fifth Circuit's rationale in *Gonzalez* is most in keeping with the Supreme Court's decisions: In order for municipal liability to attach, a plaintiff must offer evidence of not simply a decision to choose among alternatives, but a "decision by the city itself to violate the Constitution."[164]

VIII. CONCLUSION

Municipal liability under § 1983 has undergone significant changes over the last twenty years. The Supreme Court's decisions in this area have been fractured and contiguous, leaving practitioners and the lower courts with a great deal of uncertainty. The complexity of the issue of municipal liability under § 1983 has caused some commentators, and not a few judges, to call for a repudiation of *Monell* and the imposition of respondeat superior liability. The makeup of the current Supreme Court does not make that occurrence likely in the near future.

---

162. 103 F.3d 495 (6th Cir. 1996).

163. *Doe*, 103 F.3d at 508.

164. *Gonzalez*, 996 F.2d at 759, quoting City of Canton, 489 U.S. at 494 (O'Connor, concurring).

Chapter 5

FOURTH AMENDMENT FEDERALISM? THE COURT'S VACILLATING MISTRUST AND TRUST OF STATE SEARCH AND SEIZURE LAWS*

*by Kathryn R. Urbonya***

---

* Reprinted with permission from *Seton Hall Law Review,* where this article first appeared. *See* 35 SETON HALL L.R. 911 (2005).

** The author would like to thank the College of William and Mary for its grant and the research assistance provided by Lauren Eade, Robert Pealo, Shaun Richardson, and Alicia Tracy.

I. INTRODUCTION

The word "federalism" conveys many different ideas, and is a term broad enough to encompass the odd phrase "Fourth Amendment federalism." The Supreme Court's Fourth Amendment jurisprudence has suggested a peculiar interest in deferring to modern state search and seizure laws when determining what constitutes a reasonable police practice. Under this idea of "federalism," the Court has viewed current state laws as a source to define the scope of the Fourth Amendment. This interweaving of state practices with federal protections raises important federalism questions, particularly when the context involves criminal law enforcement. State legislators during their campaigns have often promised to strongly support law enforcement interests, with little interest in promising to repeal criminal laws that infringe current contemporary values. In addition, some state court judges today may similarly campaign to preserve law enforcement powers in light of the Court's recent acknowledgment of their new freedom to publicly discuss controversial issues. As a result, the Court's deference to state search and seizure practices may fail to safeguard a politically unpopular group—alleged criminals.

When police officers search and seize individuals, they may face questioning in court about whether their actions violated the Fourth Amendment to the U.S. Constitution[1] and state law. In deciding whether they crossed the federal constitutional line, the U.S. Supreme Court has explicitly considered state search and seizure practices both at the time of the Fourth Amendment's

1. U.S. Const. amend. IV.

enactment and current state practices. Understandably, the Court has cited early state practices to characterize what the Framers of the Constitution may have intended the scope of the Fourth Amendment to be. When interpreting the Fourth Amendment, the Court has both trusted and mistrusted modern state policing policies: sometimes the Court has declared them unconstitutional, and at other times, the Court has oddly used them as a source in defining the scope of federal protection.

When the Court selectively (and extensively) incorporated the Bill of Rights by its construction of the Due Process Clause of the Fourteenth Amendment, it declared that federal procedural safeguards applied to states' criminal proceedings.[2] The Warren Court continued to expand this federal presence by broadly construing the Fourth Amendment,[3] only to be later checked by the Burger and Rehnquist Courts, who constructed doctrines narrowing protections for criminal defendants.[4] In addition, the Burger and Rehnquist Courts explicitly noted that state courts could interpret their state constitutions to provide greater protection to criminal defendants.[5] They also informed states that if they granted broader rights, their highest state

---

2. *See, e.g.,* David A. Harris, *Addressing Racial Profiling in the States: A Case Study of the "New Judicial Federalism," in* CONSTITUTIONAL CRIMINAL PROCEDURE, 3 U. PA. J. CONST. L. 367, 368 (2001).
3. *See, e.g.,* Stewart F. Hancock, Jr., *The State Constitution: A Criminal Lawyer's First Line of Defense,* 57 ALB. L. REV. 271, 279 (1993) ("During the Warren Court era, federal courts suddenly assumed the leading role as protectors of the people from intrusions by state and local governments. . . . In many states, the Federal Constitutional decisions were more protective than the state decisions, and thus in those states, criminal cases were decided on federal grounds.").
4. *See, e.g.,* James A. Gardner, *State Courts as Agents of Federalism: Power and Interpretation in State Constitutional Law,* 44 WM. & MARY L. REV. 1725, 1782 & n.215 (2003) (declaring that the "United States Supreme Court has decisively halted the expansion of federal protection of individual rights," with "[t]his process . . . most notable in the decisions concerning the Fourth Amendment"); Stephen F. Smith, *The Rehnquist Court and Criminal Procedure,* 73 U. COLO. L. REV. 1337, 1358 (2002) ("Instead of overruling Warren Court precedents it deemed to be erroneous, the Rehnquist Court has distinguished, created exceptions to, and reinterpreted such precedents. . . . Whatever else might be said about the Court's approach, it was highly effective in producing the 'law and order' results Nixon and Reagan promised to deliver.").
5. *See, e.g.,* Nina Morrison, *Curing "Constitutional Amnesia": Criminal Procedure under State Constitutions,* 73 N.Y.U. L. REV. 880, 881 (1998) (noting that "the movement towards independent state constitutional analysis—known colloquially as 'New Federalism'—did not gather steam until 1977, when Justice Brennan called on state courts to 'step into the breach' left by the Burger Court's rights-narrowing jurisprudence") (citing William J. Brennan, Jr., *State Constitutions and the*

courts may shield their judgments from review by the Supreme Court, but only if they clearly specify that the greater protection arose from state law, not federal law. As a result, state courts gradually began interpreting their constitutions to grant greater protection for criminal defendants subject to searches and seizures.[6] By 2004, twenty-eight states had rejected a particular Fourth Amendment doctrine and had declared broader protection under state law.[7]

The significance of modern state search and seizure practices, however, evades easy characterization. For example, sometimes the Court has supported its Fourth Amendment reasonableness determination by indicating that a majority of states currently engage in the particular practice.[8] At other times, the Court has characterized the practice of a minority of states as indicating a "trend,"[9] one that harmonized with the Court's reasonableness conclusion. And sometimes modern state practices play no role because the Court has constructed its decision by either expanding or narrowing precedent.[10] In addition, the Court recently described a special role for state laws: they may create a legal obligation for suspects to identify themselves during

---

Protection of Individual Rights, 90 HARV. L. REV. 489, 503 (1977)). *See generally* James A. Gardner, *State Constitutional Rights as Resistance to National Power: Toward a Functional Theory of State Constitutions,* 91 GEO. L.J. 1003, 1029–30 (2003) (noting that "[n]ineteen state constitutions contain a Warrant Clause identical to that found in the Fourth Amendment"; but contending that there may be a "significant potential difference—between state and federal versions of protected rights: state constitutions may offer a level of protection for such liberties that exceeds the level of protection by the U.S. Constitution").

6. *See generally* Harris, *supra* note 2, at 368 ("An effort began—'movement' may be too strong a word—to keep alive the Warren Court's legacy of expanded constitutional protections for the criminally accused by utilizing state constitutional provisions.").
7. *See infra* note 353. *See generally* James N.G. Cauthen, *Expanding Rights under State Constitutions: A Quantitative Appraisal,* 63 ALB. L. REV. 1183, 1197 (2000) ("Retractions of rights by the Supreme Court . . . may explain the high level of state constitutional policymaking in the search and seizure areas. Between 1967 and 1984, the Supreme Court carved out numerous exceptions to the warrant requirement of the Fourth Amendment, thereby reducing the level of available federal protections.").
8. *See infra* text accompanying notes 135–148, 172–182, and 203–224.
9. *See infra* text accompanying notes 283 and 298–322.
10. *See, e.g.,* Thornton v. United States, 541 U.S. 615, 617 (2004) (concluding that *New York v. Belton,* 453 U.S. 454 (1981) "governs even when an officer does not make contact until the person arrested has left the vehicle"); Illinois v. Lidster, 540 U.S. 419, 423–27 (2004) (distinguishing an "information-seeking" roadblock from othe roadblock cases and applying three factors for balancing established in *Brown v. Texas,* 443 U.S. 47 (1979)); United States v. Banks, 540 U.S. 31, 35–40 (2003) (upholding officers' forcible home entry, done after waiting fifteen to twenty seconds after knocking and announcing their warrant authority, because cited Fourth Amendment precedent required case-by-case analysis); Knowles v. Iowa, 525 U.S.

an investigative stop, even though the Fourth Amendment does not itself create this requirement.[11] Although states have historically had the power to define what actions constitute a state criminal offense,[12] the Court's decisions reflect its more modern trust of state search and seizure provisions.

This interweaving of state practices with federal protections raises important federalism questions,[13] particularly when the context involves criminal law enforcement, because rarely do state legislators or state politicians campaign for more measures to protect alleged or convicted criminals.[14]

113, 118–19 (1998) (refusing "to extend" the "bright-line rule" of *United States v. Robinson,* 414 U.S. 218 (1973), to a vehicle search incident to a traffic citation); Maryland v. Wilson, 519 U.S. 408, 410 (1997) (extending the rule of *Pennsylvania v. Mimms,* 434 U.S. 106 (1977) (per curiam) to allow officer to order passenger of lawfully stopped car out of vehicle).

11. *See infra* text accompanying notes 243–272.
12. *See, e.g.,* Randy E. Barnett, *The Proper Scope of the Police Power,* 79 NOTRE DAME L. REV. 429, 494 (2004) (contending that when the Supreme Court in *Lawrence v. Texas,* 539 U.S. 558 (2003), struck down Texas's criminal statute banning same-sex sodomy, it "reject[ed] the view of the police power as unlimited and plenary"; contending that the statute interfered with an individual's "rightful exercise of liberty"). By contrast, when the Court declared that Congress lacked authority under the Commerce Clause, Article I, Section 8, to enact the Gun-Free School Zone Act of 1990, a criminal law, it emphasized "first principles," which included a "healthy balance of power between the States and the Federal Government." United States v. Lopez, 514 U.S. 549, 552 (1995). Justice Kennedy in his concurrence noted that more than "40 states [had] criminal laws outlawing the possession of firearms on or near school grounds." *Id.* at 581 (Kennedy, J., concurring).
13. For example, the Court extensively looked to legal sources outside the U.S. Constitution when it held that a Texas statute violated the substantive due process component of the Fourteenth Amendment because it criminalized same-sex sodomy, overruling its decision in *Bowers v. Hardwick,* 478 U.S. 186 (1986). Lawrence v. Texas, 539 U.S. 558, 578 (2003). The *Lawrence* Court noted that five states had "declined to follow [*Bowers*] in interpreting provisions in their own state constitutions parallel to the Due Process Clause of the Fourteenth Amendment." *Id.* at 576.
14. *See, e.g.,* Atkins v. Virginia, 536 U.S. 304, 315–16 (2002). In striking down the death penalty as applied to mentally retarded offenders, the *Atkins* Court noted the historic difficulty of passing legislation protecting criminals:

    > Given the well-known fact that anticrime legislation is far more popular than legislation providing protections for persons guilty of violent crime, the large number of States prohibiting the execution of mentally retarded persons (and the complete absence of States passing legislation reinstating the power to conduct such executions) provides powerful evidence that today our society views mentally retarded offenders as categorically less culpable than the average criminal.

    Id. See also Tennessee v. Lane, 541 U.S. 509, 535 n.2 (2004) (Souter, J., concurring) (noting that some of the state eugenic laws enacted in the 1920s "persist to this day").

In addition, the politics of state court judges may become a more prominent issue after the Court's decision to strike down a provision that limited state-elected judges from vigorous campaigning.[15]

This chapter examines the Court's interest in modern state laws as an aid in assessing Fourth Amendment reasonableness. Part II highlights the Court's mistrust of state criminal search and seizure procedures when it declared that the Due Process Clause of the Fourteenth Amendment incorporated the Fourth Amendment and its exclusionary rule; this incorporation—arising from the Court's constructions of "liberty"—thus compelled states to conform their procedures and practices to the Fourth Amendment. This section recalls the Court's distrust of state criminal practices and the fundamental nature of due process protections for accused. Part III examines the Court's declared jurisdictional need to safeguard federal interpretive turf. It discusses the Court's creating a "plain statement" requirement in 1983 to rebut a presumption for federal jurisdiction in state court cases deciding an issue both on federal and state law. Under this requirement,

---

15. Republican Party of Minnesota v. White, 536 U.S. 765, 785–88 (2002) (holding that state statute that barred judicial candidates from announcing views on a "disputed legal and political issues" violated the First Amendment). Justice O'Connor in her concurrence cited numerous articles indicating that some judicial elections influence a judge's decision whether to impose the death penalty. *Id.* at 789–90 (citations omitted). *See also* Erwin Chemerinsky, *Judicial Elections and the First Amendment,* 38 TRIAL, Nov. 2002, at 78 (stating that "*White* will dramatically change the nature of speech in judicial elections"). Professor Chemerinksy questioned whether the *White* decision created a workable line between "expressing views about disputed legal or political issues and making statements that appear to commit them with respect to those issues." *Id.* at 81 (questioning the difference between "'I believe that *Roe* was wrongly decided and should be overruled'" and "'I believe that *Roe* was wrongly decided and, if presented with the opportunity, I would vote to overturn the decision'"). Roy A. Schotland, Republican Party of Minnesota v. White*: Should Judges be More Like Politicians?* 41 NO. 3 JUDGES' J. 7 (2002) (stating that "the impact of elections on judicial independence is amplified because so many states have such short terms for judges" and wondering whether "more states will end judicial contestable elections altogether"); Stephanie Francis Ward, *Judging the Judge Candidates: Queries About Family Life, Religion Draw Fire in Florida County,* 3 NO. 3 A.B.A. J. E-REP. 3 (Jan. 23, 2004) (noting that Florida's governor-appointed group asked judicial candidates "how they would rule on certain matters, such as sodomy and displaying the Ten Commandments in the courtroom"); Molly McDonough, *Judges Opine on the Issues: Debate May Be Future of Judicial Campaigns,* 2 NO. 20 A.B.A. J. E-REP. 3 (May 23, 2003) (noting that prospective candidates for Pennsylvania Supreme Court positions were asked "to state their positions on abortion, gun control and tort reform").

state courts may avoid having the U.S. Supreme Court review their decisions only if they clearly state that their more protective decisions rested on independent and adequate state grounds, not the Fourth Amendment. This section reveals the Court's drawing a sharp line between federal and state interpretative powers. By contrast, Part IV examines the Court's selective use of modern state police practices to assess Fourth Amendment reasonableness; it discusses the Court's using modern state practices to both expand and narrow the protections provided by the Fourth Amendment.

The Article concludes that the Court has, at times, constructed the Fourth Amendment with a fragile floor and with an implicit understanding that individuals who seek greater protection of their liberty, privacy, and personal security need to look to state laws. Instead of considering the political unlikelihood of state legislatures passing laws to safeguard an alleged criminal's interest in liberty or of state-elected judges interpreting state laws to suppress evidence of guilt, the Court has looked to the states to aid it in assessing its independent federal duty to define the right to liberty, privacy, and personal security as safeguarded by the Fourth Amendment. This interpretive practice is odd, but revealing. It ultimately suggests that the Fourth Amendment has an evolving standard, one resembling the evolving standard for other provisions safeguarding liberty, personal security, and privacy.[16]

---

16. As with the Fourth Amendment jurisprudence, the Court has selectively cited state practices to support its constitutional determination in other contexts. For example, the Court has considered state practices in assessing the application of the death penalty, but not sentencing, under the Eighth Amendment. *Compare* Atkins v. Virginia, 536 U.S. 304, 311 (2002) ("A claim that punishment is excessive is judged not by the standards that presided . . . over the 'Bloody Assizes' or when the Bill of Rights was adopted, but rather by those that currently prevail.") *with* Ewing v. California, 538 U.S. 11, 24–28 (2003) (noting the rarity of successful challenges to state sentencing schemes). The dissent in *Ewing,* while agreeing with the standard, argued that the California three-strikes law imposed a harsh penalty that would not have been imposed by "[t]hirty-three jurisdictions, as well the federal courts." *Id.* at app. A at 53 (Breyer, J., dissenting).

Similarly, the Court has selectively invoked state practices when assessing the protection provided by the substantive due process component of the Fourteenth Amendment. *Compare* Lawrence v. Texas, 539 U.S. 558, 572 (2003) ("In all events we think that our laws and traditions in the past half century are of most relevance" in analyzing the constitutionality of a criminal statute banning same-sex sodomy) *with* Roe v. Wade, 410 U.S. 113, 140 (1973) (Even though the Court characterized modern practices as revealing a "trend toward liberalization of abortion statutes . . . by about one-third of the States," the Court admitted that the majority of states currently do not support abortion, a position contrary to the "common law, at the time of the adoption of the Constitution, and throughout the major portion of the 19th

Ultimately, the Court does define the federal standard, but one today built on a general trust, not mistrust, of states to balance the need for intrusion against a person's and society's interest in liberty, privacy, and personal security. In time, with the Court's interest in counting how many states allow or forbid various practices, states may become the ultimate protector of liberty.

The Court's interest in state laws, ones created by a separate sovereign, resembles the interest of some state courts that also consider the practices of other states. At times state courts have cited other state constitutions to justify their interpretation of their particular constitution.[17] State constitutional law scholar Alan Tarr has described a state's interests in other states as "hor-

century."). By contrast, when creating a national standard for measuring whether a punitive damages award violated the substantive due process component of the Fourteenth Amendment, the Court never mentioned the standards of other states. State Farm Mutual Automobile Ins. Co. v. Campbell, 538 U.S. 408, 422 (2003) ("A basic principle of federalism is that each State may make its own reasoned judgment about what conduct is permitted or proscribed within its borders, and each State alone can determine what measure of punishment, if any, to impose on a defendant who acts within its jurisdiction.").

In addition, the Court's selective interest in state practices has also occurred in its equal protection cases. *Compare* Loving v. Virginia, 388 U.S. 1, 6 & n.5, 11–12 (1967) (invalidating state statutes banning and punishing interracial marriage on both equal protection and substantive due grounds; noting that during the "past 15 years, 14 States ha[d] repealed laws outlawing interracial marriages" and that only sixteen States currently prohibited interracial marriage) *with* Grutter v. Bollinger, 539 U.S. 306, 342 (2003) (allowing race as a factor in law school admissions while noting that state laws in "California, Florida, and Washington" ban universities from considering an applicant's race; noting that states "'may perform their role as laboratories for experimentation to devise various solutions where the best solution is far from clear'") (quoting United States v. Lopez, 514 U.S. 549, 581 (1995) (Kennedy, J., concurring)). *See generally* Brown v. Bd. of Educ., 347 U.S. 483, 492–93, 495 (1954) (In declaring that "separate but equal" schools based on race violated the Equal Protection Clause, the Court did not cite current state practices, but instead focused on the role of modern education: "[W]e cannot turn the clock back to 1868 when the Amendment was adopted, or even to 1896 when *Plessy v. Ferguson* was written. We must consider public education in the light of its full development and its present place in American life throughout the Nation.").

17. *See, e.g.,* People v. Goldson, 682 N.W.2d 479, 489 n.10 (Mich. 2004). In *Goldson,* the Michigan Supreme Court decided that the state constitution did contain an objective good-faith exception to the exclusionary rule, which allowed officials to prove guilt by using illegally seized evidence. *Id.* at 489. In making this state constitutional law determination, the state court created a good-faith exception like the one established by the U.S. Supreme Court under the Fourth Amendment. *See infra* note 89. The state court recognized its separate sovereignty: "In interpreting our

izontal federalism."[18] This type of federalism resembles the Supreme Court's interest in state practices: both the U.S. Supreme Court and a state court interpret their own constitution, and neither must consider the separate sovereign's interpretation. Nonetheless, to give substance to the text of its constitution, these courts at times have looked outside their document for guidance. In the end, the Supreme Court and state courts render decisions under the authority of their constitution, but when the Supreme Court has looked to modern state laws to interpret the Fourth Amendment, it should not fail to scrutinize current state laws affecting an extremely unpopular minority—alleged criminal defendants, a group unlikely to be vigorously protected by state legislators or state-elected judges.

II. MISTRUSTING STATES' PROCEDURES AND PRACTICES: INCORPORATION OF THE FOURTH AMENDMENT AND THE COURT'S EXCLUSIONARY RULE

By declaring that the first ten amendments to the U.S. Constitution (the "Bill of Rights") applied only to the federal government and not to the states, the Court in 1833 drew a sharp line between limits placed on federal

---

Constitution, we are not bound by the United States Supreme Court's interpretation of the United States Constitution, even where the language is identical." *Id.* at 484–85. Nonetheless, the majority opinion rhetorically justified its interpretation of the Michigan constitution by citing interpretations of other state constitutions and state statutes, even though it declared them to be "entirely irrelevant to [its] constitutional analysis." *Id.* at 489 n.10. The majority noted that eleven state constitutions as well as the District of Columbia had a good-faith exception, and five other states had a statutory good-faith provision. *Id.* (citing the state constitution interpretations for Alabama, California, Florida, Kentucky, Louisiana, Maryland, Missouri, Ohio, South Dakota, Virginia, and Wisconsin; citing state statutory provisions for Arizona, Colorado, Illinois, Indiana, and Texas). Similarly, the dissent in *Goldson* listed the state constitutional or statutory interpretations of fourteen other states that had rejected an objective good-faith exception. *Id.* at 499 n.26 (Cavanagh, J., dissenting) (citing Connecticut, Delaware, Georgia, Idaho, Massachusetts, Montana, New Hampshire, New Jersey, New Mexico, New York, North Carolina, Pennsylvania, South Carolina, and Vermont).

18. G. Alan Tarr, Understanding State Constitutions 50–52, 98–99 (1998). In contrast to horizontal federalism is a state's practice of declaring its own constitution to mirror the federal constitution, known as a "lockstep" interpretation. *See, e.g.,* Robert F. Williams, *State Courts Adopting Federal Constitutional Doctrine: Case-by-Case Adoptionism or Prospective Lockstepping?* 46 Wm. & Mary L. Rev. 1499, 1502 (2005) (noting that in "a clear majority of cases" state courts have "decide[d] to *follow,* rather than *diverge from,* federal constitutional doctrine").

authority and state authority.[19] Although this line suggested a sharp distinction between restraints imposed on the federal government and the states, in time the doctrine of "selective incorporation" ended up giving individuals most of the protections guaranteed by the Bill of Rights, but only because the Court declared that the Due Process Clause of the Fourteenth Amendment incorporated these rights. "Liberty," as protected by the Due Process Clause of the Fourteenth Amendment, ultimately became a springboard for compelling states to conform their criminal procedures to the Fourth Amendment. The Court's landmark decisions in *Wolf v. Colorado*[20] and *Mapp v. Ohio*[21] reveal the Court's vacillating views of state practices. Initially the Court respected states' views of adequate remedies for illegal police actions, but later it mistrusted the states' remedial schemes.[22]

In *Wolf,* the Court applied the Fourth Amendment to the states, but not the federal exclusionary rule, which bars the government from using illegally seized evidence in its case-in-chief to prove guilt. By refusing to impose the exclusionary rule on the states, the Court relied upon the practices of a majority of states, which had rejected the exclusionary rule. In contrast, the *Mapp* Court twelve years later reversed *Wolf* in part by declaring that the exclusionary rule did apply to the states. It explained that the state practices it had relied on in *Wolf* were "not basically relevant to"[23] deciding whether the federal exclusionary rule applies to the states. An examination of these contrasting decisions and their aftermath lays the foun-

---

19. Barron v. Mayor & City Council of Baltimore, 32 U.S. 243, 250 (1833). *See also* Weeks v. United States, 232 U.S. 383, 393, 397 (1914) (applying Fourth Amendment and the exclusionary rule to unreasonable searches and seizures by federal officials, but not to the actions of municipal police officers). Because the *Weeks* Court did not view the Fourth Amendment to reach the action of state officials, it recognized different standards for federal and state courts, while at the same time strongly recognizing the importance of having an exclusionary rule to suppress evidence derived from illegal searches and seizures by federal officials. *Id.* at 393. The *Weeks* Court declared that without the exclusionary rule the Fourth Amendment "is of no value" and "might as well be stricken from the Constitution." *Id.*
20. 338 U.S. 25 (1949).
21. 367 U.S. 643 (1961).
22. *See generally* Barry Latzer, *Toward the Decentralization of Criminal Procedure: State Constitutional Law and Selective Incorporation,* 87 J. CRIM. L. & CRIMINOLOGY 63, 72 (1996) ("Although rarely if ever acknowledged in Supreme Court cases, undoubtedly because of the impolitic nature of the assertion, incorporation surely rested upon a measure of disrespect for state courts.").
23. *Mapp,* 367 U.S. at 651.

dation for understanding the modern Court's interest in ascertaining state practices to shape the substantive contours of the Fourth Amendment.[24]

A. Liberty as the Foundation for Incorporating the Fourth Amendment: *Wolf v. Colorado*

When the Court decided *Wolf v. Colorado* in 1949, it held that the Fourth Amendment applied to the states, but that the exclusionary rule did not. Although the Court in *Mapp* reversed that part of *Wolf* refusing to impose the exclusionary rule on the states, the *Wolf* Court's discussion of both issues—incorporation of the Fourth Amendment and the lack of need for a rule of exclusion—frame the modern Court's interpretative task in defining the scope of the Fourth Amendment. Both its view of "liberty" and its strong consideration of the states' search and seizure practices resonate with the modern Court's interpretative struggle to strike the balance of reasonableness under the Fourth Amendment.

By declaring that the Fourth Amendment applied to the states, the *Wolf* Court relied on the incorporation standard articulated in *Palko v. Connecticut*,[25] a standard also cited by the modern Court to decide whether the Due

---

24. As the Court addressed whether the Due Process Clause of the Fourteenth Amendment incorporated the provisions in other amendments, it frequently looked to state practices for guidance in determining due process. *See, e.g.,* Duncan v. Louisiana, 391 U.S. 145, 149, 161 (1968) (holding that the Due Process Clause of Fourteenth Amendment incorporated the federal jury trial guarantee of the Sixth Amendment by using the standard of whether the right was "fundamental to the American scheme of justice" and characterizing the practices of "49 of 50" states as "objective criteria" to determine the seriousness of a crime requiring a jury trial); Klopfer v. North Carolina, 386 U.S. 213, 219, 220 n.5, 222–23 (1967) (holding that North Carolina's indefinite postponement of prosecution by indictment violated the Sixth Amendment right to a speedy trial as incorporated by the Due Process Clause and noting that "every other state court" that had considered the question rejected North Carolina's practice and listing the states' nolle prossed practices); Pointer v. Texas, 380 U.S. 400, 404 n.*, 406 (1965) (holding Sixth Amendment's "confrontation guarantee" safeguarded by the Due Process Clause; citing "[s]tate constitutional and statutory provisions similar to the Sixth Amendment"); Gideon v. Wainwright, 372 U.S. 335, 344–45 (1963) (deciding that the Due Process Clause of the Fourteenth Amendment incorporated the right to counsel under the Sixth Amendment, not by considering whether the practice is "fair" in some countries, but rather whether it was "in ours"; citing to twenty-two states who requested the Court to overrule its prior denial of this right to state criminal defendants).
25. 302 U.S. 319, 325 (1937).

Process Clause of the Fourteenth Amendment protects a newly asserted liberty interest. Applying the *Palko* standard, the Court questioned whether the Fourth Amendment rights were "'implicit in the concept of ordered liberty,'"[26] signifying rights protected by the Due Process Clause of the Fourteenth Amendment. The Court viewed "liberty" as evolving, not "petrified as of any one time."[27] The Court noted that due process protects this fundamental liberty right and signifies a "living principle,"[28] one "not confined within a permanent catalogue of what may at a given time be deemed the limits or the essential of fundamental rights."[29] By viewing due process as an evolving source of protection, the Court explained that its judicial role did not involve drawing a clear line, but rather employing a "gradual and empiric process."[30]

The *Wolf* Court then characterized the Fourth Amendment's "core" as protecting a person's "privacy against arbitrary intrusion by police," a right "basic to a free society."[31] It unanimously held that the Due Process Clause of the Fourteenth Amendment incorporated the Fourth Amendment. By contrast, the Court recognized different remedial schemes for federal and state officials who conduct unreasonable searches and seizures. For federal officials, the exclusionary rule applied, a rule that the Court imposed in 1914 in *Weeks v. United States*.[32] For state officials, state remedial schemes satisfied the *Palko* standard.[33]

The Court justified its decision on two grounds: English practices and the practices of a majority of American states.[34] First, it explained that it must "hesitate to treat this remedy as an essential ingredient of the [Fourth Amendment] right" because "most of the English-speaking world does not regard [it] as vital." It looked to ten "jurisdictions within the United Kingdom and the British Commonwealth of Nations [that had] passed on the question" of exclusion, noting that "none" had applied exclusion.[35]

Second, the Court closely scrutinized states' practices both before and after *Weeks*. It noted that before *Weeks*, twenty-seven states had considered whether to apply the exclusionary rule: twenty-six opposed using the exclu-

---

26. *Wolf,* 338 U.S. at 27 (quoting *Palko,* 302 U.S. at 325).
27. *Id.* at 27.
28. *Id.*
29. *Id.*
30. *Id.*
31. *Wolf,* 338 U.S. at 27.
32. 232 U.S. 383 (1914).
33. *Wolf,* 338 U.S. at 30 n.1.
34. *Id.* at 29–31.
35. *Id.* at 30.

sionary rule, and one state "anticipated the *Weeks* doctrine."[36] The Court explained that after *Weeks*, forty-seven states weighed in on the exclusionary rule: twenty states had considered it for the first time, with six states applying the exclusionary rule and fourteen rejecting.[37] It also described the changes in the twenty-six states that had considered exclusion prior to *Weeks*: ten adopted the exclusionary rule either by "overruling or distinguishing their prior decisions"; and sixteen states still rejected the exclusionary rule; and one of these twenty-six states "repudiated its prior formulation of the *Weeks* doctrine."[38] The *Wolf* Court summarized these details: "As of today 31 States reject the *Weeks* doctrine, 16 States are in agreement with it."[39]

To remedy unreasonable searches and seizures by state officials, the Court looked to state laws to safeguard the rights protected by the Fourth Amendment. It found states' remedies adequate, "if consistently enforced."[40] These state remedies included suing police officers for trespass, suing police officers who apply for invalid warrants, suing the magistrate who acted without jurisdiction, and criminally prosecuting involved officials.[41] It also viewed community pressure against law enforcement officials as another safeguard.[42]

In the end, a majority of the *Wolf* Court deeply trusted states to protect Fourth Amendment rights. It found persuasive state practices: "We cannot brush aside the experience of States which deem the incidence of such [illegal] conduct by the police too slight to call for a deterrent remedy not by way of disciplinary measures but by overriding the relevant rules of evidence."[43] It then offered a six-and-one-half-page appendix listing all of the state practices to which it had cited.[44]

For dissenting Justices Murphy and Rutledge, trusting state practices did not comport with the *Palko* standard.[45] They rejected counting the states to decide the due process standard: "[W]e should [not] decide due process questions by simply taking a poll of the rules of various jurisdictions."[46]

---

36. *Id.* at 29.
37. *Id.*
38. *Wolf,* 338 U.S. at 29.
39. *Id.*
40. *Id.* at 31.
41. *Id.* at 30 n.1.
42. *Id.* at 32.
43. *Wolf,* 338 U.S. at 31–32.
44. *Id.* at 33–39.
45. *Id.* at 41 (Murphy, J. dissenting).
46. *Id.* at 46 (Murphy, J., dissenting).

They also described state "remedies"—both civil and criminal—as "illusory."[47] They viewed criminal prosecution by states as intertwining the illegal conduct of police officers with the actions of prosecutors and the judiciary.[48] First, they seriously doubted that a district attorney would "prosecute himself or his associates for well-meaning violations of the search and seizure clause during a raid the District Attorney or his associates have ordered."[49] Second, they thought that admitting illegally seized evidence would "have [a] tragic effect upon public respect for our judiciary" by allowing "lawlessness by officers of the law."[50] In addition, they highlighted the lack of case law addressing trespass suits against police officers.[51]

The *Wolf* Court thus separated the question of application of the Fourth Amendment from the question of exclusion as a required remedy. The Court created distinct practices in federal and state courts by relying on English practices, the practices of a majority of states, and their remedies for illegal conduct. Twelve years later, the Court in *Mapp v. Ohio*[52] not only rejected this reliance on state practices and remedies but also harmonized federal and state practices, ending the "asymmetry which *Wolf* imported into the law."[53]

B. Liberty and "Healthy" Federalism as the Foundation for Applying the Exclusionary Rule to State Search and Seizure Practices

In 1961 the *Mapp* Court reversed *Wolf* in part by holding that the exclusionary rule applied to state criminal prosecutions.[54] To justify its reversal, the Court recast the role of state practices relied on by the *Wolf* Court. The *Mapp* Court twice characterized its prior review of state practices as "not basically relevant to a decision that the exclusionary rule is an essential ingredient of the Fourth Amendment"[55] as incorporated by the Due Process Clause of the Fourteenth Amendment. It also characterized state practices as "factual considerations,"[56] which had changed by 1961. In addition, it

---

47. *Id.* at 42 (Murphy, J., dissenting).
48. *Wolf,* 338 U.S. at 42, 46.
49. *Id.* at 42.
50. *Id.* at 46.
51. *Id.* at 44.
52. 367 U.S. 643 (1961).
53. *Id.* at 670 (Douglas, J., concurring).
54. *Id.* at 657.
55. *Id.* at 651.
56. *Id.*

offered a different view of liberty, while still using the *Palko* Court's "implicit in the concept of ordered liberty" standard.[57]

The Court undermined the relevance of state practices in several ways. First, it described the *Wolf* Court's citing of state practice as a factual grounding, a grounding that had shifted since *Wolf*.[58] In describing how state practices had changed, the majority and dissenting opinions highlighted different aspects of state practices. The *Mapp* majority cited states' practices *since* the *Wolf* decision: "now, despite the *Wolf* case, more than one-half of those since passing upon it, by their own legislative or judicial decision, have wholly or partly adopted or adhered to the *Weeks* rule" of exclusion.[59] For its source, the *Mapp* majority cited the detailed appendix in *Elkins v. United States*, a 1960 decision that listed each state's practice before *Weeks*, before *Wolf*, and after *Wolf*.[60] While conceding that more states since *Wolf* had adopted the exclusionary rule, the dissent, by contrast, countered with a "recent survey" that "indicate[d] that at present one-half of the States still adhere to the common-law non-exclusionary rule, and one, Maryland, retains the rule as to felonies."[61]

Second, both the majority and the dissent declared that state practices offered little guidance in deciding the constitutional question of whether the exclusionary rule applied to the states. The *Mapp* Court stated that these "factual considerations . . . , while not basically relevant to the constitutional consideration, could not, in any analysis, now be deemed controlling."[62] Similarly, the dissent declared that states practices were "beside the point, as the majority itself indeed seems to recognize."[63] It viewed the question before the Court as a constitutional question, one in which "the disparity of views among the States on this point" reveal "that the judgment involved is a debatable one."[64]

Third, the *Mapp* Court disagreed with the *Wolf* Court's view of states' having adequate remedies.[65] Instead it highlighted California's adoption of the exclusionary rule because "'other remedies [had] completely failed to

57. *Mapp,* 367 U.S. at 655.

58. *Id.* at 651.

59. *Id.*

60. *Id.* (citing Elkins v. United States, 364 U.S. 206, app. at 224–32 (1960)).

61. *Id.* at 680 (Harlan, J., dissenting) (citing Berman & Oberst, *Admissibility of Evidence Obtained by an Unconstitutional Search and Seizure,* 55 Nw. U. L. Rev. 525, 532–33 (1960)).

62. *Mapp,* 367 U.S. at 653.

63. *Id.* at 680 (Harlan, J., dissenting).

64. *Id.* (Harlan, J., dissenting).

65. *Id.* at 651.

secure compliance with the constitutional provisions.'"[66] In this context, the failures of other states now became relevant.[67] The *Mapp* Court cited twenty-three state statutes, noting that "[l]ess than half of the States have any criminal provisions relating directly to unreasonable searches and seizures."[68]

The *Mapp* Court thus used state practices in contrasting ways: It declared them not relevant to the constitutional question, but relevant in overruling the *Wolf* Court's rejection of the exclusionary rule. To answer the constitutional question, the Court relied on its prior *Palko* standard and its view of "'healthy federalism.'"[69] Although six justices voted to suppress illegally seized evidence,[70] a majority of the Court did not clearly specify

---

66. *Id.* (citing People v. Cahan, 282 P.2d. 905, 911 (1955)). When selecting an important state for consideration, the justices have highlighted those states that support their views of the exclusionary rule. For example, the dissent in *Elkins v. United States,* 364 U.S. 206 (1960), decided one year before *Wolf,* mentioned the same California case later cited by the majority in *Wolf,* but countered with the state practice of New York. Rios v. United States, 364 U.S. 206, 242 (1960) (Frankfurter, J., dissenting). He used New York's practice and other state practices to refute the *Elkin* Court's characterization of states' adoption of the exclusionary rule as "'seemingly inexorable.'" *Id.* (citing *Wolf,* 364 U.S. at 219):

> [W]hat impresses me is the obduracy of high-minded state courts, like that of New York under the leadership of Judge Cardozo, in refusing to adopt the federal rule of exclusion. Indeed, this impressive insistence of States not to follow the *Weeks* exclusionary rule was the controlling consideration of the decision in *Wolf* not to read it into the requirement of "due process" under the Fourteenth Amendment. As the material the Court has collected shows, fully half the States have refused to adhere to our *Weeks* rule, nearly fifty years after this Court has deemed it appropriate for the federal administration of criminal justice.

Id. The Court's interest in state practices to shape the scope of its *federal* supervisory powers reveals its underlying concern with "healthy federalism," as implicated by the "silver platter doctrine." *See infra* text accompanying notes 76–86.

67. *Mapp,* 367 U.S. at 652 (stating that the "experience of California that . . . other remedies have been worthless and futile is buttressed by the experience of other States").
68. *Id.* at 652 & n.7.
69. *Id.* at 657 (quoting *Elkins,* 364 U.S. at 221).
70. Justice Clark wrote the opinion for the Court joined by Justices Brennan and Warren; Justices Black and Douglas wrote separate concurring opinions; and Justice Stewart concurred on suppressing the evidence, but joined the dissent in part. Thus, six voted to suppress the illegally seized evidence. *Id.* at 654–72. Justice Harlan dissented, joined in full by Justices Frankfurter and Whitaker. *Id.* at 672 (Harlan, J., dissenting).

whether the Constitution required exclusion or whether the Court only created the remedy to effectively safeguard Fourth Amendment interests.[71]

When applying the *Palko* standard, the Court reiterated that *Wolf* had viewed the Fourth Amendment as protecting "privacy."[72] Now, however, it viewed exclusion as "an essential part of the right to privacy."[73] The Court declared that "without that rule freedom from state invasions of privacy would be so ephemeral and so neatly severed from its conceptual nexus with the freedom from all brutish means of coercing evidence as not to merit this Court's high regard as a freedom 'implicit in the concept of ordered liberty.'"[74] The *Mapp* Court invoked the *Wolf* Court's discussion of privacy to expand its reach to the exclusionary rule. This evolving privacy and liberty interest, "'basic to a free society,'"[75] now included the exclusionary rule as a remedy.

The *Wolf* Court also justified its extension of the exclusionary rule by invoking "'healthy federalism,'" as characterized in *Elkins v. United States*.[76] In *Elkins*, the Court had invoked its federal supervisory powers to bar federal officials from using evidence seized by state officials who conducted unreasonable searches and seizures. Ironically, in addressing this issue known as the "silver platter doctrine,"[77] the *Elkins* Court split five to four, in large part because the justices had dramatically different views of what constituted "healthy federalism."

---

71. The progeny of *Weeks* and *Mapp,* however, now clearly state that the Constitution does not compel exclusion in all circumstances when officers conduct unreasonable searches and seizures. *See, e.g.,* United States v. Leon, 468 U.S. 897, 905–06 (1984). In *Leon,* the Court described its inconsistent characterizations of foundation for the exclusionary rule:

> Language in opinions of this Court and of individual Justices has sometimes implied that the exclusionary rule is a necessary corollary of the Fourth Amendment, *Mapp v. Ohio,* . . . or that the rule is required by the conjunction of the Fourth and Fifth Amendments. [citing Justice Black's concurrence in *Mapp*] . . . These implications need not detain us long. The Fifth Amendment theory has not withstood critical analysis or the test of time, . . . and the Fourth Amendment "has never been interpreted to proscribe the introduction of illegally seized evidence in all proceedings or against all persons." *Stone v. Powell,* 428 U.S. 465, 486 (1976).

Leon, 468 U.S. at 905–06.

72. *Mapp,* 367 U.S. at 655–56.
73. *Id.* at 656.
74. *Id.* at 655 (quoting Palko v. Connecticut, 302 U.S. 319 (1937)).
75. *Id.* at 656 (quoting *Wolf,* 338 U.S. at 27).
76. *Id.* at 657 (quoting *Elkins,* 364 U.S. at 221).
77. *Elkins,* 364 U.S. at 208 n.2.

For the *Elkins* majority "healthy federalism" meant "avoid[ing] . . . needless conflict between state and federal courts."[78] It viewed federal officials' attempt to use such state-seized evidence as "defeat[ing] the state's effort to assure obedience to the Federal Constitution."[79] While encouraging "cooperation between state and federal law enforcement officers,"[80] the *Elkins* majority viewed its rejection of the silver platter doctrine as protecting against state officials' "inducement . . . and evasion" of the Fourth Amendment standard.[81] It declared that a federal court, when considering whether state officials conducted an unreasonable search or seizure, "must make an independent inquiry, whether or not there has been such an inquiry by a state court, and irrespective of how any such inquiry may have turned out."[82] More significantly, the *Elkins* majority stated, "The test is one of federal law, neither enlarged by what one state court may have countenanced, nor diminished by what another may have colorably suppressed."[83]

In contrast, "healthy federalism" for the *Elkins* dissent meant trusting state officials and, through comity, deferring to a state court ruling that officials unlawfully seized evidence.[84] It highlighted the facts of the cases before the Court, in which state courts had suppressed evidence.[85] More important to modern litigation, the dissent emphasized that some states give individuals greater protection than that provided by the Fourth Amendment.[86] From its perspective, the majority's rule would "encourage state illegalities" because a federal court could admit evidence "directly contrary to state law."[87] For the dissent, the Court's decision applying the exclusionary rule to the states was "pregnant with new disharmonies between federal and state authorities and between federal and state courts."[88]

---

78. *Id.* at 221.
79. *Id.*
80. *Id.*
81. *Id.* at 222.
82. *Elkins,* 364 U.S. at 224.
83. *Id.*
84. Rios v. United States, 364 U.S. 206, 243, 245–47 (1960) (Frankfurter, J., dissenting).
85. *Id.* at 247 (Frankfurter, J., dissenting).
86. *Id.* at 245 (Frankfurter, J., dissenting) ("So comity plays no part at all, and the fruits of illegal law enforcement may well be admitted in federal courts directly contrary to state law.").
87. *Id.* (Frankfurter, J., dissenting). Justice Frankfurter viewed the Court's ruling as allowing state officials to give federal officials evidence seized in violation of state law more protection than the Fourth Amendment. He argued that under the majority's rule a "state officer who disobeys [a state regulation] needs only to turn his evidence over to the federal prosecutor, who may freely utilize it under today's innovation in disregard of the disciplinary policy of the State's exclusionary rule." *Id.* at 245–46 (Frankfurter, J., dissenting).
88. *Rios,* 364 U.S. at 243.

Yet, for the *Mapp* Court, "healthy federalism" arose from having both state and federal officials' evidence suppressed if their actions violated the Fourth Amendment. It politely excused federal officials as "being human" when they had previously complied with requests from state officials in non-exclusionary states to give them evidence that federal officials could not use in federal court.[89] By harmonizing the exclusionary rule to apply to the actions of both federal and state officials, the *Mapp* Court viewed its ruling as promoting "[f]ederal-state cooperation in the solution of crime."[90] To allow for different standards, the Court stated, would be "to breed legitimate suspicion of 'working arrangements' whose results are equally tainted."[91]

The *Mapp* Court, however, never hinted how to address the *Elkins* dissent's concern about states that grant greater protection than that provided by the Fourth Amendment. For now, it viewed healthy federalism to signify equal application of the exclusionary rule to federal and state officials for violations of the Fourth Amendment. Modern federal courts, however, have seen this harmony disappear as states grant greater protection under their constitutions and statutes than that provided by the Fourth Amendment.[92]

---

89. *Mapp,* 367 U.S. at 658.

90. *Id.*

91. *Id.*

92. *See, e.g.,* James W. Diehm, *New Federalism and Constitutional Criminal Procedure: Are We Repeating the Mistakes of the Past?* 55 MD. L. REV. 223, 250 (1996). Professor James Diehm has described how the harmony that *Mapp* created disappeared when state courts began to interpret their state constitutions and statutes to provide greater rights than the Fourth Amendment. *Id.* at 252–53. He noted three types of conflicts: federal criminal prosecutions using evidence derived from state officials; state prosecutions using evidence derived from federal officials; and state prosecutions using evidence derived from states with different standards than the prosecuting state. *Id.* With these conflicts, "criminal procedure has come full circle," according to Diehm:

> Compelling reasons may exist not to apply the law of the forum, but the failure to do so can also lead to problems. If a state court does not apply its more stringent state standards to federal officers, similarly situated state defendants will be treated differently, the admissibility of evidence will be determined by the badge of the officer rather than the legality of the act, and silver platter abuses will be encouraged. Similar problems develop in interstate situations where the court may choose to apply the law of another state. These were exactly the injustices noted by pre-*Mapp* authors that led to the Court's decision in *Mapp.*

Id. at 252–53. As of 1996, Diehm has discerned that "most federal courts" and "many scholars" support applying federal standards in federal courts. *Id.* at 251. For state prosecutions, he stated that "many state courts" seemed compelled to apply federal standards to federal officials' testifying in state court. *Id.* at 252.

By applying the Fourth Amendment and its exclusionary rule to the states, the Court thus viewed the Due Process Clause of the Fourteenth Amendment to protect privacy as "implicit in the concept of ordered liberty." The Court initially gave the states time to decide whether the exclusionary rule applied in their proceedings; but after time, it characterized the states' trend as one toward inclusion, despite a vociferous dissent's rejecting this characterization and offering a different view of healthy federalism. It viewed the exclusionary rule to be a needed and effective remedy.

With the *Mapp* decision harmonizing exclusionary practices in 1961, the Burger and Rehnquist Courts began narrowing both the scope of the Fourth Amendment and the exclusionary rule.[93] Prompted by Justice Brennan[94] and other justices,[95] state courts eventually interpreted their state

---

93. For example, the modern Court significantly limited the exclusionary rule by creating a good-faith exception in *United States v. Leon,* 468 U.S. 897, 913 (1984). Under this exception, prosecutors could use in their case-in-chief evidence from an unreasonable search and seizure if police officers had acted in "objective good faith" in obtaining the evidence. *Id.* at 919 n.20. To create this exception, the Court explicitly invoked a "costs and benefits" standard, a standard implicit in the Court's general reasonableness balancing standard under the Fourth Amendment. *Id.* at 913. In this context, however, the Court did not cite state practices to support its new limitation. Instead it cited concurring and dissenting opinions from the Court and *one* opinion from the en banc Fifth Circuit, which had explicitly created a good-faith exception. *Id.* at 913 n.11. The *Leon* Court's extension grew to apply to other objectively unreasonable violations of the Fourth Amendment; these exceptions extended the prosecutors' ability to use illegally seized evidence to prove guilt. *See, e.g.,* Arizona v. Evans, 514 U.S. 1, 15–16 (1995) (holding that if a court clerk made a computer error that led a police officer to mistakenly believe that an arrest warrant for a stopped driver existed, the exclusionary rule would not apply to the evidence the officer seized in reliance on this judicial officer); Illinois v. Krull, 480 U.S. 340, 356–57, 360 n.17 (1987) (holding that if a police officer acted within the scope of a state statute, which may be unconstitutional, his actions were objectively reasonable and the prosecution may use evidence to prove guilt); Massachusetts v. Sheppard, 468 U.S. 981, 984 (1984) (applying *Leon*'s newly created good-faith exception to the exclusionary rule to a magistrate's "technical error" in issuing a search warrant). In *Leon, Evans,* and *Krull,* the Court characterized the purpose of the exclusionary rule to deter unreasonable conduct by police officers, not errors made by judges, clerks, or state legislative bodies. *Leon,* 468 U.S. at 916–17; *Evans,* 514 U.S. at 14; *Krull,* 480 U.S. at 350. As a result, locating the source of unreasonable conduct significantly affected the Court's decision to apply or not to apply the exclusionary rule.

94. *See, e.g.,* Justice William J. Brennan, Jr., *State Constitutions and the Protection of Individual Rights,* 90 HARV. L. REV. 489 (1977).

95. *See, e.g.,* Hans Linde, *First Things First: Rediscovering the States' Bill of Rights,* 9 U. BALT. L. REV. 379 (1980). For a detailed summary of the numerous justices encouraging the state courts to interpret their constitutions and statutes, *see* WAYNE R. LAFAVE, 1 CRIMINAL PROCEDURE § 2.11(a) (2003).

constitutions and statutes to provide greater protection than that provided by the Fourth Amendment. State courts thus wrote opinions referring to state provisions as well as the Fourth Amendment. When these cases came to the U.S. Supreme Court, the Court addressed its jurisdiction to review decisions that not only discussed the Fourth Amendment but also relied on state law. In 1983, in *Michigan v. Long*,[96] the Court opted for a rule that diminished the influence of state court opinions and strongly safeguarded federal interpretative turf.[97]

III. PROTECTING FEDERAL INTERPRETATIVE TURF: THE "PLAIN STATEMENT" REQUIREMENT AND ITS AFTERMATH

In *Michigan v. Long*,[98] the Court admitted that the selective incorporation doctrine had created a strong federal presence in state criminal proceedings by requiring states to comply with most of the provisions in the Bill of Rights. As a result, the *Long* Court declared a special need to clarify when it has jurisdiction from a state court judgment that referred both to the Fourth Amendment and state law. It also characterized its prior jurisdictional case law as inconsistent and the issue as "vexing."[99] It created a new presumption favoring review by the U.S. Supreme Court:

> [W]hen . . . a state court decision fairly appears to rest primarily on federal law, or to be interwoven with the federal law, and when the adequacy and independence of any possible state law ground is not clear from the face of the opinion, we will accept as the most reasonable explanation that the state court decided the case the way it did because it believed that federal law required it to do so.[100]

Under the Court's rule, a state court may block review by the Court if it writes a "plain statement in its judgment or opinion that the federal cases

96. 463 U.S. 1032 (1983).

97. *See, e.g.*, Michael Esler, Michigan v. Long: *A Twenty Year Retrospective,* 66 ALB. L. REV. 835, 855 (2003) (stating that *Long* "has been most successful in expanding the meaning of what constitutes federal legal grounds"). For a discussion of *Long,* see *infra* text accompanying notes 99–126.

98. *Long,* 463 U.S. at 1042 n.8 ("It is not surprising that this Court has become more interested in the application and development of federal law by state courts in the light of the recent significant expansion of federally created standards that we have imposed on the States.").

99. *Id.* at 1038.

100. *Id.* at 1040–41. One year after *Long,* the Court replaced the "and" with an "or" in the phrase "and when the adequacy and independence of any possible state law ground is not clear from the face of the opinion." Ohio v. Johnson, 467 U.S. 493, 497 n.7 (1984).

. . . do not themselves compel the result that the court has reached."[101] By creating this rule, the Court protected its federal interpretative turf.

The Court attempted to draw a sharp line between interpretations of the Fourth Amendment by the Court and by state courts. The Court viewed its three prior approaches as undermining "federal-state relations."[102] Under those approaches, the Court previously had dismissed the case for lack of clarity, retained jurisdiction and sought clarification from the state court, or determined on its own when the state court's decision rested on an independent and adequate state ground.[103] It viewed its rule of presumptive jurisdiction as providing "state judges with a clearer opportunity to develop state jurisprudence unimpeded by federal interference."[104]

Although the Court underscored that the new jurisdictional rule would fulfill an "important need for uniformity in federal law,"[105] it nevertheless allowed for an exception. Under the exception, the Court could take a different action in "certain circumstances" when "necessary or desirable."[106]

In deciding that it would presume jurisdiction from state court judgments regardless of whether the state court had accepted or rejected the federal claim, the *Long* Court explicitly rejected dissenting Justice Stevens' view that the Court should not review cases when a state court has protected a criminal defendant's asserted federal right.[107] For Justice Stevens, the Court's "primary role . . . is to make sure that persons who seek to *vindicate* federal rights have been fairly heard."[108] The Court, however, rejected this type of limited jurisdiction because it had a different perspective on federalism. For the majority, federalism signified a strong need for a uniform view of federal law;[109] for the dissent, federalism signified that states constituted a separate sovereign, one free from the actions of another as long as it protected the rights safeguarded by the other sovereign.[110] The dissent dramati-

---

101. *Long,* 463 U.S. at 1041.
102. *Id.* at 1039.
103. *Id.* at 1038–39.
104. *Id.* at 1041.
105. *Id.* at 1040.
106. *Long,* 463 U.S. at 1041 n.6. After *Long,* the Court in a per curiam decision nevertheless remanded for clarification, without explicitly invoking this exception. Capital Cities Media, Inc. v. Toole, 466 U.S. 378, 379 (1984) (per curiam). Justice Ginsburg has indicated that she supports this exception. Arizona v. Evans, 514 U.S. 1, 26 (1995) (Ginsburg, J., dissenting).
107. *Long,* 463 U.S. at 1042 n.8.
108. *Id.* at 1068 (Stevens, J., dissenting).
109. *Id.* at 1040, 1042 n.8.
110. *See id.* at 1068 (Stevens, J., dissenting).

cally distinguished between sovereigns by characterizing the Supreme Court's presumptive review as similar to the U.S. Supreme Court's reviewing a judgment from the Republic of Finland's court that had acquitted a criminal defendant by interpretation of the U.S. Constitution.[111] For the dissent, a state court's protecting a criminal defendant's asserted constitutional rights resembled a judgment similar to the hypothetical ruling from the Republic of Finland.[112] By contrast, the *Long* Court viewed federalism as affording it a necessary role to define the boundaries of constitutional protections.[113]

The *Long* Court also protected its interpretative turf by rejecting the dissent's argument that review would squander "scarce federal judicial resources."[114] The majority viewed the presumptive jurisdiction rule as improving "both justice and judicial administration."[115] By requiring a "plain statement" from the state court, the majority explained that it would "avoid the danger of . . . rendering advisory opinions."[116]

Despite the Court's concerns about advisory opinions, the Court's decisions since *Long* have frequently had no effect on the particular case in which it had granted review. State courts, as recognized by the *Long* Court,[117] have, on remand, nevertheless decided in favor of criminal defendants by applying more protective state constitutions or statutes.[118]

Since the *Long* Court created this presumptive jurisdictional rule, state courts have more frequently interpreted their state search and seizure provisions as offering greater protection than that provided by the Fourth Amendment.[119] The meaning of the *Long* rule depends upon one's view of federalism.

---

111. *Id.*

112. *Long,* 463 U.S. at 1072.

113. *See id.* at 1041.

114. *Id.* at 1067 (Stevens, J., dissenting).

115. *Id.* at 1041.

116. *See id.*

117. *Long,* 463 U.S. at 1041.

118. *See, e.g., Evans,* 514 U.S. at 32 (Ginsburg, J., dissenting) (noting that after the *Long* decision, state courts reinstated their prior judgments in "26.7%" of cases reversed and remanded by the Supreme Court); Pennsylvania v. Labron, 518 U.S. 938, 951 n.8 (1996) (Stevens, J., dissenting) (noting that state courts "on many occasions" have affirmed "the original holding on state-law grounds" after reversal and remand by the U.S. Supreme Court). *See also* Robert F. Williams, *Introduction: The Third Stage of the New Judicial Federalism,* 59 N.Y.U. ANN. SURV. AM. L. 211, 221 (2003); *but see id.* at 219–20 (listing state courts that upon reversal and remand changed their interpretation of state law to mirror the federal standard).

119. *See infra* note 353.

Some scholars have declared that the Court "has applied the 'plain statement' rule without difficulty,"[120] while nonetheless stating that state courts have "no need . . . to draw a sharp distinction between" federal and state questions.[121] Some scholars have seen the *Long* rule as one forcing state court justices to be accountable for their decisions,[122] with fearful state-elected judges interpreting their state laws to be in "lockstep" with federal law.[123] Others have viewed the Court's rule as allowing state courts to enter a territory with "hidden dangers."[124] And others surmised that the Court hoped that states would not expand their laws, but would rather interpret their laws to mirror the Court's interpretations.[125]

Even though the *Long* rule protected federal interpretative turf, the Court has ironically at times looked to modern *state* laws to shape the contours of the Fourth Amendment. Because the Court has selectively invoked modern state practices to ascertain the Fourth Amendment scope, such a practice does not negate the turf guarded by the *Long* rule. Rather, this practice highlights the principle that the Fourth Amendment has an evolving standard of reasonableness.

---

120. Charles Alan Wright & Mary Kay Kane, Federal Practice & Procedure: Federal Practice Deskbook §114 n.107 (2002); *see also* Michael E. Solimine, *Supreme Court Monitoring of State Courts in the Twenty-First Century,* 35 Ind. L. Rev. 335, 341 (2002) ("Difficulty in compliance with the plain statement rule likewise cannot be seriously contended.").
121. Wright & Kane, *supra* note 120, at §114 n.100.
122. *See, e.g.,* Stewart G. Pollock, *The Court and State Constitutional Law, in* The Burger Court: Counter-Revolution or Confirmation? 244, 245 (Bernard Schwartz ed., 1998) (citing Michael Esler, *State Supreme Court Commitment to State Law,* 78 Judicature 25, 30 (1994)); Solimine, *supra* note 120, at 342 (citing Ann Althouse, *Variations on a Theory of Normative Federalism: A Supreme Court Dialogue,* 42 Duke L.J. 979, 989 (1993)).
123. Solimine, *supra* note 120, at 342 (citing Edward Hartnett, *Why Is the United States Supreme Court Protecting State Judges from Popular Democracy?* 75 Tex. L. Rev. 907, 981–82 (1997)).
124. Pollock, *supra* note 122, at 246.
125. Solimine, *supra* note 120, at 340. In an opinion decided shortly before the *Long* decision, Justice Burger blamed Florida law for the "untoward result" that a Florida state statute had created by requiring suppression of more than "100 pounds of marihuana discovered aboard a fishing vessel." Florida v. Cassal, 462 U.S. 637, 637 (1983) (Burger, C.J., concurring). Although Chief Justice Burger concurred because he viewed state law to constitute an independent and adequate ground barring review, he urged voters to change the law in order to have a "rational law enforcement" system. *Id.* at 639.

IV. SELECTIVELY TRUSTING STATES TO ENACT CONSTITUTIONALLY REASONABLE POLICE PRACTICES

In several important decisions assessing the reasonableness of officers' seizing and arresting suspects, the Court has attempted to justify its determination in part by citing modern state practices. In these decisions, the Court has extensively analyzed state practices as a factor in determining reasonableness. The Court has viewed state practices as relevant to its task of defining Fourth Amendment reasonableness. Ironically, the Court has used state practices in different manners. Sometimes it has used the practice of the majority of states to support its reasonableness determination, and sometimes it has ascertained the states' "trend" away from a majority of practices. The Court has also explicitly trusted state legislatures when interpreting the scope of the exclusionary rule. In addition, the Court has also refused to closely scrutinize state officials' allocation of policing resources when considering the means they selected to further a law enforcement goal. The Court's interest in current state police standards suggests a unique type of "Fourth Amendment federalism," one in which the Court's rhetorical deference suggests a trust in the states. The Court's decisions, however, do not uniformly reflect a deep trust in states. It has limited its trust by using state practices as a factor and, more importantly, it has *selectively* deferred to state laws.

Yet, in other Fourth Amendment decisions, the Court has not mentioned state practices in deciding Fourth Amendment reasonableness.[126] The Court's

---

126. During the Court's 2003–2004 term, the Court generally interpreted precedent to justify its Fourth Amendment interpretations. *See* Thornton v. United States, 124 S. Ct. 2127, 2132 (2004) (distinguishing and extending precedent to uphold search of a vehicle incident to the arrest of a "recent occupant"); United States v. Flores-Montano, 541 U.S. 149, 152–56 (2004) (citing old and modern federal statutes and extending precedent to uphold government's suspicionless authority to disassemble and search gas tank at border; states' practices would not logically be relevant to government's interest in safeguarding borders); Groh v. Ramirez, 540 U.S. 551, 562–64 (2004) (justifying decision by citing Fourth Amendment particularity requirement and precedent; holding search warrant facially invalid and denying qualified immunity to police officer who sought and executed the warrant); Illinois v. Lidster, 540 U.S. 419, 425–28 (2003) (distinguishing precedent and looking to "community hostility" to limit official's use of roadblocks in which officers stop and question drivers about past crimes); Maryland v. Pringle, 540 U.S. 366, 372–74 (2003) (extending precedent to uphold officer's probable cause determination that car occupant had possessed an illegal drug, despite the presence of other individuals in the car stopped for speeding); United States v. Banks, 540 U.S. 31, 36 n.2, 38 (2003)

selective use of state practices resembles its earlier interpretive struggles in deciding whether the Fourth Amendment and the exclusionary rule applied to the states by the Due Process Clause of the Fourteenth Amendment. In the end, the Court's selective use of state practices underscores the evolving protections provided by the Fourth Amendment.

A. Citing State Laws and Constitutions to Justify Important Arrest Rules

The Court has looked to state practices in constructing important arrest rules. Although the Court has not characterized these practices as dispositive in deciding the reasonableness of an arrest, it has used them to support its ultimate determination. In three significant decisions spanning the period from 1976 to 2001, the Court examined state practices and pronounced broad, foundational principles for seizing and arresting suspects. In 1976, the Court held in *United States v. Watson*[127] that officers did not need a warrant or exigent circumstances to arrest a suspect in public when the officers had probable cause to believe that he had committed a felony.[128] Four years later, in *Payton v. New York*,[129] the Court held that officers did need an arrest warrant to enter a suspect's home, even when they had probable cause to believe that the suspect had committed a felony.[130] Recently, in *Atwater v. Lago Vista*,[131] the Court expressed deep trust in state laws and held that an officer acted reasonably when he arrested a driver for violating traffic laws, even when state law provided only a fine as a penalty for the offenses.[132] By citing the practices of a majority of states, the Court underscored the need for not only a workable rule for police officers but also one with extensive support from the states.

(citing in a footnote state practices about "no-knock warrants," which were irrelevant to the Court's holding, based on precedent, that officers acted reasonably by waiting fifteen to twenty seconds after knocking and announcing their search warrant authority to look for drugs in a residence); *but see* Hiibel v. Sixth Judicial Dist. Ct., 542 U.S. 177, 187–91 (2004) (citing current state statutes as well as precedent).

127. 423 U.S. 411 (1976).
128. *Id.* at 423–24.
129. 445 U.S. 573 (1980).
130. *Id.* at 600–01.
131. 532 U.S. 318 (2001).
132. *Id.* at 354.

1. *A Majority of States Supporting Court's Warrantless Arrest Rule:* United States v. Watson

In *Watson*, the Court upheld a federal statute[133] that had authorized postal officials, who have probable cause to believe that a suspect "has committed or is committing such a felony," to make a warrantless arrest.[134] In upholding this statute, the Court used numerous sources to construct its reasonableness determination. It looked to old and current federal statutes, the "ancient common-law rule"[135] as reflected in its precedents, old and current state practices, and a model code proposed by the American Law Institute.[136] It used state practices to support its viewing the common-law rule as a foundational Fourth Amendment rule.[137] For the Court, the common law allowed an officer "to arrest without a warrant for a misdemeanor or felony committed in his presence . . . if there was reasonable ground for making the arrest."[138] The Court used state court decisions from 1814 to 1866 to show that "the common-law rule . . . generally prevailed in the States."[139] It also characterized modern state practices as continuing to adhere to the common-law rule, stating that the rule had "survived substantially intact . . . in almost all of the States in form of express statutory authorization."[140] With the *Watson* Court citing not only state practices and the common law but also federal statutes and a proposed model statute, state practices emerged as only a factor in deciding the important Fourth Amendment arrest rule.

By relying on these sources, the Court had to diminish the force of its own precedent, which had at times expressed a strong preference for warrants.[141] The Court's handling of its precedents highlights the Court's deference to the judgments of the states, Congress, and the American Law Institute:

> [W]e decline to transform this judicial preference [for a warrant] into a constitutional rule when the judgment of the Nation and

---

133. 18 U.S.C. § 3061(a)(3) (1970), *amended by* Pub. L. 100-690 (1988).
134. *Watson,* 423 U.S. at 414–15, 424.
135. *Id.* at 418.
136. *Id.* at 415–22.
137. *Id.* at 422–23.
138. *Id.* at 418.
139. *Watson,* 423 U.S. at 419–20 (internal citations omitted).
140. *Id.* at 421–22.
141. *Id.* at 423.

> Congress has for so long been to authorize warrantless public arrests on probable cause rather than to encumber criminal prosecutions with endless litigation with respect to the existence of exigent circumstances, whether it was practicable to get a warrant, whether the suspect was about to flee, and the like.[142]

Ironically, as the Court invoked the practices of the states to justify its reasonableness determination, it nonetheless mentioned a federal statute specifically enacted to create "a federal standard independent of the vagaries of state laws."[143] Thus, in one section, reliance on state practices furthered its determinations, yet in another, reliance on state practices undermined federal need for uniformity.

A concurring opinion by Justice Powell similarly invoked the common law and state practices, but admitted what the majority did not: Its opinion created an "anomaly" by allowing officers to arrest without warrants but requiring warrants for many searches.[144] Justice Powell candidly stated, "But logic sometimes must defer to history and experience."[145] Justice Powell cited the wisdom of state courts, legislatures, and "law enforcement agencies" as expressing a need for warrantless arrests under these circumstances.[146]

Reliance on these sources for assessing reasonableness engendered a strong dissent, one that criticized the Court for not using its own "reasoned analysis"[147] to decide the constitutionality of a police practice.[148] It criticized the Court's use of the common law because the common law and current law categorized felonies and misdemeanors differently.[149] More important,

---

142. *Id.* at 423–24.

143. *Id.* at 421 (citing 18 U.S.C. § 3053 (1948), which allowed marshals to make warrantless arrests).

144. *Watson,* 423 U.S. at 427–28 (Powell, J., concurring).

145. *Id.* at 429 (Powell, J., concurring).

146. *Id.* at 430 (Powell, J., concurring) ("Both the judiciary and the legislative bodies of this Nation repeatedly have placed their imprimaturs upon the practice and, as the Government emphasizes, law enforcement agencies have developed their investigative and arrest procedures upon an assumption that warrantless arrests were valid so long as based on probable cause.").

147. *Id.* at 433–34, 442–43 (Marshall, J., dissenting).

148. *Id.* at 438 (Marshall, J., dissenting).

149. *Watson,* 423 U.S. at 439–42 (Marshall, J., dissenting). The dissent also declared that even if the categorizations of felonies and misdemeanors were the same at common law and today, the Court would still have an independent duty to balance interests. *Id.* at 442 (Marshall, J., dissenting) (stating that "the Court's unblinking literalism cannot replace analysis of the constitutional interests involved").

the dissent invoked *Marbury v. Madison*.[150] It stated, "The Court's error on this score is far more dangerous than its misreading of history, for it is well settled that the mere existence of statutes or practice, even of long standing, is no defense to an unconstitutional practice."[151]

2. *States' Movement Toward an Arrest Warrant Requirement to Enter Home:* **Payton v. New York**

Despite the dissent's strong criticism of *Watson*'s sources for deciding reasonableness, the Court in *Payton v. New York*[152] similarly grounded its Fourth Amendment arrest rule, but this time it characterized the sources as less clear in deciding reasonableness. In *Payton*, the Court interpreted the Fourth Amendment to strike down two New York statutes that allowed police officers to arrest felons in their homes without using an arrest warrant.[153] In deciding that the officers needed an arrest warrant,[154] the Court considered the same sources for constructing this arrest rule, yet characterized the sources as providing less clarity than they did in *Watson*. It viewed *Watson* as considering three sources—the common law, state practices, and federal statutes.[155]

In examining the common law to characterize what the Framers might have intended, the Court stated that the "relevant common law [did] not provide the same guidance that was present in *Watson*."[156] It then diminished the common law's significance by characterizing it as not "definitively settl[ing]" the Fourth Amendment arrest issue.[157] It also undermined the common law's importance by inconsistently characterizing its role in assessing Fourth Amendment reasonableness. For the *Payton* Court, the common law was not only "obviously relevant," but could also be "entirely dispositive . . . of what the Framers of the Amendment might have thought to be reasonable."[158] By contrast, it also characterized the Fourth Amendment as

---

150. *Id.* at 443 (Marshall, J., dissenting) (citing Marbury v. Madison, 5 U.S. 137 (1803)).
151. *Id.* (Marshall, J., dissenting).
152. 445 U.S. 573 (1980).
153. *Id.* at 603.
154. The *Payton* Court specifically left open whether the Fourth Amendment allows warrantless entries of suspects' residences when they have both probable cause and exigent circumstances. *Id.* at 583. It noted that the lower courts had not addressed the issue of exigent circumstances. *Id.*
155. *Id.* at 590.
156. *Payton,* 445 U.S. at 597.
157. *Id.* at 598.
158. *Id.* at 591.

reflecting "contemporary norms and conditions."[159] It undercut the force of the common law as a source by stating that it had "not simply frozen into constitutional law those law enforcement practices that existed at the time of the Fourth Amendment's passage."[160]

With the common law providing little guidance, the *Payton* Court considered *Watson*'s use of state practices in deciding reasonableness.[161] In *Payton*, the Court deftly undercut its prior consideration of how a majority of states viewed the issue. The Court candidly admitted the majority rule did not harmonize with its warrant requirement. It stated, "A majority of the States that have taken a position on the question permit warrantless entry into the home to arrest even in the absence of exigent circumstances."[162] It initially summarized state statutes in this manner: Twenty-four permitted warrantless entries, fifteen did not, and eleven had not decided.[163] Despite this majority rule, the Court nonetheless used state court decisions that struck down these state statutes to support a different characterization: a current "significant decline during the last decade in the number of States permitting warrantless entries for arrest."[164] It also re-characterized the majority rule into a minority rule by including those states that had not considered the issue.[165] It stated, "Only 24 of the 50 States currently sanction warrantless entries into the home to arrest, . . . and there is an obvious declining trend."[166]

The Court also considered state constitutions to support its warrant requirement for the Fourth Amendment. It noted that seven states had interpreted their state constitutions to require warrants, and it characterized these interpretations as revealing the "depth of the principle."[167] It stated, "That is significant because by invoking a state constitutional provision, a state court immunizes its decision from review by this Court."[168] The Court used these interpretations to support the importance of requiring a warrant under the Fourth Amendment.[169]

---

159. *Id.* at 591 n.33.
160. *Id.*
161. *Payton,* 445 U.S. at 598–600.
162. *Id.* at 598.
163. *Id.* at 598–99.
164. *Id.* at 599.
165. *See id.* at 600.
166. *Payton,* 445 U.S. at 600.
167. *Id.*
168. *Id.*
169. *Id.* at 598–600.

In addition, the *Payton* Court selectively used evolving state practices to construct an evolving Fourth Amendment.[170] It viewed the word "reasonable" as "amorphous" and that "custom and contemporary norms necessarily play . . . a large role in the constitutional analysis."[171]

In considering the third *Watson* factor, congressional acts, the *Payton* Court noted that none had specifically authorized warrantless entries into a home.[172] And it briefly mentioned a model code provision by the American Law Institute that barred such entries only as to nighttime entries.[173] The majority in *Payton* neither distinguished nor embraced this model code provision.

The Court's characterization of each of the *Watson* factors, however, did not match the dissent's.[174] For the dissent, the common law clearly did not require an arrest warrant to enter a residence;[175] the states' "consensus" did not support the Court's warrant requirement;[176] and the lack of express federal statutory authorization for homes did not negate authorization to arrest without a warrant.[177] With the common law clear from the dissent's perspective, Congress had "intended" for the common-law rule to apply.[178]

Although the justices in *Payton* interpreted the common law differently, state practices, and federal, they nonetheless considered them as groundings for their Fourth Amendment determination. In crafting these arrest rules, the Court in both *Payton* and *Watson* cited current state practices as support for its rules. The Court's recent decision in *Atwater v. City of Lago Vista*[179] reflects a similar grounding, one that created a broad arrest rule while noting that statutes, not the Fourth Amendment, can better specify limits on arrest powers.[180]

---

170. *Id.* at 600.
171. *Payton,* 445 U.S. at 600.
172. *Id.* at 601.
173. *Id.* at 581 n.14.
174. *Id.* at 603–16 (White, J., dissenting).
175. *Id.* at 611, 616 (White, J., dissenting) (stating that "warrantless arrest entries were . . . firmly rooted at common law"; criticizing majority for "ignor[ing] the carefully crafted restrictions on the common-law power of arrest entry").
176. *Payton,* 445 U.S. at 614 (White, J., dissenting).
177. *Id.* at 614 (White, J., dissenting).
178. *Id.* at 615 (White, J., dissenting).
179. 532 U.S. 318 (2001).
180. *Id.* at 352 ("It is of course easier to devise a minor-offense limitation by statute than to derive one through the Constitution, simply because the statute can let the arrest power turn on any sort of practical consideration without having to subsume it under a broader principle.").

3. *A Majority of States Allowing Arrests for Minor Offenses:* **Atwater v. City of Lago Vista**

In *Atwater v. City of Lago Vista*,[181] the Court created an expansive Fourth Amendment arrest rule. It held that an officer acted reasonably within the meaning of the Fourth Amendment by arresting a driver without a warrant for committing offenses that provide only for fines, not for incarceration.[182] Even though the Court declared that the officer had "(at best) exercis[ed] extremely poor judgment,"[183] it nonetheless viewed its judicial role as providing a broad Fourth Amendment principle. To justify its reasonableness determination, the Court cited the same sources it used in *Watson* and *Payton* as well as others: pre-founding practices in English common law and statutes and modern state and federal arrest statutes.[184] In the end, the Court's decision expressed deep trust in state legislatures to craft sound limits on arrest powers.

By embracing a broad Fourth Amendment arrest power, the Court rejected two limiting rules proposed by the arrested driver: first, that officers may make warrantless arrests for misdemeanors only if they involve a "breach of the peace;"[185] and, second, that officers may not arrest without a warrant "when conviction could not ultimately carry any jail time and when the government shows no compelling need for immediate detention."[186]

With respect to the first rule, the driver had urged the Court to embrace her construction of the common law. The Court, however, disagreed with the driver that the common law had a "breach of peace" requirement.[187] The Court cited pre-founding- and founding-era sources describing the common law,[188] declaring that "early English statutes" had "riddle[d] . . . [her] supposed common-law rule with enough exceptions" to undermine her construction of what the Fourth Amendment Framers would have intended.[189] In addition, the Court characterized early state practices as consistent with its view of the common law, noting they too permitted warrantless arrests for "nonviolent misdemeanors."[190] The Court ironically stated that even though "the Fourth Amendment did not originally apply to the States,"[191]

---

181. *Id.* at 354–55.
182. *Id.*
183. *Id.* at 346–47.
184. *Atwater,* 532 U.S. at 331–35.
185. *Id.* at 327.
186. *Id.* at 346.
187. *Id.* at 327.
188. *Id.* at 327–40.
189. *Id.* at 335.
190. *Atwater,* 532 U.S. at 338.
191. *Id.* at 338–39.

early state practices are not "irrelevant in unearthing the Amendment's original meaning."[192]

The Court also cited the *Watson* Court's discussion of federal statutes to undercut the first proposed rule. It noted that early Congressional statutes allowed for broad, warrantless arrest powers.[193] It reiterated that the Second Congress had given "United States marshals the same power as local peace officers to make warrantless arrests."[194] By viewing early practices as inconsistent with the proposed rule, the *Atwater* Court then looked to modern law. It discerned "two centuries of uninterrupted (and largely unchallenged) state and federal practice permitting warrantless arrests for misdemeanors not amounting to or involving breach of the peace."[195]

In a lengthy appendix, the Court cited arrest statutes from fifty states harmonious with its broad arrest principle.[196] For the Court, the presence of these modern statutes provoked an unusually condescending tone: "Small wonder, then, that today statutes in all 50 States and the District of Columbia permit warrantless misdemeanor arrests by at least some (if not all) peace officers without requiring any breach of the peace."[197] For the Court, modern statutes supported its construction of English and American common law that officers may arrest for a misdemeanor committed in their presence.

The Court also considered the driver's second proposed rule, which would have barred arrests for offenses involving only a fine and that did not signify a "compelling need for immediate detention."[198] The Court, characterizing the rule as an invitation to create a "modern arrest rule"[199] limited to the facts of the case, candidly admitted that if it were to do so, the driver "might well prevail."[200] The Court instead declared that it would not "mint a new rule of constitutional law"[201] by balancing interests to determine the reasonableness of this particular arrest. Instead the Court wrote expansively about the need to trust states and protect police officers from lawsuits.[202]

The Court viewed states as acting reasonably in drawing lines for authorized arrests. It cited eight state statutes that had restricted "warrantless arrests

---

192. *Id.* at 339.
193. *Id.*
194. *Id.* (citing United States v. Watson, 423 U.S. 411, 420 (1976)).
195. *Atwater,* 532 U.S. at 340.
196. *Id.* at 355–60.
197. *Id.* at 344.
198. *Id.* at 346.
199. *Id.*
200. *Atwater,* 532 U.S. at 346.
201. *Id.* at 345–46.
202. *Id.* at 351.

for minor offenses."[203] The Court broadly defined arrest powers permissible under the Fourth Amendment in part because it viewed state legislatures as better suited to drafting limitations: "It is of course easier to devise a minor-offense limitation by statute than to derive one through the Constitution, simply because the statute can let the arrest power turn on any sort of practical consideration without having to subsume it under a broader principle."[204]

It further trusted the states and police officers to arrest only when needed because of the financial burdens on limited state resources.[205] Such self-policing, the Court implied, had already occurred because it discerned a "dearth of horribles demanding address."[206] It also trusted officers not to conduct arbitrary arrests.[207]

The Court also rejected balancing interests because that approach would not provide officers with a bright-line rule to administer.[208] The Court explained that a bright-line, broad-categorical rule would safeguard officers' decisions to arrest when they believed that circumstances indicated a need for an arrest.[209] A more narrow arrest power, the Court contended, would end up subjecting officers to too many lawsuits, which would undermine their ability to decide whether to arrest an offender.[210] The Court boldly declared as inadequate the potent affirmative defense of qualified immunity,[211] which gives officers immunity from suit as well as a defense to liability as long as they did not violate "clearly established" law.[212] The Court did not, however, explain its conflicting characterizations of the driver's proposed balancing standard for arrests: On the one hand, a balancing standard would have not given officers enough clarity; but on the other hand, it would have created clearly established law, forcing them to lose their qualified immunity defense.[213]

The Court added that the only times officers could face liability would be when they conduct arrests in "'an extraordinary manner, unusually harm-

---

203. *Id.* at 352.
204. *Id.*
205. *Atwater,* 532 U.S. at 352 ("It is, in fact, only natural that States should resort to this sort of legislative regulation, . . . [because] it is in the interest of the police to limit petty-offense arrests, which carry costs that are simply too great to incur without good reason.").
206. *Id.* at 353.
207. *Id.* at 353 n.25.
208. *Id.* at 354 (quoting Dunaway v. New York, 442 U.S. 200, 208 (1979)).
209. *Id.* at 350–51.
210. *Atwater,* 532 U.S. at 350.
211. *Id.* at 351 n.22.
212. *Id.* at 367.
213. *See id.* at 350–51.

ful to [a person's] privacy or . . . physical interests.'"[214] While noting that arrests may be "humiliating" as well as "inconvenient," the Court described the driver's particular arrest as not "so extraordinary as to violate the Fourth Amendment."[215]

The *Atwater* Court thus trusted the states and police officers to authorize and conduct reasonable arrests for minor offenses. The Court viewed state legislatures as a better institution to craft limiting rules. It also viewed states' limited policing and financial resources as a check on this broad arrest discretion. By refusing to balancing the privacy and physical interests of a particular individual who commit minor offenses against the government's need to arrest, the Court ultimately limited rights under the Fourth Amendment.

Thus, in assessing whether state arrest rules complied with the Fourth Amendment, the Court in *Watson*, *Payton*, and *Atwater* in part looked to state practices, sometimes invoking the practices of a majority of states and sometimes characterizing the state practices as reflecting a particular "trend." The Court's rhetorical invocation of state practice perhaps suggested that its interpretation of the Fourth Amendment would not disrupt sound policing practices.

The Court recently expressed even greater trust in state legislatures in *Hiibel v. Sixth Judicial District Court*,[216] as it crafted a relationship between state law and the Fourth Amendment that allows states to expand the scope of a police officer's authority during an investigatory stop. In affirming its trust in state legislatures, the Court this time safeguarded a practice authorized by a minority of state legislatures.[217]

B. Citing a Minority of State Laws to Justify a Broader Investigatory Stop Rule: *Hiibel v. Sixth Judicial District Court*

A divided Court in *Hiibel v. Sixth Judicial District Court*[218] authorized states to expand their investigatory powers. In a fact-specific holding, the

---

214. *Id.* at 354 (quoting Whren v. United States, 517 U.S. 806, 818 (1996)).

215. *Atwater,* 532 U.S. at 355.

216. 542 U.S. 177, 187 (2004).

217. *Id.* at 182.

218. *Id.* at 187. Justice Kennedy authored the majority opinion, declaring a state statute valid under the Fourth and Fifth Amendments to the U.S. Constitution. *Id.* at 180–90. Justice Stevens dissented, arguing that the statute violated the Fifth Amendment. *Id.* at 191–95 (Stevens, J., dissenting). Justice Breyer, joined by Justices Souter and Ginsburg, dissented, contending that the statute violated the Fourth Amendment. *Id.* at 197–99 (Breyer, J., dissenting).

Court determined that a Nevada statute, as interpreted by the state's highest court, did not violate the Fourth Amendment when it required an individual to disclose his name to a police officer who had reasonable suspicion that he had engaged in criminal activity.[219] In upholding the state statute, the Court balanced the government's interest against the individual's interests[220] as it had done in *Terry v. Ohio*,[221] which created a reasonable suspicion standard for both forcible investigatory stops and pat-downs of suspects.[222] More importantly, it constructed this balance with a large thumb on the states' side of the scale, trusting states to have wise policing practices.

In *Hiibel*, two state statutes led to a suspect's conviction for resisting a public officer: one statute imposed on a suspect during a *Terry* stop the legal obligation of disclosing his or her name,[223] and the other statute criminalized "willfully resist[ing], delay[ing] or obstruct[ing] a public officer in discharging or attempting to discharge any legal duty of his office."[224] When

---

219. *Id.* at 187–89.

220. *Id.* at 187–88.

221. 392 U.S. 1, 24–27 (1968).

222. For a discussion of *Terry,* see *infra* text accompanying notes 235–237 and 243–245.

223. NEV. REV. STAT. 171.123 (2003). The statute provides as follows:

> 1. Any peace officer may detain any person whom the officer encounters under circumstances which reasonably indicate that the person has committed, is committing or is about to commit a crime. . . . .
> 3. The officer may detain the person pursuant to this section only to ascertain his identity and the suspicious circumstances surrounding his presence abroad. Any person so detained shall identify himself, but may not be compelled to answer any other inquiry of any peace officer.
> 4. A person may not be detained longer than is reasonably necessary to effect the purposes of this section, and in no event longer than 60 minutes.

Id.

224. NEV. REV. STAT. 199.280 (2003). Under the statute, individuals commit a felony if they also use a weapon to resist, obstruct, or delay; otherwise, such conduct would constitute a misdemeanor:

> A person who in any case or under any circumstances not otherwise specially provided for, willfully resists, delays or obstructs a public officer in discharging or attempting to discharge any legal duty of his office shall be punished:
> 1. Where a dangerous weapon is used in the course of such resistance, obstruction, or delay, for a category D felony. . . .
> 2. Where no dangerous weapon is used in the course of such resistance, obstruction or delay, for a misdemeanor.

Id.

Larry Hiibel refused to tell his name to an officer who had reasonable suspicion that he had committed an assault, he was charged with and convicted of resisting a public officer, a misdemeanor.[225] Mr. Hiibel challenged his conviction, alleging that the state's identification requirement violated both the Fourth and Fifth Amendments[226] to the U.S. Constitution.[227] The Court upheld his conviction,[228] and it dramatically deferred to state police power as it construed the Fourth Amendment.

When interpreting the Fourth Amendment, the Court had to confront dicta from numerous decisions that indicated a suspect may remain silent without penalty during an investigatory stop.[229] The Court surprisingly characterized this dictum as consistent with suspects' obligation to disclose their names. It did so by assigning different roles for the Fourth Amendment and for state law. The Court explained that "the Fourth Amendment does not impose obligations on the citizen but instead provides rights against the government. As a result, the Fourth Amendment itself cannot require a suspect to answer questions."[230] For the Court, "the source of the legal obligation" was "Nevada state law, not the Fourth Amendment."[231]

The Court's dichotomy, at some level, resembled classic roles for the Fourth Amendment and state law with respect to a state's power to define

---

225. *Hiibel,* 542 U.S. at 180–81. The officer also arrested Mr. Hiibel for domestic battery, but the state dismissed this charge prior to trial. Hiibel v. Sixth Judicial Dist. Ct., 59 P.3d 1201, 1203 n.1 (Nev. 2002), *aff'd, Hiibel,* 542 U.S. at 190.

226. The Court's analysis of the Fifth Amendment falls outside the scope of this Chapter.

227. *Hiibel,* 542 U.S. at 182.

228. *Id.* at 189–91. For his misdemeanor conviction, Hiibel received a fine of $250 and incurred a $70 administrative fee. Brief in Opposition to the Petition for Writ of Certiorari at 4, Hiibel v. Sixth Judicial Dist. Ct., 59 P.3d 1201 (Nev. 2002) (No. 03-5554).

229. *Hiibel,* 542 U.S. at 186–87. In *Hiibel,* eight justices acknowledged dicta in opinions indicating that a suspect during an investigatory stop may remain silent. The majority opinion dismissed language in two decisions, and three dissenting justices cited four decisions. The majority referred to Justice White's concurring opinion in *Terry v. Ohio,* 392 U.S. 1, 34 (1968) (White, J., concurring), and *Berkemer v. McCarty,* 468 U.S. 420, 439 (1984). *Hiibel,* 542 U.S. at 187–88. The dissent included *Kolender v. Lawson,* 461 U.S. 352, 365 (1983) (Brennan, J., concurring), and *Illinois v. Wardlow,* 528 U.S. 119, 125 (2000), in addition to *Terry* and *Berkemer. Hiibel,* 542 U.S. at 198 (Breyer, J., dissenting).

230. *Hiibel,* 542 U.S. at 187–88.

231. *Id.*

substantive crimes,[232] to grant arrest powers,[233] and to select appropriate penalties. Yet, the Court gave the Fourth Amendment a limited role in this context. The Court's discussion ultimately reflected deep trust in state legislatures, even though it did purport to subject the mandatory identification statute to Fourth Amendment scrutiny.

While addressing the Fourth Amendment standard for investigatory stops, the Court revisited the balancing model it used in *Terry v. Ohio*,[234] which broke new ground in 1968 when the Court interpreted the Fourth Amendment to have a reasonable suspicion standard for investigatory stops and frisks.[235] Under *Terry*, the Fourth Amendment permits officers to forcibly stop individuals when they have reasonable suspicion to believe that "criminal activity may be afoot"; it also declared that officers may "conduct a carefully limited search of the [suspect's] outer clothing" if the officers have reasonable suspicion that the suspect is "armed and presently dangerous."[236] The *Terry* Court derived this standard by balancing the government's need for investigatory stops against an individual's "inestimable right of personal security."[237]

Yet, when the *Hiibel* Court applied this balancing standard, the Court did not characterize an individual's interest in maintaining silence, other than nominally noting that the demand for identification did not lengthen the stop, nor change "its location."[238] It did, however describe the government's interest in knowing a suspect's name as an "important government"

---

232. *See, e.g.,* Berkemer v. McCarty, 468 U.S. 420, 436 (1984) ("Under the law of most States, it is a crime either to ignore a policeman's signal to stop one's car or, once having stopped, to drive away without permission.").

233. *See, e.g.,* Atwater v. City of Lago Vista, 532 U.S. 318, 337 (2001) ("During the period leading up to and surrounding the framing of the Bill of Rights, colonial and state legislatures, like Parliament before them, regularly authorized local peace officers to make warrantless misdemeanor arrests without conditioning statutory authority on breach of the peace.") (internal citations omitted); *Berkemer,* 468 U.S. at 437 n.26 ("State laws governing when a motorist detained pursuant to a traffic stop may or must be issued a citation instead of taken into custody vary significantly, but no State requires that a detained motorist be arrested unless he is accused of a specified serious crime, refuses to promise to appear in court, or demands to be taken before a magistrate.") (internal citations omitted).

234. 392 U.S. 1, 30 (1968).

235. *Hiibel,* 542 U.S. at 185–91.

236. *Terry,* 392 U.S. at 30.

237. *Id.* at 8–9.

238. *Hiibel,* 542 U.S. at 188.

interest.[239] In giving weight to the government's side of the scale, the Court was concerned that a suspect may have a "record of violence or mental disorder.[240] In the area of domestic assault cases, the Court listed specific concerns of officer safety and "possible danger to the potential victim."[241] The Court also declared that "identity may inform an officer that a suspect is wanted for another offense."[242]

The *Hiibel* Court also invoked *Terry*'s two-part inquiry that framed its balancing of interests: a police officer's actions "must be 'justified at its inception, and . . . reasonably related in scope to the circumstances which justified the interference in the first place.'"[243] For the Court, the officer's demand for identification furthered the investigatory stop because the officer had reasonable suspicion of criminal activity, as opposed to a forcible stop without such suspicion.[244] The Court concluded that the balancing "principles of *Terry* permit a State to require a suspect to disclose his name in the course of a *Terry* stop."[245] In short, the Fourth Amendment did not require disclosure; it only permitted a state law to authorize mere disclosure.

Although the *Hiibel* Court considered the constitutionality of the Nevada statute, it also cited other "stop and identify" statutes enacted in a minority of states.[246] It characterized these statutes as combining "vagrancy laws" with the limits *Terry* created.[247] By citing these statutes, the Court rhetorically needed to address decisions that had struck down vagrancy laws as void for vagueness,[248] even though the suspect did not raise this issue in

---

239. *Id.* at 186.

240. *Id.*

241. *Id.*

242. *Id.* Ironically, in discussing the Fifth Amendment, the Court declared that identity disclosure was not "incriminating," except in "unusual circumstances." *Hiibel,* 542 U.S. at 191. The Court expressly deferred to the "Nevada Legislature's judgment . . . that the disclosure would [not] tend to incriminate [a suspect]." *Id.*

243. *Id.* at 185 (quoting United States v. Sharpe, 470 U.S. 675, 682 (1985) (quoting *Terry,* 392 U.S. at 20)).

244. *See id.* at 189.

245. *Id.* at 187.

246. *Hiibel,* 542 U.S. at 182–83.

247. *Id.*

248. *Id.* at 183–84. The Court referred to the statute in *Brown v. Texas,* 443 U.S. 47, 52 (1979), which violated the Fourth Amendment because the stop did not involve reasonable suspicion as required by *Terry. Hiibel,* 542 U.S. at 184. The Court also mentioned *Kolender v. Lawson,* 461 U.S. 352, 360 (1983), which declared a California statute facially void for vagueness because requiring a suspect to provide "credible and reliable" identification did not provide a sufficiently clear standard for compliance. *Hiibel,* 542 U.S. at 184–85.

Hiibel.[249] The Court quickly distinguished its case by noting that unlike prior decisions, this case involved a statute that required police officers to have reasonable suspicion for a forcible stop, and it interpreted the Nevada Supreme Court's opinion as clearly interpreting the statute's requirements.[250] The Court quoted the lower court opinion, which interpreted the statute to require a suspect to "state his name to an officer."[251] The *Hiibel* Court added its own interpretation to the lower court's construction when it assumed that the statute did not require a suspect to have a "driver's license or any other document."[252]

As the Court examined state statutes in twenty states, it referred to similarities and differences. It broadly described the similarities: "[A]ll permit an officer to ask or require a suspect to disclose his identity."[253] As it discussed the differences, it briefly noted their historical sources, such as the Uniform Arrest Act and the Model Penal Code.[254] It also described variations in the legal significance given to a defendant's failure to provide identification: Some states made nondisclosure a misdemeanor, some made it a "civil violation," and others used it as a "factor" in ascertaining whether a person is loitering.[255] Regarding other states, the Court, without any citation to specific statutes or cases, tersely stated that "a suspect may decline to identify himself without penalty."[256]

The cited statutes, however, imposed greater disclosure requirements than did the specific holding in *Hiibel*. For example, some statutes stated that an officer may "demand" or require a person during an investigatory stop to

---

249. *Id.*

250. *Id.*

251. *Id.* (quoting *Hiibel,* 59 P.3d at 1206).

252. *Hiibel,* 542 U.S. at 185. The Nevada Supreme Court never mentioned "a driver's license or any other document for identification." *See Hiibel,* 59 P.3d at 1206. When officers have probable cause for a vehicle violation, some states have afforded officers discretion in deciding what constitutes sufficient documentation. *See, e.g.,* People v. McKay, 41 P.3d 59, 72 (Cal. 2002) (upholding officer's discretion to arrest a person who had been riding his bicycle in the wrong direction, even though he disclosed his name and birth date, because he failed to comply with a California statute requiring person to provide "a driver's license or other satisfactory evidence of his identity for examination") (citing CA. VEH. CODE § 40302(a) (West 2000)).

253. *Hiibel,* 542 U.S. at 183.

254. *Id.*

255. *Id.*

256. *Id.*

provide an address,[257] to explain conduct,[258] to give "identification if available,"[259] or to state business abroad and destination.[260] The statutes that referred to loitering arguably raised classic void for vagueness problems, such as criminalizing the actions of a person who "[l]ingers, remains or prowls in a public place or the premises of another without apparent reason and under circumstances that warrant alarm or concern for the safety of persons or property in the vicinity."[261] The loitering statutes characterized as a suspicious circumstance a suspect's refusal to identify as well as failure to give a "reasonably credible account of his presence and purpose."[262] One of the cited loitering statutes provided that "[f]ailure to identify or account for oneself, absent other circumstances, however, shall not be grounds for arrest."[263] In addition, one state statute focused on the "petty misdemeanor" of concealed identity. "Concealing identity consists of concealing one's true name or identity . . . with intent to intimidate, hinder, or interrupt any public

---

257. Ark. Code Ann. § 5-71-213(a)(1) (Michie 2004); Colo. Rev. Stat. § 16-3-103(1) (2003); Del. Code Ann. tit. 11, § 1902(a) (2003); 725 Ill. Comp. Stat. 5/107-14 (2004); Kan. Stat. Ann. § 22-2402(1) (2003); La. Code Crim. Proc. Ann. art. 215.1(A) (West 2004); Mo. Rev. Stat. § 84.710(2) (2003); Neb. Rev. Stat. § 29-829 (2003); N.H. Rev. Stat. Ann. § 594:2 (2003); N.Y. Crim. Proc. Law § 140.50(1) (McKinney 2004); N.D. Cent. Code § 29-29-21 (2003); R.I. Gen. Laws § 12-7-1 (2003); Utah Code Ann. § 77-7-15 (2003); Wis. Stat. § 968.24 (2003).
258. Ark. Code Ann. § 5-71-213(a)(1); Colo. Rev. Stat. § 16-3-103(1); 725 Ill. Comp. Stat. 5/107-14 (2004); Kan. Stat. Ann. § 22-2402(1); La. Code Crim. Proc. Ann. art. 215.1(A); Neb. Rev. Stat. § 29-829; N.Y. Crim. Proc. Law § 140.50(1); N.D. Cent. Code § 29-29-21; Utah Code Ann. § 77-7-15; Wis. Stat. § 968.24.
259. Colo. Rev. Stat. § 16-3-103(1).
260. Del. Code Ann. tit. 11, § 1902(a); Mo. Rev. Stat. § 84.710(2); N.H. Rev. Stat. Ann. § 594:2; R.I. Gen. Laws § 12-7-1.
261. Ark. Code. Ann. § 5-71-213(a)(1). The Court cited five loitering or prowling statutes, all similar to the Arkansas statute. *Id.* Del. Code Ann. tit. 11, § 1321(6) (2003); Fla. Stat. ch. 856.021(2) (2003); Ga. Code Ann. § 16-11-36(b) (2003); N.H. Rev. Stat. Ann. § 644:6 (2003). These statutes also provided a defense when an officer failed to give a suspect the opportunity to speak. *See, e.g.,* Ark. Code. Ann. § 5-71-213(d) (Michie 2004) ("It shall be a defense to prosecution under . . . this section that the law enforcement officer did not afford the defendant an opportunity to identify himself and explain his presence and conduct.").
262. Ark. Code Ann. § 5-71-213(a)(1).
263. N.H. Rev. Stat. Ann. § 644:6.

officer . . . in a legal performance of his duty."[264] By contrast, one state statute indicated an officer "may request" a person's name, address, and an explanation of conduct as well as a "driver's license and the vehicle's registration and proof of insurance."[265] In the end, only a few statutes may be constitutional, under the Fourth, Fifth, and Fourteenth Amendments, if the Court were to later refuse to extend *Hiibel*'s reasoning to other contexts.[266]

The Court did not canvas the "stop and identify" statutes from all states, but instead cited statutes listed in an amicus brief[267] that ironically contended that the Nevada identification statute violated the Fourth Amendment. Although the omitted statutes both barred[268] and allowed compelled disclosure of identity,[269] the Court never referred to similar ordi-

---

264. N.M. STAT. ANN. § 30-22-3 (Michie 2004). The New Mexico Court of Appeals has interpreted this statute as imposing more than disclosure of one's name during a lawful traffic stop, an event signifying that an officer had probable cause as opposed to just reasonable suspicion. State v. Andrews, 934 P.2d 289, 293 (N.M. Ct. App. 1997). The *Andrews* decision specifically left open "other situations." *Id.* The decision, however, also contains broad statutory interpretative language as well:

> Identity is not limited to name alone. The use of the disjunctive word "or" indicates that failing to give either name or identity may violate the statute . . . . There would be no reason for the legislature to include the word "identity" if it carried the same meaning as "name." . . . Given the language of the statute, we hold that [the speeding driver] was prohibited from concealing information pertaining to his "identity," which in this case necessarily includes more than just a correct name.

Id. at 291. *See generally* State v. Dawson, 983 P.2d 421, 423, 426 (N.M. Ct. App. 1999) (upholding a person's conviction under this statute for delay in revealing a name when the officer had reasonable suspicion or "even probable cause" for lacking a license plate; stating that "[o]ne could infer that concealment for any period of time, however short, violates the statute").

265. MONT. CODE ANN. § 46-5-401 (2003) (permitted "if person is the driver of a vehicle").

266. Although Justice Breyer in his dissent did not refer to these broader statutes, he nonetheless questioned whether the Court would later permit states to grant officers the authority to compel responses to other questions. 542 U.S. at 197–98 (Breyer, J., dissenting). He specifically referred to compelled disclosure of a "license number" and address and wondered whether an officer can "keep track of the constitutional answers." *Id.*

267. Brief of the Cato Institute as Amicus Curiae in Support of Petitioner at Appendix, Hiibel v. Sixth Judicial Dist. Ct., 542 U.S. 177 (2004) (No. 03-5554).

268. 8 GUAM CODE ANN. § 30.20 (2003). Guam's investigatory stop statute states that a "person shall not be compelled to answer any inquiry of the peace officer." *Id.*

269. *See, e.g.,* CAL. PENAL CODE § 647(e) (West 2003). After the U.S. Supreme Court declared an older California loitering statute facially unconstitutionally vague in *Kolender v. Lawson,* 461 U.S. 352, 361 (1983), the California legislature did not repeal the statute, but did adopt gender-neutral language and changed "such" to "this":

nances,[270] despite their inclusion in the amicus brief's list.[271] By granting states the authority to decide whether to create this "legal obligation" to disclose, the Court thus failed to address the lack of uniformity that will now exist between states and the municipalities within.[272]

Ironically, this lack of uniformity may be short lived if states currently lacking a stop and identify statute enact one for investigatory stops or amend

---

> Every person who commits any of the following acts is guilty of disorderly conduct, a misdemeanor: . . . . "Who loiters or wanders upon the streets or from place to place without apparent reason or business and who refuses to identify himself or herself and to account for his or her presence when requested by any peace officer so to do, if the surrounding circumstances would indicate to a reasonable person that the public safety demands this identification."

CAL. PENAL CODE § 647(e). The Court also did not cite two statutes from Guam, one that addressed investigatory stops and the other the offense of loitering. 8 GUAM CODE ANN. § 30.10 (2003) (investigatory stops); 9 GUAM CODE ANN. § 61.30 (2003) (a loitering statute that makes refusal "to identify" a circumstance for an officer to consider when deciding whether loitering has occurred, provided that the officer gave the suspect an opportunity to "identify himself and explain his presence and conduct"). Another loitering statute from the Virgin Islands also imposed an identification duty. 14 V.I. CODE ANN. § 1191(1) (2003) (punishing an individual who "loiters, remains or wanders in or about a place without apparent reason and under circumstances which reasonably justify suspicion that he may be engaged or about to engage in crime, and, upon inquiring by a police officer, refuses to identify himself or fails to give a reasonably credible account of his conduct and purpose").

270. *See, e.g.,* Brief of the Cato Institute as Amicus Curiae in Support of Petitioner at Appendix, *Hiibel* (No. 03-5554) (citing and quoting from CHICAGO, ILL., MUN. CODE § 2-84-310 (2003) (during certain investigatory stops, officer "may demand the name and address of [a suspect] and an explanation of his actions")); ST. PAUL, MINN. CODE § 225.11 (2003) (during investigatory stops for felonies or an "offense involving the use of a weapon of any kind, [an officer] may demand of [the suspect] his name, address, and an explanation of his actions"); MO. ANN. STAT. § 84.710 (West 2003) (during investigatory stops, an officer may "demand" a suspect's "name, address, business abroad and whither he is going"); ARLINGTON, VA. CODE § 17-13 (2003) (officer may in a public place demand a suspect's identification to further public safety, depending on "surrounding circumstances").

271. Brief of the Cato Institute as Amicus Curiae in Support of Petitioner at Appendix, *Hiibel* (No. 03-5554).

272. An amicus brief urged the Court to strike down the Nevada statute, citing "the cumulative effect that the patchwork of state, county, and local ordinances will have upon the right to remain silent." *Id.* at 16. This brief described a new burden that lawyers face after *Hiibel:*

> Justice Robert Jackson once remarked that "[a]ny lawyer worth his salt will tell suspects in no uncertain terms to make no statement to police officers under any

other related statutes.[273] States may also choose to interpret their obstruction statutes to contain *Hiibel*'s "legal obligation." Before *Hiibel*, some states interpreted their obstruction statutes to require disclosure of one's name during an investigatory stop,[274] some states had refused to do so,[275] others had

---

circumstances." If the Nevada statute (and others like it) are sustained, such advice will no longer be sound.

Id. (internal citations omitted). *See generally* Risbridger v. Connelly, 275 F.3d 565, 569 n.3 (6th Cir. 2002) (noting the difference between Michigan's obstruction statute and East Lansing's obstruction ordinance: The statute "proscribe[s] only actual or threatened physical interference with an officer," and the ordinance "makes it unlawful to assault, obstruct, resist, hinder, or oppose an officer, does not as whole imply that physical interference is required to establish a violation").

273. *See, e.g.,* Adams v. Praytor, No. Civ.A.303CV0002N, 2004 WL 1490021, at *4 n.1 (N.D. Tex. July 1, 2004). In *Adams,* a federal district court both cited *Hiibel* and noted that Texas's failure-to-identify statute applied only to individuals already arrested: "*Hiibel* addresses the topic of what the Constitution permits, not what Texas statutes make unlawful. Here, the Texas Penal Code did not make [the individual's] failure to identify himself unlawful" when the officer arrested him for failing to identify himself. *Id.* at *6 n.2 (citing TEX. PENAL CODE ANN. § 38.02 (Vernon 2003)). Under the Texas identification statute, a state may prosecute the failure to disclose one's "name, residence address, or date of birth" after officers "lawfully arrest the person and request the information." TEX. PENAL CODE ANN. § 38.02(a) (Vernon 2003).

274. *See, e.g.,* Oliver v. Woods, 209 F.3d 1179, 1188–89 (10th Cir. 2000). In *Oliver,* the Tenth Circuit Court of Appeals upheld a suspect's conviction under Utah's obstruction statute and noted that the Utah identification statute (later cited by the *Hiibel* Court) did not provide for any "criminal sanctions." *Id.* at 1188 n.8. Instead of using Utah's identification statute to create a "legal obligation" to disclose one's name during an investigatory stop, the Tenth Circuit relied *only* on the obstruction statute. *Id.* at 1188–89 (citing UTAH CODE ANN. § 76-8-305 (2004)). The Utah obstruction statute provided in part as follows:

> A person is guilty of a class B misdemeanor if he has knowledge, or by the exercise of reasonable care should have knowledge, that a peace officer is seeking to effect a lawful arrest or *detention* of that person or another and interferes with the arrest or *detention* by: . . . .
>
> (3) the arrested person's or another person's refusal to refrain from performing any act that would impede the arrest or *detention.*

UTAH CODE ANN. § 76-8-305 (2004) (emphasis added). The *Oliver* Court interpreted Utah's obstruction statute to apply to the lawful detention of an investigatory stop and a suspect's refusal to identify himself. 209 F.3d at 1189.

By considering New Mexico's concealed identity statute, the Tenth Circuit has also upheld a conviction for a suspect's refusal to disclose his name during an investigatory stop. Albright v. Rodriguez, 51 F.3d 1531, 1537 (10th Cir. 1995) (quoting N.M. STAT. ANN. § 30-22-3, which criminalizes the concealing of one's identity "with intent to obstruct the due execution of the law or with intent to intimidate, hinder or interrupt any public officer or any other person in a legal performance of his duty").

Similarly, a federal district court, without using a state identification statute, stated that Georgia's obstruction statute would support a conviction for obstruction when a person refuses "to provide identification" during an investigatory stop. Gainor v. Douglas County, 59 F. Supp. 2d 1259, 1282 (N.D. Ga. 1998).

275. *See, e.g., Adams,* 2004 WL 14900021, at *4 n.1 (stating that the Texas statute prohibiting interfering with a peace officer's duties has an explicit exception for failing to identify: "'It is a defense to prosecution under this section that the interruption, disruption, impediment, or interference alleged consisted of speech only'") (quoting TEX. PENAL CODE ANN. § 38.15(d) (Vernon 2003)); State v. Woodring, Nos. 96-0831-CR, 206 Wis.2d 678, 558 N.W.2d 706, 1996 WL 653703, at *1–2 (Wis. Ct. App. Nov. 12, 1996) (stating that the obstruction statute does not apply even when officers have probable cause to believe that a person trepassed and refused to provide identification; citing Wisconsin Jury Instruction on obstruction; the court also noted that "'[f]urther expansion to cover simple refusal to answer questions should be done, if done at all, only by direct and carefully focused legislative action'"); Henes v. Morrissey, 533 N.W.2d 802, 807–08 (Wis. 1995) (even though the state identification statute indicated that an officer may "demand" a suspect's name, the Wisconsin Supreme Court interpreted the state obstruction statute to bar officers from elevating their "reasonable suspicion that [a suspect] committed the car theft [into] to probable cause that he obstructed their investigation" simply because the suspect refused to identify himself) (citing WIS. STAT. § 968.24 (2003) (identification statute cited in *Hiibel*) and WIS. STAT. § 946.41 (2003) ("resisting or obstructing officer" statute)). The *Henes* Court further noted that the suspect had not given false information, had not fled when seeing the officers, had not acted violently; the suspect had simply remained silent when asked for identification. *Id.* at 808. *See generally* United States v. Brown, 731 F.2d 1491, 1494 (11th Cir. 1984) (stating that the suspects' "refusal to furnish identification—which they were entitled to do if indeed this was a *Terry* stop . . . may have created suspicion that they had actually used false names, but falls far short of probable cause" to believe that they violated Georgia's false name statute; the court noted that the suspects had responded to an officers' request to see their airline tickets, which contained the false names used to identify themselves to the officers).

By contrast to decisions construing state statutes to strike down convictions arising from a suspect's refusal to identify, some courts interpreted the Fourth Amendment to bar such convictions. After *Hiibel,* these decisions do not necessarily resolve the question whether a particular state statute created the "legal obligation" to disclose as permitted in *Hiibel.* For example, before *Hiibel,* the Ninth Circuit Court of Appeals examined the two Nevada statutes at issue in *Hiibel,* declaring that they could not support a conviction for obstruction as applied to the facts of the case because they violated the Fourth Amendment. Carey v. Nevada Gaming-Control Bd., 279 F.3d 873, 879 (9th Cir. 2002). Because *Hiibel* specifically declared that the Nevada identification statute comported with the Fourth Amendment, *Carey* no longer has vitality. *Hiibel,* 542 U.S. at 187–88. Other decisions compelled disclosure under certain circumstances,[276] and others had left the question open.[277] Because obstruction and similar statutes currently exist in all states, *Hiibel* will dramatically impact state authority in states that interpret their statutes to contain a legal duty to disclose one's name.[278]

By trusting the states to create appropriate legal obligations, the Court did not mention how individuals will know when they have a Fourth Amendment right to be silent during an "encounter" as opposed to an investigatory stop.[279] Under the Court's Fourth Amendment jurisprudence, no state statute could compel and punish individuals for failing to disclose their

---

decided on Fourth Amendment grounds will still require inquiry as to whether a particular state statute created a "legal obligation" to disclose. *See, e.g.,* Martinelli v. City of Beaumont, 820 F.2d 1491, 1494 (9th Cir. 1987) (holding that a jury instruction stating that person could be prosecuted under a California obstruction statute for refusal to identify oneself during an investigatory stop violated the Fourth Amendment).

276. *See, e.g.,* State v. Srnsky, 582 S.E.2d 859, 868 (W. Va. 2003) ("[T]he charge of obstructing an officer may be substantiated when a citizen does not supply identification when required by express statutory direction or when the refusal occurs after a law enforcement officer has communicated the reason why the citizen's name is being sought in relation to the officer's official duties." The court also noted that "motorists are statutorily required as a condition of using public roadways to comply with orders of law enforcement officers.") (citing W. VA. CODE ANN. § 17C-2-3 (Michie 2004)).

277. *See, e.g.,* Shepard v. Ripperger, No. 02-1939, 57 Fed.Appx. 270, 2003 WL 192101, at *2 (8th Cir. 2003) (granting officers qualified immunity because the law was not "clearly established about whether refusing to identify oneself [during an investigatory stop] provides probable cause for arrest" under the Iowa statute barring interfering with official acts).

278. *But see* People v. Brito, No. 200NY013984, 2004 WL 1488404, at *1 (N.Y. Crim. Ct. 2004). In *Brito,* a New York state court interpreted its obstruction statute to apply to individuals "committing felonies or misdemeanors, and not traffic infractions." *Id.* at *2. Yet, when the passenger, who had not worn her seat belt, refused to identify herself, the court upheld the officer's authority to arrest her for the seat-belt violation. *Id.* (citing Atwater v. City of Lago Vista, 532 U.S. 318 (2001)).

279. *See, e.g.,* Holt v. State, 487 S.E.2d 629, 632–33 (Ga. Ct. App. 1997). In *Holt,* the Georgia Court of Appeals held that, under the state's false identity statute, because an officer lacked reasonable suspicion of criminal activity, he could not lawfully arrest a passenger in a lawfully stopped car for giving him a false name and birth date. *Id.* By contrast, the dissent viewed the facts as raising reasonable suspicion, viewing the arrest as valid under the state statute. *Id.* at 635 (Smith, J., dissenting). *See also* Iowa v. Hauan, 361 N.W.2d 336, 340–41 (Iowa 1984). In *Hauan,* officers executed a search warrant at a private club and restaurant, looking for evidence of illegal liquor sales and prostitution. *Id.* at 337–38. The officers informed the patrons of their investigation and asked their names. *Id.* Officers arrested a patron who refused to disclose his identity, contending that he violated a state statute criminalizing interfering with official acts. *Id.* at 338. The Iowa Supreme Court reversed the

names when an officer lacks reasonable suspicion of criminal activity.[280] A request in this context would be a consensual encounter.[281] Yet, if the officer has reasonable suspicion of criminal activity and forcibly stops individuals, then their refusal to disclose their names—if a state statute or ordinance create a legal obligation—might constitute obstruction. In short, the Court's decision allows police officers who have reasonable suspicion of one criminal offense to convert reasonable suspicion into probable cause for another offense—obstruction. Yet, citizens do not know what information police officers possess during a stop.

The Court thus trusted states (and impliedly municipalities) to decide whether to create the legal obligation to disclose one's identity to an officer during an investigatory stop. Yet, almost two decades prior to *Hiibel*, in *Tennessee v. Garner*,[282] the Court only rhetorically deferred to state practices while it more sharply limited states' authority to use deadly force in seizing suspects.

C. Constructing a "Trend" in State Practices to Limit Deadly Seizures: *Tennessee v. Garner*

In *Tennessee v. Garner*, the Court also invoked modern state police practices in determining the reasonableness of using deadly force to seize suspects.[283] In doing so, the Court carefully framed the practices of states to suggest that they supported the Court's new standard:

---

individual's conviction, relying on dicta in both *Terry* and *Berkemer,* which was characterized by the *Hiibel* majority as describing only the Fourth Amendment, not legal obligations imposed by a state statute. *Id.* at 340. For a discussion of the dicta, *see supra* note 230 and accompanying text. Because the officers lacked reasonable suspicion, the Iowa court upheld the patron's right to remain silent: "This is not a country where an individual must present his or her green card and proper papers at the whim of a law officer, or face jail." *Hauan,* 361 N.W.2d at 341. Ironically, the dissent invoked *Terry,* stating that officers had reason to believe that a patron may be a witness or "a possible defendant," one that does not need to know the "nature of the investigation." *Id.* (Donielson, J., dissenting).

280. *See, e.g., Srnsky,* 582 S.E.2d at 868 (holding "that refusal to identify oneself to a law enforcement officer does not, standing alone, form the basis for a charge of obstructing a law enforcement officer in performing official duties").

281. *See, e.g.,* State v. Smith, No. 03-1062, 683 N.W.2d 542, 2004 WL 1336301, at *4 (Iowa 2004) (stating that after officer completed a traffic citation for the driver, his request of a passenger to provide identification occurred during a consensual encounter, which led to the discovery of an outstanding warrant and an illegal drug on the passenger).

282. 471 U.S. 1 (1985).

283. *Id.* at 15–20.

> [I]f the suspect threatens the officer with a weapon or there is probable cause to believe that he has committed a crime involving the infliction or threatened infliction of serious physical harm, deadly force may be used if necessary to prevent escape, and if, where feasible, some warning has been given.[284]

The Court also justified its standard by citing the deadly force policies from the "majority of large cities."[285] Additionally, the Court used state and municipal practices as a tool in balancing interests.[286] For the Court, the government's self-imposed limit on the use of deadly force tipped the balance scale toward safeguarding an individual's "fundamental interest in his own life."[287]

The *Garner* Court examined a Tennessee statute, which provided that "[if], after notice of the intention to arrest the defendant, he either flees or forcibly resists, the officer may use all the necessary means to effect the arrest."[288] The Court noted that the Tennessee Supreme Court had interpreted the statute to prohibit officers from using deadly force to arrest misdemeanants.[289] When evaluating the constitutionality of the Tennessee statute, the Court noted that it reflected the common-law rule, which permitted officers to use deadly force to seize fleeing felons.[290]

The tragic facts of *Garner* aided the Court in striking down the Tennessee statute as applied to these circumstances. While investigating a nighttime burglary of a residence, a police officer heard the house door slam and watched a person run across the backyard, stopping at a six-foot-high fence.[291] Using a flashlight, the officer saw a youth's "face and hands" and "figured that [the suspect] was unarmed."[292] The officer shouted "police, halt!"[293] When Garner began climbing the fence, the officer shot him in the head;[294] the fifteen-year-old Garner later died.[295] The officer's shooting complied with both the Tennessee statute[296] and the common-law rule.[297]

---

284. *Id.* at 11.
285. *Id.* at 18.
286. *Id.* at 19–20.
287. *Garner,* 471 U.S. at 9.
288. *Id.* at 4–5 (citing TENN. CODE ANN. § 40-7-108 (1982)).
289. *Id.* at 5 n.5 (citing Johnson v. State, 114 S.W.2d 819 (1938)).
290. *Id.* at 12.
291. *Id.* at 3.
292. *Garner,* 471 U.S. at 3.
293. *Id.* at 4.
294. *Id.*
295. *Id.* at 4 nn.2–3.
296. *Id.* at 4.
297. *Garner,* 471 U.S. at 12.

The Court declared that this deadly seizure violated the Fourth Amendment by explicitly rejecting the common-law rule[298] as well as early state practices.[299] The Court admitted that it had previously used both the common law and early state practices to evaluate law enforcement procedures under the Fourth Amendment.[300] The Court characterized these older practices as conflicting with modern police practices, which are more protective of a suspect's interest in life.[301] The Court seemed to justify scrutiny of modern practices on three grounds. First, modern practices informed the Court as to how to assess the gravity of the states' interests in seizing suspects.[302] Second, they revealed a dramatic reclassification from the common law as to what currently constitutes a misdemeanor or a felony.[303] Finally, they revealed a "sweeping change" in technology.[304]

To describe modern police practices, the Court canvassed all states; but in doing so, it carefully skewed the math to support its holding.[305] It listed twenty-three states as having the common-law rule,[306] twenty-two as not using the common-law rule,[307] and four states with unclear positions.[308] The Court admitted that "[i]t cannot be said that there is a constant or overwhelming trend away from the common-law rule."[309] Despite this admission, the Court summarized state practices by declaring that the common-law practice "remains the rule in *less than half the States*."[310] In short, the four undeclared states, which may have, through time, ultimately adopted the common-law rule, did not count. Instead the Court made this statement, knowing that the states had split on the issue, with twenty-three in favor of and twenty-two against the common-law practice.

---

298. *Id.* (admitting that it had "often looked to the common law in evaluating" Fourth Amendment reasonableness).

299. *Id.* (noting that "[m]ost American jurisdictions also imposed a flat prohibition against the use of deadly force to stop a fleeing misdemeanant, coupled with a general privilege to use such force to stop a fleeing felon").

300. *Id.* at 15–16.

301. *Id.* at 15–19.

302. *Garner,* 471 U.S. at 19.

303. *Id.* at 14.

304. *Id.* at 13–15 (noting that "[t]he common-law rule developed at a time when weapons were rudimentary").

305. *Id.* at 15–18.

306. *Id.* at 16–17 & nn.15–16.

307. *Garner,* 471 U.S. at 16–17 & nn.17–19.

308. *Id.* at 17 & n.20.

309. *Id.* at 18.

310. *Id.* (emphasis added).

To bolster its construction of modern state police practices, the Court also cited a number of other sources: deadly force policies in "large cities";[311] the policy of the Federal Bureau of Investigation;[312] the association that accredits police departments;[313] and, most important, the Model Penal Code, which the Court ultimately adopted as the Fourth Amendment standard for the use of deadly force, a construction explicitly adopted by two states and similar to statutes in eighteen other states.[314] In addition, the Court cited research indicating that "only 7.5% of departmental and municipal policies explicitly permit the use of deadly force against any felon . . . [while] 86.8% explicitly do not."[315] After listing and characterizing state and municipal practices, the Court explicitly used them to shape its assessment of the Fourth Amendment standard: "In light of the rules adopted by those who must actually administer them, the older and fading common-law view is a dubious indicium of the constitutionality of the Tennessee statute."[316]

The Court also explained that modern police practices aided balancing interests, a task necessarily implied by the Fourth Amendment reasonableness standard.[317] The majority acknowledged the importance of providing officers with the law enforcement tools they need: "We would hesitate to declare a police practice of long standing unreasonable if doing so would severely hamper effective law enforcement."[318] Nonetheless, the Court characterized the government's interests as less weighty as a result of the self-imposed limitations by states and cities.[319] By doing so, the Court candidly admitted that it presumed that some suspects would elude capture.[320] The Court tersely stated, "It is not better that all felony suspects die than that they escape."[321]

The Court also justified rejecting the common-law rule by looking to other current practices, specifically, the changes in offense classifications and the weapons officers have to seize suspects.[322] The common-law rule

---

311. *Id.* at 18–19.
312. *Garner,* 471 U.S. at 18, 21.
313. *Id.* at 18.
314. *Id.* at 16–17. The court of appeals in *Garner* had declared that the Model Penal Code "accurately state[d] Fourth Amendment limitations on the use of deadly force against fleeing felons." *Garner v. Memphis Police Dep't.*, 710 F.2d 240, 247 (6th Cir. 1983) (citing MODEL PENAL CODE § 3.07(2)(b) (Proposed Official Draft 1962)).
315. *Garner,* 471 U.S. at 19 (citations omitted).
316. *Id.*
317. *Id.*
318. *Id.*
319. *Id.*
320. *Garner,* 471 U.S. at 11.
321. *Id.*
322. *Id.* at 14–15.

assumed that felons needed immediate capture, which would have involved "hand-to-hand" struggles.[323] The assumption of danger, according to the Court, did not relate to either the modern offense classifications or to the weapons officers may currently use.[324] The Court compared the "physical threat" present in the misdemeanor of driving while intoxicated to the danger arising from white-collar felonies.[325] In addition, the Court noted that officers did not begin using "handguns . . . until the latter half of the [nineteenth] century."[326] As a result, the common-law rule, if applied to today, would result in greater physical harm to suspects.[327]

The *Garner* Court thus attempted to justify its balance of interests by relying on current policing practices. For the dissent, the Court not only failed to assess the dangerousness of a nighttime burglary of a home, but it also departed from the common-law rule, still in place "in nearly half of the States."[328] More dramatically, the dissent questioned the majority's interest in state practices: "But it should go without saying that the effectiveness or popularity of a particular police practice does not determine its constitutionality."[329] The dissent cited an Eighth Amendment case addressing a state's structuring of the death penalty process: "The Eighth Amendment is not violated every time a State reaches a conclusion different from a majority of its sisters over how best to administer its criminal laws."[330] Yet, the dissent ironically invoked current state practices when declaring that the Court should not require states to provide social science research in support of its practice, particularly when the practice "continues to be accepted by a substantial number of the States."[331] In addition, the dissent also failed to mention that its cited Eighth Amendment case, which extensively canvassed state practices, nonetheless recognized an independent federal duty to assess constitutionality.[332]

---

323. *Id.* at 14.
324. *Id.* at 14–15.
325. *Garner,* 471 U.S. at 14 n.12.
326. *Id.* at 15.
327. *Id.*
328. *Id.* at 23 (O'Connor, J., dissenting).
329. *Id.* at 28 (O'Connor, J., dissenting).
330. *Garner,* 471 U.S. at 28 (O'Connor, J., dissenting) (quoting Spaziano v. Florida, 468 U.S. 447, 464 (1984)).
331. *Id.* (O'Connor, J., dissenting).
332. *Spaziano,* 468 U.S. at 464 (stating that "[a]lthough the judgments of legislatures, juries, and prosecutors weigh heavily in the balance, it is for us ultimately to judge whether the Eighth Amendment is violated by a challenged practice") (citations omitted).

V. CONCLUSION: INTERWEAVING RESPECT FOR STATES WITH THE NEED FOR FEDERAL INDEPENDENT CHECK ON ABUSIVE PRACTICES

The Supreme Court's Fourth Amendment jurisprudence has suggested a peculiar interest in deferring to modern state search and seizure laws when determining what constitutes a reasonable police practice. Under this idea of "federalism," the Court has viewed current state laws as a source to define the scope of the Fourth Amendment. This interweaving of state practices with federal protections raises important federalism questions, particularly when the context involves criminal law enforcement. State legislators during their campaigns have often promised to strongly support law enforcement agendas, with little interest in promising to repeal criminal laws that infringe current contemporary values. In addition, state court judges today may similarly campaign to preserve law enforcement powers in light of the Court's recent acknowledgment of their new freedom to address controversial issues. As a result, the Court's deference to state search and seizure practices may fail to safeguard a politically unpopular group—alleged criminals. In the end, the Court's viewing of contemporary state practices resembles the horizontal federalism practiced by state courts, that is, those that look to other state constitutions as a guide when interpreting their own sovereign constitution. Both the Supreme Court and state courts ultimately view the practices of a distinct sovereign as an aid in giving meaning to the broad language of their constitutions.

Initially the Court drew a bright line between federal and state protections when it declared in 1833 that the Bill of Rights applied only to the federal government. This clear line disappeared as the Court limited state criminal processes by selectively incorporating most of the protections in the Bill of Rights under the Due Process Clause of the Fourteenth Amendment. When the Court in 1949 first applied the Fourth Amendment to the states in *Wolf v. Colorado*, it also refused to impose on state criminal processes the exclusionary rule, a federal protection established in the 1914 decision of *Weeks v. United States*, which barred federal officials from using illegally seized evidence to prove a suspect's guilt.[333] The *Wolf* Court relied on the practices of the majority of states, looking at state laws both before and after the *Weeks* decision.[334] The Court stated, "As of today 31 states reject the *Weeks* doctrine, 16 States are in agreement with it."[335] The *Wolf* Court also trusted that states had adequate processes to check police abuse.

---

333. *Wolf,* 338 U.S. at 33.
334. *Id.* at 29.
335. *Id.*

The Court's view of state search and seizure practices changed in 1961 when the Court overruled *Wolf* in *Mapp v. Ohio*, thus making the exclusionary rule applicable to the states.[336] In its reversal, the *Mapp* Court declared that the state practices relied on in *Wolf* were "not basically relevant to" its decision whether the exclusionary rule applied.[337] It viewed the practices cited by the *Wolf* Court as providing an historical factual grounding.[338] The *Mapp* Court then declined that recent state practices (i.e., those since the *Wolf* decision) provided a better perspective.[339] It noted that "more than one-half" of states had "wholly or partly adopted or adhered to the *Weeks* rule [of exclusion]."[340] Yet, both the majority and the dissent in *Mapp* recognized that state practices were not "controlling"[341] and "beside the point."[342] Instead the *Mapp* majority looked to the inadequacies of state remedies.[343] In this state-remedy context, the Court canvassed the states, noting that "[l]ess than half of the States have any criminal provisions relating directly to unreasonable searches and seizures."[344] *Mapp* thus ended the "asymmetry which *Wolf* imported into the law."[345] The Fourth Amendment and its exclusionary rule now applied to both federal and state officials.

The *Mapp* Court viewed this harmony between federal and state courts as an example of the "healthy federalism"[346] described in *Elkins v. United States*, decided one year before *Mapp*. *Elkins* had banned federal officials from using evidence seized by state officials in violation of the Fourth Amendment.[347] By not allowing federal officials to receive on a "silver platter" this evidence from state officials (for whom the exclusionary rule did not apply), the *Elkins* Court proclaimed its ban to be wise federalism. Despite this ban, the Court nevertheless drew a sharp line when it declared that the federal court "must make an independent inquiry, whether or not there has been such an inquiry by a state court."[348] More directly, the Court stated, "The test is one of federal law, neither enlarged by what one state

---

336. *Mapp,* 367 U.S. at 660.
337. *Id.* at 650.
338. *Id.* at 651.
339. *Id.* at 653.
340. *Id.* at 651.
341. *Mapp,* 367 U.S. at 653.
342. *Id.* at 680 (Harlan, J., dissenting).
343. *Id.* at 652.
344. *Id.* at 651–53, 652 n.7.
345. *Id.* at 670 (Douglas, J., concurring).
346. *Mapp,* 367 U.S. at 657 (citing *Elkins,* 364 U.S. at 221).
347. *Elkins,* 364 U.S. at 213.
348. *Id.* at 224.

court may have countenanced, nor diminished by what another may have colorably suppressed."[349]

The bright line in *Elkins*—a federal court's authority to determine whether state officials violated federal law—did not, however, for the dissent, signify trust in state officials.[350] The dissent also forecasted future disharmony when states grant greater protection than that provided by the Fourth Amendment.[351] The dissent noted that a difficult question remained unanswered: whether federal officials could use state-seized evidence obtained in compliance with the Fourth Amendment but in violation of state laws that provided greater search and seizure protection.[352]

With many states granting greater protection under their state constitutions,[353] the Court again sought to draw an important line in *Michigan v. Long*, which addressed both federal and state search and seizure protections. For the *Long* Court, federalism allowed review of state court judgments that did not contain a "plain statement" that judgment rested on state law rather

---

349. *Id.*

350. *Id.* at 241.

351. *Id.* at 245–47.

352. *Elkins,* 364 U.S. at 245–46.

353. Many states have granted their citizens greater search and seizure protection under their state constitutions than that provided by the Fourth Amendment. *See, e.g.,* **Alaska:** State v. Jones, 706 P.2d 317, 324–25 (Alaska 1985) (determining that the state constitution requires close scrutiny of warrants based on hearsay, ALASKA CONST. art. I, §§ 14, 22, and rejecting the Court's totality of circumstances doctrine articulated in *Illinois v. Gates,* 462 U.S. 213, 230–31 (1983)); **Arkansas:** State v. Sullivan, 74 S.W.3d 215, 221 (Ark. 2002) (determining that the state constitution prohibits pretextual arrests, ARK. CONST. art. II, § 15, and rejecting the Court's foreclosure of inquiries into police officer's subjective motivations when they have probable cause as established by *Whren v. United States,* 517 U.S. 806, 813 (1996)); **California:** People v. Chapman, 679 P.2d 62, 71 (Cal. 1984) (determining that person had "a reasonable expectation of privacy in the unlisted information which the telephone company disclosed to the police," CAL. CONST. art. I, § 13, and impliedly rejecting the Court's decision of no expectation of privacy for a telephone record in *Smith v. Maryland,* 442 U.S. 735, 745–46 (1979)); **Colorado:** People v. Mason, 989 P.2d 757, 759 (Colo. 1999) (determining that the state constitution safeguards individuals' "reasonable expectation of privacy in their personal telephone toll records and banking transaction records held by third-party banking and telephone service companies," COLO. CONST. art. II, § 7, and rejecting the Court's determination of no expectation of privacy in phone records in *Smith v. Maryland,* 442 U.S. 735, 745–46 (1979) and no expectation of privacy for bank records in *United States v. Miller,* 425 U.S. 435, 442 (1976)); Tattered Cover, Inc. v. City of Thornton, 44 P.3d 1044, 1059 (Colo. 2002) (determining that the state constitution requires law enforcement to have a compelling need for purchase records of a

bookstore customer before granting a warrant, COLO. CONST. art. II, § 7, and rejecting the Court's holding that the First Amendment places no special limitation on the ability of the government to seize expressive materials under the Fourth Amendment, Zurcher v. Stanford Daily, 436 U.S. 547, 565–66 (1965)); **Connecticut:** State v. Oquendo, 613 A.2d 1300, 1309–10 (Conn. 1992) (stating that the state constitution protects against unlawful attempts to take a presumptively innocent person into custody, CONN. CONST. art. I, §§ 7, 9, and rejecting the Court's holding that seizure requires either physical force or submission to the assertion of authority, California v. Hodari D., 499 U.S. 621, 626–27 (1991)); **Delaware:** Jones v. State, 745 A.2d 856, 864, 868–69 (Del. 1999) (determining that an officer had seized a suspect who refused to comply with his orders to stop and remove his hands from his pockets, DEL. CONST. art. I, § 6, and rejecting the Court's holding that seizure requires either physical force or submission to the assertion of authority, California v. Hodari D., 499 U.S. 621, 626–27 (1991)); **Hawaii:** State v. Cuntapay, 85 P.3d 634, 641 (Haw. 2004) (stating that the state constitution guarantees short-term social guests a protected expectation of privacy and that its plain view doctrine requires inadvertent discovery of evidence, HAW. CONST. art. I, § 7, and rejecting the Court's more limited expectation of privacy for home visitors in *Minnesota v. Carter,* 525 U.S. 83, 91 (1998), and the Court's elimination of the inadvertent discovery requirement from the plain view exception, Horton v. California, 496 U.S. 128, 138–41 (1990)); State v. Lopez, 896 P.2d 889, 901 (Haw. 1995) (determining that the state constitution requires citizens to have *actual* authority over premises to legally provide consent to searches, HAW. CONST. art. I, § 7, and rejecting the Court's doctrine of apparent authority as articulated in *Illinois v. Rodriguez,* 497 U.S. 177, 184 (1990)); **Idaho:** State v. Guzman, 842 P.2d 660, 671–72 (Idaho 1992) (determining that the state constitution does not have a good-faith exception to the exclusionary rule, IDAHO CONST. art. I, § 17 and rejecting the Court's creation of this exception in *United States v. Leon,* 468 U.S. 897, 909 (1984)); **Indiana:** State v. Gerschoffer, 763 N.E.2d 960, 971 (Ind. 2002) (impliedly interpreting the state constitution to require closer scrutiny by courts of government decisions to establish sobriety checkpoints as well as the manner of conducting them, IND. CONST. art. I, § 11, and not adopting the Court's deference in evaluating sobriety checkpoints, Michigan Dep't of State Police v. Sitz, 496 U.S. 444, 455 (1990)); State v. Stamper, 788 N.E.2d 862, 867 (Ind. App. 2003) (determining that an individual had a constitutionally protected reasonable expectation of privacy in trash placed at curb, IND. CONST. art. I, § 11, and impliedly rejecting the Court's determination of no reasonable expectation of privacy in *California v. Greenwood,* 486 U.S. 35, 40–41 (1988)); **Louisiana:** State v. Tucker, 626 So. 2d 707, 713 (La. 1993) (stating that a seizure may occur when officers create a situation suggesting an "imminent actual stop," one that is "'virtually certain' to result from the police encounter," LA. CONST. art. I, § 5, and rejecting the Court's interpretation that a seizure requires either physical force or submission to the assertion of authority, California v. Hodari D., 499 U.S. 621, 626–27 (1991)); **Massachusetts:** Commonwealth v. Balicki, 762 N.E.2d 290, 297–98 (Mass. 2002) (stating that the state constitution contains an inadvertent requirement for the plain view doctrine, MASS. CONST. art. XIV, and rejecting the Court's elimination of the inadvertent discovery requirement from the plain view exception in *Horton v. California,* 496 U.S.

126, 138–41 (1990)); **Michigan:** Sitz v. Dep't of State Police, 506 N.W.2d 209, 210 (Mich. 1993) (determining on remand from the U.S. Supreme Court that the state constitution forbids sobriety checkpoints because they are warrantless and suspicionless searches and seizures, MICH. CONST. art. I, § 11, and rejecting the Court's deference in applying search and seizure concerns to sobriety checkpoints, Michigan Dep't of State Police v. Sitz, 496 U.S. 444, 455 (1990)); **Minnesota:** Ascher v. Comm'r of Pub. Safety, 519 N.W.2d 183, 187 (Minn. 1997) (striking down sobriety checkpoints because officers lack "objective individualized articulable suspicion of criminal wrongdoing *before*" stopping a driver (emphasis added), MINN. CONST. art. I, § 10, and rejecting the Court's upholding of suspicionless sobriety checkpoints in *Michigan Department of State Police v. Sitz,* 496 U.S. 444, 455 (1990)); *In re Welfare of B.R.K.* 658 N.W.2d 565, 578 (Minn. 2003) (concluding that "short-term social guests" have a legitimate expectation of privacy under MINN. CONST. art. I, § 10, even if the Court did not later interpret *Minnesota v. Carter,* 525 U.S. 83, 91 (1998), to provide one); **Montana:** State v. Bauer, 36 P.3d 892, 897 (Mont. 2001) (determining that a police officer violated the state constitution by arresting a person "for a non-jailable offense when there [were] no circumstances to justify an immediate arrest," MONT. CONST. art. II, §§ 10, 11, and rejecting the Court's condoning of warrantless arrest for minor criminal offenses, such as a misdemeanor seat-belt violation, Atwater v. City of Lago Vista, 532 U.S. 318, 354 (2001)); State v. Clayton, 45 P.3d 30, 34 (Mont. 2004) (determining that under the state constitution, the seizure standard is whether "a reasonable person would have felt that he was not free to leave," MONT. CONST. art. II, §§ 10, 11, and rejecting the Court's interpretation that seizure requires either physical force or submission to the assertion of authority, California v. Hodari D., 499 U.S. 621, 626–27 (1991)); State v. Hamilton, 67 P.3d 871, 876 (Mont. 2003) (determining that a person who lost a wallet retained a constitutionally protected expectation of privacy that prevented police from searching the wallet any more than was necessary to determine the rightful owner, MONT. CONST. art. II, §§ 10, 11, and rejecting the Court's doctrine that the State's interest in an inventory search outweighed the defendant's privacy interest articulated in *Illinois v. Lafayette,* 462 U.S. 640, 645–47 (1983)); State v. Tackitt, 67 P.3d 295, 302 (Mont. 2003) (determining that the state constitution requires "particularized suspicion as a prerequisite for the use of a drug-detecting canine," MONT. CONST. art. II, §§ 10, 11, and rejecting the Court's statement that such use did not constitute a search, City of Indianapolis v. Edmond, 531 U.S. 32, 40 (2000)); **Nevada:** Camancho v. State, 75 P.3d 370, 374 (Nev. 2003) (determining that the state constitution requires "both probable cause and exigent circumstances for police to conduct a warrantless search of an automobile incident to a lawful custodial arrest," NEV. CONST. art. I, § 18, and rejecting the Court's decision allowing automobile search of the passenger compartment after arrest of the driver, *New York v. Belton,* 453 U.S. 454, 459 (1981)); State v. Bayard, 71 P.3d 498, 502 (Nev. 2003) (stating that under the state constitution, "absent special circumstances requiring immediate arrest, individuals should not be made to endure the humiliation of arrest and detention when a citation will satisfy the state's interest," NEV. CONST. art. I, § 18, and rejecting the Court's condoning of warrantless arrest for minor criminal offenses in *Atwater v. City of Lago Vista,* 532 U.S. 318, 354 (2001)); **New Hampshire:** State v. Goss, 834 A.2d 316, 319 (N.H.

2003) (determining that an individual had a constitutionally protected reasonable expectation of privacy in trash placed at curb, N.H. CONST. pt. I, art. 19, and rejecting the Court's determination of no reasonable expectation of privacy in trash, California v. Greenwood, 486 U.S. 35, 40–41 (1988)); State v. Sterndale, 656 A.2d 409, 411–12 (N.H. 1995) (determining that citizens did not have reduced expectations of privacy in automobiles, N.H. CONST. pt. I, art. 19, and rejecting the Court's automobile exception to the warrant requirement, United States v. Ross, 456 U.S. 798, 809 (1982)); **New Jersey:** State v. Bruns, 796 A.2d 226, 232 (N.J. 2002) (determining that the state constitution entitles criminal defendants to challenge searches and seizures made incident to traffic stops as unconstitutional when they demonstrate a "proprietary, possessory or participatory interest in either the place searched or the property seized," N.J. CONST. art. I, § 7, and rejecting the Court's reasonable expectation of privacy standard articulated in *Rakas v. Illinois,* 439 U.S. 128, 143 (1978)); State v. Carty, 790 A.2d 903, 912 (N.J. 2002) (holding that the state constitution makes consent searches following lawful motor vehicle stops invalid unless there was "reasonable and articulable suspicion to believe that an errant motorist or passenger has engaged in, or [was] about to engage in, criminal activity," N.J. CONST. art. I, § 7, and impliedly rejecting the Court's exclusive focus on whether valid consent occurred in *Ohio v. Robinette,* 519 U.S. 33, 40 (1996)); State v. McAllister, 840 A.2d 967, 975 (N.J. Super. Ct. App. Div. 2004) (stating that an individual had a constitutionally protected reasonable privacy interest in bank records, N.J. CONST. art. I, § 7, and rejecting the Court's doctrine that bank customers do not have a reasonable expectation of privacy in banking records, United States v. Miller, 425 U.S. 436, 443 (1976)); **New Mexico:** State v. Gomez, 932 P.2d 1, 11–12 (N.M. 1997) (determining that the state constitution requires both probable cause and exigent circumstances before conducting a warrantless automobile search, N.M. CONST. art. II, § 10, and rejecting the Court's doctrine that probable cause alone justifies automobile searches, United States v. Ross, 456 U.S. 798, 809 (1982)); **New York:** People v. Scott, 593 N.E.2d 1328, 1336–38 (N.Y. 1992) (holding that the state constitution recognizes a reasonable expectation of privacy when "landowners fence or post 'No Trespassing' signs on their private property or, by some other means, indicate unmistakably that entry is not permitted," even in land outside the curtilage, N.Y. CONST. art. I, § 12, and rejecting the Court's determination that land outside the curtilage did not enjoy privacy interests, Oliver v. United States, 466 U.S. 170, 178 (1984)); **North Carolina:** State v. McHone, 580 S.E.2d 80, 84 (N.C. Ct. App. 2003) (determining that the state constitution does not permit a good-faith exception to the exclusionary rule, N.C. CONST. art. I, § 20, and rejecting the Court's doctrine of a good-faith exception, United States v. Leon, 468 U.S. 897, 909 (1984)); **Ohio:** State v. Brown, 792 N.E.2d 175, 178–79 (Ohio 2003) (determining that the state constitution prohibits warrantless arrests for minor misdemeanors unless one of a few stated exceptions apply, OHIO CONST. art. I, § 14, and rejecting the Court's condoning of warrantless arrests for minor criminal offenses in *Atwater v. City of Lago Vista,* 532 U.S. 318, 354 (2001)); **Oregon:** State v. Dixson, 766 P.2d 1015, 1022 (Or. 1988) (determining that the state constitution guarantees citizens the right to be free from intrusive forms of government scrutiny, including in the land outside an individual's curtilage, OR. CONST. art. I, § 9, and rejecting the Court's holding that land outside the curtilage

than on federal law.[354] To ban review by the Supreme Court, state courts had to clearly specify that their decisions rested on independent and adequate state grounds.[355] If ambiguity existed, the *Long* Court presumed

does not enjoy privacy interests, Oliver v. United States, 466 U.S. 170, 178 (1984)); **Pennsylvania:** Commonwealth v. Matos, 672 A.2d 769, 776 (Pa. 1996) (determining that the state constitution protects against attempts to take presumptively innocent persons into custody, PA. CONST. art. I, § 8, and rejecting the Court's seizure requirement of compliance with an officer's show of authority, California v. Hodari D., 499 U.S. 621, 626–27 (1991)); Theodore v. Delaware Valley Sch. Dist., 836 A.2d 76, 96 (Pa. 2003) (stating that the state constitution affords students a heightened sense of privacy that requires courts to closely examine a school's need to drug-test students participating in extracurricular activities or who drive to school, PA. CONST. art. I, § 8, and rejecting the Court's finding that random, suspicionless drug testing did not constitute unreasonable search and seizure, Bd. of Educ. of Indep. Sch. Dist. No. 92 of Pottawatomie County v. Earls, 536 U.S. 822, 838 (2002)); **Tennessee:** State v. Jacumin, 778 S.W.2d 430, 436 (Tenn. 1989) (stating that the state constitution requires warrants to meet the more heightened standard "voiced in *Aguilar* and *Spinelli,*" TENN. CONST. art. I, § 7, a standard the Court replaced with the more relaxed totality of circumstances approach articulated in *Illinois v. Gates,* 462 U.S. 213, 230–31 (1983)); **Utah:** State v. Thompson, 810 P.2d 415, 418 (Utah 1991) (determining that the state constitution protects a person's "right to be secure against unreasonable searches and seizures" of his or her bank records, UTAH CONST. art. I, § 14, and rejecting the Court's doctrine that bank customers do not have a reasonable expectation of privacy in banking transaction records, United States v. Miller, 425 U.S. 436, 443 (1976)); **Vermont:** State v. Sprague, 824 A.2d 539, 541, 544–45 (Vt. 2003) (determining that under the state constitution, a "police officer must have a reasonable basis to believe that the officer's safety, or the safety of others, is at risk or that a crime has been committed before ordering a driver out of a stopped vehicle" during a "routine traffic stop," VT. CONST. ch. I, art. 11, and rejecting the Court's balancing test between the public interest and the individual's right to be free from arbitrary police interference, articulated in *Pennsylvania v. Mimms,* 434 U.S. 106, 111 (1977)); **Washington:** State v. Rankin, 92 P.3d 202, 206 (Wash. 2004) (en banc) (determining that an officer's "mere request for identification from a passenger for investigatory purposes constitutes a seizure unless there is a reasonable basis for the inquiry," WASH. CONST. art. I, § 7, and rejecting the Court's doctrine that no seizure occurs when officers request, as opposed to demand, answers to questions, United States v. Mendenhall, 446 U.S. 544, 553–54 (1980)); **West Virginia:** State v. Perry, 324 S.E.2d 354, 357–59 (W.Va. 1984) (determining that the state constitution, in some circumstances, requires officers to give arrested motorists an opportunity to make "an alternative disposition" of their vehicles to avoid searches of their contents during impoundment, W. VA. CONST. art. III, § 6, and rejecting possible limitations arising from the Court's inventory doctrine, established in *South Dakota v. Opperman,* 428 U.S. 364, 372–73 (1976)).

354. *Long,* 463 U.S. at 1042.
355. *Id.*

review.[356] For the *Long* Court, federalism indicated a strong need for a uniform view of federal law.[357] By contrast, the dissent interpreted the *Long* rule as ignoring the sovereignty of the states.[358] Ultimately, the *Long* rule, coupled with the Burger Court's narrowing of the Fourth Amendment protections, gave state courts a clear path for shielding their decisions from review by using a plain statement.

Despite safeguarding its interpretive turf in construing and applying both the Fourth Amendment and its exclusionary rule, the Court has, at times, invoked modern state search and seizure practices in evaluating Fourth Amendment issues beyond the question of incorporation. When the Court canvassed state practices during the incorporation debate, it did so in light of the standards it created, examining the meaning of "liberty" and later considering what was "fundamental to the American scheme of justice."[359] By contrast, when the Court has cited modern state police practices, it has selectively used them to project meaning onto the Fourth Amendment.[360] Even though no coherent theory can explain when the Court will invoke current state practices to define the contours of the Fourth Amendment, an examination of those cases in which the Court has invoked modern state practices reveals both its selective deference to current practices and an implicit need for guidance in constructing sound policing practices.

Sometimes the Court has sought to support its Fourth Amendment interpretation by citing the practices of a majority of states, and sometimes the Court has constructed a "trend" in state practices.[361] By contrast, the Court has also looked to the practice of a minority of states to create a new investigatory power for states.[362] In short, the Court's citation of modern state statutes suggests a rhetorical deference to state search and seizure practices.

Several of these decisions have established important search and seizure rules. In *United States v. Watson*, the Court upheld the power to arrest without a warrant when a felony has occurred in an officer's presence, even in the absence of exigent circumstances.[363] The Court used current state practices, which were consistent with the common-law rule, to undercut its decisions that had expressed a strong preference for warrants.[364] And Justice

---

356. *Id.*
357. *Id.* at 1040.
358. *Id.* at 1068 (Stevens, J., dissenting).
359. *See supra* Part II.A.
360. *See supra* Part IV.
361. *See supra* Parts IV.A, IV.C.
362. *See supra* Part IV.B.
363. *Watson,* 423 U.S. at 423–24.
364. *Id.* at 419.

Powell cited the wisdom of "law enforcement agencies" to support the arrest rule.[365] Similarly, the Court in *Payton v. New York* used "contemporary norms and conditions" to undermine a common-law rule, as it decided that an officer needed an arrest warrant to enter a suspect's home.[366] At one point, the Court described an evolving standard for the Fourth Amendment: It refused to believe that the common law had "simply frozen into constitutional law those law enforcement practices that existed at the time of the Fourth Amendment's passage."[367]

By contrast, the Court in *Tennessee v. Garner* construed state law and municipal practices as rejecting a common-law rule.[368] By limiting police officers' authority to use deadly force, the Court explained that many states and cities had indicated that such limits did not intrude on their interest in effective law enforcement.[369] In short, while limiting authority, the Court rhetorically constructed a "trend" that appeared harmonious with states' and cities' self-imposed restrictions.

Other recent Fourth Amendment decisions also reveal the Court's continued interest in state practices. In *Atwater v. City of Lago Vista*, the Court listed statutes from all states, using these state practices to uphold an officer's discretionary authority to arrest for fine-only traffic offenses.[370] To justify its determination, the Court showed tremendous deference to state legislatures, suggesting that it was not interested in seriously questioning a state's authority to decide the circumstances in which officers may arrest individuals for committing offenses subject to a fine-only penalty. For example, the *Atwater* Court explained that the Washington Metro Transit Authority had permitted a D.C. officer to arrest a person for "eating french fries" in a subway station, but noted that the Authority had changed its policy to provide for citations.[371] In 2004, after *Atwater*, the Authority arrested a person "for chewing the last bite of her candy bar after she walked through the fare gates."[372] Even though this arresting officer exercised federal authority, the *Atwater* decision broadly supported a legislative body's decision to grant arrest authority.

---

365. *Id.* at 430 (Powell, J., concurring).
366. *Payton,* 445 U.S. at 591 n.33.
367. *Id.*
368. *Garner,* 471 U.S. at 14.
369. *Id.* at 19.
370. *Atwater,* 532 U.S. at 354.
371. 532 U.S. at 353 n.23.
372. Lyndsey Layton, *Mouthful Gets Metro Passenger Handcuffs and Jail,* WASH. POST, July 29, 2004, at A01.

The Court in *Hiibel v. Sixth Judicial District Court* similarly expanded state police power, but this time by citing the practices of a minority of states. The Court upheld a state's authority to compel a suspect to disclose his name during an investigatory stop.[373] The Court noted that the state had the power to convict him for obstruction of an officer's duty when a suspect refused to disclose his name. To sustain this power, the Court characterized the legal duty to disclose as arising from two state statutes: one state statute required suspects to tell officers their names during investigatory stops,[374] and the other provided criminal penalties for obstruction.[375] The Court listed state statutes that contained specific name disclosure references, whether during investigatory stops or as an element of the criminal offense of loitering.[376] The Court never mentioned the plethora of state obstruction statutes—a new possible source for this duty to disclose one's name—nor the frequency of their discretionary use (as with the arrest and obstruction charge of eighty-six-year-old television reporter Mike Wallace for his driver's parking violation).[377]

These Fourth Amendment cases reveal the Court's selective invocation of current state laws, whether used to expand or limit state power. Only rarely has the Court explained their relevance. In *Garner*, the Court stated that canvassing modern practices helped it to assess the gravity of law enforcement interests: to strike the best balance of interests under the Fourth Amendment for determining when officers may reasonably use deadly force. And, in *Atwater*, the Court used current state statutes to indicate states' adherence to a broad common-law arrest power. The *Atwater* Court also impliedly used these modern statutes to indicate the wisdom of state officials, who had only rarely used their arrest powers for petty offenses.

The Court's interest in current state policing practices and its turf-protecting *Long* decision in part parallels the interpretive struggle of state courts interpreting their constitutions. Some state courts have looked outside their state constitutions to give meaning to their own constitutions, known as "horizontal federalism." As with the Supreme Court, these state courts have final authority to interpret their constitutions, yet they also have examined other states to aid them in their interpretations. These state courts

---

373. *Hiibel,* 542 U.S. at 190–91.

374. *Id.* at 181–82.

375. *Id.* at 182.

376. *Id.*

377. Associated Press, *NYC Mayor to Probe Arrest of Mike Wallace, at* http://www.nytimes.com/apoline/arts/AP (Aug. 11, 2004); Joshua Robin, *City Probe on Wallace Cuffing,* NEWSDAY (New York), Aug. 27, 2004, at A10.

understand their sovereignty, noting that even if the language of their constitutions mirrors the language of the U.S. Constitution, they remain free to create new interpretations. Other state courts, still maintaining their sovereignty, have declared that their constitutions provide no greater protection than that provided by the federal Constitution. These state courts have adopted a "lockstep" interpretive approach. In short, independent sovereign courts in both the federal and state system have looked outside their constitutions for interpretive guidance.

The difficulty of constitutional interpretation—how to give meaning to a text not designed to be a code of regulations—may in part explain the Supreme Court's interest in current state laws. The Court, however, has selectively invoked these modern laws, at times trusting the wisdom of state legislatures and sometimes mistrusting them. In the end, the Court's vacillating trust and mistrust of state legislatures and courts suggests an evolving standard of reasonableness for Fourth Amendment issues, one reflecting a peculiar kind of "Fourth Amendment federalism."

Chapter 6

THE CONSTITUTIONAL RIGHTS OF PUBLIC EMPLOYEES

by Mary Massaron Ross

I. INTRODUCTION

Employment decision making in the public sector differs fundamentally from employment decision making in the private sector because public employees are protected by the Constitution. Justice Holmes once wrote an opinion holding that the Massachusetts Constitution did not protect the constitutional right of a public employee to speak freely since his job was conditioned on his agreement to suspend his free speech rights.[1] Justice Holmes assumed that there is a difference for constitutional purposes between the government as a lawmaking body and the government as a proprietor or employer.[2] Whatever the merits of that approach, the federal courts long ago took a different path.[3] Public employers act as an arm of the state in their capacity as an employer. Thus, their conduct is limited by the Constitution. The complex analysis employed to resolve public employment disputes that center around constitutional rights provides a fertile ground for 42 U.S.C. § 1983 litigation.[4]

II. DUE PROCESS RIGHTS OF PUBLIC EMPLOYEES

In order to bring a claim against a government employer on the basis of due process, the plaintiff must establish that he or she has a constitutionally cog-

---

1. McAuliffe v. New Bedford, 155 Mass. 216, 29 N.E. 517 (1892).
2. *See* discussion in G. Edward White, Justice Oliver Wendell Holmes: Law And Inner Self at 285–86 (1993).
3. "[T]he theory that public employment which may be denied altogether may be subjected to any conditions, regardless of how unreasonable, has been uniformly rejected. . . . It is too late in the day to doubt that the liberties of religion and expression may be infringed by the denial of or placing of conditions upon a benefit or privilege." Keyishian v. Board of Regents, 385 U.S. 589, 605–06 (1967).
4. Section 1983 provides in pertinent part:

   > Every person who, under color of law of any statute, ordinance, regulation, custom, or usage, of any State or Territory or the District of Columbia, subjects or causes to be subjected, any citizen of the United States or other person residing within the jurisdiction thereof to the deprivation of any rights, privileges, or immunities secured by the Constitution and laws, shall be liable to the party injured in an action at law, sued in equity, or other proper proceeding for redress.

   Section 1983 does not apply to private conduct or to actions by federal agencies or federal officials. Wheeldin v. Wheeler, 373 U.S. 647, 650 n.2 (1963). Employees bringing an action against federal agencies or officials may sue directly those allegedly responsible. Bivens v. Six Unknown Named Agents of Fed. Bureau of Narcotics, 403 U.S. 388 (1971).

nizable property or liberty interest. Thus, the existence of this interest is a threshold question, often decided on the basis of early motion practice.

A. What Is a Property Interest in the Employment Context?

Property interests are not created by the Due Process Clause of the U.S. Constitution. They arise from state law.[5] The independent source of a property right may be a statute, policy, practice, regulation, or guideline.[6] State law defines the expectation or entitlement, but federal law determines whether the practice "rises to the level of a 'legitimate claim of entitlement' protected by the Due Process Clause."[7] The rules or understanding need not be formal or explicit; "agreements implied from words and conduct in the light of surrounding circumstances" may be sufficient to invoke constitutional protections.[8] A benefit is not a protected entitlement if officials have discretion to grant or deny it.[9]

To establish a protected interest in a government job, the employee must point to a statutory or contractual right that supports a legitimate claim to continued employment.[10] Lesser rights, such as an interest in terms and conditions of employment, may not rise to the level of a constitutionally cognizable property interest.[11]

The Third Circuit's opinion in *Portman v. County of Santa Clara*[12] illustrates the distinction between the deprivation of a benefit, which does not automatically give rise to a protected property interest, and a protected form of tenure, which does. A state employee argued that he had a protected property interest in accrued sick pay and medical benefits. Despite the existence

---

5. Board of Regents of Stage Colleges v. Roth, 408 U.S. 564 (1972).
6. Bishop v. Wood, 426 U.S. 341, 347 (1976), *overruled in part by* Cleveland Bd. of Educ. v. Loudermill, 470 U.S. 532 (1985); McCammon v. Indiana Dep't of Financial Institutions, 973 F.2d 1348, 1350 (7th Cir. 1992).
7. Memphis Light, Gas & Water Div. v. Craft, 436 U.S. 1, 9 (1978).
8. Perry v. Sindermann, 408 U.S. 593, 602 (1972).
9. *See, e.g.,* Kentucky Dep't of Corrections v. Thompson, 490 U.S. 454, 462–63, 109 S. Ct. 1904, 104 L. Ed. 2d 506 (1989).
10. Bailey v. Floyd County Bd. of Educ., 106 F.3d 135 (6th Cir. 1997).
11. Gilbert v. Homar, 520 U.S. 924, 1997 "[W]e have not had occasion to decide whether the protections of the Due Process Clause extend to discipline of tenured public employees short of termination. Petitioners, however, do not contest this preliminary point, and so without deciding it we will, like the District Court, '[a]ssum[e] that the suspension infringed a protected property interest.'").
12. 995 F.2d 898 (9th Cir. 1993).

of a genuine issue of material fact as to the former employee's right to the benefits under state law, the *Portman* court concluded that the deprivation of benefits did not amount to the deprivation of a constitutionally protected property interest.[13] An accumulation of sick leave and medical insurance is not a protected property interest.[14]

Provisions that merely establish disciplinary procedures are also distinguishable from those that create a right to continued employment.[15] They do not ordinarily create a constitutionally protected property right. A deprivation of due process rights typically occurs when an employee is fired. Courts have been hostile to claims based on other lesser employment decisions.[16] The reassignment or transfer of an employee does not ordinarily implicate a protected property interest, although some courts have found a

---

13. *Portman,* 995 F.2d at 906. The *Portman* court reviewed cases from other jurisdictions. In dicta, the court suggested that while most benefits are not constitutionally protected, the entitlement to retirement or disability benefits probably is protected. *Id.*
14. Ramsey v. Board of Educ., 844 F.2d 1268 (6th Cir. 1988). *See* Henry H. Perritt, 2 Employee Dismissal Law And Practice, § 6.10, at 19–25 (3d ed. 1992). *See also* Charles v. Baesler, 910 F.2d 1349, 1353–55 (6th Cir. 1990). The Sixth Circuit's analysis is that state-created property interests are all protected by procedural due process, but substantive due process protections are afforded only to a more limited subset of those interests, a subset defined by federal constitutional principles. *Charles,* 910 F.2d at 1353. *See also* McKinney v. Pate, 20 F.3d 1550, 1555–58 (11th Cir. 1994), *cert. denied,* 513 U.S. 1110 (1995) (holding substantive due process rights are created by the Constitution while rights created by state law need only be protected by observing the elements of procedural due process). The protected property interest may be taken away as long as the employer gives the process that is due. In contrast, substantive due process claims based on fundamental rights cannot be denied or impinged upon regardless of the procedures used. Copeland v. Philadelphia Police Dep't, 840 F.2d 1139, 1144–48 (3d Cir. 1988), *cert. denied,* 490 U.S. 1004 (1989).
15. Campbell v. City of Champion, 940 F.2d 1111 (7th Cir. 1991). The employment handbook relied upon by a public employee contained no promissory language, but set forth progressive discipline procedures. Relying upon Lim v. Central DuPage Hosp., 871 F.2d 644, 648 (1989), the court held that a contract that "merely creates a right to procedure does not create a property interest within the meaning of the due process clause." *Id. See also* Campbell v. Mercer, 926 F.2d 990 (10th Cir. 1991) (only substantive restrictions on the employer's discretion are relevant to the existence of a constitutionally cognizable interest).
16. Ferraro v. City of Long Branch, 23 F.3d 803, 805–06 (3d Cir. 1994); Maples v. Martin, 858 F.2d 1546, 1550 (11th Cir. 1988); Volk v. Coler, 845 F.2d 1422, 1430 (7th Cir. 1988); Kelleher v. Flawn, 761 F.2d 1079, 1087 (5th Cir. 1985).

demotion to be sufficient.[17] Employees typically have no right to a particular assignment even if it involves a loss of rank, status, or salary.[18] A constructive discharge may amount to the deprivation of a protected property interest.[19]

But no due process rights exist where the public employer can demonstrate that its employee voluntarily resigned. In *Lenz v. Dewey*,[20] the Tenth Circuit held that a bank president (operating a bank under the control of state regulators) relinquished any property interest he may have had in stock ownership and a directorship of the bank's holding company by voluntarily resigning from a holding company's board. Offered the choice between resignation from the holding company board with payment of his stock or termination without stock payment, the bank president resigned. The economic compulsion inherent in the choice did not amount to a constructive discharge; the decision was voluntary and deprived the plaintiff of any actionable claim.

1. Formal Creation of a Property Interest

The strongest basis for finding a property interest is to point to a right created by a statute, ordinance, or contract. Courts scrutinize the terms of these measures to see if they provide the employee with a right to continued employment. If state law prohibits firing a public employee except for cause, courts have generally recognized a protected property interest, which cannot be taken away without procedural due process.[21] A unilateral expectancy of continued employment does not give rise to a constitutionally protected interest.[22] The analysis basically tracks the approach used by many state courts in resolving wrongful termination claims. Those who work at the will of their employers may be fired without notice under traditional contract law. Those who can be fired only for a "just cause" have an enforceable contract under state law. At-will employees lack a right to continued

---

17. *Compare* Anglemyer v. Hamilton County Hosp., 58 F.3d 533, 538–39 (10th Cir. 1995) *with* Sonnleitner v. York, 304 F.3d 704, 715–16 (7th Cir. 2002) (transfer and demotion can be an actionable deprivation of property).

18. *Anglemyer,* 58 F.3d at 539–40. *See also* Hon. Harvey Brown and Sarah V. Kerrigan, *42 U.S.C. 1983: The Vehicle for Protecting Public Employees' Constitutional Rights,* 47 Baylor L. Rev. 619, 632–35 (1995).

19. *See, e.g., Bishop,* 426 U.S. at 350; Rathjen v. Litchfield, 878 F.2d 836, 838 (5th Cir. 1989).

20. 64F.3d 547 (10th Cir. 1995).

21. Cleveland Bd. of Educ. v. Loudermill, 470 U.S. 532 (1985).

22. *Bishop,* 426 U.S. at 345–47.

employment that amounts to a protected property interest; however, if they have a right to their jobs under state law, then the government must provide due process before they are terminated.

Property interests may also be created by formal contracts. Several types of contracts have been found to create property interests protected by the Fourteenth Amendment.[23] The first is a contract that confers a protected status, such as a tenure contract providing for permanent employment. The second is a contract explicitly providing that the employee may be terminated only for cause. In *Sanguigni v. Otisburg Board of Public Education,*[24] the plaintiff, a public high school teacher asserting a property interest in her coaching positions, argued that when she was removed from coaching, she was deprived of procedural due process. She claimed that the collective bargaining agreement gave her a protected property interest, but the court found that the collective bargaining contract was not a tenure contract or one for just cause employment. The court suggested that she might have fared better if she had alleged that she worked under an informal agreement providing her with tenure as coach. The third is a contract for a definite term.[25] In *Archer v. Sanchez,*[26] a university fired an employee without notice after only six months of a one-year term contract. Although the personnel manual provided that the employee served at the university president's pleasure, the plaintiff argued that the university had to provide notice and a hearing before firing him during his term. The Tenth Circuit agreed with the plaintiff because "his employment contract for a specific term is recognized under New Mexico law as a property right which cannot be taken away without some procedural protection reflecting fundamental fairness."[27]

2. *Informal Creation of a Property Interest*

A de facto tenure system, such as where there are "mutually explicit understandings" that include a promise of continued employment, may amount to a protected property interest.[28] These understandings have been found in policies, handbooks, or oral promises. Difficult problems of proof may arise where the claim is based upon unwritten policies or customs. Claims based on such informal agreements require a careful analysis of state law. In the

---

23. Sanguigni v. Otisburg Bd. of Public Educ., 968 F.2d 393 (3d Cir. 1992).
24. 968 F.2d 393 (3d Cir. 1992).
25. Archer v. Sanchez, 933 F.2d 1526 (10th Cir. 1991).
26. 933 F.2d 1526 (10th Cir. 1991).
27. *Archer,* 933 F.2d at 1530.
28. *Perry,* 408 U.S. 593.

decade of the 1980s the traditional rule permitting termination at will was whittled down extensively and riddled with exceptions.[29] More recently, the balance has tipped the other way.[30] Because state law provides the basis for determining whether a protected right exists, at the outset of any procedural due process litigation, it is critical to evaluate the scope of protection afforded an employee under state law.

In *Perry v. Sindermann*,[31] the U.S. Supreme Court ruled that a de facto tenure system gave rise to a constitutional claim. On the same day, the Court rejected a potential claim based on the nonrenewal of a one-year term contract.[32] These rulings teach that a due process claim must be predicated on the deprivation of an expectation of continued employment rather than a hope or expectancy. The Supreme Court's affirmance of *Vail v. Board of Education*[33] illustrates the tension between the protection of property interests in employment and the notion advocated by Judge Posner in dissent, that every breach of contract claim should not give rise to a federally litigated constitutional claim.[34]

The *Vail* court held that the Supreme Court's ruling in *Parratt v. Taylor*[35] governed only where the loss of property was due to a "random and unauthorized act by a state employee."[36] The Court rejected Judge Posner's suggestion that the plaintiffs' right was "just a right to a particular remedy—damages."[37] Since a state court breach of contract action was available, Judge Posner took the position that no due process deprivation had occurred.[38]

---

29. For a discussion of the employment at will rule, its erosion, and the current status of state law, *See* PERRITT, *supra,* note 14 at §§ 1.1–1.76.
30. *See, e.g.,* Rowe v. Montgomery Ward, 437 Mich. 627, 473 N.W.2d 268 (1991), overruling Toussaint v. Blue Cross & Blue Shield of Michigan, 408 Mich. 579 N.W.2d 880 (1980) because "the theory it had recognized was a transparent invitation to the factfinder to decide not what the 'contract' was, but what 'fairness' requires").
31. 408 U.S. 564 (1982).
32. *Roth,* 408 U.S. 564.
33. 706 F.2d 1435 (7th Cir. 1983), *aff'd by an equally divided court,* 466 U.S. 377 (1984).
34. *Vail,* 706 F.2d at 1449–56.
35. 451 U.S. 527 (1981). In *Parratt,* the U.S. Supreme Court ruled that procedural due process claims arising from the random and unauthorized deprivation of a property interest may be satisfied by an adequate post-deprivation judicial remedy. The Supreme Court refined its analysis in Daniels v. Williams, 474 U.S. 327 (1986), holding that negligence was not sufficient to amount to a due process deprivation.
36. Logan v. Zimmerman, 455 U.S. 422 (1982).
37. *Vail,* 706 F.2d at 1453.
38. *Id.* at 1453–54.

Later decisions by the Seventh Circuit continued to reject Judge Posner's approach. In *Cushing v. City of Chicago*,[39] for example, the Seventh Circuit held that the availability of a state court contract action based on an employee's claim that he was entitled to medical benefits did not bar a procedural due process claim. Because the employer could readily provide a predeprivation hearing, its failure to do so gave rise to a claim. The court distinguished *Zimmerman v. Burch*,[40] because the city's refusal to pay the plaintiff's medical benefits was not random and unauthorized but allegedly resulted from a city policy.

But the availability of a state breach of contract action and its impact on due process claims remains unclear. In *McKinney v. Pate*,[41] the Eleventh Circuit reinstated a jury verdict. Two members of the panel concurred, pointing out that the court's prior decisions were inconsistent with Supreme Court due process jurisprudence. These judges embraced the view that Judge Posner unsuccessfully advocated in *Vail*, that the termination of a public employee implicates procedural, not substantive, due process. Based on this reasoning, the court dismissed the claim because adequate state remedies were available.[42] Thereafter, in an en banc opinion, the Eleventh Circuit adopted the views of the concurrence.[43]

Practitioners should check the law in their circuit on this point. Defense counsel should consider raising the argument that adequate state post-termination remedies mandate dismissal of the due process claim.[44]

B. What Process Is Due Before Depriving a Public Employee of a Property Interest?

Established principles of due process require, as a prerequisite to the intentional deprivation of a protected property interest, that the government provide notice and an opportunity for a hearing. In *Cleveland Board of Education v. Loudermill*,[45] the Court summarized essential "notice" and "opportunity to respond" requirement as follows:

---

39. 3 F.3d 1156 (7th Cir. 1993).
40. 489 U.S. 113 (1990).
41. 985 F.2d 1502 (11th Cir. 1993), *cert. denied,* 513 U.S. 1110 (1995).
42. *McKinney,* 985 F.2d at 1507–11.
43. McKinney v. Pate, 994 F.2d 772 (11th Cir. 1993) (en banc). *See also* Charles v. Baesler, 910 F.2d 1349, 1353–54 (6th Cir. 1990).
44. For an in-depth discussion of the Parratt v. Taylor doctrine, *see* Martin A. Schwartz and John E. Kirklin, 1A Section 1983 Litigation: Claims & Defenses, at 361–89 (3d ed. 1997).
45. 470 U.S. 532 (1985).

> The opportunity to present reasons, either in person or in writing, why proposed action should not be taken is a fundamental due process requirement. The tenured public employee is entitled to oral or written notice of the charges against him, an explanation of the employer's evidence, and an opportunity to present his side of the story.[46]

Emphasizing the importance of the employee's interest in retaining his or her job, the *Loudermill* Court pointed out that the opportunity for the employee to present his or her side of the case was "of obvious value in reaching an accurate decision."[47]

In most cases, a public employer should provide pretermination procedures to afford due process to an employee before termination. But the pretermination hearing did not need to be "elaborate."[48] Whether it is adequate depends on the government's interest in imposing the deprivation immediately, the private interest of those affected by the government's conduct, the risk of erroneous deprivations as a result of the challenged procedures, and the probable value of additional or different procedural safeguards.[49] A public employee who is given post-termination administrative procedures must be given only oral or written notice of the charges against him or her, an explanation of the employer's evidence, and an opportunity to present his or her side of the story.[50] When post-termination administrative procedures are available, pretermination procedures function only as an initial check against mistaken decisions to determine whether there are reasonable grounds to believe the charges against the employee are true and support the proposed action. The pretermination process need not resolve the propriety of the discharge.[51] By recognizing that less than a full-blown pretermination hearing was adequate for due process purposes, the Supreme Court struck a balance between an employee's interest in retaining employment and presenting her side of the story, and the public employer's interest in quickly removing an unsatisfactory employee.[52]

This minimal pretermination process differs from the more complete procedural safeguards required in a judicial proceeding.[53] The right to call

---

46. *Loudermill,* 470 U.S. at 546.
47. *Id.* at 543.
48. *Id.* at 546. *See* Mathews v. Eldridge, 424 U.S. 319.
49. *Mathews,* 424 U.S. at 335.
50. *Loudermill,* 470 U.S. at 546.
51. *See* Linton v. Fredrick County Bd. of County Comm'rs, 964 F.2d 1436 (4th Cir. 1992).
52. *Loudermill,* 470 U.S. at 546.
53. Fred S. Friendly, *Some Kind of Hearing,* 123 V. Pa. L. Rev. 1267 (1975).

witnesses and present evidence, the right to counsel, an unbiased tribunal, a record of the evidence, the right to cross-examine adverse witnesses, and other procedural protections for decision making may ultimately be required at a post-termination hearing.[54] Numerous federal courts have considered whether the process provided to an employee meets the *Loudermill* standard. A sample of these opinions confirms that the requirements for a pretermination hearing are minimal.[55] That being the case, public employers should consider treating all public sector discharges as ones requiring due process.

In *Farhat v. Jopke*,[56] the Sixth Circuit explained that the pretermination hearing is to provide an initial check against mistaken conclusions, "essentially, a determination of whether there are reasonable grounds to believe that the charges against the employee are true and support the proposed action."[57] According to the Sixth Circuit, in the pretermination stage, the employee does not have a right to, and the Constitution does not require, a neutral and impartial decision maker. The "right of reply" before the official responsible for the discharge is sufficient.[58] On the other hand, a university professor who used the words "nigger" and "bitch" in teaching a course on social deconstructivism was speaking on a matter of public concern.[59] In *Vukadinovich v. Board of School Trustees of the Michigan City Area Schools*,[60] a teacher sued the school board claiming that the circumstances surrounding his termination violated his constitutional right to procedural due process. After being notified that the board would consider canceling his employment contract, the teacher formally requested a hearing. The school board's private lawyer presided over the hearing without objection and made rulings concerning the admissibility of evidence, but did not act as a prosecutor for the school administration or participate in the school board's deliberations. During the hearing, both the school administration and the teacher presented evidence, questioned witnesses, and argued their respective positions.

The Tenth Circuit rejected the teacher's complaint that the hearing was conducted by the school board's lawyer and held that the plaintiff failed to

54. Schaper v. City of Huntville, 813 F.2d 709, 716 (5th Cir. 1987); Wells v. Dallas Indep. Sch. Dist., 793 F.2d 679, 683 (5th Cir. 1986).
55. *See, e.g.,* Delahoussaye v. City of New Iberia, 937 F.2d 144, 151 (5th Cir. 1991).
56. 370 F.3d 580 (6th Cir. 2004).
57. *Id.* at 595, citing *Loudermill.*
58. *Id.,* citing Duchesne v. Williams, 849 F.2d 1004, 1006–07 (6th Cir. 1988), *cert. denied,* 489 U.S. 1081, 109 S. Ct. 1535, 103 L. Ed. 2d 840 (1989).
59. Hardy v. Jefferson Community College, 260 F.3d 671 (6th Cir. 2001).
60. 978 F.2d 403 (7th Cir. 1992), *cert. denied,* 114 S. Ct. 133 (1993).

overcome the presumption of honesty and integrity attributed to those who serve as adjudicators. The court followed the Supreme Court's holding in *Withrow v. Larkin*,[61] a case in which the Court held that performing dual roles in an adjudicative setting does not, without more, violate due process.[62]

Because the pretermination hearing is not "adjudication," the decision maker need not be impartial.[63] But a biased post-termination proceeding is not constitutionally adequate.[64] Nor does subsequent review of post-termination proceedings cure the defect.[65] Post-termination adversary-trial type hearings are available to ferret out bias, pretext, deception, or corruption that may have caused the complained-of decision. Post-termination hearings can be state judicial proceedings, collective bargaining grievance procedures, or arbitration hearings.[66]

Although it is safer to provide a hearing in person, courts have approved notice and a hearing by memo. In *Williams v. Texas Tech University Health Sciences Ctr.*,[67] the court found that a former public employee received the minimal process required when he was informed in writing of the complaints against him, had the opportunity, and did respond. A tenured professor, in charge of research in the department of surgery, was compensated by salary and fringe benefits, a portion of which came from an income plan for faculty members. The department's chair decided that the professor had not generated enough grant money and notified him that funds from the income plan would no longer be available to him. The Fifth Circuit ruled that the professor had received the requisite procedural protection. The record revealed that the department chair had sent the plaintiff a memo warning that he would not receive funds from the income plan, and the plaintiff had responded. The minimal process required by *Mathews v. Eldridge*[68] had been satisfied.[69]

---

61. 421 U.S. 35 (1975).
62. *See also Myrick,* 810 F.2d at 1387.
63. Walker v. City of Berkeley, 951 F.2d 182, 183 (9th Cir. 1991). *See also* Hicks v. City of Watonga, 942 F.2d 737, 746 (10th Cir. 1991).
64. Clements v. Airport Auth. of Washoe County, 69 F.3d 321, 333 (9th Cir. 1995).
65. *Clements,* 69 F.3d at 321.
66. *See, e.g.,* Maples v. Martin, 858 F.2d 1546, 1551 (11th Cir. 1988); Lewis v. Hillsborough Transit Auth., 726 F.2d 668 (11th Cir. 1984), *cert. denied,* 469 U.S. 822 (1984); Archuleta v. Colorado Dep't of Inst., Div. of Youth Serv., 936 F.2d 483 (10th Cir. 1991).
67. 6 F.3d 290 (5th Cir. 1993), *cert. denied,* 510 U.S. 1194 (1994).
68. 424 U.S. 319 (1976).
69. *Williams,* 6 F.3d at 293.

The Eighth Circuit also approved a notification by letter that was coupled with the opportunity for a response. In *Simons v. City of Grand Forks*,[70] the plaintiff sued after he was dismissed from his position as city assessor. Before his termination, the plaintiff received a letter from the mayor stating that he was considering recommendations made by the civil service commission as a result of grievances filed against the plaintiff. The plaintiff responded to this letter as requested by the mayor. He then received a termination letter that listed eight reasons for the termination and advised the plaintiff of his right to post-termination review.[71]

The sole issue on appeal was whether the pretermination procedure satisfied due process. The court concluded that it did.[72] The mayor's letter provided clear written notice to the plaintiff of the allegations and afforded him complete access to all evidence used in making the decision. The court found that the plaintiff had ample time to present his side and eventually responded in writing to the allegations. As a result, dismissal of the procedural due process claims was appropriate.

A thirty-minute meeting with a supervisor may be enough to satisfy the requirements of due process. In *Browning v. City of Odessa, Tex.*,[73] a firefighter with an exemplary record—until he experienced personal problems with a co-worker—was fired. After the assistant fire chief recommended that the plaintiff be terminated, the fire chief told the firefighter of the circumstances that led to the dismissal recommendation and allowed him to respond. After this hearing, the firefighter was demoted and placed on probation. He was then discharged because he protested and refused to return to work. The Sixth Circuit pointed out that the fire chief had notified the plaintiff of the proposed termination, discussed the reasons, and allowed plaintiff to present any arguments in his favor. Even though the meeting between the fire chief and the firefighter lasted for only thirty minutes, nothing more was required since the plaintiff had the option of a full evidentiary post-termination hearing. He failed to exercise this option, a choice that the court took into account when it ruled.

Although a minimal pretermination hearing is generally required, courts have occasionally approved discharges with no pretermination hearing. The Supreme Court approved a suspension with no hearing in advance after criminal felony charges had been brought.[74] If an important governmental

---

70 985 F.2d 981 (8th Cir. 1993).

71. *Williams,* 985 F.2d at 982.

72. *Id.* at 983.

73. 990 F.2d 842 (6th Cir. 1993).

74. Gilbert v. Homar, 520 U.S. 924 (1997).

interest is at stake, a substantial assurance exists that the deprivation is not baseless or unwarranted, and a need for prompt action justifies postponing the hearing, a post-termination hearing may suffice. *Ambus v. Granite Bd. of Educ.*[75] illustrates this situation. A tenured teacher at a high school was terminated with no notice or hearing after the school board became aware that the teacher had been arrested for distributing marijuana. The teacher claimed he was deprived of his right to procedural due process and argued that a post-termination procedure was insufficient. Relying upon *F.D.I.C. v. Mellen*,[76] the Tenth Circuit approved the school board's procedure. The school board presented substantial evidence that, before suspending the teacher, the assistant superintendent had verified that the teacher had indeed been arrested on drug charges. Because an arrest and the filing of charges by the government requires probable cause, the school had a sufficient basis for a temporary deprivation of a property interest without a prior hearing. The Court held that the substantiated knowledge that the teacher had been arrested for drug sales raised a substantial government interest justifying immediate suspension without pay. The plaintiff had been notified before the suspension and was informally provided with an opportunity to correct any erroneous information on which the suspension and subsequent termination were based.

While the lack of a pretermination hearing was approved in *Ambus*, this represents the exception and not the rule. *Loudermill* itself suggests some hearing is required before the employee is fired.[77] Even if the deprivation is ultimately approved, the lack of constitutionally adequate procedures supports an award of nominal damages.[78]

C. What Is a Liberty Interest in the Employment Context?

The U.S. Supreme Court first recognized a liberty interest in employment in the case of *Meyer v. Nebraska*,[79] where it established "the rights of an individual . . . to engage in any of the common occupations of life."[80] The Supreme Court expanded this notion to give rise to a protected liberty interest.[81] To qualify as a liberty interest, and thus invoke the procedural guarantees

---

75. 975 F.2d 1555 (10th Cir. 1992).
76. 486 U.S. 230, 240 (1988).
77. *Loudermill,* 470 U.S. at 544–45.
78. Knudson v. City of Ellensburg, 832 F.2d 1142, 1149 (9th Cir. 1987).
79. 262 U.S. 390 (1923).
80. *Id.*
81. Paul v. Davis, 424 U.S. 693 (1976).

contained in the Due Process Clause, "a right or status previously recognized by state law [must be] distinctly altered or extinguished" by state action.[82] To establish a deprivation of a liberty interest without due process of law, a public employee must show (1) a false statement; (2) of a stigmatizing nature; (3) attending his or her discharge; (4) made public; (5) by the governmental employer; (6) without a meaningful opportunity for an employee name-clearing hearing.[83]

The concept of liberty protected by the Due Process Clause has long included occupational liberty—"the liberty to follow a trade, profession or other calling."[84] The courts have not recognized a right not to be stigmatized, but an interest in liberty from stigmatization without procedural protections.[85] Injury to reputation alone is not protected.[86] The courts have consistently drawn a distinction between occupational liberty and the right to a specific job. "It stretches the concept too far to suggest that a person is deprived of 'liberty' when he simply is not rehired in one job but remains as free as before to seek another."[87] It is the liberty to pursue a calling or occupation, and not the right to a specific job, that is secured by the Fourteenth Amendment.[88]

Defamation that is incident to the government's refusal to reemploy an individual can implicate a liberty interest. A liberty interest is involved if "(1) the individual's good name, reputation, honor or integrity are at stake by such charges as immorality, dishonesty, alcoholism, disloyalty, communism or subversive acts or (2) the State imposes a stigma or other disability on the individual which forecloses other opportunities."[89] Liberty is not infringed when the individual is only somewhat less attractive to some other employers, as through a label of incompetence or poor management skills.[90] There must be permanent exclusion from or protracted interruption of employment.[91]

---

82. *Paul,* 424 U.S. at 711.
83. Warren v. Crawford, 927 F.2d 559, 565 (11th Cir. 1991).
84. Wroblewski v. City of Washburn, 965 F.2d 452, 455 (7th Cir. 1992).
85. Wells v. Doland, 711 F.2d 670, 676 (5th Cir. 1983).
86. *Paul,* 424 U.S. 693.
87. *Roth,* 408 U.S. at 5775.
88. Lawson v. Sheriff of Tippecanoe County, 725 F.2d 1136, 1138 (7th Cir. 1984).
89. *Wroblewski, supra* at 456, quoting Perry v. FBI, 781 F.2d 1294, 1300 (7th Cir. 1986).
90. *Id.,* quoting Munson v. Friske, 754 F.2d 683, 693 (7th Cir. 1985).
91. *Id.*

The stigmatizing information must be equivalent to charges of "dishonesty or immorality" that might seriously damage an employee's reputation.[92] Charges that carry the stigma of moral turpitude may implicate a liberty interest, but charges of incompetence or inability to get along with others do not.[93] Statements that the terminated employee was overpaid do not rise to the level of those that implicate a liberty interest.[94] Statements that the employee had poor work habits, was incompetent, or inefficient do not amount to stigma.[95]

Public disclosure of the allegedly stigmatizing information is usually required. *Johnson v. Martin*[96] is illustrative of this rule. A probationary police officer was required to provide a urine sample for drug testing. The results of the officer's test showed positive for the presence of drugs. Following disciplinary proceedings in which the plaintiff denied using drugs, he was fired. The police officer sued, claiming that the police department's actions discharging him and placing the information in his personnel file damaged his reputation in the community. He claimed his constitutionally protected liberty interest in his reputation was violated.

The Seventh Circuit held that the police officer could not prove public disclosure of the allegedly stigmatizing information. The officer conceded that the drug-testing results had not been disseminated to any potential future employer. He argued, however, that the stigmatizing information contained in his personnel file "will as a matter of logic and common sense have an adverse effect on . . . [his] ability to obtain future employment in the field of law enforcement as well as other areas."[97] In rejecting this conclusion, the Seventh Circuit relied upon the Supreme Court's decision in *Bishop v. Wood*.[98] The Supreme Court explained that if the reasons for the

---

92. Russillo v. Scarborough, 935 F.2d 1167 (10th Cir. 1991).

93. Wheaton v. Webb-Petette, 931 F.2d 613 (9th Cir. 1991).

94. Erickson v. Pierce County, 960 F.2d 801 (9th Cir. 1992), *cert. denied,* 506 U.S. 1035 (1992).

95. *See, e.g.,* Russillo v. Scarborough, 935 F.2d 1167, 1172 (10th Cir. 1991); Munson v. Friske, 754 F.2d 683, 693 (7th Cir. 1985); *Erickson,* 960 F.2d 801; Mitchell v. Glover, 996 F.2d 164, 167 (7th Cir. 1993); Stritzl v. United States Postal Serv., 602 F.2d 249, 252 (10th Cir. 1979).

96. 943 F.2d 15 (7th Cir. 1991).

97. *Johnson,* 943 F.2d at 16.

98. 426 U.S. 341 (1976). *See also* Simpkins v. Sandwich Community Hosp., 854 F.2d 215 (7th Cir. 1988) (employee accused of improper recordkeeping regarding drugs; charges not made public, so no liberty interest implicated). *But see* Burris v. Willis Indep. Sch. Dist., Inc., 713 F.2d 1087, 1092 (5th Cir. 1983).

discharge have not been made public, the communication "cannot properly form the basis for a claim that petitioner's interest in his 'good name, reputation, honor, or integrity' was thereby impaired."[99]

The mere reporting of defamatory accusations of a third party does not make a governmental agency or official liable for the deprivation of a protected liberty interest. In *Melton v. City of Oklahoma*,[100] a police officer, discharged after being accused of perjury in a departmental criminal investigation, argued that his liberty interest was violated by the publication of two stories revealing accusations of perjury made against the officer by the FBI. The statements attributed to the supervisor and published in the press did not stigmatize the officer, because nothing that the supervisor reported was false. The supervisor neither accepted the FBI accusation of perjury as truth nor did he himself accuse the plaintiff of perjury.[101]

A temporal relation between the remark and the termination is required. Thus, the Seventh Circuit concluded that a remark made long after the former employee's discharge did not violate any liberty interest.[102] Likewise, the First Circuit held that a defamatory remark made well after the discharge failed to implicate a liberty interest in employment.[103] The Second Circuit agreed with this approach in *Salpaugh v. Monroe Community Hosp.*[104] The court held that the trial court had improperly dismissed the plaintiff's claim that her liberty interest had been violated by comments made to a prospective employer. The Second Circuit criticized the district court for failing to determine whether the statements were made during the termination process, which would amount to a protected liberty interest, or after the plaintiff was terminated, in which case there would not be a protected liberty interest.

D. What Process Is Due Before Depriving a Public Employee of a Liberty Interest?

If a court finds that the statements were sufficiently stigmatizing to give rise to a protected liberty interest, then the public employee is entitled to due process. In *Board of Regents v. Roth*,[105] the U.S. Supreme Court held that

99. *Bishop,* 426 U.S. at 348.
100. 928 F.2d 920 (10th Cir. 1991), *cert. denied,* 502 U.S. 906 (1991).
101. *Id.*
102. Sudeikis v. Chicago Transit Auth., 774 F.2d 766 (7th Cir. 1985).
103. Laureano-Agosto v. Garcia Caraballo, 731 F.2d 101 (1st Cir. 1984).
104. 4 F.3d 134 (2d Cir. 1993), *cert. denied,* 510 U.S. 1164 (1994).
105. 408 U.S. 564 (1972).

the hearing necessary to protect an employee's liberty interest is one that provides the person with "an opportunity to clear his name."[106] This hearing need not be separate from the hearing provided before depriving the plaintiff of a property interest. The pretermination hearing under *Loudermill*[107] may be sufficient to protect both interests.[108]

There is no need for hearing if the employee admits the truth of the statements or charges.[109] But otherwise the employee is entitled to a public hearing at which to clear his or her name.[110] If provided upon the request of the public employee, a name-clearing hearing can cure any violation.[111] The loss of employment coupled with stigmatizing statements, absent an opportunity to clear the employee's name, amounts to the deprivation of a liberty interest.[112] If the employee insists on a public hearing at which the charges are disseminated, then the employer is not responsible for the public dissemination of the information at that hearing.[113]

E. Substantive Due Process

The scope and parameters of a substantive due process claim in the public employment context are unclear. The Supreme Court has increasingly limited substantive due process claims because "guideposts for responsible decision-making in this unchartered area are scarce and open-ended."[114] In *Collins v. City of Harker Heights, Tex.*,[115] the Court explained that the "doctrine of judicial self-restraint requires us to exercise the utmost care whenever we are asked to break new ground in this field."[116] The *Collins* Court set forth an analytical framework requiring the Court "to focus on the allegations in the complaint to determine how petitioner describes the constitutional right at stake and what the city allegedly did to deprive her husband of that right."[117]

---

106. *Roth,* 408 U.S. at 573, n.12.
107. *Loudermill,* 470 U.S. 532.
108. Schleck v. Ramsey County, 939 F.2d 638 (8th Cir. 1991).
109. *See* Codd v. Velger, 429 U.S. 624 (1977).
110. Rosenstein v. City of Dallas, 876 F.2d 392, 396, n.8 (5th Cir. 1989); Chilingirian v. Boris, 882 F.2d 200, 205–06 (6th Cir. 1989).
111. Arrington v. County of Dallas, 970 F.2d 1441, 1447 (5th Cir. 1992).
112. *Id.*
113. Campos v. Giullot, 743 F.2d 1123 (5th Cir. 1984).
114. Regents of Univ. of Mich. v. Ewing, 474 U.S. 214, 225–26, 106 S. Ct. 507, 513–14, 88 L. Ed. 2d 523 (1985).
115. 503 U.S. 115, 112 S. Ct. 1061, 117 L. Ed. 2d 261 (1992).
116. *Id.*
117. *Id.*

The *Collins* Court employed this analysis to reject an argument that a substantive due process claim could be predicated on a governmental employer's duty to provide its employees with safe working conditions.[118] The Court explained that substantive due process does not encompass garden-variety state tort actions:

> We also are not persuaded that the city's alleged failure to train its employees, or to warn them about known risks of harm, was an omission that can properly be characterized as arbitrary, or conscience shocking, in a constitutional sense. Petitioner's claim is analogous to a fairly typical state-law tort claim: The city breached its duty of care to her husband by failing to provide a safe work environment. Because the Due Process Clause "does not purport to supplant traditional tort law in laying down rules of conduct to regulate liability for injuries that attend living together in society," Daniels v. Williams, 474 U.S., at 332, 106 S. Ct., at 665, we have previously rejected claims that the Due Process Clause should be interpreted to impose federal duties that are analogous to those traditionally imposed by state tort law, see, e.g., *id.,* at 332–333, 106 S. Ct., at 665–666; Baker v. McCollan, 443 U.S. 137, 146, 99 S. Ct. 2689, 2695, 61 L. Ed. 2d 433 (1979); Paul v. Davis, 424 U.S. 693, 701, 96 S. Ct. 1155, 1160, 47 L. Ed. 2d 405 (1976).[119]

According to the Court, this limitation is particularly important in the public employment context because "state law, rather than the Federal Constitution, generally governs the substance of the employment relationship."[120] Yet substantive due process claims have been recognized where predicated on arbitrary conduct or where the government employer's policies interfere with fundamental rights. Conduct challenged as arbitrary is subject to a rational basis test, an approach that normally makes it easy for the government to prevail.[121] Conduct challenged because it interferes with a fundamental right is subject to strict scrutiny, an approach that is much more likely to result in a victory for the public employee. The test is whether the challenged government action would shock the conscience.[122]

---

118. *Id.* at 125–126.
119. *Id.* at 128.
120. *Id.,* citing Bishop v. Wood, 426 U.S. 341, 350, 96 S. Ct. 2074, 2080, 48 L. Ed. 2d 684 (1976); Board of Regents of State Colleges v. Roth, 408 U.S. 564, 577–78, 92 S. Ct. 2701, 2709–10, 33 L. Ed. 2d 548 (1972).
121. *See, e.g.,* Tonkovich v. Kansas Bd. of Regents, 159 F.3d 504, 528 (10th Cir. 1998).
122. Uhlrig v. Harder, 64 F.3d 567 (10th Cir. 1995).

Even substantive due process claims that are subject to a rational basis test may sometimes survive the challenge. *Pence v. Rosenquist*[123] illustrates this principle. The *Pence* court held that school officials lacked any rational basis for refusing to let a person with a mustache, no matter how neatly trimmed, drive a school bus.[124] The record failed to show that the "plaintiff's mustache negatively affected his driving skills, or relationship with his passengers, nor that it tended to generate any kind of problem which endangered their health or safety."[125] The policy was, therefore, so irrational that it was arbitrary in a constitutional sense.[126] The *Pence* court rejected the notion that a government employee's liberty interest in his or her choice of personal appearance was so insignificant as to preclude a claim.[127]

If the government employer can show some legitimate reason for the regulations, however, they will be upheld. In *Lowman v. Davis*,[128] the Eight Circuit upheld a hair-length regulation against a challenge that it lacked a rational basis. The state park management grounded the hair-length requirement in its need to make members of the park management team more identifiable to the public, make it more likely that park officials would be obeyed, and promote an esprit de corps among team members.[129] The *Lowman* court accepted the proffered reasons over a strong dissent that pointed to the absence of logical or factual support for a connection between the regulation and the stated goals.[130] Likewise, in *Tardif v. Quinn*[131] the school's termination of a nontenured high school teacher for wearing too-short skirts survived a challenge on constitutional grounds. The court affirmed the lower court's ruling, emphasizing its narrow scope of review.[132] To succeed, the public employer must demonstrate that the regulation furthers a legitimate government interest.

---

123. 573 F.2d 395 (7th Cir. 1978). *See also* Lowman v. Davies, 704 F.2d 1044 (8th Cir. 1983).
124. *Pence,* 573 F.2d at 398.
125. *Id.*
126. *Id.* at 399.
127. The *Pence* court withdrew the holding of a prior case rejecting such claims, Miller v. School Dist. No. 167, Cook County, Ill., 495 F.2d 658 (7th Cir. 1974), in favor of a rule providing for case-by-case evaluation of the rational relationship between the government policy and claimed public purpose. *Pence,* 573 F.2d at 399–401.
128. 704 F.2d 1044 (8th Cir. 1983).
129. *Lowman,* 704 F.2d at 1046.
130. *Id.*
131. 545 F.2d 761 (1st Cir. 1976).
132. *Tardif,* 545 F.2d at 763–64.

Substantive due process claims have more typically been predicated on fundamental rights such as the right to marry.[133] Despite the potential to affect the right to marry, several federal circuits have approved municipal antinepotism policies. *Waters v. Gaston County, N.C.*,[134] illustrates the reasoning in this line of cases. In *Waters*, employees who sought to marry in violation of an antinepotism policy challenged their public employer, contending that the policy intruded on their constitutional right to marry.[135] The policy prohibited employees from marrying each other if they were employed in the same division or unit or if one had supervisory authority over the other.[136] The *Waters* court acknowledged that the policy affected the marriage, but allowed it because it did not forbid marriage altogether or require permission of the government to marry.[137] Fundamental rights were not therefore involved.[138] The policy passed constitutional muster under a rational basis test since it fostered workplace goals such as avoiding conflicts between work and family obligations, reducing favoritism, limiting interoffice dating, and decreasing the likelihood of sexual harassment in the workplace.[139]

More often than not, the claims are dismissed at the motion stage because the court determines that no constitutionally cognizable substantive due process claim exists. Courts have rejected substantive due process claims predicated on the government employer's decision not to renew an employment contract[140] or to provide a negative employment review.[141] Courts have also rejected substantive due process claims based on the failure to protect a government employee in a potentially dangerous setting

---

133. *See, e.g.,* Littlejohn v. Rose, 768 F.2d 765, 769–72 (6th Cir. 1985), *cert. denied,* 475 U.S. 1045 (1986) (denial of public employment because of involvement in constitutionally protected behavior such as decision to seek a divorce states a claim).
134. 57 F.3d 422 (4th Cir. 1995).
135. *Waters,* 57 F.3d at 424.
136. *Id.*
137. *Id.*
138. *Id.*
139. *Id.* at 426–27. *See also* Parks v. City of Warner Robins, Ga., 43 F.3d 609, 613–15 (11th Cir. 1995); Shawgo v. Spradlin, 701 F.2d 470, 482–83, *cert. denied,* 464 U.S. 965 (5th Cir. 1983); Wright v. Metrohealth Medical Ctr., 58 F.3d 1130, 1134–38 (6th Cir. 1995), *cert. denied,* 516 U.S. 1158 (1996); Parsons v. County of Del Norte, 728 F.2d 1234 (9th Cir.), *cert. denied,* 469 U.S. 846 (1984).
140. Howard v. Columbia Public Sch. Dist., 363 F.3d 797 (8th Cir. 2004).
141. Yates v. District of Columbia, 324 F.3d 724 (DC Cir. 2003).

such as a prison[142] or a mental hospital.[143] When another textual source of constitutional protection is available, courts are likely to dismiss the substantive due process claim as duplicative.[144]

III. FIRST AMENDMENT CLAIMS

Applying the First Amendment right to free speech in the employment setting creates both practical problems and doctrinal difficulties. Courts have struggled to balance the government employer's need for efficiency, workplace discipline, harmony, and productivity with the traditional tolerance of "verbal tumult, discord, and even offensive utterance," as "necessary side effects of . . . the process of open debate" that is protected by the Constitution.[145] The Supreme Court has recognized that "when an employee counsels her coworkers to do their job in a way with which the public employer disagrees, her managers may tell her to stop, rather than relying on counter-speech."[146] Likewise, the First Amendment does not prohibit managerial discipline based on an employee's expressions made pursuant to official responsibilities.[147] Yet, the Court recognizes the value of protecting government employees who seek to participate in public debate. The tension between these overarching themes has led to the judicial use of balancing tests, and a reluctance to make rulings that intrude too far into the workplace. As a result, the holdings to be found in decisional authority tend to be narrow and fact-based. This results in difficult choices for government employers, for whom "taking any action" may be risky.[148]

The protection of government employees' free speech rights can be traced to *Keyishian v. Board of Regents*,[149] where the Court held that even if a public employee can be fired without cause, the employee's right to free expression cannot be infringed by denying or placing conditions on the

---

142. Sperle v. Michigan Dep't of Corrections, 297 F.3d 483 (6th Cir. 2002); Fraternal Order of Police Dep't of Corrections Labor Comm. v. Williams, 375 F.3d 1141 (D.C. Cir. 2004).
143. *Uhlrig,* note 121, *supra.*
144. Brandenburg v. Housing Auth. of Irvine, 253 F.3d 891 (6th Cir. 2001) (claim based on violation of former executive director of government housing authority's substantive due process rights was duplicative of First Amendment retaliation claim).
145. Cohen v. California, 403 U.S. 15, 24–25 (1971).
146. Waters v. Churchill, 511 U.S. 661 (1994).
147. Garcetti v. Ceballos, 126 S. Ct. 1951, 2000 WL 1458026 (U.S. 2006).
148. Walsh v. Ward, 991 F.2d 1344 (7th Cir. 1993).
149. 385 U.S. 589 (1967).

benefit or privilege of the public employment.[150] *Keyishian* represented the culmination of a line of cases decided during the Cold War, which involved government efforts to require loyalty oaths from all public employees.[151] The Supreme Court stepped in to prevent government employers from searching out suspected communists by delving into their political activities and ordering public workers to pay political obeisance to the government.

A public employer may not discharge an employee on a basis that infringes his constitutionally protected speech or associations. In bringing a case based on the violation of a public employee's First Amendment rights, the terminated employee must establish that the conduct at issue was entitled to constitutional protection.[152] The employee must then prove that the constitutionally protected conduct was a substantial or motivating factor behind the termination.[153] The employer may then show by a preponderance of the evidence that it would have made the decision to terminate even if the employee had not engaged in the protected conduct.[154] The premise underlying the causation rule is that the "constitutional principle at stake is sufficiently vindicated if . . . [the] employee is placed in no worse a position than if he had not engaged in the conduct."[155]

A. Freedom of Speech

A state or other governmental entity cannot condition public employment on a basis that infringes the employee's constitutionally protected interest in

---

150. *Keyishian,* 385 U.S. at 606.

151. *See, e.g.,* Garner v. Board of Public Works of Los Angeles, 341 U.S. 716 (1951) (upholding ordinance requiring employees to take a loyalty oath and sign an affidavit disclosing whether they had ever been a member of the Communist Party); Adler v. Board of Educ., 342 U.S. 485 (1952) (upholding statute making membership in a subversive group a basis for denying employment to public school teachers); Wieman v. Updegraff, 344 U.S. 183 (1952) (holding state employees could not be required to take an oath that they have not innocently associated with subversive groups); Shelton v. Tucker, 364 U.S. 479 (1960) (striking down ordinance that required teachers to disclose every organization to which they had belonged during preceding five years).

152. Mt. Healthy City Sch. Dist. Bd. of Educ. v. Doyle, 429 U.S. 274, 287 (1977); Erickson v. Pierce County, 960 F.2d 801 (9th Cir. 1992); Garrett v. Barnes, 961 F.2d 629 (7th Cir. 1992).

153. *Mt. Healthy,* 429 U.S. at 287.

154. *Id.*

155. *Id., Mt. Healthy,* 429 U.S. at 286. *See also* Padilla-Garcia v. Rodriguez, 212 F.3d 69 (1st Cir. 2000); Sanchez-Lopez v. Fuentes-Pujols, 375 F.3d 121 (1st Cir. 2004).

freedom of expression.[156] The employee's right to freedom of speech is not absolute. To determine whether a public employer has infringed upon an employee's protected right of free speech, the court applies a multilevel analysis.

Two questions "guide interpretation of the constitutional protections according to public employee speech."[157] The first question is whether the employee spoke as a citizen on a mater of public concern.[158] If not, the Supreme Court has adopted a categorical rule that denies an employee a "First Amendment cause of action based on his or her employer's reaction to the speech."[159] If the answer is yes, then the possibility of a claim exists and the court must determine whether the employer "had an adequate justification for treating the employee differently from any other member of the general public."[160] *Garcetti v. Ceballos*[161] refined and narrowed the rest for a plaintiff to succeed with a First Amendment claim in the employment context.

If an employee is speaking not as a citizen, but in his or her capacity as an employee, that ends the First Amendment analysis and no claim exists.[162] The Court specifically held that "when public employees make statements pursuant to their official duties, the employees are not speaking as citizens for First Amendment purposes, and the Constitution does not insulate their communications from employer discipline."[163] The Court insisted that its decision was consistent with prior decisions.[164] Reasoning that employers have a heightened need to create substantive consistency and clarity in official communications warranted this categorical rule.[165] At the same time, the Court cautioned that it had not yet needed to "articulate a comprehensive framework for defining the scope of an employee's duties in cases where there is room for serious debate."[166] It rejected any "suggestion that employers can restrict employees' rights by creating excessively broad job descriptions."[167] The Court announced in dicta that the "proper inquiry is a

---

156. Pickering v. Board of Educ., 391 U.S. 563 (1968); Perry v. Sindermann, 408 U.S. 593 (1972); Rankin v. McPherson, 483 U.S. 378 (1987).
157. 2006 WL 1458026 *5.
158. *Id.*
159. *Id.*
160. *Id.*
161. 126 S. Ct. 1951, 2006 WL 1458026 (U.S. 2006).
162. *Id.* at *8.
163. *Id.*
164. *Id.* at 9.
165. *Id.* at *8.
166. *Id.* at *10.
167. *Id.*

practical one."[168] It then emphasized that formal job descriptions are not dispositive since "the listing of a given task in an employee's written job description is neither necessary nor sufficient to demonstrate that conducting the task is within the scope of the employee's professional duties for First Amendment purposes."[169] The Court also expressly observed that arguably different constitutional interests are implicated in an academic setting because of academic freedom and that it was not deciding whether the same analysis would be applied there.[170]

To determine whether a public employer has infringed upon an employee's protected right of free speech, the court applies a multi-level analysis. The court must decide, as a matter of law, whether the speech at issue touches on a matter of public concern.[171] To determine this, the court looks to the time, place, and manner of the speech in question.[172]

If the speech addresses a matter of public concern, the court applies the *Pickering* balancing test to weigh the interest of the employee "as a citizen, commenting upon matters of public concern," against the "interest of the state, as an employer, in promoting the efficiency of the public services it performs through its employees."[173] If the employee's interest in making the statement outweighs the state's interest, then the employee bears the burden of proving that his or her speech was a motivating factor in the employment decision.[174]

If the employee satisfies this burden, then the employer must prove by a preponderance of the evidence that it would have reached the same decision in the absence of the protected conduct.[175] In conducting this analysis, the focus should be on what the employer thought was said and not on what the trier of fact ultimately determines to have been said.[176]

1. Matter of Public Concern

The First Amendment has been held to protect only some speech in the government employment setting. Courts try to protect speech that is related to

168. *Id.*
169. *Id.*
170. *Id.*
171. Rankin v. McPherson, 483 U.S. 378, 384 (1987); Connick v. Myers, 461 U.S. 138 (1983).
172. *Rankin,* 483 U.S. at 384–85.
173. Pickering v. Board of Educ., 391 U.S. 563, 568 (1968); Perry v. Sindermann, 408 U.S. 593 (1972); Rankin v. McPherson, 483 U.S. 378 (1987).
174. *Mt. Healthy,* 429 U.S. 274.
175. *Id.* at 287.
176. Waters v. Churchill, 511 U.S. 661, 114 S. Ct. 1878, 128 L. Ed. 2d 686 (1994).

the employee's role as a citizen and not speech that is only of concern to the employee. The court will analyze the content, form, and context of the given statement to determine whether it could "be fairly considered as relating to any matter of political, social or other concern to the community."[177] If the speech is of general interest, on topics such as disclosure of public officials' wrongdoing or waste and inefficiency of the particular governmental entity, it will likely be considered a matter of public concern. In applying the "content, form, and context" analysis, the Supreme Court has directed courts to consider whether the speech at issue was made in the employee's role as citizen or as employee.

> [W]hen a public employee speaks, not as a citizen upon matters of public concern, but instead as an employee upon matters only of personal interest, absent the most unusual circumstances, a federal court is not the appropriate forum in which to review the wisdom of a personnel decision taken by a public agency allegedly in reaction to the employee's behavior.[178]

Courts pay particular interest to the context to prevent plaintiffs from recharacterizing their speech more broadly after the fact. "[R]etrospective embellishment cannot transform personal grievances into matters of public concern."[179] Judge Posner explained that chit-chat is not protected, but speech need not be earth-shattering to fall under the First Amendment:

> [T]he Supreme Court . . . did not mean matters of transcendent importance, such as the origins of the universe or the merits of constitutional monarchy; they meant matters in which the public might be interested, as distinct from wholly personal grievances—which . . . are too remote from central concerns [of the First Amendment] to justify judicial interference with the employment relation . . . and casual chit-chat, which is not protected by the First Amendment at all.[180]

Content is the most important factor. Note that the subject may be a matter of public concern, and statements about the subject will not be protected; for example, an employee who complains about secondhand smoke

---

177. *Connick,* 461 U.S. at 146–48.

178. *Id.* at 147.

179. Dodds v. Childers, 933 F.2d 271, 274 (5th Cir. 1991). *See also* Hyland v. Wonder, 972 F.2d 1129 (9th Cir. 1992), *cert. denied,* 508 U.S. 908 (1993); Schad v. Jones, 415 F.3d 671, 674–78 (7th Cir. 2005).

180. Dishnow v. School Dist. of Rib Lake, 77 F.3d 194, 197 (7th Cir. 1996).

is not engaging in protected speech when his complaints are purely on his own behalf and in his own interest.[181]

A further illustration of this distinction can be seen in the courts' conflicting approach to speech about sexual harassment. Some courts have focused on the speaker's motivation and thus held that sexual harassment complaints are not protected, since they have a "private and informal flavor." When the specific statements related solely to a personal problem, these courts have held that the speech does not merit First Amendment protection.[182] The Third Circuit criticized this approach in *Azzaro v. County of Allegheny*.[183] The *Azzaro* court disagreed with earlier opinions that gave controlling significance to the speaker's motive in making the challenged statement.[184] The *Azzaro* court found several lessons to the contrary in *Connick*. First, the community has an interest in the "free exchange of information and ideas relating to matters of public concern."[185] That interest is implicated by private speech as well as public.[186] Second, *Connick* suggests that such information is likely to be of public concern. For example, speech about racial discrimination in the assignment of school personnel, the district attorney's failure to discharge its responsibilities in investigating and prosecuting crimes, and actual or potential wrongdoing are matters of public concern.[187] Third, *Connick* teaches that the speaker's motive is not dispositive of whether speech relates to a matter of public concern.[188] In the Third Circuit's view, if a "complainant reports sexual harassment by a public official, her speech touches on a matter of public concern, even if motivated by purely personal considerations because it exposes the potential malfeasance of a public official."[189]

Although sexual harassment has sometimes been treated as an unprotected personal grievance, an employee's statements to a news reporter about racial or sexual harassment are likely to be protected. The injection of

---

181. Brown v. Disciplinary Comm. of Edgerton Volunteer Fire Dep't, 97 F.3d 969, 974 (7th Cir. 1996). *See also* Smith v. Fruin, 28 F.3d 646, 653 (7th Cir. 1994), *cert. denied,* 513 U.S. 1083 (1995).
182. Saulpaugh v. Monroe Community Hosp., 4 F.3d 134 (2d Cir. 1993), *cert. denied,* 510 U.S. 1164 (1994); Woodward v. City of Worland, 977 F.2d 1392 (10th Cir. 1992), *cert. denied,* 509 U.S. 923 (1993).
183. 110 F.3d 968 (3d Cir. 1997) (en banc).
184. *Azzaro,* 110 F.3d at 979.
185. *Id.* at 977.
186. *Id.*
187. *Id.* at 978. *See, e.g.,* Brennan v. Norton, 350 F.3d 399, 414–15 (3d Cir. 2003).
188. *Azzaro,* 110 F.3d at 977.
189. *Id.*

the speech into a public forum may transform it from a personal grievance to a matter of public concern.[190] But if an employee contacts the media, the press release or public comment does not always make the speech a matter of public concern.[191] Nor must speech be made publicly in order to be protected.[192] In *Givhan v. Western Line Consolidated School District*,[193] the Court held that even private speech could be protected in some cases.[194] The line between protected and unprotected speech in this area is a thin one, and practitioners should scrutinize the facts with care.

Courts have recognized certain subject matters as "inherently of public concern."[195] Speech regarding illegal campaign activity, criminal misuse of public funds, wastefulness, and inefficiency in managing governmental entities are inherently matters of public concern.[196] Even when such speech is uttered in private to the employee's supervisor, it retains its public character. But the argument that any activity that occurs within a government office is a matter of public concern has been routinely rejected.[197]

In *Dorsett v. Board of Trustees for State Colleges & Univ.*,[198] the court specifically analyzed this issue regarding educational institutions:

> In public schools and universities across this nation, interfaculty disputes arise daily over teaching assignments, room assignments, administrative duties, classroom equipment, teacher recognition, and a host of other relatively trivial matters. A federal court is simply not the appropriate forum in which to seek redress for such harm.[199]

---

190. Matulin v. Village of Lodi, 862 F.2d 609, 613–14 (6th Cir. 1988); *See also* Rode v. Dellarciprete, 845 F.2d 1195, 1202 (3d Cir. 1988).
191. Rahn v. Drake Ctr., 31 F.3d 407 (6th Cir. 1994), *cert. denied,* 115 S. Ct. 2578 (1995).
192. Givhan v. Western Line Consol. Sch., 439 U.S. 410, 414 (1979).
193. 439 U.S. 410, 99 S. Ct. 693, 58 L. Ed. 2d 619 (1979).
194. *Id.* at 414.
195. Roth v. Veteran's Admin., 856 F.2d 1401, 1405 (9th Cir. 1988).
196. Chateaubriand v. Gaspard, 97 F.3d 1218, 1222 (9th Cir. 1995).
197. Caine v. Hardy, 943 F.2d 1406, 1416 (5th Cir. 1991), *cert. denied,* 503 U.S. 936 (1992). *See also* Thomson v. Scheid, 977 F.2d 1017 (6th Cir. 1992), *cert. denied,* 508 U.S. 910 (1993); Wallace v. Texas Tech Univ., 80 F.3d 1042 (5th Cir. 1996). Brooks v. University of Wisconsin Bd. of Regents, 406 F.3d 476, 480–81 (7th Cir. 2005).
198. 940 F.2d 121 (5th Cir. 1991).
199. *Dorsett,* 940 F.2d at 123.

Federal courts have upheld speech rights when a professor criticized the public school curriculum (and its supporters) for reflecting bias against minorities. Likewise, a school guidance counselor's articles in a local newspaper and comments to the media were protected speech because the counselor was "participating in a public debate on matters of interest to the public."[200]

First Amendment rights may be afforded in cases where an employee refuses to speak.[201] In *Langford v. Lane*, an employee was fired after she refused to tell her employer what grievances she planned to air at a public meeting the next day. The court held that the worker's refusal to speak was afforded First Amendment protection under the *Connick* framework. "[T]he protection of the First Amendment extends equally to the right to speak freely and the right to refrain from speaking at all."[202]

Insults and profanity do not generally amount to speech on a matter of public concern.[203] Calling the dean of a university a Hitler or engaging in rude or insulting speech is not protected.[204] Expressive conduct may amount to protected speech. For example, a police officer "wearing a blackened face, dressed in bib overalls and a black curly wig, and carrying a watermelon," might be engaged in protected speech if the costume was intended to express a message.[205] The officer's claim was ultimately rejected since he testified that he did not intend to comment on any issue of interest to the public; he wanted to entertain the other guests at the party.[206] On the other hand, an off-duty police officer who wore a blackened face and a wig during a public musical show was engaged in protected speech since the performances were a "form of artistic expression" of interest to the public.[207] Wearing a flag patch to protest discrimination or a peace pin to support peace were protected.[208]

False statements may be protected speech.[209] At a minimum, "absent proof of false statements knowingly or recklessly made by him, a teacher's

---

200. Dishnow v. School Dist. of Rib Lake, 77 F.3d 194, 196–97 (7th Cir. 1996).
201. *See* Langford v. Lane, 921 F.2d 677 (6th Cir. 1991).
202. *Id.* at 680 (quoting Wooley v. Maynard, 430 U.S. 705, 714 (1977)).
203. City of San Diego v. Roe, 543 U.S. 77, 125 S. Ct. 521, 160 L. Ed. 2d 410 (2004) (police officers offering homemade sexually explicit videos for sale for online auction site was not protected).
204. McBride v. City of Roanoke, 871 F. Supp. 885 (W.D. Va. 1994); Landrum v. Eastern Ky. Univ., 578 F. Supp. 241 (E.D. Ky. 1984).
205. Tindle v. Caudell, 56 F.3d 966 (8th Cir. 1995).
206. *Tindle,* 56 F.3d at 970.
207. Bergler v. Battaglia, 779 F.2d 992 (4th Cir. 1985), *cert. denied,* 476 U.S. 1159 (1986).
208. Leonard v. City of Columbus, 705 F.2d 1299 (11th Cir. 1983), *cert. denied,* 468 U.S. 1204 (1984); Smith v. United States, 502 F.2d 512 (5th Cir. 1974).
209. *Pickering, supra,* 391 U.S. at 566–74.

exercise of his right to speak on issues of public importance may not furnish a basis for his dismissal from public employment."[210] Courts have disagreed about how to apply this analysis.[211] The Seventh Circuit held and the Tenth Circuit suggested in dicta that false statements are protected absent proof that the inaccuracies were knowing or reckless.[212] The First, Fifth, and Ninth Circuits have rejected a per se rule in favor of a rule that considers recklessness as to the truth as part of the *Pickering* balancing test.[213]

2. Pickering *Balancing Test*

Once a public employee demonstrates that the speech addressed is a matter of public concern, the employee's interest in speaking on matters of public concern must be balanced against "the interest of the state, as an employer, in promoting the efficiency of the public services it performs through its employees."[214]

The courts consider a number of factors in completing this balancing of interests:

1. The need for harmony in the office or workplace;
2. Whether the government's responsibilities require a close working relationship to exist between the plaintiff and co-workers when the speech in question has caused or could cause a relationship to deteriorate;
3. The time, manner and place of the speech;
4. The context in which the dispute arose;
5. The degree of public interest in the speech; and
6. Whether the speech impeded the employee's ability to perform his or her duties.[215]

---

210. *Id.* at 574.

211. *Compare* Brenner v. Brown, 36 F.3d 18, 20 (7th Cir. 1994); *with* Wulf v. City of Wichita, 883 F.2d 842, 859, n.24 (10th Cir. 1989); and Brasslett v. Cota, 761 F.2d 827, 840–41 (1st Cir. 1985); and Moore v. City of Kilgore, 877 F.2d 364, 376 (5th Cir.), *cert. denied,* 493 U.S. 1003 (1989).

212. *See Brenner,* 36 F.3d at 20; *Wulf,* 883 F.2d at 859, n.24.

213. Johnson v. Multnomah County, Or., 48 F.3d 420, 423–24 (9th Cir.), *cert. denied,* 115 S. Ct. 2616 (1995); *Brasslett,* 761 F.2d at 840–41; American Postal Workers Union v. United States Postal Serv., 830 F.2d 294, 305–06 (D.C. Cir. 1987); *Moore,* 877 F.2d at 376.

214. Pickering v. Board of Educ., 391 U.S. 563, 568 (1968).

215. Stever v. Independent Sch. Dist. No. 625, 943 F.2d 845, 850 (8th Cir. 1991) (citing Bowman v. Pulaski County Special Sch. Dist., 723 F.2d 640, 644 (8th Cir. 1983)). *See also* Martinez v. City of Opa-Locka, 971 F.2d 708 (11th Cir. 1992).

Other relevant considerations include "whether the statement impairs discipline by superiors or harmony among co-workers, has a detrimental impact on close working relationships for which personal loyalty and confidence are necessary, impedes the performance of the speaker's duties or interferes with the regular operation of the enterprise."[216] The "inappropriate or controversial character of the statement is irrelevant to the question whether it deals with a matter of public concern."[217] Courts give great deference to the government employer's judgment when close working relationships are essential to fulfilling the job responsibilities.[218]

The content of public expression must be assessed to determine if the statements impede the employee's job performance or interfere with the operations of the government employer.[219] Sometimes the public nature of the speech is enough to tip the balance. In *McMullen v. Carson*,[220] an employee of the sheriff's office said in a televised news broadcast that he was a Ku Klux Klan recruiter. Public outrage made his "discharge . . . necessary to prevent a deleterious effect on the Sheriff's ability to enforce the law in the community."[221] Private expression may invoke additional factors such as whether the speech threatens the "employing agency's institutional efficiency . . . not only by the content of the employee's message but also by the manner, time, and place in which it is delivered."[222]

Pickering balancing involves a case-by-case analysis of the government interests and the protected speech.[223] The Eleventh Circuit evaluated a police officer's right to conduct a letter-writing campaign that was critical of the police department without giving the department the opportunity to investigate her complaints internally before going public.[224] Although the officer had an interest in expressing her opinion on the alleged malfeasance of her superiors, it was outweighed by the police department's need to maintain a close working relationship within the department. The court gave substantial weight to the fact that the department was a quasi-military organization with a need to protect confidentiality, the esprit de corps, and the discipline required in such groups.[225] The department regulation did not bar

---

216. *Rankin,* 483 U.S. at 388.
217. *Id.* at 386–88.
218. Brandenburg v. Housing Auth. of Irvine, 253 F.3d 891, 899 (6th Cir. 2001).
219. *Givhan,* 439 U.S. at 415, n.4.
220. 754 F.2d 936 (11th Cir. 1985).
221. *McMullen,* 754 F.2d at 937.
222. *Id.*
223. Busby v. City of Orlando, 931 F.2d 764, 774 (11th Cir. 1991).
224. *Busby,* 931 F.2d at 669–770.
225. *Id.* at 773–75.

the officer from voicing her complaints; it merely delayed her right to go public until an internal investigation was complete.[226] Presumably, a complete bar to such speech would not have passed muster.

In *Moore v. City of Wynnewood*,[227] the Tenth Circuit applied *Pickering* to hold that the government interests outweighed those of the speaker. A former deputy chief of police, demoted for criticism of the department's race relations, sued. His insider's perspective on the department's racial problems was important to the public debate, but the city had "a strong interest in controlling the speech of its employees when they purport to speak for the city or one of its departments."[228] The officer wore his uniform and was on duty at the city council meeting when he spoke. He left his post to attend the meeting "despite being the only officer on duty" at the time.[229] These factors coupled with the need for close working relationships in the department tipped the balance in favor of the city.[230] The *Moore* court refused to make the city prove that the speech actually disrupted the department. Although the government cannot rely on "purely speculative allegations" that speech will disrupt operations, it need not "wait for speech to actually disrupt core operations before taking action."[231] The department's small size and the officer's leadership position increased the likelihood that the speech would interfere with the officer's ability to function.[232]

Normally, the government must prove its interests and the harm that allegedly flows from speech.[233] The Third Circuit required proof of actual disruption in *Zamboni v. Stamler*.[234] In its view, a finding of potential disruption is not enough. The record must contain proofs that the speech impeded the speaker's proper job performance or interfered with the regular operations of the school.[235]

The weight given to the disruptive effect of speech depends, in part, on the responsibilities of the employee.[236] If an employee "serves in a sensitive

---

226. *Id.* at 774.
227. 57 F.3d 924 (10th Cir. 1995).
228. *Moore,* 57 F.3d at 933–34.
229. *Id.* at 934.
230. *Id.* at 934–35.
231. *Id.* at 934. *See also* Jeffries v. Harleston, 52 F.3d 9 (2d Cir.), *cert. denied,* 116 S. Ct. 173 (1995).
232. *Moore,* 57 F.3d at 934–35.
233. Anderson v. McCotter, 100 F.3d 723 (10th Cir. 1996); Considine v. Board of County Comm'rs of the County of Adams, 910 F.2d 695 (10th Cir. 1990).
234. 847 F.2d 73, 78–79 (3d Cir. 1988), *cert. denied,* 488 U.S. 899 (1988).
235. *Zamboni,* 847 F.2d at 79.
236. *Rankin,* 483 U.S. at 388.

capacity that requires extensive public contact, the employee's private speech may pose a substantial danger to the agency's successful functioning."[237] A police officer whose job involved building community support for the department and fostering credibility with all constituent groups of a multiethnic city could be fired for making statements critical of immigrants and deploring the need to speak Spanish.[238] The officer made his comments while preaching a sermon; but the remarks were published in the press. His speech fell outside the scope of the First Amendment because it posed a substantial danger to the police department's successful accomplishment of its mission.[239]

A probation officer's public criticism of the police department and local court system during a call-in radio show did not outweigh the government's interest in promoting the efficiency of its judicial system.[240] Since loyalty and confidence are critical to the probation officer's position, and his statements potentially injured the probation officer's relationship with other law enforcement agencies, the government could reasonably conclude that he could no longer perform his duties effectively.[241]

The government employer's conduct must be judged in light of the speech as the employer interpreted it. In *Waters v. Churchill*,[242] the Court held that substantial weight must be afforded to the right of the "government's interest in achieving its goals as effectively and efficiently as possible."[243] The *Waters* Court, evaluating a government employer's discharge of an employee based on mistaken facts, approved the use of personnel procedures that differ from evidentiary rules and required courts to "look to the facts as the employer reasonably found them to be."[244] The *Waters* Court ruled that "[i]f an employment action is based on what an employee supposedly said, and a reasonable supervisor would recognize that there is a substantial likelihood that what was said was protected, the manager must tread with a certain amount of care."[245]

The Court's approach is intended to protect employers from situations in which "reasonable employers would disagree about who is to be

---

237. Sims v. Metropolitan Dade County, 972 F.2d 1230 (11th Cir. 1992).
238. *Sims,* 972 F.2d at 1234–38.
239. *Id.* at 1238. *See also* Jeffries v. Harleston, 52 F.3d 9 (2d Cir.), *cert. denied,* 516 U.S. 862 (1995).
240. Jefferson v. Ambroz, 90 F.3d 1291 (7th Cir. 1996).
241. *Jefferson,* 90 F.3d at 1297.
242. 511 U.S. 661, 114 S. Ct. 1878, 128 L. Ed. 2d 686 (1994).
243. *Waters,* 511 U.S. at 674–75.
244. *Id.* at 677.
245. *Id.*

believed, or how much investigation needs to be done, or how much evidence is needed to come to a particular conclusion."[246] Liability will not result from mistaken though reasonable conduct. Government employers may "rely on hearsay, on past similar conduct, on their personal knowledge of people's credibility, and on other factors that the judicial system ignores."[247] *Waters* carves out a broader sphere of action for government employers. They may, for example, prohibit employees from being rude, a standard that would be too vague if applied to the public at large.[248] The *Waters* Court gives "substantial weight to government employers' reasonable predictions of disruption."[249]

Some courts, unsympathetic to the trouble resulting from a critical employee's gripes, have found a strong interest in ensuring government discretion and control over the management of its employees. In *Williams v. Alabama State University,*[250] the court recognized the employer's "prerogative to remove employees whose conduct hinders efficient operation."[251] The *Williams* court resolved the case on immunity grounds, an easy out where the issue is close. But the language suggests a far-reaching right to terminate troublesome employees. It would be unwise for a government employer to count on such a favorable application of the balancing test.

Because *Pickering* is a fact-specific test, the government employer is entitled to immunity unless the balance "would lead to the inevitable conclusion that the discharge of the employee was unlawful."[252] Because the rule turns upon a fact-intensive balancing test, it can rarely be considered 'clearly established' for purposes of the Harlow qualified immunity standard.[253] Judge Easterbrook acknowledged the difficulties inherent in administering a balancing approach, noting that litigation is both expensive and error-prone, in *Walsh v. Ward.*[254]

---

246. *Id.*
247. *Id.* at 676.
248. *Id.* at 671.
249. For an interesting discussion of the *Waters* opinion, *see* E.J. Velazquez, *Waters v. Churchill: Government-Employer Efficiency, Judicial Deference, and the Abandonment of Public-Employee Free Speech by the Supreme Court,* 61 Brooklyn L. Rev. 1055 (1995).
250. 102 F.3d 1179 (11th Cir. 1997).
251. *Williams,* 102 F.2d at 1184.
252. Dartland v. Metropolitan Dade County, 866 F.2d 1321, 1323–24 (11th Cir. 1989).
253. Bartlett v. Fisher, 972 F.2d 911 (8th Cir. 1992); *But see* Burnham v. Ianni, 119 F.3d 668 (8th Cir. 1997) (en banc) (rejecting qualified immunity claim because of inadequate factual support for claimed harmful effect on government mission).
254. 991 F.2d 1344 (7th Cir. 1993).

The question of whether speech is on a matter of public concern and the balancing of the speaker's First Amendment interest against the government's interests are both legal determinations for the court.[255] It is reversible error to instruct a jury to perform the *Pickering* balancing test.[256] The court should instruct the jury which speech is protected and ask it to determine whether the protected speech was a substantial factor in the detrimental employment decision—and, if so, whether the employer would have reached the same decision in the absence of that speech.[257] The failure to object to instructions submitting the question of what speech is protected to the jury waives the issue.[258] Government defendants must ask the court on the record to make a finding that speech is not on a matter of public concern and to balance the interests of the parties.[259] Otherwise, they will not be in a position to appeal from the failure to do so.

3. Causation

Once an employee establishes speech on a matter of public concern and persuades the court that *Pickering* balancing prohibits taking an adverse employment action based on the speech, he must then show that his protected speech was a substantial or motivating factor in the adverse action.[260] The rule of causation adopted by the Supreme Court in *Mt. Healthy City School District Boardd of Education v. Doyle* requires the plaintiff to show that the government employer would not have reached the same decision in the absence of the protected conduct. The plaintiff must allege facts showing that his protected speech motivated the adverse employment action. The government agency may then show that it would have reached the same decision even absent the protected conduct.[261]

At a minimum, these showings require the plaintiff to demonstrate that the employer knew about and disagreed with the protected speech.[262] An extended period of time between the protected speech and the adverse employment action undercuts the existence of any causal link.[263] Showing

---

255. Gardetto v. Mason, 100 F.3d 803 (10th Cir. 1996).
256. *Gardetto,* 100 F.3d at 817.
257. *Id.* at 816–18.
258. Feldman v. Philadelphia Hous. Auth., 43 F.3d 823, 831 (3d Cir. 1994).
259. Dishow v. School Dist. of Rib Lake, 77 F.3d 194, 197–98 (7th Cir. 1996).
260. *Mt. Healthy,* 429 U.S. 274.
261. *Id.*
262. O'Connor v. Chicago Transit Auth., 985 F.2d 1362 (7th Cir. 1993).
263. *Id.* at 1368.

that the adverse employment decision followed protected speech, by itself, however, is insufficient.[264]

In the absence of evidence that the government employer knew about the protected speech, summary judgment is in order.[265] When opposing a motion for summary judgment, the employee must point to specific nonconclusory facts reasonably linking her protected speech to employer discipline.[266] The employee may not "rely on the mere fact that an adverse employment action followed speech that the employer would have liked to prevent."[267] The employee must link the speech to the adverse employment action.[268]

This determination is ordinarily a question of fact.[269] Courts have struggled with the requirements for a prima facie case.[270] Temporal proximity must normally be coupled with other evidence that is sufficient to support an inference of retaliation.[271] Because the ultimate fact of retaliation turns on the defendants' state of mind, it is particularly difficult to establish by direct evidence.[272] A plaintiff will typically prove her case with circumstantial evidence.[273] Often, this is accomplished by persuading the jury that the employer's explanation for the adverse action is pretextual.[274] This can be done by showing that a discriminatory motive more likely motivated the employer, or that the employer's explanation is unworthy of credence.[275]

---

264. Barnard v. Jackson County, 43 F.3d 1218, 1226 (8th Cir.), *cert. denied,* 116 S. Ct. 53 (1995).
265. Cabrol v. Town of Youngsville, 106 F.3d 101, 108 (5th Cir. 1997).
266. Bailey v. Floyd County Bd. of Educ., 106 F.3d 135, 144–45 (6th Cir. 1997).
267. *Bailey,* 106 F.3d at 145, citing Collyer v. Darling, 98 F.3d 211, 229 (6th Cir. 1996); Wright v. Illinois Dep't of Children & Family Serv., 40 F.3d 1492, 1500 (7th Cir. 1994).
268. *Bailey,* 106 F.3d at 145.
269. Matulin v. Village of Lodi, 862 F.2d 609, 613 (6th Cir. 1988).
270. *See* Bartlik v. U.S. Dep't of Labor, 73 F.3d 100 (6th Cir. 1996).
271. *See, e.g.,* Durant v. Independent Sch. Dist. No. 16 of LeFlore County, Okla., 990 F.2d 560, 564 (10th Cir. 1993); Burkybile v. Board of Ed. of the Hastings on Hudson Union Free Sch. Dist., 411 F.3d 306 (2d Cir. 2005); Hughes v. Derwinski, 967 F.2d 1168, 1174–75 (7th Cir. 1992). *See also* Clark County Sch. Dist. v. Breedon, 532 U.S. 268 (2001) (causation for retaliation under Title VII could not be shown by pointing to temporal connection between complained-of conduct and EEOC right to sue letter sent three months earlier).
272. Ramirez v. Oklahoma Dep't of Mental Health, 41 F.3d 584, 595–96 (10th Cir. 1994).
273. Harrington v. Harris, 108 F.3d 598, 606 (5th Cir. 1997).
274. *Harrington,* 108 F.3d 598.
275. Amburgey v. Corhart Refractories Corp., Inc., 936 F.2d 805, 813 (5th Cir. 1991).

The Supreme Court has recognized that a government employer may have mixed motives.[276] To prevail, the government employer must show that it would have made the same decision based on legitimate reasons.[277] If the employer's dual motivations arose at different times, the employer must establish that it would have taken the same action at the same time.[278] If an employee is discharged because of protected speech, a First Amendment violation has occurred even if some other circumstance occurs or comes to the employer's attention that would have resulted in a decision to fire the employee. But the later circumstance cuts off liability for damages and avoids the remedy of reinstatement.[279]

Although many defendants do not want to instruct the jury on a mixed-motive defense, the Seventh Circuit says that if the plaintiff offers one motive for the action and the defendant says it was based on something else, "the jury should be told what to do if it concludes that the employer had both motives."[280] Courts have distinguished mixed-motive cases from pretext cases.[281] Some courts take the position that in a pretext case, the burden of proof never shifts.[282] But if there is credible evidence of both permissible and impermissible factors influencing the challenged decision once the plaintiff proves an impermissible factor motivated the employer, the burden shifts to the employer to prove as an affirmative defense that it would have made the same decision anyway.[283] Defense counsel should carefully evaluate the evidence to decide whether to pursue a pretext or mixed-motive defense. The theory chosen may affect the jury instructions and the burden of proof. Practitioners should carefully review the abundant case law governing jury instructions and burden of proof in the context of employment discrimination. Although some courts have borrowed from Title VII, the Age Discrimination in Employment Act (ADEA), and other bodies of law to

---

276. Price Waterhouse v. Hopkins, 490 U.S. 228, 109 S. Ct. 1775, 104 L. Ed. 2d 268 (1989) (dual motivation defense in employment discrimination context).

277. *Price Waterhouse,* 490 U.S. at 251; *Mt. Healthy,* 429 U.S. at 287.

278. Sagendorf-Teal v. County of Rensselaer, 100 F.3d 270, 275 (2d Cir. 1996).

279. McKennon v. Hashville Banner Publ'g Co., 513 U.S. 352 (1995) (after-acquired evidence does not bar all relief under ADEA but can limit damages and render reinstatement and front pay inappropriate).

280. Gooden v. Neal, 17 F.3d 925, 928–29 (7th Cir. 1994), *cert. denied,* 573 U.S. 816 (1994).

281. *See Price Waterhouse,* 490 U.S. at 260.

282. Mary Ann Luciano v. Olsten Corp., 110 F.3d 210 (2d Cir. 1997).

283. *Luciano,* 110 F.3d at 218.

resolve instructional issues in the context of First Amendment analysis,[284] the Seventh Circuit rejected that approach in *Gooden v. Neal*.[285]

B. Freedom of Association

Except under limited circumstances, a public employer may not terminate an employee because of political beliefs or associations. The U.S. Supreme Court has addressed this issue on three occasions and determined that a violation of the First Amendment occurs when governmental employees are discharged on the basis of their political beliefs or associations. This represents a break with American political history, a history typified by New York Senator William Marcy's statement that "to the victor belong the spoils of the enemy."[286] Traditionally, when a new president, governor, sheriff, or other public official took office, he or she cleaned house by firing the employees of the predecessor and replacing them with his or her own cronies.[287] Gradually, civil service reform efforts replaced some patronage jobs with a bureaucratic merit-based system.[288] But these efforts left some of the patronage system in place.

Then, in 1976, the Supreme Court expanded First Amendment protection to bar discharge or threats of discharge of employees solely because of their partisan political affiliation or nonaffiliation.[289] In *Elrod v. Burns*, the Supreme Court criticized patronage as a restraint on freedom of belief and association.[290] In *Elrod*,[291] several non-civil-service employees of a sheriff's office sued when they were dismissed or threatened with dismissal because they were not affiliated with the current political party. The Supreme Court

---

284. Hawkins v. Hennepin Tech. Ctr., 900 F.2d 153 (8th Cir. 1990); Sagendorf-Teal v. County of Rensselaer, 100 F.3d 270, 275 (2d Cir. 1996). *See* SCHWARTZ & KIRKLIN, *supra* n.44 at 206–27.

285. 17 F.3d 925, 928 (7th Cir.), *cert. denied,* 513 U.S. 816 (1994). *But see* McMillian v. Svetanoff, 878 F.2d 186, 190, n.3 (7th Cir. 1989).

286. Brian L. Porto, *The Constitution & Political Patronage: Supreme Court Jurisprudence and the Balancing of First Amendment Freedoms,* 13 PACE L. REV. 87 (1993) (citing MARTIN TOLCHIN & SUSAN J. TOLCHIN, TO THE VICTOR . . .: POLITICAL PATRONAGE FROM THE CLUBHOUSE TO THE WHITE HOUSE 323 (1971)).

287. In fact, the concept of judicial review was first announced in connection with deciding the propriety of just such an attempt in Marbury v. Madison, 1 Cranch 137, 2 L. Ed. 60 (1803).

288. Porto, *supra* note 286 at 89–91.

289. Elrod v. Burns, 427 U.S. 347 (1976).

290. *Elrod,* 427 U.S. at 354–58.

291. *Id.*

examined the interest of government efficiency and effectiveness and reasoned that such dismissals were not the least-restrictive means to those ends. In the Court's view, the "need to ensure that policies which the electorate has sanctioned are effectively implemented" could be met by limiting patronage dismissals to policymaking employees only.[292]

The *Elrod* Court did not enunciate a clear line for determining when an employee occupies a policymaking position. The most important factor is the nature of the employee's responsibilities. Employees who are non-policymaking usually have limited responsibility. Non-policymaking employees are those who cannot easily undermine the goals of the party. In contrast, an employee in a policymaking position most likely has responsibilities that are broadly defined and allow for the exercise of substantial discretion:

> In determining whether an employee occupies a policy making position, consideration should also be given to whether the employee acts as an advisor or formulates plans for the implementation of broad goals.[293]

Under *Elrod*, patronage dismissals must be limited to policymaking positions. All other such dismissals are unconstitutional under the First and Fourteenth Amendments. The Court rejected the argument that patronage dismissals contribute to the democratic process by helping partisan politics. In the Court's view, "any contribution of patronage dismissals to the democratic process does not suffice to override [the] severe encroachment of first amendment freedoms."[294] This conclusion has elicited sharp criticism from political scientists and legal scholars, who fear it will weaken political parties and democratic accountability to the voters.[295]

Four years after *Elrod*, the Supreme Court refined its analysis of patronage dismissals involving a policymaking or confidential employee.[296] The Court replaced the inquiry into whether the employee was a policymaker or confidential employee with a functional test that looks for a connection between the employee's political views and the ability to perform the spe-

---

292. *Id.* at 357.
293. *Id.* at 368.
294. *Id.* at 372–73.
295. *See* J. Moeller, *The Supreme Court's Quest for Fair Politics,* 1 Constitutional Commentary 203–23 (1984); K.J. Meier, *Ode to Patronage: A Critical Analysis of Two Recent Supreme Court Decisions,* 41 Pub. Admin. Rev. 558–63 (1981); M.A. Fitts, *The Vices of Virtue: A Political Party Perspective on Civic Virtue Reforms of the Legislative Process,* 136 U. Pa. L. Rev. 1567–45 (1988).
296. Branti v. Finkel, 445 U.S. 507 (1980).

cific responsibilities of the job.[297] In *Branti v. Finkel*, two assistant public defenders were terminated by a newly appointed public defender because they were Republicans. They sued. The *Branti* Court's analysis is instructive. Assistant public defenders can effectively perform their office without political allegiance to the public defender's party. Since the assistant public defender represents clients, his allegiance must be to them and not to partisan and political concerns. Further, the assistant public defender's access to confidential information arises more out of the attorney-client relationship than partisan political activity. The *Branti* Court altered the test formulated in *Elrod* and concluded that the assistant public defenders should not be discharged based on their political affiliations.[298] The Court noted that "under some circumstances, a position may be considered political even though it is neither confidential nor policymaking in character."[299] For example, speechwriters and other assistants to a political officeholder may not be policymakers or confidential employees, but party affiliation is an appropriate requirement for the effective performance of their jobs.[300]

An employee who performs primarily ministerial functions and has little autonomy or discretion in performing his job is not subject to patronage dismissal.[301] *Billingsley v. St. Louis County*[302] illustrates the application of the *Branti* test to a county council administrative assistant who was fired for refusing to participate in her boss's election campaign. A clerk involved in mailing procedures and ordering office supplies could not be fired for her political associations because her "duties did not encompass areas that would be influenced by . . . [her] political views."[303] On the other hand, a staff legal assistant who advised the city clerk on legal and personnel matters and represented him in judicial and administrative hearings could be replaced on political grounds.[304] The administrative assistant at issue in *Billingsley* fell between the two extremes. Since the county council administrative assistant

---

297. *Branti,* 445 U.S. at 517.

298. *Id.*

299. *Id.* at 518.

300. *Id.*

301. Matlock v. Barnes, 932 F.2d 658, 664 (7th Cir. 1991), *cert. denied,* 502 U.S. 909 (1991); Soderbeck v. Burnett County, 752 F.2d 285, 288 (7th Cir. 1985), *cert. denied,* 417 U.S. 1117 (1985).

302. 70 F.3d 61 (8th Cir. 1995).

303. *Billingsley,* 70 F.3d at 63 (citing Bornes v. Bosley, 745 F.2d 501, 505 (8th Cir. 1984), *cert. denied,* 471 U.S. 1017 (1985)).

304. *Id.* at 63–64 (citing Bauer v. Bosley, 802 F.2d 1058 (8th Cir. 1986), *cert. denied,* 481 U.S. 1038, 107 S. Ct. 1976, 95 L. Ed. 2d 816 (1987)).

was the sole intermediary between the elected official and his clients, received telephone calls from constituents and communicated the elected official's response, and dealt with sensitive legislative issues, a reasonable official could have assumed she could be replaced.[305]

Labels or job titles are not controlling. The question is whether the hiring authority can demonstrate that party affiliation is an appropriate requirement for the effective performance of the public office involved.[306] Thus, generalizations cannot be made on the basis of one court's conclusion that a particular position is confidential.[307] Even if a bailiff or deputy sheriff or correctional officer is subject to patronage dismissal, it does little to advance the argument to point to earlier opinions dealing with bailiffs, sheriffs, or correctional officers without discussing the job responsibilities.[308] This point is significant both as a guide to the proofs necessary in a patronage case and for consideration of any qualified immunity defense. Since it is the particular duties of the jobholder rather than his or her job title that controls, immunity is likely to be available in close cases.[309] But the Sixth Circuit warned that there need not be a separate patronage decision on the particular position before qualified immunity can be denied.[310] Thus, government employers should tread with care in this area where the lines are blurred or if the question is a close one.

The Sixth Circuit has outlined four categories of public occupations that are validly subject to patronage considerations.[311] The categories are

> Category One: positions specifically named in relevant federal, state, county, or municipal law to which discretionary authority with respect to the enforcement of that law or the carrying out of some other policy of political concern is granted;
>
> Category Two: positions to which a significant portion of the total discretionary authority available to category one position-holders

305. *Id.* at 64.

306. Baker v. Hadley, 167 F.3d 1014, 1018–21 (6th Cir. 1999); Flenner v. Sheahan, 107 F.3d 459 (7th Cir. 1997).

307. Meeks v. Grimes, 779 F.2d 417, 420 n.2 (7th Cir. 1988).

308. *Flenner,* 107 F.3d at 463–65.

309. *See, e.g.,* Beauregard v. Olsen, 85 F.3d 1402, 1405 (11th Cir. 1996); Parrish v. Nikolits, 86 F.3d 1088 (11th Cir. 1996), *cert. denied,* 520 U.S. 1228 (1997); Pounds v. Griepenstroh, 970 F.2d 338, 341 (7th Cir. 1992), *cert. denied,* 507 U.S. 910 (1993); Rakovich v. Wade, 850 F.2d 1180, 1209 (7th Cir.), *cert. denied,* 488 U.S. 968 (1988).

310. McCloud v. Testa, 97 F.3d 1536, 1556 (6th Cir. 1996).

311. *McCloud,* 97 F.3d at 1556, 1557.

> has been delegated; or positions not named in law, possessing by virtue of the jurisdiction's pattern or practice the same quantum or type of discretionary authority commonly held by category one positions in other jurisdictions;
>
> Category Three: confidential advisors who spend a significant portion of their time on the job advising category one or category two position-holders on how to exercise their statutory or delegated policymaking authority, or other confidential employees who control the lines of communications to category one positions, category two positions or confidential advisors; [and]
>
> Category Four: positions that are part of a group of positions filled by balancing out political party representation, or that are filled by balancing out selections made by different government agents or bodies.[312]

The categories provide a road map for litigating a patronage dismissal. The government employer should look for relevant statutes or policies giving the employee discretionary authority to enforce the law or carry out some policy of political concern to the public. If the government can demonstrate that the employee is a confidential advisor or communicator for the policymaker, patronage considerations are probably permissible. Finally, if the government can show that the position is filled by a representative of a political party or agency, patronage will be allowed.

More recently, in *Rutan v. Republican Party of Illinois*,[313] the U.S. Supreme Court extended First Amendment protection to employment practices other than dismissals, which were based on political patronage. The Court held that the rule of *Elrod* and *Branti* extends to promotion, transfer, recall, and hiring decisions based on party affiliation and support.[314] In *Rutan* petitioners sued, alleging that the governor used a hiring freeze procedure to establish a political patronage system that limited state employment and beneficial employment decisions to those supported by the Republican Party. Of the three petitioners, one had been denied promotions for several years; another was denied a promotion and later a transfer because he did not have the support of the local party officials; and the third was repeatedly denied state employment, again because he was without the support of party officials.

---

312. *See also* Mumford v. Basinski, 105 F.3d 264, 272 (6th Cir. 1997).

313. 497 U.S. 62, 110 S. Ct. 2729, 111 L. Ed. 2d 52 (1990).

314. *Rutan,* 497 U.S. at 78.

The Supreme Court reviewed the *Elrod* and *Branti* decisions and underscored its earlier conclusion that there are various ways a governmental employer can meet its agenda:

> A government's interest in securing effective employees can be met by discharging, demoting or transferring staff members whose work is deficient. A government's interest in securing employees who will loyally implement its policies can be adequately served by choosing or dismissing certain high-level employees on the basis of their political views.[315]

In the *Rutan* Court's view, the democratic process is no more furthered by other patronage-related employment decisions than by patronage dismissals. The Court noted that political parties have survived the decline in patronage-related employment. The Court also found that patronage-related employment decisions "impair the elective process by discouraging free political expression by public employees."[316] These conclusions are not free from doubt. Justice Powell, in his *Branti* dissent, pointed out that successful "implementation of policy often depends upon the cooperation of public employees who do not hold policymaking posts."[317] But the Court nevertheless expanded *Elrod-Branti* by holding that the First Amendment prohibits patronage hiring, transfer, demotion, or discharge.[318]

The *Elrod-Branti* analysis has been consistently applied when the court determines that the motivation for terminating an employee was solely for political affiliation.[319] But the circuits have not agreed on the proper analysis for cases involving both speech and political association.[320] If the employee was discharged because of his political affiliation and political activity (speech and association mixed), the analysis differs depending upon the jurisdiction.

The Sixth Circuit has distinguished political candidacy from political affiliation and held that the former could be a basis for firing an employee, in *Carver v. Dennis*.[321] Retention of a government job cannot be based on

---

315. *Id.* at 74.
316. *Id.*
317. *Branti,* 445 U.S. at 529–30 (Powell, Jr., dissenting).
318. *Rutan,* 497 U.S. at 78.
319. *See, e.g.,* Stough v. Gallagher, 967 F.2d 1523 (11th Cir. 1992).
320. Curinga v. City of Clairton, 357 F.3d 305, 310–12 (3d Cir. 2004); Rodriguez v. Munoz, 808 F.2d 138, 143–44 (1st Cir. 1986) (hybrid speech and affiliation case poses difficulty).
321. 104 F.3d 847, 853 (6th Cir. 1997). *See also* Brazil-Breashears v. Bilandic, 53 F.3d 789, 791 (7th Cir.), *cert. denied,* 516 U.S. 869 (1995) (right to run for office is not fundamental but is subject to balancing tests).

political beliefs or affiliations, but discharging an employee for announcing her candidacy against her boss was permissible. While this holding seems startling in light of the broad protection given employees in other cases, the result is as much to do with the record as anything else. The Sixth Circuit found no evidence that the basis for the plaintiff's termination was her exercise of her right to speak out on matters of public concern.[322] There was no evidence that the employee "either held or voiced any opinions or anything."[323] Nor were there allegations that by running for office she was advancing the political ideas of a particular set of voters. Since running for office is not, itself, a fundamental right, the plaintiff's First Amendment rights were not implicated.[324] A neutral rule prohibiting or limiting government employees from running for political office while on the public payroll is likely to be enforced. Courts distinguish restrictions on candidacy from those based on an employee's political views.

There is a split regarding whether political differences must be partisan to be protected by the First Amendment. The Ninth Circuit has held that *Elrod-Branti* does not protect an employee who personally opposes the incumbent in a nonpartisan election.[325] But the Sixth Circuit found it clearly established that *Elrod-Branti* protects nonideological factions of the same party from patronage retaliation.[326] Firing someone out of personal pique is unlikely to be protected; firing someone for their political leanings even if they are nonpartisan is more likely to give rise to a claim.

The Supreme Court has recognized that the First Amendment protects the right of association in two lines of cases.[327] The clearest and broadest protection has been afforded to political or social associations. The First Amendment protects the freedom to engage in association for the advancement of beliefs and applies to political, economic, religious, or cultural matters.[328] While patronage cases involving political or social affiliations have resulted in the most frequent litigation, the right of association has been applied to protect intimate human relations implication in lifestyle choices,

---

322. *Carver,* 104 F.2d at 852.

323. *Id.*

324. *Id.* at 852–53. *See also* Bart v. Telford, 677 F.2d 622, 624 (7th Cir. 1982) (incumbent mayor could require city employee to take a leave of absence to run for mayor).

325. Thomas v. Carpenter, 881 F.2d 828, 831 (9th Cir. 1989), *cert. denied,* 494 U.S. 1028 and 497 U.S. 1003 (1990).

326. McCloud v. Testa, 97 F.3d 1536, 1537 (6th Cir. 1996); Monks v. Marlinga, 923 F.2d 423 (6th Cir. 1991). *But see* Correa v. Fischer, 982 F.2d 931 (5th Cir. 1993) (no First Amendment violation when new county attorney fired member of former county attorney's staff because he disliked his predecessor).

327. City of Dallas v. Stanglin, 490 U.S. 19, 22–24 (1989).

328. Roberts v. United States Jaycees, 468 U.S. 609 (1984).

nepotism policies, and other interests.[329] The right to associate may extend to the right to meet with others on a personal or social basis.[330]

The protection afforded to social or personal relationships can be seen in *Wilson v. Taylor*.[331] A police officer, fired for dating the adopted daughter of a convicted felon who was reputedly a member of organized crime, sued. The court held that the relationship was protected under the First Amendment. The city did not argue that even if dating were protected, a law enforcement officer's rights could be curtailed due to the nature of police work. So the court did not answer this question.

In *Swank v. Smart*,[332] the Seventh Circuit held that the First Amendment did not protect a police officer discharged, at least in part, because of conversations with a seventeen-year-old college student while the officer was off duty. Judge Posner's opinion provides an excellent discussion of the parameters of lifestyle claims. Because the speech between the officer and the teenage student was not on a matter of public concern, no free speech claim existed. The officer took pains to emphasize that no intimate association of the kind to which a right of privacy attaches had taken place. Thus, no fundamental right was involved. As a result, the test for the government conduct was whether it was arbitrary. The court held that it was not. While at least some family relationships fall within the ambit of the First Amendment right of association, not all such relationships do.[333] The precise boundaries of the right of intimate association remain to be developed.

In other opinions addressing off-duty conduct, courts have held that the First Amendment does not provide a right to continued government employment in a capacity that is undermined by the employee's off-duty expressive conduct. In *Sims v. Metropolitan Dade County*,[334] the court considered whether supervisors of the county department of community affairs were protected by immunity for their action in suspending an employee for his off-duty remarks expressing frustration at being required to speak Spanish at restaurants and urging blacks to boycott certain establishments. The court

---

329. *See, e.g., Roberts,* 468 U.S. 609 (1984); Wallace v. Texas Tech Univ., 80 F.3d 1042, 1051 (5th Cir. 1996).

330. Wilson v. Taylor, 733 F.2d 1539, 1544 (11th Cir. 1984).

331. 733 F.2d 1539 (11th Cir. 1984).

332. 898 F.2d 1247 (7th Cir.), *cert. denied,* 498 U.S. 853 (1990).

333. *See, e.g.,* Rode v. Dellarciprete, 845 F.2d 1195, 1204–05 (3d Cir. 1988) (brother-in-law relationship not an intimate association that is protected). *See also* Walters v. Village of Oak Lawn, 548 F. Supp. 417, 419 (N.D. Ill. 1982) (loss of consortium not constitutionally protected).

334. 972 F.2d 1230 (11th Cir. 1992).

held that the nature of the employee's job, the public employer's purpose of avoiding racial and cultural resentment, and belief that the off-duty statements would undermine the employer's ability to accomplish its purpose all meant that the employer's discharge of the employee was appropriate.

C. Freedom to Petition

The First Amendment petition clause protects an employee's right to petition the government for a redress of grievances.[335] This basis for protection has often been ignored, perhaps because free speech analysis is often available and reaches the same result.[336] The Supreme Court has not "discussed the scope of the constitutional right to petition in the context of an allegedly retaliatory discharge of a public employee."[337] But the Court's teachings suggest that an employer cannot retaliate against an employee for filing a lawsuit or a grievance.[338]

Courts have generally applied the *Connick* requirement that speech be on a matter of public concern to claims involving retaliation for the filing of grievances or lawsuits.[339] The right to petition is subject to the same analysis as the right to free speech.[340] Courts subsume the right to petition the government into that of free speech.[341] They have been unsympathetic to the argument that the petition clause provides broader protection.[342]

Occasionally, courts have rejected the *Connick* requirement.[343] *Stellmaker v. DePetrillo*[344] illustrates this broader interpretation of the petition clause. A teacher complained that she had been demoted for filing a grievance against

---

335. Genas v. State of New York Dep't of Correctional Serv., 75 F.3d 825 (2d Cir. 1996); Boyle v. Burke, 925 F.2d 497, 505 (1st Cir. 1991).

336. *See* discussion in Margo Pave, *Public Employees and the First Amendment Petition Clause: Protecting the Rights of Citizen-Employees Who File Legitimate Grievances and Lawsuits Against Their Government Employers,* 90 N.W. U. L. Rev. 304 (1995).

337. San Filippo v. Bongiovanni, 30 F.3d 424, 435 (3d Cir. 1994), *cert. denied,* 513 U.S. 1082 (1995).

338. Renfroe v. Kirkpatrick, 722 F.2d 714, 715 (11th Cir.), *cert. denied,* 469 U.S. 823 (1984); Yatvin v. Madison Metro Sch. Dist., 840 F.2d 412, 419–20 (7th Cir. 1988).

339. *See, e.g.,* Rathjen v. Litchfield, 878 F.2d 836 (5th Cir. 1989).

340. Valot v. Southeast Local Sch. Dist. Bd. of Educ., 107 F.3d 1220 (6th Cir. 1997).

341. Belk v. Town of Minocqua, 858 F.2d 1258 (7th Cir. 1988).

342. Day v. South Park Indep. Sch. Dist., 768 F.2d 696, 697–701 (5th Cir. 1985), *cert. denied,* 474 U.S. 1101 (1986).

343. *San Filippo,* 30 F.3d 424.

344. 710 F. Supp. 891 (D. Conn. 1989).

the director and superintendent of the school district. The government raised *Connick* and argued that the grievance did not touch on a matter of public concern. But since the retaliation was not due to speech, the court bypassed *Connick's* requirement and looked to other petition clause cases for guidance. Because these cases extended First Amendment protection to petitions raising "employment conditions and even personal injury claims," the *Stellmaker* court ruled for the plaintiff.[345] The parameters and requirements for a petition clause case have not yet been clearly enunciated, but practitioners should not overlook the theory in appropriate cases.

IV. FOURTH AMENDMENT

Workplace searches are subject to the Fourth Amendment.[346] Under the Fourth Amendment, a public employer engages in a search whenever it invades a space in which an employee has a reasonable expectation of privacy. The Supreme Court has provided a framework for analyzing whether searches and seizures pertaining to office space and personal effects are unreasonable in *O'Connor v. Ortega*.[347] While a psychiatrist at a state hospital on administrative leave pending review of charges against him was absent, his office was searched and officials seized various personal items from his desk and file cabinets. The Supreme Court pointed out that a public employee's expectation of privacy in his or her office or personal space might be "reduced by virtue of actual office practices and procedures, or by legitimate regulation," but the Fourth Amendment does apply.[348]

Where a school guidance counselor's desk was searched by a school board member after hours to try to find out the identity of the person who had drawn a cartoon ridiculing the policies of the school board, a Fourth Amendment right to privacy was implicated.[349] The school board member gained access to the office after hours with the help of a janitor with a passkey. The court found that the counselor had a reasonable expectation of privacy in his office, which was not open to the public, and the superintendent of schools agreed that the desk was considered private.

---

345. *Stellmaker,* 710 F. Supp. at 892. *See also* Fuchilla v. Prockop, 682 F. Supp. 247 (D. N.J. 1987); McCoy v. Goldin, 598 F. Supp. 310, 315 (S.D. N.Y. 1985).

346. For an excellent overview of workplace privacy issues, including those arising under the Fourth Amendment, see James Baird, David D. Kadue, & Kenneth D. Sulzer, Public Employee Privacy: A Legal and Practical Guide to Issues Affecting the Workplace (1995).

347. 480 U.S. 709 (1987).

348. *O'Connor,* 480 U.S. at 717.

349. Gillard v. Schmidt, 579 F.2d 825 (3d Cir. 1978).

If no specific regulation or practice alerts a public worker to the possibility of a search, the employee probably has a reasonable expectation of privacy in a desk or locker.[350] A police officer, whose locker was secured with a private lock, had a reasonable expectation of privacy when the department failed to show that it routinely opened such lockers without permission.

If an employee's desk is frequently invaded by others, the employee lacks exclusive control of the area, or legitimate regulations authorize others to be within the area, then the employee lacks any reasonable expectation of privacy and the Fourth Amendment does not come into play.[351] *Schowengerdt v. United States* illustrates these principles. The Ninth Circuit held that a government employee lacked a reasonable expectation of privacy in his office, desk, or credenza because his employer had extensive security procedures in place. The office environment was characterized by frequent office searches and surveillance for compliance with security precautions. And the employer used trained security investigators to monitor the workplace. As a result, the employee lacked any Fourth Amendment privacy right.[352]

An employer may reduce expectations of privacy by announcing a policy of searching lockers, work areas, and other internal spaces.[353] The Sixth Circuit held that a search of employees' lockers did not violate the Fourth Amendment where the employer's regulations permitted lockers to be searched at any time, and the employees signed a waiver stating that their lockers were subject to inspection at any time.[354] Likewise, the Ninth Circuit Court of Appeals held that no Fourth Amendment privacy interest was implicated where postal regulations permitted searches by supervisors and inspectors. Any Fourth Amendment expectation of privacy that might otherwise have arisen was eliminated by the postal regulations.[355]

But a sign or warning will not always eliminate a Fourth Amendment expectation of privacy.[356] Employees of a commuter railroad facility retained

---

350. United States v. Speights, 557 F.2d 362 (3d Cir. 1977).

351. *See* Schowengerdt v. United States, 944 F.2d 483 (9th Cir. 1991), *cert. denied,* 503 U.S. 951 (1992). *See also* Stewart v. Evans, 351 F.3d 1239, 1243–44 (D.C. Cir. 2003).

352. *See also* Shaul v. Cherry Valley-Springfield Cent. Sch. Dist., 363 F.3d 177 (2d Cir. 2004).

353. American Postal Workers Union v. United States Postal Serv., 871 F.2d 556 (6th Cir. 1989).

354. *American Postal Workers,* 871 F.2d 556.

355. United States v. Bunkers, 521 F.2d 1217 (9th Cir.), *cert. denied,* 423 U.S. 989 (1975).

356. *See* McGann v. Northeast Illinois Reg'l Commuter R.R., 8 F.3d 1174 (7th Cir. 1993).

a reasonable expectation of privacy in their cars, despite signs posted authorizing such searches. Although the employees saw the signs and could have parked elsewhere, the sign did not inform employees "of the grounds for the search, the extent of the search or the frequency or regularity of the searches."[357] The Seventh Circuit held that the employees would "have modestly but not drastically, diminished expectations of privacy."[358] Since no searches had previously taken place, the court found "only a vague possibility that they might be searched."[359] This finding suggests that regular searches may be necessary in order to eliminate the expectation of privacy that would otherwise exist.

While the Seventh Circuit warns against playing "wolf" with warnings about searches, the Sixth Circuit has held that once a policy permits searches, they need not be carried out to negate an expectation of privacy. In *American Postal Workers Union v. United States Postal Service*,[360] a collective bargaining agreement permitted random and unannounced locker inspections. The past failure to implement this provision did not mean it could not be carried out. This result, while grounded on the lack of an expectation of privacy, may also have been based on implied consent since the collective bargaining agreement provided for searches. If a union consents to drug testing of public employees as part of a collective bargaining agreement, the employee will not be able to raise a Fourth Amendment claim.[361]

Drug testing of public employees is sometimes permissible.[362] The Supreme Court has made clear that the collection and testing of urine is a search under the Fourth Amendment.[363] Whether the urine test is permissible depends on the reasonableness of the search and the reasonableness of the manner of the search. *Skinner v. Railway Labor Executives Ass'n* held that neither a warrant nor probable cause are necessary "when 'special needs, beyond the normal need for law enforcement, make the warrant and probable-cause requirement impracticable.'"[364] The court must evaluate

---

357. *McGann,* 8 F.3d at 1180.
358. *Id.* at 1182.
359. *Id.*
360. 871 F.2d 556, 560–61 (6th Cir. 1989).
361. Bolden v. Southeastern Pa. Transit Auth., 953 F.2d 807 (3d Cir. 1991), *cert. denied,* 504 U.S. 943 (1992). *See* Andrew M. Sauder, *Bargaining Away Fourth Amendment Rights in Labor Dispute Resolution:* Bolder v. SEPTA, 38 VILL. L. REV. 1133 (1993).
362. Skinner v. Railway Labor Executives Ass'n, 489 U.S. 602, 633 (1989); National Treasury Employees Union v. Von Raab, 489 U.S. 656, 677 (1989).
363. *Von Raab,* 489 U.S. at 665.
364. *Skinner,* 489 U.S. at 619.

whether the government interest "justifies the privacy intrusions absent a warrant or individualized suspicion."[365] In *Skinner*, the Court held that workers engaged in safety-sensitive tasks could be subjected to drug testing without a warrant or probable cause. Likewise, in *Von Raab* the Court upheld such testing for suspicionless drug testing of customs officers who were directly involved in drug interdiction or required to carry a firearm. A court must balance the government's interest against the employee's expectation of privacy. Factors considered include the government's interest in safety, the employee's knowledge of the drug testing program, whether the policy and test results are used for criminal prosecution or kept confidential, and the government's need to maintain public confidence in public employees.

Reasonableness is tested under two prongs. First, is the search justified in its inception? Second, is it related in scope? A drug test or workplace search is justified at its inception if there are reasonable grounds for expecting misconduct.[366] Proof of an existing drug problem is unnecessary.[367] The search must be related in scope to the circumstances for which it was justified.[368] When a drug-testing policy requires reasonable suspicion before testing, it satisfies the second prong of the reasonableness standard because the intrusion is not excessive in light of the nature of the suspected drug use.[369]

The justification for a workplace search need not amount to the probable cause required to obtain a search warrant. In *Ortega*, the Supreme Court explained that an employer may search the workplace with "reasonable grounds for suspecting that the search will turn up evidence that the employee is guilty of work-related misconduct, or that the search is necessary for a non-investigatory work-related purpose."[370] Reasonable suspicion may be based on objective facts such as observed behavior suggesting drug use or inferences based on facts.[371] It depends on both the content of the information provided and its degree of reliability.[372] Direct observation or physical evidence that an employee's ability to perform his job was

---

365. *Id.* at 621.
366. *O'Connor,* 480 U.S. at 726.
367. Harmon v. Thornburgh, 878 F.2d 484, 487–88 (D.C. Cir. 1989), *cert. denied sub nom* Bell v. Thornburgh, 493 U.S. 1056 (1990).
368. New Jersey v. T.L.O., 469 U.S. 325, 340–42 (1985).
369. *New Jersey,* 469 U.S. at 342.
370. *O'Connor,* 480 U.S. at 726.
371. *See, e.g.,* Copeland v. Philadelphia Police Dep't, 840 F.2d 1139, 1144 (3d Cir. 1988), *cert. denied,* 490 U.S. 1004 (1989).
372. Benavidez v. City of Albuquerque, 101 F.3d 620, 624 (10th Cir. 1996).

impaired because of drug use is not necessary.[373] Information that would lead a reasonable person to suspect the employee of on-the-job drug use or impairment is enough.[374] The source of the information may be a person with a close personal relationship[375] or an informant's report.[376]

The government's interest in testing may be compelling enough to justify testing without individualized suspicion.[377] If the employee is engaged in a safety-sensitive task, drug testing may be permitted without a warrant or probable cause.[378] Courts will scrutinize the testing policy or regulation to ensure that it curtails discretion in the administration of the tests.[379]

Random drug testing has been upheld for police officers because the police industry is a highly regulated quasi-military organization whose members are armed.[380] The administrative search exception to the Fourth Amendment permits random urinalysis testing to ensure confidence in the police department.[381] Random drug testing is also permitted for public employees in safety-sensitive positions. Workers involved in the nuclear power industry; railroad industry; or other transportation areas, such as bus drivers, may be subject to such tests.[382] But it is the government employer's burden to show that drug use by its employees poses a danger to the public.[383]

---

373. *Benavidez,* 101 F.3d at 624.
374. *Id.*
375. Garrison v. Department of Justice, 72 F.3d 1566, 1569–70 (Fed. Cir. 1995).
376. *Garrison,* 72 F.2d at 1570.
377. *Von Raab,* 489 U.S. at 668; *Skinner,* 489 U.S. at 634. *See, e.g.,* Carroll v. City of Westminster, 233 F.3d 308 (4th Cir. 2000).
378. Greenawalt v. Indiana Dep't of Corrections, 397 F.3d 587 (7th Cir. 2005) (probing psychological examination was not a search; but if it had been one, it may have been problematic because employee did not have contact with prisoners, was not armed, and was not privy to state secrets in her job as a researcher).
379. *See, e.g.,* McDonnell v. Hunter, 809 F.2d 1302, 1309 (8th Cir. 1987).
380. Policeman's Benevolent Ass'n of N.J. v. Township of Washington, 850 F.2d 133 (3d Cir. 1988), *cert. denied,* 490 U.S. 1004 (1989); McDonnell v. Hunter, 809 F.2d 1302 (8th Cir. 1987).
381. *Policeman's Benevolent Ass'n,* 850 F.2d at 134, 141–42.
382. Bolden v. Southeastern Pennsylvania Transit Auth., 953 F.2d 807 (3d Cir. 1991), *cert. denied,* 504 U.S. 943 (1992).
383. Taylor v. O'Grady, 888 F.2d 1189 (7th Cir. 1989) (remanding drug-testing challenge in prison context to determine whether employees subjected to testing had regular access to inmate population, had a reasonable opportunity to smuggle in drugs, or had access to firearms); Aubrey v. School Bd. of Lafayette Parish, 148 F.3d 559, 562–63 (5th Cir. 1998).

Courts have also upheld drug testing as part of the job application process. In *Middlebrooks v. Wayne County*,[384] the Michigan Supreme Court found that urinalysis testing was permissible in connection with a job application. The position sought entailed riding a lawn mower on highway medians and embankments, driving front-end loaders, and operating other heavy equipment. Even though county general service workers are less regulated than railroad employees or commercial drivers are, the job duties pose a greater threat to the public than do the operation of normal cars, vans, and trucks.[385] Since the record showed applicants were provided notice of the testing, were not arbitrarily selected for testing, and the information was used only for determining suitability for the job, the testing was upheld.

The Fourth Amendment limits the scope of the search. The search is permissible when the measures adopted for it are reasonably related to the objectives of the search and not excessively intrusive in light of the purpose for the search. Courts look at whether urine samples are tested only for specified drugs, whether samples must be provided under the direct observation of a monitor, whether the tests are provided in a hospital environment by a medical professional, and whether the information is kept confidential.[386]

Sometimes Fourth Amendment claims are coupled with generalized right to privacy allegations that may also be analyzed under the First Amendment. In *O'Brien v. DiGrazia*,[387] the court considered claims brought by police officers who had been suspended for failing to fill out a questionnaire seeking financial information. The court held that even if the Fourth Amendment was applicable to the request to fill out the questionnaire, the order requiring a list of sources of income, assets, and copies of income tax returns was not so lacking in justification as to be unreasonable.

Some courts have found a privacy interest that bars unnecessary or overbroad investigations into an employee's sexual practices or private life.[388] Government lawyers should review employment questionnaires with care to determine whether they comply with case law in this area.

---

384. 446 Mich. 151, 521 N.W.2d 774 (1994).

385. *Middlebrooks,* 521 N.W.2d at 778–81.

386. *See Von Raab,* 489 U.S. at 662–71; *Skinner,* 489 U.S. at 622–26. For a more detailed discussion of drug testing, *see* DAVID EVANS, DRUG TESTING LAW, TECHNOLOGY, AND PRACTICE (West 1990).

387. 544 F.2d 543 (1st Cir. 1976), *cert. denied,* 431 U.S. 914 (1977).

388. Thorne v. El Segundo (Thorne I), 726 F.2d 459 (9th Cir. 1983), *cert. denied,* 469 U.S. 979 (1984); Thorne v. El Segundo (Thorne II), 802 F.2d 1131 (9th Cir. 1986); Schowengerdt v. General Dynamics Corp., 823 F.2d 1328 (9th Cir. 1987).

V. FIFTH AMENDMENT

The Fifth Amendment has potential application to a public employer's internal investigations. The U.S. Supreme Court has ruled that public employers may discipline employees who refuse to answer questions that directly relate to job performance but may not require employees to waive their constitutional protection with respect to the use of answers in a criminal prosecution of the employee.[389]

The Supreme Court has held that interrogations of public employees must comply with the Fifth Amendment guarantee against compelled self-incrimination.[390] Thus, public employers may not require their employees to provide a questionnaire asking about the private use of illegal drugs if the information may be disclosed to law enforcement agencies.[391] Nor may city officials require their employees to waive the constitutional privilege against compelled self-incrimination as a condition of employment.[392] The Third Circuit distinguished a questionnaire during the application process on the basis that it was not compulsory.[393] An employee has no right to lie or make a false statement to his employer; but denying charges and their underlying facts may not be used as a basis for a falsification charge.[394]

VI. CONCLUSION

The careful balancing required to determine the parameters of constitutional rights in the public employee setting remains a fertile ground for litigation. With few bright-line rules, especially in the area of free speech, public employers and those representing them may find it difficult to predict the outcome of a dispute. And the constitutional overlay complicates decision-making that would be routine in the private sector. These challenges require careful lawyering and advice that is based on a multi-level analysis.

---

389. Gardner v. Broderick, 392 U.S. 273 (1968).
390. United Sanitation Men's Ass'n v. Commission of Sanitation, 392 U.S. 280 (1968).
391. American Fed'n of Gov't Employees v. United States R.R. Bd., 742 F. Supp. 450 (N.D. Ill. 1990).
392. Hester v. City of Milledgeville, 598 F. Supp. 1456 (M.D. Ga. 1984).
393. Fraternal Order of Police v. City of Philadelphia, 859 F.2d 276 (3d Cir. 1988).
394. King v. Erickson, 89 F.3d 1575, 1584 (Fed. Cir. 1996).

Chapter 7

THE SECTION 1983 LAND USE CASE

by Thomas E. Roberts

I. INTRODUCTION

Section 1983 can be used to seek redress for various constitutional and federal statutory claims that arise as a consequence of land use regulations. While property rights cases now form the bulk of land use cases under § 1983, the statute was originally viewed by some courts as a vehicle only to redress what were characterized as "personal rights." It was not until 1972 that the Supreme Court expressly held that property rights fell within the purview of § 1983.[1]

Property rights claims are based on the due process clause of the Fourteenth Amendment and the takings clause of the Fifth Amendment, as applied to the states through the Fourteenth Amendment. Confusion between these two claims has existed since 1922, when the Supreme Court created the regulatory takings doctrine. The Supreme Court went a long way toward clarifying the differences between these claims with its opinion in the 2005 case of *Lingle v. Chevron, USA Inc.*[2] That opinion also lays out in clear terms the various types of regulatory takings claims, and it is a recommended starting point for someone new to the area, or someone who, like many, has suffered from a confused state of mind about takings law.

1. Lynch v. Household Finance Corp., 405 U.S. 538 (1972).
2. 125 S. Ct. 2074 (2005).

The Fifth Amendment regulatory takings claim is likely the most common land use claim filed; yet ironically, it is the one land use claim that does not need the aid of § 1983, since the Fifth Amendment's takings clause constitutes a "self-executing" right to seek compensation if the government takes property.[3] There are, however, reasons to use § 1983, and they will be discussed below.[4]

Many land use claims are also based on the equal protection clause, and occasionally, the privileges and immunities clause, of the Fourteenth Amendment. An important distinction to keep in mind is that a denial of either of these rights does not require establishing a property right.

Land use cases also involve First Amendment free speech rights typically arising with sign regulation and sexually oriented business regulation, and First Amendment free exercise and establishment clause cases arising from zoning limitations on, and preferences granted to, religious uses. Increasingly, the First Amendment right to petition the government is raised in complaints against government actions allegedly taken in retaliation to a landowner's complaints against the government in other matters. These claims also do not require establishment of a property right.

Many aspects of a § 1983 land use claim are no different from any other claim brought under the statute, so that discussions in this book of immunities, attorney's fees, and discovery are applicable to land use claims. Yet, in several respects distinct issues arise with land use claims. This chapter will, therefore, begin with these procedural distinctions, and then move on to the substantive law of the various types of claims that might be brought.

II. PROCEDURAL AND OTHER GENERAL ISSUES IN LAND USE CLAIMS

A. Availability and Exclusivity of Action

Section 1983 is likely the only procedural vehicle available for most constitutionally based land use claims, since the Supreme Court has been chary of implying direct causes of action under the Fourteenth Amendment.[5] One

---

3. First English Evangelical Lutheran Church v. County of Los Angeles, 482 U.S. 304 (1987).
4. *See* discussion, *infra,* Part II(A).
5. The Court has held that direct suits are available against the federal government for conduct violative of the Fourth Amendment, Bivens v. Six Unknown Agents, 403 U.S. 388 (1971), and for the due process clause of the Fifth Amendment. Davis v. Passman, 442 U.S. 228 (1979). Direct actions against state or local governments based on the Fourteenth Amendment may or may not be implied. *See* Rogin v. Bensalem Twp., 616 F.2d 680 (3d Cir. 1980).

exception is the Fifth Amendment's just compensation clause, which is self-executing,[6] and an action in inverse condemnation lies to permit the recovery of just compensation without the aid of statutory authorization.[7] This is not true if the claim is that the government action fails to promote a public use.[8] However, even when compensation is sought for an otherwise valid taking, § 1983 will be preferable in most takings cases due to the availability of attorneys' fees.[9]

When suing on a statute, as opposed to the U.S. Constitution, a party must show more than the mere violation of federal law. Section 1983 permits suits based on "rights," not, as the Court has said, "broader or vaguer 'benefits' or 'interests.'"[10] Consequently, a plaintiff must show that a statute creates an individually enforceable right. Also, some federal statutes such as the Fair Housing Act[11] and the Telecommunications Act may create private causes of action, and in some instances, those statutory rights may preclude § 1983 suits.[12]

---

6. First English Evangelical Lutheran Church v. County of Los Angeles, 482 U.S. 304, 315 (1987). Curiously, some courts have said that the existence of § 1983 precludes a direct action. *See* Azul-Pacifico, Inc. v. City of Los Angeles, 973 F.2d 704 (9th Cir. 1992), *cert. denied,* 506 U.S. 1081 (1993); This reasoning deprives the phrase "self-executing" of meaning. These courts say that the availability of § 1983 means no direct causes of action will be implied under the Constitution; but the Fifth Amendment takings clause, with its self-executing remedy, ought not be included in a ban against implied causes of action.
7. For detailed discussion of the mandatory compensation remedy, *see* Thomas E. Roberts, *Procedural Implications of Williamson County/First English in Regulatory Takings Litigation: Herein of Reservations, Removal, Diversity, and Supplemental Jurisdiction,* Rooker-Feldman, *and Res Judicata,* 31 Envtl. L. Rptr. 10353 (April 2001).
8. Section 1983 is likely necessary in that case since the cause of action would not fall under the "self-executing" compensation clause. *See* discussion, *infra,* at Part II(B).
9. 42 U.S.C.A. § 1988. Plaintiffs seeking longer statutes of limitations may try to bring a direct action. Usually this is unsuccessful. Azul-Pacifico, Inc. v. City of Los Angeles, 973 F.2d 704 (9th Cir. 1992), *cert. denied,* 506 U.S. 1081 (1993).
10. Gonzaga Univ. v. Doe, 536 U.S. 273, 283 (2002).
11. 42 U.S.C. § 3613(a)(1)(A).
12. A close examination of the interplay between different statutes is necessary. Discussing when § 1983 is available in the fair housing context, *see* Thompson v. U.S. Dept. of Housing and Urban Development, 348 F. Supp. 2d 398 (D. Md. 2005), and Wallace v. Chicago Housing Authority, 298 F. Supp. 2d 710 (N.D. Ill. 2003).

As a general proposition, the Court will likely find the existence of a comprehensive remedial scheme in a statute to infer an intent to preclude suits under § 1983. The Supreme Court, however, has rejected the argument that the availability of a private cause of action conclusively establishes congressional intent to preclude suits based on § 1983. Rather, the Court has held that the "ordinary inference that the remedy provided in the statute is exclusive can surely be overcome by textual indication, express or implicit, that the remedy is to complement, rather than supplant, § 1983."[13] For example, in *Middlesex County Sewerage Authority v. National Sea Clammers Assoc.*,[14] the Court found the remedies under the Clean Water Act to be sufficiently comprehensive to preclude suits under § 1983.

Recently, in *City of Rancho Palos Verdes v. Abrams*,[15] the Court held that a § 1983 action was not available to enforce the rights created by the Telecommunications Act.[16] There, the plaintiff, having been denied a permit to construct a radio tower on his property, brought suit in federal court seeking an injunction under the Telecommunications Act and damages under § 1983. The § 1983 suit was necessary since the Telecommunications Act does not include a damage remedy or allow attorneys' fees. Importantly, however, the Act has its own special features that suggest exclusivity. Thus, the Telecommunications Act requires courts to hear private suits on an expedited basis. It also has a short, thirty-day limitation period. Allowing enforcement of the Telecommunications Act through § 1983 would, said the Court, "distort the scheme of expedited judicial review and limited remedies created by [the Act.]"[17]

In certain instances § 1983 may be used along with other federal statutory rights of action. The Religious Land Use and Institutionalized Persons Act[18] creates a right of action for a person seeking to enforce religious land use rights. RLUIPA statutory claims are often combined with § 1983 claims

---

13. City of Rancho Palos Verdes v. Abrams, 125 S. Ct. 1453, 1459 (2005).
14. 453 U.S. 1 (1981).
15. 125 S. Ct. 1453 (2005).
16. 47 U.S.C. § 332(c)(7).
17. 125 S. Ct. at 1461.
18. 42 U.S.C. § 2000cc-2(a).

asserting First Amendment violations.[19] Both statutes authorize attorneys' fees.[20]

B. Under Color of Law

Section 1983 applies only to persons "who, *under color of* any statute, ordinance, regulation, custom, or usage, of any State. . . ." This section discusses that requirement in the land use context. The "color of" requirement of § 1983 means the same thing as state action under the Fourteenth Amendment.[21] Whether the action is taken pursuant to a law or custom is a separate question from whether the action, albeit by a private person, was *under color of* law.[22] Individual government officials' actions are "under color of state law" when the government official acts within the scope of his or her duties.[23] An official's actions are also actionable if taken "while clothed with the authority of state law."[24] As stated by the Supreme Court, "[m]isuse of power, possessed by virtue of state law and made possible because the wrongdoer is clothed with the authority of state law, is action taken 'under color of' state law."[25]

Problems arise when private parties act by order or consent of the state. Numerous cases raise the question of lessees of government property, licensees, homeowner's associations, neighborhood groups or other citizens petitioning or pressuring the government to act, permit holders, and government contractors or consultants. To meet the color of law requirement, the private party's action must have been made possible because she "was clothed with the authority of the state,"[26] or as the courts often say, that the act was "fairly attributable to the state." It is the relationship between the

---

19. *See, e.g.,* Fifth Ave. Presbyterian Church v. City of New York, 293 F.3d 570 (2d Cir. 2002).
20. RLUIPA does not make reference to attorneys' fees; but Congress, when enacting RLUIPA, also amended 42 U.S.C. § 1988 to allow attorneys' fees in RLUIPA cases.
21. United States v. Price, 383 U.S. 787, 794 n.7 (1966). Since the state action/color of law test is the same, cases cited in this discussion may be based on the Fourteenth Amendment or § 1983 without express notation.
22. Regarding law and custom, *see* discussion in Part II(C) of this chapter.
23. Monroe v. Pape, 365 U.S. 167 (1961).
24. *Id.* at 184.
25. United States v. Classic, 313 U.S. 299, 326 (1941).
26. West v. Adkins, 487 U.S. 42 (1988).

action taken and the government that matters, not the relationship between the private actor and the government.[27]

In contrast to actions against governmental entities,[28] some courts apply a heightened pleading requirement to complaints against private parties, demanding more than conclusory allegations.[29]

1. Lobbying the Government

Neighbors who lobby against land development approval do not become state actors, and attempts to sue them under § 1983 have failed.[30] Such conduct is protected by the First Amendment.[31] In *City of Cuyahoga Falls v. Buckeye Community Hope Foundation*,[32] the Supreme Court held that comments by citizens in the petitioning process do not constitute state action.

2. Lessees

Lessees of state property may, but do not necessarily, act under color of law. Two recent cases illustrate the dividing line. In *Lee v. Katz*,[33] the Ninth Circuit found that a private organization that leased a city park, a traditional public forum, acted as the state where the city virtually ceded all power to the organization. In contrast, in *Lansing v. City of Memphis*,[34] the Sixth Circuit held that a street festival organizer given nonexclusive power over certain

---

27. Young v. Halle Housing Associates, L.P., 152 F. Supp. 2d 355, 364 (S.D.N.Y. 2001).
28. Leatherman v. Tarrant County, 507 U.S. 163 (1993) (no heightened pleading requirement).
29. *See* Kasper v. City of Middletown, 352 F. Supp. 2d 216 (D. Conn. 2005) (though private entity may be found liable under § 1983, if it is willful participant in joint activity with State or its agents, merely conclusory allegation of such concerted activity does not suffice to state § 1983 claim against the private entity). *But see* Miranda v. Clark County, 319 F.3d 465 (9th Cir. 2002) (no heightened pleading requirement).
30. Chapel Farm Estates, Inc. v. Moerdler, 2003 WL 21998964 (S.D.N.Y. 2003); Bethany Bldg., Inc. v. Dungan Civic Ass'n, 2003 WL 1847603 (Pa. Com. Pl. 2003).
31. *See* R.R. Presidents Conference v. Noerr Motor Freight, Inc., 365 U.S. 127 (1961); and United Mine Workers v. Pennington, 381 U.S. 657 (1965).
32. 538 U.S. 188 (2003).
33. 276 F.3d 550 (9th Cir. 2002), *cert. denied sub nom,* Oregon Arena Corp. v. Lee, 536 U.S. 905 (2002).
34. 202 F.3d 821 (6th Cir. 2000).

city streets, also a traditional public forum, did not become a state actor because the city retained ultimate control of the streets. The difference between *Lee* and *Lansing* is that the lease in the former case authorized the lessee to create rules for public access, while the lease in the latter case required the lessee to comply with all directives of the police department.[35]

3. Mere Permit Holders

More than acquisition of a government permit is necessary to become a state actor. Thus, where private landowners trespassed on another's property while connecting to a town's water supply pursuant to a permit authorizing such connection, an action against the trespassers might lie in tort but will not lie under § 1983.[36]

4. Consultants

A consultant who drafts an ordinance for a city does not thereby become a state actor.[37] Likewise, an architect hired to advise a city on whether development applications meet the city's design standards does not, by giving his opinion, act under color of law.[38]

5. Homeowner Associations

The sometimes stringent rules of homeowner's associations have led some commentators to suggest that such associations are quasi-governmental and that they should be subject to constitutional restraints. The courts have generally rejected these claims. In *Kalian at Poconos, L.L.C. v. Saw Creek Estates Community Ass'n, Inc.*,[39] the court refused application of the public

---

35. *See also* United Auto Workers v. Gaston Festivals, Inc., 43 F.3d 902 (4th Cir. 1995) ("If a party obtaining a permit to use public property for a specific event were constitutionally required to admit unconditionally everyone seeking admission, it would be virtually impossible to hold the event for which the permit was obtained."); Diener v. Reed, 232 F. Supp. 2d 362 (M.D. Pa. 2002).
36. Cassaboon v. Town of Somers, 359 F. Supp. 2d 320 (S.D.N.Y. 2005).
37. Omnipoint Communications, Inc. v. Comi, 233 F. Supp. 2d 388 (N.D.N.Y. 2002).
38. R-Goshen LLC v. Village of Goshen, 289 F. Supp. 2d 441 (S.D.N.Y. 2003). *See also* Florida Country Clubs, Inc. v. Carlton, Fields, Ward, Emmanuel, Smith and Cutler, P.A., 98 F. Supp. 2d 1356 (M.D. Fla. 2000) (private law firm was not state actor due to its actions as attorney for city).
39. 275 F. Supp. 2d 578 (M.D. Pa. 2003).

function analysis as applied to a community association where the association had the authority to maintain the roads and utilities and to collect dues to fund such maintenance. This, the court found, was distinguishable from the leading public function case of *Marsh v. Alabama*,[40] involving the classic company town where a person was "arrested" for distributing religious literature in violation of a company rule. *Kalian at Poconos* involved a claim that the association's assessment of fees deprived the lot owner of property. If a homeowner's association were to restrict the exercise of speech rights, the court pointed out that a different result might obtain.[41]

6. Recipients of Government Funding

Receipt of government funding and compliance with various governmental regulations does not convert a private party into a state actor.[42] In *Young v. Halle Housing Associates, L.P.*,[43] residents sued their landlord, a nonprofit corporation; the landlord's employees; and the state; claiming that the landlord's ban on overnight guests violated various constitutional rights. The state action rationale was that the landlord received substantial state and federal funding and was required by the state to lease a certain percentage of its units to homeless persons and provide certain other services to residents. The court found no state action. The state had not participated in the promulgation or enforcement of the rule, which was entirely of the making of the landlord.

C. Official Policy: Statute, Ordinance, Custom, or Usage

Section 1983 land use litigation almost always involves the actions of local governmental entities. Municipal corporations and other political subdivisions, and individuals acting for them are liable if an alleged injury or deprivation is the "natural consequence of [an official] policy or custom."[44] There

---

40. 326 U.S. 501 (1941).
41. *Id.* at 590 ("This case does not involve an outsider who unwittingly ran afoul of some privately-imposed rule."). *See, generally,* "Proof of Homeowner Association Acting as Quasi Governmental Entity Whose Conduct Constitutes State Action Requiring Declaration of Rights Under Homeowner Association Restriction Prohibiting Political Signs," 76 Am. Jur. Proof of Facts 3d 89 (June 2005).
42. Young v. Halle Housing Associates, L.P., 152 F. Supp. 2d 355, 362 (S.D.N.Y. 2001).
43. 152 F. Supp. 2d 355, 364 (S.D.N.Y. 2001).
44. Smith v. Ambrogio, 456 F. Supp. 1130, 1135 (D. Conn. 1978).

is no precise definition of "policy."[45] A single action by a city official may suffice. In *Pembaur v. City of Cincinnati*,[46] the Court held that a municipality is liable "where and only where a deliberate choice to follow a course of action is made from among various alternatives by the official or officials responsible for establishing final policy with respect to the subject matter in question."[47] Random acts or isolated incidents are normally not sufficient to show a policy or custom.[48]

In land use cases, a municipality may be liable not only through the adoption of a zoning ordinance but also by taking other official action, such as where a city council denies or revokes a development or building permit.[49] The action of a building inspector taken pursuant to authority from the board of adjustment has been held to be official policy.[50] The powers granted to a planning director and to a planning commission also have been held sufficient to cause their actions in issuing permits to be official policy for § 1983 liability purposes.[51] However, where a mayor vetoed a zoning ordinance in an attempt to bribe a developer, it was held not to be official policy of the city.[52] The mayor was not the final policymaker in zoning matters, as the city council had the power to override the veto.

D. Exhaustion of Remedies and Land Use Exceptions

Generally, a plaintiff need not exhaust state judicial or administrative remedies before seeking redress under § 1983.[53] The Civil Rights Act exists to

---

45. *See* Steven Stein Cushman, *Municipal Liability under § 1983: Toward a New Definition of Municipal Policymaker,* 34 B.C. L. Rev. 693 (1993); Michael T. Burke & Patricia A. Burton, *Defining the Contours of Municipal Liability Under Title 42 U.S.C. § 1983:* Monell *Through* City of Canton v. Harris, 18 Stetson L. Rev. 511 (1989).
46. 475 U.S. 469 (1986).
47. *Id.* at 483.
48. Florida Country Clubs, Inc. v. Carlton, Fields, Ward, Emmanuel, Smith and Cutler, P.A., 98 F. Supp. 2d 1356, 1363 (M.D. Fla. 2000).
49. Bateson v. Geisse, 857 F.2d 1300 (9th Cir. 1988). *See also* WAM Properties, Inc. v. Desoto County, Florida, 758 F. Supp. 1468 (M.D. Fla. 1991) (council authorization of a lawsuit for code violations constituted an act of official governmental policy).
50. Video Intern. Production, Inc. v. Warner Amex Cable Communications, Inc., 858 F.2d 1075 (5th Cir. 1988), *cert. denied,* 491 U.S. 906 (1989). *See also* Rodrigues v. Village of Larchmont, 608 F. Supp. 467 (S.D.N.Y. 1985) (board of zoning appeals decisions are official policy).
51. Hutchison v. City of Huntington, 479 S.E.2d 649 (W.Va. 1996).
52. Manor Healthcare Corp. v. Lomelo, 929 F.2d 633 (11th Cir. 1991).
53. *See, e.g.,* Beaulieu v. City of Alabaster, 338 F. Supp. 2d 1268 (N.D. Ala. 2004) (exhaustion of state administrative remedies is not prerequisite to filing suit under § 1983 based on First Amendment challenge to sign ordinance).

provide a remedy that is supplementary to any state remedies. Requiring exhaustion of those state remedies, the Court has held, would thwart the purpose of the statute.[54] Two significant cautionary points to this rule apply in the land use context, and both stem from the case of *Williamson County Regional Planning Commission v. Hamilton Bank*.[55] First, for a cause of action to be ripe, the state action must be final; and to achieve finality, a meaningful development application must be made. Second, with respect to takings claims, a claimant must seek compensation from the state.

E. Final Decision Ripeness

While exhaustion of administrative remedies is not required, finality of decision is. Confusion between the two has led to the filing of numerous unripe cases, with much wasted time. In *Celentano v. City of West Haven*,[56] for example, the property owner "insisted emphatically" that he, like other § 1983 civil rights litigants, did not need to seek final action, citing as authority *Patsy v. Florida Board of Regents*,[57] where the Supreme Court held that there is no exhaustion requirement applicable to § 1983 actions. Yet, in *Williamson County*, the Court expressly distinguished *Patsy* and held that as-applied takings claims differ from other constitutional claims, noting that while exhaustion of administrative remedies is not required, a final decision by the initial decision maker is required.

Some confusion is understandable in light of the difficulty of ascertaining when a decision is final. Land use regulation and permitting schemes typically involve multiple boards, commissions, and councils, all of which may be included in *Williamson County*'s "initial decision maker." Multiple applications for permission are commonplace. Thus, it is not obvious how many applications for development must be made, to whom they must be made, and whether it is necessary to apply for development permission when to do so seems fruitless.[58]

Exhaustion of remedies, which is not necessary, refers to use of procedures to provide redress to an injured party. Finality, which is necessary, asks whether the government has reached a definitive position that inflicts injury. While these terms are "conceptually distinct,"[59] the distinction blurs in practice. Under the final-decision rule, multiple applications for development

---

54. Patsy v. Florida Board of Regents, 457 U.S. 496 (1982).
55. 473 U.S. 172 (1985).
56. 815 F. Supp. 561 (D. Conn. 1993).
57. 457 U.S. 496 (1982).
58. *See, generally,* Thomas E. Roberts, *Ripeness and Forum Selection in Fifth Amendment Takings Litigation,* 11 J. Land Use & Envtl. L. 37 (1995).
59. *Id.* at 192.

may need to be made and a variance sought to render a case ripe. *Williamson County* provides a good example. The Court said the developer would not be required to appeal the planning commission's rejection of a plat to the board of adjustment, since the board had the power only to review, not participate, in that decision. The Court said the property owner, however, had to go to both the Board of Adjustment and the Planning Commission to seek variances because those bodies had the power to relieve the property owner of the alleged hardships.

Williamson County sets a strict standard: If a variance is theoretically available, one must apply for it. Resort to a board of adjustment is not required if the board has only the power to review application of the regulation. It is required if the board possesses the power to waive or grant a variance from the regulations. The developer in *Williamson County*, after eight years or so of going back and forth with various county agencies, commissions, and boards, likely thought applying for a variance would be a waste of time; but the Court implicitly found that irrelevant.

While many courts have applied the final decision rule strictly per the letter and spirit of *Williamson County*, the more recent cases have relaxed the rule so that mere theoretical availability of a variance does not conclusively establish the obligation to seek one. The question of whether an injury has occurred that creates a justiciable matter, and whether to file yet one more time for permission, is very much fact-based. In *Palazzollo v. Rhode Island*,[60] the Court found two applications had clearly shown that the state would not allow any development.[61] It would have been futile to ask again even for a smaller development. In another case, where the zoning board indefinitely continued a landowner's permit applications and threatened to bring suit to force her to move her home and pay the cost, the court found the action ripe.[62] If an injury has occurred, the case is ripe even though no final decision had been handed down on the permit application. Thus, where a property owner charged that the county retaliated against him for publicly criticizing the county by delaying his permit to develop, the retaliation case was ripe even though the permitting process was incomplete since the retaliation claim did not depend on the ultimate outcome of the permitting process.[63]

---

60. 533 U.S. 606 (2001).
61. Actually, there were four applications, two in the plaintiff's name and two in his corporate capacity.
62. Lauderbaugh v. Hopewell Township, 319 F.3d 568 (3d Cir. 2003).
63. Carpinteria Valley Farms, Ltd. v. County of Santa Barbara, 344 F.3d 822 (9th Cir. 2003).

The Supreme Court has said that the "finality requirement is concerned with whether the initial decision maker has arrived at a definitive position on the issue that inflicts an actual, concrete injury."[64] Yet, identifying the initial decision maker is no easy task. In fact, the plural "decision makers," rather than the singular, more accurately expresses the requirement since it may include the local legislative body, the planning commission, the building inspector, *and* the board of adjustment. Depending on local procedure, resort to all four (the legislative body, the planning commission, the building inspector, and the board of adjustment) may be required to make a decision final. Typically, a request for a rezoning to the legislative body is not necessary, but it may be necessary where the current zoning classification is somewhat dated.[65]

Meaningful, as opposed to "exceedingly grandiose," development applications must be made. In *MacDonald, Sommer & Frates v. Yolo County*,[66] the Court found a 159-lot subdivision, which it characterized as an "intense type of residential development," was not meaningful. Looking back at prior cases, the Court observed that the "'five Victorian mansions'" sought in *Agins v. City of Tiburon*[67] and the nuclear power plant in *San Diego Gas & Electric Co. v. City of San Diego*[68] were of the nonmeaningful, grandiose variety. The proposed fifty-five–story office tower atop Grand Central Station in the *Penn Central Railroad Co. v. City of New York*[69] case was also likely "grandiose" in the ripeness sense, since the Court there noted that the landmark commission might have approved a smaller tower. This meaningful application requirement creates a dilemma since it encourages a developer to downsize its request without going so far as to render the project economically unfeasible. It may have the effect of promoting negotiation and compromise by a developer, just as the fear of monetary liability may cause the government to do the same.

This final decision ripeness requirement applies to as-applied takings claims, as well as to substantive due process claims and equal protection

---

64. *Williamson County,* 473 U.S. at 192.
65. *See* Hernandez v. City of Lafayette, 643 F.2d 1188 (5th Cir. 1981).
66. 477 U.S. 340 (1986).
67. 447 U.S. 255 (1980).
68. 450 U.S. 621 (1981).
69. 438 U.S. 104 (1978).

claims.[70] It is not applicable to facial[71] or physical[72] takings claims since, by definition, the action is ripe or final upon adoption of the ordinance or invasion by the state. The *Williamson County* rule has also been applied to First Amendment claims,[73] though the rule is more relaxed in that setting.[74]

F. Seeking Compensation from the State

The second qualification to the non-exhaustion rule, more accurately labeled a bar to federal court, is that a claimant must seek compensation in state court. (Note: Claims against the United States must be filed in the Court of Federal Claims.) Again, the requirement stems from the *Williamson County* case, where the Court, noting the long-standing rule that post-condemnation compensation satisfies the Fifth Amendment, reasoned that there is no violation of the takings clause until the state refuses to pay compensation. It then held that a property owner must use available state procedures to seek compensation. All takings claims, physical and regulatory, facial and as-applied, are subject to the requirement that the property owner seek compensation from the state by way of an action in inverse condemnation.[75]

While the Court phrases the requirement of seeking compensation from the state in terms of ripeness, the preclusive effects accorded to a state court judgment generally will bar a subsequent suit in federal court. The act of ripening the claim concludes it as well. In *San Remo Hotel, L.P. v. City and County of San Francisco*,[76] the Court held that the federal full faith and credit statute compels federal court recognition of a state court's takings judgment. Unfortunately, in doing so, the Court reiterated the misleading ripeness label:

---

70. Cramer v. Vitale, 359 F. Supp. 2d 621 (E.D. Mich. 2005); Forseth v. Village of Sussex, 199 F.3d 363, 370 (7th Cir. 2000).
71. Yee v. City of Escondido, 503 U.S. 519 (1992); V. Jacobs & Sons v. Saginaw County Dept. of Public Health, 284 F. Supp. 2d 711 (E.D. Mich. 2003).
72. Sinaloa Lake Owners Ass'n v. City of Simi Valley, 882 F.2d 1398, 1402 (9th Cir. 1989), *cert. denied,* 494 U.S. 1016 (1990).
73. Murphy v. New Milford Zoning Comm'n, 402 F.3d 342 (2d Cir. 2005) (also applied to RLUIPA claim).
74. Dougherty v. Town of North Hempstead Bd. of Zoning Appeals, 282 F.3d 83 (2d Cir. 2002).
75. For a time there was some dispute about facial claims. The Ninth Circuit did not require state court action for takings claims based on the allegation that an ordinance did not substantially advance a legitimate state interest. For criticism of this rule, *see* Thomas E. Roberts, *Facial Takings Claims Under* Agins-Nectow*: A Procedural Loose End,* 24 U. Haw. L. Rev. 623 (2002). In 2005, the Court held no such takings test exists. *See discussion, infra, regarding* Lingle v. Chevron USA Inc., 125 S. Ct. 2074 (2005).
76. 125 S. Ct. 2491 (2005).

> We have only one narrow question to decide: whether we should create an exception to the full faith and credit statute, and the ancient rule on which it is based, in order to provide a federal forum for litigants who seek to advance federal takings claims that *are not ripe until* the entry of a final state judgment denying just compensation. See *Williamson County*.[77]

The Court determined no exception was justified. This unanimous decision was not surprising. There is no justification for duplicative litigation (and no Justice could offer one) that would allow a federal district court to second-guess a decision of a state court, thereby undermining the integrity of the courts, not to mention overusing limited resources.

Whether a state court judgment precludes subsequent lower federal litigation depends on the law of the state issuing the judgment. Rules of claim and issue preclusion vary from state to state, and where state law provides for no preclusive effect a federal action may proceed.[78] In *Wisznia v. City of Albuquerque*,[79] plaintiff appealed a permit denial to state court asserting that the city had misinterpreted its zoning code and that the action of the city was arbitrary. While that appeal was pending, plaintiffs' lease was terminated based on the city's action. The plaintiffs then filed a § 1983 action in state court seeking damages. The city removed the case to federal court. In the meantime the plaintiffs had dismissed their state appeal challenging the correctness of the zoning permit denial because they had lost the land, making their claim moot. The city then argued in federal court that the constitutional § 1983 claims were barred by res judicata. The Tenth Circuit found that the city's removal constituted a waiver of its res judicata defense and, even absent waiver, the defense was invalid since under state law a case dismissed due to mootness is not on the merits, and res judicata does not apply.

Wisznia is the exception, and typically a federal court suit is not permitted. While the result (one suit rather than two) is defensible, the sticky point is the "unripe" language the Court uses in explaining the *Williamson County* obligation to sue in state court. Having state courts adjudicate takings claims defers to state and local government in an area historically viewed as quintessentially local, and it is collateral review that is barred. Appellate review, however, exists.

Four justices issued a concurring opinion in *San Remo*, indicating dissatisfaction with the *Williamson County* compensation requirement. The

---

77. *Id.* at 2500 (emphasis added). When the Court speaks of exceptions to ancient rules, the reader gets a big clue as to how the decision is going to come out.
78. The *Rooker-Feldman* rule could still bar suit in federal court. *See, infra,* Part III(E).
79. 135 Fed. Appx. 181 (10th Cir. 2005).

rule, while defensible, is not unassailable. Neither the language of the Fifth Amendment nor the rationale of inverse condemnation compels the conclusion that compensation must first be sought from the state by way of litigation. The cause of action could be said to arise when the action complained of is final under prong one of *Williamson County*, or the Court could modify the prong-two rule to say that the cause of action arises when the property owner simply demands compensation and the state refuses to pay.[80] At least one lower court has so held.[81]

The Court should either stop using the ripeness label and either recognize that the Fifth Amendment is unique in compelling state court adjudication of federal takings claims on their merits, or overrule the second prong of *Williamson County* and earlier cases to find that a cause of action is ripe once a decision is final.

A similar "compensation" requirement exists for procedural due process claims. As with the Fifth Amendment, a post-deprivation remedy by way of a cause of action in state court may cure a potential due process violation. Under *Parratt v. Taylor*[82] and *Hudson v. Palmer*,[83] a damage action for random, unauthorized acts of state officials must be pursued in state court.[84] Again, once a state court adjudicates an issue, the federal courts must give it full faith and credit.[85] The Supreme Court has suggested that the *Parratt-Hudson* rule applies only to procedural due process,[86] but some courts have applied it to substantive due process as well.[87]

---

80. A demand letter, nothing more.
81. Dickinson Leisure Industries, Inc. v. City of Dickinson, 2004 WL 1774865 (S.D. Tex. 2004). The case is not good authority inasmuch as it fails to abide by the prevailing rule of *Williamson County.*
82. 451 U.S. 527 (1981).
83. 468 U.S. 517 (1984).
84. *See* Frederic S. Schwartz, *The Post-Deprivation Remedy Doctrine of* Parratt v. Taylor *and Its Application to Cases of Land Use Regulation,* 21 Ga. L. Rev. 601 (1987).
85. 28 U.S.C. § 1738.
86. *See, e.g.,* Albright v. Oliver, 510 U.S. 266 (1994) (Stevens, J., dissenting) (*Parratt* is categorically inapplicable to substantive due process).
87. Weimer v. Amen, 870 F.2d 1400 (8th Cir. 1989) (finding *Parratt* applicable); New Burnham Prairie Homes, Inc. v. Village of Burnham, 910 F.2d 1474, 1481 (7th Cir. 1990). Most courts, however, reject the application of *Parratt* to substantive due process. *See* Cozzo v. Tangipahoa Parish Council—President Government, 279 F.3d 273 (5th Cir. 2002). *But see* Doe v. Dept. of Public Safety *ex rel.* Lee, 271 F.3d 38 (2d Cir. 2001) (expressing concern that the *Parratt* rule not be avoided by labeling a claim as substantive rather than procedural).

The preclusive effects of compliance with the compensation rule of *Williamson County* have led to a variety of evasive efforts to reach a federal forum. These include attempting to reserve the right in state court to litigate the federal claim after the state action is completed, suing in federal court on a non-takings federal claim then asking the court to take supplemental jurisdiction of a state law takings claim, and using diversity jurisdiction.[88]

III. LOOKING FOR WAYS TO GET TO FEDERAL COURT

While state and federal courts share concurrent jurisdiction over § 1983 claims, parties may prefer federal court for various reasons. At times the landowner wants to be in federal court, and at times it is the government that prefers a federal forum. Local conditions control this strategy decision, but reasons may include a perceived greater sympathy for the landowner (or the government) or an uncrowded docket (or a crowded one).

A. Reservation of Rights Under England

A number of takings claimants have tried to reserve the right to litigate their Fifth Amendment takings claims in federal court under the *England* doctrine. In *England v. Louisiana State Board of Medical Examiners*,[89] the Court held that a party who properly invoked federal court jurisdiction but was compelled by the federal court's exercise of *Pullman* abstention[90] to litigate in state court can reserve her right to return to federal court for consideration of federal issues after the termination of the state proceedings.[91]

---

88. These techniques are discussed, *infra,* at Part III.

89. 375 U.S. 411 (1964). *See also* Wilkinson v. Pitkin County, 142 F.3d 1319, 1324 (10th Cir. 1998); Front Royal and Warren County Industrial Park Corp. v. Town of Front Royal, 135 F.3d 275, 283 (4th Cir. 1998); Rainey Brothers Construction Co., Inc. v. Memphis and Shelby County Bd. of Adjustment, 967 F. Supp. 998, 1004 n.5 (W.D. Tenn. 1997), *aff'd,* 178 F.3d 1295 (6th Cir. 1999), *cert. denied,* 528 U.S. 871 (1999).

90. *Pullman* abstention is appropriate where there is an unsettled question of state law that, when resolved, would obviate the need for a federal constitutional decision. *See* Railroad Commission of Texas v. Pullman Co., 312 U.S. 396 (1941).

91. The *England* Court had "fundamental objections to any conclusion that a litigant *who has properly invoked the jurisdiction* of a Federal District Court to consider federal constitutional claims can be compelled, without his consent and through no fault of his own, to accept instead a state court's determination of those claims." 375 U.S. at 415 (emphasis added).

While some takings claimants have met with limited success arguing *England*, the argument has reached its end since, in *San Remo Hotel, L.P. v. City and County of San Francisco*,[92] the Court found the doctrine inapplicable to takings claims.

Emphasizing that *England* is available only when a case is properly before a federal district court, the *San Remo* Court followed the rule of *Williamson County*. That case holds that a federal district court lacks jurisdiction over a takings claim where the claimant has failed to resort to state compensation procedures, so that the *England* requirement of properly invoking federal jurisdiction in the first instance cannot be met.

Furthermore, the Court noted that an *England* reservation does not override the law of preclusion.[93] This can be seen in the case of *Dodd v. Hood River County*,[94] where the court found for the parties and the state court had agreed to allow the property owners to assert their takings claim in federal court[95] after state court adjudication of a state takings claim. The state court expressly ruled that it was considering only Oregon law in finding no taking of the plaintiffs' property. Since there was an agreement allowing the plaintiffs to split their claims, the court held the plaintiffs were not subject to claim preclusion when they sued in federal court. The court went on to hold, however, that issue preclusion prevented the Dodds from relitigating issues that had been decided adversely to them by the state court.[96]

---

92. 125 S. Ct. 2491 (2005).
93. The Court did say that the plaintiffs' facial taking claim based on the "substantially advances" test was properly before the lower court, but plaintiffs in state court had not asserted that claim and thus waived a right to rely on their reservation. This is a dubious observation by the Court, but it matters not since the Court subsequently rejected the "substantially advances" test. *See* Lingle v. Chevron U.S.A. Inc., 125 S. Ct. 2074 (2005). *See also San Remo*'s acknowledgment of this. 125 S. Ct. at 2506 n.25.
94. 59 F.3d 852 (9th Cir. 1995), *after remand decision,* 136 F.3d 1219 (9th Cir. 1998), *cert. denied,* 525 U.S. 923 (1998).
95. Query how the parties by agreement can confer jurisdiction on a court.
96. If a reservation is held to allow claim splitting, some takings issues not covered by the state's law of issue preclusion will be reached on the merits by the federal court. *See Dodd, supra.* Another case involving reservation and issue preclusion is Popp v. City of Aurora, 2000 WL 684804, 2000 U.S. Dist. LEXIS 7160 (N.D. Ill. 2000).

B. Supplemental Jurisdiction

Since equal protection or substantive due process claims can be filed in federal court without regard to the compensation requirement of *Williamson County*,[97] a property owner might file an equal protection or due process claim in federal district court and append a state takings claim to it.[98] Since this "turns *Williamson County* on its head," as one court charged,[99] and since courts have discretion in exercising supplemental jurisdiction, it may not be successful.

Appending a state takings claim easily fits within 28 U.S.C.A. § 1367(a), which provides that "the district courts shall have supplemental jurisdiction over all other claims that are so related to claims in the action within such original jurisdiction that they form part of the same case or controversy under Article III of the United States Constitution." Thus, a property owner who secures federal district court jurisdiction by asserting a due process or equal protection claim may append a state takings claim, which the court may hear through its exercise of supplemental jurisdiction.[100]

---

97. Cramer v. Vitale, 359 F. Supp. 2d 621 (E.D. Mich. 2005). There is some disagreement here. The Seventh Circuit, for example, subject's substantive due process claims to both prongs of *Williamson County. See* Forseth v. Village of Sussex, 199 F.3d 363, 370 (7th Cir. 2000). In so doing, the court fails to consider the differences between substantive due process claims that are duplicative of takings claims with those that are based on alleged arbitrary and capricious conduct. *See* JULIAN C. JUERGENSMEYER & THOMAS E. ROBERTS, LAND USE PLANNING AND DEVELOPMENT REGULATION LAW, § 10.12 (Thomson-West 2003).
98. All states have takings clauses in their constitutions, which are usually interpreted identically to the federal clause and in some instances are read more favorably to property owners.
99. "[B]ecause the federal claim is not yet ripe precisely because the state courts have not yet had an opportunity to consider the parallel state takings claim, this court would turn Williamson County upside down if it proceeded to decide SGB's state constitutional takings claim." SGB Financial Services, Inc. v. Consolidated City of Indianapolis–Marion County, 2000 WL 680412, 2000 U.S. Dist. LEXIS 7204 (S.D. Ind. 2000).
100. Geddes v. County of Kane, 121 F. Supp. 2d 662 (N.D. Ill. 2000) (plaintiffs brought equal protection, federal takings claim, and state takings claim; the federal takings claim was dismissed because the plaintiffs have not used their remedies under state law. The court, however, retained the state takings claim).

That the court can hear the claim does not mean that it will. Under § 1367(c), a federal court may decline to exercise such jurisdiction if one or more of the following circumstances exists: "(1) the claim raises a novel or complex issue of state law, (2) the claim substantially predominates over the claim or claims over which the district court has original jurisdiction, (3) the district court has dismissed the claims over which it has original jurisdiction, or (4) in exceptional circumstances, there are other compelling reasons for declining jurisdiction."[101] Normally, at least one, and perhaps several, of these will apply to *Williamson County* end-run attempts.

C. Diversity Jurisdiction

If diverse citizenship exists between the property owner and the city or county agency,[102] then a federal district court has jurisdiction to hear any claim the state court could hear by way of diversity jurisdiction.[103] In *County of Allegheny v. Frank Mashuda Co.*,[104] the Supreme Court upheld the exercise of diversity jurisdiction over a state law claim of a taking for private use. Since the petitioners could have filed such an action in state court, they were entitled, by virtue of their noncitizenship, to ask a federal court to act as a state court and apply Pennsylvania law with respect to private takings.[105]

Following this Supreme Court lead,[106] several lower federal courts in recent years have ruled on property owners' state law regulatory takings claims when their jurisdiction was founded on diversity.[107] In such a case,

---

101. 28 U.S.C.A. § 1367(c). *See* Hoagland v. Town of Clear Lake, 415 F.3d 693 (7th Cir. 2005); Manufactured Home Communities Inc. v. City of San Jose, 420 F.3d 1022 (9th Cir. 2005).
102. Counties and cities, as municipal corporations, are citizens of their state for purposes of diversity. Regents of the University of California v. Doe, 519 U.S. 425, 430 n.6 (1997) (counties); People of State of Ill. v. Kerr-McGee Chemical Corp., 677 F.2d 571 (7th Cir. 1982) (cities).
103. "In diversity cases the rights enjoyed under local law should not vary because enforcement of those rights was sought in the federal court rather than in the state court." Ragan v. Merchants Transfer & Warehouse Co., 337 U.S. 530 (1949).
104. 360 U.S. 185 (1959).
105. *Id.* at 190.
106. In addition to *Mashuda, see* Searl v. School Dist. No. 2, 124 U.S. 197 (1888) (ordering district court to exercise diversity jurisdiction in condemnation case removed from state court).
107. SK Finance SA v. La Plata County, 126 F.3d 1272, 1276 (10th Cir. 1997); Sinclair Oil Corp. v. County of Santa Barbara, 96 F.3d 401 (9th Cir. 1996); American Tel. & Tel. Co. v. Madison Parish Police Jury, 465 F. Supp. 168 (D. La. 1977).

the federal district court must act as a state court would act, and this presents no problem insofar as the takings claim is based on state law.

D. Government Removal

Plaintiffs may involuntarily secure a federal forum when municipalities remove cases under 28 U.S.C. § 1441. Removal is permissible only where the claim being removed is within the original jurisdiction of the federal court.[108] If a plaintiff brings a federal and/or state takings claim in state court and couples it with other federal claims such as equal protection or due process, removal is proper, and supplemental jurisdiction over the takings claim may exist.

In *Koscielski v. City of Minneapolis*,[109] plaintiff filed a takings claim, along with equal protection and due process claims, in state court. The city removed and sought dismissal. The equal protection and due process claims were dismissed on the merits on summary judgment. The takings claim was found unripe and dismissed. The plaintiff argued that it had done just what *Williamson County* called for—that is, it filed a claim seeking compensation in state court—and that the city, having deprived the plaintiff of the state forum by its removal, should be deemed to have waived its ripeness argument. Without explaining itself, the district court said the plaintiff had not "maintained an inverse condemnation claim at any point." Presumably, the court thought that the plaintiff needed to file a separate claim in state court labeled "action in inverse condemnation."[110] The court rejected the argument that removal constituted waiver by the city, not because the argument did not make sense but because the plaintiff had no authority to cite in support.[111]

A property owner can prevent removal by filing only a Fifth Amendment takings claim in state court. The case is not removable, since the case is not within the original jurisdiction of the court under prong two of *Williamson County*[112] and, without an equal protection or due process claim

108. "Any civil action brought in a State court of which the district courts of the United States have original jurisdiction, may be removed by the defendant." 28 U.S.C. § 1441(a).

109. 2005 WL 240930 (D. Minn. 2005).

110. This is unpersuasive reasoning by the court. There is nothing magic about the phrase "inverse condemnation." The plaintiff's state court suit, that the district court itself described as a claim for "taking without compensation," was in substance an inverse condemnation claim.

111. It is a mistake to characterize the city's action as a waiver, since ripeness is jurisdictional and not waivable; but the argument is sound. The city's action establishes the unavailability of a state forum, and the courts could recognize that as rendering a case ripe for the federal court.

112. Eggleston v. Pierce County, 99 F. Supp. 2d 1280 (W.D. Wa. 2000).

to support jurisdiction, the city ought not be able to remove. If the city does so nonetheless, and the plaintiff wants to stay in federal court, keeping quiet may not work. The court on its own motion might dismiss the case for lack of jurisdiction. At that point the plaintiff might argue that the city's act of removal establishes the unavailability of a state remedy, conferring original jurisdiction on the court.[113]

E. *Rooker-Feldman* Ban on Relitigation

Government defendants who have faced a takings claim or similar litigation in state courts have another defense similar to that of claim or issue preclusion.[114] The *Rooker-Feldman* doctrine[115] bars federal district courts from "entertaining a proceeding to reverse or modify"[116] a state court judgment or from hearing issues "inextricably intertwined"[117] with a state court decision. The basis of *Rooker-Feldman* is 28 U.S.C. § 1257, which vests appellate jurisdiction solely in the Supreme Court.[118] The rationale is that if a federal challenge succeeds only to the extent that the state court wrongly decided the issue, . . . [or] if the federal action would effectively reverse the state court decision,[119] the district court would be exercising appellate review.

Rooker-Feldman, while similar to preclusion in that it prevents relitigation,[120] has some significant differences. As Professor Sherry says, "[R]es judicata is about parties; *Rooker-Feldman* is about courts."[121] Preclusion rules exist to protect persons from being exposed to repetitious litigation by those they have defeated in prior lawsuits, and the full faith and credit statute evinces federalism concerns. While preclusion rules limit all courts (within a state, between states, and between state and federal systems) from second-guessing prior court decisions, *Rooker-Feldman* only acts to curtail federal district court jurisdiction. *Rooker-Feldman* is federal law. A state's

---

113. A similar argument prevailed in *Wisznia v. City of Albuquerque,* 2005 WL 1400385 (10th Cir. 2005), where the Tenth Circuit held that removal by a municipal defendant constituted a waiver of its res judicata defense.

114. This discussion draws heavily from JUERGENSMEYER & ROBERTS, LAND USE PLANNING AND DEVELOPMENT, *supra* note 97, § 10.28.

115. *See* Rooker v. Fidelity Trust Co., 263 U.S. 413 (1923), and District of Columbia Court of Appeals v. Feldman, 460 U.S. 462 (1983).

116. *Rooker,* 263 U.S. at 414.

117. *Feldman,* 460 U.S. at 486.

118. Rooker v. Fidelity Trust Co., 263 U.S. 413, 425 (1923).

119. Snider v. City of Excelsior Springs, 154 F.3d 809, 811 (8th Cir. 1998).

120. U.S. v. Owens, 54 F.3d 271, 274 (6th Cir. 1995).

121. Suzanna Sherry, *Judicial Federalism in the Trenches: The* Rooker-Feldman *Doctrine in Action,* 74 NOTRE DAME L. REV. 1085, 1101 (1999).

law of preclusion may not apply to bar a case, but a district court should nonetheless dismiss the case if it were asked to hear issues "inextricably intertwined" with issues already decided by a state court.

Rooker-Feldman goes to the subject matter jurisdiction of the district court and, thus, "may be raised at any time by either party or sua sponte by the court . . . [and] in that respect, it is quite unlike the affirmative and waivable defenses of collateral estoppel or res judicata."[122] The *Rooker-Feldman* determination of jurisdiction based on federal law comes first; and, if jurisdiction exists, res judicata or collateral estoppel may follow as an affirmative defense.[123] What *Rooker-Feldman* does not bar, preclusion doctrines may.[124]

Rooker-Feldman differs from abstention as well. The most frequently invoked rule of abstention, *Younger v. Harris*,[125] requires that the state proceeding be pending and that the matter involve important state interests. Neither requirement applies to *Rooker-Feldman.*

Hill v. Town of Conway[126] exemplifies *Rooker-Feldman*'s use in takings litigation.[127] There, the Second Circuit upheld the dismissal of a takings claim on the basis of *Rooker-Feldman.* The landowners had filed a subdivision plat that depicted a road. After the project was built, the town maintained the road. Then, the town filed a declaration taking the road with the state Board of Tax and Land Appeals. The board allowed the take but awarded no damages. The landowners filed two state lawsuits. One challenged the propriety of the taking. The other sought a reassessment of the damages. The landowners lost both cases. In the first case, the court held that the filing of the plat constituted a voluntary dedication of the road to the public and, alternatively, that the maintenance performed on the road resulted in dedication. The state supreme court summarily affirmed the trial court.

---

122. Moccio v. New York, 95 F.3d 195, 198 (2d Cir. 1996).

123. Long v. Shorebank Development Corp., 182 F.3d 548, 553 (7th Cir. 1999); Fayyumi v. City of Hickory Hills, 18 F. Supp. 2d 909 (N.D. Ill. 1998).

124. Fayyumi v. City of Hickory Hills, 18 F. Supp. 2d 909 (N.D. Ill. 1998).

125. 401 U.S. 37 (1971). Other abstention doctrines such as *Pullman* and *Burford* deal with matters of state law that have not been the subject of state litigation. *Colorado River,* like *Younger,* relates to ongoing proceedings. *See* Juergensmeyer & Roberts, Land Use Planning and Development, *supra*, note 97, § 10.27.

126. 193 F.3d 33 (2d Cir. 1999). For other applications, *see* Manufactured Home Communities Inc. v. City of San Jose, 420 F.3d 1022 (9th Cir. 2005); Shooting Point, L.L.C. v. Cumming, 368 F.3d 379 (4th Cir. 2004).

127. Disagreement exists with respect to the application of *Rooker-Feldman* to a federal challenge to local government conduct alleged to violate due process and equal protection, where the state court has already found the conduct appropriate. While several courts have applied *Rooker-Feldman* to such cases, the Seventh Circuit has rejected its use.

In the second case as to damages, the trial court held that the plaintiffs were barred from relitigating the issue of the first case, that is, whether a dedication had occurred. The court then found that damages were not due to one who dedicated a road. The state court rejected landowners' reliance on *Dolan v. City of Tigard*,[128] finding that dedication in *Dolan* was not voluntary. The state supreme court refused review.

Rather than seeking U.S. Supreme Court review of the state court judgment,[129] the landowners commenced suit in federal district court, seeking compensation for the taking of the road on the basis of *Dolan*. Since the relief requested in the federal action, if granted, would effectively void the state judgment, the Second Circuit held that the district court was barred from hearing the claim for compensation under the doctrine of *Rooker-Feldman*.[130]

Rooker-Feldman does not apply if the federal plaintiff lacked an opportunity to raise the federal issue in state court. Thus, in *Agripost, Inc. v. Miami-Dade County*,[131] the county revoked a waste disposal facility's permit due to neighbor complaints about noxious odors that the plant emitted. The permit revocation was appealed to a three-judge panel of the state circuit court, which affirmed based on findings that Agripost had breached its permit conditions. The state court of appeal refused review. Then Agripost filed a takings claim in federal court. The county sought dismissal on the basis of *Rooker-Feldman*, or in the alternative, on preclusion grounds. The district court rejected the applicability of either, and on its own initiative, dismissed the case as unripe since Agripost had not sought compensation from the state court.

The county appealed to the Eleventh Circuit, which affirmed the district court. *Rooker-Feldman* did not apply, since the plaintiff could not have raised the takings issue in the state circuit court, which, due to the procedural posture in which the case came to it, lacked authority to decide it.[132] The state circuit court was only to decide the validity of the permit revocation. While the state court decided the revocation was proper under state law, the Eleventh Circuit noted that it was still possible that the revocation had rendered the plaintiff's land worthless and might therefore be a taking. But,

---

128. 512 U.S. 374 (1994).

129. The state supreme court's denial of review was not appealable, but the state trial decision was.

130. *See also* Snider v. City of Excelsior Springs, 154 F.3d 809 (8th Cir. 1998) (federal plaintiffs could not challenge in federal court the result of state condemnation action).

131. 195 F.3d 1225 (11th Cir. 1999), *cert. denied,* 531 U.S. 815 (2000).

132. *Id.* at 1231.

that issue had not been before the state court. In *Rooker-Feldman* terms, the federal court is barred from hearing a matter where its judgment would contradict a prior state court ruling. Here, a finding of no economic value would not have been at odds with what the state court had found.

As the Eleventh Circuit opinion in *Agripost* indicates, if the takings issue was not—or could not have been—litigated in state court, the takings claim must still be dismissed by the federal court, but on *Williamson County*'s state compensation rule rather than *Rooker-Feldman* grounds. That, however, does not mean that the landowner can return to federal court after the litigation takes place in state court. At that point, a return to federal court will be barred by either *Rooker-Feldman* or preclusion.

F. Abstention

The exercise of abstention may frustrate one who seeks to challenge a local land use action in federal court.[133] While the Supreme Court says that "[a]bstention from the exercise of federal jurisdiction is the exception, not the rule,"[134] and that "abstention rarely should be invoked,"[135] lower federal courts have used the *Pullman*, *Burford*, *Younger*, and *Colorado River* doctrines to abstain from adjudicating § 1983 claims in the land use area fairly often.[136]

Under the *Pullman* abstention doctrine,[137] a federal district court may refrain from deciding constitutional questions that hinge on difficult state law issues, if a constitutional ruling would be avoided by resolution in state court of those state issues. When a federal court invokes the *Pullman* abstention doctrine, the federal action is not dismissed. Rather, it is stayed pending decision in the state court of the uncertain state law issues.[138]

A number of courts relying on the *Pullman* abstention doctrine have held that adjudication of state law issues in land use cases would alleviate the necessity of addressing federal constitutional questions. In *Stallworth v. Monroeville*,[139] for example, plaintiffs challenged the validity of a rezoning denial in state court and then filed suit in federal court alleging violations of

---

133. This discussion draws heavily from JUERGENSMEYER & ROBERTS, LAND USE PLANNING AND DEVELOPMENT, *supra* note 97, §10.27.

134. Colorado River Water Conserv. Dist. v. United States, 424 U.S. 800 (1976).

135. Ankenbrandt v. Richards, 504 U.S. 689, 705 (1992).

136. *See, e.g.,* Aaron v. Target Corp., 357 F.3d 768 (8th Cir. 2004); Esso Standard Oil Co. v. Cotto, 389 F.3d 212 (1st Cir. 2004); Habich v. City of Dearborn, 331 F.3d 524 (6th Cir. 2003).

137. Railroad Commission of Texas v. Pullman Co., 312 U.S. 496 (1941).

138. England v. Louisiana State Board of Medical Examiners, 375 U.S. 411, 422 (1964).

139. 426 F. Supp. 236 (S.D. Ala. 1976).

their Fifth and Fourteenth Amendment rights. The federal court, however, refused to hear the case, invoking the abstention doctrine. The court noted that zoning questions are "uniquely of local import" and that state courts are familiar with local law and factual nuances.[140] The court further said that the interpretation of state statutes is a matter of state law and that the state courts had not yet fully addressed the statutes in question. Where it is clear that no state law interpretation would eliminate the need to address the federal constitutional questions, *Pullman* abstention is inappropriate.[141]

Under *Burford* abstention, a federal court may decline to hear a case where a federal decision of the case would risk interfering with complex state regulatory schemes concerning important state policies for which expeditious and adequate judicial review is afforded in state courts.[142] *Burford* abstention is appropriate only "where relief being sought is equitable or otherwise discretionary."[143] Under *Burford*, plaintiffs are not able to preserve their right to return to federal court once a decision has been rendered at the state level. Rather, the federal action is dismissed.[144]

Courts differ over what comprises a complex regulatory scheme in land use cases for the purposes of *Burford* abstention. The Eleventh Circuit holds that zoning decisions must be vested in a "single forum" to qualify.[145] The fact that an enabling act provides that a city "may" appoint a board of adjustment, as the standard act does, has also been held to reveal a lack of state interest in uniformity. In contrast, the Fourth Circuit says that abstention is proper if the state has a comprehensive regulatory scheme; there is no

---

140. *Id.* at 239.

141. *See, e.g.,* Neufeld v. City of Baltimore, 964 F.2d 347 (4th Cir. 1992); Gwynedd Properties, Inc. v. Lower Gwynedd Township, 970 F.2d 1195 (3d Cir. 1992); Blodgett v. Santa Cruz County, 502 F. Supp. 204 (N.D. Cal. 1980).

142. Burford v. Sun Oil Co., 319 U.S. 315 (1943).

143. Quackenbush v. Allstate Ins. Co., 517 U.S. 706 (1996).

144. MacDonald v. Village of Northport, 164 F.3d 964 (6th Cir. 1999) (*Burford* abstention proper because Michigan law provided regulatory scheme to address disputes relating to land use); Trinity Baptist Church, Inc. v. City of Asheville, 88 F. Supp. 2d 487 (W.D.N.C. 1999) (*Burford* abstention proper because plaintiff sought equitable relief); Williamson v. Guadalupe County Groundwater Conservation Dist., 343 F. Supp. 2d 580 (W.D. Tex. 2004). *But see* Habich v. City of Dearborn, 331 F.3d 524 (6th Cir. 2003) (*Burford* abstention inappropriate).

145. Nasser v. City of Homewood, 671 F.2d 432, 440 (11th Cir. 1982). *See also* International Broth. of Elec. Workers, Local Union No. 1245 v. Public Service Commission of Nevada, 614 F.2d 206 (9th Cir. 1980); and Heritage Farms, Inc. v. Solebury Township, 671 F.2d 743, 746 (3d Cir. 1982) (*Burford* abstention inappropriate where state policy on local land use regulation not based on uniformity concerns).

requirement that a specialized state agency exist to resolve zoning disputes.[146] If the *Burford* doctrine standing alone is not met, the court may apply it in combination with the *Pullman* doctrine.[147]

A third abstention doctrine comes from *Younger v. Harris*.[148] Under the *Younger* doctrine, if a parallel proceeding in a state court is pending and that proceeding involves largely the same issues as the federal proceeding, the federal court should dismiss the case. *Younger*'s goal is to avoid friction between state and federal courts. The mere pendency of a parallel state court proceeding, however, is insufficient to trigger *Younger*. Before abstaining, the court must determine that the relief sought in federal court would in some manner directly interfere with ongoing state judicial proceedings.[149] As with *Burford* abstention, the proceeding in federal court is dismissed, and the plaintiff does not retain the right to return to federal court once the state court has issued a decision.[150]

The *Younger* abstention doctrine is applied in land use cases where a pending state court proceeding involves the same issues as the federal proceeding.[151] In *Community Treatment Centers, Inc. v. City of Westland*,[152] the court, applying *Younger*, noted that it was "well-established that for abstention purposes, the enforcement and application of zoning ordinances and land-use regulations is an important state and local interest."[153] In that case, an organization sought a special use permit to operate a prerelease center for federal prisoners. When the city denied the permit, the organization sued in state court, and while that action was pending, it sued in federal court. By the time the district court ruled on the defendant's motion to dismiss, the case had been appealed to the state intermediate appellate court. Federal interference with the state proceedings was deemed inappropriate.[154]

Younger abstention has been rejected when it appears that irreparable harm will ensue. For example, one court refused to apply *Younger* abstention

---

146. Browning Ferris, Inc. v. Baltimore County, 774 F.2d 77, 80 (4th Cir. 1985).
147. *See, e.g.*, C-Y Development Company v. Redlands, 703 F.2d 375 (9th Cir. 1983).
148. 401 U.S. 37 (1971).
149. Green v. City of Tucson, 255 F.3d 1086 (9th Cir. 2001) (en banc), *cert. denied,* 533 U.S. 966 (2001).
150. Colorado River Water Conservation District v. United States, 424 U.S. 800 (1976).
151. Columbia Basin Apartment Ass'n v. City of Pasco, 268 F.3d 791 (9th Cir. 2001) (federal court was required to abstain under *Younger* since city's state court suit was pending at time federal suit was filed, and city had strong interest in its land use ordinance).
152. 970 F. Supp. 1197 (E.D. Mich. 1997).
153. *Id.* at 1223.
154. *See also* Central Avenue News, Inc. v. Minot, 651 F.2d 565 (8th Cir. 1981).

when an action was pending in state court since it found that the residents of a group home for recovering alcoholics would suffer irreparable harm if they lost their home through the state court proceeding before the federal court could act on their constitutional claim.[155] In another case, the court found that *Younger* abstention could not be invoked where a city started criminal action in state court against a plaintiff who had a federal action pending against the city in which the district court had already held an evidentiary hearing.[156]

IV. TAKINGS CLASSIFICATIONS

A substantial body of law covers the takings issue, and the discussion of this complex area, by necessity, is compressed. Other sources are available when detailed analysis is needed.[157] The goal here is limited to setting a framework for analysis of takings issues. The first question to ask is whether the government conduct promotes a public use. If it does, then compensation may be sought under one of the four theories listed in *Lingle*.

In *Lingle v. Chevron USA, Inc.*,[158] the Supreme Court, after rejecting the use of the substantially advances due process test in takings claim, succinctly set out four possible claims:

> [W]e reaffirm that a plaintiff seeking to challenge a government regulation as an uncompensated taking of private property may proceed . . . by alleging a "physical" taking, a *Lucas*-type "total regulatory taking," a *Penn Central* taking, or a land-use exaction violating the standards set forth in *Nollan* and *Dolan*.[159]

A. Public Use or Public Purpose

In *Kelo v. City of New London*,[160] the Supreme Court affirmed long-standing precedent that interprets the phrase "public use" broadly to include public purpose. Use by the public is not necessary. In *Kelo*, the Court upheld a condemnation of private homes even though the government would lease the land taken to private persons. The goal of promoting economic develop-

---

155. Sullivan v. City of Pittsburgh, 811 F.2d 171 (3d Cir. 1987), *cert. denied,* 484 U.S. 849 (1987) (alternative holding).
156. For Your Eyes Alone, Inc. v. City of Columbus, 281 F.3d 1209 (11th Cir. 2002).
157. *See* listing in Part VI of this chapter.
158. 125 S. Ct. 2074 (2005).
159. 125 S. Ct. at 2087.
160. 125 S. Ct. 2655 (2005).

ment for taxes and jobs is a valid pubic purpose. In *Hawaii Housing Authority v. Midkiff*,[161] the Court said that a purely private taking is impermissible, but the Court went on to make it clear that low-level rational basis scrutiny is to be applied to challenges that the government's use is private. *Kelo*, elucidating on *Midkiff*, says that a one-to-one transfer of property to an identifiable person solely for the reason that the latter party may put the land to a more productive use would be "suspicious."[162] Presumably, in such a case, meaningful rational basis scrutiny would apply.[163]

An action lies in federal court under § 1983 to enjoin a taking for a private use.[164] The *Williamson County* requirement that compensation be sought in state court is not applicable to such a claim.[165] If, however, there is an ongoing state court condemnation action, a federal court may abstain.[166] If an illegal or private taking is found, it is unclear what remedy lies beyond an injunction. Compensation, it would seem, cannot be awarded because the compensation clause is triggered when taking for a public use. Where a court finds government action is for a private use, it cannot cure the illegality by awarding compensation. In such a case, the appropriate remedy may be damages under the due process clause.[167]

B. Physical Takings Claims

In *Loretto v. Teleprompter Manhattan CATV Corp.*,[168] the Court established a per se takings test for physical invasions. A cable company under city authority installed a small box on the roof of an apartment building and ran cable wires down its side. The purpose was to make cable television, as an educational medium, available to tenants. The owner-landlord alleged the invasion was a taking. Though the intrusion was minor, the Court held that a permanent physical occupation of property by the state or a third party pursuant to state authority is a taking, regardless of the scope or economic impact of the intrusion.

---

161. 467 U.S. 229 (1984).

162. 125 S. Ct. 2655, 2667.

163. *Id.* at 2670 (Kennedy, J., concurring).

164. Daniels v. Area Plan Comm'n of Allen County, 306 F.3d 445 (7th Cir. 2002); Montgomery v. Carter County, 226 F.3d 758, 766–67 (6th Cir. 2000).

165. Montgomery v. Carter County, 226 F.3d 758, 766–67 (6th Cir. 2000); Samaad v. City of Dallas, 940 F.2d 925 (5th Cir. 1991).

166. Aaron v. Target Corp., 357 F.3d 768 (8th Cir. 2004).

167. Wheeler v. City of Pleasant Grove, 833 F.2d 267 (11th Cir. 1987). *See also* San Diego Gas & Electric Co. v. San Diego, 450 U.S. 621, 656 n.23 (1981).

168. 458 U.S. 419 (1982).

The ruling was "narrow."[169] Temporary physical invasions were exempted from the per se test. Two cases the Court had previously decided afforded examples; one was the imposition of a navigational servitude on a once nonnavigable pond, made navigable with government permission. The servitude allowed public use of the pond.[170] The other involved a state law that required shopping center owners to allow third parties to exercise speech and petitioning rights. Though physical invasions resulted, they were temporary. Such invasions are not permanent and therefore are not per se takings, but are judged by the Court's *Penn Central* multifactor balancing test.[171]

In all but one instance, the Court has kept its word and construed *Loretto* narrowly.[172] The exception was the case of *Nollan v. California Coastal Commission*,[173] where the Court said that a state-required public easement along an otherwise private beachfront, allowing the public to pass "to and fro" was permanent for the purposes of *Loretto* even though it did not allow people to station themselves permanently on the land. Thus, a classic right-of-way easement to pass back and forth is permanent for purposes of the rule of *Loretto*.

While expanding *Loretto*'s definition of "permanent" in favor of property owners, a second aspect of *Nollan* acknowledged an important exception favoring government. Interpreted literally, *Loretto* raised the specter that conditions imposed in the permitting process that resulted in physical occupations, such as subdivision exactions of land for schools or roads, were per se takings. The Court, however, said that requiring the easement as a condition for issuing a land use permit would avoid the conclusion that a taking had occurred if the state could show that a nexus existed between the effects of the landowner's proposed development and the land that was being exacted for easement use.

---

169. 458 U.S. at 441. *See* Echevarrieta v. City of Rancho Palos Verdes, 103 Cal. Rptr. 2d 165 (Cal. App.), *cert. denied,* 534 U.S. 950 (2001) (ordinance that requires landowner to remove trees blocking neighbor's view, and allows state to remove if landowner refuses, is not a physical taking). *See also* Stearns Co. v. United States, 396 F.3d 1354 (Fed. Cir. 2005) ("incredible attempt to transform a regulatory taking into a per se taking" under Surface Mining Control and Reclamation Act (SMCRA)).

170. Kaiser Aetna v. United States, 444 U.S. 164 (1979).

171. Penn Central Transportation Co. v. City of New York, 438 U.S. 104 (1978), discussed *infra* at Part IV(H).

172. *See* Yee v. City of Escondido, 503 U.S. 519 (1992).

173. 483 U.S. 825 (1987).

C. *Nollan*'s Nexus and *Dolan*'s Proportionality Tests

Taking the fourth type of claim from the *Lingle* list next, since it follows and relates to the first type of claim, the Court refers to land use exactions that are assessed for their qualitative and quantitative acceptability under *Nollan* and *Dolan.* In *Nollan v. California Coastal Commission*,[174] discussed immediately above, the state defended its easement requirement, arguing it was to protect the public's ability to see the beach from the street, to prevent congestion on the beach, and to overcome psychological barriers to the use of the beach resulting from increased shoreline development. The Court had no quarrel with the legitimacy of the state's goals, but disagreed that the lateral access easement along the beachfront would promote them. Employing heightened scrutiny, the Court found the interests asserted by the state would not have been substantially advanced[175] by the easement sought. The aim of the nexus search of *Nollan* is to find a justification for singling out a property owner to contribute land for public use. When the state conditions development permission on the owner dedicating property to public use, it may do so only without paying compensation if the dedicated land is "reasonably necessary"[176] to prevent or counteract anticipated adverse public effects of the proposed development.

In *Dolan v. City of Tigard*,[177] the Court held that even if a causal connection between the adverse impact of the development project and the condition is established (the *Nollan* requirement), it still must be shown that the amount exacted is proportional to the harm. In *Dolan*, the owner of a plumbing and electric supply store sought a permit to double the store's size and pave the parking lot. For flood control reasons, the city required the owner to convey to it an affirmative easement on the portion of the lot lying within the 100-year-old floodplain adjacent to a creek and an easement on an additional 15-foot strip of land for a pedestrian and bicycle path.

---

174. 483 U.S. 825 (1987).

175. *Nollan* requires the law to "substantially advance a legitimate state interest," and the Court emphasized the word "substantially" to make it clear that low-level, rational basis scrutiny is insufficient to test the strength of the nexus. While the Court discarded the "substantially advances" test in *Lingle v. Chevron,* 125 S. Ct. 2074 (2005), it reaffirmed the *Nollan* nexus test; there is no reason to believe that anything less than a form of heightened scrutiny (either intermediate, or at least so-called rational basis with a bite) applies to physical exactions.

176. 483 U.S. at 834.

177. 512 U.S. 374 (1994).

The *Dolan* Court held the exactions were not proportional to the harm. The *Dolan* Court agreed that the paving of the parking lot would increase stormwater runoff and exacerbate flooding problems, justifying the city in requiring some mitigation response by the owner. It was not clear to the Court, however, why the city asked for an easement permitting the public to use *Dolan*'s floodplain land. Physical access did not seem necessary to control floods. The Court also agreed that the store's expansion might lead to more traffic, so that asking the owner to help the city cope with traffic problems made sense. Yet, the city had found only that the pedestrian/bicycle pathway *could* offset this increased demand. That was not good enough for the Court. The city needed to quantify the traffic increase, at least in some general way, to show that the pathway *would* offset some of the traffic.

Dolan adopts what it calls a rule of "rough proportionality."[178] While the burden is on the government to show a degree of connection, the Court does not demand a "precise mathematical calculation, but [rather] some sort of individualized determination that the required dedication is related both in nature and extent to the impact of the proposed development."[179]

Nollan spoke of requiring that the law "substantially advance a legitimate state interest," and in *Lingle v. Chevron, USA Inc.*,[180] the Court discarded the "substantially advances" test of *Agins v. City of Tiburon*.[181] However, the *Lingle* opinion distinguished *Nollan and Dolan*:

> [W]hile the Court drew upon the language of *Agins* in [*Nollan* and *Dolan*], it did not apply the "substantially advances" test that is the subject of today's decision. Both *Nollan* and *Dolan* involved Fifth Amendment takings challenges to adjudicative land-use exactions—specifically, government demands that a landowner dedicate an easement allowing public access to her property as a condition of obtaining a development permit. . . .
>
> . . . *Nollan* and *Dolan* both involved dedications of property so onerous that, outside the exactions context, they would be deemed *per se* physical takings. In neither case did the Court question whether the exaction would substantially advance *some* legitimate state interest. . . . Rather, the issue was whether the exactions substantially advanced the *same* interests that land-use authorities

178. *Id.* at 391.
179. *Id.* at 395.
180. 125 S. Ct. 2074 (2005). *See* discussion, *infra,* and at subsection H.
181. 447 U.S. 255 (1980).

> asserted would allow them to deny the permit altogether. As the Court explained in *Dolan*, these cases involve a special application of the "doctrine of 'unconstitutional conditions,'" which provides that "the government may not require a person to give up a constitutional right—here the right to receive just compensation when property is taken for a public use—in exchange for a discretionary benefit conferred by the government where the benefit has little or no relationship to the property.[182]

The Court applies heightened scrutiny[183] in *Nollan* and *Dolan* to adjudicative land use exactions. As Chief Justice Rehnquist said in *Dolan*, the burden is on a challenger to prove the invalidity of a generally applicable law, but where an adjudicative decision is made, the burden switches to the government.[184] Where property owners must bargain on a case-by-case basis, in what is essentially an adjudicatory setting, the safeguards of the open legislative process are lost, and concern arises that the individual may be compelled to give more than a fair share.

Taking their cue from *Dolan*'s emphasis on the fact that the case involved an adjudicative decision, most courts have found heightened scrutiny inapplicable to broad-based legislative conditions.[185] Where a dedication requirement is a part of legislation generally applicable to all development, courts are reluctant to review the condition with demanding scrutiny.

---

182. *Lingle,* 125 S. Ct. at 2087–87.

183. Whether the heightened scrutiny of *Nollan* and *Dolan* rises to the level of "intermediate scrutiny" in the traditional three tiers of constitutional review standards, or falls somewhere below that standard, is disputed. *See* Daniel A. Crane, Comment, *A Poor Relation? Regulatory Takings after* Dolan v. City of Tigard, 63 U. Chi. L. Rev. 199, 238, n.68 (1996). What is not disputed is that the Court rejected the lowest-level rational basis scrutiny in these cases.

184. *Dolan,* 512 U.S. at 391 n.8.

185. *See, e.g.,* Krupp v. Breckenridge Sanitation Dist., 19 P.3d 687 (Colo. 2001); Home Builders Ass'n of Central Arizona v. City of Scottsdale, 187 Ariz. 479, 930 P.2d 993 (1997), *cert. denied,* 521 U.S. 1120 (1997) (finding *Dolan* not applicable to a uniform legislative fee). For a complete listing, *see* Juergensmeyer & Roberts, Land Use Planning and Development, *supra*, note 97, § 10.5 n.15. A few courts take the position that heightened scrutiny applies to legislative as well as adjudicative acts. Home Builders Ass'n of Dayton & Miami Valley v. Beavercreek, 89 Ohio St.3d 121, 729 N.E.2d 349 (2000) (impact fees); Northern Illinois Home Builders Ass'n, Inc. v. County of DuPage, 165 Ill.2d 25, 649 N.E.2d 384 (1995) (applies to legislative road impact fee, but fee held valid).

Opinions differ over whether the heightened scrutiny of *Nollan* and *Dolan* applies in contexts other than permanent physical invasions, such as impact fees.[186] The Court has held that such scrutiny does not apply to mere regulatory denials.[187] *Lingle*'s reiteration of the rationale of *Nollan* and *Dolan* suggests they apply only to physical exactions, but that issue was not before the Court. The argument for inapplicability stresses the Court's historical concern with physical invasions and finds nothing in the opinions to justify an extension to fee cases. The argument for applicability notes the similarity of impact fees to exactions in the permitting process and finds that in both instances, the government may improperly leverage the police power to seek a benefit unrelated to the development's projected impact.

D. Non-trespassory Interference with Property

Harm from a government operation that is nuisance-like, but does not result in a physical invasion, generally is not found to be a taking. For example, in cases where noise from airplane overflights cause harm to the use of the land below, a critical fact for the courts has been whether the noise invaded the land from above. The Court found a taking in such a case in *United States v. Causby*.[188] Non-trespassory harm may be a taking if the harm is peculiar to the land and not of a community-wide nature. In *Richards v. Washington Terminal Co.*,[189] a landowner complained of injury from smoke, dust, cinders, and gases emitted from an adjoining railroad. A taking was found with respect to harm suffered from a tunnel, built by the railroad next to plaintiff's property, that used a fanning system and forced the gases and dust collected in the tunnel directly onto plaintiff's land.

E. Regulations with No Physical Invasion: *Lucas* and *Penn Central*

Likely the most frequently levied complaint in land use litigation is that government has regulated land excessively and thereby "taken" the land, for which compensation must be paid under the Fifth Amendment's takings

---

186. Finding *Nollan/Dolan* applicable to nonpossessory exactions, *see* Home Builders Ass'n of Dayton & Miami Valley v. Beavercreek, 89 Ohio St.3d 121, 729 N.E.2d 349 (2000); and Finding *Nollan/Dolan* not applicable, *see* Krupp v. Breckenridge Sanitation Dist.,19 P.3d 687 (Colo. 2001). For a complete listing, *see* JUERGENSMEYER & ROBERTS, LAND USE PLANNING AND DEVELOPMENT, *supra* note 97, § 10.5 n.23.
187. City of Monterey v. Del Monte Dunes, 526 U.S. 687, 703 (1999).
188. 328 U.S. 256 (1946).
189. 233 U.S. 546 (1914).

clause. The authors of the Fifth Amendment intended to require compensation only for physical expropriations of property.[190] The Court, however, as Chief Justice Rehnquist has said, does "not . . . read [the takings clause] literally."[191] The word "take" is read to include "excessively regulate" (nota bene: not simply regulate) or, in the classic phrase of Justice Holmes in *Pennsylvania Coal v. Mahon*, when a regulation goes "too far." The limitation on the liberal reading of the word "taking" is that a regulation be so severe that it is treated as the functional equivalent of a physical seizure.

The touchstone for deciding when a regulation constitutes a taking is what the Court sees as the clause's purpose: to prevent government "from forcing some people to alone bear public burdens which, in all fairness and justice, should be borne by the public as a whole."[192]

F. In the Beginning: *Pennsylvania Coal v. Mahon*

The Court's expansion of the takings clause to include regulations is generally viewed as having arisen in the 1922 decision, *Pennsylvania Coal v. Mahon*.[193] A Pennsylvania statute prohibited mining beneath residential areas in such a way as to cause mine subsidence. The coal company claimed that the statute was an unconstitutional taking of mineral rights since the statute effectively prohibited it from excavating the coal that the company had expressly reserved to itself in conveying the land to the Mahons' predecessor in title. The Court agreed with the coal company. Justice Holmes considered the issue a "question of degree," and warned that "[w]e are in danger of forgetting that a strong public desire to improve the public condition is not enough to warrant achieving the desire by a shorter cut than the constitutional way of paying for the change." The famous, or perhaps infamous, test he established was that "while property may be regulated to a certain extent, if regulation goes too far it will be recognized as a taking."[194] In this case the statute went too far, since it made it commercially impracticable to mine certain coal that had been expressly reserved by contract to advance a purpose that Holmes regarded as predominantly private in nature.

The next important regulatory takings decision, which yielded the test most often applied today, was *Penn Central Transportation Co. v. New York*

190. *See* Lucas v. South Carolina Coastal Council, 505 U.S. 1003, 1015 n.15 (1992).

191. Penn Central Transportation Co. v. New York City, 438 U.S. 104, 142 (1978) (Rehnquist, J., dissenting).

192. Armstrong v. United States, 364 U.S. 40, 49 (1960).

193. 260 U.S. 393 (1922).

194. *Id.* at 416.

City,[195] coming in 1978, more than fifty years after *Pennsylvania Coal*. New York City declared Grand Central Station a historic landmark, requiring the owner to seek municipal permission to make changes in the structure. After the designation, Penn Central leased the airspace above the station to a developer who planned to build a fifty-five-story office complex. When the railroad and its lessees sought a certificate of appropriateness from the city's landmark commission, permission was denied with the uncharitable characterization that the proposed tower was an "aesthetic joke." The railroad claimed that its inability to build in the airspace was a taking.

The Court admitted that the takings issue was "a problem of considerable difficulty," and that there was no "'set formula' for determining when 'justice and fairness' require that economic injuries caused by public action be compensated by the government, rather than remain disproportionately concentrated on a few persons."[196] While the Court admitted the test involved "essentially ad hoc, factual inquiries,"[197] it listed three factors for consideration: (1) the economic impact on the claimant; (2) the extent to which the regulation interfered with investment-backed expectations; and (3) the character or extent of the government action.[198]

In weighing these factors, the Court held that the historic preservation ordinance was not a taking because it left the station exactly as it had been, it did not amount to a physical invasion of the property, and it did not interfere with the original investment-backed expectations of the owners. The railroad argued that a total loss of use had occurred by focusing on the airspace alone. The Court, however, said the relevant measure was the whole parcel, and with respect to it, the record showed that the railroad was able to earn a reasonable return under its present use. The Court also said there was no proof of loss of all airspace. A smaller tower might be approved, and the transferable development rights available to the station owner mitigated the loss.[199]

While *Penn Central*'s ad hoc test can be faulted for lack of precision and predictability, the Court made matters worse in *Agins v. City of Tiburon*,[200] where it held that an ordinance designed to preserve open space did not constitute a facial taking of five acres of unimproved land by limiting the owner to building from one to five houses. In its general statement

195. 438 U.S. 104 (1978).
196. *Id.* at 124.
197. *Id.*
198. *Id.*
199. *Id.* at 137.
200. 447 U.S. 255 (1980).

of takings principles, the *Agins* Court said that "[t]he application of a general zoning law to particular property effects a taking if the ordinance does not substantially advance legitimate state interests [citing *Nectow v. City of Cambridge*], or denies an owner economically viable use of his land [citing *Penn Central*]."[201] The Court added that "[a]lthough no precise rule determines when property has been taken . . ., the question necessarily requires a weighing of private and public interests."[202] The problem with the test is the first prong, which was not a takings test. It was a substantive due process test. The Court's citation to *Nectow*, a substantive due process case from 1928, suggests the Court was not conscious of its error.

In 2005, the Court renounced the "substantially advances" test of *Agins* in *Lingle v. Chevron, USA Inc.*[203] The Court frankly conceded the test had been lifted improperly from a substantive due process case where government conduct was challenged as arbitrary. In contrast, a regulatory takings claim admits that a law advances a legitimate state goal, but claims that compensation is due because the economic impact of the otherwise valid regulation is too severe. The substantially advances test survives *Lingle*, but its place is the due process clause. In addition to clarifying the doctrinal foundation of regulatory takings, *Lingle*'s holding is significant because property owners, hoping for *Nollan*-like heightened scrutiny, are now left with a Fourteenth Amendment claim and low-level, rational basis scrutiny.

G. *Lucas* and Total Deprivation of Value or Use Claims

In 1992, the Supreme Court established a categorical rule for economic impact cases in *Lucas v. South Carolina Coastal Council.*[204] The owner of two beachfront lots was unable to build due to the application of a setback rule adopted to deter sand-dune loss and beach erosion. Accepting the state trial court's finding that the lots subject to the regulation were valueless, the Court held that where a regulation deprives real property of all economically viable use, a taking occurs unless the state can prove that the regulation does no more to restrict use than what the state courts could do under background principles of property law or the law of private or public nuisance.

Lucas was successful in his case, due to the finding that his land was "valueless"; but, since that is an unusual regulatory effect, *Lucas* claims are rarely successful. To take advantage of the *Lucas* categorical rule, one must

---

201. *Id.* at 260.
202. 447 U.S. 255, 260 (1980).
203. 125 S. Ct. 2074 (2005).
204. 505 U.S. 1003 (1992).

show a deprivation of all economically viable use, and "all" means 100% or something very close to it. In *Palazzolo v. Rhode Island*,[205] the Court rejected the argument that a 93.7% diminution in value was a categorical taking. It is unusual for a regulation to go that far.

The most important factor in determining the degree of loss is the unit of property against which the affected property is measured. The Court has held on several occasions in various contexts that the loss is not measured against the affected part of the land, but rather by reference to the whole parcel. This stance is often outcome determinative. In *Penn Central*, 100% of the airspace above Grand Central Station was "taken," but the Court said "'[t]aking' jurisprudence does not divide a single parcel into discrete segments, [but] focuses on the nature and extent of the interference in the parcel as a whole."[206] Viewing the whole parcel, the loss of the airspace still left the railroad with a reasonable use of the existing building. In *Palazzolo*, 100% of the landowners' eighteen acres of wetlands were affected, but he had two adjacent buildable acres. The economic loss using all his acreage was 93.7%, and not a total taking under *Lucas*. In *Tahoe-Sierra Preservation Council, Inc. v. Tahoe Regional Planning Agency*,[207] the Court rejected so-called temporal segmentation, holding that a moratorium period, when no development is permitted, cannot be viewed alone but must be coupled with the future use of the property after the moratorium is lifted.

The "whole parcel" rule ought not to be seen as rigid, since flexible, ad hoc determinations, not rigidity, describe the Court's approach in takings cases. As the *Lucas* Court said, the question may be answered by examining "how the owner's reasonable expectations have been shaped by the State's law of property, that is, whether and to what degree the State's law has accorded legal recognition and protection to the particular interest in land."[208] While using a broad measure of the relevant parcel is the clear tendency of the courts, it is not a foregone conclusion that such will always be the case.

A second reason *Lucas* claims may fail is a successful defense by the government that background principles of state property or nuisance law justify the total restriction. For example, the Colorado Supreme Court held that its doctrine of nuisance law could preclude the spread of radioactive contamination,[209] and the Federal Circuit has found that the federal naviga-

---

205. 533 U.S. 606 (2001).

206. 438 U.S. at 130.

207. 535 U.S. 302 (2002). *See also* Sartori v. United States, 67 Fed. Cl. 263 (2005).

208. Lucas v. South Carolina Coastal Council, 505 U.S. 1003, 1016 n.7 (1992).

209. State v. The Mill, 887 P.2d 993 (Colo. 1994).

tion servitude is a background principle under *Lucas*.[210] State courts have differed, as they presumably are entitled to do, on whether filling wetlands violates their background principles.[211]

H. *Penn Central:* The Multifactor, Ad Hoc Test for Partial Economic Deprivations

If a regulation's economic effect is less than total, the *Penn Central* multifactor test is used to determine whether a taking has occurred.[212] Under *Penn Central*, as discussed above, economic impact is but one factor to consider. Other factors include the extent to which the regulation interfered with investment-backed expectations and the character or extent of the government action.

Other than where the value taken is total, mere diminution in value plays a role; but standing alone, it does not result in a taking. For example, in *Palazzolo*, the loss was 93.7%, causing the Supreme Court to reject a *Lucas* claim, saying the claim should be decided under *Penn Central*. In *Tahoe-Sierra Preservation Council, Inc. v. Tahoe Regional Planning Agency*,[213] the Court rejected the applicability of the *Lucas* test to a moratorium period, since the economic loss was not total when the future use of the property is considered. *Penn Central* was the test to use, said the Court. Another court, comparing *Lucas* and *Penn Central*, concluded that the latter provides "an avenue of redress for a landowner whose property retains value that is slightly greater than de minimis, . . . [but] it is apparent that the level of interference must be very high."[214]

The character or extent of the governmental action factor requires an assessment of the "purpose and importance of the public interest,"[215] which

---

210. Palm Beach Isles Assocs. v. United States, 208 F.3d 1374 (Fed. Cir. 2000). *See also* John R. Sand & Gravel Co. v. United States, 62 Fed. Cl. 556 (Fed. Cl. 2004) (background principles of nuisance and environmental law preclude mining).

211. *Compare* K & K Const., Inc. v. Department of Natural Resources, 217 Mich.App. 56, 551 N.W.2d 413 (1996) (state constitutional declaration regarding conservation of natural resources not a principle of property law, reversed on other grounds, 456 Mich. 570, 575 N.W.2d 531 (1998), *cert. denied,* 525 U.S. 819 (1998)) *with* Palazzolo v. Rhode Island, 533 U.S. 606 (2001).

212. Palazzolo v. Rhode Island, 533 U.S. 606 (2001).

213. 535 U.S. 302 (2002).

214. Animas Valley Sand and Gravel, Inc. v. Bd. of County Commissioners, 38 P.3d 59 (Colo. 2001).

215. Loveladies Harbor, Inc. v. United States, 28 F.3d 1171, 1176 (Fed. Cir. 1994).

then must be weighed against the loss.[216] Under the categorical takings rules of *Loretto* and *Lucas*, an inquiry into the public interest advanced by the regulation arises only by way of defense.[217] With partial economic deprivation cases, the inquiry into the public interest occurs as part of the case in chief, and the burden of proof is on the property owner.[218] Measuring the strength of the public interest presumes that "not all police power values are equal."[219] A health and safety concern should carry more weight than an aesthetic-based control.

Another factor from *Penn Central* is the degree of interference with investment-backed expectations. The term "investment-backed expectations" has not been further defined, but some guidance as to its meaning can be gleaned from the Court's applications. In *Penn Central*, the Supreme Court found that the railroad's belief that it could use the airspace above the railroad terminal did not qualify as a "distinct investment-backed expectation." It was sufficient for takings purposes, held the Court, that the railroad's primary expectation of using Grand Central Station as a railroad terminal and office building, established by sixty-five years of use, was unaffected by the landmark designation.

In *Pennsylvania Coal*, expectations played a role where the state's anti-subsidence statute abrogated an express contractual reservation of the right to remove coal free from liability for damage to the surface. The fact that *Pennsylvania Coal* was a private dispute where the surface owner bought the land with notice of the prior severance of the mineral rights suggests a high degree of expectation, on both sides to the contract, that the coal could be removed without liability for surface damage.[220]

Under *Palazzolo v. Rhode Island*,[221] constructive notice of the law in force upon acquisition of title, though not an automatic bar to a takings claim, is a factor in the assessment of reasonable expectations. Even where

---

216. Bernardsville Quarry, Inc. v. Borough of Bernardsville, 129 N.J. 221, 608 A.2d 1377 (1992).
217. *Loretto,* 458 U.S. at 440.
218. Florida Rock Ind., Inc. v. United States, 18 F.3d 1560 (Fed. Cir. 1994), *cert. denied,* 513 U.S. 1109 (1995).
219. John J. Costonis, *Presumptive and Per Se Takings: A Decisional Model for the Taking Issue,* 58 N.Y.U. L. Rev. 465, 499 (1983).
220. Frank I. Michelman, *Property, Utility, and Fairness: Comments on the Ethical Foundations of "Just Compensation" Law,* 80 Harv. L. Rev. 1165, 1212 (1967).
221. 533 U.S. 606 (2001).

a law does not predate acquisition of ownership, foreseeability of impending change and knowledge of the regulatory climate may so diminish expectations as to defeat a takings claim.[222]

V. OTHER CONSTITUTIONAL ISSUES

A. The Compensation Remedy

In *First English Evangelical Lutheran Church v. County of Los Angeles*,[223] the Court held that the remedy for a regulatory taking, as with a physical taking, is compensation. In so holding, the Court put to rest the long-debated issue of whether the "regulatory taking" theory used by the Court in *Pennsylvania Coal* was grounded in the Fifth Amendment's takings clause or in the Fourteenth Amendment's due process clause. Since *Pennsylvania Coal* was an injunction action between private parties, some claimed the Court's use of takings language was purely figurative.

If a taking is found, the government has the option to keep the excessive regulation in place and pay compensation on the basis of a permanent taking, or it may rescind the excessive regulation and pay only for the period of the take. Compensation is due for the period of time that the taking endured, and the beginning point in calculating compensation depends on whether the challenge is facial or as applied.[224] With a facial challenge, the date of enactment starts the compensation meter running, since by definition it is the mere enactment of the law that causes the taking. With an as-applied challenge, the enactment date does not start the meter running, because the landowner suffers no harm from enactment alone. The beginning date generally will be when the action is ripe and the statute of limitations begins to run.[225]

B. Substantive Due Process

Substantive due process limits the exercise of the police power by requiring that a land use regulation promote the health, safety, morals, or general welfare

---

222. Good v. United States, 189 F.3d 1355 (Fed. Cir. 1999), *cert. denied,* 529 U.S. 1053 (2000).

223. 482 U.S. 304 (1987).

224. *See* generally Gregory M. Stein, *Pinpointing the Beginning and Ending of a Temporary Regulatory Taking,* 70 WASH. L. REV. 953 (1995).

225. *Id.* at 960.

by a rational means.[226] It protects against arbitrary or capricious actions,[227] which "'may not take place no matter what procedural protections accompany them.'"[228] Courts used substantive due process during the heyday of the *Lochner* era in the early twentieth century to act as a kind of super-legislature to overturn progressive social and economic legislation. Most courts today articulate substantive due process as a theoretical constraint on government action; but, by according great deference to the legislative branch, they do not use it to strike down legislation unless fundamental rights are affected. Nonetheless, while usually unsuccessful, substantive due process continues to be a basis of complaint in many land use cases.

In 1926, the Supreme Court upheld a comprehensive zoning ordinance against a facial substantive due process challenge in *Village of Euclid v. Ambler Realty Co.*[229] Two years later, in *Nectow v. City of Cambridge*,[230] the Court found a zoning ordinance invalid in an as-applied case on substantive due process grounds.

The doctrine appeared again in a zoning case in 1977, *Moore v. City of East Cleveland*.[231] East Cleveland, in limiting residential use to "single families," had a complex definition of family that precluded the plaintiff from living with her son and two grandsons (who were also first cousins). In a divided opinion the Court, applying strict scrutiny, found the ordinance invalid on due process grounds. Conceding that it was reentering a "treacherous field," the Court could not endorse such an intrusion into family. *Moore* is a limited revival of substantive due process. At most, the Court is likely to use the strict scrutiny of *Moore* only when related persons are affected by a land use control.[232]

---

226. Sometimes the Court adds that the measure also cannot be unduly oppressive upon the affected class. *See* Lawton v. Steele, 152 U.S. 133 (1894). For a general discussion of substantive due process, *see* JOHN E. NOWAK & RONALD D. ROTUNDA, CONSTITUTIONAL LAW, ch. 11 (6th ed. 2000).

227. Nectow v. City of Cambridge, 277 U.S. 183 (1928); PruneYard Shopping Center v. Robins, 447 U.S. 74, 84 (1980); Village of Arlington Heights v. Metropolitan Housing Development Corp., 429 U.S. 252 (1977) (a landowner has a right to be free from arbitrary or irrational zoning actions).

228. Harris v. City of Akron, 20 F.3d 1396, 1405 (6th Cir. 1994).

229. 272 U.S. 365 (1926).

230. 277 U.S. 183 (1928).

231. 431 U.S. 494 (1977).

232. *See* Armendariz v. Penman, 75 F.3d 1311, 1318 (9th Cir. 1996).

Dating from its inception in *Pennsylvania Coal v. Mahon*,[233] the doctrine of regulatory takings has been confused with substantive due process. The statement in the 1980 case of *Agins v. City of Tiburon*[234] that an ordinance that did not substantially advance a legitimate state interest was a taking exacerbated the confusion. Under *Agins*, parties sought injunctive relief from allegedly arbitrary legislation as so-called takings. When the Ninth Circuit invalidated a rent control ordinance as a "taking" because it disagreed with the state legislature that the rent control ordinance would achieve its goal,[235] the Court finally stepped in. In *Lingle v. Chevron USA Inc.*,[236] objecting to the Ninth Circuit's use of heightened scrutiny to second-guess a state legislature, the Court bluntly said the *Agins* "substantially advances" test did not belong in Fifth Amendment takings jurisprudence. A challenge to legislation on the grounds that it does not substantially advance a legitimate state interest belongs in the Fourteenth Amendment where, unless it involves a fundamental right (*Moore*'s strict scrutiny), it will be reviewed under the deferential rational basis test.[237] Post-*Lingle*, one can expect the argument to be made that heightened scrutiny should be applied in substantive due process cases. This will likely be a tough sell.

Courts express the degree of deference variously, requiring that a law must "shock the conscience,"[238] or be "egregiously unacceptable,"[239] or "truly horrendous."[240] From a pure examination of the language of these formulations, it is not clear whether one standard describes conduct that is worse than the other. While one might make a substantive due process challenge, it is not wise to have high expectations. Federal courts will, on occasion, find violations of substantive due process; but usually such cases are colored by political, religious, and/or racial discrimination.[241] State courts

233. 260 U.S. 393 (1922).

234. 447 U.S. 255 (1980).

235. Chevron USA Inc. v. Cayetano, 224 F.3d 1030 (9th Cir. 2000).

236. 125 S. Ct. 2074 (2005).

237. Expect arguments asking the courts to drop deferential review under the Fourteenth Amendment.

238. Harris v. City of Akron, 20 F.3d 1396, 1401 (6th Cir. 1994).

239. United Artists Theatre Circuit, Inc. v. Township of Warrington, 316 F.3d 392 (3d Cir. 2003); Licari v. Ferruzzi, 22 F.3d 344, 347 (1st Cir. 1994).

240. Nestor Colon Medina & Sucesores, Inc. v. Custodio 964 F.2d 32, 45 (1st Cir. 1992).

241. Rarely, some involve solely economic harm. *See* JSS Realty Co., LLC v. Town of Kittery, 177 F. Supp. 2d 64 (D. Me. 2001); Elsmere Park Club Ltd. Partnership v. Town of Elsmere, 771 F. Supp. 646 (D. Del. 1991).

vary, but some are quite active in overseeing land use law through due process clauses in their state constitutions.[242] Courts that do intervene are more likely to find delaying and deceptive conduct by the government as arbitrary than to second-guess the wisdom of zoning land for a particular purpose.

The degree of deference accorded to the government may also depend on whether the challenged action is legislative or administrative. This difference is important since a court may hypothesize a rational basis for a legislative action but insist on actual proof for administrative action.[243] While courts agree that review of economic claims is deferential, some treat all zoning actions, including variances, as legislative for the purposes of reviewing the substance of an action.[244] Other courts divide acts along more traditional lines and confer less deference to administrative acts.[245] Even then, the review is described as "extremely narrow."[246]

A conflict exists among the courts as to the property interest sufficient to invoke such a claim.[247] While ownership of an interest in land is sufficient for some courts,[248] most courts require a property owner to establish a right or entitlement in a permit.[249] The latter requirement, though a majority

---

242. *See, e.g.,* Mission Springs, Inc. v. City of Spokane, 954 P.2d 250 (Wash. 1998) (improper delay); Costco Wholesale Corp. v. Orange County, 780 So.2d 198 (Fla. App. 2001), *review granted,* 791 So.2d 1100 (Fla. 2001); Orangetown v. Magee, 88 N.Y.2d 41, 643 N.Y.S.2d 21, 665 N.E.2d 1061 (1996). For a more hostile view, *see* ATC Partnership v. Town of Windham, 741 A.2d 305 (Conn. 1999), *cert. denied,* 530 U.S. 1214 (2000).

243. Shelton v. City of College Station, 780 F.2d 475, 479 (5th Cir. 1986).

244. *Id.*

245. *See* listing and discussion of cases in Pearson v. City of Grand Blanc, 961 F.2d 1211, 1220 (6th Cir. 1992).

246. *Id.*

247. *See* listing and discussion in Pearson v. City of Grand Blanc, 961 F.2d 1211, 1220 (6th Cir. 1992), characterizing the lack of uniformity as remarkable.

248. Polenz v. Parrott, 883 F.2d 551, 555 (7th Cir. 1989); DeBlasio v. Zoning Bd. of Adjustment, 53 F.3d 592 (3d Cir. 1995), *cert. denied,* 516 U.S. 937 (1995) (overruled on other grounds); *but see* Woodwind Estates, Ltd. v. Gretkowski, 205 F.3d 118 (3d Cir. 2000), where the Third Circuit finds property interest by way of the entitlement theory. *See also* American Marine Rail NJ, LLC v. City of Bayonne, 289 F. Supp. 2d 569 (D.N.J. 2003).

249. Hyde Park Co. v. Santa Fe City Council, 226 F.3d 1207 (10th Cir. 2000); Triomphe Investors v. City of Northwood, 49 F.3d 198 (6th Cir. 1995), *cert. denied,* 516 U.S. 816 (1995); Gardner v. City of Baltimore, 969 F.2d 63 (4th Cir. 1992); RRI Realty Corp. v. Incorporated Village of Southampton, 870 F.2d 911 (2d Cir. 1989).

position, is odd,[250] and the showing is difficult to make since an entitlement exists only if there is a strong likelihood or virtual assurance that the permit will be issued. If the regime vests the decision maker with discretion, there is no entitlement. Since land use permitting processes generally do confer discretion on the authorities, a developer who seeks, or needs, to establish a property right in a permit loses his case at the outset.[251] If one has no right to a permit, there is no need to determine whether the action denying it was arbitrary. Property rights in permits sometimes are found.[252]

C. Procedural Due Process

In contrast to substantive due process, which looks primarily at why a deprivation occurred, procedural due process asks how the deprivation came to be. Procedural due process rights do not attach to legislation of general applicability.[253] Thus, a critical question is whether to characterize a given land use decision as legislative or quasi-judicial.[254] If a rezoning is deemed legislative, the due process clause does not require that affected persons be given notice or a hearing.[255] Procedural due process rights attach to administrative or quasi-judicial decision making. In land use, the decisions of the various zoning boards of adjustments and planning commissions typically are viewed as administrative or quasi-judicial.[256]

---

250. The entitlement test for property stems from what were once called the Supreme Court's "new property" cases that dealt with procedural due process rights in certain government benefit programs. This new property theory is used in the land use area to shrink property rights for substantive due process purposes. *See* JUERGENSMEYER & ROBERTS, LAND USE PLANNING AND DEVELOPMENT, *supra,* note 97, § 10.12E.
251. Kelley Property Development, Inc. v. Town of Lebanon, 226 Conn. 314, 627 A.2d 909 (Conn. 1993) (one must show that the local law so narrowly circumscribes discretion that there is "a virtual assurance of approval").
252. Woodwind Estates, Ltd. v. Gretkowski, 205 F.3d 118 (3d Cir. 2000); Reserve, Ltd. v. Longboat Key, 17 F.3d 1374 (11th Cir. 1994) (a property interest in a permit after significant expenditures in reliance on governmental actions); Town of Orangetown v. Magee, 88 N.Y.2d 41, 665 N.E.2d 1061, 1068, 643 N.Y.S.2d 21, 28 (1996).
253. Bi-Metallic Inv. Co. v. State Bd. of Equalization, 239 U.S. 441 (1915). Judge Posner suggests that "'legislative due process' seems almost an oxymoron." LC & S, Inc. v. Warren County Area Plan Commission, 244 F.3d 601, 602 (7th Cir. 2001).
254. Pearson v. City of Grand Blanc, 961 F.2d 1211, 1220 (6th Cir. 1992).
255. Pro Eco, Inc. v. Bd. of Commissioners of Jay County, 57 F.3d 505. 512 (7th Cir. 1995); Jacobs, Visconsi, & Jacobs v. City of Lawrence, 927 F.2d 1111 (10th Cir. 1991).
256. *Id.*

D. Equal Protection

Equal protection complaints are made often in land use disputes since the essence of many controls, particularly Euclidean zoning, is to classify land and people. Historically, such claims, in the absence of a fundamental right or suspect class, have not fared well since the rational basis test used by the Court borders on being a rule of nonreview.[257]

An example is *Village of Belle Terre v. Boraas*,[258] where an ordinance differentiated between related and unrelated persons. It allowed only "families" to live in single-family homes and defined "family" to include any number of related persons but not more than two unrelated adults. The Court was not troubled by the law, since it saw the ordinance as merely regulating social and economic affairs and not implicating any fundamental rights of privacy or intimate association. Several state courts have refused to accept the *Belle Terre* Court's deferential posture in the context of zoning excluding unrelated persons. Applying greater scrutiny, they have invalidated such ordinances relying on state constitutional provisions of equal protection,[259] substantive due process, and privacy rights.[260]

The Supreme Court broke from its usual deferential posture in *City of Cleburne v. Cleburne Living Center, Inc.*[261] There the Court found a violation of the equal protection clause where a city zoning ordinance excluded group homes for the mentally retarded from a zone where apartment houses, fraternity and sorority houses, hospitals, and nursing homes for the aged were permitted. The Court refused to classify the mentally retarded as a "quasi-suspect" class, but nonetheless proceeded to find the ordinance invalid by examining, and refuting, the reasons the city offered for handling housing for the mentally retarded under a special classification. The Court

---

257. F.C.C. v. Beach Communications, Inc., 508 U.S. 307 (1993).

258. 416 U.S. 1 (1974).

259. Kirsch v. Prince George's County, 331 Md. 89, 626 A.2d 372 (1993) (using both federal and state constitutions to find ordinance imposing more-stringent regulations on occupancy of rental units by university students to violate equal protection); College Area Renters and Landlord Ass'n v. City of San Diego, 50 Cal. Rptr. 2d 515 (Cal. App. 1996).

260. City of Santa Barbara v. Adamson, 610 P.2d 436 (1980); New Jersey v. Baker, 81 N.J. 99, 405 A.2d 368 (1979); Charter Twp. of Delta v. Dinolfo, 351 N.W.2d 831 (Mich. 1984); Coalition Advocating Legal Housing Options v. City of Santa Monica, 105 Cal. Rptr. 2d 802 (Cal. App. 2001) (requirement that second housing unit in single-family district be occupied only by relatives or caregivers violated state constitution's right of privacy).

261. 473 U.S. 432 (1985).

said it was using the rational basis test, but it was not the "traditional" toothless test of *Belle Terre*. Justice Kennedy called it "meaningful rational basis review."[262]

The *Cleburne* opinion sparked numerous attempts by developers and others to obtain some form of heightened scrutiny. Most have been unsuccessful. Developers, asserting economic interests, have been unable to convince courts to apply *Cleburne*-like scrutiny to permit denials.[263] A shelter for battered women and a day care center were also refused such scrutiny,[264] and courts have differed over whether halfway homes for prisoners deserve more exacting scrutiny.[265] *Cleburne* scrutiny has been used to find a substantive due process violation where a palm reader was denied a permit based on the religious objections of neighbors.[266] In short, it is likely that one must be a member of a vulnerable or politically unpopular group, which is subjected to irrational fear or prejudice, in order to avail oneself of this enhanced judicial review.[267]

Where permits have been granted or denied for personal or political reasons, courts sometimes have found equal protection violations.[268] Until

---

262. Kelo v. City of New London, 125 S. Ct. 2655, 2670 (2005) (Kennedy, J., concurring); Cervantes v. Guerra, 651 F.2d 974, 982 (5th Cir. 1981) ("rationality with a bite").

263. Jacobs, Visconsi & Jacobs Co. v. City of Lawrence, 927 F.2d 1111 (10th Cir. 1991) (shopping center); Pontarelli Limousine, Inc. v. City of Chicago, 929 F.2d 339 (7th Cir. 1991) (airport livery services). *But see* Armendariz v. Penman, 75 F.3d 1311, 1326 (9th Cir. 1996).

264. Doe v. City of Butler, 892 F.2d 315 (3d Cir. 1989) (shelter case based on substantive due process but test the same); Howard v. City of Garland, 917 F.2d 898 (5th Cir. 1990) (day care).

265. Bannum v. City of St. Charles, 2 F.3d 267 (8th Cir. 1993) (no); Freedom Ranch, Inc. v. Board of Adjustment, 878 P.2d 380 (Okl. App. 1994) (no); Bannum v. City of Louisville, 958 F.2d 1354 (6th Cir. 1992) (yes).

266. Marks v. City of Chesapeake, 883 F.2d 308 (4th Cir. 1989). *See also* Love Church v. City of Evanston, 671 F. Supp. 515 (N.D. Ill. 1987) (alternative holding that treatment of religious uses did not pass deferential review).

267. *See* Powers v. Harris, 379 F.3d 1208 (10th Cir. 2004) (discussing the differences between *Cleburne*-style rational basis test and traditional rational basis test).

268. *See, e.g.,* Cordeco Development Corp. v. Santiago Vasquez, 539 F.2d 256 (1st Cir. 1976), *cert. denied,* 429 U.S. 978 (1976), where a delay in issuing permit, coupled with limitations on the permit when issued that made land worthless, was found to be a violation of equal protection where the city issued a permit to members of a politically influential family that owned neighboring land. *But see* Nestor Colon Medina & Sucesores, Inc. v. Custodio, 964 F.2d 32, 41 (1st Cir. 1992), expressing concern over use of equal protection in such cases.

recently, however, even these cases usually have failed. A potential break from this tradition came in a terse, per curiam ruling by the Supreme Court in the "class of one" *Village of Willowbrook v. Olech* case.[269] Olech sued the Village of Willowbrook, Illinois, seeking damages for the village's alleged denial of her right to equal protection. The essence of her complaint was that when she asked the village to allow her to hook her house to the public water line, the village demanded that she convey a 33-foot easement. Others similarly situated had only been asked to grant a 15-foot easement. The reason for the disparate treatment, she alleged, was that she had successfully sued the village earlier over stormwater damage and that the village, seeking revenge, was motivated by ill will.

The Court held that Olech stated an equal protection claim. It mattered not that she was a "class of one," or that she asserted no fundamental right, or that she claimed no membership in a suspect class. It was sufficient that she "alleges that she has been intentionally treated differently from others similarly situated and that there is no rational basis for the difference in treatment."[270] Though Olech had alleged that the village was motivated by ill will, the Court said the village's subjective motivation did not matter. Her complaint was sufficient without such allegation.

In a concurring opinion, Justice Breyer, worried that the Court's ruling could be read as "transforming run-of-the-mill zoning cases into cases of constitutional right,"[271] sought to limit these "class of one" cases to those involving allegations of ill will or vindictive action. While none of the other Justices joined Breyer, some lower courts have followed his view. Most notable is the Seventh Circuit, which holds that to make out a prima facie class-of-one case, a plaintiff must present evidence that "the cause of the differential treatment of which the plaintiff complains [is] a totally illegitimate animus toward the plaintiff by the defendant."[272] Some courts have taken the per curiam opinion at face value and assumed that motive is irrelevant,[273] while others have casually assumed *Olech* presents nothing new in

---

269. 528 U.S. 562 (2000).
270. 528 U.S. at 522.
271. 528 U.S. at 566.
272. Hilton v. City of Wheeling, 209 F.3d 1005, 1008 (7th Cir. 2000). *See also* Cruz v. Town of Cicero, 275 F.3d 579 (7th Cir. 2001); Albiero v. City of Kankakee, 246 F.3d 927 (7th Cir. 2001); Forseth v. Village of Sussex, 199 F.3d 363 (7th Cir. 2000).
273. City Recycling, Inc. v. State, 778 A.2d 77 (Conn. 2001). *See* Jackson v. Burke, 256 F.3d 93, 97 (2d Cir. 2001) (per curiam) (noting in dicta that proof of subjective ill will is not essential). *See* Paul D. Wilson, *What Hath* Olech *Wrought? The Equal Protection Clause in Recent Land Use Damages Litigation,* 33 URB. LAW. 729 (2001).

the way of equal protection jurisprudence[274] or have avoided the question by finding that differential treatment did not occur or that the parties were not similarly situated.[275]

Discrimination against persons on the basis of race and economic status range from the overt to the subtle. In *Buchanan v. Warley*,[276] the Court found that an ordinance that established zones on racial lines violated the due process property right of "a white man to dispose of his property to a person of color if he saw fit."[277] One is not likely to find an overt racial classification in a zoning ordinance today. The same is not true, however, with ordinances that restrict on the basis of wealth. Because racial minorities are disproportionately represented among lower-income groups, communities can practice racial exclusion simply by zoning out housing projects that cater to those of modest means. In such cases, claims of disproportionate racial impact may be made.

In the 1977 decision of *Village of Arlington Heights v. Metropolitan Housing Development Corporation*,[278] the ability to attack zoning ordinances restricting multifamily developments as racially discriminatory was dealt a major blow by the Supreme Court. There, a developer wished to build a federally subsidized public housing project on land zoned for single-family use. Arlington Heights refused to rezone the land, invoking a buffer policy that allowed multifamily zoning only when it could serve as a buffer between single-family use and industrial use. The developer, whose site did not meet that criterion, attacked the action on equal protection grounds.

The Court upheld Arlington Heights's refusal to rezone, holding that the equal protection clause requires proof of discriminatory intent rather than effect. Intent is much harder to prove than effect. Even though the failure of

---

274. Greenspring Racquet Club, Inc. v. Baltimore County, 232 F.3d 887 (4th Cir. 2000) (unpublished), *cert. denied,* 532 U.S. 957, 121 (2001); Bryan v. City of Madison, Miss., 213 F.3d 267 (5th Cir. 2000), *cert. denied,* 531 U.S. 1145 (2001).

275. Tri County Paving, Inc. v. Ashe County, 281 F.3d 430 (4th Cir. 2002); Harlen Associates v. Incorporated Village of Mineola, 273 F.3d 494 (2d Cir. 2001); Summers v. City of Raymond, 105 F. Supp. 2d 549 (S.D. Miss. 2000); McDonald's Corp. v. City of Norton Shores, 102 F. Supp. 2d 431 (W.D. Mich. 2000); American Fabricare v. Twp. of Falls, 101 F. Supp. 2d 301 (E.D. Pa. 2000); Little v. City of Oakland, 2000 WL 1336608 (N.D. Cal. 2000); Blumenthal Inv. Trusts v. City of Des Moines, 636 N.W.2d 255 (Iowa 2001). Some courts ignore *Olech. See* Vigilante v. Village of Wilmette, 88 F. Supp. 2d 888 (N.D. Ill. 2000). *See* discussion in Wilson, *What Hath* Olech *Wrought? supra,* note 273.

276. 245 U.S. 60 (1917).

277. *Id.* at 81.

278. 429 U.S. 252 (1977), *on remand,* 558 F.2d 1283 (7th Cir. 1977).

Arlington Heights to rezone would have a disproportionate impact on racial minorities, the Court held that this action could be used only as evidence of intent.

Discrimination on the basis of wealth is practiced by zoning for single-family use only (thus excluding multifamily use), precluding manufactured housing, and requiring large lots or houses so as to exclude all but the upper economic strata. These practices generally fall under the rubric of exclusionary zoning.[279] Economic discrimination effected through exclusionary zoning practices is actionable under the statutory or constitutional law of a number of states.[280] Racial discrimination in zoning can be challenged without proof of intent under the federal Fair Housing Act, where a showing of effect is sufficient to raise a prima facie case.[281]

E. First Amendment Issues Overview

Land use controls implicate rights protected by the First Amendment most frequently in the regulation of billboards and other signs, sexually oriented adult businesses, and religious uses.[282] The First Amendment right to petition the government may also be implicated in land use disputes where the government is alleged to have retaliated against those seeking zoning changes or opposing zoning changes. Generally, plaintiffs bringing retaliatory claims must allege that their conduct was constitutionally protected and that the government's retaliation was motivated by or substantially caused by their exercise of the protected conduct.[283]

1. Sign Controls

Constitutional litigation over sign regulations is of recent origin; it was not until 1976 that the Supreme Court held that the First Amendment protected

---

279. *See* JUERGENSMEYER & ROBERTS, LAND USE PLANNING AND DEVELOPMENT, *supra,* note 97, ch. 6.

280. The state approach to discriminatory zoning is best seen in the two Mt. Laurel decisions. Southern Burlington County NAACP v. Township of Mt. Laurel (Mt. Laurel I), 67 N.J. 151, 336 A.2d 713 (1975), *appeal dismissed and cert. denied,* 423 U.S. 808 (1975); Southern Burlington County NAACP v. Township of Mt. Laurel (Mt. Laurel II), 92 N.J. 158, 456 A.2d 390 (1983).

281. Huntington Branch NAACP v. Town of Huntington, 844 F.2d 926 (2d Cir. 1988).

282. *See* PROTECTING FREE SPEECH AND EXPRESSION: THE FIRST AMENDMENT AND LAND USE LAW (D. Mandelker and R. Rubin eds., 2001). For a general discussion of First Amendment issues, *see* NOWAK & ROTUNDA, CONSTITUTIONAL LAW, *supra,* note 226, 986.

283. Gagliardi v. Village of Pawling, 18 F.3d 188, 194 (2d Cir. 1994).

commercial speech. Even then, the protection conferred was limited. Commercial speech, said the Court, was not "wholly outside" the First Amendment. *Metromedia, Inc. v. City of San Diego*[284] is the leading case on the First Amendment issues. The San Diego ordinance at issue in *Metromedia* banned all billboards with two categories of exceptions. First, there were twelve exemptions for such matters as informational and governmental messages, commemorative historical plaques, religious symbols, time and temperature signs, and temporary political campaign signs.[285] Second, on-site commercial signs were exempt. In effect, the ordinance banned all off-site commercial billboards, the lifeline of the outdoor advertising industry. The Court upheld the restrictions on commercial speech but invalidated the restrictions on noncommercial speech. In doing so, the Court produced five separate opinions, making it a difficult case from which to draw guidance—a situation that persists some twenty-five years later.

Justice White's plurality opinion upheld the restriction on commercial speech under the four-part test of *Central Hudson Gas & Electric Corp. v. Public Service Commission*.[286] To be valid, a restriction on commercial speech must (1) concern a lawful activity and not be misleading; and (2) the asserted governmental interest must be substantial. If the answers to (1) and (2) are yes, then (3) the regulation must directly advance the governmental interest asserted; and (4) the regulation cannot be more extensive than is necessary to serve that interest. The plurality found all four parts satisfied.[287] The two goals furthered by the ordinance, traffic safety and aesthetics, were considered substantial. Acknowledging that the ordinance was underinclusive in that the permitted on-site commercial billboards were "equally distracting and unattractive," the Court nonetheless held the classification constitutional. The city "may [have] believe[d]," said the Court, that off-site billboards posed "a more acute problem" than on-site signs, and since the affected speech was commercial, favoring one kind of commercial speech over another was permissible.[288]

The noncommercial speech aspects of San Diego's zoning law received greater scrutiny and did not fare as well. The ordinance allowed only on-site *commercial* messages. Because it failed to provide also for on-site *noncommercial* messages (which would be no more distracting or unattractive than commercial billboards), that portion of the law was found facially unconstitutional.

---

284. 453 U.S. 490 (1981).
285. *Id.* at 495.
286. 447 U.S. 557 (1980).
287. 453 U.S. at 507.
288. *Id.* at 511–12.

This was considered impermissible content-based regulation and not a reasonable time, place, or manner restriction. "Insofar as the city tolerates billboards at all," said the Court, "it cannot choose to limit their content to commercial messages."[289]

Regulations of yard signs on residential property receive close attention of the courts. When a New Jersey town enacted a zoning ordinance prohibiting posting "for sale" signs to limit panic selling or "white flight," the Supreme Court wasted no time in striking down the control as a free speech violation in *Linmark Assoc., Inc. v. Township of Willingboro*.[290] The ordinance was not a mere restriction of time, place, and manner because reasonable alternatives for landowners wishing to sell were not available, and it was not content-neutral. Though the speech regulated was commercial, the "for sale" messages were vital community information.[291]

In *City of Ladue v. Gilleo*,[292] a city banned virtually all signs except "for sale" signs and few others. Margaret Gilleo's 8.5- by 11-inch window sign proclaiming that she was "For Peace in the Gulf" was not among the exceptions, and she sued to enjoin enforcement of the act against her. Describing the case as "in some respects . . . the mirror image" of *Linmark*, the Court held that the city banned "too much" speech. The Court, noting the nation's historic respect for "liberty in the home,"[293] viewed noncommercial sign posting from one's home as an important, unique, and "venerable means of communication." For the Court the regulation was essentially a total ban on this "distinct medium of expression," and left persons with no reasonable options to communicate quickly, directly, and cheaply with their neighbors. While cities cannot likely ban such signs, reasonable regulations that deal with location, size, number, and color are acceptable.[294]

---

289. 453 U.S. at 513. A number of courts have stricken ordinances favoring commercial billboards over noncommercial ones. *See* R. Douglas Bond, *Making Sense of Billboard Law: Justifying Prohibitions and Exemptions,* 88 MICH. L. REV. 2482 (1990).

290. 431 U.S. 85 (1977).

291. *See also* Daugherty v. East Point, 447 F. Supp. 290 (N.D. Ga.1978). Where panic selling is proved, courts may uphold the ordinance. *See, e.g.,* Barrick Realty, Inc. v. Gary, 491 F.2d 161 (7th Cir. 1974).

292. 512 U.S. 43 (1994).

293. *Id.* at 58.

294. *Id.* at 58 n.17. *See* American Legion Post 7 v. City of Durham, 239 F.3d 601 (4th Cir. 2001) (limit on size of flags, including the American flag, for aesthetics purposes held to be a valid time, place, and manner restriction); Kroll v. Steere, 759 A.2d 541 (Conn. App. 2000). *But see* Cleveland Area Bd. of Realtors v. City of Euclid, 88 F.3d 382 (6th Cir. 1996) (limiting signs to the windows of homes found invalid for not providing ample alternative channels for communication).

2. *Sexually Oriented Businesses*

Sexually oriented businesses such as adult bookstores and movie theaters, strip clubs, and massage parlors are said to "attract an undesirable quantity and quality of transients,"[295] resulting in an increase in crime, especially prostitution. As a consequence, when adult uses move into an area, property values drop, and those neighbors who are able to do so move elsewhere.[296] Singling out adult uses for special treatment raises free speech concerns. While courts accord no First Amendment protection to obscene speech, they protect nonobscene, sexually oriented speech, at least to a degree.

Adult-use zoning is usually done through either a dispersal or concentration method. The dispersal method came under review in *Young v. American Mini Theatres*,[297] where a Detroit ordinance prohibited the location of an adult movie theater within 1,000 feet of another such theater or 10 other establishments thought to produce similar effects. In a divided opinion, the Court upheld the ordinance, finding it was a valid exercise of the city's zoning power and not an impermissible prior restraint on free speech. The city did not aim the regulation at suppressing ideas. Documented studies of the effects of the regulated uses supported the law, which had the legitimate purpose of maintaining neighborhood character.[298]

The Court upheld the concentration technique in *City of Renton v. Playtime Theatres*.[299] Renton, a Seattle suburb, banned adult theaters from locating within 1,000 feet of any residential zone, single- or multifamily dwelling, park, school, or church. While the city did not expressly create an adult use zone, the effect of the distance limitations was to limit adult theaters to an area of 520 acres—5% of the city. The regulation was undeniably content-based in that one determined affected theaters by asking what kind of movies they played. Nonetheless, the Court treated the ordinance as content-neutral because it found that the predominant intent was directed at the secondary effects of the message, not the message itself. As a content-neutral ordinance, it would pass constitutional muster if it served a substantial governmental interest and did not unreasonably foreclose other avenues of communication. *Renton*'s ordinance met the test. Reasonable alternative avenues of communication must be left open, and most litigation today deals with this issue.

---

295. Young v. American Mini Theatres, Inc., 427 U.S. 50 (1976).

296. *See* Rachel Simon, *New York City's Restrictive Zoning of Adult Businesses: A Constitutional Analysis,* 23 FORDHAM URB. L.J. 187 (1996).

297. 427 U.S. 50 (1976).

298. *Id.* at 70.

299. 475 U.S. 41 (1986).

3. *Religious Uses*

Whether, and if so to what degree, land use controls must accommodate religious practices under the command of the free exercise clause is not clear. In 1963, the Court held in *Sherbert v. Verner*[300] that government regulation of conduct that substantially burdens the free exercise of religion cannot be sustained unless it has a compelling interest and uses the least restrictive means to advance this interest. Lower courts consistently found that land use regulations did not substantially burden the free exercise of religion and were thus not subject to the compelling interest test.[301]

Religious exercise claims in the land use context, which had already typically failed under *Sherbert*, became even more tenuous in 1990 when the Court held, in *Employment Division v. Smith*,[302] that the strict scrutiny test of *Sherbert* does not apply to claims challenging neutral laws of general applicability. Following *Smith*, several courts, treating zoning ordinances as laws of general applicability, refused to apply strict scrutiny and upheld the exclusion of a church from a commercial district[303] and the designation of a church as an historic landmark.[304]

The decision in *Employment Division v. Smith* provoked outcry from some who feared the end of religious freedom. In response, Congress enacted the Religious Freedom Restoration Act of 1993 (RFRA).[305] The Act purported to restore the compelling interest test of *Sherbert*, but the Court invalidated the Act in 1997. In *City of Boerne v. Flores*,[306] the Court found RFRA an unconstitutional exercise of Congress's remedial powers under Section Five of the Fourteenth Amendment.

Attempting to overcome the Court's objections to RFRA, Congress enacted the Religious Land Use and Institutionalized Persons Act of 2000 (RLUIPA).[307] RLUIPA provides that government shall not "impose or

---

300. 374 U.S. 398 (1963).

301. Lakewood, Ohio Congregation of Jehovah's Witnesses v. City of Lakewood, 699 F.2d 303 (6th Cir. 1983); Messiah Baptist Church v. County of Jefferson, 859 F.2d 820 (10th Cir. 1988); Grosz v. City of Miami Beach, 721 F.2d 729 (11th Cir. 1983).

302. 494 U.S. 872 (1990).

303. Cornerstone Bible Church v. City of Hastings, 948 F.2d 464 (8th Cir. 1991) (dismissing free exercise claim, but remanding hybrid speech-religion claim).

304. St. Bartholomew's Church v. City of New York, 914 F.2d 348 (2d Cir. 1990), *cert. denied,* 499 U.S. 905 (1991).

305. 42 U.S.C.A. §§ 2000bb *et seq.*

306. 521 U.S. 507 (1997).

307. 42 U.S.C. §§ 2000cc et seq. RLUIPA provides that "no government shall impose or implement a land use regulation in a manner that imposes a substantial burden of the religious exercise of a person . . . or institution, unless . . . it is in furtherance

implement a land use regulation in a manner that imposes a substantial burden on the religious exercise of a person, including a religious assembly or institution, unless the government demonstrates that imposition of the burden on that person, assembly, or institution (A) is in furtherance of a compelling governmental interest; and (B) is the least restrictive means of furthering that compelling governmental interest."[308]

RLUIPA litigation is substantial, and since it creates a right of action for a person seeking to enforce religious land use rights, § 1983 need not be used. But, RLUIPA statutory claims are often combined with § 1983 claims asserting First Amendment violations. RLUIPA does not make reference to attorneys' fees; but Congress, when enacting RLUIPA, also amended 42 U.S.C. § 1988 to allow attorneys' fees in RLUIPA cases.

VI. SUGGESTED READINGS

One-Volume Treatises on Land Use Law

JULIAN C. JUERGENSMEYER & THOMAS E. ROBERTS, LAND USE PLANNING AND DEVELOPMENT REGULATION LAW (Thomson-West 2003).

DANIEL R. MANDELKER, LAND USE LAW (5th ed. LEXIS 2003).

PETER W. SALSICH & TIMOTHY J. TRYNIECKI, LAND USE REGULATION: A LEGAL ANALYSIS & PRACTICAL APPLICATION OF LAND USE LAW (2d ed. American Bar Association 2004).

Takings Law Covered Exclusively

ROBERT MELTZ, DWIGHT MERRIAM, & RICHARD FRANK, THE TAKINGS ISSUE: CONSTITUTIONAL LIMITS ON LAND USE CONTROL AND ENVIRONMENTAL REGULATION (Island Press 1999).

STEVEN EAGLE, REGULATORY TAKINGS (2d ed. LEXIS 2005).

TAKING SIDES ON TAKINGS ISSUES: PUBLIC AND PRIVATE PERSPECTIVES (T. Roberts, American Bar Association 2002).

TAKING SIDES ON TAKINGS ISSUES: THE IMPACT OF TAHOE-SIERRA (T. Roberts, ed., American Bar Association 2002).

First Amendment Issues

PROTECTING FREE SPEECH AND EXPRESSION: THE FIRST AMENDMENT AND LAND USE LAW (D. Mandelker and R. Rubin eds., American Bar Association, 2001).

---

of . . . a compelling governmental interest [and] is the least restrictive means of furthering that [interest]." 42 U.S.C. § 2000cc(a)(1).

308. 42 U.S.C. § 2000cc.

Chapter 8

STUDENTS' CONSTITUTIONAL RIGHTS IN PUBLIC SCHOOLS

by Margaret-Ann F. Howie

I. INTRODUCTION

It's a chilling roll call: Red Lake, Minnesota.[1] Columbine, Colorado.[2] Santee, California.[3] Pearl, Mississippi.[4] Red Lion, Pennsylvania.[5] Public schools, once havens of academic refuge, have become sites of adolescent horror. Thus, the protection of students has become a matter of national

1. On March 21, 2005, five students, one teacher, and one security guard were killed by a fellow student, who later killed himself. *Horror in Red Lake: A school shooting, and no answers, at* http://www.usnews.com/usnews/news/articles/050404/4redlake.htm.
2. On April 20, 1999, two students killed twelve students and one teacher in their high school in suburban Denver before committing suicide. http://www.cnn.com/US/9904/21/school.shooting.02/.
3. On March 5, 2001, a student opened fire in a boys' high school bathroom, killing two; thirteen students were wounded. http://www.cbsnews.com/stories/2001/03/05/national/main276424.shtml.
4. On October 1, 1997, a student stabbed his mother and then shot fellow students with a rifle. Nine were shot; two died. http://www.cnn.com/US/9806/12/school.shooting.verdict/; http://lubbockonline.com/news/1010297/LA0540.htm. "Town Tries to Cope with School Shooting".
5. On April 24, 2003, a fourteen-year-old student shot and killed his middle school principal. http://www.cbsnews.com/stories/2003/04/25/national/main551088.shtml?CMP= ILC-SearchStories.

importance. Federal law now permits students to transfer from "persistently dangerous" schools into those with more stellar disciplinary records.[6] Although some statistics show that youth crime has decreased,[7] public perception that schools are unsafe persists. In addition to wielding its sword of statutory authority over the dragon of school violence, Congress has shown an unprecedented interest in controlling the academic performance of public schools.[8]

It is not surprising, then, that the daily lives and constitutional rights of today's public school students should be affected by the twin national interests of school safety and student success. Indeed, as a review of recent cases demonstrates, many boards of education justify the limitations on student freedom by citing the need for academic rigor and school safety.[9] Judicial responses to curtailing student rights have remained measured; most federal courts balance the rights of students against the rights of public schools to maintain order and discipline; in many cases the schools' rights may outweigh a student's rights.

This chapter presents an overview of the seminal Supreme Court decisions concerning the First and Fourth Amendment rights of public school students, as well as more recent circuit court opinions. In analyzing these cases, the chapter attempts to present a basic framework of the constitutional rights of students in our nation's public schools, recognizing that this target moves with particular agility.

---

6. The No Child Left Behind Act of 2001, 20 U.S.C. § 7912, provides, in pertinent part, that "each State . . . shall establish and implement a statewide policy requiring that a student attending a persistently dangerous public elementary or secondary school . . . or who becomes a victim of a violent criminal offense . . . while in or on the grounds of a public elementary or secondary school that the student attends, be allowed to attend a safe public elementary or secondary school."
7. *See, generally, Youth Violence: A Report of the Surgeon General, at* http://www.surgeongeneral.gov/library/youthviolence/report.html. The immediate impetus for this Surgeon General's Report was the April 1999 Columbine High School shooting. The Administration and Congress requested a report summarizing research about the causes and prevention of youth violence.
8. The No Child Left Behind Act of 2001, 20 U.S.C. § 6301 *et seq.*, requires that public schools demonstrate "adequate yearly progress" in order to avoid adverse action, which may include corrective action, reconstitution, or permitting students to transfer to academically successful schools. 20 U.S.C. § 6316.
9. *See, e.g.,* Blau v. Fort Thomas Public School District, 401 F.3d 381 (6th Cir. 2005); Boroff v. Van Wert City Board of Education, 220 F.3d 465 (6th Cir. 2000); and Butler v. Derby Unified School District No. 260, 206 F.3d 1358 (10th Cir. 2000).

II. STUDENT EXPRESSION

A. The Beginning

Its subsequent equivocation notwithstanding, the U.S. Supreme Court has unequivocally declared that students do not "shed their constitutional rights to freedom of speech or expression at the schoolhouse gate."[10]

The Supreme Court first articulated this principle in *Tinker v. Des Moines Independent Community School District*,[11] when high school students sought an injunction under § 1983 to prevent school officials from disciplining them for violating the school district's dress code. The challenged dress code prohibited students from wearing black armbands to protest the Vietnam War.

Several facts are noteworthy: In a school system of more than 18,000 students, only five were suspended for violating the dress code. No evidence of "threats or acts of violence on school premises" was found, nor was there any "evidence whatsoever of petitioners' interference, actual or nascent, with the schools' work or of the collision with the rights of other students to be secure and to be let alone."[12] Additionally, the school system did not prohibit wearing "all symbols of political or controversial significance."[13] Therefore, the regulation's sole purpose was to suppress the student's speech about Vietnam. "A particular symbol—black arm bands worn to exhibit opposition to this nation's involvement in Vietnam—was singled out for prohibition."[14] In fact, an internal school memorandum noted that "the schools are no place for demonstrations" and, if the students were dissatisfied with the political process, then "it should be handled with the ballot box and not in the halls of our public schools."[15]

The Court found this singular prohibition to be particularly reprehensible. As a result, it clearly articulated the distance that existed between the rights of the public school student and the reach of the public school administration:

> In our system, state-operated schools may not be enclaves of totalitarianism. School officials do not possess absolute authority over their students. Students in school as well as out of school are "persons"

---

10. Tinker v. Des Moines Independent Community School District, 393 U.S. 503, 506 (1969).
11. 393 U.S. 503 (1969).
12. 393 U.S. at 508.
13. 393 U.S. at 510.
14. 393 U.S. at 510–11.
15. 393 U.S. at 508 n.3.

> under our Constitution. They are possessed of fundamental rights which the State must respect, just as they themselves must respect their obligations to the State. In our system, students may not be regarded as closed-circuit recipients of only that which the State chooses to communicate. They may not be confined to the expression of those sentiments that are officially approved. In the absence of a specific showing of constitutionally valid reasons to regulate their speech, students are entitled to freedom of expression of their views.[16]

Two competing sets of rights were involved. (1) The student's: "First Amendment rights, applied in light of the special characteristics of the school environment, are available to students;"[17] and (2) the school's: "The Court has repeatedly emphasized the need for affirming the comprehensive authority of the States and of school officials, consistent with fundamental constitutional safeguards, to prescribe and control conduct in the schools."[18] Therefore, the "problem lies in the area where students in the exercise of First Amendment rights collide with the rules of the school authorities."[19]

Schools, the Court concluded, cannot suppress speech "because of an undifferentiated fear or apprehension of disturbance."[20] Rather, in order to suppress the students' speech, the Court ruled that a public school must prove that a student's First Amendment exercise would "materially and substantially" disrupt the school program.

Indeed, the *Tinker* court noted that the public school setting was the ideal venue for self-expression, especially on controversial subjects, as long as the student does not "materially and substantially interfere with the requirements of appropriate discipline in the operation of the school."[21] The Court waxed eloquent in its defense of student's rights:

> Under our Constitution, free speech is not a right that is given only to be so circumscribed that it exists in principle but not in fact. Freedom of expression would not truly exist if the right could be exercised only in an area that a benevolent government has provided as a safe haven for crackpots. The Constitution says that Congress (and the States) may not abridge the right to free speech.

---

16. 393 U.S. at 511.
17. 393 U.S. at 506.
18. 393 U.S. at 507.
19. *Id.*
20. 393 U.S. at 508.
21. 393 U.S. at 513.

> This provision means what it says. We properly read it to permit reasonable regulation of speech-connected activities in carefully restricted circumstances. But we do not confine the permissible exercise of First Amendment rights to . . . a supervised and ordained discussion in a school classroom.[22]

Subsequent cases have demonstrated, however, that the distance between the student's rights and the school's reach has never been greater. Instead, the Supreme Court has strived to substantially shorten it.

B. More Recent Cases

For instance, in *Bethel School District No. 403 v. Fraser*,[23] the Supreme Court clarified the "material and substantial disruption" standard. In *Fraser*, a high school student, in spite of warnings from teachers concerning its appropriateness, delivered a speech before the entire student body. The speech was full of graphic and sexually explicit metaphors.[24] Fraser received a three-day suspension for violating a *Tinker*-fashioned school rule prohibiting the use of obscene language, specifically "conduct which materially and substantially interferes with the educational process."[25]

The Court found there to be a "marked distinction" between the student's speech in *Fraser* and the students' armbands in *Tinker*. The Court noted that:

> [i]n upholding the students' right to engage in a nondisruptive, passive expression of a political viewpoint in *Tinker*, this Court was careful to note that the case did "not concern speech or action that intrudes upon the work of the schools or rights of other students."[26]

---

22. *Id.*
23. 478 U.S. 675 (1986).
24. Mr. Fraser's speech, part of which was reproduced in Justice Blackmun's dissent, read: "I know a man who is firm—he's firm in his pants, he's firm in his shirt, his character is firm—but most of all, his belief in you, the students of Bethel, is firm. Jeff Kuhlman is a man who takes his point and pounds it in. If necessary, he'll take an issue and nail it to the wall. He doesn't attack things in spurts—he drives hard, pushing and pushing until finally—he succeeds. Jeff is a man who will go to the very end—even the climax, for each and every one of you. So vote for Jeff for A.S.B. vice-president—he'll never come between you and the best our high school can be." 478 U.S. at 687 (Blackmun, J., dissenting). A later Court characterized the speech as "not legally obscene." *Hazelwood, infra,* note 29, 484 U.S. at 266.
25. 478 U.S. at 678.
26. 478 U.S. at 680 (citations omitted).

According to the Court, because Fraser's speech did not merit First Amendment protection, school administrators had the authority to suppress it. The First Amendment rights of schoolchildren, the Court reasoned, are not coextensive to those of adults. Therefore, "[i]t does not follow, however, that simply because the use of an offensive form of expression may not be prohibited to adults making . . . a political point, the same latitude must be permitted to children in public school. . . . '[t]he First Amendment gives a high school student the classroom right to wear Tinker's armband, but not Cohen's jacket.'"[27] However, the exercise of a student's First Amendment rights need not "materially disrupt" the school program in order for a disciplinary code to suppress that right. On the contrary, as the Court noted subsequently:

> The decision in *Fraser* rested on the "vulgar," "lewd," and "plainly offensive" character of a speech delivered at an official school assembly rather than on any propensity of the speech to "materially disrup[t] classwork or involv[e] substantial disorder or invasion of the rights of others."[28]

In *Hazelwood School District v. Kuhlmeier*,[29] the Supreme Court closed the distance created in *Tinker* through what the dissent characterized as "brutal censorship."[30] The students in that case were three high school newspaper staff members. They asserted that school officials (in particular, their principal, Robert Reynolds, and their journalism teacher, Howard Emerson) had violated their First Amendment rights when they deleted two full pages of the school newspaper. The paper was edited and written by members of the Journalism II class at Hazelwood East High School.

---

27. *Fraser,* 478 U.S. at 682–83 (citations omitted). Cohen, an adult, had been arrested for wearing, in a courthouse, a jacket that read: "Fuck the draft." Cohen v. California, 403 U.S. 15 (1971). The Court upheld Cohen's right to express his political viewpoint in a public place, regardless of the offense it caused.
28. Hazelwood School District v. Kuhlmeier, 484 U.S. 260, 271 n.4 (1988). Lower federal courts have imposed similar restrictions. *See, e.g.,* Walker-Serrano v. Leonard, 325 F.3d 412 (3d Cir. 2003) (public elementary student's free speech rights were not violated when she was prevented from distributing a petition during a class reading period or during recess on an icy playground); and Hansen v. Ann Arbor Public Schools, 293 F. Supp. 2d 780 (E.D. Mich. 2003) (school district violated the First Amendment free speech rights of high school student when she was excluded from a panel and thus could not express her religious objections to homosexuality).
29. 484 U.S. 260 (1988).
30. 484 U.S. at 289 (Brennan, J., dissenting).

Page proofs of each issue were normally submitted to the principal for prepublication review. The principal objected to two stories: one detailing three students' experiences with pregnancy, the other describing the impact of divorce on students. Although pseudonyms were used in the pregnancy story, Principal Reynolds believed that the identity of the students could be discovered from the story's content. Additionally, he was concerned about the discussion of sexual activity and birth control and its impact upon younger students at the school. Lastly, Reynolds believed that the divorce story, which identified students by name, required parental consent prior to publication. Reynolds directed the journalism teacher to exclude two pages of the newspaper even though the pages contained articles to which Reynolds did not object.

The Court, while paying necessary tribute to its holding in *Tinker*, found the principal's actions to be constitutional. It noted a marked distinction between *promotion* of student speech and *toleration* of student speech. The Court also found persuasive the level of involvement in the newspaper's production: Students received grades and academic credit; public funds were expended from the school board's budget; and the publication was to be developed within the school's educational mission. Ultimately, therefore, the school retained control over the content of the publication. "Accordingly, school officials were entitled to regulate the contents of [the school newspaper] in any reasonable manner. It is this standard, rather than our decision in *Tinker*, that governs this case."[31]

The Court went on to acknowledge that the First Amendment does not require that "a school affirmatively . . . promote particular student speech."[32] Therefore, public schools may exercise "authority over school-sponsored publications, theatrical productions, and other expressive activities that students, parents, and members of the public might reasonably perceive bear the imprimatur of the school."[33]

Because a school may exercise greater control over student expression that is part of the curriculum, a public school may rightly "disassociate itself" from speech that is ungrammatical, poorly written, or unsuitable for immature audiences.[34] Therefore, the *Tinker* standard would not apply to the school's determination to lend its name and resources to the dissemination of student expression:

---

31. 484 U.S. at 270 (citations omitted).
32. 484 U.S. at 270–71.
33. 484 U.S. at 271.
34. *Id.*

> [W]e hold that educators do not offend the First Amendment by exercising editorial control over the style and content of student speech in school-sponsored expressive activities so long as their actions are reasonably related to legitimate pedagogical concerns.[35]

The Court refused to concede that specific written regulations would be required to define educators' prepublication control.[36] Rather, the majority found all of Principal Reynolds's actions to be reasonable, including the deletion of two full pages of the newspaper. However, Justice Brennan (joined by Justices Marshall and Blackmun) disagreed:

> The Court opens its analysis in this case by purporting to reaffirm *Tinker*'s time-tested proposition that public school students "do not 'shed their constitutional rights to freedom of speech or expression at the schoolhouse gate.'" [citations omitted] That is an ironic introduction to an opinion that denudes high school students of much of the First Amendment protection that *Tinker* itself prescribed. Instead of "teach[ing] children to respect the diversity of ideas that is fundamental to the American system," [citations omitted] and "that our Constitution is a living reality, not parchment preserved under glass," [citations omitted] the Court today "teach[es] youth to discount important principles of our government as mere platitudes."[37]

In effect, Principal Reynolds's scissors severed the *Tinker*-established distance between the student's rights and the school's control.[38]

---

35. 484 U.S. at 273.
36. 484 U.S. 273 n.6.
37. 484 U.S. at 290–91 (citations omitted).
38. *But see* Dean v. Utica Community Schools, 345 F. Supp. 2d 799 (E.D. Mich. 2004) (censorship of school newspaper deemed unconstitutional, where the newspaper was deemed a limited public forum); Ashby v. Isle of Wight County School Board, 354 F. Supp. 2d 616 (E.D. Va. 2004) (school's denial of permission to student to sing a religious song at a graduation ceremony did not violate the student's rights, where school board had a compelling interest); Demmon v. Loudon County Public Schools, 342 F. Supp. 2d 474 (E.D. Va. 2004) (school district violated students' free speech rights when it removed bricks inscribed with religious symbols and messages from its "walkway of fame"); Bannon v. School District of Palm Beach County, 387 F.3d. 1208 (11th Cir. 2004) (school could restrict religious messages on school mural, where mural could not be considered a designated public forum); and Butler v. Derby Unified School District No. 260, 206 F.3d 1358 (10th Cir. 2000) (drawing of a confederate flag).

Although the Supreme Court has not revisited *Tinker* or its progeny, subsequent federal circuit cases have explored *Tinker's* limits through dress codes.[39] For example, in *Blau v. Fort Thomas Public School District*,[40] the Sixth Circuit upheld a middle school dress code. Parents had asserted that the code violated students' rights to free speech.

As described by the court of appeals, the school district's comprehensive dress code prohibited:

> [C]lothing that is too tight, revealing or baggy as well as tops and bottoms that do not "overlap"; [h]ats, caps, scarves, or sweat bands; . . . non-jewelry chains and chain wallets; clothing that is "distressed" or has "holes in it"; [v]isible body piercing (other than ears); "[u]nnaturally colored hair that is distracting to the educational process," including "blue, green, red, purple [or] orange" hair; "clothing that is too long, flip-flop sandals, or high platform shoes"; pants, shorts or skirts that are not of "a solid color of navy blue, black, or any shade of khaki, or white"; "[s]horts, skirts or skorts that do not reach mid-thigh or longer"; "bottoms made with stretch knits, flannel, or fleece such as sweatpants, jogging pants, or any type of athletic clothing" as well as "[b]aggy, sagging, or form-fitting pants"; tops that are not "a solid color" and are not "crew neck [style], polo style with buttons, oxford style, or turtleneck"; tops with writing on them and "[l]ogos larger than the size of a 'quarter' . . . except 'Highlands' logos or other 'Highlands Spirit

---

39. *See* Brandt v. Board of Education of the City of Chicago, 326 F. Supp. 2d 916 (N.D. Ill. 2004) (T-shirt designed and worn by gifted students was not protected speech); Bragg v. Swanson, 371 F. Supp. 2d 814 (W.D. W.Va. 2005) (dress code that disciplined student for wearing a confederate flag T-shirt and belt buckle deemed unconstitutionally vague and overbroad); Barber v. Dearborn Public Schools, 286 F. Supp. 2d 847 (E.D. Mich. 2003) (school unconstitutionally prohibited student from wearing a T-shirt calling President George W. Bush an "international terrorist"); West v. Derby Unified School District No. 260, 206 F.3d 1358 (10th Cir. 2003) (student drawing of a confederate flag was permissible); Boroff v. Van Wert City Board of Education, 220 F.3d 465 (6th Cir. 2000) (school district permissibly prohibited student from wearing a Marilyn Manson T-shirt); Harper v. Poway Unified School District, 345 F. Supp. 2d 1096 (S.D. Ca. 2004) (student suspended for T-shirt with the words "homosexuality is shameful" expressing his religious beliefs defeated a motion for summary judgment, having stated a claim that his First Amendment rights had been violated); and Jacobs v. Clark County School District, 373 F. Supp. 2d 1162 (D. Nev. 2005) (dress code authorized by state statute was constitutional).

40. 401 F.3d 381 (6th Cir. 2005).

Wear'"; tops that are not "of an appropriate size and fit"; and "form-fitting or baggy shirts" or "[a]ny material that is sheer or lightweight enough to be seen through."[41]

According to board policy, the objective of the dress code addressed both academic and safety concerns:

> The objective of this dress code is to provide an appropriate educational environment while allowing students to dress comfortably within limits to facilitate learning. Students' attire can have a positive or negative effect on the learning process, contribute to students' success, and generate a safe and positive learning environment. We expect students to maintain the type of appearance that is not distracting to students, teachers, or the educational process of the school.[42]

Middle school student Amanda Blau[43] complained that the dress code limited her ability to "wear clothing that she likes" and that she wished to wear clothing that looks "nice" and that "she feels good in" and that expresses her individuality.[44] Amanda denied that the dress code prohibited her from conveying any particular message.

The Sixth Circuit distinguished between the "pure speech" of *Tinker*'s black armbands and concluded that the Blau family's challenge did not involve any expressive conduct. "Under these circumstances, the Blaus have not met their burden of showing that the First Amendment protects Amanda's conduct—which in this instance amounts to nothing more than a generalized and vague desire to express her middle school individuality."[45] Moreover, the court noted that the dress code did not exist to restrict expressive conduct. Rather, the school board noted that the code should "enhance school safety, improve the learning environment, promote good behavior, reduce discipline problems, improve test scores, improve children's self-respect and self-esteem, bridge socioeconomic differences between families, help eliminate stereotypes, and produce a cost-savings from families."[46] These, concluded the court, represent important governmental interests.

---

41. 401 F.3d at 385–86.
42. 401 F.3d at 386.
43. Amanda's father, Robert, was a lawyer who filed the action on his daughter's behalf. 401 F.3d at 386.
44. *Id.*
45. *Id.* at 389 (citations omitted).
46. *Id.* at 391.

The court found persuasive testimony concerning the effect of the dress code on student achievement at the school. Citing *Hazelwood*, the court concluded that "[i]n the First Amendment arena and other arenas as well, the Supreme Court thus has frequently emphasized that public schools have considerable latitude in fashioning rules that further their educational mission and in developing a reasonable fit between the ends and means of their policies."[47] Unfortunately for Miss Blau, "the First Amendment does not protect such vague and attenuated notions of expression—namely, self-expression through any and all clothing that a 12-year-old may wish to wear on a given day."[48]

The power of *Tinker* and its progeny rests in its simple affirmation of students' rights: As our society has become increasingly aware of the violence that pervades the public schools, the simple has become complex, eliminating distance in order to ensure safety.[49] Not unlike the Biblical Samson (who became weak when his long hair was cut), that which once gave strength has been excised. A similar emasculation appears with respect to student's Fourth Amendment rights.

III. STUDENT FOURTH AMENDMENT RIGHTS

The Supreme Court's seminal case on students' Fourth Amendment rights is *New Jersey v. T.L.O.*[50] The case, which held that the exclusionary rule does not apply to the public school setting, set the standard for analyzing the legality of student searches in public schools.

Two high school girls were caught smoking in the lavatory, in violation of school rules. Both violators were questioned by Assistant Vice Principal Choplick. While T.L.O.'s co-violator admitted to smoking, T.L.O. denied that she had been smoking—but asserted firmly that she did not smoke at all. Mr. Choplick demanded to inspect T.L.O.'s purse; he immediately

---

47. *Id.* at 393.

48. *Id.* at 390.

49. *But see* Isaacs v. Board of Education of Howard County, 40 F. Supp. 2d 335 (D. Md. 1999) (African-American student did not have a constitutional right to wear a headwrap in a public high school to express her cultural heritage); Jacobs v. Clark County School District, 373 F. Supp. 2d 1162 (D. Nev. 2005) (school dress code authorized by state statute did not violate students' religious or free speech rights); and Griggs v. Fort Wayne School Board, 359 F. Supp. 2d 731 (N.D. Ind. 2005) (student disciplined under school violence policy for wearing a T-shirt demonstrating support for the U.S. Marines and depicting a rifle used by the Marines, although policy itself was constitutional, it was unconstitutionally applied to the student).

50. 469 U.S. 325 (1984).

observed a pack of cigarettes. Upon reaching into her purse for the cigarettes, he then noticed cigarette rolling papers. A thorough search ensued and uncovered a small amount of marijuana, a pipe, empty plastic bags, a roll of money in one-dollar bills, and a list of students purportedly who owed T.L.O. money. When T.L.O.'s case was referred to juvenile court for disposition of charges of possession and sale of marijuana, T.L.O. argued that Choplick's search of her purse had violated her Fourth Amendment rights.

Although the Court declined to hold that the search was illegal, it concluded that the Fourth Amendment's prohibition on illegal searches and seizures did indeed apply to searches by public school officials. In so doing, the Court majority sought guidance from *Tinker*:

> We have held school officials subject to the commands of the First Amendment. . . . If school authorities are state actors for the purposes of the constitutional guarantees of freedom of expression . . ., it is difficult to understand why they should be deemed to be exercising parental rather than public authority when conducting searches of their students. . . . Today's public school officials do not merely exercise authority voluntarily conferred on them by individual parents; rather, they act in furtherance of publicly mandated educational and disciplinary policies.[51]

The Court went on to balance the school officials' need to search against the "invasion which the search entails."[52] It determined that a student would possess a legitimate expectation of privacy in personal articles carried to school. At the same time, the Court noted that teachers and administrators possessed a "substantial interest . . . in maintaining discipline in the classroom and on school grounds."[53]

Unlike in criminal cases, however, searches in the public schools bear no warrant requirement or probable cause standard. "Rather, the legality of a search of a student should depend simply on the reasonableness, under all the circumstances, of the search."[54] The standard of reasonableness will govern the objectives of the search, and will be guided, moreover, by the nature of the infraction and the age and sex of the student. In applying the reasonableness to the facts presented, the Court concluded that Mr.

51. *Id.* at 336 (citations omitted).
52. *Id.* at 337.
53. *Id.* at 339.
54. *Id.* at 341.

Choplick's search of T.L.O.'s purse complied with the Fourth Amendment. The Court increased the school's reach, however, in subsequent decisions.

In *Vernonia School District 47J v. Acton*,[55] the Supreme Court held that random urinalysis drug tests of student athletes was constitutional; the case is a marked departure from the individualized suspicion that the Court found vital in *T.L.O.* The Petitioner school district observed a sharp increase in drug use; the district court noted that the disciplinary problems had reached "epidemic" proportions. Indeed, the school district found that athletes led the drug culture. Athletes who used drugs presented a particular concern to the school district, because of the increased risk of sports-related injury. After proposing a Student Athlete Drug Policy ("Policy") to parents (it received their unanimous approval), the school board adopted the Policy. Its stated purpose was to prevent drug use by student athletes; protect athletes' health and safety, and provide assistance programs to drug users. The Policy applied to all students participating in interscholastic athletics. Athletes were tested at the beginning of each season. During the season, 10% of the athletes were randomly tested each week. When tested, students were monitored by adults of the same sex; the samples, in turn, were forwarded to an independent laboratory and tested for the presence of amphetamines, cocaine, and marijuana. Only the superintendent, principals, assistant principals, and athletic directors had access to the results.

The Court acknowledged that *T.L.O.* was based upon individualized suspicion. First and foremost, it noted that the reasonableness of every search must be balanced between the individual's Fourth Amendment interests and the promotion of legitimate governmental interests. The Court easily disposed of the privacy interests of student athletes but reasoned that "[c]entral . . . to the present case, is the fact that the subjects of the Policy are (1) children, who (2) have been committed to the temporary custody of the State as schoolmaster."[56] In interpreting its prior holding in *T.L.O.*, the court noted that "*T.L.O.* did not deny, but indeed emphasized, that the nature of that power is custodial and tutelary, permitting a degree of supervision and control that could not be exercised over free adults."[57] Thus, "while children assuredly do not shed their constitutional rights . . . at the schoolhouse gate, the nature of those rights is what is appropriate for children at school."[58]

---

55. 515 U.S. 646 (1995).
56. *Id.* at 654.
57. *Id.* at 655.
58. *Id.* at 655–56 (citations omitted).

The Court applied a yet more relaxed reasonableness standard to the privacy interests of student athletes, and noted that there is "an element of 'communal undress' inherent in athletic participation."[59] As such, "somewhat like adults who choose to participate in a 'closely regulated industry,' students who voluntarily participate in school athletics have reason to expect intrusions upon normal rights and privileges, including privacy."[60] Lastly, the Court concluded that the character of the complained intrusion was "negligible"[61] because the results were disclosed to a limited class of persons; the test was conducted only to determine the presence of illegal drugs; and the drugs for which the urine was screened did not vary based upon the identity of the student.

Most importantly, however, the Court considered whether the governmental interest was "important enough"[62] to justify these types of searches. Although it failed to definitively state "[w]hether that relatively high degree of government concern"[63] is necessary, the Court found that the government's concern was both "compelling"[64] and immediate. It refused to find less-intrusive measures (e.g., suspicion-based testing) to be required: "In many respects . . . testing based on 'suspicion' of drug use would not be better, but worse."[65]

Nonetheless, the Court refused to hold that all suspicionless drug testing in public schools would be constitutional. Rather,

> [t]he most significant element in this case is the first we discussed: that the Policy was undertaken in furtherance of the government's responsibilities, under a public school system, as guardian and tutor of children entrusted to its care. . . . [W]hen the government acts as guardian and tutor, the relevant question is whether the search is one that a reasonable guardian and tutor might undertake.[66]

Apparently, in the view of the Court, it would not be unreasonable for a parent or guardian to subject his or her child to random drug testing.[67]

---

59. *Id.* at 657 (citations omitted).
60. *Id.*
61. *Id.* at 658.
62. *Id.* at 661 (emphasis in original).
63. *Id.* at 661.
64. *Id.* at 662.
65. *Id.* at 664.
66. *Id.* at 665.
67. Lower federal courts have addressed a number of other issues related to student Fourth Amendment rights: Cornfield v. Consolidated High School District No. 230, 991 F.2d 1316 (7th Cir. 1993) (nude strip search); Williams v. Ellington, 936 F.2d

In *Board of Education of Independent School District No. 92 of Pottawatomie County v. Earls*,[68] the Court revisited its decision in *Vernonia* and expanded upon it. In *Earls*, the Tecumseh, Oklahoma, school district adopted a Student Activities Drug Testing Policy ("Policy") that required all middle and high school students who participated in *any* extracurricular activities to consent to random urinalysis drug testing.[69] Thus, students who were members of athletic teams as well as those belonging to such diverse groups as cheerleaders, Future Homemakers of America, pom-poms, band, choir, and Future Farmers of America were subject to random testing.

Parents and students[70] sought relief under § 1983, alleging that the policy violated the Fourth Amendment. They further asserted that the school district had failed to articulate a special need for such a broad range of testing, because the "[d]rug [t]esting [p]olicy neither addresses a proven problem nor promises to bring any benefit to students or the school."[71]

Citing *Vernonia*, the Court denied relief and upheld the constitutionality of the Policy. The Court reasoned that students who participated in extracurricular activities enjoyed diminished expectations of privacy, while the

---

881 (6th Cir. 1991) (strip search); Horton v. Goose Creek Independent School District, 690 F.2d 470 (5th Cir. 1982); Doe v. Renfrow, 475 F. Supp. 1012 (N.D. Ind. 1979), *rev'd on another issue,* 631 F.2d 91 (7th Cir.) (per curiam), *cert. denied,* 451 U.S. 1022 (1982) (canine sniffing of students and lockers); Wofford v. Evans, 390 F.3d 318 (4th Cir. 2004) (Fourth Amendment was not violated when school officials failed to contact parent about questioning and detention of a ten-year-old student); Watkins v. The Millennium School, 290 F. Supp. 2d 890 (S.D. Oh. 2003) (search of third-grade student); Porter v. Ascension Parish School Board, 301 F. Supp. 2d 576 (M.D. La. 2004) (Fourth Amendment rights were not violated for search of book bag, but student's drawing of high school being soaked with gasoline and administrators being assaulted was not entitled to First Amendment protection); and Cuesta v. School Board of Miami-Dade County, 285 F.3d 962 (11th Cir. 2002) (strip search of student permissible given school's "zero-tolerance policy" toward school-related violence).

68. 536 U.S. 822 (2002).
69. *Id.* at 826.
70. Complainants Lindsay Earls and Daniel James were students at Tecumseh High School. Earls was a member of the show choir, the marching band, the Academic Team, and the National Honor Society. Daniel James sought membership to the Academic Team. *See id.* at 826.
71. *See id.* at 827. In her dissent, Justice Ginsburg cited the school district's Application for Funds under the Safe and Drug-Free Schools and Communities Act, indicating that "types of drugs [other than alcohol and tobacco] including controlled dangerous substances, are present [in the schools] but have not identified themselves as major problems at this time." *Id.* at 849–50 (Ginsburg, J., dissenting).

degree of the intrusion was deemed minimal. The majority declined to distinguish between athletic and nonathletic extracurricular activities. Rather, the Court noted that this distinction "was not essential to our decision in *Vernonia*, which depended primarily upon the school's custodial responsibility and authority."[72] Indeed, both nonathletic and athletic activities impose regulations that "do not apply to the student body as a whole."[73] The Court, again quoting *Vernonia*, reasoned that students who voluntarily subject themselves to such regulation are "[s]omewhat like adults who choose to participate in a closely regulated industry . . . [and] have reason to expect intrusions upon normal rights and privileges, including privacy."[74]

The testing procedure, which was deemed "virtually identical to that reviewed in *Vernonia*," was declared to represent a "negligible" intrusion upon students' privacy. [75] Test results were not disclosed to law enforcement agencies; the sole consequence was limitation of the student's participation in extracurricular activities. Neither academic nor disciplinary restrictions ensue.[76] Further, test results were maintained in confidential files separate from other educational records and released to school personnel only under limited circumstances.[77] The Court found persuasive the "nature and immediacy of the government's concerns" because the school district had presented specific evidence concerning the drug abuse problem in its schools.[78] While a problem need not be "particularized or pervasive" to justify suspicionless testing,[79] the urgency of the Court's rhetoric is clear:

---

72. *Id.* at 831.
73. *Id.* at 832.
74. *Id.* at 832 (citations omitted).
75. *Id.* at 832.
76. Following a positive test result, a student may continue to participate in the activity, but must show proof of drug counseling and must submit to an additional drug test in two weeks. A second positive test resulted in a fourteen-day suspension from the activity, and the student must complete four hours of substance abuse counseling and submit to monthly drug testing. After a third positive test result, a student was to be suspended from participating in any extracurricular activity for the remainder of the school year or for eighty-eight school days, whichever is longer. *See id.* at 833–34.
77. *Id.* at 833.
78. *See id.* at 834. Testimony at the district court level revealed incidents of drug use: that some students appeared to be under the influence of drugs; that a drug dog had found marijuana near the school parking lot; that police officers had found drugs or drug paraphernalia in a car driven by a Future Farmers of America member; that the school board had received community complaints concerning a "drug situation." *See id.* at 835.

> The drug abuse problem among our Nation's youth has hardly abated since *Vernonia* was decided in 1995. In fact, evidence suggests that it has only grown worse. As in *Vernonia*, "the necessity for the State to act is magnified by the fact that this evil is being visited not just upon individuals at large, but upon children for whom it has undertaken a special responsibility of care and direction." The health and safety risks identified in *Vernonia* apply with equal force to Tecumseh's children. Indeed, the nationwide drug epidemic makes the war against drugs a pressing concern in every school.[80]

The Fourth Amendment, however, has its limits—even in the quest for safer schools. In *Gruenke v. Seip*,[81] the Third Circuit ruled that a swim team coach violated a team member's Fourth Amendment rights when he required her to take a pregnancy test.[82] Similarly, in *Doe v. Little Rock School District*,[83] the court of appeals struck down the random searching of students' persons and "bookbags, backpacks and purses and similar containers." Lastly, in *Doe v. State of Hawaii Department of Education*,[84] the action of taping a second-grade student to a tree in order to discipline him violated the Fourth Amendment.

IV. CONCLUSION

In 1859, Americans understood what they expected from community and public school relationships. Social conventions, as described by the Supreme Court of Vermont, were vastly different:

> [T]he defendant was the teacher of a district school in Burlington, and that the plaintiff, whose age was about eleven years, was one of

---

79. The Court declined to design a formula upon which to base the need for a drug testing program. "[I]t would make little sense to require a school district to wait for a substantial portion of its students to begin using drugs before it was allowed to institute a drug testing program designed to deter drug use." *See id.* at 836.
80. *Id.* at 834 (citations omitted).
81. 225 F.3d 290 (3d Cir. 2000).
82. The facts show that the student's pregnancy was confirmed by one of the four (4) tests she took, two of which occurred on school grounds. In Cuesta v. School Board of Miami-Dade County, Florida, 225 F.3d 290, 297–98 (11th Cir. 2000), the Eleventh Circuit ruled that a student's constitutional rights were not violated by a strip search because the school's zero-tolerance policy did not lead to the alleged constitutional violation.
83. 380 F.3d 349 (8th Cir. 2004).
84. 334 F.3d 906 (9th Cir. 2003).

> his pupils; that one day, about an hour and a half after the close of school in the afternoon, and after the plaintiff had returned home from school, and while he was driving his father's cow by the defendant's house, in the presence of the defendant and of some of his fellow pupils, the plaintiff called the defendant *Old Jack Seaver*; that the next morning, after school had commenced . . . the defendant, after reprimanding the plaintiff for his insulting language the evening before, whipped him with a small rawhide. The testimony on the part of the plaintiff tended to show that this whipping was severe and excessive, while that of the defendant tended to prove the contrary.[85]

The millennium, on the other hand, has been marked by terrorists and technology; war and peace; floods and famine. It is not equally clear to Americans how public schools fit into society's new paradigm. Our public schools, as a reflection of the changing world in which we live, represent our national ideal. At the same time, our public schools represent our hopes for succeeding generations. It stands to reason, then, that in the judicial context, our public schools represent both parent and public entity, both intimately involved with us and distantly removed from us. As the courts determine which of these roles best fits the public schools, the analysis of the students' rights changes.[86] This is not to conclude that the trends observed have changed dramatically in recent years.[87]

As is evident from the case law presented in this chapter, the most obvious interpretation often changes. However, this mercurial nature of legal

---

85. Lander v. Seaver, 32 Vt. 114 (1859).

86. Oddly enough, the increased use of technology in the public schools has not created a substantial difference in the First Amendment analysis. *See, e.g,* Mahaffey v. Aldrich, 236 F. Supp. 2d 779 (E.D. Mich. 2002); Beussink v. Woodland R-IV School District, 30 F. Supp. 2d 1175 (E.D. Mo. 1998); and Emmett v. Kent School District No. 415, 92 F. Supp. 2d 1088 (W.D. Wash. 2000).

87. Students will continue to press the boundaries of their constitutional rights. They are not, however, the only parties who assert their rights under § 1983. In Association of Community Organizations for Reform Now v. New York City Department of Education, 269 F. Supp. 2d 338 (S.D.N.Y. 2003), a community organization sued two local school districts alleging violations of the No Child Left Behind Act (NCLB). The district court declined to extend the reach of § 1983 to NCLB. Note, additionally, that third parties have asserted § 1983 actions for denial of First Amendment rights in the public schools. *See, e.g.,* Child Evangelism Fellowship of Maryland, Inc. v. Montgomery County Public Schools, 373 F.3d 589 (4th Cir. 2004) *rev. and rem.,* 368 F. Supp. 2d 416 (D. Md. 2005).

decision making is not disturbing.[88] Rather, we know how far we must go to reach our ideal. As W.E.B. DuBois noted, "[t]o make . . . in . . . education that ever necessary combination of the permanent and the contingent—of the ideal and of the practical in workable equilibrium—has been . . . as it ever must be in every age and place, a matter of infinite and frequent mistakes."[89]

88. On the contrary, this is quite comforting. We have moved from Plessy v. Ferguson, 163 U.S. 537 (1896) (separate but equal), to Brown v. Board of Education of Topeka, 347 U.S. 497 (1954) (separate is unconstitutional).

89. William Edward Burghardt DuBois, The Souls of Black Folk 124 (New American Library 1982).

Chapter 9

INDIVIDUAL IMMUNITY DEFENSES UNDER SECTION 1983

by Robert F. Brown

I. INTRODUCTION

While the text of § 1983 ostensibly creates a cause of action against "every person" who, while acting under color of state law, deprives another of a federal or constitutional right, "every person" does not include all persons. The U.S. Supreme Court has created special immunity defenses for certain classes of individual defendants who are sued in their individual capacities. These persons may be entitled to an absolute immunity from suit and damages, or may assert a qualified immunity from suit and damages, depending on the particular functions exercised by the individuals to avoid liability. This chapter outlines these immunity defenses as they have developed in § 1983 lawsuits. The focus of this chapter is the substantive considerations that provide the sources of these defenses. Procedural matters related to the use of these defenses are discussed in Chapters 1 and 2.

II. RECOGNITION AND EVOLUTION OF IMMUNITY DEFENSES

Section 1983 was enacted to deter public officials from abusing their authority in a manner that deprives persons of their federally protected rights and to provide a remedy to victims of unconstitutional acts.[1] Section

1. *See* Carey v. Piphus, 435 U.S. 247, 253–54 (1978).

1983, however, contains no language addressing either absolute or qualified immunity for public officials alleged to have violated § 1983. Rather, individual immunity defenses from § 1983 liability are judicially created doctrines that stem from the common law as it existed when Congress enacted the Civil Rights Act of 1871, Section 1 of which is now codified as § 1983. These historically recognized common-law immunities were driven by public policy and designed to protect public officials from litigation that might tend to chill the officials' proper exercise of discretion and divert the attention of public officials from their duties by unnecessary and time-consuming litigation.[2] As stated by the Supreme Court in *Owen v. City of Independence*,[3] "Where the immunity claimed by the defendant was well established at common law at the time § 1983 was enacted, and where its rationale was compatible with the purposes of the Civil Rights Act, we have construed the statute to incorporate that immunity."

A. Source of Federal Immunities

The Supreme Court has consistently recognized individual immunity defenses that were well established in 1871 when Congress enacted the Civil Rights Act of 1871. Regardless of strong policy considerations, the Court has not, however, provided immunities from § 1983 actions where such immunities did not exist in 1871.[4]

In developing the federal immunities applicable in § 1983 litigation, the Supreme Court has chosen not to be influenced by the various state law doctrines of immunity for governmental entities and government officials. Rather, the Supreme Court has held that federal law controls the immunity analysis under § 1983 even if the matter in question is pending in state court.[5] Pursuant to the Supremacy Clause of the U.S. Constitution, federal laws are enforceable in state courts, and state courts are charged with the

2. *See, e.g.,* Wood v. Strickland, 420 U.S. 308, 319–20 (1975); Pierson v. Ray, 386 U.S. 547, 554–55 (1967).
3. 445 U.S. 622, 638 (1980).
4. *See, e.g.,* Tower v. Glover, 467 U.S. 914, 922 (1984) (where no immunity was available in 1871 providing public defenders an absolute immunity from liability for intentional misconduct that deprives clients of their federal rights, even strong public policy reasons do not support providing public defenders such immunity under § 1983).
5. *See* Howlett v. Rose, 496 U.S. 356, 369 (1990) ("A state court may not deny a federal right, when the parties and controversy are properly before it, in the absence of a 'valid excuse.'").

parallel responsibility of enforcing those laws according to their regular modes of procedure.[6]

> No one disputes the general and unassailable proposition relied upon by the [state] Supreme Court below that States may establish the rules of procedure governing litigation in their own courts. By the same token, however, where state courts entertain a federally created cause of action, the "federal right cannot be defeated by the forms of local practice."[7]

Since immunity under the Civil Rights Act is a question of federal law, state courts are obligated to recognize and apply federal law regarding immunities to suits brought under § 1983.[8]

B. Distinction Between Immunity from Damages and Immunity from Injunctive Relief

There is a distinction between immunity from damages and immunity from injunctive relief. For example, in *Supreme Court of Virginia v. Consumers Union of the United States*,[9] the Supreme Court held that the Virginia Supreme Court and its Chief Justice could be sued under § 1983 for injunctive relief in their capacities as enforcers of the Virginia Supreme Court's disciplinary rules for lawyer advertising, which rules had been challenged on First Amendment grounds.[10] The Court held that the Virginia Supreme Court could not, however, be sued for injunctive relief in its legislative capacity in promulgating the challenged rules or in its judicial capacity in adjudicating the constitutionality of the rules.[11]

Similarly, in *Pulliam v. Allen*,[12] the Supreme Court held that judges are not absolutely immune from injunctive relief under § 1983.[13] The Court, noting that actions in prohibition and mandamus had historically been used at common law to enjoin judicial actions, held that the lack of absolute

---

6. *Id.* at 367.
7. Felder v. Casey, 487 U.S. 131, 138 (1988) (quoting Brown v. Western R. Co. of Alabama, 338 U.S. 294, 296 (1949)).
8. *See* Martinez v. State of California, 444 U.S. 277, 284 n.8 (1980).
9. 446 U.S. 719 (1980).
10. *Id.* at 736.
11. *Id.* at 731–34.
12. 466 U.S. 522 (1984).
13. *Id.* at 541–42.

immunity from injunctive relief for judicial actions, as compared to immunity from damage suits, would not have a chilling effect on judicial independence.[14]

In 1996, however, Congress, in reaction to the holdings in *Consumers Union* and *Pulliam*, amended § 1983 by adding at the end of the first sentence the phrase "except that in any action brought against a judicial officer for an act or omission taken in such officer's judicial capacity, injunctive relief shall not be granted unless a declaratory decree was violated or declaratory relief was unavailable."[15] As a result, the judicially created rule that had held that judges were subject to injunctive relief was effectively overruled by congressional fiat, so that judges are now absolutely immune from injunctive relief liability for their judicial acts unless declaratory relief does not remedy the challenged judicial conduct.

C. Individual-Capacity versus Official-Capacity Suits

In *Kentucky v. Graham*,[16] the Supreme Court attempted "to unravel once again the distinction between personal and official capacity suits."[17]

> Personal-capacity suits seek to impose personal liability upon a government official for actions he takes under color of state law. Official-capacity suits, in contrast, "generally represent only another way of pleading an action against an entity of which an officer is an agent." As long as a government entity receives notice and an opportunity to respond, an official-capacity suit is, in all respects other than name, to be treated as a suit against the entity. It is *not* a suit against the official personally, for the real party in interest is the entity. Thus, while an award of damages against an official in his personal capacity can be executed only against the official's personal assets, a plaintiff seeking to recover on a damage judgment in an official-capacity suit must look to the government entity itself.[18]

Consequently, individuals sued in their official capacities only are not entitled to assert individual immunity defenses.

---

14. *Id.* at 536–40.
15. Pub. L. No. 104-317, § 309(c), 1996.
16. 473 U.S. 159 (1985).
17. *Id.* at 163.
18. *Id.* at 165–66 (citations omitted) (emphasis in original).

D. Functional Approach to Immunity Analysis

The Supreme Court utilizes a functional approach in determining whether a particular class of individual defendants is entitled to assert an absolute immunity or qualified immunity defense:

> Running through our cases, with fair consistency, is a "functional" approach to immunity questions other than those that have been decided by express constitutional or statutory enactment. Under that approach, we examine the nature of the functions with which a particular official or class of officials has been lawfully entrusted, and we seek to evaluate the effect that exposure to particular forms of liability would likely have on the appropriate exercise of those functions. Officials who seek exemption for personal liability have the burden of showing that such an exemption is justified by overriding considerations of public policy, and the Court has recognized a category of "qualified" immunity that avoids unnecessarily extending the scope of the traditional concept of absolute immunity.[19]

Utilizing a functional analysis, the Supreme Court has determined that state, regional, and local legislators (when acting in a legislative capacity); judges (when acting within their jurisdiction); and prosecutors (when acting as advocates in the criminal process) are all absolutely immune from liability for damages under § 1983.[20] Under a functional approach, determining what type of immunity applies to a particular official in a given case turns on the nature of the act being performed, rather than on the position or title held by the official. For example, state and regional legislators, when acting administratively rather than legislatively, are protected only by the affirmative defense of qualified immunity.[21] Moreover, prosecutors, when acting in an investigative capacity rather than as advocates in a criminal process, are not entitled to absolute immunity but are entitled only to assert the defense of qualified immunity.[22]

A critical distinction between absolute immunity and qualified immunity is that absolute immunity does not look to the reasonableness of the

---

19. Forrester v. White, 484 U.S. 219, 224 (1988).
20. *See* Tenney v. Brandhove, 341 U.S. 367, 379 (1951) (state legislators); Lake Country Estates, Inc. v. Tahoe Reg'l Planning Agency, 440 U.S. 391, 405–06 (1979) (regional legislators); Bogan v. Scott-Harris, 523 U.S. 44, 49 (1998) (local legislators); Stump v. Sparkman, 435 U.S. 349, 356–57 (1978) (judges); Imbler v. Pachtman, 424 U.S. 409, 427 (1976) (prosecutors).
21. *See Lake Country Estates,* 440 U.S. at 402–06.
22. Burns v. Reed, 500 U.S. 478, 492–96 (1991).

defendant's actions; rather, an absolute immunity analysis is complete once it is determined that the defendant's function entitles that defendant to an absolute immunity, regardless of the defendant's subjective or objective good faith. As is explained below, the functional approach to immunity analysis has extended absolute immunity beyond even legislators, judges, and prosecutors to other individual defendants who are engaged in legislative, judicial, or prosecutorial acts.

III. ABSOLUTE IMMUNITY

Under a functional approach, absolute immunity protects certain government officials for their official acts regardless of the legality or constitutionality of the acts. Courts have consistently recognized two policy rationales justifying the recognition of absolute immunity: (1) The fear of damages may chill an official's exercise of discretion; and (2) the process of defending civil rights claims may divert the official's attention from his or her duties.[23]

A. Legislators

Federal law is well settled that legislators are entitled to an absolute immunity from suit under § 1983 for conduct in furtherance of their legislative duties.[24] Utilizing a functional approach, however, the Court has limited the application of absolute legislative immunity to acts within the sphere of legitimate legislative activities.[25]

The landmark case of *Tenney v. Brandhove*[26] discusses the historical antecedents of legislative immunity. Justice Frankfurter wrote that legislators

> are immune from deterrents to the uninhibited discharge of their legislative duty, not for their private indulgence but for the public good. One must not expect uncommon courage even in legislators. The privilege would be of little value if they could be subjected to

---

23. *See Bogan,* 523 U.S. at 52.
24. *See Id.* at 48–49; *Owen* 445 U.S. at 663 n.6; *Lake Country Estates,* 440 U.S. at 402–06; and *Tenney*, 341 U.S. at 379.
25. *See Lake Country Estates,* 440 U.S. at 402–06 (court used functional approach to determine that a bistate regional planning agency created by California and Nevada was entitled to absolute legislative immunity for its adoption and enforcement of a regional land use plan); and *Tenney,* 341 U.S. at 379 (state legislators absolutely immune from liability for damages when they act "in a field where legislators traditionally have power to act").
26. 341 U.S. 367 (1951).

> the cost and inconvenience and distractions of a trial upon a conclusion of a pleader, or to the hazard of the judgment against them based upon a jury's speculation as to motives.[27]

This language was repeated favorably in *Lake Country Estates, Inc. v. Tahoe Regional Planning Agency*.[28] Justice Frankfurter in *Tenney* quoted language from *Coffin v. Coffin*,[29] in describing the parameters of absolute legislative immunity:

> I will not confine it to delivering an opinion, uttering a speech, or haranguing in debate; but will extend it to the giving of a vote, to the making of a written report, and to every other act resulting from the nature, and in the execution, of the office; and . . . securing to every member exemption from prosecution, for everything said or done by him, as a representative, in the exercise of the functions of that office, without inquiring whether the exercise was regular according to the rules of the house, or irregular and against their rules.[30]

> Recognizing this venerable tradition, the Supreme Court held in 1959 in *Tenney* that state legislators are entitled to absolute immunity from liability under § 1983 for their legislative activities.[31] In 1979, this immunity was extended to regional legislators in *Lake Country Estates*,[32] and in 1998 to local legislators in *Bogan*.[33]

B. The Functional Approach: Legislative versus Administrative Acts

Under the functional approach, only those persons whose actions are legislative in nature are entitled to the protection of absolute legislative immunity.[34] Legislators are absolutely immune while passing laws, hold-

---

27. *Id.* at 377.
28. 440 U.S. 391, 405 (1979).
29. 4 Mass. 1, 27 (1808).
30. *Tenney,* 341 U.S. at 379.
31. *Id.*
32. *Lake Country Estates,* 440 U.S. at 402–06.
33. *Bogan,* 523 U.S. at 48–49.
34. *See, e.g., Bogan,* 523 U.S. at 54–55 (local legislators); *Lake Country Estates,* 440 U.S. at 402–06 (regional legislators); *Consumers Union,* 446 U.S. at 731–34 (state supreme court justices in promulgating lawyer conduct rules); Gravel v. United States, 408 U.S. 606, 616–21 (1972) (legislative aides when performing acts for which a legislator would be immune).

ing committee meetings, or when acting "in a field where legislators traditionally have power to act."[35] Absolute legislative immunity attaches to all actions taken "in the sphere of legitimate legislative activity."[36] Legislative immunity has been found for budgeting decisions,[37] ordinance enactment,[38] zoning decisions,[39] and other matters held to be legislative in nature.[40]

When local legislators are acting with respect to a specific situation that does not amount to policymaking, however, they may not have legislative

---

35. *Tenney,* 341 U.S. at 379.
36. *Bogan,* 523 U.S. at 54.
37. *Bogan,* 523 U.S. at 55–56 (city council's adoption of budget that eliminated employee's position was a legislative act and thus local legislators were entitled to absolute immunity from suit); Woods v. Gamel, 132 F.3d 1417, 1419–20 (11th Cir. 1998) (county commissioners' act of approving county budget for all county expenses, pursuant to state law, was "legislative act," because act was policymaking of general application, and commissioners were thus entitled to legislative immunity for that act in § 1983 action brought by county jail inmates alleging inadequate conditions); and Aitchison v. Raffiani, 708 F.2d 96, 98–100 (3d Cir. 1983) (mayor and city council were absolutely immune for eliminating position of assistant building inspector).
38. R.S.W.W. v. City of Keego Harbor, 397 F.3d 427, 437–38 (6th Cir. 2005) (passage of sign ordinance was a legislative act entitling city council members to absolute immunity); and Mears v. Town of Oxford, 762 F.2d 368, 371 (4th Cir. 1985) (town commissioners who passed ordinance limiting marina expansion were acting in a legislative capacity and were absolutely immune).
39. Biblia Abierta v. Banks, 129 F.3d 899, 903–04 (7th Cir. 1997) (aldermen were entitled to absolute legislative immunity for introducing and voting for zoning ordinances that would prevent churches from purchasing property in aldermen's wards); Shoultes v. Laidlaw, 886 F.2d 114, 117 (6th Cir. 1989) (mayor and city council who voted for unconstitutional zoning ordinance held absolutely immune); Bruce v. Riddle, 631 F.2d 272, 279 (4th Cir. 1980) (members of county council were absolutely immune in passing rezoning ordinance); and Gorman Towers, Inc. v. Bogoslavsky, 626 F.2d 607, 611–14 (8th Cir. 1980) (city board of directors were absolutely immune for passing zoning amendment).
40. Whitener v. McWatters, 112 F.3d 740, 741 (4th Cir. 1997) (legislative body's discipline of one of its members is a core legislative function protected by legislative immunity); Schultz v. Sundberg, 759 F.2d 714, 717 (9th Cir. 1985) (senate president was absolutely immune in compelling legislator to attend session through use of senate sergeant at arms and state troopers); Agromayor v. Goldberg, 738 F.2d 55, 58–60 (1st Cir. 1984) (Puerto Rico Speaker of the House was absolutely immune in refusing to hire individual of rival political party as a legislative press officer); Kuzinich v. City of Santa Clara, 689 F.2d 1345, 1349 (9th Cir. 1982) (members of local legislative bodies had complete immunity from suits based on their legislative acts); and Green v. DeCamp, 612 F.2d 368, 372 (8th Cir. 1980) (state senators who released committee report to media were entitled to legislative immunity).

immunity. For example, in the land use area, a vote to change zoning laws or to establish general rules for the use of property may be a legislative act, but an individual decision on a single parcel of land may not be a legislative act. The mere fact that the complained-of action occurred by way of a vote does not automatically mean the action is legislative. A number of federal appellate courts have recognized that "[a]lthough a local legislator may vote on an issue, [the act of voting] alone does not necessarily determine that he or she was acting in a legislative capacity."[41]

The U.S. Supreme Court has not outlined any definitive test for determining when a particular action taken by a local official is considered legislative and when it is not. Nevertheless, the Fifth and First Circuits have adopted two tests to aid in this determination.[42] The first test focuses on the nature of the facts used to reach a given decision. Under that test, if the underlying facts on which a decision is based are "legislative facts," such as generalizations concerning a policy or state of affairs, then the decision is legislative. If, on the other hand, the facts used in the decision making are more specific, such as those that relate to particular individuals or situations, then the decision is administrative.[43]

The second test focuses on the "particularity of the impact of the state action." Under this test, if the action involves establishment of a general policy, it is legislative. If it singles out specific individuals and affects them differently from others, it is administrative.[44] Other federal appellate courts have adopted the same or similar tests for determining the scope of absolute legislative immunity.[45]

---

41. Brown v. Griesenauer, 970 F.2d 431, 437 (8th Cir. 1992); and Crymes v. DeKalb County, Ga., 923 F.2d 1482, 1485 (11th Cir. 1991). *See also* Roberson v. Mullins, 29 F.2d 132, 134 n.3 (4th Cir. 1994) (recognizing that member of local governmental body does not necessarily act in legislative capacity when participation takes form of a vote).

42. *See* Hughes v. Tarrant County, 948 F.2d 918, 921 (5th Cir. 1991); and Cutting v. Muzzey, 724 F.2d 259, 261 (1st Cir. 1984).

43. *Hughes,* 948 F.2d at 921; and *Cutting,* 724 F.2d at 261. *See also Acevedo-Garcia v. Vera-Monroig,* 204 F.3d 1, 9 (1st Cir. 2000); and Bryan v. City of Madison, 213 F.3d 267, 273–74 (5th Cir. 2000).

44. *Hughes,* 948 F.2d at 921; and *Cutting,* 724 F.2d at 261. *See also Acevedo-Garcia,* 204 F.3d at 9; *Bryan,* 213 F.3d at 273–74.

45. *See, e.g.,* Harhay v. Town of Ellington Bd. of Educ., 323 F.3d 206, 211 (2d Cir. 2003); Kaahumanu v. County of Maui, 315 F.3d 1215, 1220 (9th Cir. 2003) ("We determine whether an action is legislative by considering four factors: (1) 'whether the act involves ad hoc decisionmaking, or the formulation of policy;' (2) 'whether the act applies to a few individuals, or to the public at large'; (3) 'whether the act is

C. Judges

Absolute judicial immunity was recognized as part of the common law well before the adoption of the Civil Rights Act of 1871.[46] In *Pierson v. Ray*, the Supreme Court recognized absolute judicial immunity for damages under § 1983: "The immunity of judges for acts within the judicial role is . . . well established, and we presume that Congress would have specifically so provided had it wished to abolish the doctrine [when it enacted § 1983]."[47] It was not until the Supreme Court's 1978 decision in *Stump v. Sparkman*,[48] however, that the Court articulated two limits on judicial immunity. The Court held that (1) acts in the clear absence of a court's jurisdiction are not entitled to immunity, although immunity does extend to acts in mere excess of jurisdiction, and (2) only judicial acts are protected.[49]

The Supreme Court has articulated at least three policy bases justifying absolute judicial immunity from § 1983 suits: (1) the recognition of the common-law history of immunity for judges; (2) the desire not to chill judicial discretion, undermine the finality of judicial proceedings, or unfairly punish judges from exercising discretion; and (3) the availability of alternative methods of addressing judicial abuse by way of appeal, judicial conduct proceedings, criminal prosecution, and the will of the electorate for elected judges.[50]

D. The Functional Approach: Judicial versus Nonjudicial Conduct

The functional approach to absolute judicial immunity protects judges at all levels as well as those who act like judges.[51] Only judicial acts, however,

---

formally legislative in character'; and (4) 'whether it bears all the hallmarks of traditional legislation.'"); *Roberson,* 29 F.3d at 135; *Brown,* 970 F.2d at 437; Acevedo-Cordero v. Cordero-Santiago, 958 F.2d 20, 23 (1st Cir. 1992); *Crymes,* 923 F.2d at 1485; Ryan v. Burlington County, N.J., 889 F.2d 1286, 1290–91 (3d Cir. 1989); and Cinevision Corp. v. City of Burbank, 745 F.2d 560, 580 (9th Cir. 1984), *cert. denied,* 471 U.S. 1054 (1985).

46. *See* Bradley v. Fisher, 13 Wall. 335 (1871).

47. 386 U.S. 547, 554–55 (1967).

48. 435 U.S. 349 (1978).

49. *Id.* at 356–62. *See also* Mireles v. Waco, 502 U.S. 9, 11 (1991).

50. *See Pierson,* 386 U.S. at 554–55; *Stump,* 435 U.S. at 355–57.

51. *See, e.g.,* Butz v. Economou, 438 U.S. 478, 512–13 (1978) (absolute immunity extended to hearing examiners).

are protected by absolute immunity.[52] In determining whether conduct constitutes a judicial act, the Supreme Court has stated that

> the factors determining whether an act by a judge is a "judicial" one relate to the nature of the act itself, *i.e.*, whether it is a function normally performed by a judge, and to the expectations of the parties, *i.e.*, whether they dealt with the judge in his judicial capacity.[53]

The Supreme Court has upheld judicial immunity even in extreme circumstances.[54] Lower courts have also upheld such immunity in a variety of circumstances.[55] Even judges acting outside of, or in excess of, their juris-

---

52. *See, e.g.,* Cleavinger v. Saxner, 474 U.S. 193, 203–06 (1985) (hearing officers in a prison disciplinary proceeding functioned as adjudicators in an administrative matter and were entitled only to qualified immunity).
53. *Stump,* 435 U.S. at 362.
54. *See, e.g., Mireles,* 502 U.S. at 11–12 (judge was acting within his judicial function when he ordered deputies to physically bring lawyer who was late into his courtroom and excessive force was allegedly applied; judge had absolute judicial immunity since ordering lawyer who was physically present in the courthouse to come to his courtroom was a judicial function); and *Stump,* 435 U.S. at 357–60 (judge of court of general jurisdiction who ordered sterilization of fifteen-year-old girl was absolutely immune even if Indiana law did not authorize his acts).
55. *See, e.g.,* Harvey v. Waldron, 210 F.3d 1008, 1012 (9th Cir. 2000) (absolute judicial immunity applied to protect justice of the peace from § 1983 liability to owner of antique business for issuing ex parte order to destroy or dispose of antique gaming devices seized from owner's property, inasmuch as issuance of order was function that justice of the peace had jurisdiction to perform, and therefore immunity applied even if order was erroneous and its effect was injurious to owner, and irrespective of claimed motivation); Cooper v. Parrish, 203 F.3d 937, 945 (6th Cir. 2000) (state court chancellor was acting in his judicial capacity when he allegedly engaged in ex parte contact with state prosecutors and gave them legal advice regarding ways that they could improve their public nuisance case against nightclubs, given that chancellor was judge of court in which public nuisance action was ultimately filed and communications, although possibly improper under state law, were related to chancellor's general judicial functions, including his authority to issue ex parte restraining order prior to commencement of action); Myers v. Vogal, 960 F.2d 750 (8th Cir. 1992) (judge who sentenced juvenile as adult was still acting within his jurisdiction and was entitled to absolute judicial immunity); John v. Barron, 897 F.2d 1387, 1391–92 (7th Cir. 1990) (judge was absolutely immune in removing trustee of charitable trust); Mills v. Criminal Dist. Court No. 3, 837 F.2d 677 (5th Cir. 1988) (trial judge was absolutely immune against allegations of denial of a fundamentally fair trial); Glick v. Koenig, 766 F.2d 265, 269 (7th Cir. 1985) (judge who allegedly conspired with prosecutor in speeding-ticket case was entitled to absolute immunity); Halloway v. Walker, 765 F.2d 517, 522–23 (5th Cir. 1985) (judge was absolutely immune for placing company in receivership and running company improperly);

diction are entitled to absolute judicial immunity unless the judge is acting in *clear excess* of his territorial jurisdiction.[56]

Judges are not typically entitled to immunity, however, when acting outside of their judicial offices. For example, in *Zarcone v. Perry*,[57] a judge ordered a sandwich vender brought before him in handcuffs because he sold "putrid" coffee. In the resulting civil rights suit, the judge was held not to have been performing a judicial act and the jury's verdict of $80,000 in

---

Adams v. McIlhany, 764 F.2d 294, 297–99 (5th Cir. 1985) (judge who sentenced woman to thirty days in jail for contempt because she had accused the judge of accepting bribes was absolutely immune); Emory v. Peeler, 756 F.2d 1547, 1551 (11th Cir. 1985) (judge who singled out and chastised juror for not voting for death penalty was absolutely immune); Green v. Maraio, 722 F.2d 1013, 1017–18 (2d Cir. 1983) (judge who allegedly told court reporter to alter trial transcript after criminal defendant was sentenced was absolutely immune, as was the court reporter who acted pursuant to the judge's explicit instructions); Scott v. Hayes, 719 F.2d 1562, 1566–67 (11th Cir. 1983) (judge who ordered party in divorce proceeding to have vasectomy as a condition of obtaining a favorable property settlement was absolutely immune).

56. *See, e.g.,* Gallas v. Supreme Court of Pennsylvania, 211 F.3d 760, 770 (3d Cir. 2000) (judge was entitled to absolute judicial immunity from claim by former court administrator that judge invaded his privacy by issuing order releasing to newspaper a petition for protection from abuse filed by administrator's wife, even if order was issued orally; issuance of order releasing court record to public was judicial act, fact that order was issued ex parte did not mean that act was not judicial, and any violation of rule allowing release of information only for use in judicial proceeding established at most that judge acted in excess of jurisdiction, not that she acted in clear absence of jurisdiction); Rosenthal v. Justices of the Supreme Court of California, 910 F.2d 561, 565–66 (9th Cir. 1990) (even if judge acts outside of jurisdiction, judge still has absolute judicial immunity so long as acts themselves are judicial); King v. Love, 766 F.2d 962, 965–66 (6th Cir. 1985) (municipal court judge who acted in excess of his jurisdiction by jailing driver was still absolutely immune since court had subject matter jurisdiction over the underlying offense); Billingsley v. Kyser, 691 F.2d 388, 389 (8th Cir. 1982) (judge who amended plaintiff's criminal sentence while plaintiff's appeal was pending was immune even though the judge had lost jurisdiction over the matter); Turner v. Raynes, 611 F.2d 92, 93–94 (5th Cir. 1980) (Texas justice of the peace with limited criminal jurisdiction was absolutely immune even if he convicted plaintiff of nonexistent crime). *Contra* Maestri v. Jatkofsky, 860 F.2d 50, 53 (2d Cir. 1988) (town judge, who could hear criminal cases only in his own town and in towns immediately adjacent, was not entitled to absolute immunity when he heard a case beyond those limits and issued arrest warrants for acts that took place in a town not within his jurisdiction); Dykes v. Hosemann, 743 F.2d 1488, 1496–97 (11th Cir. 1984) (judge acting in clear and complete absence of personal jurisdiction loses judicial immunity).

57. 572 F.2d 52 (2d Cir. 1978).

compensatory damages and $60,000 in punitive damages was subsequently upheld.[58] In a rather striking case, the Sixth Circuit concluded in *Archie v. Lanier*[59] that "[w]e hold that stalking and sexually assaulting a person, no matter the circumstances, do not constitute 'judicial acts.' The fact that, regrettably, Lanier happened to be a judge when he committed these reprehensible acts is not relevant to the question of whether he is entitled to immunity. Clearly he is not."[60]

Judges are not absolutely immune when they act in an administrative capacity,[61] or when they act as supervising employers.[62] A judge acting in other capacities is not entitled to judicial immunity. For example, a judge who acts as a prosecutor, preparing complaint forms and then acting on them as a judge, is immune for his judicial acts, but not for the prosecutorial acts.[63] A

---

58. *Id.* at 54–55. *See also* Harris v. Harvey, 605 F.2d 330, 336 (7th Cir. 1979) (where judge initiated criminal proceedings against black police officer based upon racially improper motives and made racial remarks to press, he was not entitled to absolute immunity, and jury's award of $60,000 in compensatory damages and $200,000 in punitive damages was accordingly upheld).
59. 95 F.3d 438 (6th Cir. 1996).
60. *Id.* at 441.
61. *See, e.g.,* Kurowski v. Krajewski, 848 F.2d 767, 773–74 (7th Cir. 1988) (state court judge did not have absolute immunity from civil liability arising from his firing of public defenders on basis of their political beliefs); Atcherson v. Siebenmann, 605 F.2d 1058, 1063–64 (8th Cir. 1979) (judge who allegedly unlawfully terminated employee was entitled only to assert qualified immunity defense); and *King,* 766 F.2d at 968–69 (judge who deliberately misled an officer about the identity of the person named in a warrant, which led to that person's arrest, committed a nonjudicial act for which no judicial immunity was available).
62. *See, e.g.,* Forrester v. White, 484 U.S. 219, 229–30 (1988) (state court judge was acting in an administrative capacity when he demoted and dismissed probation officer and, thus, was not absolutely immune from § 1983 damages suit brought by disgruntled ex-employee); Meek v. County of Riverside, 183 F.2d 962, 966–67 (9th Cir. 1999) (decision to fire subordinate judicial employee was administrative decision and, thus, because alleged actions of municipal court judges in voting to terminate court commissioner and thereby force him to retire were administrative rather than judicial acts, judges were not entitled to absolute judicial immunity from commissioner's civil rights action alleging that he was terminated in retaliation for exercising his First Amendment right to campaign for judicial office); and Goodwin v. Circuit Court of St. Louis County, 729 F.2d 541, 545 (8th Cir. 1984) (judge who allegedly transferred female hearing officer on the basis of her sex was not entitled to absolute immunity).
63. *See* Barnes v. Winchell, 105 F.3d 1111, 1118–18 (6th Cir. 1997) ("[D]espite its breadth, the doctrine of absolute judicial immunity does not protect a judge performing the purely prosecutorial functions involved in initiating criminal prosecutions. This is especially true where the judge initiates criminal prosecutions based

judge acting as a legislator, issuing court rules, is absolutely immune in the legislative capacity but not in enforcing the rules, which is an administrative capacity.[64]

E. Others Who May Perform Judge-Like Functions

Executive officials performing judge-like functions are also immune,[65] as are parole officers acting in a judicial capacity.[66] Persons acting pursuant to court order or in conjunction with judicial activities are typically entitled to

---

on the judge's private interests, completely separate from cases brought to court independently by the parties. Nonetheless, this exception to absolute judicial immunity when a judge engages in purely prosecutorial functions is narrow."); Lopez v. Vanderwater, 620 F.2d 1229, 1234–35 (7th Cir. 1980).

64. *Consumers Union,* 446 U.S. at 731–34.

65. *See, e.g., Butz,* 438 U.S. at 513–14 (administrative law judge and hearing examiner in Agriculture Department were acting in a judicial capacity when they attempted to revoke plaintiff's registration with the department and, thus, were absolutely immune); Scott v. Schmidt, 773 F.2d 160, 164–65 (7th Cir. 1985) (members of Illinois Racing Board were acting in a judicial capacity in suspending and denying horse owner's racing license where owner allegedly took a bribe to fix a horse race and, thus, were absolutely immune); Mills v. Killebrew, 765 F.2d 69, 72 (6th Cir. 1985) (lawyers who served on mediation panel were entitled to absolute immunity); Vakas v. Rodriquez, 728 F.2d 1293, 1296–97 (10th Cir. 1984) (members of Kansas Board of Healing Arts hearing disciplinary charges against doctors were absolutely immune); Sprecher v. Graber, 716 F.2d 968, 972–73 (2d Cir. 1983) (SEC officials enjoyed absolute immunity insofar as alleged misconduct in connection with SEC investigation fell within scope of judicial or prosecutorial functions); Simons v. Bellinger, 643 F.2d 774, 777–78 (D.C. Cir. 1980) (unauthorized practice of law committee of bar association had absolute immunity in determining compliance with laws and rules governing practice of law); and Ashbrook v. Hoffman, 617 F.2d 474, 476–77 (7th Cir. 1980) (commissioners appointed by the court to conduct a partition sale of the divorced plaintiffs' property were sufficiently related to the judicial process to entitle them to quasi-judicial absolute immunity from federal suit for damages arising from their conduct in handling sale and in distributing proceeds of sale).

66. *See, e.g.,* Montero v. Travis, 171 F.3d 757, 761 (2d Cir. 1999) ("[W]e join our sister circuits and hold directly that parole board officials, like judges, are entitled to absolute immunity from suit for damages when they serve a quasi-adjudicative function in deciding whether to grant, deny or revoke parole," citing Anton v. Getty, 78 F.3d 393, 396 (8th Cir. 1996); Littles v. Board of Pardons & Paroles Div., 68 F.3d 122, 123 (5th Cir. 1995) (per curiam); Walrath v. United States, 35 F.3d 277, 281–82 (7th Cir. 1994); Russ v. Uppah, 972 F.2d 300, 303 (10th Cir. 1992); Fuller v. Georgia State Bd. of Pardons & Paroles, 851 F.2d 1307, 1310 (11th Cir. 1988); Johnson v. Rhode Island Parole Bd. Members, 815 F.2d 5, 8 (1st Cir. 1987); Anderson v. Boyd,

absolute immunity. For example, state officials charged with the duty of executing a facially valid court order enjoy absolute judicial immunity.[67] Court clerks acting in a ministerial role, however, are entitled only to qualified immunity with respect to certain functions.[68] Persons who are an

---

714 F.2d 906, 908–10 (9th Cir. 1983)); Farrish v. Mississippi State Parole Bd., 836 F.2d 969, 973–76 (5th Cir. 1988) (parole board members were absolutely immune in deciding whether to grant or deny parole); Nelson v. Balazic, 802 F.2d 1077, 1078 (8th Cir. 1986) (parole board members who paroled individual who subsequently kidnapped, raped, and sodomized plaintiffs were absolutely immune for their decision to parole the perpetrator); Evans v. Dillahunty, 711 F.2d 828, 830–31 (8th Cir. 1983) (regional parole commissioner, who rejected parole panel's recommendation, resulting in prisoner spending four extra months in prison, acted within scope of his official duties in reviewing the recommendation and, therefore, was entitled to absolute immunity); and Sellars v. Procunier, 641 F.2d 1295, 1302–03 (9th Cir. 1981) (state parol board officials are entitled to absolute immunity from suits by prisoners for actions taken when processing parole applications since, under "functional comparability" test, parole board officials perform functionally comparable tasks to judges when they decide to grant, deny, or revoke parole, and parole board officials face same risk of constant unfounded suits by those disappointed by parole board's decisions). *But see* Jones v. Moore, 986 F.2d 251, 253 (8th Cir. 1993) (parole officer was absolutely immune in revoking parole, but not in issuing false violation report); Harper v. Jeffries, 808 F.2d 281, 284 (3d Cir. 1986) (parole board members were absolutely immune when carrying out adjudicatory functions, but not when performing executive or administrative functions); Ray v. Pickett, 734 F.2d 370, 373–74 (8th Cir. 1984) (probation officer, in filing report with the U.S. Parole Commission to secure a parole violator's warrant, was not functioning in an adjudicatory or prosecutorial capacity, and thus was not entitled to absolute immunity in suit claiming intentional falsification of report); and Anderson v. Boyd, 714 F.2d 906, 908 (9th Cir. 1983) (absolute immunity does not extend to the knowing dissemination of false information concerning a parolee to persons ou side the parole system).

67. *See* Valdez v. City and County of Denver, 878 F.2d 1285, 1287–88 (10th Cir. 1989). *See also* Carroll v. Gross, 984 F.2d 392, 393 (11th Cir. 1993) (members of the Florida State Bar were acting as agents of the Florida Supreme Court in connection with disciplinary proceeding and were entitled to absolute immunity); and Turney v. O'Toole, 898 F.2d 1470, 1473–74 (10th Cir. 1990) (superintendent and psychologist at public mental health facility were entitled to absolute quasi-judicial immunity from juvenile's civil rights action insofar as action was based upon fact of juvenile's confinement pursuant to court order, even assuming order was infirm as matter of state law, but such immunity did not extend to any liability arising from placement of juvenile in maximum security ward; superintendent and psychologist were qualifiedly immune only for any liability arising from placement).

68. *See* Antoine v. Byers & Anderson, 508 U.S. 429, 436–37 (1993) (court reporter was not absolutely immune from damages liability for failing to produce transcript of federal criminal trial; tasks performed by court reporter were not discretionary and were not functionally comparable to that of judge); Snyder v. Nolen, 380 F.3d 279,

integral part of the judicial system are also absolutely immune.[69] For example, grand jurors exercising discretionary judgment on the basis of evidence

---

287–88 (7th Cir. 2004) (state court clerk who, on his own initiative, refused to file prison inmate's pro se marital dissolution pleadings, under mistaken belief that counsel was required to prosecute action, was not entitled to absolute quasi-judicial immunity in inmate's § 1983 action alleging denial of his constitutional right of access to the courts; clerk was not acting in functionally comparable way to a judge, since his duty under state law was purely ministerial one of maintaining official record, and secondly there was no evidence that clerk had acted at direction of any judicial officer); and Henriksen v. Bentley, 644 F.2d 852, 856 (10th Cir. 1981) (clerks entitled only to qualified immunity when exercising ministerial and nondiscretionary duty to file court papers). *But see* Kincaid v. Vale, 969 F.2d 594, 601 (7th Cir. 1992) (court clerks were entitled to absolute immunity against § 1983 action brought by two inmates who alleged that clerks had deprived them of their constitutional right to access to courts by refusing to file inmates' civil suit in Indiana Superior Court; clerks' acts were done at judicial direction, and were not mechanical functions integral to judicial process); Rogers v. Bruntrager, 841 F.2d 853, 856 (8th Cir. 1988) (court clerks held to have absolute immunity from actions for damages arising from acts they are specifically required to do under court order or at a judge's direction); and McCaw v. Winter, 745 F.2d 533, 534 (8th Cir. 1984) (court clerk who followed judge's order in selecting jury was absolutely immune).

69. *See, e.g.,* Wilson v. Kelkhoff, 86 F.3d 1438, 1443–44 (7th Cir. 1996) (prisoner review board members are entitled to absolute immunity for activities that are analogous to those performed by judges, such as decision to grant, deny, or revoke parole, as well as activities that are inexorably connected with execution of parole revocation procedures and are analogous to judicial action; thus, not only actual decision to revoke parole but also activities that are part and parcel of decision process justify absolute immunity); Davis v. Bayless, 70 F.3d 367, 373 (5th Cir. 1995) (court-appointed receivers act as arms of the court and are entitled to share the appointing judge's absolute immunity provided that the challenged actions are taken in good faith and within the scope of the authority granted to the receiver); Fleming v. Asbill, 42 F.3d 886, 889 (4th Cir. 1994) (guardian ad litem was entitled to quasi-judicial immunity on all civil rights claims arising from guardian's actions during child custody dispute, even if guardian lied to judge in open court); Millspaugh v. County Dept. of Public Welfare, 937 F.2d 1172, 1176 (7th Cir. 1991) (social service worker initiating child abuse proceeding was absolutely immune); Property Management & Investments, Inc. v. Lewis, 752 F.2d 599, 602 (11th Cir. 1985) (court-appointed receiver was entitled to absolute immunity in performing acts within the scope of his authority and in carrying out judge's orders); and Kurzawa v. Mueller, 732 F.2d 1456, 1458 (6th Cir. 1984) (state employees who were responsible for prosecution of child neglect and delinquency petitions in state courts, and psychologist and psychiatrists whose findings following examination of child were used by Department of Social Services and state courts to determine what environment best suited interests of child, all of whom were integral parts of judicial process, were entitled to absolute immunity in action brought by parents individually and as next friends of their son alleging violation of their civil rights).

presented to them in grand jury proceedings are entitled to absolute immunity.[70] Additionally, law enforcement officers acting pursuant to court orders are typically entitled to absolute immunity.[71]

F. Prosecutors

Prosecutors generally enjoy absolute immunity when performing prosecutorial acts.[72] As discussed below, however, prosecutors are not absolutely immune for all actions taken. Following a functional approach, the courts have held that while prosecutors are entitled to immunity for traditional litigation activities, they are not absolutely immune for activities such as office administration, criminal investigations, or press releases.

Imbler articulated a number of justifications for immunizing prosecutors for their prosecutorial acts. Those justifications, which are substantially similar to those advanced to justify absolute judicial immunity, include (1) the recognition of the common-law history of immunity for prosecutors; (2) policy considerations designed to protect prosecutors from unfounded litigation that would divert attention from their duties and effect independent decision making; and (3) the availability of alternative checks on prosecutor's activities by various posttrial and appellate procedures and professional disciplinary review mechanisms.[73]

G. The Functional Approach: Advocacy versus Investigative Acts

Prosecutors are absolutely immune when performing prosecutorial acts such as initiating the prosecution, presenting the case in court, and taking

70. *See* DeCamp v. Douglas County Franklin Grand Jury, 978 F.2d 1047, 1050–51 (8th Cir. 1992) (members of grand jury had absolute immunity against § 1983 claims against them arising from grand jurors' "co-authoring" of report issued following investigation of child abuse and other charges; grand jurors' comments in report involved exercise of discretionary, quasi-judicial function).
71. *See, e.g., In re* Foust, 310 F.3d 849, 855 (5th Cir. 2002) ("Law enforcement officers have absolute immunity for enforcing the terms of a court order but only qualified immunity for the manner in which they choose to enforce it."); Valdez v. City & County of Denver, 878 F.2d 1285, 1289 (10th Cir. 1989) ("Officials must not be called upon to answer for the legality of decisions which they are powerless to control."); and Henry v. Farmer City State Bank, 808 F.2d 1228, 1239–40 (7th Cir. 1986) (explaining that appeal is the sole avenue for challenging an unconstitutional court order).
72. *See Imbler,* 424 U.S. at 430–31; *Burns,* 500 U.S. at 490–91.
73. *See Imbler,* 424 U.S. at 424–27.

appeals.[74] Similarly, prosecutors are immune for their decisions to prosecute or not prosecute.[75] Activities associated with prosecutorial decisions are also

---

74. *See, e.g., Imbler,* 424 U.S. at 430–31; Reid v. State of New Hampshire, 56 F.3d 332, 336–37 (1st Cir. 1995) (prosecutors who prosecuted sexual assault action against former defendant had absolute immunity to former defendant's civil rights action, which alleged that prosecutors knowingly withheld exculpatory evidence in direct violation of trial court's discovery orders; under *Imbler,* prosecutors have absolute personal immunity for knowing suppression of exculpatory information, even if exculpatory information is suppressed in violation of trial court orders or is suppressed long after a defendant's conviction); Hansen v. Black, 885 F.2d 642, 646 (9th Cir. 1989) (city prosecutor entitled to absolute immunity for charging arrestee with violation of city ordinance); Ryan v. Bilby, 764 F.2d 1325, 1328 (9th Cir. 1985) (prosecutor involved in taxpayer's prosecution for failure to file tax returns was absolutely immune for damages under § 1983); Siano v. Justices of Mass., 698 F.2d 52, 57–58 (1st Cir. 1983); (county district attorney entitled to prosecutorial immunity from allegations that he initiated prosecution in bad faith and used tactics during trial that violated the criminal defendant's rights to due process and a fair trial); Lee v. Willins, 617 F.2d 320, 322 (2d Cir. 1980) (prosecuting lawyers entitled to prosecutorial immunity from § 1983 action based upon alleged falsification of evidence and coercion of perjured testimony); and Henzel v. Gerstein, 608 F.2d 654, 657 (5th Cir. 1979) (alleged unlawful acts of prosecutors—including filing information without investigation, filing charges without jurisdiction, filing a baseless detainer, offering perjured testimony, suppressing exculpatory evidence, refusing to investigate complaints about prison system, and threatening defendant with further criminal prosecutions—were all acts protected by prosecutorial immunity).
75. *See, e.g.,* Higgason v. Stephens, 288 F.3d 868, 877 (6th Cir. 2002) (prosecutor was entitled to absolute immunity in civil rights action brought by son who was indicted for attempted murder of his mother, although criminal case was dismissed with prejudice, and although jury in criminal case, had case gone to trial, may have ultimately agreed with son that there was no evidence to support charge; prosecutor was absolutely immune for his professional evaluation of evidence assembled, and for his presentation of that evidence to grand jury); Pinaud v. County of Suffolk, 52 F.3d 1139, 1149–52 (2d Cir. 1995) (prosecutor who presented case to grand jury and accepted plea agreement was entitled to absolute immunity for those acts, but not for delaying for three weeks the transfer of the prisoner back to federal custody after all state charges had been dismissed); Brummett v. Camble, 946 F.2d 1178, 1181 (5th Cir. 1991) (prosecutor was entitled to absolute immunity even if he had interest in bank that initiated complaint and even if he knew the charges were baseless); Newcomb v. Ingle, 944 F.2d 1534, 1536 (10th Cir. 1991) (decision not to prosecute entitled to absolute immunity); Fields v. Soloff, 920 F.2d 1114, 1119 (2d Cir. 1990) (prosecutors were absolutely immune in presenting case to grand jury and in deciding whom to prosecute); Celia v. O'Malley, 918 F.2d 1017, 1019–20 (1st Cir. 1990) (prosecutors were absolutely immune in prosecuting case without seeking indictment from grand jury); and Webster v. Gibson, 913 F.2d 510, 513–14 (8th Cir. 1990) (prosecutor was absolutely immune in failing to file information, even if ordered to do so by the court).

protected,[76] including immunity for plea-bargaining activities[77] as well as immunity in preparing for trial and in presenting the case in court.[78]

---

76. *See, e.g.,* Cousin v. Small, 325 F.3d 627, 634–35 (5th Cir. 2003) (prosecutor who allegedly instructed State's witness to implicate defendant falsely in murder trial was acting as an advocate rather than as an investigator, and therefore prosecutor was entitled to absolute immunity from defendant's civil rights claims; prosecutor's interview with witness was intended to secure evidence that would be used in presentation of the state's case at the pending trial of an already identified suspect, not to identify a suspect or establish probable cause); Anderson v. Simon, 217 F.3d 472, 475–76 (7th Cir. 2000) (county prosecutor's decision not to charge prisoner until lineup could be held was prosecutorial rather than administrative decision, and prosecutor thus was absolutely immune from § 1983 claim by prisoner's widow alleging that delay in charging, after prisoner stated that he wanted to kill himself, led to prisoner's suicide and violated his Fourth and Fourteenth Amendment rights; prosecutor's review of evidence and determination that additional evidence was necessary to support charge were necessary part of his role as advocate); Grant v. Hollenbach, 870 F.2d 1135, 1138–39 (6th Cir. 1989) (prosecutor bringing child abuse charges who allegedly conspired with complainant was entitled to absolute immunity); Baez v. Hennessey, 853 F.2d 73, 74–75 (2d Cir. 1988) (signing by assistant district attorney of erroneous indictment that grand jury did not return was prosecutorial act for which he was absolutely immune); Umphlet v. Connick, 815 F.2d 1061, 1062–63 (5th Cir. 1987) (district attorney was entitled to prosecutorial immunity from liability in § 1983 action for enforcement of state statute); Morrison v. City of Baton Rouge, 761 F.2d 242, 246–48 (5th Cir. 1985) (prosecutor who maliciously presented evidence to a grand jury in a manner calculated to clear a suspect of wrongdoing was absolutely immune); Powers v. Coe, 728 F.2d 97, 103–04 (2d Cir. 1984) (prosecutor who presented matter to the grand jury in breach of an agreement not to prosecute was absolutely immune); Lerwill v. Joslin, 712 F.2d 435, 441 (10th Cir. 1983) (city attorney who had power to file only criminal charges based on a violation of city ordinances was absolutely immune for wrongfully filing state felony charge); Gray v. Bell, 712 F.2d 490, 502–03 (D.C. Cir. 1983) (prosecutor was immune in presenting evidence to grand jury); and Dellums v. Powell, 660 F.2d 802, 805–07 (D.C. Cir. 1981) (U.S. Attorney General was absolutely immune in ordering prosecution of Vietnam War demonstrators).
77. *See, e.g.,* Krohn v. United States, 742 F.2d 24, 29–30 (1st Cir. 1984) (federal prosecutor had absolute immunity from allegations that he conspired to convert plaintiff's property by striking deal with defense counsel to learn the location of plaintiff's safe-deposit box); McGruder v. Necaise, 733 F.2d 1146, 1148 (5th Cir. 1984) (prosecutor who offered to drop criminal charges against arrestee if he would dismiss a civil suit against the county jail was absolutely immune); and Taylor v. Kavanagh, 640 F.2d 450, 453–54 (2d Cir. 1981) (prosecutor was absolutely immune in plea-bargaining role).
78. *See, e.g., Burns,* 500 U.S. at 490–91 (prosecutor was absolutely immune in presenting application for search warrant, but not in advising police on investigation); and Geter v. Fortenberry, 849 F.2d 1550, 1554 (5th Cir. 1988) (act of setting a trial date was a prosecutorial act requiring absolute immunity).

Acts of prosecutors not directly related to the decision to prosecute or the presentation of cases are typically not entitled to absolute immunity. For example, if a prosecutor acts in other ways, such as conducting investigations, making representations to the court, or issuing press releases, he or she may be entitled to a qualified immunity but not to absolute immunity.

Prosecutors who are involved in investigative functions are not usually entitled to absolute immunity.[79] Similarly, prosecutors are not entitled to

79. *See, e.g.,* Kalina v. Fletcher, 522 U.S. 118, 129–30 (1997) (prosecutor was not entitled to absolute prosecutorial immunity with respect to her actions in executing certification for determination of probable cause in connection with filing of charges against accused in which accused alleged that certification contained false statements; act of filing certification was not one of traditional functions of advocate, as neither federal nor state law required that prosecutor make certification, and it could have been made by any competent witness); Buckley v. Fitzsimmons, 509 U.S. 259, 274–75 (1993) (prosecutor's alleged misconduct when endeavoring to determine whether a boot print at a crime scene had been left by a suspect was an investigatory, administrative function rather than a prosecutorial function, for which the prosecutor was entitled to only qualified immunity in suspect's subsequent § 1983 suit); Rowe v. City of Fort Lauderdale, 279 F.3d 1271, 1279 (11th Cir. 2002) (even if prosecutor knowingly proffered perjured testimony and fabricated exhibits at trial, he was entitled to absolute immunity from liability for doing so; however, to the extent he stepped out of his prosecutorial role to perform the investigative functions normally performed by a detective or police officer, prosecutor did not have absolute immunity); Houston v. Partee, 978 F.2d 362, 365–66 (7th Cir. 1992) (prosecutors who discovered exculpatory evidence after person was convicted and did not disclose it to the defense had no absolute immunity, since they were acting in an investigative capacity); McSurely v. McClellan, 697 F.2d 309, 319–20 (D.C. Cir. 1982) (alleged conduct of prosecutor in participating in a public meeting for the purpose, known to him to be unconstitutional, of preventing plaintiffs from disseminating ideas, preparing flagrantly unconstitutional arrest and search warrants, participating in raid on plaintiff's home which went far beyond warrant, and conspiring with representatives of Senate subcommittee to transfer to them documents that had been illegally seized and were irrelevant to the subcommittee's business, and that were required by court order to be returned to plaintiffs or retained in safekeeping, did not implicate state prosecutor's protected advocate function, and thus was not protected by absolute immunity from suit); Marrero v. City of Hialeah, 625 F.2d 499, 505–06 (5th Cir. 1980) (prosecutor participating in illegal search and seizure was not entitled to absolute immunity); Hampton v. Hanrahan, 600 F.2d 600, 633–34 (7th Cir. 1979) (prosecutors who arranged for police raid on Black Panther headquarters were not entitled to absolute immunity); and Jacobson v. Rose, 592 F.2d 515, 524 (9th Cir. 1978) (where district attorney ordered and joined with sheriff's office in implementing illegal wiretap, he was not entitled to absolute immunity).

absolute immunity for exercising law enforcement functions,[80] for giving legal advice,[81] or in making public statements.[82]

A prosecutor's out-of-court treatment of seized evidence or property is not protected by absolute immunity.[83] Additionally, when prosecutors order the destruction of exonerating material, they are not entitled to absolute immunity.[84]

H. Others Who Perform Prosecutorial-Like Functions

Persons performing prosecutorial-like functions are entitled to immunity.[85] Social workers initiating or "prosecuting" child neglect or child

---

80. *See, e.g.,* Latimore v. Widseth, 986 F.2d 292, 294–95 (8th Cir. 1993) (prosecutor was not absolutely immune in disclosing to media that prisoner would be a witness in a case when that prisoner was subsequently attacked by other inmates); Buckley v. Fitzsimmons, 919 F.2d 1230, 1244 (7th Cir. 1990) (no absolute immunity for coercive interrogation of defendants by prosecutor); Day v. Morganthau, 909 F.2d 75, 77–78 (2d Cir. 1990) (prosecutor who ordered person arrested for trespassing was not entitled to absolute immunity); and Price v. Moody, 677 F.2d 676, 678 (8th Cir. 1982) (no immunity if prosecutor orders mistreatment of prisoner).
81. *See, e.g., Burns,* 500 U.S. at 491–92 (prosecutor giving legal advice to policeman on how to conduct investigation was not entitled to absolute immunity); and Benavidez v. Gunnell, 722 F.2d 615, 617 (10th Cir. 1983) (no absolute immunity when prosecutor gave legal advice to police).
82. *See, e.g., Buckley,* 509 U.S. at 277–78 (press statements by prosecutors not subject to absolute immunity); and Stepanian v. Addis, 699 F.2d 1046, 1048 (11th Cir. 1983) (federal prosecutor's statements made at a press conference announcing criminal indictment were not subject to absolute immunity).
83. *See* Coleman v. Turpen, 697 F.2d 1341, 1346 (10th Cir. 1982) (participation in illegal sale of seized property was not protected by absolute immunity).
84. *See* Henderson v. Fisher, 631 F.2d 1115, 1120 (3d Cir. 1980) (prosecutor who allegedly failed to preserve exculpatory evidence was not entitled to absolute immunity).
85. *See, e.g.,* Ostrzenski v. Seigel, 177 F.3d 245, 251 (4th Cir. 1999) (physician conducting peer review at behest of Maryland Board of Physician Quality Assurance was entitled to absolute quasi-judicial immunity from reviewed physician's § 1983 claim alleging due process violations; reviewing physician was performing function analogous to prosecutor reviewing evidence to determine if charges should be brought, and absolute immunity was necessary to foster atmosphere in which reviewing physician could exercise professional judgment without fear of retaliation); and Wang v. New Hampshire Bd. of Registration in Medicine, 55 F.3d 698, 701–02 (1st Cir. 1995) (administrative board members initiating professional misconduct charges against a doctor were entitled to absolute prosecutorial immunity).

abuse proceedings have generally been held to have absolute immunity.[86] The cases, however, are not entirely consistent.[87] Activities that have attributes of prosecutorial-like conduct may also be protected.[88]

86. *See, e.g.,* Doe v Lebbos, 348 F.3d 820, 826 (9th Cir. 2003) (social worker's alleged failure to investigate possible exculpatory evidence and fabrication of evidence in dependency petitions, if proven, had requisite connection to judicial process to be protected by absolute immunity from § 1983 action filed by child and child's father, where such actions were part of initiation and pursuit of child dependency proceedings); Miller v. Gammie, 335 F.3d 889, 898 (9th Cir. 2003) (en banc) (critical decision to institute proceedings to make a child a ward of the state is functionally similar to the prosecutorial institution of a criminal proceeding; the decision, therefore, is likely entitled to absolute immunity); Millspaugh v. County Dept. of Public Welfare, 937 F.2d 1172, 1175–76 (7th Cir. 1991) (social service worker initiating child abuse proceeding was absolutely immune); Vosburg v. Department of Social Services, 884 F.2d 133, 135–38 (4th Cir. 1989) (in filing a petition for removal of a child from her home, as opposed to conduct in investigating the possibility that removal petition should be filed, Virginia state social workers were acting in a prosecutorial rather than an investigative or "policing" capacity and thus were absolutely immune from any liability arising from the decision to file a removal petition); Salyer v. Patrick, 874 F.2d 374, 378 (6th Cir. 1989) (social worker investigating child abuse case was absolutely immune); Meyers v. Contra Costa County Dept. of Social Serv., 812 F.2d 1154, 1157–58 (9th Cir. 1987) (absolute immunity provided for social welfare workers who were investigating child abuse); Coverdell v. Department of Social and Health Services, 834 F.2d 758, 762–63 (9th Cir. 1987) (social workers prosecuting child abuse cases are absolutely immune); and Kurzawa v. Mueller, 732 F.2d 1456, 1458 (6th Cir. 1984) (social service department employee enjoys absolute immunity in removing child from home and placing it in foster home).

87. *See, e.g.,* Snell v. Tunnell, 920 F.2d 673, 690–92 (10th Cir. 1990) (social workers who sought pre-petition conditional protective custody order as part of their investigation into neglect at private home being operated as emergency shelter were entitled to only qualified immunity from § 1983 civil rights liability); Hodorowski v. Ray, 844 F.2d 1210, 1213–15 (5th Cir. 1988) (conduct of child protective service workers in temporarily removing children from parents' home without first obtaining court order was more akin to function of police than prosecutor, so that workers were not protected by absolute prosecutorial immunity from civil rights liability arising from removal but rather were entitled only to qualified immunity); and Austin v. Borel, 830 F.2d 1356, 1360–63 (5th Cir. 1988) (child protection workers who allegedly filed false charges against parents were not entitled to absolute immunity).

88. *See, e.g.,* Spear v. Town of West Hartford, 954 F.2d 63, 66 (2d Cir. 1992) (city manager's decision to initiate a lawsuit in pursuit of city's governmental interests was similar to the filing of an administrative complaint and, thus, was entitled to absolute immunity); Hamill v. Wright, 870 F.2d 1032, 1037 (5th Cir. 1989) (director

I. Witnesses

Witnesses testifying at trial are entitled to absolute immunity.[89] As described below, however, the circuits are split as to whether witness immunity should be extended to those testifying at proceedings other than trial, such as probable cause and grand jury hearings.

The Supreme Court in *Briscoe* articulated two bases for justifying absolute immunity for witnesses testifying at trial. One, the common law had historically recognized immunity for witnesses; and two, public policy dictated that witnesses should not fear testifying truthfully for fear of a subsequent lawsuit based upon their testimony.[90]

Some circuits hold that witnesses are entitled to immunity for their testimony at proceedings other than trial.[91] Some circuits, however, have refused

---

of county's domestic relations office was entitled to full prosecutorial immunity from civil rights claim based upon his decision to bring contempt proceedings against parent for failure to pay child support); Werle v. Rhode Island Bar Association, 755 F.2d 195, 198–99 (1st Cir. 1985) (members of state bar unauthorized practice of law committee were acting as public prosecutors and were entitled to absolute immunity); Walden v. Wishengrad, 745 F.2d 149, 152–53 (2d Cir. 1984) (lawyer employed by county social services department who prosecuted child protective orders in family court was acting as a prosecutor and was absolutely immune); Demery v. Kupperman, 735 F.2d 1139, 1142–45 (9th Cir. 1984) (deputy attorney general prosecuting an administrative complaint against a doctor to revoke his medical license was absolutely immune in allegedly inducing witnesses to testify falsely); and Malachowski v. City of Keene, 787 F.2d 704, 712 (1st Cir. 1981) (policeman who initiated juvenile delinquency proceeding in his capacity as juvenile officer was acting like a prosecutor and was entitled to absolute immunity).

89. *See* Briscoe v. LaHue, 460 U.S. 325, 334 (1983); and Franklin v. Terr, 201 F.3d 1098, 1101 (9th Cir. 2000) (psychiatrist was absolutely immune from liability for damages under § 1983 based on allegation that she conspired to present her own and another witness's perjured testimony at plaintiff's criminal trial since her alleged conspiratorial behavior was inextricably tied to her testimony, where plaintiff was tried for twenty-year-old murder based in part on his daughter's recovered memory, and plaintiff alleged that psychiatrist conspired with daughter by incorporating information obtained from daughter into her own testimony and by providing daughter with description of the sort of details that would make her testimony more persuasive).
90. *Briscoe,* 460 U.S. at 333–34.
91. *See* Scarbrough v. Myles, 245 F.3d 1299, 1305 (11th Cir. 2001) (police officer was protected by absolute immunity from imposition of liability under § 1983 based on testimony he gave during preliminary hearing); Williams v. Hepting, 844 F.2d 138, 141–43 (3d Cir. 1988) (witness entitled to absolute immunity for alleged perjured testimony given in preliminary criminal hearing); Alioto v. City of Shively, 835

to extend absolute witness immunity to proceedings other than testifying at trial.[92] One apparent rationale between the divergent cases denying absolute immunity and those granting absolute immunity is the distinction between being a fact witness and being a complaining witness; that is, fact witnesses could lie and defame at common law with immunity in order to protect the integrity of the judicial process, but complaining witnesses were never afforded such immunity for malicious prosecution.[93] While this may be a distinction without a difference with respect to law enforcement officials, it is a distinction that appears to have been drawn by some circuits.

F.2d 1173, 1174 (6th Cir. 1987) (police officers were absolutely immune from civil rights liability for their alleged conspiracy to give false and incomplete testimony in grand jury proceedings); Holt v. Castaneda, 832 F.2d 123, 127 (9th Cir. 1987) (extending absolute witness immunity to adversarial pretrial proceedings); and Kincaid v. Eberle, 712 F.2d 1023, 1024 (7th Cir. 1985) (granting absolute immunity to grand jury witnesses).

92. *See, e.g.,* Newsome v. McCabe, 319 F.3d 301, 304 (7th Cir. 2003) (police officers who allegedly instructed identifying witness in homicide investigation to pick specific suspect out of lineup and then warned witness that he risked jail time if he informed prosecutors of officers' manipulation were not entitled to absolute immunity owing to their concealment of exculpatory evidence); Keko v. Hingle, 318 F.3d 639, 642 (5th Cir. 2003) (physician sued for allegedly conspiring to violate defendant's civil rights in connection with murder prosecution was not entitled to absolute immunity for expert report that was offered not as evidence at trial, but at hearing to obtain warrant for defendant's arrest, in which physician concluded that bite marks found on victim's body undoubtedly came from defendant); Paine v. City of Lompoc, 265 F.3d 975, 982–83 (9th Cir. 2001) (absolute witness immunity does not shield an out-of-court, pretrial conspiracy to engage in non-testimonial acts such as fabricating or suppressing physical or documentary evidence or suppressing the identities of potential witnesses); White v. Frank, 855 F.2d 956, 961 (2d Cir. 1988) (police officers who act as complaining witnesses do not have absolute immunity); Anthony v. Baker, 767 F.2d 657, 660 (10th Cir. 1985) (refusing to extend absolute witness immunity to grand jury witnesses); San Filippo v. United States Trust Co., 737 F.2d 246, 255 (2d Cir. 1984) (no absolute immunity for alleged conspiracy between prosecutor and witnesses to secure false testimony before grand jury); and Wheeler v. Cosden Oil & Chemical Co., 734 F.2d 254, 261 (5th Cir. 1984) (denying absolute immunity to witness who testified at probable cause hearing).

93. Curtis v. Bembeneck, 48 F.3d 281, 284 (7th Cir. 1995) (police officer's absolute immunity from § 1983 liability for testimony given at trial extended to liability for allegedly perjured testimony given during preliminary hearing to determine whether probable cause existed to support warrantless arrest, and during hearing on motion to quash arrest and suppress evidence; policy consideration that witness might shade testimony in order to avoid liability applied with equal force to witness testimony in

IV. QUALIFIED IMMUNITY

The Supreme Court has held that government officials performing discretionary functions are entitled to qualified immunity from suit and damages where "their conduct does not violate clearly established statutory or constitutional rights of which a reasonable person would have known."[94] The critical issue is not whether a defendant actually infringed upon a plaintiff's rights: "Even defendants who violate constitutional rights enjoy a qualified immunity that protects them from liability for damages unless it is further demonstrated that their conduct was unreasonable under the applicable standard."[95] To aid in that determination, the Court has reaffirmed that "whether an official protected by qualified immunity may be held personally liable for an allegedly unlawful action turns on the 'objective legal reasonableness' of the action . . . assessed in light of the legal rules that were 'clearly established' at the time it was taken."[96] For the relevant legal standards to be "clearly established," the "contours" of the right alleged to have been violated "must be sufficiently clear that a reasonable official would understand that what he is doing violates that right."[97] Under the *Harlow* standard, "a defense of qualified immunity may not be rebutted by evidence that the defendant's conduct was malicious or otherwise improperly motivated. Evidence concerning the defendant's subjective intent is simply irrelevant to that defense."[98]

A. The Evolution of Qualified Immunity

The doctrine of qualified immunity, like the absolute immunities discussed earlier in this chapter, is a judicially created doctrine that recognizes the

---

trial and adversarial pretrial settings, and plaintiff's argument that officer was akin to complaining witness and thus was not immune was inapplicable where plaintiff failed to state claim for malicious prosecution); and Enlow v. Tishomingo County, Miss., 962 F.2d 501, 512 (5th Cir. 1992) ("In resolving questions of immunity, the common law distinguished between defamation actions and actions for malicious prosecution, cloaking with absolute immunity a witness in the former but not the latter.").

94. Harlow v. Fitzgerald, 457 U.S. 800, 818 (1982); and Mitchell v. Forsyth, 472 U.S. 511, 526 (1985). *See also* Groh v. Ramirez, 540 U.S. 551, 563–65 (2004); Hope v. Pelzer, 536 U.S. 730, 739–41 (2002); Saucier v. Katz, 553 U.S. 194, 200–03 (2001); and Crawford-El v. Britton, 523 U.S. 574, 587–92 (1998).
95. Davis v. Scherer, 468 U.S. 183, 190 (1984).
96. Anderson v. Creighton, 483 U.S. 635, 639 (1987) (citations omitted).
97. *Id.* at 640.
98. *Crawford-El,* 523 U.S. at 588.

common-law immunity of public officials for their "good faith" actions. The public policy behind such qualified immunity includes attracting competent individuals to public sector jobs, encouraging individuals to serve in elected offices, allowing public officials to exercise unfettered discretion in serving the public good, and avoiding exposing public officials to unnecessary litigation that would distract them from their civic responsibilities.[99] This concept of good-faith qualified immunity has evolved from a two-pronged, objective and subjective test to a one-pronged, objective test.

B. *Wood v. Strickland* and the Subjective Test

In *Wood v. Strickland*,[100] the Supreme Court defined qualified immunity in § 1983 actions as including both an objective and subjective element. The Court, in a case involving the liability of school board members for disciplinary actions against students, articulated the standard as follows:

> [A] school board member is not immune from liability for damages under § 1983 if he knew or reasonably should have known that the action he took within his sphere of official responsibility would violate the constitutional rights of the student affected, or if he took the action with the malicious intention to cause a deprivation of constitutional rights or other injury to the student.[101]

Under the two-pronged *Wood* test, public officials could be held liable under § 1983 for violations of federal law when their conduct was either objectively unreasonable or in subjective bad faith.

The use of a subjective good-faith standard in the application of qualified immunity, however, proved problematic because it triggered an examination of the public official's subjective state of mind at the time of the alleged unconstitutional act. Such a factual determination obviously frustrated the intent of qualified immunity to quickly resolve insubstantial lawsuits by way of a motion to dismiss or a motion for summary judgment.

C. *Harlow v. Fitzgerald* and the Objective Test

In *Harlow v. Fitzgerald*,[102] the Supreme Court recognized this problem and significantly redefined the standard for qualified immunity by abandoning the subjective prong of the qualified immunity test and holding that § 1983

99. *Id.* at 590.
100. 420 U.S. 308 (1975).
101. *Id.* at 322.
102. 457 U.S. 800 (1982).

defendants would be liable for damages only when their conduct violated clearly established federal law.[103] The Court discussed the parameters of its newly defined objective qualified immunity test as follows:

> [W]e conclude today that bare allegations of malice should not suffice to subject government officials either to the costs of trial or to the burdens of broad-reaching discovery. *We therefore hold that government officials performing discretionary functions generally are shielded from liability for civil damages insofar as their conduct does not violate clearly established statutory or constitutional rights of which a reasonable person would have known.*
>
> Reliance on the objective reasonableness of an official's conduct, as measured by reference to clearly established law, should avoid excessive disruption of government and permit the resolution of many insubstantial claims on summary judgment: *On summary judgment, the judge appropriately may determine, not only the currently applicable law, but whether that law was clearly established at the time an action occurred. If the law at that time was not clearly established, an official could not reasonably be expected to anticipate subsequent legal developments, nor could he fairly be said to "know" that the law forbade conduct not previously identified as unlawful.* Until this threshold immunity question is resolved, discovery should not be allowed. If the law was clearly established, the immunity defense ordinarily should fail, since a reasonably competent public official should know the law governing his conduct. Nevertheless, if the official pleading the defense claims extraordinary circumstances and can prove that he neither knew nor should have known of the relevant legal standard, the defense should be sustained. But again, the defense would turn primarily on objective factors.
>
> By defining the limits of qualified immunity essentially in objective terms, we provide no license to lawless conduct. The public interest in deterrence of unlawful conduct and in compensation of victims remains protected by a test that focuses on the objective legal reasonableness of an official's acts. Where an official could be expected to know that certain conduct would violate statutory or constitutional rights, he should be made to hesitate; and a person who suffers injury caused by such conduct may have a cause of

---

103. *Id.* at 818–19.

> action. But where an official's duties legitimately require action in which clearly established rights are not implicated, the public interest may be better served by action taken "with independence and without fear of consequences."[104]

The Court's reasoning in *Harlow* was later elaborated upon in *Crawford-El.*

> Two reasons that are explicit in our opinion in *Harlow*, together with a third that is implicit in the holding, amply justified *Harlow*'s reformulation of the qualified immunity defense. First, there is a strong public interest in protecting public officials from the costs associated with the defense of damages actions. That interest is best served by a defense that permits insubstantial lawsuits to be quickly terminated. Second, allegations of subjective motivation might have been used to shield baseless lawsuits from summary judgment. The objective standard, in contrast, raises questions concerning the state of the law at the time of the challenged conduct—questions that normally can be resolved on summary judgment. Third, focusing on "the objective legal reasonableness of an official's acts," avoids the unfairness of imposing liability on a defendant who "could not reasonably be expected to anticipate subsequent legal developments, nor . . . fairly be said to 'know' that the law forbade conduct not previously identified as unlawful." That unfairness may be present even when the official conduct is motivated, in part, by hostility to the plaintiff.[105]

D. Breaking Down the *Harlow* Standard

The Supreme Court has stated that "government officials performing *discretionary functions* generally are shielded from liability for civil damages insofar as their conduct does not violate clearly established statutory or constitutional rights of which a reasonable person would have known."[106] The discretionary versus ministerial function dichotomy in decision making, however, has rarely been used as a disqualifier for undertaking a qualified immunity analysis.

---

104. *Id.* (emphasis added, citations and footnotes omitted).

105. *Crawford-El,* 523 U.S. at 590 (citations and footnotes omitted).

106. *Harlow,* 457 U.S. at 818 (emphasis added).

For example, in *Horta v. Sullivan*,[107] the First Circuit downplayed the importance of discretionary versus ministerial functions in a qualified immunity analysis.

> [In] spite of the reference to discretionary functions [in *Harlow*], it has never since been clear exactly what role, if any, this concept is supposed to play in applying qualified immunity. Judge Cummings, writing for the Seventh Circuit, warned that "it would be unwise to engage in a case by case determination of Section 1983 immunity based upon the ministerial versus the discretionary nature of the particular official act challenged."[108]

Other circuits also have recognized the danger in rejecting qualified immunity claims merely on the basis of a determination that the functions involved are ministerial rather than discretionary.

> The distinction between ministerial and discretionary duties of public officials has a long history. However, the plaintiffs have cited, and we can find, no recent case other than that before us in which a court has rejected qualified immunity simply because the official in question was performing a ministerial duty.[109]

In *Davis v. Scherer*,[110] the Supreme Court dramatically circumscribed the viability of the ministerial duty exception to qualified immunity. In *Davis*, the plaintiff, a discharged employee of the Florida Highway Patrol, sued certain public officials of the Florida Department of Highway Safety and Motor Vehicles under § 1983, alleging that his due process rights had been violated.[111] The trial and appellate courts had denied the public officials' qualified immunity because they had not followed certain administra-

---

107. 4 F.3d 2 (1st Cir. 1993).

108. *Id.* at 11 (quoting Coleman v. Frantz, 754 F.2d 719, 727 (7th Cir. 1985)).

109. McIntosh v. Weinberger, 810 F.2d 1411, 1432 (8th Cir. 1987), *partially vacated and remanded on other grounds sub. nom.* Turner v. McIntosh, 487 U.S. 1212 (1988) (citation omitted). *See also* Ricci v. Key Bancshares of Maine, Inc., 768 F.2d 456, 464 (1st Cir. 1985) ("[B]reaking down discretionary acts . . . into discretionary and ministerial components would seem to vitiate much of the protection of discretionary action which absolute immunity was designed to provide."); and *Horta,* 4 F.3d at 15 ("[I]t would be the rare case indeed where an officer is denied qualified immunity because the officer is found to have engaged in 'ministerial' rather than 'discretionary' conduct.").

110. 468 U.S. 183 (1984).

111. *Id.* at 185–87.

tive regulations in discharging the plaintiff and, therefore, were held not to have acted in a discretionary capacity.[112] In rejecting this contention, the Supreme Court stated as follows:

> Appellee's contention mistakes the scope of the "ministerial duty" exception to qualified immunity in two respects. First, as we have discussed, breach of a legal duty created by the personnel regulation would forfeit official immunity only if that breach itself gave rise to the appellee's cause of action for damages. This principle equally applies whether the regulation created discretionary or ministerial duties. Even if the personnel regulation did create a ministerial duty, appellee makes no claim that he is entitled to damages simply because the regulation was violated. . . .
>
> . . . [T]he District Court's findings that appellants ignored a clear legal command does not bear on the "ministerial" nature of appellants' duties. *A law that fails to specify the precise action that the official must take in each instance creates only discretionary authority; and that authority remains discretionary however egregiously it is abused.*[113]

The Court also held that "[o]fficials sued for constitutional violations do not lose their qualified immunity merely because their conduct violates some statutory or administrative provision."[114] The Court reasoned that the officials could lose their immunity only if the breach of the state regulation, rather than a constitutional duty, gave rise to the plaintiff's damages claim.[115]

The narrow application of the ministerial duty exception to qualified immunity also has been recognized by the Fifth Circuit in *Gagne v. City of Galveston*:[116]

> Although the Supreme Court's qualified immunity opinions have given special attention to the need to avoid inhibiting the ardor of public officials whose positions entail the exercise of discretionary

---

112. *Id.* at 188–89.

113. *Id.* at 196 n.14 (emphasis added).

114. *Id.* at 194.

115. *Davis,* 468 U.S. at 194 n.12 ("For the reasons that we discuss, officials sued for violations of rights conferred by a statute or regulation, like officials sued for violation of constitutional rights, do not forfeit their immunity by violating some other statute or regulation. Rather, these officials become liable for damages only to the extent that there is a clear violation of the statutory rights that give rise to the cause of action for damages.").

116. 805 F.2d 558, 559–60 (5th Cir. 1986), *cert. denied,* 483 U.S. 1021 (1987).

> authority, the Court has never implied that the immunity defense is lost when an official is engaged in routine tasks. Indeed, any such suggestion was firmly rejected in footnote 14 of *Davis v. Scherer*, where the Court emphasized that the so-called "ministerial duty" exception to qualified immunity is extremely narrow in scope. . . . Thus, if an official is required to exercise his judgment, even if rarely or to a small degree, the Court would apparently not find an official's duty to be ministerial in nature.[117]

In *Sellers v. Baer*,[118] the Eight Circuit has even gone so far as to opine that the ministerial exception is a "dead letter," collecting opinions expressing skepticism as to whether a distinction should be drawn between discretionary and ministerial duties for purposes of a qualified immunity analysis.[119]

E. Conduct That Does Not Violate Clearly Established Statutory or Constitutional Rights of Which a Reasonable Person Would Have Known

The doctrine of qualified immunity shields an official performing discretionary functions from liability for damages under § 1983 so long as the official's conduct does not violate clearly established constitutional or statutory rights of which a reasonable person would have been aware. Whether an official can be held personally liable for taking an allegedly unlawful action turns on the "objective legal reasonableness" of the action, assessed in light of the legal rules that were "clearly established" at the time the action was taken.[120] To be clearly established, the "contours" of the right allegedly violated must be sufficiently clear that a reasonable official would understand what he is doing violates that right.[121]

The appropriate inquiry is whether a reasonable official could have thought that he acted in accordance with the Constitution in taking the action of which is being complained.[122] As noted by the Supreme Court in *Hunter*, "the court should ask whether the [government official] acted rea-

117. *Id.* at 559–60.
118. 28 F.3d 895 (8th Cir. 1994).
119. *Id.* at 902.
120. *See Harlow,* 457 U.S. at 818–19.
121. *See Anderson,* 483 U.S. at 640.
122. *See* McCleary v. Navarro, 504 U.S. 966 (1992); and Hunter v. Bryant, 502 U.S. 224, 228 (1991).

sonably under settled law in the circumstances, not whether another reasonable, or more reasonable, interpretation of the events can be constructed . . . years after the fact."[123]

This deferential standard is also applicable in a summary judgment context: "If, upon viewing the evidence in the light most favorable to the non-movant, reasonable public officials could differ on the lawfulness of the defendant's actions, the defendant is entitled to qualified immunity."[124] The qualified immunity standard "gives ample room for mistaken judgments."[125]

To properly apply the test for qualified immunity, a court must determine whether the law, as applied to a specific factual situation, was clearly established in such a way that the officials involved should have known that their decision or actions violated constitutional rights or federal law. Simple negligence on the part of a public official is not enough.[126]

> That qualified immunity protects government actors is the usual rule; only in exceptional cases will government actors have no shield against claims made against them in their individual capacities. Unless a government agent's act is so obviously wrong, in the light of pre-existing law, that only a plainly incompetent officer or one who was knowingly violating the law would have done such a thing, the government actor has immunity from suit.[127]

F. What Is a Clearly Established Right, and How Is It Determined?

In *Anderson v. Creighton*,[128] the Supreme Court required increased fact specificity from plaintiffs alleging that a public official had violated clearly established law. The Court clarified the qualified immunity standard by rejecting the notion that public officials were expected to be able to give concrete application to lofty, abstract principles of constitutional law:

---

123. *Hunter,* 502 U.S. at 228.

124. Harper v. Harris County, 21 F.3d 597, 600 (5th Cir. 1994).

125. Malley v. Briggs, 475 U.S. 335, 343 (1986). *See also Hunter,* 502 U.S. at 229 ("[A]ccommodation for reasonable error exists because 'officials should not err always on the side of caution' because they fear being sued.") (citing Davis v. Scherer, 468 U.S. 183, 196 (1984)).

126. *See* Daniel v. Williams, 474 U.S. 327, 328 (1986); and Davidson v. Cannon, 474 U.S. 344, 346–47 (1986).

127. Lassiter v. Alabama A&M Bd. of Trustees, 28 F.3d 1146, 1149 (11th Cir. 1994).

128. 483 U.S. 635 (1987).

> The operation of [the *Harlow*] standard . . . depends substantially upon the level of generality at which the relevant "legal rule" is to be identified. For example, the right to due process of law is quite clearly established by the Due Process Clause, and thus there is a sense in which any action that violates that cause (no matter how unclear it may be that the particular action is a violation) violates a clearly established right. Much the same could be said of any other constitutional or statutory violation. But if the test of "clearly established law" were to be applied at this level of generality, it would bear no relationship to the "objective legal reasonableness" that is the touchstone of *Harlow*. Plaintiffs would be able to convert the rule of qualified immunity that our cases plainly establish into a rule of virtually unqualified liability simply by alleging violation of extremely abstract rights. *Harlow* would be transformed from a guarantee of immunity into a rule of pleading.[129]

The Court has held that qualified immunity must be analyzed at an "objective, albeit fact-specific" level of abstraction:

> [O]ur cases establish that the right the official is alleged to have violated must have been "clearly established" in a more particularized, and hence more relevant, sense: The contours of the right must be sufficiently clear that a reasonable official would understand that what he is doing violates that right.[130]

The objective reasonableness of the action in question is to be assessed in light of the constitutional norms that were "clearly established" at the time the action was taken.[131]

G. How Is the Law Clearly Established?

It is unquestioned that Supreme Court precedent directly on point establishes clearly settled law of which a reasonable public official either knows or should know.[132] What constitutes "clearly established law" outside of

---

129. *Id.* at 639.

130. *Id.* at 640.

131. *Id.* at 639–40.

132. *See, e.g., Groh,* 540 U.S. at 563–65 (Federal agent who had prepared and executed warrant for search of plaintiffs' ranch could not have reasonably believed in validity either of warrant itself, which utterly failed to describe persons or things to be seized in clear contravention of explicit Fourth Amendment command, or of search conducted pursuant thereto, and was not entitled to qualified immunity from liability in action for violating ranch owners' Fourth Amendment rights.)

Supreme Court precedent, however, is simply not clearly established. The question of which, and how many, courts must speak on an issue has not been addressed by the Supreme Court. For example, the Sixth Circuit has interpreted "clearly established law," other than black-letter statutory provisions, to mean law that has been established by decisions of (1) the U.S. Supreme Court; (2) the U.S. Court of Appeals in which the incident occurred; (3) other U.S. Courts of Appeals; or (4) the highest state court in the state where the action arose.[133]

Some cases suggest that Supreme Court precedent or case law from the defendant's own jurisdiction is necessary to clearly establish a constitutional right, while others rely on case law from other jurisdictions.[134] Some courts of appeals have granted immunity despite case law favoring the plaintiff simply because the number of such cases was insufficient.[135] If the relevant precedents conflict either within the defendant's own jurisdiction or among

---

133. *See* Robinson v. Bibb, 840 F.2d 349, 351 (6th Cir. 1988).

134. *Compare* Azeez v. Fairman, 795 F.2d 1296, 1301–02 (7th Cir. 1986) (noting that "the State of Illinois is not bound to comply with every constitutional ruling by every district judge in the United States" and referring to "[t]he test *in this circuit* for a prison regulation challenged on religious grounds") (emphasis added) *with* LeClair v. Hart, 800 F.2d 692, 695 (7th Cir. 1986) (denying immunity even though "the Supreme Court has never passed upon the precise type of recording which is involved in this case" because "the lower courts have encountered no difficulty in . . . cases involving analogous circumstances" and Ward v. County of San Diego, 791 F.2d 1329, 1332 (9th Cir. 1986) (in the absence of binding precedent, courts should look to all available cases, including those from other circuits)). *See also* Jenkins by Hall v. Talladega City Bd. of Educ., 115 F.3d 821, 827 n.4 (11th Cir. 1997) (en banc) ("In this circuit, the law can be 'clearly established' for qualified immunity purposes only by decisions of the U.S. Supreme Court, Eleventh Circuit Court of Appeals, or the highest court of the state where the case arose."); and McClendon v. City of Columbia, 305 F.3d 314, 327–28 (5th Cir. 2002) (in the Fifth Circuit, in determining whether a right was "clearly established" under qualified immunity analysis, it is appropriate for a court to look to the law of other circuits when neither the Fifth Circuit nor the Supreme Court has spoken).

135. *See, e.g.,* Walnut Properties, Inc. v. City of Whittier, 861 F.2d 1102, 1113 (9th Cir. 1988), *cert. denied,* 490 U.S. 1006 (1989) (referring to three federal court of appeals decisions and three federal district court decisions as only a "few cases"); Ohio Civil Service Employees Ass'n v. Seiter, 858 F.2d 1171, 1177–78 (6th Cir. 1988) ("[A] mere handful of decisions of other circuit and district courts, which are admittedly novel, cannot form the basis for a clearly established constitutional right in this circuit."); and Coleman v. Frantz, 754 F.2d 719, 730 n.15 (7th Cir. 1985) (requiring "case law which clearly and consistently recognized the constitutional right").

various jurisdictions, almost all courts conclude that the right asserted by the plaintiff is not clearly established.[136]

Lower courts conflict as to whether dictum and opinions issued over dissents are relevant in determining whether a right is clearly established.[137]

H. When Is the Law Clearly Established?

In determining whether the law is "clearly established," courts must look to specific, concrete examples that shed an illuminating light on the factual scenario under review.

> For the law to be clearly established to the point that qualified immunity does not apply, the law must have earlier been developed in such a concrete and factually defined context to make it obvious to all reasonable government actors, in the defendant's place, that "what he is doing" violates federal law. Qualified immunity is a doctrine that focuses on the actual, on the specific, on the details of concrete cases.[138]

Some cases suggest that there must be a bright line that the officials have clearly transgressed,[139] and that preexisting law must dictate that the official's decision or actions violated well-established constitutional rights.[140]

---

136. *See, e.g., Walnut Properties,* 861 F.2d at 1113 (granting immunity despite admitting that six federal decisions supported plaintiff, with none to the contrary); and Benson v. Allphin, 786 F.2d 268, 275 n.16 (7th Cir.), *cert. denied,* 479 U.S. 848 (1986) (suggesting that rights can never be clearly established if the circuits conflict until the Supreme Court resolves the issue).
137. *Compare* Hall v. Medical College of Ohio at Toledo, 742 F.2d 299, 309 (6th Cir. 1984), *cert. denied,* 469 U.S. 1113 (1985) (dismissing earlier cases as dictum, and noting that relevant Supreme Court opinion was issued by divided Court) *with* LeClair v. Hart, 800 F.2d 692, 694 n.3 (7th Cir. 1986) (holding that split decisions are equally authoritative as unanimous ones).
138. *Lassiter,* 28 F.3d at 1149–50 (citation omitted).
139. *See, e.g.,* Hodge v. Jones, 31 F.3d 157, 167 (4th Cir. 1994) (Under thc doctrine of qualified immunity, "officials are not liable for bad guesses in gray areas; they are liable for transgressing bright lines."); Post v. City of Fort Lauderdale, 7 F.3d 1552, 1557 (11th Cir. 1993) ("If case law, in factual terms, has not staked out a bright line, qualified immunity almost always protects the defendant."); and Barts v. Joyner, 865 F.2d 1187, 1190, 1194 (11th Cir. 1989) ("The *Harlow* decision sets up a bright-line test that is a powerful constraint on causes of action under § 1983," and "the line is not to be found in abstractions—to act reasonably, to act with probable cause, and so forth—but in studying how these abstractions have been applied in concrete circumstances.").
140. *See Lassiter,* 28 F.3d at 1150 ("For qualified immunity to be surrendered, pre-existing law must dictate, that is, truly compel (not just suggest or allow or raise a question

The Supreme Court, however, has made it clear that a case on all fours factually is not needed for a defendant to lose the assertion of qualified immunity. As noted in *Hope v. Pelzer*:[141]

> As we have explained, qualified immunity operates "to ensure that before they are subjected to suit, officers are on notice their conduct is unlawful." For a constitutional right to be clearly established, its contours "must be sufficiently clear that a reasonable official would understand that what he is doing violates that right. This is not to say that an official action is protected by qualified immunity unless the very action in question has previously been held unlawful, but it is to say that in the light of pre-existing law the unlawfulness must be apparent."[142]

I. Who Is the Reasonable Person to Whom *Harlow* Refers, and to What Extent Does Actual Knowledge of a Violation of Rights Play in an Objective Analysis?

While *Harlow* protects discretionary conduct that does not violate clearly established statutory or constitutional rights of which "a reasonable person would have known,"[143] neither *Harlow* nor any subsequent Supreme Court precedent has discussed who is the reasonable person to whom Harlow refers. Is the reasonable person a reasonable public official in the abstract, or a reasonable person in the defendant's position? Some lower courts refer to what is reasonable for a defendant in that defendant's position.[144] These cases seem to imply that the court should consider the defendant's position in determining whether that defendant acted reasonably. The author is aware of no case, however, that directly discusses this issue.

Another issue not answered in *Harlow* is whether there is a subjective prong involved when a defendant has actual knowledge of a violation of

---

about), the conclusion for every like-situated, reasonable government agent that what defendant is doing violates federal law *in the circumstances*") (emphasis in original). *See also* Alexander v. University of North Florida, 39 F.3d 290, 291 (11th Cir. 1994) (to avoid qualified immunity, a plaintiff must point to preexisting law that "dictates" and "compels" the conclusion that the defendants violated the constitution).

141. 536 U.S. 730 (2002).

142. *Id.* at 739 (quoting *Saucier,* 533 U.S. at 206; and *Anderson,* 483 U.S. at 635).

143. *Harlow,* 457 U.S. at 818.

144. *See, e.g.,* Auriemma v. Wise, 910 F.2d 1449, 1455 (7th Cir. 1990) ("reasonable police chief of a large metropolitan police force"); Abel v. Miller, 824 F.2d 1522, 1531 (7th Cir. 1987) ("a reasonably competent prison official"); and Schlegel v. Bebout, 841 F.2d 937, 945 (9th Cir. 1988) ("a reasonable PUC official").

rights, even if the rights are not clearly established. After *Harlow*, there was considerable case law that indicated that in determining whether a government official acted reasonably, the subjective intent of the official was to be ignored and the court was to look only to a test of objective legal reasonableness.[145] The Supreme Court in *Saucier*[146] clarified this aspect of the qualified immunity defense, that is, whether the defense applies *even if* the defendant knew that what he did violated the plaintiff's constitutional rights.[147]

In *Saucier*, the Supreme Court clarified that the qualified immunity defense, available in an excessive force case, is to be reviewed by a district court under a different analysis than is the review of the case on the merits. The Court's opinion underscores the strength of the defense, in that these two aspects of the case (review of the merits, then review of whether qualified immunity is nonetheless available) are to be separately analyzed:

> Officers can have reasonable, but mistaken, beliefs as to the facts establishing the existence of probable cause or exigent circumstances, for example, and in those situations courts will not hold that they have violated the Constitution. Yet, even if a court were to hold that the officer violated the Fourth Amendment by conducting an unreasonable, warrantless search, *Anderson* [*v. Creighton*, 483

---

145. *See Anderson,* 483 U.S. at 641 (despite that courts may inquire into "information possessed" by the defendant, the defendant's "subjective beliefs . . . are irrelevant"); Mitchell v. Forsyth, 472 U.S. 511, 517 (1985) (in *Harlow,* "this Court purged qualified immunity doctrine of its subjective components"); *Lassiter,* 28 F.3d at 1150 ("The subjective intent of government actor defendants plays no part in qualified immunity analyses."); *Post,* 7 F.3d 1552 at n.6 ("Qualified immunity invokes an objective standard; that is, if a reasonable person in the defendant's place could have acted the same way, the defendant's subjective intent is irrelevant."); American Civil Liberties Union of Maryland, Inc. v. Wicomico County, Maryland, 999 F.2d 780, 784 (4th Cir. 1993) ("The existence of qualified immunity generally turns on the objective legal reasonableness of the actions; without regard to the knowledge or subjective intent of the particular official.") (citations omitted); Cartier v. Lussier, 955 F.2d 841, 843 (2d Cir. 1992) ("A subjective inquiry into an official's personal belief is rejected in favor of an objective analysis of what a reasonable officer in defendant's position would believe."); and Courson v. McMillian, 939 F.2d 1479, 1487 (11th Cir. 1991) ("The Supreme Court has developed an objective-reasonableness test for evaluating actions of a government official claiming qualified immunity. . . . The use of this test precludes the determination by district courts of subjective good faith in government officials' conduct in section 1983 actions.").
146. Saucier v. Katz, 553 U.S. 194 (2001).
147. *Id.* at 205–06.

> U.S. 635 (1987)] still operates to grant officers immunity for reasonable mistakes as to the legality of their actions. The same analysis is applicable in excessive force cases, where in addition to the deference officers receive on the underlying constitutional claim, qualified immunity can apply in the event the mistaken belief was reasonable.[148]

It can certainly be argued that while a defendant's subjective state of mind is not relevant to determine whether there is a violation of clearly established law, the defendant's actual subjective knowledge may be important for determining whether that defendant is liable for violating clearly established law if that public official knew that he had violated clearly established law, even where an objective, reasonable defendant would not have known that he was violating clearly established law. The author is aware of no case that directly addresses this issue, and those that mention it do so only in passing.[149]

J. The Extraordinary Circumstances Exception

In *Harlow* the Supreme Court, without discussion, indicated that there could be "extraordinary circumstances" where defendants who violated clearly established law proved that they should not have known of the relevant legal standard:

> If the law was clearly established, the immunity defense ordinarily should fail, since a reasonably competent public official should know the law governing its conduct. Nevertheless, if the official pleading the defense claims *extraordinary circumstances* and can prove that he neither knew nor should have known the relevant

---

148. *Id.* at 205.

149. *Compare* Perry v. Larson, 794 F.2d 279, 284 n.1 (7th Cir. 1986) ("it would be illogical to extend good faith immunity to a government official who has intentionally violated an individual's constitutional rights") and Fujiwara v. Clark, 703 F.2d 357, 359 n.3 (9th Cir. 1983) (noting that the *Harlow* standard "has elements of subjectivity" because qualified immunity is available only if the defendant "neither knew nor should have known of the relevant legal standard") *with* Kompare v. Stein, 801 F.2d 883, 887 (7th Cir. 1986) ("[i]t is irrelevant whether a particular defendant knew at the time she acted . . . that her actions violated someone's constitutional rights") and Bothke v. Flour Engineers & Constructors, Inc., 834 F.2d 804, 811 (9th Cir. 1987) (the defendant's "'subjective beliefs' about the lawfulness of her conduct are 'irrelevant'").

legal standard, the defense should be sustained. But again, the defense would turn primarily on objective factors.[150]

The most common assertion of the extraordinary circumstances exception is when public officials rely on the advice of legal counsel as authority for their actions.[151] Other cases strongly suggest that mere reliance on a lawyer's advice cannot be used as a shield from liability for actions that violate the constitution and clearly established law.[152]

---

150. *Harlow,* 457 U.S. at 819 (emphasis added).

151. *See* Cox v. Hainey, 391 F.3d 25, 34 (1st Cir. 2004) (state trooper's consultation with local prosecutor regarding presence of probable cause before he made arrest was factor that could be considered in determining whether he was entitled to qualified immunity in arrestee's civil rights action for false arrest); Kijonka v. Seitzinger, 363 F.3d 645, 648 (7th Cir. 2004) (police officer was entitled to qualified immunity in arrestee's § 1983 action alleging that officer arrested him for assault without probable cause; officer consulted county prosecutor before making arrest and thus had reasonable basis for believing that he had probable cause to make arrest); Pritchett v. Alford, 973 F.2d 307, 316 (4th Cir. 1992) ("mistaken official advice by legal counsel" given as an example of extraordinary circumstances that might insulate defendant from liability even if the defendant violated clearly established law); and V-I Oil Co. v. State of Wyoming, Dept. of Environmental Quality, 902 F.2d 1482, 1489–90 (10th Cir. 1990) (even though the defendant violated clearly settled Fourth Amendment law when he searched the plaintiff's business premises, the defendant was entitled to qualified immunity given the extraordinary circumstances presented by high-ranking government lawyers advising the defendant that the search was lawful).

152. *See* Buonocore v. Harris, 134 F.3d 245, 253 (4th Cir. 1998) (Although reliance on counsel's advice may indeed be factor to be considered in deciding whether defendant has demonstrated "extraordinary circumstance" that entitles defendant to qualified immunity despite defendant's violation of clearly established law, reliance on legal advice alone does not, in and of itself, constitute extraordinary circumstance sufficient to prove entitlement to exception to general rule of § 1983 liability where law is clearly established.); Melton v. City of Oklahoma City, 879 F.2d 706, 730–31 (10th Cir. 1989) (court rejected police chief's defense of good-faith reliance on advice of city attorney where law was clearly established, stating that "[a]dopting the proffered position would immunize officials from liability via the simple expedient of consulting counsel"); Watertown Equip. Co. v. Norwest Bank Watertown, 830 F.2d 1487, 1495 (8th Cir. 1987) (reliance on their lawyer's advice did not make bank and its vice president qualifiedly immune under § 1983 from liability to lender where the law was clearly established that the actions complained of were unlawful); Kompare v. Stein, 801 F.2d 883, 887 (7th Cir. 1986) ("It is irrelevant

V. CONCLUSION

Immunity defenses available to individuals are judicially created in response to the practical effect § 1983 suits have upon governmental employees and officials. While some plaintiffs may become frustrated with use of these defenses, and while some defendants may abuse these defenses during the course of a lawsuit by asserting extreme or untenable positions, the Supreme Court's repeated endorsements of these defenses makes it clear that they are here to stay. The § 1983 practitioner, therefore, is wise to appreciate and understand the underlying jurisprudence that has shaped these defenses. While defensive in nature, these issues likewise shape a plaintiff's case and strategy. Whether representing plaintiff or defendant, these important aspects of § 1983 litigation practice cannot be ignored.

---

whether a particular defendant knew at the time she acted (or failed to act) that her actions violated someone's constitutional rights. The question is whether the state of the law was such that a reasonable person would have known her actions were unconstitutional.") (citation omitted); Wentz v. Klecker, 721 F.2d 244, 248 (8th Cir. 1983) (rejecting advice of counsel as defense to § 1983 liability since "state employees may not rely on their ignorance of even the most esoteric aspects of the law to deny individuals their due process rights"); and Bier v. Fleming, 717 F.2d 308, 312 (6th Cir. 1983) (reversed trial court's rejection of qualified immunity defense, premised upon defendant's failure to follow the advice of counsel, because the law in question was not clearly established).

TABLE OF CASES

McDonald's Corp. v. City of Norton Shores, 102 F. Supp. 2d 431 (W.D. Mich. 2000) 411 n.275

McDonnell v. Hunter, 809 F.2d 1302 (8th Cir. 1987) 360 nn.379–80

McDuffie v. Estelle, 935 F.2d 682 (5th Cir. 1991) 202 n.365

McEwen v. Delta Air Lines, 919 F.2d 58 (7th Cir. 1990) 111 n.160

McFadden v. Sanchez, 710 F.2d 907 (2d Cir. 1983), *cert. denied,* 464 U.S. 961 (1983) 134 n.274

McGann v. Northeast Illinois Reg'l Commuter R.R., 8 F.3d 1174 (7th Cir. 1993) 357 n.356, 358 n.357

McGreevy v. Stroup, 413 F.3d 359 (3d Cir. 2005) 230–231

McGruder v. Necaise, 733 F.2d 1146 (5th Cir. 1984) 458 n.77

McIntosh v. Weinberger, 810 F.2d 1411 (8th Cir. 1987), *partially vacated and remanded on other grounds sub nom.* Turner v. McIntosh, 487 US. 1212 (1988) 468 n.109

McKenna v. Wright, 386 F.3d 432 (2d Cir. 2004) 53 n.277

McKennon v. Hashville Banner Publ'g Co., 513 U.S. 352 (1995) 346 n.279

McKinley v. City of Mansfield, 404 F.3d 418 (6th Cir. 2005) 28 n.152

McKinney v. Pate, 20 F.3d 1550 (11th Cir. 1994), *cert. denied,* 513 U.S. 1110 (1995) 314 n.14

McKinney v. Pate, 985 F.2d 1502 (11th Cir. 1993), *cert. denied,* 513 U.S. 1110 (1995) 318 & n.42

McKinney v. Pate, 994 F.2d 772 (11th Cir. 1993) (en banc) 318 n.43

McKinnon v. City of Berwyn, 750 F.2d 1383 (7th Cir. 1984) 195 n.327

McKnett v. St. Louis & San Francisco Railway, 292 U.S. 230 (1934) 149

McLain v. Real Estate Board, 444 U.S. 232 (1980) 96 n.89

McMath v. City of Gary, Indiana, 976 F.2d 1026 (7th Cir. 1992) 108, 121 n.211

McMillian v. Monroe County, 520 U.S. 781 (1997) 22, 33, 131 n.254

McMillian v. Svetanoff, 878 F.2d 186 (7th Cir. 1989) 347 n.285

McMullen v. Carson, 754 F.2d 936 (11th Cir. 1985) 340 & n.221

McPherson v. Coombe, 174 F.3d 276 (2d Cir. 1999) 6 n.10

McSurely v. McClellan, 697 F.2d 309 (D.C. Cir. 1982) 459 n.79

Mears v. Town of Oxford, 762 F.2d 368 (4th Cir. 1985) 447 n.38

Medical Laundry Servs. v. Board of Trustees of Univ. of Ala., 906 F.3d 571 (11th Cir. 1990) 18 n.79

Meek v. County of Riverside, 183 F.2d 962 (9th Cir. 1999) 452 n.62

Meeks v. Grimes, 779 F.2d 417 (7th Cir. 1988) 350 n.307

INDEX

E

F

L

M

N

O

P